ACTS OF WILL

The thought and the form are equal in the order of time, but in the order of genesis the thought is prior to the form. The poet has a new thought: he has a whole new experience to unfold; he will tell us how it was with him, and all men will be the richer in his fortune. For, the experience of each new age requires a new confession, and the world seems always waiting for its poet.

—R. W. Emerson, "The Poet," *Essays*

The happiness of my existence, its unique character perhaps, consists in its fatefulness: To speak in a riddle, as my own father I am already dead, as my own mother I still live and grow old. This double origin, taken as it were from the highest and lowest rungs of the ladder of life, at once a decadent and a beginning, this, if anything, explains that neutrality, that freedom from partisanship in regard to the general problems of existence, which perhaps distinguishes me.

—F. Nietzsche, *Ecce Homo*

Biography is as little an objective science as history . . . the main purpose is the picture of the creative personality and not merely of the man of actuality, and the two portraits can naturally never be wholly identical. The effort to make them so is, however, the avowed or unavowed tendency not only of the biographer, but of the artist himself and of his public, present and future. . . . That in every age the poet's life should be revalued and re-edited to suit the ideology of that age is only natural. . . .

—O. Rank, *Art and Artist*

ACTS OF WILL
The Life and Work of Otto Rank

E. James Lieberman, M.D.

THE FREE PRESS
A Division of Macmillan, Inc.
NEW YORK

The Free Press
A Division of Macmillan, Inc.
866 Third Avenue, New York, N.Y. 10022

Collier Macmillan Canada, Inc.

Printed in the United States of America

printing number
1   2   3   4   5   6   7   8   9   10

Library of Congress Cataloging in Publication Data

Lieberman, E. James
  Acts of will.

  Bibliography: p.
  Includes index.
  1. Rank, Otto, 1884–1939.   2. Psychoanalysts—
Biography.   I. Title.
RC339.52.R36L54   1985   150.19′5′0924 [B]   84–21121
ISBN 0–02–919020–7

TEXT ACKNOWLEDGMENTS

The following have generously granted permission to use extended quotations from copyrighted works:

Helene Rank Veltfort, Estelle Simon, and Columbia University Library for the published and unpublished writings of Otto Rank.

Anita Faatz for excerpts from *Journal of the Otto Rank Association*.

Sigmund Freud Copyrights Ltd. for unpublished letters of Sigmund Freud to Otto Rank.

Judith Dupont for unpublished letters of Sandor Ferenczi.

Mervyn Jones for letters of Ernest Jones.

Ernst Federn and Margarete Nunberg for excerpts from Otto Rank's *Minutes of the Vienna Psychoanalytic Society*, Volume One, edited by Herman Nunberg and Ernst Federn, Translated by M. Nunberg, NY: International Universities Press, Copyright 1962 by Herman Nunberg, M.D., Ernst Federn.

Excerpts from *The Diary of Anais Nin*, Volumes One and Two, edited by Gunther Stuhlmann, copyright © 1966 and 1967 by Anais Nin. Reprinted by permission of Harcourt Brace Jovanovich, Inc. and Peter Owen Ltd., London.

Selection from Ramon Guthrie's poetry copyright 1970 by Ramon Guthrie and reprinted by permission of Persea Books, Inc., from *Maximum Security Ward and Other Poems*, copyright 1984 by Sally M. Gall.

Excerpts from *Art and Artist* by Otto Rank, translated by Charles Francis Atkinson, copyright © 1932 by Alfred A. Knopf, Inc.

PHOTO ACKNOWLEDGMENTS

Helene Rank Veltfort: 1, 2, 3, 10, 13, 18, 28, 30, 31, 34

Anita Faatz/The Otto Rank Association: 24, 27, 33

The Otto Rank Collection, Columbia University: 5, 6

Museen der Stadt Wien: 7, 14

Österreichische Nationalbibliotek Bild-Archiv: 4

Sigmund Freud Copyrights/Mary Evans Picture Library: 8, 11, 15

Rupert Pole/Anais Nin Foundation: 21, 22, 23

Mervyn Jones: 9

The New York Psychoanalytic Institute: 12, 16

The Rank–Wilbur papers/EJL: 25, 32

Ned L. Gaylin: 17

Wilda Peck O'Hanlon: 19

American Jewish Archives: 20

The University of Pennsylvania School of Social Work: 26

Estelle Buel Rank Simon: 29

Time Magazine, June 23, 1958. Copyright 1958 Time Inc. All rights reserved. Reprinted by permission from *Time:* 35

Map of Vienna: Redrawn by Emily Scherer, Audio Visual Department, George Washington University School of Medicine, from Erstes Illustrierter Monumental Plan, Vienna 1913 and advertising map of Ost Credit-Anstaˡᵗ n.d., both in Map Division, New York Public Library.

To the memory of my father

Benjamin Lieberman, M.D.

1902–1984

who loved both the present and the past in medicine;

and to

Pauline M. Shereshefsky, M.S.S.W.

mentor and friend

who introduced Otto Rank

ever so gently

CONTENTS

LIST OF PHOTOS

PREFACE

As a reader who feels burdened by a surfeit of books, I must justify the production of yet another. Otto Rank gave up writing for a time, saying, "There is already too much truth in the world—an overproduction which apparently cannot be consumed!"

I agree. However, the truth about Rank himself can scarcely be found in print. Apart from Jessie Taft's memoir and a few articles by others, the literature is dominated by half-truths about him, at best. His complete works have not been published in a collected edition; one must know both German and English to read all his books, since he wrote in both languages and some works have never been translated. Several major works have been out of print for some time. After Rank left Freud and psychoanalysis, he neither entered another professional mainstream nor developed more than a small cadre of disciples. The fruits of his most creative period, the last fifteen years of his life, have yet to be discovered by most connoisseurs and teachers of the subjects he addressed: psychotherapy, religion, education, art, and social psychology.

As a psychiatrist in mid-career with only a sketchy knowledge of the history of psychotherapy, I was casting about for roots when a study group on Otto Rank was established in Washington in 1976. Pauline Shereshefsky, who had studied with Jessie Taft and Virginia Robinson, introduced me to the group. I found the members congenial and the reading exacting and exciting.

The paucity of good material about Rank and the abundant errors about him in the literature amazed me.

With the centennial of his birth approaching, I decided to do a biography. The research represented a change of pace and a chance to reflect, an opportunity to see the world through the eyes of an important yet almost forgotten psychotherapeutic mentor. I would try to discover why his message had fallen on deaf ears for so long, why psychoanalysis, psychiatry, and psychology fought against or simply failed to understand one of the most creative philosophers of helping. Rank presents difficulties as a writer, but not more than many others before and since who enjoy a large following. Unfortunately his chief rival, Ernest Jones, held enormous power long after Rank's death, not only in the politics of the international psychoanalytic movement, but as the author of the standard biography of Freud. At last we can set at least part of the record straight.

That a comprehensive biography of the man appears only now may seem to suggest that he was a minor figure, perhaps one of Freud's lesser disciples. On the contrary: Otto Rank was virtually his adopted son and contributed more than anyone else to Freud and the psychoanalytic movement for twenty years. His critique of the limitations of psychoanalysis is echoed by writers on existential psychology, relationship therapy, and creativity, most of whom are unaware that Otto Rank said the same things half a century ago. In some areas, like anthropology, his name is known on account of his early work, but general readers and scholars alike are less aware of the major contributions of his later years—especially *Art and Artist,* one of the great psychohistorical works of this or any epoch. Perhaps until now Rank was too far ahead of his time to be properly judged. I hope this book will prompt people in diverse fields to join with those who already know Rank to assess his lasting (not just historical) importance.

Otto Rank was skeptical about biography, at least that which purports to explain the sources of creativity, heroism, saintliness, or genius. That which makes the artist cannot be traced to universal complexes or unusual life events. Rank himself wavered, like many artists, between creative work and whole-hearted engagement in living. Finally he resolved the dilemma, saying that creating one's personality, one's life, becomes the artist's task in the post-Freudian world.

The life Rank lived may be studied as an example of one who loved books but came to know their limits, of an artist by temperament who learned the difference between art as enhancement of life, as escape, and as fulfillment. Rank's concerns with birth, death, and immortality—the nature and preservation of the soul—are as fresh as when he wrote his masterworks some fifty years ago.

Rank was an intensely private man, scrupulously discreet in his professional and personal life. At times this admirable trait frustrated me as a biographer. The fair-haired son *and* the ugly duckling of the psychoanalytic movement, Rank knew more about Freud than anyone else but did not retaliate with gossip or backbiting even though the Freudian establishment labeled him mentally ill. Rank was no martyr, but he did not like to fight in the arena of politics. Now he is being discovered or rediscovered in the work of Carl Rogers, Rollo May, Paul Goodman, Anais Nin, Carl Whitaker, Esther Menaker, Ernest Becker, Jessie Taft, Fritz Perls, Robert Jay Lifton, Irvin Yalom, and many others. For me it is a labor of love to assist in this celebration of a genius who, it appears, was also an exemplary human being.

Every presentation involves interpretation, and I take responsibility willingly for my biases. I regret any errors, omissions, or misstatements of fact, and hope to be corrected by knowledgeable readers. There are as many ways to recount a life as there are to conduct a symphony. Rank is like a composer whose work is rarely played. He needs no apology—only more interpreters and a larger audience.

Washington, D.C.
April, 1984

ACKNOWLEDGMENTS

Only at the end of this work did I realize what may be an important subliminal influence, with an ironic twist. During my psychiatric residency in Boston, 1959–63, I was in close proximity to, but never met, several figures of importance in this story: Beata Rank, Helene and Felix Deutsch, Ives Hendrick, and George Wilbur. In those days I knew nothing of Otto Rank; he was scarcely mentioned, much less discussed or taught. Recently I learned from Herbert I. Harris, my own analyst in Cambridge, that he had been supervised in a control case by Beata Rank. Although known as a staunch Freudian, Rank's first wife admired him and much of his work and it is perhaps not far-fetched to say that she transmitted a bit of his influence to me. She taught, supervised, or analyzed a number of people with whom I studied in those days.

Researching this biography has been a great pleasure, especially when it brought me into contact with people. I cannot thank them sufficiently but will acknowledge many of them here. I have listed separately those informants who knew Rank even slightly, but wish to express my special gratitude to his widow, Estelle Simon, and his daughter, Helene Rank Veltfort, for their trust and cooperation. It should be understood that no one authorized this biography and I am responsible for any errors: none of my informants reviewed the manuscript.

INFORMANTS WHO KNEW OTTO RANK

Frances Levinson Beatman
Julia Ann Bishop
Kay Campbell Braugham
Anna Freud
Dorothea Gilbert
Rose Green
Hugh Guiler (Ian Hugo)
Dorothy Hankins
Marianne Hauser
Margaret Liebman
Sandor Lorand
Ruth Mellor
Henry A. Murray
Karl Menninger
Emil Oberholzer, Jr.
Mary Plowden
Marguerite Pohek
Frederick Praeger

Clara Rabinowitz
Victor Rubenstein
Irving Ryckoff
Nelly (Mrs. Hanns) Sachs
Ethel Wannemacher
  Seidenman
Max Silverstein
Estelle Buel Rank Simon
Editha Sterba
Richard Sterba
Harold Stevens
George Stevenson
Everett Taft
Beatrice Taussig
Gladys Townsend
Annie Federn Urbach
Helene Rank Veltfort

LIBRARIES

Above all, I wish to thank the Rare Books and Manuscripts Division, Columbia University Library (Kenneth A. Lohf and staff), curators of the Otto Rank Collection, composed of papers originally donated by Estelle Buel Rank to Jessie Taft who placed them at Columbia in 1957. There they have been open—without restrictions—to qualified scholars. Major additions have been made by Estelle Rank, by the Directors of the Otto Rank Association, and by Anita Faatz, who gave not only Rank's letters to Jessie Taft and Virginia Robinson, but also their important papers. I also made use of the Lionel Trilling papers and the Marion Kenworthy papers at Columbia, and, through the Oral History Collection, the reminiscences of Theodore Reik, Abraham Kardiner, and Sandor Rado which were recorded by Bluma Swerdloff.

The following have been of great help: The Library of Congress (Ronald Wilkinson); the A. A. Brill Library of the New York Psychoanalytic Society (Ellen Gilbert, Ruth Reynolds); The New York Public Library; The Countway Library of Medicine

(Mary E. Van Winkle); the Archives of the History of American Psychology (John Popplestone); and the libraries of The American Psychiatric Association (Zing Jung); the University of Pennsylvania School of Social Work (Evelyn Butler); The New York Hospital—Cornell Medical Center (Eric T. Carlson); The Lifwynn Foundation (Alfreda S. Galt and Hans Syz); The University of California at Los Angeles (Dale Treleven); The Washington School of Psychiatry (Gloria Parloff); Yale University (Christa Sammons); the University of Texas Humanities Research Center (Cathy Henderson); the Leo Baeck Institute (Fred Bogin); The National Archives; the Boston Psychoanalytic Society (Ann Menashi); the Washington Psychoanalytic Society (Patricia Driscoll); the University of Wyoming (Gene Gressley).

ORGANIZATIONS

The Otto Rank Association, founded in 1965, directed through its eighteen productive years by Anita Faatz, provided a supportive base for this work. Miss Faatz generously allowed me access to her files before they became part of the Rank Collection at Columbia University, and gave invaluable guidance. The local ORA branch, founded by Marilyn Pollin, gave me my start on this project, and I wish to thank all those who have helped along the way. Sanford Gifford kindly invited me to be a guest member of the Committee on History and Archives of the American Psychoanalytic Association. The Anais Nin Foundation (Rupert Pole) was especially helpful with photographs. The Audio Visual Department of the George Washington University School of Medicine, John Gach Books, and Goodspeed's Book Shop made my task easier.

SPECIAL ASSISTANCE

The following helped me with translations: Eva Salomon, Gretl Wölfel Cox, David Berger, Sam M. Silverman, Werner Low, Sophie Feuermann, and George Wilbur; nevertheless I am responsible for the final versions. Drena Owens got my research off to an excellent start, and Molly Abramowitz lent her expertise to the bibliography. Kitty Moore, Robert Cohen, and

Eileen DeWald edited: only we know what a difference they made. Carol Keegan proofread with great care.

These and others have helped with ideas, advice, generous permission to quote from pertinent sources, and various forms of support, including: Marjorie Boulton, F. Harry Brown, Norman Braugham, Stanley and Lydia Burnshaw, Richard Centing, Rachael Dunaway Cox, Suzanne Derrick, Peter F. Drucker, Pat Durkin, Samuel Eisenstein, Philip Freund, Isadore From, Ned Gaylin, Muriel Gardiner, Susannah Gourevitch, Phyllis Grosskurth, Martin Grotjahn, Carol Hall, Zelda Heller, Richard Henshaw, Philip Jason, William M. Johnston, Jack Jones, Rochelle Kainer, Florence Kaslow, Walter Kendrick, Dennis Klein, Alfred A. Knopf, Esther Kovenock, Robert Kvarnes, Francois Lafitte, Lovell Langstroth, Jr., Susan Lanser, Zigmond Lebensohn, Anna Leifer, Max Lerner, Jane Cook Lewis, Sophie Freud Loewenstein, Rollo May, Ralph Melnick, Esther Menaker, Jennie Montgomery, Fifi Salem O'Connor, Wilda Peck O'Hanlon, Andrew Paskauskas, Elsie Behrend Paull, Helen Swick Perry, Paul Roazen, Norman Reider, Henrik Ruitenbeek, Polly Salmon, Sharon Spencer, Melvin Stern, Grace Stern, Irving Stone, Keith Sward, Taylor Stoehr, Humphrey Tonkin, Muriel Waddington, Will Wadlington, Ruth Gilpin Wells, Emilio Weiss, Carl Whitaker, and Joseph Wortis.

Frustrations can be acknowledged, too. K. R. Eissler's restrictions upon the Sigmund Freud Archives have done little to protect anyone and have allowed grievous mischief by one or two who gained access. Rank's letters to Anais Nin were not made available to me and the papers of Ernest Jones in London and of pioneer American analysts in New York were not accessible. Eventually these sources may open up, but they will probably not much change the story of Otto Rank.

Finally I wish to thank my wife, Susan, and our children, Karen and Daniel, for their support and tolerance during nearly two years of writing.

A READER'S GUIDE

Lengthy quotations are indented. Italic type indicates letter or manuscript-diary extract. Roman type is used for extracts from books and articles.

The Appendix section, preceding the notes and bibliography, is intended to orient general readers as well as researchers in the geography, chronology, and family relationships of the story.

The majority of footnotes (indicated in the text by superscript numbers) are reference citations. A few amplify the text and are easily identifiable by their length.

Unlike English, German is phonetic: pronunciations of letters are constant. The letter "a" in German is pronounced as in "father" or as the "o" in "rock," which is virtually a homonym of "Rank." The temptation to anglicize Rank (to rhyme with "thank") should be resisted, as it has been for Jung. Incidentally, the names Freud, Adler, Jung, and Rank have the following meanings: joy, eagle, young, and slender or winding, respectively.

The umlaut, which may appear over the vowels a, o, and u, blends an "ee" sound with the marked vowel; thus "für" sounds between "fur" and "fear." Ordinary as well as proper nouns are capitalized. In particular:

Gasse = alley or lane; Strasse = street or avenue.
Verlag ("fer-LAHG") = publishing house
Gymnasium (hard "g" always) = academic high school, completed

at about 18, and equivalent to about the first two years of American colleges
Wien (pron. "veen") = Vienna; Wiener = Viennese
Zeitscrift ("z" pron. "ts") = Chronicle (lit., "timewrit")
Jahrbuch (pron. "yar-buch") = Yearbook, Annual
The name Lueger (mayor of Vienna) is pronounced "lu-AY-ger."
Seelenglaube (pron. "ZAY-len-glaub-e") = soul–belief

Among the problems in translating Rank and Freud, one of the most important concerns the word "soul." In German, *Seele* means soul, mind, heart, human being, and the center of something—e.g., the bore of a gun, soundpost of a violin, or core of a cable. (*Seelenkunde,* literally "soul science," is an older word for psychology.) Unfortunately the English equivalent for its adjective, *seelisch,* has fallen into disuse (soulish, soular, soulical), leaving only psychic(al) or spiritual. Despite its origin, "psyche" lacks heart, and Freud is mechanistic enough without such a burden. "Spiritual" has a religious connotation not in keeping with Rank or Freud; its use has misled some readers to suppose that Rank had a Jungian mystical-religious streak. I have sometimes used "soular," a good "old" word, homophonous with a familiar term connoting warmth and energy, but not likely to be confused in context.

INTRODUCTION

Beyond Freudian Psychology

Jocasta

    *It is because I wish you well that I give you this counsel—
and it's the best counsel.*

Oedipus

    Then the best counsel vexes me, and has for some while since.

Jocasta

        O Oedipus, God help you!

God keep you from the knowledge of who you are!
               —Sophocles, *Oedipus Rex*[1]

In 1929 Dr. Otto Rank, at age 44, was making a rather good living as a psychotherapist in Paris, with a supplemental practice in New York. That year his most notorious book, *The Trauma of Birth*, appeared in English translation. After two decades as Freud's devoted helper and most creative student, Rank had been independent for less than five years. At that point, lecturing at Yale University, Rank said that someday after he retired he might write a history of the psychoanalytic movement.[2]

No one before or since was better qualified to write it. Rank had served as Secretary of the Vienna Psychoanalytic Society and Freud's closest colleague from 1906 to 1924. He was one of a handful of men who attended all of the first nine Congresses of the International Psychoanalytic Association. He co-edited two journals and next to Freud was the most important psycho-analytic author.

But Rank died young, before he could retire. He never wrote his history. Most of what he said about the subject was virtually ignored during the heyday of psychoanalysis because Rank had become an outsider, a dissident. To my knowledge, no historian has ever commented on Otto Rank's presentation of the origins of psychoanalysis. Psychoanalysts themselves have been poor historians of their profession. The Freud edifice constructed by Ernest Jones has been scrutinized and found wanting by some well-qualified outsiders: Paul Roazen, political scientist; Frank Sulloway, historian of science; and Ronald Clark, biographer. (Psychiatric historians like Franz Alexander and Henri Ellenberger completed their worthy projects too soon to benefit from Roazen's original research, and even he did not have access to documents released in the last decade).

Distortions in history die hard, especially when few people care enough to correct them. For example, Jones, quoting Edoardo Weiss (the pioneer Italian analyst), asserts that Mussolini intervened with Nazi authorities on Freud's behalf. Years later Weiss himself published a denial: He had told Jones emphatically that the rumor about Mussolini was *false*.[3] Unfortunately such corrections overtake errors belatedly, if at all.

Another example shows the danger of careless abridgement. In his eulogy for Karl Abraham, Freud wrote, "So high a place had he won for himself that, of all who have followed me through the dark pathways of psychoanalytic research, there is only one whose name could be put beside his." Freud's willingness to stir up sibling rivalry at a funeral is noteworthy. How surprising, then, to find Ferenczi's name at the end of the provocative sentence in a recent abstract of the eulogy. The explanation is simple: The abstract was made from the Standard Edition of Freud's works, which contains extensive footnotes. The footnote so casually incorporated into the abstract said, "Freud no doubt had Ferenczi in mind."[4] Perhaps. But he could *also* have had Rank in mind, among others. The simplification falsifies Freud's distinctive style, if not his whole intent. And it will be disseminated far more than either of the primary sources.

As will become evident later, Freud's relationship with his mentor, Josef Breuer, was so conflicted that it led—in Rank's opinion—to distortions, on Freud's part, of the historical record

and of psychoanalytic theory. Rank's brief and poignant introduction to that story sets the stage for an understanding of his
own relationship to Freud.

> Psychoanalysis was born in the year 1881. Its father was the late
> physician Dr. Josef Breuer, who for nearly ten years kept secret
> the birth of this illegitimate child. Dr. Breuer then abandoned the
> child because it might appear a bastard of scientific medicine, of
> which he himself was a representative, and of psychotherapy, which
> is still under suspicion at the present time. It was then that it found
> a tender and loving foster mother in the person of Sigmund Freud.
> He reared the neglected and misunderstood being, and developed
> it into what we know today as psychoanalysis. It is now full grown
> and self-reliant. It leaves behind it a very interesting past.[5]

The ten years of secrecy refers to the delay in publication
of Breuer's case. His patient, Anna O., developed pseudocyesis
(false pregnancy), and attributed fatherhood to Breuer, which
frightened him away. Freud, unintimidated, drew on his background in hypnosis and explained the intense affect in the patient
as "transference" derived from childhood relationships, not to
be taken personally by the doctor.

Rank labeled psychoanalysis a "bastard," the unplanned offspring of prestigious scientific materialism and the discredited
metaphysics of Mesmer and faith healers. Yet there is more to
Rank's metaphor: It represents part of his own biography. Freud
has been called many things, but only his foster son called him
a mother! Otto Rank could not have done so unaware of its
symbolic meaning.

A child unloved and intimidated by his father, Otto Rosenfeld
(Rank) might as well have been taken in as a foster child by
his mother, a warm, intelligent, and caring woman. His brother
Paul, three years older, was favored with an academic career
leading to a law degree. Despite his frail health, Otto had to
attend trade school and work long hours. At 21, Rank, who disowned his father in name and act, met Freud, who nurtured
him to maturity.

Freud's psychoanalytic theory focused on the father as both
guide and threat to the son, while the mother was the boy's
unattainable sex object. There was an active (male) and a passive
(female) parent. Freud decided that this model of parental roles
fit neatly into the Oedipus legend, but in so doing he left out

some major themes while stretching the framework to include others. Oedipus valued the parents he knew but not his biological ones, who had cast him away. A motif that Freud only began to explore but which Rank fully developed can be summarized: In human affairs, relationship outweighs biology. To put it in Rank's words:

> In *The Trauma of Birth* I compared the creative drive of the artistic individual to the creation of the individual himself—not merely in the physical but also the soular sense of the "rebirth" experience, which I regard psychologically as the singular *creative act of the person*. Thereby not only is the individual, the "soular I," born from the biological "somatic I," but the person is both creator and creature at once; from creature he actually becomes the creator— in the ideal case, of his self, his personality.[6]

FATHER, MOTHER, AND SON: THE OEDIPUS MYTH

The classic Sophocles play concerns a royal couple, Laius and Jocasta, who are told by an oracle that their newborn son is destined to kill his father and marry his mother. Laius orders Jocasta to have the child put to death. Its feet bound ("Oedipus" means swollen foot), the infant is given to a shepherd, who, instead of exposing the child on the mountainside, gives it to another shepherd. He in turn finds a childless couple who become loving parents to their foundling son.

As a young man, Oedipus has his fortune told by an oracle and hears the same dire prophecy of patricide and incest. He immediately leaves the home of his beloved foster parents to protect them from the prophesied horror. On the road he meets a group of travelers; a dispute erupts about right of way and Oedipus kills two men in the ensuing fight. Later he comes to the Sphinx, half-woman, half-lion, who held Thebes in the grip of famine. The one who could solve a riddle would defeat her, but should he fail he dies. "What goes on four legs in the morning, two at noon, and three in the evening?" was the riddle.

"Man" is the answer that overthrows the Sphinx, saves Thebes, and makes Oedipus king and new husband of the widowed Jocasta. Years later another famine comes, relief from which depends on delving into a mystery of the double crime of patricide and incest. With obsessional zeal, Oedipus pursues an inquest which leads him to his own past. The fact of Laius's

death in a fight on the road, and the testimony of the old shepherds about the infant they saved, make the proud and stubborn
Oedipus conscious of his unwitting guilt. Jocasta begs for a halt
to the inquest, saying that chance rules life and foresight is not
possible; she pleads for living and opposes pursuing knowledge
that would destroy the innocent. Finally stricken with both the
historical truth and Jocasta's suicide, Oedipus blinds himself and
goes into exile.

The play concerns biological and adoptive parenthood, gener-
ational conflict, mortality, anger, the power of truth to help and
hurt, predestination versus will, and the making and breaking
of family ties. Freud's Oedipal theme—the son's hostility toward
father and his lust toward mother—is subliminal in the play, if
not imaginary.

Oedipus and Laius shared a certain arrogance and combative-
ness; hence their fatal fight. (By contrast, Freud's real-life father,
harassed by anti-Semitic ruffians in the village street, would not
risk life and limb to fight. Young Sigmund, on being told of
this, was disappointed in his father.) Laius and Oedipus, respectively, heard a prophecy and moved to quash it, and those very
efforts led to its fulfillment. But the motives of the two were
wholly different. Laius sacrificed his only child to save himself.
An anguished mother and two shepherds chose to flout the regal
order, which flouted the divine "order." For his part, Oedipus
tried to escape the prophecy *un*selfishly: By leaving them he
sought to protect his (psychologically) real parents.[7]

In this tale, an innocent son escapes a homicidal father. The
son later acts to spare the beloved couple he perceived as his
parents—and they were his true parents from the standpoint
of relationship. Oedipus in fact reveals nothing resembling patricidal feeling. While Freud's theory of repression allows us to
interpret actions as more telling than words, even Freud did
not claim that Oedipus had any idea who he killed, or who he
married. Freud emphasized the play's determinism, the folly
of evasion, the necessity for solving riddles no matter how terrible the answer. He dismissed emotional in favor of biological
reality, choosing self-knowledge ahead of life itself. His theory
justifies the father's fear as a response to the son's rage; there
is no paternal guilt. Freud ignored Jocasta's plea to accept and
live life. Having made the son guilty, Freud then exonerated
him—not as a priest offering absolution, but as a scientist offering
consolation.

Rank, in contrast, interpreted the expressed infanticidal wish of Laius as the father's desperate reach for immortality, the denial of his starkly finite biological substance. Rank reinterpreted Oedipus in terms beyond psychoanalysis. Salvation, he agreed with Freud, comes not through priestly intervention with God. But he took issue with Freud's willingness to sacrifice the son on the altar of science—knowing—for the father's immortality. Rank was probably the first Freudian to identify and put to use the mother in himself. With Jocasta he argued against Oedipus and Freud: *Living is better than knowing when the two are in conflict.*

Freud revised Oedipus into a universal template for the family, normal and neurotic. Freud, not Sophocles, found every son rife with sexual love for his mother and jealous hatred toward his father, both emotions repressed in the unconscious with a force equal to their instinctual energy. Freud accepted the deterministic faith in the oracle and the futility of conscious willing. He subordinated present experience to the ominous future and the ineluctable past. Like the tragic Oedipus, Freud valued objective, rational "truth" above an equally valid emotional reality.

Freud overlooked the play's theme of adoptive versus biological parenthood, the former characterized by love without any "biological immortality" motive, the latter by sacrifice of child for the sake of parent. Without denying the importance of biological origins, the story teaches that emotional disengagement leads to confusion and tragedy. *Absence of relationship leads to a form of ignorance which cannot be overcome rationally.* Jocasta's wisdom, ignored by Oedipus and Freud but heard by Rank, divined the terrible cost of too much hindsight, foresight, and insight. Appropriately, Oedipus blinded himself.

Rank never called himself a feminist, nor did he explicitly espouse a maternal identity. His psychology recognized gender differences in social life and personal expression—not at the level of penis envy and womb envy but in terms of individuality, immortality, intimacy, and creativity. As a creative writer he needed a muse; as a therapist—or friend—he could *be* the muse. Thus without blurring his sexual identity he integrated positive elements of both sexes.

Rank's experience as husband and father brought new insight. He appreciated, even envied, the closeness he felt between mother and child—Beata and Helene. In analytic work with patients, Rank found their transference feelings toward the mother to be stronger, more basic, than the paternal transference emphasized by Freud. Thus with fatherhood and professional maturity, Rank came upon an essential difference with Freud: a maternal element. (The original Mentor of Greek myth, to whom Odysseus entrusted his son, was sometimes inhabited by Athena, so the prototypical advisor was not lacking a womanly aspect.) If the maternal side of Freud had been stronger, he not only would have understood women better, but he might have allowed his protégé to separate more freely. Instead of nurturing Rank's self-creation, Freud withdrew as though it were a threat.

In 1924, at age 68, Freud faced a slow death from cancer of the palate. At the peak of success, he could no longer work at the peak of his powers. Meanwhile Rank's star had risen. His personal and professional breakthrough, his trauma of birth, came as Rank turned 40. (At precisely that age, in 1896, Freud had a similar experience: He worked out his theory of dreams while losing both his elderly father and his dearest mentor, Josef Breuer.) Rank, separated from his mortal mentor, now became the deep explorer of the soul, confronting riddles Freud had left unsolved.

Regarding Rank's break with Freud, virtually all the attention of historians has been paid to changes in Rank, to account for his deviance. A well-known analyst wrote, "For three years (1923–26) Freud hoped that Rank's new attitude was curable."[8] But some major changes in Freud just before and during those years have gotten short shrift. With Rank and Ferenczi, Freud was for several years a staunch supporter of "wild analyst" Georg Groddek—to the consternation of Jones, Pfister, and others. Again showing a liberal side, Freud championed the active therapy of Ferenczi and Rank, only later to back down under pressure from Jones and Abraham precisely as he did with Rank's birth trauma theory. It would appear that Freud's wavering and his poor handling of conflict in the inner circle contributed as much to Rank's departure as any theoretical difference between the two men.

HISTORY OF A LIBEL

In 1926 Otto Rank left Freud's inner circle, the "Ring" or Committee, to make his own way in Paris and New York. The departure of Freud's favorite son was promptly interpreted by Rank's rivals as a sign of his own emotional instability, and Ernest Jones sent out word to that effect. But many American professionals including psychiatrists continued to seek out Rank for analysis and supervision.

Then, at a major conference in 1930 the eminent Dr. A. A. Brill slandered Rank before a large audience, denouncing his ideas as a product of mental disturbance. Rank was dropped from the roster of the American Psychoanalytic Association; analysts who had been trained by him had to resign from the APA or be reanalyzed by an approved Freudian. Freud himself vacillated between expressions of admiration for Rank's contributions to psychoanalysis and condemnation of his maverick ideas and behavior.

To the extent that Rank expressed himself politically in these times, he opposed the fascism of Hitler, Mussolini, and Franco. Yet in 1939 Erich Fromm—not an establishment Freudian—published an article labeling Rank's "will therapy" as a Nazi-style totalitarian philosophy.

Upon Rank's death that same year, Ernest Jones described his late rival as a mentally sick man. In his subsequent biography of Freud, Jones relentlessly pursued this theme.

> Rank in a dramatic fashion presently to be described, and Ferenczi more gradually toward the end of his life, developed psychotic manifestations that revealed themselves in, among other ways, a turning away from Freud and his doctrines. . . .
>
> I had known that Rank had suffered much in childhood from a strongly repressed hostility to his brother, and that this usually covered a similar attitude toward a father. This was now being unloaded on to me, and my dominant concern was how to protect Freud from the consequences. . . .
>
> It became plain that a manic phase of his cyclothymia was gradually intensifying.[9]

Comparing Rank with Carl Jung, Jones said, "The outstanding difference in the two cases is of course that Jung was not afflicted by any of the mental trouble that wrecked Rank and so was able to pursue an unusually fruitful and productive life." Unfortunately this testimony became widely accepted even in New York, where—as Jones himself later admitted in a complete reversal—Rank had a highly successful career. Reviewing the Jones work in *The New York Times*, critic Lionel Trilling exaggerated the falsehood, stating that Rank and Ferenczi both died insane.[10]

In 1958 Jessie Taft's fine memoir *Otto Rank* was reviewed in the mass media. Although it effectively refuted Jones, reviews of her book in *Time* magazine and The *New York Post* carried on the libel: "Ernest Jones, the peppery little Welshman, was perhaps the first to realize that Rank was deeply disturbed . . . a victim of manic-depressive psychosis." Dr. Walter Alvarez, the widely syndicated medical columnist, diagnosed the adolescent Rank as "a typical schizoid or mildly schizophrenic person. . . . Like so many men of this type, who one finds in mental hospitals, he soon was feeling that he belonged to the group of heroes. . . . See what sort of a man it was who presented some of our psychiatrists and social workers with many of the weird theories of mental illness on which they now base their teachings and behavior."[11]

Marthe Robert represents a second wave of historians who discredited Rank in Europe and America. "The practice of excessively short treatments could easily lead to charlatanism," she wrote, "especially as Rank, who was not a doctor, preferred to address 'lay' analysts and thus opened the doors of the profession to all comers."[12] Rank *was* a doctor—a clinical psychologist, not a physician. And *Freud* was the strongest advocate for nonmedical (lay) therapists; he hoped to prevent the domination of psychoanalysis by psychiatry. In this he was thwarted by the efforts of Jones and Brill, the most powerful psychoanalysts in the English-speaking world, where analysis flourished after World War II.

Karl Menninger, perhaps the most influential American psychiatrist and psychoanalyst, wrote: "The three months of analysis advocated by Otto Rank proved to be a farce for some and a tragedy for others."[13] But Rank never advocated a fixed length of time for treatment, only that an ending be kept in focus.

Some correctives appeared in books favorable to Rank by Ira Progoff, Paul Roazen, and Ronald Clark, and articles by Jack Jones, Max Lerner, and Philip Freund. But the denunciations continue in recent psychoanalytic writings: "Clinical evidence of a narcissistic disturbance in Rank's personality can be found in the patterning of his mood swings, in his lifelong tendency of grandiose isolation, and in the quality of his object relations." This posthumous analysis suggests that Rank suffered from "a dangerous fragility in his self-representation along with a looming threat of self-fragmentation," and that "isolation and insulation from human contact was apparent throughout his life."[14] As recently as 1983, in a biography of the late Anna Freud, who did *not* regard Rank as mentally ill, the author echoes Jones in citing Rank's "eventual paranoia and psychotic collapse."[15]

Considering the duration and extent of the attack on Rank, it stands out among examples of psychoanalytic character assassination. He was demeaned in public and private, in plain words and in jargon, in professional and lay circles. It is hard to imagine a stigma greater than to be labeled mentally ill by leading authorities in psychiatry and psychoanalysis. Rank did not fight back directly: he tried to find assistance in disseminating his views but did not defend or counterattack. (I have found no mention of Ernest Jones, for example, in Rank's publications or correspondence after 1925.) The sorry result of the stigma has been the virtual disappearance of the works of Otto Rank. For a whole generation only a few hardy souls studied his books, and even fewer taught his ideas in universities and clinics.

THE RANKIAN REVIVAL

The late Ernest Becker, a professor of sociology, was one of those exceptions. He came upon Rank relatively late, but his last two books—*The Denial of Death* (Pulitzer Prize, 1974) and *Escape from Evil*—brought his discovery to a wide and enthusiastic audience. "You cannot merely praise much of his work," Becker said, "because in its stunning brilliance it is often fantastic, gratuitous, superlative; the insights seem like a gift. . . . Rank's thought always spanned several fields of knowledge." Becker recognized the problems, too: "Rank is very diffuse, very hard to read, so rich that he is almost inaccessible to the general reader."[16]

Although Rank did not live into the nuclear age, Becker shows how his ideas touch our present dilemmas with characteristic subtlety and force. Thus in a sentence is distilled an explanation of "overkill," be it in primitive warfare or the irrational arms race of today: "To be stronger than enemies who wish your death is to be stronger than death itself."[17] Demagogues through the ages have seduced multitudes by promising to defeat (or defend against) an evil enemy that symbolizes death itself.

The modern era brought the democratization of immortality: The photograph, sound recordings, radio, newsreels, and magazines gave a sense of permanence to images and events of ordinary life. Science and technology opened new paths to eternity as the traditional routes—established religion, royalty, and tribal or racial identity—were obstructed by doubt and change. Rank witnessed the advent of the telephone, the automobile, radio, cinema, the airplane—devices which made common folk feel in command of destiny. But he also saw the unprecedented destruction wrought by World War I. Although he died before the holocaust and the leveling of cities which came with World War II, Rank's teaching about life fear and death fear needs no revision. It can help us face constructively the marvels and threats of the nuclear age, when we can obliterate all the trophies and tokens of immortality, all human history, even the future.

On a less global scale, the psychology of Otto Rank is being discovered—sometimes unwittingly reinvented—by leading scholars and therapists. "Knowingly or unknowingly, every therapist assumes that each patient has within him the capacity to change through willful choice. The therapist, using a variety of strategies and tactics, attempts to escort the patient to a crossroads where he can choose. . . . The interpretive remarks of the therapist can all be viewed in terms of how they bear on the patient's will." So states psychiatrist Irvin Yalom, a recognized authority on group and existential psychotherapy who readily acknowledges his debt to Rank. The late Silvano Arieti made similar points, but apparently arrived at his position without knowing Rank's work.[18]

Like Arieti, Judd Marmor, a third psychiatrist of international renown, represents a progressive force in psychoanalysis. Unlike Arieti, he recognizes Rank's role. "In some ways Otto Rank may well be the most important historical forerunner of the brief dynamic psychotherapy movement . . . [He] laid the groundwork for the subsequent recognition of the predominant importance in personality development of the pre-oedipal years, particularly the early mother-child relationship. It is unfortunate that the issue of disloyalty to Freud has cast a heavy shadow over the value of Rank's achievements. . . . We can now perceive that Rank was the prime theoretical precursor of these developments [including the concept of separation and individuation] without in any way denigrating the later creative contributions of people like Rene Spitz, Margaret Mahler, or John Bowlby."[19] The density of Rank's writing may excuse the ignorance of general readers, but professionals constantly confront texts of equal difficulty; it is only surprising how often we ignore past luminaries to follow those who gain the limelight for the moment.

RANK—PERSONAL AND PROFESSIONAL

Difficult though Rank's writing may be, his teaching and therapy were easy to enjoy and assimilate. I spoke with a number of his former patients and students who remembered him vividly and with great affection.

One woman was rather nonplused on meeting Rank for the first time. She had somehow expected a tall, handsome Teuton: "When he opened the door I was so surprised: he was a small man [Rank stood about five feet four inches tall] with a potbelly, his thick glasses made his eyes look as though they were bulging. Then after a short while with him I forgot all about that. His personality became so important." Quite unathletic, Rank made up in brains and charm what he lacked in looks; no one ever claimed he was handsome, but many found him an attractive person.

He was gentle and humorous. His therapy was straightforward, respectful, honest, a conversational partnership. Rank told her he learned as much from every patient as the patient did from him. "I never try to cure. I utilize the neurosis," he once said. As for his books, he said, "Read them if you want to, but forget them, don't act on them. Read *Huckleberry Finn*—everything is there!"

"With Rank there was no dogma," she told me. "Everything was open from minute to minute. Nothing was imposed on you. Rank was not looking for disease, he was not trying to eradicate anything. He wanted you to open up and be as you might want to be but didn't dare to. He had an overwhelming force but it did not take away from anything else—it gave you a force of your own. Talking about my husband (who also was in treatment with Rank) he said, 'You might not like what he turns out to be.' I felt this as a subtle suggestion to let go of any preconceived idea of what he was. I must allow the process of finding out to go forward without imposing any restraint on it."

When she and her husband considered educating their son for a time at home, Rank discouraged the idea. "He must go to school. We don't know what he is going to have to fit into when he is thirty, but *that* he will have to fit in is sure." Freedom within structure was the guiding principle.[20]

For Rank, each therapeutic encounter was a slice of life. The analytic hour may not be typical of life, but what happens within its limits includes an intensification of feeling in a real relationship: an art work, no mere artifact. Rank cultivated and celebrated that intense here-and-now reality which classical analysis avoided. His discovery might be called "psychopoiesis" in contrast to psychoanalysis. Like the artist who works within the borders of his canvas to enhance a portion of experience, or the poet who transcends his own complaint about the poverty of language, Rank seized Freud's invention, the analytic hour, and fashioned from that excellent tool a new instrument for the creation of personality.

To patients' vulnerability—love, anger, pain, joy—Rank responded humanely, within clinical bounds. While discovering the mother in himself Rank also recognized the limit to the protective, healing touch of maternal love: the need to separate, the trauma of birth. Rank taught that each analytic hour, a partial life, contains union and separation, as does the whole therapeutic relationship on a larger scale. Those who practice Rankian therapy do not hide from the patient's affect, nor do they hide relevant feelings from the patient. Feelings are to be taken as real until proven otherwise, rather than the reverse, which psychoanalysis teaches.

One of his students found Rank to be very different in person from his writings—informal, human, warm. This young man recalled asking Rank about a case reported by Jessie Taft involving therapy with a provocative child. Taft had allowed the child near a window from which he could have jumped and hurt himself. Some people criticized her for not setting firmer limits. "I put the question to Rank: What was his position?"

Rank answered: "The therapist may do whatever he believes is pertinent to the process and *moment of therapy* with a particular individual, as long as he takes responsibility for and deals helpfully with what he precipitates in the patient." Characteristically, Rank did not give a simple directive, but offered a guiding principle, leaving the choice to the listener.[21]

AT THE FRONTIER

These memories of Rank date back to the late 1930s, the end of his life. He planned to obtain citizenship in his new homeland and retire to California with his American bride of three months, when he succumbed to complications of an infection.

Rank was the first from the Freudian circle to penetrate—and be penetrated by—America. His interest in American culture dates back to his youth, when he wrote about Twain and Emerson in his diary. (Emerson also had a major influence on Nietzsche, one of Rank's intellectual mentors.) One of Rank's teachers at the University of Vienna was steeped in the psychology of William James. Before he graduated, Rank translated into German a psychoanalytic article by Harvard neurologist James Jackson Putnam.[22]

An American by choice in his last years, Rank strongly identified himself with Huckleberry Finn. He took the nickname "Huck," calling himself the twin of the idealistic, earthy hero of Twain's great novel. Although Rank didn't say why he saw a resemblance, one can suppose that his approach to liberating poor enslaved souls was direct, emotional, and practical like Huck's with "nigger" Jim. Tom Sawyer, by contrast, preferred an elaborate, bookish strategy to free the slave—an approach hedged with emotional detachment, like Freud's. Questions of propriety, personal involvement, and style all enter in, just as they do in therapy. Freeing the trapped or downtrodden human will was Rank's special mission. He felt it could only be done with honesty, humor, humility, and a will of one's own.

As leading advocate in modern psychology for the conscious will, the present, and the reality of caring and catalysing, Rank became the pioneer relationship therapist, an existential pathfinder. He brought to therapy the Kierkegaardian motto, "Life can only be understood backwards; it can only be lived forwards."

Having begun with birth, and having made the present moment the focus of therapy, Rank confronted the future with his concept of will. This concept, more than any other issue, separates Rank from therapists before and since. With it he moved away from Freudian determinism to the idea of choice, within limits. Rankian psychology combines responsibility with freedom in creating one's own personality. In this creative process—a psychological rebirth—the therapist serves as midwife. If with respect to Freud one can say, "The unexamined life is not worth living," then on behalf of Rank one can say, "The uncreative life is not worth living."

Tension exists in psychological theory—as in life—between knowing and experiencing. Freud pulls toward one pole, Rank toward the other. So it is with their differences about past and present, father and mother, wish and will, science and art. That the two were joined for so long testifies to the strength of complementary ideas in two individuals whose goal—a new depth psychology—was the same. But the two men, closer to each other than Otto to his father or Sigmund to his sons, could not stay together.

Considering his humble roots, poor physical health, and lack of medical credentials, Rank did well in the competitive world beyond the prickly but protective Freudian circle. The resistance he encountered after the break was fierce, but Rank met it as a free spirit, disciplined but no longer a disciple. To the question, Was the separation choice or necessity? follows the answer: For Rank, the student of creative will, it was mainly choice, but he could not stay the same; Freud, an apostle of determinism, vacillated, wishing it were different, but he could not change.

CHAPTER 1

An Adolescent Diary

Thou shalt not give birth reluctantly.
—Otto Rank's Eighth Commandment

"**I** was born with hair complete, the third child of weak but apparently healthy parents," wrote Otto Rank in his adolescent diary. Born Otto Rosenfeld on April 22, 1884, Rank was the second son of Simon and Karoline Fleischner Rosenfeld. The family lived in a small apartment on Czerningasse, a narrow lane near the main street of Leopoldstadt. "Leopold City," separated from old Vienna by a canal of the Danube, was the main settling place for Jewish immigrants in Vienna. Sigmund Freud had lived there as a schoolboy. Simon Rosenfeld had moved there from Burgenland, an eastern province near Hungary. Karoline, like Freud, was from Moravia, now part of Czechoslovakia.

Simon, an artisan jeweler, married Karoline in a Jewish ceremony on August 31, 1880, when he was 31 and she 23. A son, Paul, was born nine months later on May 30. Their second child, Elisabet, was born in September of the following year; she died within a few months. When Otto, their last child, was born, Simon was already 35 and Karoline (born the same year as Freud) was 27.[1] (A Rank family tree appears in the Appendix, p. 415.)

Few details remain of Rank's early years. What evidence exists comes from the diaries Rank started when he was 18½.

1

At that age, he summarized his early years in a sentence: "I followed the usual course from first bath to teething, and the usual childhood diseases and unpleasantness such as measles, diphtheria, school, and so forth, in quick succession, only to fall back broken at the first milestone of my dangerous path."

The milestone to which Rank refers was rheumatic fever. Caused by a streptococcal infection, rheumatic fever affects patients diversely, with results ranging from sore throat and joint problems to heart disease. Poor nutrition and overcrowded conditions increase the risk of contracting the disease. Without penicillin, recurrences of the disease are likely. Rank, an unhealthy child, continued to have bouts of rheumatic fever throughout his adolescence, and it contributed to his premature death.

Rank mentions his parents only in passing in the diaries. His father is described as an alcoholic, quiet before drinking and boisterous afterwards, leaving the impression of an inaccessible man. His mother, he says, was satisfied to see her boys decently fed and clothed. A childhood friend gives a warmer picture of the family: "In September 1889, I came from my Moravian birthplace to Vienna, and my friendship with the brothers Paul and Otto began that first day. We children attended the primary school in the Czerningasse, Leopoldstadt. Otto's parents took great care of the young lads, and his mother, especially, was very close to him."[2] Otto's reticence in talking about his parents in his diaries may belie the close relationship he seems to have had at least with his mother.

Rank appears to have had a good relationship with his older brother, Paul. "My brother is so full of the joy of life, without thoughts of the opposite (that is real optimism), that I am quite unable to contemplate his death, and find the thought of it much more painful than the thought of my own dying. That is surely remarkable!"

The two boys usually spent a few weeks every year with their mother's relatives in the country (Moravia). There, just as at home, they were primarily left to themselves—"or, what was worse, to the handymen and maids." Otto felt they lacked parental guidance in many areas—education, religion, perhaps social relationships—yet thought it helped to instill independence in them. Their independence eventually got them into trouble with their father. The brothers had their opinions on many matters and let them be known. Paul, "one of those people whose candor helped rather than harmed," forged a path for his younger brother. When their father asserted his authority, he usually met with hard resistance from Paul and Otto. There were clashes between the father and both sons, but Otto does not describe them. Eventually, there was a complete falling out, after which Paul and Otto no longer even greeted him. An "idyllic" family life followed: blessed silence, punctuated occasionally by screaming arguments, mostly between Paul and Simon. Otto and his mother could not stand the noise and fled from it if possible. Later, Otto went out almost nightly and when home, would plead for quiet so that he could study. This was usually respected.

Otto remarked in his diary that school was his only diversion. Paul went to the Gymnasium (academic high school), while Otto had to enter technical school in preparation for a trade. The older son was given preference in being allowed the better education, leading to a career in law. Otto resented being deprived of academic opportunities: "A second son cannot choose his calling because it must be different from his brother's." Otto pursued learning on his own, reading Schopenhauer, Nietzsche, Ibsen, and many others.

Rank had a good record at Bürgerschule (middle school) and, at the age of 14, went on to technical school and trained for a job in a machine shop. He worked at a shop job arranged by his uncle, "a consummate Philistine and workhorse," but was completely uninterested and bored. Otto still suffered from rheumatic symptoms, and the shop work was too strenuous for him physically. He was transferred to the office. The bouts of joint pain and fatigue then became less frequent, occurring only after great exertion or in damp weather.

"So I grew up, left to myself, without education, without friends, without books," Rank wrote in his diary. Given his parents' modest background, they could not have supplied the intellectual stimulation he needed. He spent much time alone and felt pangs of friendlessness at times. When he was older, he found the lack of friends "no longer deep, for I have learned that friends are mostly props or burdens, in either case bad." Paul, three years older, preferred to associate with comrades his own age, while Otto was drawn more to grown men than to schoolboys. Twice, Otto found himself in traumatic situations, according to his diary. He bitterly alludes to an erotic experience at age 7 with a "friend." At 20, the diarist Rank curses this man for seducing him. "Given my extraordinary curiosity and desire for knowledge and my deep-seated propensity for experimenting, the cornerstone of my later suffering was laid then; it was also the gravestone of my joy." In another incident, Otto says one man took a special liking to him and "thought to show it by enlightening me on some already-mentioned phenomena. Then I really had subjects enough besides school but, as I feared, too little strength for other 'diversion.'"

From his diary we learn that at the age of 15 Otto suddenly awoke to culture, reading voraciously and attending theater and concerts. Paul helped his younger brother—then an apprentice locksmith—by getting student tickets. The first performance they attended was Schiller's *The Maid of Orleans,* which so impressed Otto that he became a steady patron of the performing arts. From then until he was almost 19 (1899 through 1902) Otto rarely spent an evening at home. "The evening illusion of the theater cast a veil over the raw reality of the day," he wrote.

Rank read widely—from Stendahl and Dostoevsky to the works of popular writers of the day, such as the German playwright Frank Wedekind, who satirized middle-class morality and espoused more liberal sexual attitudes. But Rank found his mentors in the nineteenth-century pioneers of a new self and social consciousness: especially Ibsen and Nietzsche. Apparently Otto Rosenfeld took the pen name Rank from a character in Ibsen's *A Doll's House.*[3]

At 19 Otto informally adopted his non-Jewish name and changed his religious registration to *konfessionslos,* "unaffiliated." The Rosenfelds were not a religious family. Apparently there was not even a bar mitzvah. "My parents lived, as Jews now live even in the towns, keeping to one or two Holy Days, customs, usages, and prejudices, leaving the rest to dear God." Among Viennese Jewish writers who had changed their names were Felix Salten, Peter Altenberg, and Egon Friedell. Conversion from Judaism—a bigger step than Rank took at the time— was common for occupational and social reasons, notable examples including Alfred Adler, Hermann Broch, Karl Kraus, Gustav Mahler and Arnold Schönberg. Otto Weininger's conversion to Catholicism had a more ideological basis. Rank's disaffiliation

expressed his intellectual and social independence from traditional religion. The name change separated him from his father
and his Jewish forefathers. Thus he began to create a different
self, a new personality, a destiny of his own.

Rank does not explain why he changed his name from "rose
field" to "slender." The adjective *rank* sounds very much like
rang, "struggled." As a noun *Rank* is sometimes used in the
sense of "crookedness, winding course, tendril, intrigue, trick,
artifice." The young wordsmith must have known these less familiar meanings, which befit the tortuous path and grim milestones of which he wrote.

Ibsen's Dr. Rank was a sympathetic older man, a warm but
sad physician who befriended Nora in *A Doll's House.* Having
supported her personal growth and human rights, Dr. Rank declared his love for Nora, only to be rebuffed. He also diagnosed
general paralysis (neurosyphilis) in himself: "My poor innocent
spine must do penance for my father's wild oats." In the nineteenth century it was thought that heredity and/or degenerate
living caused the disease. Otto Rank feared that his own father,
Simon, exhibited symptoms of such degeneracy, another reason
for Otto to identify with Ibsen's liberal, noble, but hapless doctor.

Rank had little faith in organized religion, and he was tortured by his fear of death, lying awake many nights in childhood
agonizing over the problem. "Especially that never-never-never
coming again, and the impossibility of thinking it through to
the end, flooded me with terrible anxiety." He became convinced that he suffered from syphilis, as in this diary entry when
he was 19: "Today I confirmed slight symptoms in myself of
BRAIN PARALYSIS (I find the words sound so beautiful, says
Oswald Alving)." In Ibsen's *Ghosts,* Alving is the young man
who goes blind in his mother's arms from syphilis, his father's
legacy.

This grim diagnosis re-presented itself to Rank when his father, who often complained of headaches, went into what
seemed a drunken frenzy. Otto was alone in the house with
him when Simon began to bellow hoarsely and beat the table
with his hands until they were bloody. Huddled in a corner,
Otto stared, motionless. Later he reflected on his own constitutional weakness—"from birth perhaps not a single part was completely right"—aggravated by lack of good parental care, and
concluded that he had the dread disease and would slowly die,

blind and demented. For a time he found it hard to maintain his sanity. Within a few weeks—probably feeling better physically—he passed this crisis with a newfound equanimity that left him able to shrug off "petty human needs."

Another incident occurred when Rank first heard that Nietzsche had died of syphilis.

February 16 [1904]. Paralytics usually are, before the outbreak of the last stage of this loathsome disease, highly gifted minds. (Nietzsche, Hugo Wolf. Ibsen lets Oswald Alving, very nicely observed, be an artist.) I believe that happens because the fight they instinctively wage against the disease strengthens the resistance of the menaced organ (brain) and speeds, improves, and refines its function from fear of approaching incapacity.

Otto Rank's diaries consisted of four slender notebooks of lined pages filled with neat black script. They were carefully copied, sometimes months later, from pocket-sized memo books full of penciled thoughts, quotations from reading, references, and cryptic scribbles. A fifth book contains Rank's poems from the same period: January 1, 1903, to July 1905.

Rank modeled his diaries after others he had read: Playwright Friedrich Hebbel (1813–1863) is one diarist he mentions. The two and one-half years of self-observation, from ages 18½ to 21, were intended for Rank's own study and for some vaguely defined posterity, a readership who, Rank said, "may find more than expected."

Certainly Rank changes, in the diaries, from a self-conscious and self-critical introvert to a more confident and self-possessed young man. As the diary progresses, we see Rank gain perspective, showing more empathy, becoming less aloof and rigid. He began to view life with a more disciplined, sober, and moderate response. Wordiness characterized Rank's youthful writing and, to some extent, all his writing. He gives a hint about this in saying that coming to the point leaves him indifferent. This idea foreshadows what he later called "life fear." If one ceases to trust one's feelings because they change, one will withdraw from people, or engage them in a relationship with caution. Later, Rank learned to trust and accommodate change in himself and others.

In the flush of growing self-confidence tempered with humor and a sense of paradox, Rank wrote his own version of the Ten

Commandments, including, "Thou shalt have no God"; "Fathers and Mothers! Honor your children and love them"; "Thou shalt not covet thy neighbor's wife, for there are plenty of others"; and "Thou shalt not be so bold as to want to tell the 'truth.'"

Rank's diaries differ from Freud's famous self-analysis, undertaken at the much later age of 40. *The Interpretation of Dreams* presents Freud's scientific expedition into his own unconscious. Rank sought a more philosophic understanding of life and the mind, an artist's attempt to discern the design of human development in a godless world. No less profound than that of his fellow atheists Nietzsche and Freud, Rank's existential quest moves along the edge of the psychological abyss of meaninglessness. Rank questioned human existence when he was not scorning it, as he followed the philosophers who looked deeply into themselves and, like Nietzsche and Kierkegaard at times, nearly went over the edge into madness or despair. Can one see, learn, feel too much? Can the self-conscious life be lived? These questions stayed with Rank and became part of his later teachings about the creative life and art, about how psychology affects its theorists and practitioners and society in general. Rank, like Kierkegaard and Nietzsche, drove himself to the end point of thought and feeling. "My thoughts behave like circles on water. A little stone makes a dot, from which thoughts spread ever outward until they break on the shores of the unthinkable." Finally, he confronted the paradoxical imperative to live self-consciously. In the diaries, and later in his life, Otto Rank found existential truth in the present, in which living and understanding, experiencing and knowing, unite for some elusive moment. He found that insight and self-consciousness can heal, but can also hurt; dwelling on life's grimness and absurdity defeats life. Religion no longer worked for Rank, and he sought meaning and consolation first in art, then in creative human existence.

The diaries oftentimes read like a stream of consciousness. One does not always know the events in Otto's world and cannot understand the significance of his reactions. The diaries tell little of his personal life. Many pages are filled with notes about his attitudes toward music, women, sickness, death, literature, and, of course, philosophy. Some of the entries read like adolescent yearnings; others foreshadow his later theories. But the diaries are important documents of Rank's thinking life and provide a sketch of the world as he perceived it.

MODELS AND MENTORS

Otto Rank began his diary on January 1, 1903, with a parable entitled "Life and Death." The tale concerns a giant who is busily grinding coffee beans with sadistic pleasure: Their noisy demise amuses him greatly. He replenishes the supply and changes hands when one tires from grinding. Some beans manage to escape the final chute a little longer than others. This is young Rank's caricature of the human condition, a parody of life by a grim observer outside Vienna's gay coffeehouses, where life was viewed as hopeless but not serious.

Rank was isolated, showing his poems and essays to no one, telling no one he was a writer: "I could not bear a confidant." He struggled to be self-critical and self-conscious: "To test every word under the microscope and under the hammer, before writing it down. And even then to doubt its origin and meaning." He goes on to say:

> Many times I read a thought of mine as if it were that of another; it does not occur to me that I could have written something, and I would like to meet the man who authored it. Am I in another state when I write? Is it a higher one?
>
> I see in myself not a steady development but growth by leaps and bounds. I really have periods for certain states. For months I do nothing and then suddenly get into feverish activity. It's like that for me in many other things . . . I believe that in loneliness every idle person starts to think—provided he doesn't hang himself from boredom first.

Just after his nineteenth birthday, there is an entry in the diary in which Rank expresses his despair of ever living fully and creatively, and says his pride will make him die rather than muddle through: "But no middle ground; no cattle-life!" He cannot abide mediocrity. Claiming that Europe has become effeminate and weak, he looks back longingly to a time when the great minds explored life during antiquity and the Renaissance. He then goes on to praise the novel *Max Havelaar* by Multatuli (1820–87), the Dutch author and critic of colonial life in Java. (Sigmund Freud, when once asked to list ten good books, put Multatuli first, along with Kipling, Twain, and Zola.) Rank compared Multatuli's humor to that of Mark Twain, who later became Rank's favorite author. Many of Twain's works had been translated into German, and Twain had lived in Vienna for a year. A celebrity there during Rank's adolescence, Twain wrote about the turmoil in Vienna regarding which languages would be official in the Hapsburg Empire.

An apprentice machinist, Rank pursued academic learning on his own. Much of his diary consists of comments about works he has read, leaving a valuable record of the development of Rank's intellect. He recorded quotations from writers he admired in the diary, which is also his "commonplace book." Rank read Charles Darwin's *Origin of Species* (in German), grasping it readily, the fundamental principles being "almost self-explanatory." Although he found much of it of interest only to specialists, Rank admired Darwin's erudition, modesty, and "real English collector's patience." Can a theory like Darwin's stand apart from a philosophical system? Rank thought not, but noted that Darwin avoided anything intangible or metaphysical, such as the origin of the mind or of life itself. We see here Rank's lifelong concern with ideology, unconscious as well as conscious. The widespread resistance to Darwin Rank ascribed to scientists' envy and popular prejudices. "His colleagues' envy ceased with Darwin's death; the prejudices of a people are lost only with their own death."

Although Rank wrote about many writers, artists, and composers in his diaries, three stand out as intellectual mentors. Rank studied the lives as well as the works of Arthur Schopenhauer (1788–1860), Henrik Ibsen (1828–1906), and Friedrich Nietzsche (1844–1900), whose writings also inspired Rank to study the music of Richard Wagner. Rank compared his development with theirs, growing intellectually and emotionally through acquaintance with the works of great men. Just as societies of average people unconsciously prepare for the coming of a hero or savior, "so must I slowly and unconscious of the goal, plow through a mass of ordinary works in order to reach the solid ones." Of these nineteenth-century geniuses, Ibsen was still living as Rank wrote his tribute, while Nietzsche had died three years before, when Otto was 16.

Schopenhauer was the first of the three to change the way Otto looked at the world. From Schopenhauer he quotes: "Only befogged as it is by the thought of humanity as the highest and only goal can the human intellect call man beautiful in contrast to animals and in regard to the rest of nature."

Rank left Schopenhauer "for a rough journey until at the

right moment I met Henrik Ibsen." Soon Rank came to regard Ibsen as the writer "who best understands and describes human beings." In the play *Wild Duck* Otto recognized his own parents in the main characters, Hjalmar and Gina Ekdal. In a diary entry of October 12, 1903, Otto exclaims "Tragedy of Hjalmar's son—I. Hjalmar's son."

Hjalmar is a caricature of selfishness whose devoted, sensitive only child—Hedvig, 14—lives and dies for his approval. Hjalmar's extreme narcissism blots out concern for others, most importantly his wife and daughter. A hypochondriac and procrastinator, Hjalmar boosts his weak ego with promises about an invention that will make him rich and famous. His modest, tolerant, and industrious wife Gina keeps the family going. Young Hedvig consoles and indulges her childish father despite his insensitivity to her needs. Thus Hjalmar completely forgets Hedvig and returns from a banquet with empty pockets, though he promised to bring back some delicacies. Reminded of this, he hands her a menu: "It's not a great treat, all that fancy stuff . . . read the menu and later on I'll tell you what the different courses taste like." The cupboard at home was almost bare, but Hjalmar had Gina feeding him shortly after his return.

Hedvig is going blind, a tragedy for which Hjalmar pities himself. A turning point occurs when, under pressure from a meddling friend who insists that "truth" is always therapeutic, Gina admits to Hjalmar that she is not sure whether he or another man is Hedvig's biological father. Hjalmar uses this revelation to separate himself from Gina and the innocent child, who then shoots herself. Like *Oedipus Rex*, Ibsen's *Wild Duck* dramatizes the effect of too much truth, or truth brutally applied. It suggests also that a man like Hjalmar—Rank's father—cannot be helped by insight.

Marriage, parenthood, heredity, sight and blindness, the "life lie" or consoling illusion of the average person, and the consequences of intervention by a truth fanatic are themes which make the play rich and still vital today. For Rank, Ibsen provided not only a trenchant analysis of his family, but also a negative view of "truth" as confrontational therapy. The Ekdals, like the family of Oedipus, have essential secrets and delicately balanced illusions. Ibsen's message pervades Rank's therapeutic philosophy, which, unlike Freud's, respects the need for illusions and the hazards of unmitigated self-consciousness.

Rank reflects, in another entry which links playwright, actor, and philosopher:

For a long time I had serious thoughts of suicide which, as Nietzsche says, helped me get past many a night and many a day. Then in reaction came a tremendous love of life and creative joy, which swept me into activity. I definitely decided then to become an actor, and this idea took such hold that I immediately began to study some roles. Vividly I recall how I memorized Faust and declaimed it well instinctively, but with relatively little understanding. Too shy to exhibit my abilities to associates, I never came to exercise the actor's art and so finally lost interest in it. I have noticed generally, and especially in this case, that projects which fulfill me, states into which I commit myself wholly, very soon lose their influence over me. At first I thought that was progress, development, pursuit of the higher; but now I don't trust my moods and wanderings, since I know they are unstable and unreliable.

Friedrich Nietzsche, Rank's "model, leader, and guide," perhaps the most dynamic psychologist before Freud, developed his own working concept of the unconscious. Oddly, Freud always claimed never to have read Nietzsche, yet many of his ideas suggest Nietzschean influences. The German philosopher was well known, though not accepted by academicians during his lifetime. His writings stirred younger intellectuals in the 1890s, when Nietzsche was deranged and dying.

Rank believed his generation was nourished by Nietzsche. "I virtually bathed in Nietzsche's genius, and got a charmed, weather-tight and bullet-proof skin to shield me against attacks from without as I go along my way." Through psychoanalysis Rank eventually came to grips with the human paradox inherent in living self-consciously, but Nietzsche first led him to the brink of self-conscious—existential—ecstasy and despair. Mankind may end, Nietzsche said, by everyone going crazy. "That may have been the situation at the beginning," Rank mused; "then the circle would be closed. But where is the culmination? Moreover, everyone may be crazy already; we have no criterion for that." Rank was to study Nietzsche for many years, turning away from him only when he began to work with Freud.

Much of Rank's energy was directed toward absorbing and understanding the work of these mentors. He does not disparage those who reformulate thoughts expressed by others before them, noting that the average writer lives by spinning out the thoughts of weightier men: He must work back through the original creative process and start afresh. According to Rank, the rest of mankind needs this repetition of important thoughts: "If you repeat something to the mob often, they finally believe it . . . and in the final analysis mankind is a mob." He notes that sometimes one of these thought restorers becomes famous, thus raising the status of the idea, which may then even become attributed to him (Rank's example: Columbus and Amerigo Vespucci). Rank deplored, however, those who make popular slogans out of misunderstood ideas from great minds, displaying cheap intellectual elitism. He discusses the transmission of cultural values in a passage on genius and popular taste.

> *Nietzsche: "Children do not learn from authority or teaching that this melody sounds beautiful." But, that it should sound beautiful to them. If you ask the average person who talks with awe and admiration of Shakespeare, Goethe, or Beethoven wherein lies the importance of these men, he will stutter embarrassedly, stumble, and finally not know what to say. At best he will respond that their works are "just beautiful," that he "likes them." But he also likes the daily vomit of undigested mental food, called* feuilleton *[the section containing light articles, serials, or features] in his favorite newspaper. Whence comes that appreciation? The first opinion, authority; the second, his own taste.*

Although of humble origins, Rank, like many of the philosophers he read, was himself an elitist, and felt the pull of genius. He wrote about self-confidence, "the first condition for greatness," coupled with realism, humility, and humor. In the diary, he offers a ladder of mankind's development, in order from the lowest to the highest:

1. Religiosity. *Smeared with tar, because customs or prejudices are usually pasted on.*
2. Respect for art. *Covered with a sticky sweetness which soon cloys and disgusts.*
3. Worship of women. *Most hang on this rung their whole lives. It is smeared with sweet fly poison, at first intoxicating but later cruelly lethal. One must be light of foot, heart, mind, and free, to be able to slip away.*
4. Inertia. *Here sit the practical people.*
5. Disgust. *Grumblers, sick and morose.*
6. Knowledge. *The learned.*
7. Skepticism. *Skeptics and psychologists.*

8. Philosophy. *Here, on the last and highest, stands the philosopher, if such a one exists. Seldom does one climb so high. That air is too rare and thin, the thoughts also. His powers fail before then.*

THE VIENNA OF RANK AND WEININGER

Otto Rank's Vienna was the cosmopolitan center of Europe. It has been compared to The Athens of Pericles, and to Florence under the Medici. After a long development from pre-Roman outpost to seat of the Holy Roman Empire to capital of the far-flung Hapsburg Empire, Vienna had become a mecca for students of music, art, and medicine. A crossroads city on the Danube, a southeastern conduit from Europe to the Ottoman Empire, Vienna held together a diverse realm of nationalities and ethnic groups and a Babel of tongues, customs, costumes, and currencies. The Hapsburg Empire stretched from Belgrade to Brussels and from Milan to Breslau, having grown since the Middle Ages more by prudent matrimony than by military prowess. Perhaps because languages did not meld—eight were official in parliament when Rank was a youth, and many more unofficial—music, which needed no interpreter, charmed and moved the populace and made Vienna famous.

In 1800 Beethoven conducted the premiere of his First Symphony in Vienna. One hundred years later Freud published his epochal book, *The Interpretation of Dreams*. The one changed music as the other changed psychology. The century between these cultural milestones witnessed revolutionary changes in everyday life, thought, and feeling. Scientific and technological developments included canned food and the camera, the railway and bicycle, the typewriter and fountain pen, the machine gun and anesthetics, and the light bulb, telegraph, gramophone, and telephone. Mozart had died by 1800, but Haydn, Beethoven, and Schubert composed into the century in Vienna, and Brahms, Richard Strauss, Hugo Wolf, Schönberg, and Lehar were active in Rank's time. Like music, medicine thrived in the city, attracting physicians from around the world, including thousands from America. A remarkable group of Viennese physicians were also artists and musicians, and Arthur Schnitzler left medicine to be a playwright. Mathematics, poetry, philosophy, theater, and criticism all flourished. So did anti-Semitism and the beginnings of Zionism.

As of Freud's arrival in 1860 there were about half a million people in Vienna; the population had grown by 300,000 when Otto Rosenfeld was born. The 14,000 Jews present at mid-century multiplied ten-fold by 1900, many of the new arrivals refugees from Russian pogroms in 1881.[4] Hapsburg Emperor Franz Josef came to power in 1848, reigning over a monarchy which lost substantial territory to the new German and Italian nations. His Austro-Hungarian kingdom suffered a terrible shock in 1889 when Crown Prince Rudolph, the hope of the liberal constituencies, died with his mistress in an apparent murder and suicide. When the international celebrity Mark Twain came to Vienna in 1897, he found things so astir politically as "would set any country but Austria on fire from end to end." Yet people could waltz away any thoughts of war or revolution and cleverly say, "It is dis-union which has held our empire together for centuries."[5] Rank, like Freud, grew up speaking German, the dominant language, while belonging to the Jewish minority in an overwhelmingly Catholic nation.

Politically Vienna of the "Gay Apocalypse," as Hermann Broch called it, was a study of change and resistance to change. The fin-de-siècle period combined stagnation and ferment, tired ritual and fierce new imagination. Vienna could dress like a queen, act like a strumpet, and feel quite neurotic. It was a city that "suffered from reminiscences," like Freud's hysterical patients.

During this period of technological and cultural upheaval, changes in politics and religion disconnected generations from their past. Nationalism flowered while traditional belief systems were shaken. The assimilation of individuals and groups was offset in part by a new ethnic sensitivity. Individuals like Otto Rank, lacking father and faith, sought a beacon, a steady direction.

As Rank reached adulthood, the young Viennese philosopher Otto Weininger (1880–1903) produced a literary bombshell: *Sex and Character*. It created a sensation in Europe and beyond, affecting Freud, Strindberg, Rank, and, not least, Adolf Hitler. Rank's diary entry of February 22, 1904, describes Weininger's work with adulation, noting that every argument presented mirrored Rank's ideas and experience: "there it was in my own words." The book appeared in the summer of 1903; a few months later, at 23, Weininger shot himself. *Sex and Character* went into two dozen posthumous printings and many translations.

A scholarly diatribe on the weakness and self-hatred of women and Jews, the book urges freedom from sexual bondage through abstinence. For Weininger, whose erudition and brilliance sweep the reader along, Wagner was the greatest man since Christ, and *Parsifal* the greatest work in world literature. Raising women from slave to animal to human, Weininger wrote, required that male and female abjure the degrading act of sex and move toward a utopia—"until the two be one, until from man and woman a third self, neither man nor woman, is evolved."[6]

Weininger's fame spread, helped along by Strindberg and the drama of his own suicide. The book mentions the work of Josef Breuer and Sigmund Freud on hysteria, and may have introduced young Rank, among others, to the fledgling science of psychoanalysis. Freud had actually met Weininger and read his thesis in manuscript. Later Freud denied knowing him, only to be caught lying about his involvement with the student philosopher. Otto Rank was not the first young genius to approach Freud with a manuscript. The first, Weininger, represents a heretofore unrecognized link between Rank and his future mentor.

Rank soon outgrew his strong affinity for Weininger. His own attitudes toward women and sex were never as extreme. In the early papers of his diary, Rank regards woman as little more than seducer of man and producer of babies: "Who knows a famous woman composer, painter, sculptor, poet, philosopher?" Girls, he observed scornfully, learn theories of piano playing and man-catching and then "perform." He also wrote, with somewhat more subtlety: "The woman is born to acting. In recognition of this fact, Shakespeare only permits men to play in his theater, since he wanted to make an art of acting. With women it is nature." Viewed from the present, statements like these have led to charges that Rank was a male chauvinist. However, he came to value experience over art, which he felt often served as a masculine substitute for living.

Nearing his twentieth birthday, Rank makes it clear he has not yet been close to a girl. He suffered a transient phobia of touching anyone without wearing gloves. That pathological fear of germs and intimacy probably stemmed from his traumatic early introduction to sex. Meanwhile, Otto had allowed chiefly abstractions to excite him: literature, philosophy, drama, music, art, science. That spring the smell and sight of flowers began to stir him.

But Otto found a way to resist sexual passion: He would imagine the beloved's body in an unappetizing state. His adolescent struggle with erotic feeling took a less elegant form than Weininger's but was less extreme and more workable. The very need for such resistance reveals the strength of Rank's sexual drive, and his growing attraction to women. Probably he was resisting masturbation as well, a practice that in those days was still blanketed with medical as well as moral prohibition, and which Rank thought had contributed to Nietzsche's demise. Discussing sexual intercourse, Rank creates a somber dualism: Every pleasure is balanced by pain, and vice versa.

> *Every coitus, the momentary pleasurable sinking into the unconscious feeling of eternity, into Nothingness, is compensated by a death (that of the child) and the momentary painful sinking away into the selfsame unconscious nothingness. Death, the insoluble riddle which life bestows on man. Curiosity and thirst for knowledge will not let him rest; he knows how to get the answer from life—he dies.*

Already Rank was expressing ambivalence about living fully in the passing moment. He felt the universal human imperative toward immortality. Without religion, he found in art a way of preserving part of the self for posterity rather than exhausting it in living. Eventually as Rank's own experience balanced his erudition, Rank found art to be overvalued at the expense of life. In an undated, early romantic essay on meeting a girl, he poignantly expresses the internal conflict between living fully and savoring the event in memory—but without being sure he actually lived it.[7]

On March 19, 1904, Rank took a position in a Vienna machine shop earning 31 Heller (six cents) an hour. He writes of suffering horribly, waking up mornings feeling empty and aimless, and wanting to go to sleep again "at once and forever." At the same time he began to analyze, and remove himself from, two favorite authors. Both Weininger and Nietzsche, Rank decided, admire what they lack and want; what they have, they deprecate. Thus Weininger's sensitive, feminine endowment made him anti-woman. Rank pursued the analysis further:

Great men are usually woman-haters because sensuality, only a momentary stimulus, does not fill their lives as with the average man (as with all women), but hems it in, limits and degrades. But after fulfillment they realize the complete absurdity, aimlessness, and shame of these desires and rage against the woman instead of their own senses, themselves. Ascetics never were enemies of women. Illustrious men project their rejection of lust upon the woman who allays it, only to have it flare up the more violently. Wagner seems always to have composed right after intercourse.

From Schopenhauer's will to live, via Nietzsche's will to power, to Weininger's will to value. One sees that the life of the philosophers becomes more powerful and worthless.

A normal man is done in thirty years. Life brings him nothing new any more. Fortunate are the souls to whom every day of existence is a new birth until their death.

In this passage, Rank offers a dazzling glimpse of his own future development. He uses the concept of projection to explain Weininger's frantic, belabored, indeed hysterical attack on women, making them the sole source and provocation of sex. Rank's own view of coitus may be somber, his reserve toward women still strong, but he no longer shares Weininger's phobia. The keen edge of Rank's analysis cuts to the core of Weininger's fear. Rank admired the power of philosophical thought at the same time that he saw the loss of value—the worthlessness— in the philosopher's life. In tracing the philosophical development of "will," Rank leads directly to his own eventual use of the term, which is notably absent from Freudian psychology. The notion of continuing rebirth of personality is another important, embryonic Rankian concept. About this time, Rank described his mind at work.

True leisure, the mother of every important work, I have not yet managed. Every time I want to formulate something from the empty chaos of thoughts, a peculiar feeling overcomes me. . . . It is the exact opposite of freedom of will, a mixture of disgust with life and creative joy, indifference and interest, thoughts of death and plans for the future. It seizes me like dizziness, as if my head were a dark room, in which, at the midnight hour, spirits carry on their being. So I trace in my brain the thought-arrows shooting around, and, along with the highest, the most trivial things fly through my consciousness like shadows. Especially in the evening before going to sleep I have these attacks, as I would like to call them, and listening to music, when the images follow each other quicker than the notes. The condition reminds me of dreams, which I have very often. At best I protect myself from them through physical work.

ART AND THE ARTIST

Considering that he lived in turn-of-the-century Vienna, it is surprising that Rank did not say more in his diary about art and politics. He did write about drama, as noted, and music, which he called "the most sensuous art. It is a matchmaker among the arts and between people." Rank felt that only two other composers match Wagner's dramatic power and unity of word and tone: Bizet with *Carmen,* and Leoncavallo with *Pagliacci.* These operas meet Schopenhauer's test of greatness, Rank says, because he himself could imagine supplying other texts: Great music stands independent of words.

Rank was ambivalent about Wagner, who created a new dramatic art form but whose music, he wrote, "is a substratum of his sexuality. Heavy, German, sick, mindless passion. How releasing is Mozart's delicate, witty coquetry." Having just heard Hugo Wolf's opera *Corregidor,* Rank said, "Light Wagner, bright, gay, gifted . . . too bad that Nietzsche could not hear it." Rank believed that Nietzsche could not free himself from Wagner—all the less, the more passionately he asserted that he was free. The love of music is something Rank had in common with Schopenhauer and Nietzsche, but not with Freud.

Throughout the diary, Rank expresses both his humility in the face of genius and his confidence that he too is an artist.

I am an artist, even if I fail to bring forth a single work of art. I lack the practical skill and the theoretical basis to be a musician, painter, or sculptor and the general, historical, and linguistic education for poet and philosopher. Well, the skills might be acquired; the rest I have. It seems too late for acquiring these skills systematically; moreover, beginning in youth, because of ignorance, and at ripe manhood, because of knowledge, I have lacked perseverance and focus on a small area. I have tasted too many fruits.

Rank's mind was already a cornucopia, overflowing with ideas and interests. Instead of choosing an art, he would study the artist type, that is himself, one who has a creative gift and drive even if he or she never produces a work of art in the conventional sense. Self-consciousness, he says, is the artist's only good fortune.

Before he had ever read Freud, Rank began to analyze his dreams.

> *Last night I dreamt that fire had broken out in the house where I live. I am on the top floor. There is no escape. I burn up completely, with all my possessions. No one knows I have ever lived. Vanished without a trace. It cannot be thought through. As I awoke, I was still within the dream realm and undertook to write it down. Now, if the house had really burned down last night? And I think about writing it down!*

Rank wants his life to make a difference to someone. Its tracks must be preserved tangibly: in possessions, in works. That means the diary, a play, and some poems. The yearning for immortality became the central point in Rank's understanding of the artist. At this time—he was not yet 20—tangible creation had more meaning for him than human relationships. With amazement Rank observes himself as recorder as well as dreamer, watches himself writing down the dream as though he might have done the same in the midst of a real fire: Art loomed larger than life.

Classic Freudian dream interpretation would uncover a wish, and would use sexual symbolism. The house would be seen as the mother, the fire as sexual passion, the destruction his castration for the Oedipal crime. Nevertheless, Rank's pre-Freudian self-observation—which is not a full dream interpretation—remains a vivid visual poem, a creative condensation of life, death, and immortality. (The German word for poem, *Dichtung,* comes from the verb "to condense.")

A distinction may be made between the science and art of dream interpretation. Freud's science, easily mastered by Rank the artist, reduces the dream to elements of unconscious—often unconscionable—wishing. The dreamer enacts a drama scripted by family and biology; his or her uniqueness becomes no more than a variation on the Oedipal theme. By contrast, artistic interpretation proceeds outward from the dreamer's unique self rather than inward to a predetermined instinctual core. The artist sees and develops what is knowingly wished and willed, not only what is hidden from consciousness.

Freud's use of the Oedipal template for psychoanalysis reflects the creative use of his own experience, which included an unusual family constellation. With a mixture of observation and allegory, he formed a theory of the human family that was widely accepted as scientific fact. Similarly, Rank's awareness of his own striving for immortality in an uncertain universe led him to postulate *that* as the artist's driving force. Freud's Oedipal libido and Rank's need for immortality were personal imperatives articulated by great minds into generalized "truths." The two men complement each other well: a scientist with artistic temperament, and an artist who was intrigued by science.

Lamenting the job that consumed his days and tortured his soul, all for a pittance, Rank passed his twentieth birthday in despair. The previous fall he had written, "At birth one is *given* life; with suicide one first *takes* it. Therefore an act of distinction!" Celebrating this negative act of will was for Rank a declaration of independence from life which contains the seed of a new affirmation. Now, in April 1904, he exclaims "I came near to killing myself. I see no other way out. Why didn't I do it?"

In this mood Rank drafted a long letter to an unnamed friend and potential benefactor, evidently a man to whom he had sent some of his writing. Perhaps it was his family doctor, Alfred Adler, who was involved in a small discussion group on psychoanalysis with Sigmund Freud. Adler's office was on Czerningasse, where Otto was born, and only a short walk from Rothe Kreuzgasse, the Rosenfelds' address during this period.

In the letter, perhaps never even sent, Rank asks that this confession of his suffering be kept secret: "There is nothing more painful for a person than to have to reveal to a stranger, as I am now compelled to do, his innermost thoughts and feelings, like the retina of his soul, in which his whole being is reflected." Otto described his frustration in technical school and the period of feverish activity which followed graduation. Then, in one day, "as if in an ecstasy," he wrote down a four-act play. He felt his genius breaking through; he was like a tool without a will of his own, "a lightning rod of God." There were periods of dryness and exhaustion, which he came to know as the norm for creative people.

In order to feed and clothe himself, Rank continues, he started working in a machine shop, hoping it would leave time and energy for writing. But "I am the kind of man who can do nothing superficial but must follow everything into the last nook and cranny, and each task begun occupies me fully until it is done." Because he could not clear his mind of the awful job, he fell into terrible moods. "I traversed the road to the shop like one condemned who is led into slavery and not simply executed."

Rank thought that he had learned more in the last five years than all mankind had in its whole existence. "But the almost sick brain activity which occurred over a few days last month exceeded all that had gone before. . . . My head hurt terribly, I had fever and was close to madness. . . . I could not even give free rein to my pain." Dissembling with a mask, to appear normal, was the worst part.

Rank calls this confession "the image of a quivering human soul under the microscope, an interesting case for experimental psychologists." He proposed leaving the job and his parents as soon as possible in order to avoid a violent conclusion, and beginning his own career as a writer. He begged the man for a loan, 1,000 Kroner (about $200; over a year's wages for Rank). That would partly support a year in Paris, where he could learn French while earning fees teaching German and then doing translations. He notes that important French psychologists have only partly been translated into German. The draft letter concludes with thanks for any answer, since the person addressed is "the only human being to whom I could turn."

Otto did not go to Paris. When spring arrived, just after he turned twenty, Rank's dark mood had lifted: "The perfume of flowers acts like all pleasant impressions received through the sense organs, bringing sexual excitement. Does sexuality actually move through all nature or does only man find it, or only I?" The isolated romantic felt a strong, sensual pull into life, a force not yet governed by his will, and to some extent a disturbing challenge.

Rank had changed. He began to accept sexual feeling and question it tenderly. He no longer resembled the phobic, self-hating Otto Weininger. Rank writes further of the "anti-sexuality of genius," which exists because such men do not need a child to complete themselves; they turn the unused procreative energy partly to controlling sexual desire, but mainly to their works. He generalizes, saying that the genius rarely has children, but if he does, they resemble him little.

Otto Rank's identity, his evolving self-definition, starts from the depths and reaches for the heights. Born with a poor constitution to a boorish, hostile father and a sensitive, caring mother, Otto cut his weak ties to his past, setting himself apart from his religion and changing his name. A humanist condemned to work with machines to support a seemingly empty life, Rank pursued meaning through books and the arts, and managed to nourish a hungry soul. (Beethoven overwhelmed him; after Rank heard the Ninth Symphony and "staggered" home, all he could write was "There are names—Beethoven!") Rank's passion for music and philosophy distinguished him from his next mentor, Sigmund Freud, who had a strong aversion to both.

Rank's formidable intellect brought him pleasure mixed with pain. He became more moderate, mellower, more complex. He made imaginary companions of authors and artists. His feelings toward women steadily changed from scorn and disgust to wary attraction; he could write of Don Juan, "Not the wild sensualist, but the man who seeks the ideal of woman and cannot find it."

Transcending his brief but consuming attachment to the brilliant misogynist, Otto Weininger, Rank saw as much hypocrisy in men as in women. "Men fear coitus as such (and the forbidden much more), and they call it morality. Man has preached monogamy to woman." Rank concluded that while man's sexuality is a need, woman's is her essence. Because it is higher for her she can also degrade it more. Rank calls man's sexual side "the semblance of will;" woman's "is will." In every woman, Weininger saw a prostitute. Rank saw nothing *less* feminine than the prostitute, "the man among women." Anticipating a major principle of his later teaching, Rank bowed to the power and mystery of emotional attachment: "The man can never think as deeply about love as the woman can feel." This can be taken as a statement of humility and perhaps envy. It speaks to the limits of Nietzsche, Ibsen, Weininger, Freud, and Rank himself.

Death, like sex, terrified Rank in childhood and youth and then became a tolerable thought, even a form of release. He had already entered his last will, *"Mein Testament,"* in his diary.

> As it is possible that I shall not survive my dying day, and the slight physiological change called death can come at any hour, I state here for this unpredictable event my firm and solemn will. Above all I do not want printed announcements to publicize my death. . . . should the news of my death be placed in a paper

> . . . I commission my brother, whom I name as the unrestricted sole executor, heir, and legal successor, to make the following correction. . . . : It is untrue that they who published the notice are deeply moved over my "departure". . . Further, it is unimportant that I was "deeply loved" by them; indeed I never made such an absurd demand, yet, as I must correct it, I was only tolerated by them. Further, the title "vocation" under my name is incorrect—much better to say I was never "called," but a series of needs and accidents dragged me into this business.
>
> Further, it is senseless to impart to "all friends and acquaintances" that "after great, long suffering" or "after brief, slight suffering" or otherwise have I "gently" passed away or "entered sleep." For to measure suffering by length or weight is an affair of small merchant souls, and few people dare to fix in words the substance of their sorrow. But if suffering is a synonym for illness, which is not always appropriate, the length and type of my sickness would only interest doctors. As for the "gentle sleep in the Lord," that can happen to an old woman on the fifteenth rosary. Evidently one "passes on" unpeacefully with noisy organ chords into the house or hotel of the dear God. Good for sleeping, prompt service, prices to suit.
>
> Further, it is of no consequence that my "earthly shell" be "consigned to eternal rest." It is more in order that a rummage dealer (maybe the one person who is interested in my death) buy it, and that my cadaver, as I hope, be burned in a crematorium. Wreaths are to be refused, though not in the mind of the deceased, since no one has fathomed that. Dry foliage, brushwood, and wilted flowers, however, are to be accepted for fueling the fire. Whether the management of the crematorium agrees, I know not.
>
> *Otto R.*

As a therapist Rank later became known for his focus on the ending. As a theorist he viewed each separation, starting with birth, as a painful beginning which human beings must both endure and embrace. As an existentialist Rank focused on living fully in the limited time between beginnings and endings, facing the anxiety and accepting the pain of transience and separation.

"I am a poet!" he exclaimed. "And I might rejoice, that I have already borne so much pain." One of his poems, "To the Old Year," expresses the glory of having ripened quickly, but continues: "What ripens early also dies early." Then: "A shadow, yes . . . without it there would be no light. And the lightning that struck me—did it not illuminate the dark?" The last of the five stanzas says, "I will never be satisfied; always struggle, fight, strive. Peace is the happiness of crowds for whom life is eating and slumber."

Rank embraced the difficult life as the only life. One might think he had no choice, but he made choice the paramount concern, so that living became an act of will. "Thou shalt not give birth reluctantly," he offered as a new commandment to parents: The gift of life ought not be marred by hesitation. Although the newborn receives it helplessly and passively, there comes a time when he or she can choose actively. For Rank, this meant contemplating and rejecting death as a choice. He was excited, challenged, hurt, and frightened by life but he viewed the peace of passive resignation as a living death.

Rank said (to the unknown benefactor) that he could do nothing superficially, that every task had to be carried to completion. If Rank was burdened with a compulsion to persevere he also saw it as a boon. "I have an iron diligence," he wrote in the diary, "the envy of many colleagues, and what I begin I finish effectively and with zeal."

That sentence—it could be Otto Rank's epitaph, a condensed biography—explains much of how this brilliant, long-suffering young man became a leader in the psychological revolution of the twentieth century. Many did envy him. He worked and lived enthusiastically. He transmuted the givens of life by acts of powerful will.

CHAPTER 2

Self-made Soul

Art is life's dream-interpretation.
—Otto Rank, *Diary*,
December 3, 1904

At the age of 20, Otto Rank came to terms with his own identity. He allowed parts of the past to die, so that he could take hold of the present and create a future. Rank made peace with his father, and with his own sexuality and mortality. His diary no longer echoes the hostility toward women that obsessed Otto Weininger. In 1904 Rank moved away from Nietzsche, discovered Freud, and matured from adolescent philosopher into a serious but not humorless young adult, ready to take control of his life. Depending more on experience, less on the ideas and art of others, Rank developed his own personality as a creative endeavor, a work of art in the new era of psychology. Conscious self-formation marks the epitome of Rank's self-study—an act of will. It compares in significance with Freud's self-analysis, which produced *The Interpretation of Dreams*, a work consciously motivated by science as opposed to art, but nonetheless also a creative act of will.

Apparently both a cause and a result of Rank's maturing perspective was a new recognition of his father. Despite justifiable anger and disappointment about his upbringing, Otto now pays respect to Simon Rosenfeld in the diary by accepting paternal traits in himself. Rank now sees that his development proceeded "out of the tendencies of my father" (May 3, 1904).

25

My father's importunate self-praise; my indestructible belief in my abilities.

My father's effort to be witty, his persistent want and embellishment of a striking remark; my preference for clever turns of phrase and the expression of my pleasure thus, in the form.

My father's attempts in reporting a conversation to imitate the tone and bearing of the speakers, to characterize them; my dramatic talent.

His fear of death; my problem.

His appearance of endured, assumed pessimism and his profligate optimistic nature; my apparent optimism behind which is hidden a deep suffering in life.

His dirty sexual appetite; my purified (after a long battle) refined sensuality.

My father's drive to follow (imitate); my fabulous ability to accomodate.

His shrewdness (affected wisdom); my wisdom.

His self-will (caprice); my character.

I could give a longer list of examples. In short I possess his qualities, either projected on the globe, completely built up, softened, often increased to the extreme, or on the contrary, refined. I expiate his mistakes since I transform them into virtues.

Rank's self-hatred has given way to self-acceptance, even pride. His ability to relate some virtues to his formerly despised father indicates a real reconciliation. Within himself the son has separated that of his father which he will keep and that which he will let go. With older, wiser eyes Otto views Simon as a flawed yet respectable character. As in a mirror, Otto reflects the image: respectable but still flawed.

This understanding proceeded out of a remarkable self-analysis. Rank moved from the vicarious perception of his father through Ibsen's psychological caricature to a more complete internalized perception of his own. Rank let Simon Rosenfeld step off the stage into life, so that both father and son became more real. Had Simon been all bad, simply negative, there would have been less cause for conflict within Rank. But having changed his name, left his nominal faith, and set his sights on a career, Otto could look back, emancipated, and see more of a paternal legacy than rage, fear, neglect, and brain disease. Having finally separated from the pathetic but frightening father of his childhood, Rank found a way—and the will—to attach himself once again. Rank's therapeutic triumph recalls that of Mark Twain, who, returning from college, was struck by how much his father had learned in four years!

Another epiphany occurred when Rank seriously contemplated taking his own life. He had previously written about the dignity of suicide as a noble choice in a world where so much of life is accidental and meaningless. But only at this point (May 14) did he make a real choice. Oppressed by the daily grind, and perhaps by loss of hope for a stipend for travel, Rank bought a weapon—he doesn't say what kind—to kill himself. Unlike Weininger, however, he did not use it. "Afterwards," he wrote, "there grew in me the greatest lust for life and courage toward death."

In his moment of crisis, Rank, like other sensitive, self-conscious artists, accepted life with its ending. Having made death a choice, Rank made living an act of will. Choosing a second life, as it were, represents a psychological rebirth. As expressed in a contemporary phrase of psychologist William James, such a person—the divided self, the "sick soul,"—must be twice-born to live happily.[1] Unlike Weininger, a psychological stillbirth, Rank emerged from his self-made womb a soul-artist and sexual man, capable of happiness. Later Rank says: "Life is just an experiment for discovering the secret of death."

Rank sought a soul-father in books, music, and theater, having found his own wholly inadequate. He returned from these mentors to confront his real father at home, in this process becoming much more human. The limitations of everyday life could now evoke humor. "I draw in my tired nerves in the evening and crumple up like an empty balloon." Rank's workaday world of grinding wheels and pounding hammers enervated him. The people he knew did not attract him: Mostly "confined, small, narrow and suffering" they nevertheless provoked Rank to express himself: "Things that long fermented inside that I would not let out . . . now escape from me laughing."

His preoccupation with death continued, but Rank's reflections show more courage, generosity, and openness, less fear and gloom. Referring to his brother Paul, Rank ponders: "We are just as little extant after death as before birth . . . I feel the idea of your death more painfully than the thought of my own. Is that love?"

As Rank's feeling grew to include love, his thought moved

from philosophers to heroes. Napoleon became the subject of a projected biography, which he outlined in the diary. A psychological study, it was to pass lightly over love intrigues. It was to be written in forceful German prose: "French is too light and fine. German words—blows of a club." Rank saw Napoleon's empire as psychologically based, the man as representative of all men of action. He fell because he wanted to control everything himself, but the achievement was his alone. Rank contrasts Napoleon with Hamlet, who enters the scene lacking a worldview, only to be paralyzed by dour reflection. Napoleon acts, and learns from the effects of action; he, like Hamlet, considered the world bad, but believed he could set it right.

There is a parallel here to the later evolution of differences between Freud and Rank. The classical psychoanalyst is reflective, disengaged, and rather pessimistic. Freud had little hope of changing the world; he even professed little interest in changing many patients through analysis. Rank became a more active therapist, enthused about the possibilities of change, both individual and social.

DISCOVERING FREUD

Perhaps Rank first encountered Freud in Weininger's book, or in the newspaper *Neue Freie Presse,* in which Freud wrote some reviews, and which favorably reviewed his *Psychopathology of Everyday Life* (1904). Freud gave a lecture in April at the B'nai B'rith (a Jewish fraternal organization) in which he argued that women's intellectual inferiority was not biological, but psychosocial in origin. Rank may have attended the talk or heard about it.[2] But he first mentions Sigmund Freud on October 17, 1904, as "Freud: *Interpretation of Dreams.*" Within the next two weeks Rank quotes Freud about time and causality in dreams, mentioning the terms "association," and "the unconscious."

Many of the diary entries now refer to dreams; thus, youth is "like a dream, in which a man remembers himself" and: "The dream begins when the dreamer's thoughts become unpleasant (when inner thoughts become oppressive, then art begins, also)." Rank's writing was becoming more aphoristic and succinct, like Freud's. At work on a novel, reflecting on creativity in the diary, Rank says: "Composing (writing poetry) is nothing other than dreaming awake (artistic dreams, willed dreams). The dream 'composes' also; it creates the events, lifts out the essential . . . in poetic creation, the poet as in the dream says much that he would not otherwise, and also veils and displaces as in dreams: He lets it be said by other people." And a profound summation:

> *Life is a dream. Meaning is fate, waking is death. Man's dream is convention, hypocrisy, lies. Truth struggles against it; if it gains the upper hand, the man dies . . . His dream figures are society; his wishes, the will. . . . When Nietzsche could interpret the dream of his life, he began to love his fate.*

Here Rank expresses three existential ideas of lasting importance. First, too much truth or self-consciousness destroys man. Second, will exists, Freud's mechanistic determinism notwithstanding. Third, interpretation makes sense of the apparently meaningless. Meaning—given, found, or created—enables one to love life and live it. We create meaning because we cannot exist without it. Of all creatures, only humans anticipate death, and only humans make interpretations.

Rank began to analyze his own dreams. One took place in a trade school class, another concerns a debt concealed from a friend, the third involves a physical fight with an unknown opponent. All three feature Otto himself. The first is the most complete and coherent: Rank is called upon to solve an engineering problem at the blackboard. In the dream the best student in the class, Rank draws the design upside down, and fears he will be kept back for his mistake. Then he takes the problem to his classmate Johann Stur. Rank's interpretation: The dream expressed his wish for self-respect. Rank wanted to outshine Stur, who was actually the best student. The inverted drawing showed his wit and willfullness. It also (Rank does not say this) expressed his contempt for trade school and the life it led to.

Freud made dream interpretation a tool for the physician, removing it from the control of soothsayers and the superstitious. While Freud had scientific goals, Rank immediately considered the new method in the context of art. Week after week toward the end of 1904 he reveled in the new material, using the diary to record both his agreement and his incipient differences with Freud. Dreams lead back to childhood memories, Rank noted, memories that are barred from awareness until brought across the threshold of consciousness by interpretation. Rank idealized dreaming as a creative life-phase which has to die by waking. The mental turmoil of an unacceptable unconscious is creatively developed by the artist in his work as it is by the dreamer in sleep. Rank modified Freud's main conclusion, that dreams express hidden wishes: "The dream can only be directed to the fulfillment of wishes in the truest sense, and cannot fulfill man's deepest striving nor the core of his highest life." A single dream can in effect fulfill a wish, but "highest willing" requires application of a whole life. Another entry reads: "In a dream the wishes are the driving element, in life the will itself." Freud did not dwell on such exalted ideas. To him the instinct-driven unconscious lay dominant beneath a thin veneer of civilization—man's highest achievement, a costly, fragile product of what he called sublimation.

Perhaps the first flower of Rank's contribution to psychoanalysis, and later to psychology and philosophy as a whole, is expressed in his epigram "Art is life's dream interpretation." Dated December 3, 1904, it suggests that like dreaming, art both conceals and reveals; like psychoanalysis it helps to cure illness but also to understand what is normal and universal. On the same day Rank wrote "I see my fate hovering over me; it treatens to crush me at any moment if I should dare to pit myself against it."

NIETZSCHE: CONSCIOUSNESS, WILL, AND DEATH

Contrary to long-standing misconception, Nietzsche's *Übermensch* (superior person) has nothing to do with the Nazi "super race," nor was Nietzsche anti-Semitic. Rather, he would have admired men like Freud and Gandhi, who combined passion, discipline, will, intellect, and—usually—kindness. Nietzsche's Dionysian will—an exhuberant, creative affirmation of life—was, of course, interpreted differently by such diverse students as Alfred Adler, Otto Weininger, and Otto Rank.

Rank describes vividly in the diary his shock at the news that syphilis had caused Nietzsche's death. "Hitherto I had taken him for a man who was brought into the world by a suffering, nervous father addicted to drink . . . sensitive and instinctively shy . . . diverted to masturbation by his disgust for woman."

Rank strongly identified with Nietzsche, who died in 1900 after a decade of insanity. Earlier Rank had assumed that the death was due to a combination of factors: The legacy of a degenerate father, masturbation, and "unwholesome, grinding, enervating mental activity." On November 28 he exclaims "But syphilis! I could not grasp it. Probably because it shattered my pretty theories."

Having dealt with the indignity of Nietzsche's madness, Rank reflects back to when he was 7, thirteen years before:

> *On Czernin Street in the evening, in our house, the two rooms, one behind the other, dining room and bedroom. The connecting door was opened wide against the wall and my mother sat on the threshold between the rooms and wept. My father strode through both rooms with huge comedian steps and raged. I cowered in a dark corner of the bedroom and trembled with fear.*

This episode, like the later one when Simon beat his hands bloody on the table, led Otto to conclude that his father—and he, also—had brain disease. Less fearful now in young manhood, Otto accepted his father's traits with a modicum of respect, and he tempered Simon's bombast with a comedian image as though to quiet his childhood terror. Rank suffered not the plague of syphilis but he endured and transcended the emotional plague that results when a child must be more mature than his parent.

That Nietzsche's sickness could be so tawdry perplexed Rank, who felt his own heterogeneous soul balance close to the edge of sanity. Nietzsche said that ambivalence was a precondition for self-analysis. He, Kierkegaard, and Rank were well endowed in that respect. Their ambivalence toward father and sexual women brought turmoil, deep analysis, and monumental self-expression. Ironically, scientists discovered the role of the father and the sexual woman as transmitters of syphilis, the biological plague of minds, just as Rank was struggling with his heritage, his masculinity, and his own sense of genius.

Although suspected to exist earlier, the microorganism causing syphilis was not discovered until 1905; only in 1913 was it demonstrated in the brains of victims of general paresis.[3] However, since the syphilis spirochete crosses the placenta, newborns also contracted the disease—a parental sin visited upon generations to come. Given these complex routes of contagion, the delayed consequences (years to decades), and the fact that not every partner of a syphilitic contracts the disease, it is no wonder that unproved theories abounded up to the time of Rank's maturity. Ibsen wrote of the dismal inheritance of brain paralysis in his *A Doll's House, Wild Duck,* and *Ghosts,* all favorite plays of Otto Rank. Nietzsche's father died with a softened brain, and Nietzsche, who was virtually sexually abstinent, speculated about the inheritance of madness. He also viewed insanity as one logical outcome for a sensitive man facing the world without illusions.

In the nineteenth century, science had revolutionized biology. Notions of heredity and evolution were built upon new knowledge of plants and animals, gleaned from the microscopic study of cells and bacteria. Some fundamental ideas which today seem very old emerged only after 1850: "Every cell comes from a cell" (Virchow, 1855); Pasteur's proof that bacteria come only from other bacteria; Darwin's theory of natural selection, *On the Origin of Species,* was published in 1859. Gregor Mendel set down the genetic secrets of garden peas in 1866, and Galton worked out aspects of human genetics, including studies of genius and of twins. The genetic transmission of hemophilia had been known since 1820; that of color blindness since 1876.

Philosophers and mystics rode the tide or were swamped by the waves of science in these decades. One theory, perhaps by coincidence, finds an echo in the will of Nietzsche and Rank: "Orthogenesis" posits an inner force that guides organisms along their evolutionary path. That force can push a species beyond its adaptive tolerance, into extinction.[4]

To Rank, Nietzsche's syphilis reduced his madness from a self-created mental illness—a price of, and refuge for, genius—to a miserable sexual accident. Like Kierkegaard before and Rank after him, Nietzsche suffered from ill health most of his life. All three were preoccupied with the relationship between body and soul. Nietzsche's favorite philosophers—Socrates, Pascal, Spinoza, and Schopenhauer—were all "primarily concerned with the cure of sick souls," and for Nietzsche "a genuine philosopher was essentially a physician of the interior self." Nietzsche believed that the well won't care for the sick; true healers also had to be sick. Furthermore, he wrote, moral innovators had to cultivate madness, real or feigned. Ultimately Rank accepted in Nietzsche what Freud could not: Consciousness is often pathological; philosophy and art are therapeutic.[5]

Despite Freud's disavowal of Nietzsche, a passage like the following shows a kinship between the philosopher and the psychoanalyst:

Men were thought of as free—in order that they might be judged and punished; but consequently every action had to be regarded as voluntary, and the origin of every action had to be imagined as lying in consciousness. In this way the most fundamentally fraudulent characteristic of psychology was established as the very principle of psychology itself.[6]

Catholic and other theology could not penalize sin if human action was involuntary, will-less, as when governed by an unconscious. Religion fostered the psychology which Nietzsche attacked philosophically, and Freud scientifically. Without will there is no responsibility, without responsibility, no sin. (Original sin was not in essence sexual, but was rather the defiant assertion of human will against God's.) Before Freud, will had a place in psychology equal to that of emotion and intellect. With Freud the will virtually disappears, swallowed up by the unconscious and biological determinism. Despite major differences, Nietzsche and Freud have in common their respect for the irrational and the unconscious. This new psychology clashed powerfully with established religion.

Nietzsche and Freud differ profoundly, however. Although just twelve years younger than the German philosopher, Freud adopted a scientific view of the psyche. In the nineteenth century that meant cause led to effect, and mechanisms could be found to explain the relationship. If an observer had enough scientific knowledge, the human mind would yield its secrets. Laws of nature govern the operation of the universe—everything from snowflakes to the conduct and consciousness of *homo sapiens.* Nothing in nature is free to determine itself. To Freud, will belonged to outworn moral philosophy and pre-scientific psychology, a romantic illusion employed to ward off harsh truths. Despite his own formidable will, Freud put most willing down as wishful thinking.

This doctrine offended both the religious and the romantics, for whom will was a dignifying, consoling idea withal its burden of responsibility for sin. The radical removal of will caused as much controversy as Freud's emphasis on sex, discussion of which was nothing new in medical circles. (*Psychopathia sexualis* [1886] by the Viennese psychiatrist Richard Krafft-Ebing, had been translated into seven languages and reached its twelfth edition by 1902. But Krafft-Ebing, who both criticized and supported Freud at times, was a Catholic who viewed sex as properly a procreative function.)[7] Although Nietzsche celebrated will in his philosophy, his religious iconoclasm equalled Freud's. Nietzsche argued from subjective ground, from his inner experience of will as wonderful and terrifying. He was an artist, a philosopher-poet. Freud argued objectively, using inner experience as case material.

Rank's diary at the end of 1904 shows his skillful juxtaposition, not to say integration, of will and wish, or conscious and unconscious motivation. Rank, the great reader, had found Freud, the great writer. Encompassing both Freud and Nietzsche, Rank set out on a new path to study the soul, its creativity and its sickness.

LOVE, ART, AND DREAMS

To begin the new year 1905, Rank quotes Kierkegaard in his diary: "Every man who takes cognizance of himself knows what no science knows, for he knows how he himself is." This states the subjective argument which Nietzsche articulated further; Freud, of course, began with self-knowledge but generalized it as a science rather than as art or philosophy.

Rank was now describing positive feelings in the diary, including erotic ones, and he was focusing less on illness and death (although still suffering head, leg, and foot pains). He recalls how, in youth, he felt happiest going to sleep with thoughts of being a mighty magician, picturing great "(sexual)" things he could do. Rank imagined the growth of a child inside the mother's body and her various emotions and sensations, comparing this to carrying a creative work inside himself. He decides that woman is unfit for artistic production because she stands closer to nature than man, whose yearning for the completeness of nature draws him to art.

Meanwhile, Rank completed three stories which he liked. Different settings of one dream, they "had to be written (as dreams must be dreamed) just as they are." The dream (and presumably each story) ends when something is going to happen against his will; on waking, the obstacle to the will is gone. As he did in maturity, so even then Rank gave the conscious—waking, willful—mind priority over the unconscious.

Relating the story to its source in his inner life, Rank noted that there is always something in creative work that is not for the crowd, perhaps not even for fellow artists, unless it is pointed out by the artist's artist, an "interpreter . . . more gifted than the artist himself." Was that Sigmund Freud? Reading *Interpretation of Dreams* one encounters a brilliant storyteller, whose weird but charming tales come out of the creative sleep of ordinary people. An artist among dreamers, Freud interpreted the deeper meaning that is not for the crowd.

Grounded in a new creative optimism, Rank sketched his ultimate philosophy of life.

> *The most beautiful thing in an artist's life is that which he cannot work out. An artist, whose creative work would be his life! The peak! If the whole man, whole life, is not contained in every moment of life as the sea in its drops, then life makes no sense! What does nature make of the myriad lost days, hours, lives? How much advantage the least of the living has over the greatest of the dead!*
>
> *To best describe something, think of a person you love and to whom you want to tell it.*

For the first time Otto Rank sounds like a lover—of life, and of someone. In the diary he recalls again the fantasy of performing magic while falling asleep, one which he still experiences. His thoughts go to a waking dream, then to a real dream which, however, ends with sound sleep. Since he labeled the magic "sexual" just a few weeks earlier, we know there was a woman in mind in the silence of the night. In an undated manuscript, "Diary of a Stillborn," probably of this period Rank tells of a young man's romantic interlude with a woman. But he could not hold on to her, only to the memory.

Rank continues to reflect on his own creative work (January 28): He is not cut out simply to write novels, poems, or essays; he had already "looked too deep into the workings of the world." Still, he could not define another goal, but watched carefully the "struggle between science and fantasy in me." Freud, too, had struggled to resolve an inner conflict between the scientific and the speculative study of the inner life. Freud and Rank combined art and science, the romantic and the positivist, but in different proportions. In 1905, nearing 21, Rank came to the crossroads in life that Freud had reached at 17. Rank read Freud on dreams at a critical moment, just as Freud had heard an essay on nature attributed to Goethe. All three were men of great intellect coupled with powerful but restrained passions. Rank marked his discovery of Freud with an exclamation in the diary (February 15): "A medically proven artist!"

Rank began his first psychoanalytic essay early in 1905, on the artist. Fragments and references appear in the diary, interspersed with personal reflections on reading, music, compassion for animals, and other topics. Rank's appreciation for Freud's epochal discoveries in *Interpretation of Dreams* was matched by his struggle to keep faith with his old mentors and to find a balance among them. In late March, Rank opined that Schopenhauer was the greatest of all men: "In him, according to his own theory, the intellect reached such clarity about itself that it recognized its dependence on the will." Taking Schopenhauer's doctrine as the most beautiful hypothesis ever, but as no more than a hypothesis, Rank considered the personal consequences of deep insight: "If Schopenhauer's teaching were right, would there not be a total transformation (rebirth) in everyone who recognized its 'truth'? The person who perceives the *core of his innermost being*, the goal and limits of all life, cannot go on living in the same way he has heretofore. But perhaps the fact that, in spite of this knowing, he can, just proves the rightness of the Schopenhauerian doctrine of 'Primacy of Will'; the intellect is now secondary for once and may not *in all* its expressions keep raising itself above the will."

At age 20, self-taught philosopher Otto Rank first stated what he elaborated long after completing his formal education and serving as apprentice to Freud. In the ideological contest between will and intellect as governing forces, Rank cast his vote for the primacy of will. Insight achieved through intellect can change a life, paralyze the knower, or be pushed aside. If will is primary, then intellect yields to it so that life, for better and for worse, can be lived.

Rank respected intellect, with the caveat that it could paralyze and petrify the creative mind. Conversely, Freud respected irrational emotion, in himself and others, and set out to master it scientifically, with intellect. In Rank's psychoanalytic study of the artist he wanted to find the sources of creativity without destroying them. By becoming the first Freudian to analyze art and the artist, Rank also positioned himself to protect the artist's soul from annihilation by overzealous dissection.

Rank was likewise protecting his own soul, his capacity to

will and live creatively. In music, which Freud never analyzed, Rank found a haven. He called music "only the reiteration of the excited unconscious" and quoted Schopenhauer: "Music is not the image of an idea, but the image of the will itself." Rank's musical soul might well have resisted the analytic probing of the physician-interpreter. But Rank was not content with passive protection. Asserting the primacy of will in relation to life and art, Rank secured the basis for existential optimism in his inner battle. On March 28, 1905 he wrote:

> *Everything comes from "living." How can one merely write, as long as he still expects to live? Art until now has been falsely motivated. Life itself must be formed artistically, wholly in and of itself, not placed next to another artistic or artist's life. Real living must be created so that it has need of no other life, no art, beyond itself.*

Rank continued to express his own beliefs through his reactions to books. During this period he read the letters of Elizabeth and Robert Browning, Emerson's essays, and Shakespeare's sonnets (all in German). He quotes Leonardo da Vinci: "The greater the man, the deeper his love." Rank recorded some passages in French, psychoanalyzed the Wagnerian Ring operas at length, and explored some early writings on dreams referred to in Freud's work.

Steeped in Wagner's music, Rank studied his biography and wrote about Wagnerian heroes, myths, and dramatic art. Rank esteemed Wagner highest among the species "artist," empathizing with the composer's "constant dissatisfaction with the life of the present," even under favorable conditions—"the suffering of genius."

> *Just as the dreamer opposes negating voices (suppression) not only with affirming promises and hopes, but by treating wishes as facts, so the artist not only counters oppressive, threatening life with his power of resistance, his abilities, his individuality, his genius, but he embodies that all in doing, in the art work. Great artists always had to struggle and suffer. In the dream, wishes are guided through the burning point of the will and generalized. In art work it is the task of genius to lift out of individual wishes the genuine, universally human.*
>
> *The outer world (convention) is for the artist what the censor is for the dreamer. The solitude into which the artist flees compares*

with the peaceful rest the person seeks in sleep, wearied of strug-
gling with the outer world: Then the "person" dreams, the artist
creates.

Dramatic art is the interpretation of the life dream: *the seeming*
loosely connected ongoing scenes made understandable to all . . .

In the dream we feel only our own emotions. Through music
the emotions (inner self) of every single person are revealed.

In dreaming, when wish fulfillment is thwarted, we change the
scene or wake up. At a play it is always possible for us to switch
back to reality if the illusion has taken us too far; we then see it
was only a play (dream).

Not surprisingly, Freud was immediately taken with this young
man, whose draft essay on the artist must have included many
of the ideas expressed at this time in the diary.

In the diary Rank becomes more open and more personal.
Where before there was lamentation about sex, he now acknowledges a positive power. The best sedative would be coitus, "the
real wish fulfillment," but the imagined is also a means "for
wiping out consciousness." He is enthralled with introspection,
the most exciting, rewarding experience of all: "Joy streams
through me in such moments. But I cannot entice these moments
at will, they come over me from time to time as though to
strengthen me, so I can endure."

Without naming them, Rank reveals that there are three people he values. One whom he sees daily has things Otto lacks:
skill, courage, blind optimism, iron will, ambition. It is satisfying
just to be with him. The second, a married man with children,
is seen less often. There is high-level discourse, but he is older,
settled, of firm opinions, his character *"frozen;* completely my
opposite." But Otto was learning tranquility from him. The third
is not seen at all. "I long for him the most; same age, much
like me, in much superior; flexible mind, keen judgment, iron
industry, admirable understanding."

What I lack, I love in the three. I am alone, all alone. *(No one*
can think through that to the end who has not felt it through to
the end.) I have no one with whom I speak, no one to whom I
can write. Most and the best stays in me, as nourishment (in the
good and bad sense), the rest is diary.

It was April, 1905. The third book ends with a flurry of quotations and thanks to "I. H. V." for guiding Rank to a knowledge

of practical psychology. "The diversity in me is the most wonderful thing I know."

THE SOUL DIVER

The fourth and last diary, beginning April 10, 1905, shortly before Rank's 21st birthday, covers less than three months. It begins provocatively: Why record thoughts at all? The few great thoughts worth preserving are unforgettable, so there is no reason to write them down! Shortly thereafter the diary becomes a register of quotations, a commonplace book filled with names ranging from Lao-Tse to Luther, along with Seneca, Ruskin, Voltaire, Kant, and even the Talmud. Despite his alienation from Judaism, Rank enjoyed the wisdom of the rabbis. Example: "If a stone falls on a jug, poor jug; if a jug falls on a stone, poor jug. Always, poor jug!" The only use of English in the diary: "Hell is paved with good intentions" [Samuel Johnson, 1775]. In one passage Rank improves on the famous iceberg metaphor of the mind.

> *April 19. The "soular" in man is like the sea, the surface of which symbolizes consciousness. Data that come into consciousness change like the waves which rise on the surface. In general, always the same part of the soular entity—its surface—is active, while the inner, the deep, rests motionless and only occasionally a few bubbles come up. Perhaps a few storms occur which are powerful enough to stir the sea from its profoundest depth—so that for once the innermost would come up? No! But there are divers!*

Schopenhauer compared consciousness to the surface of the earth, the interior being unknown. Another comparison likens the mind to an iceberg, the larger part (the unconscious) being under the surface. The iceberg metaphor comes from G. T. Fechner (1801–1887), German psychophysicist, whose theories greatly influenced Freud.[8] Rank's metaphor makes the unconscious deep, translucent, and inviting to the intrepid, active explorer.

As Rank was self-taught, he came relatively late to Goethe. Rank comes alive in quoting passages from Goethe's *Sayings*, as the maxims closely matched his own thoughts, even his own words. There is joyous anticipation of "the woman who is made for me," appreciation for the beauty of dawn, the mixed perfume of flowers in the park, and his nature as a poet, which perhaps resulted from his being alone so long. He is not sure he will remain a poet, and observes (with Goethe? he queries) that one cannot combine living and thinking simultaneously; alternating them is best. At about this time, Rank began to come out of his isolation and make social contacts.

In the diary, Rank puzzles over the memory of blind people, who do not have pictures with which to associate sounds; his examples are bird calls, of the cuckoo and the stork, which he had recently heard for the first time. The blind person has to concoct surrogate images, unnecessary for the normal person: "Therein lies the superiority of a blind person . . . he is forced to go to the bottom . . . where the sighted sees no more. The blind poet: the *Seer* Homer: the inner eye at cost of the outer." (In *Oedipus* the seer is blind and the hero blinds himself, finally, after seeing too much.) Later Rank was to write a major study of Homer.

For a man who would spend his life in three different language environments—German, French, and American English—the following is notable: "A foreign language is more useful before one completely masters it: for making things concise. If you have something to impart in your mother tongue, try expressing it in the foreign language and you will be astonished, how much superfluous has fallen away."

Having reached 21, Rank devoted himself to an essay on the artist, an ambitious attempt toward a psychological understanding of the motives and social role of the creative type. He placed the artist psychologically between the dreamer and the neurotic, sprinkling epigrams of his own among dense paragraphs, e.g., "Instinct is the unconscious of animals" and "Religion is the synthesis of poetry and philosophy." The writing is clear and self-assured, with references to wide-ranging authority. Rank talks about the rules of art: how the artist knows the rules, although an art work cannot be created by following them. Then does the hysteric know the rules by which his illness is formed? "Perhaps not entirely, for then he would be the doctor."

Rank felt that suffering was inevitable for the artist. One cannot spare the creative individual "that terrible conflict with the world," nor can the conflict be introduced deliberately. "You cannot 'bring up' an artist." In creating, the artist hovers between life and death; he chooses between suicide and creating, between hysteria and art.

Reflecting on Ibsen, Rank now placed him somewhere between good and bad. Good dramatists make their characters develop before our eyes, while bad ones describe them. Only the sophisticated appreciate some of Ibsen's teachings (such as the need for "life lies," illusions). The average playgoer hears a message directed to others and applauds. The only ones who really understand it are above average, and they don't need to be told.

MEETING FREUD

A draft letter dated May 1905, separate from the diary, seems to be addressed to Freud and refers to a visit to Alfred Adler the preceding October. Rank read *Interpretation of Dreams* for the first time then, followed by *Studies on Hysteria* (1895), by Breuer and Freud. In April, the letter goes on, Rank went back to Adler to borrow *Interpretation of Dreams* and, with deepened psychological understanding, analyzed twenty-two of his own dreams. The novice then proposed an alternative interpretation to one of Freud's own dreams; we do not know whether he had the audacity to send the letter, but he may well have. Like Freud, he loved ideas and loved to share them; both men put diplomacy second to "truth" on some occasions. In the diary on May 4, Rank refers to "Prof. Freud"; nowhere else does he use a title in this way, which suggests that he had met the father of psychoanalysis personally by then.

The date of this crucial meeting cannot be fixed more precisely than the spring of 1905. Ernest Jones, Freud's official biographer, misstated the year and the title of the manuscript: "In 1906 Otto Rank presented himself to Freud with an introduction from Adler and the manuscript copy of his little book *Art and Artist.*" Anais Nin, relating what she heard from Rank much later, said he was taken by a friend to Dr. Adler because of lung trouble, where Otto spoke so thoughtfully of Freud that Adler brought him to the Professor, whose pupil Rank became in 1905. Freud himself gives no year: "One day a young man who had passed through the technical training school introduced himself with a manuscript which showed very unusual comprehension." Freud either forgot or snubbed Adler in this history, written after their bitter quarrel.[9]

In late spring, Rank makes enthusiastic, probing, ebullient entries in the diary. Reveling in Freud's work, Rank expands on it to meet his own concerns. "The people are the unconscious, the poet its consciousness." Recalling the rush of thoughts during creative periods, Rank compares that "higher state" to the more passive one of hypnosis, which excludes criticism. He links poet, hypnotist, and interpreter of psychoses with this mental state, comparing his own writing process to that of free association and the phenomenon of resistance. On May 13 he ecstatically declares that he can see everything clearly, "the world process is no longer a riddle . . . I can explain *everything*. What shall I do with the rest of my life?" And a few days later he noted that the world process moves not in a circle but in a mounting spiral, and "in every saying there is a chain of the unconscious; you can analyze *everything*."

The notion of cure appears too, but it is more of a Nietzschean than a Freudian concept. Rank compares the therapeutic function of the dream interpreter to the actor who transmits the playwright's vision to the audience. Rank extends this notion of a group or societal "cure" to the newspaper ("the most popular cure: where one can read everything forbidden"), and to wars, religion, and art. He sketches a psychology of religion (June 6):

Old Testament: *the human is bisexual; man gives birth to woman.* New Testament: *the human is heterosexual: woman gives birth to man. But the man thus born becomes God, becomes bisexual again, enters Paradise, raising himself to solitude away from union (sexual).*

Rank was at this point reading Freud's recent works. The diary mentions erogenous zones and forepleasure, themes of Freud's *Three Essays on the Theory of Sexuality* (1905). Still, in the midst of discussing hysteria, cure, and sex as a driving force, Rank asserts his own ideas, e.g., "Religion is a generalized philosophy; philosophy is an individualized religion." Since *Three Essays* first appeared in the summer of 1905, Rank evidently had access to a manuscript or galley proofs; his special tie with Freud began, as we have seen, in the spring of 1905. In a footnote in his first book, Rank mentions attending a lecture by "the Viennese physician Dr. Alfred Adler (April 1905) at the Teachers' Temperance Union." Recalling his first book, *The Artist* (1907),

Rank said that it was written in 1905, and subsequently revised
with changes suggested by Freud.[10]

The diary winds down with fragments, ideas, and epigrams,
including some chaff, confusing but never dull, from the *Artist*
manuscript. There is one personal revelation, in an entry written
April 16 but transcribed later:

> *When a person knows the compass and extent of his capacity to
> grow, he ought really to die. The masters never come to know them-
> selves completely: so for them death comes too soon. The more
> timely one dies, the earlier was he ripe, perfected. What then has
> one to await, who really knows himself? For what should his life
> continue? (Today, 19 July 1905 I would answer "living"; at that
> time [April] I believed the highest "living" consisted in mental
> creativity.) Instead of "Know Thyself," I would write over the gates
> of the temples of modern thinkers: "Seek to Know Thyself." The
> search—that's the most important thing.*

There is a fifth notebook, of poems, written during the same
three year period, the subjects of which include mother, aunt,
female friend, death, exhilaration at learning, and, quoted here,
a cap for the diary with a pun on "Rank," which as a verb means
"to creep/climb around, as tendrils."

Hauptmotto zur Gesamtausgabe der Tagebücher

*Soll ich Euch einen Spruch zur Widmung
    des Buches voran stell'n?
Sehet: mein ganzes Sein
    als* Otto Rank *sich's darum.*

Motto for the Collected Edition of the Diaries

*Shall I give you a saying to dedicate this book?
Look: my whole being as* Otto Wraps *around.*

—Verse 56, August 21, 1905

With this playful ending which goes back to the beginning like
the palindromic Otto, the bold young man marks his arrival as
an artist at the threshold of life.

"Every great thinker," he wrote near the end of the diary,
"considers himself the pinnacle of 'evolution.' That belief is the
noblest kind of 'egotism.' " Otto Rank had found a new mentor,
benefactor, and father-surrogate in Sigmund Freud, one of those
great thinkers and noble egotists.

CHAPTER 3

Sigmund Freud

> The uppermost idea with Hellenism is to see things as they really
> are; the uppermost idea with Hebraism is conduct and
> obedience.
>
> —Matthew Arnold, *Culture and Anarchy*, 1869

No longer can one person absorb the whole corpus of writing
by and about Sigmund Freud. His published work comprises
some two million words—twice as much as that of Shakespeare's
output. Freud wrote a yet unscaled mountain of letters, almost
all by hand; some 900 to Martha Bernays during four years of
courtship, and perhaps 2,500—still unpublished—to Sandor Ferenczi, next to Rank his favorite disciple. There are dozens of
Freud biographies, scores of reminiscences, and countless critiques. Not only the field of psychology but everything that psychology touches has been changed in this century by this man
and his followers: literature and the arts, the social sciences,
philosophy, religion, politics, and our understanding of history.

A man of protean interests and Promethean will, Freud loved
to read and found diverse mentors, from Hannibal to Goethe.
Looking back in time, one finds an enormous range of influences
on Freud, just as, looking forward from the beginning of this
century, one finds little his ideas have not touched. Besides the
classics (he was at home in Greek and Latin, and knew some
Hebrew) and the great German writers, Freud knew enough
Spanish to read Cervantes, enough French to study with Char-

cot, and enough English to delight in Shakespeare, Dickens, George Eliot, Disraeli, Thackeray, and Twain; he also translated a volume of John Stuart Mill into German. Freud hoped at an early age to be a statesman or lawyer, then abruptly changed at 17 to an interest in biology and medicine. He prolonged his medical studies by doing laboratory research, and his first published papers were on anatomy.

Authorities on Freud differ about the sources of his ideas and the reasons for his monumental impact. Some consider him a poet in scientist's garb, others the reverse. All agree he was an exceptional writer and speaker. Somewhere between the extremes—that he was a biologist masquerading as a psychologist, or the other way around—all would agree that he digested and crystallized the old and creatively synthesized the new. Freud was both a product of his time and a prime mover of history. The nature of his contribution to human understanding is still not fully understood, nor has its worth been agreed upon.

A personality of so many sides and strengths yields something to a study of his weak spots. Freud acknowledged at least three: a lack of understanding of philosophy and of music, both of which he tried to avoid, and the inability to judge character, which is surprising but is supported by evidence. Although at 17 Freud told a friend he had read Nietzsche, later he spurned his own strong philosophical leanings in favor of the scientific side of his personality. Freud's well-known lack of musicality has been interpreted as a sign that he could only enjoy what he could analyze. Freud attended the opera more than once, and could whistle a tune, so it was not a matter of tone deafness. "I feel no need for a higher moral synthesis in the same way that I have no ear for music," he wrote. "But I do not consider myself a better man because of that."[1] He kept away from synagogues and concert halls and had to brace himself to bear the presence of musicians in a Viennese café.

Freud was born on May 6, 1856, in Moravia (now Czechoslovakia), in the same area and the same year as Otto Rank's mother, Karoline Fleischner. Sigmund was the first child of his mother, Amalie, and the third of his father, Jakob, who had two sons from an earlier marriage. Jakob was 40, Amalie 20 when they married, just nine months before their son's birth. Jakob, a wool merchant, was already a grandfather at the time, so "Sigi" became an uncle at birth: His nephew John, a year old, lived nearby, and became Sigi's inseparable companion for three years. Five sisters and two brothers issued from the marriage within a decade. Freud was concerned with hereditary weakness and found evidence of "neuropathological taint" in one branch of the family, to which he attributed a "tendency to neurasthenia" in himself and in his favorite sister, Rosa. Freud's first brother died soon, when Sigi was nineteen months and could remember, with mixed pleasure and guilt, the first loss of a rival.

Nephew John was a special object of Freud's love and hate in early childhood. Freud wrote, "An intimate friend and a hated enemy have always been indispensable to my emotional life; I have always been able to create them anew, and not infrequently my childish ideal has been so closely approached that friend and enemy have coincided in the same person; but not simultaneously, of course, as was the case in my early childhood."[2] Fliess and Jung most clearly exemplify this pattern in Freud's adulthood, along with, to a lesser extent, Breuer, Adler, Stekel, and Rank.

Freud's first sister, Anna, was born when he was two-and-a-half; her birth coincided with the abrupt departure of his Czech-Catholic Nannie (to jail, for stealing). "Freud never liked that sister," Jones wrote, but Freud's youngest and favorite child had the same name.[3] With Sigmund's mother halfway in age between him and Jakob, the family constellation constituted a riddle for the boy. For a time young Freud thought Jakob and Nannie were the senior couple or grandparents, while half-brother Emanuel and Amalie were his parents. He had to reconcile this logical pairing with the fact that Jakob and Amalie shared a bed.

"Goldene Sigi" as she called him, was his mother's favorite; thus Anna's music lessons came to an end to placate her 10-year-old scholar-brother; his study room was private but not soundproof, so the piano had to go. By this time, 1866, the family had been in Vienna for six years, living in the heavily Jewish Leopoldstadt, where Rank was to spend his youth a generation later. Freud started Gymnasium a year early (at ten) and stood first in his class. For the final examination Freud had to translate a portion of Sophocles' *Oedipus Rex*, the play which held his attention from then on. An essay, "On Nature," led him away from law to medicine. The essay, attributed to Goethe, portrays nature as a challenging but rewarding female; thus, "One obeys her laws even if one resists them; one works with her even if one wants to work against her. . . . She has isolated everything in order to draw all together. With a draft or two from love's beaker she compensates for a life of toil and trouble."[4]

Sigmund's half-brothers had emigrated to England, and he made his first visit there at the age of 19, in 1875. A lover of the language, Freud read widely in English throughout his life. He visited England only once more before emigrating to London in 1938, the year before his death, a reluctant refugee from Nazi-controlled Austria.

Young Freud's choice of medicine as a career was well suited to his inquisitive mind. It was also an idealistic way to relieve the suffering of humanity. Later, self-analyzed, he denied altruistic, therapeutic motives: "My innate sadistic disposition was not a very strong one, so that I had no need to develop this one of its derivatives."[5] For Freud the analyst, strong altruism exists mainly as a reaction to unconscious sadism.

Freud believed that many traits derive from opposite impulses in the unconscious: "Reaction formation" is the term he used to describe that defense against unacceptable wishes. Applied simplistically—which even Freud did—the idea puts all goodness in a bad light and vice versa. Thus: Helping masks the wish to hurt, heroism masks cowardice, passivity hides aggression. (In response to a question about how much philosophy he had read, Freud answered, "Very little. As a young man I felt a strong attraction towards speculation and ruthlessly checked it."[6]) Under this much-abused approach to human understanding, little can be accepted at face value, and the observer acquires a cynical and pessimistic bias.

Biographer Ernest Jones describes a marked shift in Freud's personality in late adolescence, from a combative, active lad who admired military heroes to an intense scholar who valued understanding more than action. Freud gave up his fantasy of becoming a statesman not because he lost ambition, but because he found another source of power: solving riddles of the human condition.

Freud studied medicine between ages 17 and 25 (1873–81). He spent several years in the physiology laboratory of Ernst Brücke, his most influential teacher. This great scientist painted for recreation, studied art history, optics, and philology, and was a museum curator. Other influential teachers were psychiatrists Theodor Meynert, a brain anatomist and poet who disdained "treatment of the soul," and Richard von Krafft-Ebing, author of the famous text on sexual psychopathology, who pioneered in the study of syphilis and paresis.

The philosophical climate of those years combined strange partners. Scientific positivism, associated with the French philosopher Auguste Comte (1798–1857), led away from theological and metaphysical explanations to observable phenomena, the data of science. Science and technology produced many changes in society and the landscape and promised many more. Medicine made progress in such basic areas as bacteriology, embryology, and the understanding of the nervous system. The introduction of anesthesia gave new scope to surgery, but asepsis became widespread only late in the century. Psychiatry as a medical specialty originated in the early 1800s, but, of course, little could be done "scientifically" for the insane. Tuberculosis and syphilis disabled and killed multitudes. These and other scourges (like malaria) gave up their secrets to science and became treatable only after Freud's medical training. Numerous treatments of the time, like nonsterile surgery and bloodletting, actually harmed patients, while a few, like digitalis and vaccination, helped. Most "remedies" neither helped nor harmed, and the wise physician realized that nature did most of the healing. From this awareness came the doctrine of therapeutic nihilism, that diagnosis was everything and treatment almost nothing.

According to the positivist extreme, man should eventually have enough knowledge to grasp the position of every atom in the universe. Then, applying the laws of physics, he could explain every event in history and foretell everything to come! Many of Freud's teachers subscribed to that kind of materialistic, mechanistic ideal. Freud himself thought mental illness would someday be reduced to a matter of biochemistry. What he learned from Meynert was a static psychopathology based on brain anatomy. Meynert's approach used the most advanced microscopes and tissue-preparation technology, but his theorizing, though touted as science, was as fanciful as any romantic philosophy. Critics rightly put it down as "brain mythology" and "speculative anatomy." Even Freud scoffed at those who tried to link psychiatric diagnosis with the colors—the staining characteristics—of specific brain tissue under the microscope.[7] Given this context, Freud's subsequent experiments with cocaine and his use of hypnosis were bold steps away from static anatomy into dynamic physiology, psychology, and therapeutics.

SEEKING A BREAKTHROUGH

In 1882, at age 26, Freud became engaged to the beautiful Martha Bernays, 21, of Hamburg. Their wish to marry helped him decide to leave the laboratory for the more lucrative practice of medicine (neurology). Freud hoped for a therapeutic discovery that would bring fame and fortune. On April 21, 1884, the eve of Otto Rosenfeld's birth, Sigmund wrote Martha of his prospering practice.

> *I have been reading about cocaine, the effective ingredient of coca leaves, which some Indian tribes chew in order to make themselves resistant to privation and fatigue. A German has tested this stuff on soldiers and reported that it really rendered them strong and capable of endurance. I have now ordered some of it and for obvious reasons am going to try it out on cases of heart disease, then on nervous exhaustion . . . There may be any number of other people experimenting on it already; perhaps it won't work. But I am certainly going to try it, and, as you know, if one tries something often enough and goes on wanting it, one day it may succeed. We need no more than one stroke of luck of this kind to consider setting up house. But, my little woman, do not be too convinced that it will come off this time. As you know, an explorer's temperament requires two basic qualities: optimism in attempt, criticism in work.*[8]

In July, Freud published a paper extolling the benefits of cocaine in various conditions, from asthma to morphine addiction. He called it a stimulant and aphrodisiac. Unfortunately, the morphine addict he treated soon became a cocaine addict. Meanwhile, two colleagues picked up and pursued an idea of his that led them to discover the use of cocaine as a local anesthetic. Freud continued to promote cocaine for various ills, only to be criticized by Meynert and Krafft-Ebing, among others, on grounds that its harmful effects outweighed any therapeutic value.

Despite the need for money in order to marry, Freud decided

to go to Paris to study with the great neurologist Jean-Martin Charcot. With the support of Brücke and Meynert he won a traveling grant for six months, beginning in October 1885. Freud considered this Paris sojourn the opportunity of his life. He returned to Vienna imbued with Charcot's dramatic psychological approach to hysteria.

The passionate courtship continued, meanwhile, having survived Sigmund's jealousy and tyrannical possessiveness toward Martha. Freud pressed her to share his dislike of her mother and her brother, Eli. He even boycotted the wedding of his sister Anna and Eli. In his biography, Jones notes this lack of diplomacy, "an art in which Freud never achieved much eminence."[9] In a rare display of self-doubt, Freud expressed his fierce but unwarranted jealousy of Martha's cousin Max, a musician and imagined rival, and forbade her to speak of him by name. "I think there is a general enmity," Freud wrote her, "between artists and those engaged in the details of scientific work. We know that they possess in their art a master key to open with ease all female hearts, whereas we stand helpless at the strange design of the lock and have first to torment ourselves to discover a suitable key to it."[10] Judging by his love letters, Sigmund found the key more through passion than analysis. The two married in 1886. Within a decade they had six children, three girls and three boys.

Within that same decade, Freud, a neurologist fascinated by hypnosis, created the science and art of psychoanalysis. He introduced the term in 1896, borrowing "analysis" from chemistry. With Josef Breuer, one of Vienna's most respected physicians, Freud produced *Studies on Hysteria* in 1895. The book presents the famous case of Anna O., first treated by Breuer in 1880. Amnesic for German, Anna O. spoke in English, naming Breuer's cathartic method "the talking cure." Breuer lent Freud money and referred patients to him over a number of years. Despite— or perhaps because of—Freud's indebtedness, the friendship did not last. Their work together was favorably reviewed, and William James abstracted part of it—resulting in the first mention of Freud in America.[11]

In 1896 Freud's theory held that traumatic sexual events in a person's childhood were the cause of psychoneurosis: The child had been molested by an adult, usually a family member. The event might be forgotten, but at puberty or afterwards something could revive it or its representation, which then acted as a trauma. If the child had participated at all actively, with pleasure, then there would be self-reproach expressed as obsessional neurosis. Passively experienced trauma caused hysterical neurosis. Hence males, who were more often in the active category, suffered more from obsessions, while hysteria afflicted more females.

Within a year the theory was a shambles. Freud decided he had been fooled by his patients' "memories," many or most of which proved to be fantasies. Jakob Freud died in October 1896, after Freud had broken with Breuer and was deep in self-analysis, involving interpretation of his own dreams. Freud found the psychological model of the human family in the Oedipus myth while reacting to his father's death, "the most important event," he wrote, "the most poignant loss, of a man's life."[12] Freud was then using free association and dream analysis with patients and confiding in his close friend Dr. Wilhelm Fliess, a surgeon in Berlin.

FRIENDS AND RIVALS

Two years younger than Freud, Fliess became his confidant in the mid-1890s. Freud's letters to him, like those to Martha and later to Jung and others, combine passion with intellectual virtuosity. Fliess provided emotional and scientific support which Freud reciprocated with respect to his comrade's theories on bisexuality and periodicity. Fliess believed that each person has a feminine cycle of twenty-eight days and a masculine one of twenty-three days. With imaginative permutations of these numbers one could "explain" or "predict" many things, including one's life expectancy. But this pseudoscientific exercise was an illusory triumph of positivism. Freud wrote Fliess excitedly about his discovery of the role of childhood sexual trauma and his conviction that he could cure hysteria and obsessional neurosis in some cases. "As a young man," Freud wrote revealingly, "my only longing was for philosophical knowledge, and now that I am changing over from medicine to psychology I am in the process of fulfilling this wish."[13] Fliess, Freud's peer, was the transitional person between those who taught Freud—Brücke, Meynert, Breuer, Charcot—and those taught by Freud after the turn of the century.

Despite his strong philosophical bent, Freud tightly controlled any tendency to speculate. Though he gave artists the edge in courting women, Freud disdained unscientific types as "people who have no occasion to submit their inner life to the strict control of reason."[14] Of course, one man's reason can be another man's fancy. Fliess's numbers only masqueraded as science, like Meynert's psychiatric mapping of the brain and Freud's use of the Oedipus myth. The Viennese *Künstler-Arzt*—artist-physician—was a well-known phenomenon in those times, but art and medicine kept to separate paths. Brücke had his art and philology, Breuer his music; Meynert wrote poetry, Arthur Schnitzler became a leading playwright, and famed surgeon Theodor Billroth was a fine pianist and intimate of Brahms. Freud's nonscientific interests were literature and collecting ancient artifacts, a hobby that merged science with art and paralleled his interest in the archeology of the mind.

As an adolescent, Freud identified strongly with a character from Cervantes; biographers have overlooked its significance.[15] The character, Cipion, appears in "The Colloquy of the Dogs" (1613), a picaresque tale in which a vagabond mongrel tells his story to a compassionate canine listener. Freud and Eduard Silberstein were high school friends who studied Spanish together. From the "Colloquy," Sigmund became Cipion, the quiet commentator, while Eduard was Berganza, the garrulous one. The two, guard dogs at a hospital, had the gift of speech for only a day, and Cipion instructed Berganza to tell his life story first. Cervantes' two characters—the sage commentator and the charming, sometimes maudlin hysteric—interact within strict time limits. Cipion never gets his turn to confess or regale; as in the "talking cure," there is no reciprocity. Cervantes' tale unfolds a charming parody of the human colloquy called psychoanalysis.

Freud neither concealed this remarkable identification (he wrote to Martha about it in 1884), nor did he refer to it in writing on the origin of psychoanalysis. Rather, Freud focused on whether he or Breuer deserved credit: "I have never heard that Breuer's great share in psychoanalysis has earned him a corresponding measure of criticism and abuse; and as it is long ago now since I recognized that to stir up contradiction and arouse bitterness is the inevitable fate of psychoanalysis, I conclude that I must be the real originator of all that is particularly characteristic in it."[16] Breuer had told Freud of his work with

Anna O. in 1882; the case impressed Freud, and after his return
from Paris the two men collaborated. From hypnotism and the
cathartic method Freud elaborated psychoanalysis, using free
association and dream interpretation in place of the older techniques. This creative shift came in the 1890s, during which time
he broke with Breuer, probably his most important mentor.
Meanwhile, Freud forged a strong attachment to Fliess, whose
sexual theories matched Freud's in boldness if not in durability.
Though far off in Berlin, Fliess appears to have become Freud's
closest colleague since Eduard Silberstein.

In September 1897, Freud confided the error of his seduction
theory of neurosis in one of many letters to Wilhelm Fliess. This
reversal temporarily daunted his confidence in curing patients,
whose visits to 19 Berggasse (his home and office since 1891)
provided Freud's hard-earned livelihood as well as much research material. His self-analysis went forward, with dream interpretation the dominant element since his discovery, in 1895,
that unconscious (repressed) wishes provided the key to the
meaning of dreams. Patient hours fluctuated from a few to a
dozen daily. Freud worried about poverty at times as he pressed
on with the writing of *The Interpretation of Dreams.* The book,
at once a scholarly treatise and a selective autobiography, appeared late in 1899. By then Freud felt isolated from the medical
community; whether or not his pique was justified, he refused
to present his work to physicians because of their mixed reactions
to his earlier formulations. Freud did lecture on his ideas to
audiences at B'nai B'rith. After 1902, when his (assistant) professorship finally came through at the University of Vienna, he
lectured there. The title "Professor," used by Freud's colleagues
thereafter, gave his practice and his new psychology a major
boost in prestige-conscious Vienna.[17]
Freud's relationship with Fliess, beset with increasing tension, finally came apart. Freud's approach to the mind became
increasingly psychological, while the Berlin surgeon pressed for
a biological emphasis, elaborating his pet themes of periodicity
and bisexuality. Freud lamented that he could not yet fit together
the organic and the psychological, concluding that "I have nothing, either theoretical or therapeutic, to work on, and so I must
behave as if I were confronted by psychological factors only."[18]
Freud voiced envy of the originality, beauty, and "simple

coherence" of Fliess's work, convinced that its publication would bring immediate acclaim regardless of its ultimate worth. By contrast, publication of *The Interpretation of Dreams* left Freud frustrated with the gap between the problem and his attempted solution, "and it will be a fitting punishment for me that none of the unexplored regions of the mind in which I have been the first mortal to set foot will ever bear my name or submit to my laws."[19]

The two men met in the summer of 1900. Sigmund stated, as though he had originated the thought, that the solution to the problem of neuroses must be based on the presumption of bisexuality. Wilhelm responded that the idea was his own, but when he had broached it two years before, Freud had rejected it! Freud pondered the matter for a week until his amnesia cleared; Fliess had been right. Freud's frankness in presenting the episode in his *Psychopathology of Everyday Life* (1901) is commendable. He admitted how painful it was to be asked to "surrender one's originality." Freud's admission, however, fell short of an apology. He did not endear himself to Fliess, or regain his trust.[20]

In October 1900 Freud was analyzing Hermann Swoboda, a 27-year-old psychologist. The patient observed that fantasies of defeat as well as victory could be pleasurable. Freud told him that our being "now incubus and now succubus vis-à-vis events" is to be explained by our bisexual constitution. Smitten with the idea, Swoboda forthwith told his friend Otto Weininger that Freud attributed man's dualism to an organically bisexual disposition. Weininger, then 20 and working on his doctoral thesis, seized and elaborated the idea as his own: One could no longer separate humans (or other organisms) into two sex categories. "Let it be noted clearly that I am discussing the existence not merely of embryonic sexual neutrality, but of a permanent bisexual condition." Thus he introduced his "new" conception in the manuscript which became *Sex and Character* (1903). Although there were references to both Freud and Fliess in the book's lengthy appendix, they did not relate to this theme, the main platform of the work. Weininger's book was a sensation, aided by his suicide in October 1903. He left his books and papers to his friend Hermann Swoboda.[21]

Early in 1904 a book appeared by Swoboda on periodicity in relation to both body and mind (since developed into the

"science" of biorhythms). The book was brought out by Deuticke, publisher of Freud's and Fliess's books. Swoboda briefly
acknowledged Fliess's work, but claimed to have made his discoveries independently and asserted priority on their psychological application. Freud renewed the shriveled correspondence
with Fliess in April, mentioning Swoboda's book, "the intellectual originator of which I am in many respects, although I
wouldn't want to be the author." Freud called Swoboda his "pupil." In the same letter he proposed collaboration with Fliess
on a new journal.[22]

On July 20, 1904, Fliess, very upset, wrote Freud about *Sex
and Character.* "Weininger obtained knowledge of my ideas
through you," Fliess charged, naming "pupil" Swoboda as intermediary. He pleaded for a candid explanation. By return mail
Freud agreed that "Weininger broke into private property with
a key he picked up by chance." This time he called Swoboda
a patient, not a pupil, brushing the whole thing off as a normal
discussion in treatment about bisexuality, a theme that could
also be found in Krafft-Ebing. Freud denied any part in Weininger's infringement: "I did not read his book before publication."
Freud promised to credit Fliess in his own forthcoming book
as the one from whom he first learned the importance of bisexuality.

Fliess played his trump card by return mail. He had learned
from his brother-in-law Dr. Oskar Rie, a Viennese pediatrician
and Freud's colleague, that Weininger had met Freud and discussed the controversial manuscript with him before its publication. Fliess rebuked Freud for failing either to warn him or to
stop Weininger. "We might have asked for a better reason for
our correspondence than this debate over a plagiarist. Let us
hope that the future will bring us one."[23]

Trapped, Freud once again confessed to Fliess and analyzed
the fault. He had read the Weininger manuscript, recognizing
Fliess as the source of the bisexuality idea. Then he simply told
Weininger not to publish the book because it was nonsense.
Recalling the earlier conflict with Fliess, this time Freud ana-
lyzed his behavior as expressing his own wish to steal the idea.
He admitted giving Fliess's ideas away through Swoboda. "I have
often secretly reproached myself, as I now do openly, with my
generosity or carelessness in making free with your property."
Having confessed and analyzed the fault—a large one—Freud

tried to justify himself. It would have been futile, he claimed, to try to stop Weininger, who could have maintained that the idea was his own. Then Freud expatiated upon the history of ideas: Forgetfulness, unconscious plagiarism, even deception are inevitable, and "you cannot take out a patent on ideas." He doubted anyone would take *Sex and Character* too seriously, and chided Fliess for only finding time to correspond "on such a trivial matter."[24]

This reaction made Fliess furious. Freud had made his offense into a trivial matter, and then reproached the victim! In a manner that proved to be characteristic, Freud confessed his unconscious wish, forgave himself, and expected the injured party to forget the offense. Freud viewed psychoanalysis as a rigorous discipline, requiring confrontation of difficult truths. It can also be used as a weapon against opponents and a shield for oneself. Rank was perhaps the first to point out that psychoanalysis, like other intellectual movements, is a consoling ideology for its adepts. Thus Freud confessed to the high priest—himself—and received absolution. That was supposed to satisfy Fliess.

Otto Weininger had in fact brought his manuscript to Freud in the fall of 1901, a year after Swoboda passed on the idea of bisexuality. Freud did not like what he read. But he described the visitor as "a slender, grown-up youth with grave features and a veiled, quite beautiful look in his eyes . . . a personality with a touch of genius." Much later Freud wrote that he was the first to read the manuscript and the first to condemn it. "In the manuscript Otto Weininger gave me to read there were no depreciatory words about the Jews and much less criticism of women." Without mentioning Fliess, Freud scolded Weininger: "You have opened the lock with a stolen key."[25]

The situation exploded in 1906, when pamphlets were published on Fliess's behalf attacking Weininger and Swoboda for plagiarism. Freud's incriminating correspondence was printed without his authorization. Swoboda sued Fliess unsuccessfully. Freud defended himself, Swoboda, and Weininger against the "slander" by Fliess. "I myself did not know Weininger before he wrote his book," Freud wrote to journalist Karl Kraus.[26]

This claim, blatantly false and easily disproved, almost defies explanation. Perhaps Freud made a petty distinction between Weininger's *manuscript* and his published book. Swoboda was on Freud's side by then, Weininger was dead, and Oskar Rie might have been sorry enough about his role to have backed away from Fliess. Freud's memory for some things was short. He was also desperate then and very angry, describing Fliess to Kraus as a brutal and petty personality.

Although crediting Fliess here and there in his publications, Freud omits mention of him in his autobiographical essay. Fliess is awarded the dubious distinction of having triggered Freud's theory of paranoia—that it follows from a repressed homosexual relationship: "My one-time friend Fliess," he later wrote Jung, "developed a dreadful case of paranoia after throwing off his affection for me, which was undoubtedly considerable. I owe this idea to him, i.e., to his behavior. One must try to learn something from every experience."[27]

To protect himself from public reproach, Freud distorted the truth and sacrificed a relationship. His self-reproach for carelessness, for being an accomplice in theft, did not make him repent. The unhappy Fliess was left distrusting Freud, and for good reason. Diagnosing adversaries, as Freud did with Fliess, became a frequent practice in the political arena of psychoanalysis. From the beginning, Freud's science was a tool for divining the source of illness. Even when it matured into a general psychology, psychoanalysis remained focused on the base elements in human functioning and their modification or socialization. Diagnosis, the psychoanalytic scalpel, was wielded all too soon in political combat as well as in the pursuit of knowledge and the art of healing.

Freud's emotions were as strong as his formidable intellect. His closest friendships were as passionate, while they lasted, as his attachment to ideas. When a serious flaw developed in a theory or in a friendship, he abandoned either with decisive vigor. The apology Freud offered mattered less to him than his unflinching acknowledgment of base motive. Having confessed envy, hostility, or some other fault, Freud forgave himself and expected his friend to do the same. In this case, having failed to receive the absolution he required, Freud charged Fliess with hysterical or paranoid exaggeration of trivia.

Even Ernest Jones acknowledges Fliess as Freud's intimate friend for a decade, and begrudingly admits that the Weininger episode was "perhaps the only occasion in Freud's life when he was for a moment not completely straightforward." But Jones agrees with Freud that the episode was trivial, and praises him for "manfully" confessing that he wished to steal Fliess's ideas.[28] Freud and Jones in concert disposed of opponents on several occasions. Adler, Stekel, and Rank were to suffer a similar ostracism and they were at Freud's side when the Fliess episode erupted in the Viennese press.

RANK INTERPRETS FREUD

In Freud's life as in his theory, knowing dominated being. Rank began that way but changed. By the time he published his first manuscript, Rank had raised a question which remained central for him: Can one live fully and self-consciously? Unlike Freud, Rank valued subjective engagement—reality—over objective knowledge—truth. Rank's philosophy placed being, the ontological, ahead of knowing—the epistemic. In Matthew Arnold's sense, Rank identified with the Hebraic ethical imperative, Freud with the Hellenic scientific ideal. Freud's pessimistic determinism not only diminished his therapeutic zeal, but also blunted the ethical sensitivity that accompanied Rank's individual will.

Rank's analysis of Freud began early—around the time they first met. Among his youthful papers is a draft letter, probably never sent, supplementing and criticizing Freud's interpretation of his own "Frau Doni" dream. In his diary, as we have seen, Rank had argued that an artist cannot be "brought up," but can only be forged in a fearsome conflict with the world. In reinterpreting Freud's dream, Rank takes issue with Freud's mention of a poetic son, his eldest: "F's son cannot become a great poet because he protected him up through puberty from all real harm. But on the other hand, from the psychological riches and keen insight of the father, from his half-poetic, half-scientific talents (studies-stories), his perception of people and relationships, it could well be possible! And that would be most interesting (the first case of its kind!)."

The genius as touted by young Otto required a traumatic life history, one which he found in the biographies of many poets and in his own. Rank respected Freud and, while probably envying his son such a father, wondered whether such a blessing would deny the son life's hard-won insights, an artistic gift, or philosophical depth.

Rank concluded that Freud's reference to a poetic son reflected Freud's wish for immortality! The only children in the
Frau Doni dream were two little girls. The dream occurred
on the eve of his eldest son's birthday. Freud interpreted it to
mean he was pleased to be a father. Turning the tables on his
future mentor, Rank decided that Freud ignored his own wish
fulfillment in the dream. Rank's interpretation: Freud wished
not to have children. Freud disposed of his wife in the guise
of the recently deceased Frau Doni, and envied P., a rival, his
freedom from parenthood and his highly successful career. Rank
wrote that Freud's interpretation was "scientific disguise," hid-
ing rather than revealing the unconscious. Freud's sense of satisfaction on awakening from "Frau Doni" can be attributed to
something quite different from having children. Rank saw it
as a comfortable evasion of the unpleasant wish to be rid of
them. Freud's quest for immortality embodied the wish to make
a mark on the world himself—with his genius, not his genes.

Rank regarded the introductory Latin motto of *The Interpretation of Dreams* as a metaphor for Freud's unsuccessful struggle
to resolve doubt and fear. "If I cannot move the heavens above,"
the motto says, "I will stir the powers below." Applied to Freud's
condition by the 21-year-old self-taught analyst, it meant, "If I
cannot convince people of the correctness of my theory, I will
at least soothe my unconscious."

Although he was to serve as Freud's devoted secretary and
wholeheartedly took to the role of pupil, Rank started with a
critical perspective on Freud and never lost it, as evidenced
by his assertiveness in meetings of the Vienna Society. Endowed
with a great mind, raised by a sensitive mother amidst hard
knocks and loneliness, Rank came to accept suffering as a condition for creativity. Encountering Freud, Rank tested whether
a great thinker could both protect a son and stimulate his genius.
Rank accepted surrogate fatherhood from Freud, aware of the
older man's gifts and also at least some of his blind spots. Inspired
and chary at the same time, Rank launched his filial relationship
with a father who may indeed have wanted immortality without
paternity.

Compulsively honest, Freud did not hide his ambivalence
about family life. Once, in a doubled-edged denial, he said he
could have become famous at an early age if not for Martha.
He left his research on cocaine in 1884 to visit her, leaving it

for a colleague to discover the drug's use as a local anesthetic. "But I bore my fiancée no grudge for her interruption of my work."

Freud complained, if only mildly, about the burden of raising a large family, which was incompatible with the demands of a research career. Six children between the ages of 10 and 18 lived at home, along with Martha and her younger sister, Minna, whom Freud valued as an intellectual and traveling companion. At 49 Sigmund Freud had six siblings plus the two half-brothers in England, his mother, and a total of eighteen nieces and nephews. (A chart of Freud's family in 1905 appears in the Appendix, p. 416.) More than once he expressed disappointment with his sons, whose careers did not impress or please him. And although he analyzed himself as a son—thereby launching the Oedipus complex—he scarcely touched on his feelings or his performance as a father.

THE END OF FREUD'S ISOLATION

Freud described the interval between his work with Breuer and the formation of a small group of disciples as a decade of "splendid isolation."[30] He thus expunged Fliess from the record, although it is true that Freud had no special friend in Vienna during those years.

Wilhelm Stekel, who had been in brief analysis with Freud, suggested a weekly meeting of a few Viennese colleagues to discuss psychoanalysis. This group consisted of Max Kahane, Rudolf Reitler, and Alfred Adler, all physicians. In autumn 1902 the five doctors met at 19 Berggasse for a discussion of the psychological implications of smoking, and the lively session, with Freud as leader, was repeated and formalized as the Wednesday Psychological Society. The Society expanded to twenty, but usually no more than a dozen attended. Nonphysicians included music critics Max Graf and David Bach, publisher Hugo Heller, and Otto Rank, who began to record the minutes of this group, the embryonic Vienna Psychoanalytic Society, in October 1906.

Before Rank arrived with his manuscript, Freud had already met at least two outstanding young scholars with manuscripts: Otto Weininger and Hermann Swoboda. The first he had dismissed, though not without admiration. The other he treated, tutored, and shrugged off. Swoboda never joined Freud's Wednesday group, but he was more concerned with Fliessian periods than with psychoanalysis. When Rank, the unschooled locksmith, came to Freud, he was greeted with enthusiasm. "We induced him to go through the *Gymnasium* and the University," Freud wrote, "and to devote himself to the nonmedical side of psychoanalysis. The little society acquired in him a zealous and dependable secretary, and I gained in Otto Rank a faithful helper and co-worker."[31]

By the time Rank joined the group, they were a devoted band who followed the Professor in awe, having memorized the new "Bible" of psychoanalysis, Freud's *Three Essays on Sexuality* (1905). (This book and *The Interpretation of Dreams* were the only ones Freud kept updating through the years.) Freud was also getting some notice in the press, through summaries of the Wednesday sessions prepared by Stekel.

Freud's daily routine consisted of seeing patients from 9:00 A.M. to 8:00 P.M. with a long break for lunch and a vigorous walk around the Ringstrasse. He did his professional writing and correspondence, all by hand, until about 1:00 A.M. On Saturday nights there was a regular game of cards. Freud smoked twenty cigars daily most of his long life and slept seven hours a night, soundly.

Sigmund Freud had started a therapeutic revolution. Neurotics once seen by neurologists who neither cared nor helped much might now be listened to intently. It was therapeutic for the patients just to encounter physicians who were both interested and professional. These patients often burdened their regular doctors, who tolerated or perhaps welcomed them if they had status and money. Freud recruited such patients to study and treat their problems. He had physician friends in spite of his controversial ideas, but he needed a broad referral base; his contact with nonmedical intellectuals was helpful. Freud embraced a wide circle of friends and interests although he was a marginal man in certain respects: a Jew who disdained religion, a physician who shunned the medical society, a philosopher who avoided philosophers. His coveted title of Professor helped his practice, through which Freud rescued a class of patients who suffered form medical opprobrium as well as from symptoms of hysteria, anxiety, compulsions, depression, impotence, and guilt. With a mixture of pride and humility he led them away from a sterile neurology toward a fruitful psychotherapy. Grandiose dreams of glory and paranoid sensitivity to attack might be expected to accompany a brilliant and determined prophet like Freud on his long march to the promised land: a whole new scientific psychology.

FREUD AND HIS CONTRADICTIONS

Freud's psychoanalytic ideology, as we have noted, consoled him for his lapses in diplomacy and ethics. As the premier psychoanalyst he was the supreme judge of himself and others. In 1924 he claimed in regard to the Fliess-Weininger matter: "In my answer to Fliess I reproached myself and expressed my regret at the chain of events in a rather exaggerated way, including a self-tormenting reference to the role played by the unconscious."[32] This conveys no apology, no sense that Fliess must be asked for forgiveness.

If Freud reproached himself without much shame, he also praised himself without much pride. The Freudian view places responsibility for good and bad in human affairs mostly beyond our control. Surprisingly, Freud found his intellect wanting but his conduct faultless. In a letter to the American neurologist James Jackson Putnam, Freud expressed satisfaction with having been "a very moral human being."

> *I believe that when it comes to a sense of justice and consideration for others, to the dislike of making others suffer or taking advantage of them, I can measure myself with the best people I have known. I have never done anything mean or malicious, nor have I felt any temptation to do so, with the result that I am not in the least proud of it. . . .*

> *When I ask myself why I have always aspired to behave honorably, to spare others and to be kind wherever possible, and why I didn't cease doing so when I realized that in this way one comes to harm and becomes an anvil because other people are brutal and unreliable, then indeed I have no answer. Sensible this certainly was not. In my youth I didn't feel any special ethical aspirations, nor does the conclusion that I am better than others give me any recognizable satisfaction![33]*

Freud was playing devil's advocate to challenge Putnam's idealism. He concluded his argument with a characteristically humble boast: "If the knowledge of the human soul is still so incomplete that my poor mental faculties have managed to produce such ample discoveries, it is evidently premature to declare oneself for or against such assumptions as yours."

Sigmund Freud felt more confident of his goodness than his greatness, but he could only be satisfied—if at all—by being great. Genius knows its own limitations best, but Freud's dissatisfaction with his intellect comes as a surprise. So does his easily cleared conscience, through which he denied responsibility and fault in relation to Breuer, Fliess, Adler, Rank, and others with whom he was first close, then distant or hostile. Perhaps he took the Hebraic goodness in himself for granted, while striving toward a Hellenic ideal.

A great deal has been written about Freud's Jewishness, but no simple statement can be made about it. An atheist, he maintained his Jewish identity socially but, like Rank, was assimilated to the extent that the family observed Christmas and Easter, not the Jewish holidays; his son Martin never set foot in a synagogue until his wedding day.[34] Freud was a fearless opponent of some forms of anti-Semitism, at least twice risking injury to shout down rabble-rousers. A father–son dialogue from *The Interpretation of Dreams* reveals how Jakob Freud fell in the estimation of Sigmund, then about ten years old.

> "When I was a young man," he said, "I went for a walk one Saturday in the streets of your birthplace; I was well dressed, and had a new fur cap on my head. A Christian came up to me and with a single blow knocked off my cap into the mud and shouted: 'Jew! Get off the pavement!' " "And what did you do?" I asked. "I went into the roadway and picked up my cap," was his quiet reply. This struck me as unheroic conduct on the part of the big, strong man who was holding the little boy by the hand. I contrasted this situation with another which fitted my feelings better: the scene in which Hannibal's father, Hamilcar Barca, made his boy swear before the household alter to take vengeance on the Romans.[35]

But Freud's indignation did not prevent him from tolerating anti-Semitism in order, as he saw it, to advance the psychoanalytic movement, which he feared might become a "Jewish national affair." He undervalued Jewish adherents and overvalued Gentiles, most notably Carl Jung but also, it now appears, Ernest Jones. Otto Rank and Sandor Ferenczi suffered insults from Jones which Freud made them tolerate. In 1934, Jones was so upset with a manuscript written by the Viennese analyst Isidor Sadger that, in order to suppress it, he suggested Sadger be put in a concentration camp. (The suggestion was not followed, but neither was the manuscript published.)[36] Freud was understandably slow himself to recognize the gravity of the Nazi threat, and Jones helped arrange his flight from Nazi Vienna in 1938.

According to one theory, creativity depends on the ability to hold opposite ideas in the mind simultaneously, to live and work with contradictions. "No mind can engender till divided in two," wrote W. B. Yeats. Sigmund Freud not only coped with ambivalence; he raised it to a new level of conciousness. Reaction formation, denial, repression, and dream work are some of the terms he used to accommodate the phenomenon of opposites that he observed in himself and others: Disgust conceals attraction, altruism conceals sadism, behind the fear lies the wish, etc. Many people cannot tolerate such oxymorons in their lives; they feel out of control, or "crazy." Their notion of sanity stifles creativity. Freud's elucidation of the dynamic unconscious enabled people to cope better with normal inconsistency and to be more creative as a result.

Freud's own powerful impulses and emotions found their match in his intellect and self-control. He checked his passion for philosophy with the detachment of a chemist, his yen for deductive reasoning with a disciplined inductive approach. Sometimes he fooled himself, as when he denied ambition, malice, and idealism, and when he claimed to be unruffled by critics. He labeled himself an obsessive, but he showed signs of (controlled) anxiety, paranoia, homosexuality, and hysteria as well and probably used all to advantage, as he did his own dreams. As with any powerful new tool, psychoanalysis was used roughly at first and mistakes were made, even by its inventor.

From his concern with archeology to his wish for a statue of himself in the university courtyard, Freud worked out his ambivalent relationship with the past. Ambition for greatness suggests a preoccupation with the future, but in his case the key fantasy concerns becoming a part of history, an indispensable figure who first solved the riddle of life. It was part of his struggle with mortality, his search for permanence. For Freud, who seemed to use every hour productively, the momentary present was almost hidden, sandwiched between past and future. The present took its meaning from the larger perspective, the non-present, from which Freud derived his higher motive, his drive for success and permanence.

If Freud's issue was an ambivalent relationship to history, Rank's was an ambivalent relationship to the present. Living in the moment, choosing life by facing death, were for him important themes. The term "existential" fits Rank. But for Freud, the present moment was a window to the past; consciousness was merely the tip of the iceberg, most of which is hidden: a weak ego struggles between the powerful forces of id and super-ego. Unlike Rank, Freud spoke scornfully of the ego, which he compared with "the clown in the circus who is always putting in his oar to make the audience think that whatever happens is his doing."[37]

With Freud, reason struggles to overcome impulses; science disarms the explosive unconscious, which must be approached the way a bomb squad approaches a ticking box. If you disarm the bomb, life can go on. Rank came to view the explosive differently. Ticking is a sign of life. The ego has real power as the heroic or artistic will. Too many people shut off its energy in order to live—neurotically; a high price. The alternative is to risk explosions—small ones, preferably. That is better than the bland security of the living dead.

Freud and Rank forged a strong bond lasting two decades. A psychological explosion finally split that bond, and the after-effects are still being felt. The causes of the break can be seen more clearly now, sixty years later.

CHAPTER 4

The "Little Society"

*Sow an act, and you reap a habit. Sow a habit, and you reap
a character. Sow a character, and you reap a destiny.*
—Author unknown. Attributed to Thackeray in Rank's Diary.

The year 1905, when Rank met Freud, was marked by several
important historical events. Norway separated from Sweden. Japan's military humiliated Russia, and President Theodore Roosevelt mediated their peace treaty. Albert Einstein, then 26,
published his theory of relativity. Zoologist Fritz Schaudinn identified the spirochete which causes syphilis. The first neon signs
appeared, and the London subway opened.

Viennese creativity flourished: Franz Lehar's *Merry Widow*
and Richard Strauss's *Salomé* were first presented, as was a new
play by symbolist poet Hugo von Hofmannsthal. A modest political reform to protect racial minorities in Austria provided for
voting by language affiliation. The upshot was that German-
speaking Viennese Jews had to cast their ballots for the Christian
Socialists, who happened to be anti-Semitic.[1] That same year
Freud published a major book on sex and a study of wit, heavily
based on his favorite Jewish jokes. These, he observed, were
self-critical, democratic, irreverent, fatalistic and—witness the
bittersweet "reform"—politically paranoid.

Rank's arrival at Freud's office in the spring began an historic
association of two great minds and personalities which lasted

67

twenty years, the closest professional relationship either man ever had. It was a filial, tutorial, and then collegial relationship between "Herr Rank," 21, and "Herr Professor," 49. The generation gap between them showed itself in the German script each wrote: modern vs. Gothic. Rank was three years older than the Freuds' first-born, Mathilde, and eleven years older than Anna, the youngest (once said to be Freud's choice for Rank's wife); he was junior by eighteen years to Alexander, Freud's only brother and youngest sibling. A locksmith, philosopher-poet, and interpreter of dreams, the self-educated young Otto found ready acceptance in Freud's family and his study circle—more than ample consolation for his failure to get a travel stipend to Paris. Otto's relationship to Freud as adopted son has often been suggested, but Martha is said to have adopted him in her way as Sigmund's youngest brother.[2]

Rank probably first attended sessions of the Wednesday Psychological Society in 1905, before any minutes were taken. Drs. Paul Federn and Alfred Meisl had joined in 1903 and Eduard Hitschmann and Adolf Deutsch in 1905, along with schoolteacher and author Philipp Frey. Rank entered Gymnasium (academic high school) in October, taking pre-University courses, including Latin, Greek, mathematics, and science.[3] He was six years older than the average entrant, and his grasp of literature, the arts, philosophy, psychology, and history must have set him far above most of his classmates.

THE SECRETARY

When Freud turned 50 on May 6, 1906, he received a remarkable gift from his "little society." They gave him an engraved medal with his profile on the front and a portrait of Oedipus on the back. Next to Oedipus, in Greek, were these words from Sophocles: "Who divined the famed riddle and was a man most mighty." Freud was staggered by the gift, explaining that he had as a medical student imagined his own bust among those of the great scientists honored in the courtyard of the University of Vienna. In Freud's fantasy, the bust had the same inscription from Sophocles that Federn had chosen for the medal.

By 1906 Freud had an international reputation as the author of five books and some seventy articles in a variety of journals. His monograph *Three Essays* was reviewed favorably in Europe and (by Adolf Meyer) in the United States. He was lauded as far west as St. Louis by Morton Prince, who spoke at the Universal Exposition (1904) along with a rival of Freud, French psychiatrist Pierre Janet. Freud began corresponding with English sexologist Havelock Ellis in 1898 and with Swiss psychiatrist Carl Jung in 1906. An indefatigable correspondent, Freud was now receiving—and answering immediately, in longhand—several letters a day from readers around the globe.[4]

Otto Rank's minutes of the Wednesday Psychological Society constitute the first record of the psychoanalytic movement. Only recently published, the four large volumes cover nine years of what became the Vienna Psychoanalytic Society, from 1906 to 1915. Rank was not only hired as salaried secretary, he also was initiated as a full-fledged member of the group by virtue of his opening presentation in October 1906.

By this time Rank had moved from Leopoldstadt to 8 Simondenkgasse, in the IXth District, a pleasant walk through the Lichtenstein Garden to 19 Berggasse. Ironically, Rank's little street, "memorial to Simon," honors his father's name. Freud's home and office stood about halfway up the sloping five-block "Hill [Berg] Street," which runs parallel to and four blocks from the western edge of the Ringstrasse, where Freud liked to walk. He could reach the Danube Canal, down the hill, in two minutes. Alfred Adler, a convert to Protestantism, lived in the largely Jewish Leopoldstadt; the only other member in that District (II) was Wilhelm Stekel.

It was the custom for each new member to present some work to introduce himself. Rank's manuscript on the artist had been accepted for publication, and Freud must have shared it with the group already. In the year and a half since meeting Freud, Rank had addressed another major topic: "The Incest Motif in Literature and Legend." Because of its length he was to present the material on three successive Wednesdays while he took minutes on the discussion portion of the meetings.

The fifth academic year of The Society began on October 10, 1906. The minutes declare: "Prof. Dr. Freud chairs the meetings, Otto Rank acts as salaried secretary." The meetings started at 8:30 P.M. for preliminary business. The presentation began at nine. Afterwards members would discuss the paper with the order of speakers decided by lot, except that Freud usually spoke last.

Present at the meeting, besides Freud and Rank, were (with

age, if known, in parentheses) Drs. Adler (36), Adolf Deutsch, Federn (35), Hitschmann (35), Kahane, and Reitler (40) and Mr. Frey. Most of the members stood about halfway in age between the new Secretary, 22, and the Professor, 50. Of the total roster, then seventeen members, about half attended each session in Freud's apartment, sitting around a table well supplied with cigars and cigarets. An admiring member said he found one fault with the Professor: "He can only think in a cloud of tobacco smoke."[5]

Rank already had achieved something remarkable. His forthcoming monograph *The Artist* [*Der Künstler*] was the first psychoanalytic book to be published by a member of the group other than Freud. His massive book *The Incest Motif in Poetry and Legend* (1912) was essentially written before his presentation in 1906; although he delayed publication of the 685-page tome, he was eager to talk about it with the Wednesday group.

THE INCEST MOTIF

In reviewing world literature and mythology, Rank did not find simple incest to the extent suggested by the girth of his published book. Rather, in an elegant, imaginative, perhaps facile analysis Rank showed that the blatant incest of *Oedipus Rex* becomes modified over centuries, disguising the incest theme.[6]

Rank began with Freud's observation that the incest theme in ancient myth corresponds with typical incest dreams; the same mental forces that cause the dream generate the myth. The child's incestuous wishes appear unequivocally. As civilization progressed, however, overt fantasies remained alive only in a few individuals, among them artists. The poet, impelled by powerful unconscious motives, takes this material and recreates it artistically to express both the hidden, forbidden wish and defenses against it.

The universality of the incest theme in literature attests to its power and diverse manifestations. Cultural development proceeds through time with increasing repression of erotic impulse and fantasy. New forms, although disguising the theme, still derive their power for the artist and the audience from the same forbidden impulses.

Two thousand years after Sophocles' *Oedipus* the theme appears completely changed in Shakespeare's *Hamlet*. Hamlet cannot kill his uncle, now his mother's husband, because his father's murderer expressed Hamlet's own hidden infantile wish. Hamlet is no better than the one he wants to punish.

After two more centuries, the motif appears transformed again in Schiller's *Don Carlos*. In *Oedipus* we see the direct expression of incest, with Hamlet reflecting the reverse, i.e., jealous hatred of the mother. Don Carlos desires his stepmother, not a blood relation. Ultimately Don Carlos dies at the command of his father.

Such transformations of the incest theme, Rank said, will not surprise those who are familiar with unconscious mental processes. He spoke of the striking similarity between artistic creation, dreaming, and the artfully constructed symptoms of psychoneurosis. But he cautioned his audience not to conclude that the artist is neurotic. Although artistic creations have something in common with the expressions of the neurotic, the former are also part of normal or superior psychological functioning. Freud's pioneering exploration of dreams took place amidst the sufferings of neurotics, whose exaggerations and inhibitions helped elucidate normal emotion. The boundary between normal and neurotic tends to be blurred, with mixed forms and finely graduated differentiation.

Writer Irving Stone offered this impression of the moment:

> Otto Rank finished his presentation on the dot of ten. The maid arrived from the upstairs kitchen with coffee and a tray of plain cake covered with nuts. She placed the tray in the center of the oval table. The men rose, put hot milk or whipped cream in their coffee, moved about the room chatting and chaffing each other amiably for a few moments before picking a number out of a bowl on the table and returning to their seats. Otto Rank now transformed himself from a budding scholar into a secretary who had a talent for reproducing an entire discussion as faithfully as though it had been recorded on one of the phonographs recently invented by an American named Thomas A. Edison.[7]

From Rank's minutes one can recreate comments and rebuttal conversationally. Given Freud's concern for style as well as content, oral or written, and his supervisory role with respect to the new Secretary, he must have scrutinized and set the standard for the early minutes. Members could check the accuracy of their own reported comments, and they could borrow the minutes to catch up on a missed meeting.[8] A first-person rendition of the third-person minutes follows:

FREY: "The paper is fragmentary and vague. In fact, Rank, it is not really a paper, but an excerpt of your manuscript. I cannot grasp a logical outline for your theme. There are so many isolated details. Another problem is the tendency to interpret everything according to Freud's method, so you read too much into the material, and interpret too much. Some of what you interpret symbolically can be taken literally. For example, why interpret Oedipus' taking the belt and sword from Laius as a symbol of castration of the father and taking possession of the mother? Oedipus did not know that Laius *was* his father. You ought to be content with making what is probable more plausible; don't overreach."

REITLER: "I don't feel the paper was extensive enough to give a clear idea of its scope. One area you might pursue is the role of penitence in the legends of the saints, since penitence is so closely related to hysteria. The gradations you postulate, in which repression operates least in the dream, more in the myth, and most in the drama, in art, should be reversed. You pointed out the paternal hate against Don Carlos; there is another example: God the Father killed His Son Jesus—indirectly, it is true—His Son Who, together with God the Father, is part of the Trinity. Finally, on a lighter level, may I call your attention to incestuous themes in student songs?"

HITSCHMANN: "I find the paper to be no more than a rather superfluous extension of Freud's discovery of the Oedipus situation. Love between relatives does not always have incestuous roots, but may be simply familial or parental love. Incest is pathological; that's why, if I may mention Lombroso, poet-geniuses are so attracted to it. I will concede that unconscious factors influence the choice of material and the interest of the audience, as well. Lastly, let me warn you, Rank, not to get so far out on a limb in looking at such broad topics. You'll end up in a heap on the ground if you don't admit other points of view."

FEDERN: "I disagree with you, Hitschmann. This is an important contribution. I was amazed to learn that incestuous impulses were so ubiquitous. A discussion of the phylogenetic development of incest would be helpful, that is, historical development in primeval society and in the family. I assume that the prohibition evolved with the family unit. Since incest between father and daughter is not as strictly forbidden as that between mother and son, the former is a less frequent topic in literature."

FREUD: "Herr Rank, you will understand if I speak directly to what I perceive as the shortcomings of this paper. You do not know how to stay within the limits of the subject and how to outline the topic clearly. For instance, it was unnecessary to bring in the Orestes and Clytaemnestra myths or Hartmann's medieval poetry, although you made some skillful connections with the main theme. A second failing is that you are satisfied when you yourself understand the matter in question; you do not consider what is needed to demonstrate your insights and results to the listener. You should briefly outline the most important results of your research and use examples to illustrate them. The scheme I have in mind uses Oedipus as the core and model; you then group the material around this core, and also develop a series to take the theme from the core outward to its farthest ramifications. It is true that the farther you move out from the core, the less certain the interpretations become, and it is a matter of personal style and skill to stop before you go too far. Another point: in some places you used 'repression' when the idea was displacement, or mitigation. Lastly, we should remember the frequent occurrence of incest among the 'Gods.' Everything which was later forbidden and finally sanctified was originally allowed and then renounced. Hence the double meaning of the word *sacer* (which means both 'holy' and 'accursed')."

ADLER: "Your work concerns itself with the disclosure of a nucleus, and you should be content with doing that rather than giving detailed interpretations. The paper is important in confirming experience gained from the psychoneuroses; beginners could learn much from it. I had a woman patient who untied her belt during hysterical seizures. Your interpretation brought out the sexual meaning of this act. Another woman, awaking from a dream, found she had bitten her finger til it bled. Analysis led to the interpretation of the finger as a penis, as in your interpretation of Orestes biting off his finger. Now, my dear Otto, I must object to the superficial attempt to explain crime. To say that every criminal act has sexual roots explains nothing. The frequent indication in myths and legends that parents are aware of their child's criminal inclinations must be attributed to the poet's instincts; he carries his awareness into the myth."

KAHANE: "You will find another case of incest in Shake-speare's *Pericles*. Some of your interpretations remind me of someone overstretching an elastic band. For example your ideas about parental affection for their children. I'd like to point out that there is a good deal of sex envy on the part of parents, and the prohibition of masturbation and intercourse imposed upon their children originates not in morality but in sex envy."

FREUD: "Thank you for an interesting presentation and dis-cussion. Before we close, I will take a moment to report a case showing the impact of sexual trauma. For a week and a half I have been treating a female hysteric. In her first session she related an exhibitionistic scene from her fourth year: she un-dressed in front of her brother, who became very indignant. Later, she had an almost incestuous relationship with this brother. From her eleventh year on they would show their bod-ies to each other, observing the progress of their development. Between 11 and 14, she had intimate bodily contact with him, without using their hands. They would lie on top of each other attempting intercourse. All these are *conscious* memories. Dur-ing a session in which not much progress was being made, she began to talk of everyday happenings. She said that she was an excellent *spot remover* and a passionate fruit grower, espe-cially *apples*. She spoke of a conversation with her father. He spoke of a certain German lady's breasts as 'godly' or 'pious' (*fromm*) and found fault with her dress, which exposed them. She said to her father that he would not have minded seeing the breasts, had they been less pious (pious breasts: pear-shaped breasts: *pomme au poire*)."

KAHANE: "Pious, because at night they fall to their knees!"

Rank survived his initiation ceremony well enough, his de-tailed and objective minutes showing he could not only take criticism but record it faithfully. The presentation and discussion continued for two more weeks, dramatically demonstrating the contemporary state of psychoanalysis. Attendance went up from nine at the first meeting to thirteen at the next two, including Dr. Stekel, musicologists Graf and Bach, and Rank's first pub-lisher, Hugo Heller.

Rank replied to his critics firmly and directly. He found most of the objections to be about form rather than substance. The shortcomings are inherent in the work, he said, the purpose of which was to show the correspondence of phenomena in myth and art with some of those in the psychoneuroses. In order to lead the listener from literature to the frontiers of psychoanalysis, he had tried to compile most of the cases of incest found in literature, while also attempting bold efforts at interpretation. To connect these extremes was difficult enough in a book, and could not be attempted in a short paper. Terms had to be clarified. (For example, "repression" and "suppression" had not yet been defined as unconscious and conscious processes, respectively.) Rank took issue with negative points raised by Federn and Adler, who were otherwise the most supportive.

Adler felt that art had been overrated as a factor in the development of society, and that Rank's work would not encourage progress in art. It might, by making too much conscious, inhibit creative artists and even endanger the mental stability of whole populations. On the other hand, there might be compensation from fields other than art, resulting from expansion of the sphere of consciousness.

Rank's presentation took three sessions, the last of which opened with a reference to an attack on Freud in *Waage* [*Scale*], a monthly magazine. The Fliess-Weininger-Swoboda affair had become public: Rank became aware of the whole matter then, if he had not been before. The minutes merely mention the topic. Stekel reported that a Vienna group would be formed to fight the penal code affecting homosexuals.

Freud then spoke at length on Rank's topic, introducing case material and asserting a priority: He, not Rank, had first made the distinction between conscious repression ("defense") and unconscious organic repression. He went on to say that Rank should not use early Greek gods such as Uranos and Chronos as examples, since it was too easy to object that they had no sexual option besides incest!

The following passage suggests that Freud and Rank compared their own childhoods. "Concerning the relation between choice of subject matter and the poet's life, Freud points out— as he had already said to Rank in private—that where hate for a brother and love for a sister appear in a poet's work and there is no evidence of similar circumstances in the poet's own life, one should find out whether there had been a child in the family who died at an early age. Suppression (of the death) at an early stage in his life might lead to the transformation of his feelings into poetry."[9] Freud's younger brother died when Sigmund was less than two. Rank's infant sister died before his birth.

Hitschmann asked whether Rank included cases of incest from Ibsen's plays. (He did so in the book.) Hitschmann feared that awareness of mental processes might inhibit creativity, but two others disagreed on grounds that enough obscurity will remain in the human mind to provide for artistic expression. Heller noted that by uncovering the incest motif one deprived the poet of its use, but the loss of one motif does not bring art to an end.

In characteristically provocative words, Stekel criticized Rank's work as diligent but schoolboyish. "Everything in this book is seen through spectacles colored by Freudian teachings, without going beyond Freud."[10] Another speaker was worried that publication of the book, because of its vulnerability to critics, might hurt psychology, and Freud's work in particular.

Rank concluded his response by saying that art must perish when the unconscious is made conscious. "Artists are the ones who attain the highest degree of consciousness among their contemporaries, and therefore it is *in them* that such transition takes place. To Federn's remark that incestuous relations are inescapable in the case of Cain and Abel: These myths were in fact a creation of much later cultural periods. The incestuous feelings of these periods were projected onto the myths of early times. I think this also refutes Professor Freud's objection concerning Uranos and Chronos."

Rank took them on, including Freud, with aplomb. He held his ground, with the intermittent support of group members. The criticism, heady and sometimes harsh, had none of the meanness which almost disrupted the Society later on. In light of Rank's later theory of the birth trauma and the universal wish to return to the womb, Freud's closing remark, as Rank wrote it, merits quotation:

> FREUD, at the end of the meeting, tells of a disguised form of the dream of incest with the mother. The dreamer relates: He and his family, father, brothers, and sisters, are in front of the entrance to a house. The father and the others enter and ascend a narrow passageway. Finally he, too, goes inside. He has the vague recollection of *having been in there once before* [emphasis in original]. Note that the dreamer enumerates the whole family with the exception of the mother. If one inverts the sentence that all

the others go inside, i.e., that he alone goes inside, the narration becomes meaningful. It is then the mother's vagina, for this is the place where he has been once before.[11]

PSYCHOANALYTIC "GROUP DYNAMICS"

Rank's minutes recreate much of the group process in this first psychoanalytic forum, led by Freud at the peak of his powers if not of his fame. Freud's inversion of the incest dream—which could just as well be a womb dream—illustrates his facile interpretive process, a mixture of imaginative manipulation and scientific conviction. The group meetings reveal Freud's interest in diverse issues and his mastery of a huge intellectual terrain, from aesthetics to astronomy. Adler's political sensitivity comes through, as does Stekel's irascible flair and Federn's gentleness.

The Wednesday Society was a proving ground for Freud and Rank both. Between 1902, when the first disciples came, and 1906, when Freud warmed to Jung, only his local colleagues shared ideas and reactions with the pioneer. Nonmedical intellectuals were more receptive than most physicians, and Freud staunchly supported the principle that that one need not be a physician in order to practice psychoanalysis. Although diverse occupationally, the Society was all male and nearly all Jewish in the first few years. In no sense were the members narrow or parochial, however, and what they shared was curiosity, excitement, intellectual independence, a striving for recognition, mostly liberal values, and a socially marginal position in Catholic and politically anti-Semitic Vienna. The center of an admiring group, Freud could and did contend with the independent and sometimes flatly critical comments of some members. His ability to confront Freud gave Rank standing to confront anyone in the group, while proving that he was not his mentor's puppet.

In this formative period, readers of Freud became familiar with the unconscious as the dynamic force in all mental life, abnormal and normal; with the wish-fulfilling character of dreams and its various disguises; with the forbidden, repressed sexual wish as the source of neurosis; and with the libido and infantile sexuality (oral, anal, and genital phases). Freud had given up hypnosis and catharsis and developed psychoanalysis, a method of study and treatment in which the patient just talked, freely associating for an hour on the couch. Transference—feelings from early relationships projected onto the analyst—guided the analyst's understanding and interpretations. Although the Oedipal paradigm had been briefly mentioned in *Interpretation of Dreams,* the Oedipus complex came later (1910), as did the system of id, ego, and super-ego (1923).

In November 1906 Adler presented on "organ inferiority" as the basis of neurosis, a preview of his forthcoming book. Freud praised him, but preferred "variability" to "inferiority." Adler's was a theory of overcompensation, e.g., ear problems predispose to a musical career, eye defects to art, and childhood illness produces doctors. Rank agreed with Adler on artists and musicians, but thought that among poets skin and eye problems are defenses against exhibitionism, and "these poets quite easily become the victims of real eye or skin diseases, for which they are predisposed." The facility with which the pioneer analysts linked mind and body suggests the positivist zeal that led Meynert to assign roles to the various brain tracts; this was highly speculative psychophysiology. In closing, Rank recorded a piece of kitchen wisdom from the home of his mentor, where he often dined: "Freud remarks that cooks very frequently incline to psychoneurotic disturbances (especially to paranoia) and that good cooks are always severely abnormal. (He mentions his own cook, who invariably cooks particularly well when a period of illness is imminent.)"[12]

In the next session Frey talked about conceit, or megalomania, in everyday life. Among others, he cited the example of Hjalmar Ekdal from *Wild Duck.* Frey thought that to open the eyes of megalomanics would undermine such people's struggle for existence; they could not live with insight. Rank disagreed on the grounds that it is impossible to open their eyes! (Little did the others know that Rank was speaking of a subject very close to home, his own father.)

On the wearing of uniforms to overcome inferiority (soldiers and psychiatrists had been mentioned as examples), Rank suggested that the "increased self-confidence lies in the awareness of the effect on the opposite sex." In this session Reitler mentioned a paranoid patient who accused him of assaulting her; she wrote Freud to complain about Reitler, his pupil, stressing that he was impotent! Such strong sexual feeling toward the doctor, which alarmed Breuer and prompted Freud to develop the theory of transference, was by now quite familiar. Freud summed up the state of the art: "In curing neuroses one takes hold of the floating part of the patient's libido and transfers it to one's own person. The translation of the unconscious material into consciousness is performed with the help of the transference. The cure, therefore, is effected by means of a conscious love. In paranoia, however . . . there is no love. The patient, like the child, believes only one he loves."[13]

Dr. Isidor Sadger joined the group and gave a presentation on the Austrian poet Nickolaus Lenau. Lenau died in a mental institution of general paresis, which Sadger noted results from syphilis. Freud said that Lenau was an onanist (masturbator) throughout life; also, that neurotics do not suffer anxiety as a consequence of coitus interruptus the way normals do. This illustrates Freud's entrenched negative attitude toward masturbation, combined with his need to link anxiety to a physical etiology. Havelock Ellis and Albert Moll led the progressive trend away from the medical dictum that onanism leads to insanity, but Freud held to a conservative line, even alienating his son Oliver, who sought reassurance on the subject and got a stern warning from his father instead.[14]

Stekel disputed Freud's view of such matters, asserting that the causes of neurosis derive from the psyche, not from heredity, syphilis, or sexual frustration. Some of the others charged Stekel with indulging in metaphysics, citing the high incidence of syphilis in the families of hysterics and other neurotics. But Stekel was more right than his colleagues, including Freud. Another prescient comment by Stekel anticipates later writers, especially Rank: Modern man can be characterized as "haunted by anxiety. Due to a superabundance of hygienic restrictions, which are meant to preserve his life, he does not live at all; it is precisely his anxiety which makes him ill." He attacked Freud's theory for "giving new life to an old superstition."[15] But Stekel was too flamboyant and undisciplined to gain much respect; he was said to invent cases to support his theories.

The next day (December 6), Freud wrote Jung that he was suffering the torment of an innovator, being regarded among his own supporters as a crank or fanatic. Freud was still smarting from Stekel's attack, even though it had been rebuffed. The letter goes on to agree with Jung that claims for the therapeutic benefits of psychoanalysis are premature, and would invite a flood of unqualified practitioners and then a backlash of criticism. Freud would say only that "this method is more fruitful than any other." He explained that "our cures are brought about through the fixations of the libido prevailing in the unconscious (transference) . . . Transference provides the impulse necessary for understanding and translating the language of the unconscious; where it is lacking, the patient does not make the effort or does not listen when we submit our translation to him. Essentially, one might say, the cure is effected by love. And actually transference provides the most cogent, indeed, the only unassailable proof that neuroses are determined by the individual's love life."[16]

The assertion that love is the critical therapeutic element becomes muted in later analytic teaching, perhaps because of the very danger to which Jung fell prey, as will be seen. Freud meant, of course, the patient's *transference* love for the analyst, who must be able to receive and use it objectively, unselfishly. The analyst's feeling for the patient, if amounting to more than professional regard, was correspondingly labeled "counter-transference." Not until much later was the power of reciprocated love considered as a therapeutic tool, chiefly by Ferenczi.

RANK AND THE ARTIST

Rank's first publication, *The Artist* (1907), was subtitled "Toward a Sexual Psychology." Revised with Freud's help, the little book runs to only fifty-six densely written pages. Rank chose an epigram from Shakespeare and put it on the front cover, in English: "Is it possible, he should know what he is, and be that he is?" This expresses Rank's concern: art and life both pale as the unconscious becomes conscious. Years later Rank said that Shakespeare's question contains the whole problem of psychoanalysis: self-consciousness in its complex relationship to experience and self-creation.[17]

In the book, Rank compares and contrasts artist, dreamer, and neurotic. The dreamer, on waking, spontaneously returns to reality; the neurotic cannot let go the fantasy in spite of every effort. By his capacity to create, to actively use the fantasy, the artist's regression to fantasy ends with a productive return to reality. Rank set the creative type on an artistic continuum between dreamer at the low end and neurotic at the high end, along with dramatist, philosopher, and prophet (founder of religion). The neurotic represents a highly evolved, though unsuccessful, attempt to resolve the major psychological problems of existence.

The artist, according to Rank, transforms unconscious impulses (repressed sex) into an admired product, the work of art, which gratifies, even heals, the admiring audience. But when art no longer suffices to control the audience's impulses or passions, a savior is required who delivers them from sin by taking on their suffering, atoning for them, "to free them from the will toward culture, toward pleasure." The savior or prophet is an idealized, strengthened artist, who provides a psychotherapeutic cure for the masses greater than that which the artist provides for the few. The cure of the neurotic, by contrast, has to be performed case by case, individually: "He is the complete egotist, his opposite is the prophet who suffers for the people, and the artist stands between the two."

Rank seems to straddle a line between Freud and Stekel. "Every nervous illness is produced by the 'mental,' which wants to go back to its origin, to the 'physical.' In the most outspoken form of psychoneurosis—hysteria—the mental, as if for revenge, rides into the body on false pathways: The affects are converted and cause disturbances." Rank sees in the hysteric a collision of cultural extremes: A strong, many-sided libido meets the ultimate rejection of sexuality. Symptoms emerge as a compromise. "The neurotic feels the conflict between his first and second nature with its whole cultural impact as a personal schism with which, of course, his psyche cannot cope; he can only help himself by denying the conflict, by repressing . . . The neurotic wants, if one may say, to digest the painful, the artist spits it out, the dreamer sweats it out." Religion is unconscious mass psychotherapy; art is unconscious individual therapy.[18]

Small wonder that Freud chose this young writer to be his assistant. Rank based his search and his synthesis on Freudian theory but probed new domains: not only art, but cultural evolution generally. He was struggling with the mixed blessing of self-consciousness. The artist needs an illusion, the faith that his is the highest art; psychoanalysis may undermine that illusion. The artist listens to inner voices, closed off to everything external. Dramatic artists like Ibsen and Wagner blend actor and poet. Their characters are analyzed and described, so the artist merges with the clinician-scientist. Rank envisaged a continuing evolution from artist to physician, where the creative become healing-artists for the recipients, neurotics. Neurosis is the basis for a general widening of consciousness, and the abnormal shows the normal the way to liberation—through the individual psyche to an understanding of the universal psyche. Suffering makes him whole, illness leads to knowledge. Once the injudiciously repressed unconscious has become conscious, the unartistic superior man will master his instinctual drives and guide them well. Rank mixed a heady dose of Nietzsche into the essay.

Freud sent Rank's book to Jung, who remarked, "Herr Rank is another who simply takes the broadened conception of sexuality for granted, in such a way that even I, who have been studying your thought intensively for more than four years, have difficulty in understanding this conception. The public Herr Rank writes for won't understand it at all." Rank's book was reviewed in a Viennese paper in April 1907, as he turned 23.[19] It had little impact on the public; a few scholars took note of it.

Reflecting on this first effort a quarter-century later, Rank said it anticipated some developments in psychoanalysis as well as his own mature viewpoint. He called it the first synthesis of a psychoanalytic world-view, and the first application thereof to the history of culture. It was also the first attempt at a "doctrine of the impulses (*Trieblehre*) with a definite tendency toward *monism* (such as later proclaimed by Jung . . .)." In this work he conceived the idea of an inner resistance, a kind of "self-inhibition instinct," opposed to Freud's externally (father-) derived inhibition. The emphasis is on the general features of the creative type, on what he has in common with the neurotic and the normal (dreamer).[20]

LIBIDO AND INSTINCT

The first international visitor to the Wednesday Psychological Society in the new year (1907) was Max Eitingon, a just-graduated physician from Bleuler's clinic in Switzerland, where Jung worked. Afflicted with stuttering, Eitingon pursued a medical career not expecting to do clinical work. He became enamored of psychoanalysis under the influence of Carl Jung. From a wealthy Russian Jewish family, Eitingon was a cultured, kind, reserved man who later became one of Freud's inner circle.[21]

There were twenty-five scientific sessions of the Wednesday Society during the calendar year, with a long intermission between May and October. Rank made no presentation during the year, probably a concession to his studies, although he took part in discussions.

The first scientific session of 1907, on January 23, concerned the instincts of hunger and love. At that time Freud separated the sexual and self-preservation instincts. Although never clearly defined, libido stood for the energy of the sexual instinct; libido was to love as hunger was to the nutritional (self-preservation) instinct. Libido did not include all the instincts; it could not be reduced to a single energy source. Eventually Jung parted with Freud over this point, but here, in the presence of Jung's emissary, Max Eitingon, the Vienna group heard Otto Rank challenge the Professor's dualism.

Rank cited his attempt to show the monistic root of hunger and love in the first part of his sexual psychology [*The Artist*]. He challenged the view that "hunger" drives the prostitute into her trade and the man to the performance of homosexual acts. That notion, based on social factors, Rank found outmoded and superficial. In his book Rank speaks of libido as an urgent desire, a reaction to an inner disturbance, i.e., displeasure, which it seeks to remove. He traces the primal, singular energy source via Schopenhauer to the Greek philosophers Anaxagoras and Empedocles, who taught that plants grow from an inner desire. This source is the primordial libido, from which the various drives differentiate in time.[22] Here Rank's later concept of will appears in embryonic form.

The following session, one of the most important of the Vienna Society, included a long theoretical discussion by Freud. Therapy cannot be directed against the symptom, he said, but by removing resistances helps the patient to develop himself. Only transference can remove resistances: The patient gives them up "*to please us.* Our cures are cures of love." The task remains of removing personal resistance to transference. He pointed out the similarity to hypnosis, to him a kind of trickery, while psychoanalysis produced permanent change in the patient.

The others' positions varied from therapeutic nihilism (only prophylaxis is effective, not treatment) to Adler's assertion that therapy is a form of psychological training, to Stekel's doctrine that the patient must be shown the mechanism of repression and must become his own therapist. Admitting that he lacked clinical experience, Rank observed, "Between the illness and its cure, the symptom and its resolution, there is, one might say, the normal life of the patient; there his social, religious, artistic instincts come to the fore, and it is from here that one can start, even if one has not actually practiced psychotherapy." Others remarked that the line between normal and neurotic is hazy, and that the analysis of normals would be a good idea. Kahane, in an elegant but strange metaphor of psyche as organ and neuroses as diseases of metabolism, said the psyche lives on charges it receives (like a battery). "Presumably the first charge is the affect of anxiety engendered in the passage through the birth canal (dyspnea)."[23] Here is a remarkable anticipation—recorded in Rank's hand—of the birth trauma principle.

JUNG VISITS VIENNA

In early March, Dr. Carl Jung, 31, his wife, Emma, and Dr. Ludwig Binswanger visited Vienna from Switzerland. Freud and Rank met Jung for the first time. Jung had read and criticized Rank's book, and Freud had written him, "I know of only one who might be regarded as your equal in understanding, and of none who is able and willing to do so much for the cause as you."[24] Rank qualifies for the honor; he was not yet able to do much for the cause, but Freud regarded him very highly. Jung must have wondered if the diminutive Secretary could be his chief rival. Rank was small, about five feet four inches tall. Freud was three inches taller. Jung towered above them both at six feet two. Freud and Jung, already engrossed in warm and stimulating correspondence, intensified their relationship in hours and hours of animated talk.

The Swiss psychiatrists were present at the Wednesday Society meeting on March 6. Alfred Adler presented and Jung supported him, calling the doctrine of organ inferiority "a brilliant idea." Afterwards Binswanger was dismayed by the caustic way in which Freud referred to his own Viennese "gang" of followers (*"diese Bande"*).[25] Freud had little respect for them and perhaps needed to set himself apart to impress his visitors. Not only did the Swiss add an international dimension to psychoanalysis, but they were from a respected psychiatric hospital and were non-Jews.

Jung reflected later: "Freud was the first man of real importance I had encountered . . . extremely intelligent, shrewd, and altogether remarkable." But Jung found himself resisting Freud's sexual theory; to him it seemed a dogma, a substitute for the religion and philosophy which Freud disparaged. "Wherever, in a person or in a work of art," Jung later complained, "an expression of spirituality (in the intellectual, not the supernatural sense) came to light, he suspected it, and insinuated that it was repressed sexuality." Freud warned Jung against incursions of the occult; to Jung this meant anything that smacked of religion or philosophy. For his part, Freud found Jung to have an exceptional breadth of knowledge, real intellectual dynamism, great imagination, and a fine understanding of the psychoanalytic approach.[26]

Late in April, Stekel held forth brilliantly on the psychological origin of anxiety. A provocateur, he mentioned Fliess and Swoboda in his argument, thus challenging Freud: "Anxiety neurosis cannot be traced back to coitus interruptus alone, but the mental conflict must be taken into account." Stekel asserted that instincts are not isolated, that both death and life instincts accompany the sex instinct, and the stronger the life instinct the more developed is the feeling of anxiety. Here Stekel anticipated Freud's later Thanatos, and Rank's life-fear. Adler remarked that he would trace anxiety back to childhood, but not to the process of birth, as Freud does. The minutes of the meeting, which ran late, overflow with ideas. Rank's only comment was a protest that the presentation was too hurried.[27]

In May, new member Fritz Wittels presented a paper opposing women in medicine as constituting a betrayal of their feminine calling. He was called one-sided and warped, but even his critics agreed that studying might harm women, and that as physicians they should not handle men's genitals. Freud refuted Wittels' extremism but admitted that the woman gains nothing by studying and her collective lot will not improve thereby. Rank elaborated an idea from Freud that the study of medicine is a way to settle in reality the child's question of where babies come from. The philosopher broadens the (sexual)

question obsessively: "From where does man come? The world?"
Theologians confront the question directly, but the medical student's approach is the least neurotic.[28] It was perhaps a year later that Rank decided with Freud's encouragement, to pursue a nonmedical doctorate.

The Freud-Jung relationship warmed over the spring and summer. In his letters, Freud declared a new optimism about the future: "I am as replaceable as everyone else," he wrote, and nominated Jung "to continue and complete my work. . . . Every time we are ridiculed, I become more convinced than ever that we are in possession of a great idea. In the obituary you will some day write for me, don't forget to bear witness that I was never so much as ruffled by all the opposition."[29] Again, Freud's wishes altered his memory. Not only did he ruffle easily, but Freud bore grudges with undisguised bitterness.

Jung waxed ecstatic: "Anyone who knows your science has veritably eaten of the tree of paradise and become clairvoyant." For Jung, a pastor's son, the Eden metaphor conveys a tinge of guilt: forbidden fruit. Freud went off for a three-month summer vacation, begging Jung to keep writing: "Your letters have become a necessity for me." Freud's own passionate letters to Jung compare with those to Martha during their courtship and to Fliess at the height of their collaboration. (Neither Adler nor Rank evoked such passion; being of Viennese-Jewish origin, they bore a double stigma in Freud's eyes.) Vivid homosexual symbolism emerges as Freud exhorted Jung to use the hysterical element in himself, the part that makes him such an impressive teacher: "And when you have injected your own personal leaven into the fermenting mass of my ideas in still more generous measure, there will be no further difference between your achievement and mine."[30]

At this time, Karl Abraham, M.D., 30, Jung's sometime colleague, began corresponding with Freud. Jung grew jealous, describing the Berlin psychiatrist as intelligent but cold and stealthy. Freud, supporting Abraham for his work on the sexual problem, delicately asked Jung whether the German doctor was Jewish: "By the way, is he a descendant of his eponym?"[31] (He was.)

Freud viewed Jung as better suited for propaganda than himself, "for I have always felt that there is something about my personality, my ideas and manner of speaking, that people find strange and repellent, whereas all hearts open to you. If a healthy man like you regards himself as a hysterical type, I can only claim for myself the 'obsessional' type, each specimen of which vegetates in a sealed-off world of his own."[32] But Freud was a commanding speaker for lay as well as professional audiences. Perhaps he didn't stomach propaganda well, so he transferred that burden as best he could, especially if a non-Jew could help. But he would not call Jung healthy for long.

A first, informal meeting on psychoanalysis was planned for Salzburg in 1908. Freud wondered if he should attend. Jung insisted on it, and Freud then urged that Bleuler be made the chairman. Behind the self-effacement lay a strategy, a campaign for scientific immortality.

Although some writers claim that Freud's sex life ended before he was 40, a letter to Jung from this period suggests otherwise. Freud met with Eitingon during a stay in Italy, and noted that he, Eitington, was again involved with a woman. "Such practice is a deterrent from theory. When I have totally overcome my libido (in the common sense), I shall undertake to write a 'Love-life of Mankind.' "[33]

Jung admitted that his veneration for Freud had the quality of a religious crush, which troubled him because of its erotic implications. As a boy, Jung related, he was sexually victimized by a man he once admired. As a brilliant doctor, Jung felt disgust at the admiration (transference) of his colleagues, and he feared that Freud felt the same toward him. With a cynicism remarkable for a healer of souls, Jung wrote, "Every intimate relationship turns out after a while to be sentimental and banal or exhibitionistic." Freud, for his part, worried less about erotic than religious transference on Jung's part: "It could end only in apostasy. . . . I shall do my best to show you that I am unfit to be an object of worship." This was not the first time Freud worried about Jung. According to Binswanger, who accompanied Jung to Vienna, Freud asked the two men to share their dreams with him. Freud interpreted Jung's as a wish to dethrone and supplant him.[34]

Like Jung, Rank also reported, but in more veiled language, a seduction by a trusted older man. Like Jung, Rank (again, in his diary) reviled human foibles and revered a few great men. As brilliant and devoted but rather independent-minded followers of Freud, they shared certain ideas (unitary libido: the monistic view) and an inclination toward philosophy, myth, art, cultural development, and the human soul. But Jung was the scion of doctors and a minister, well-schooled, a handsome giant; Rank was a poor Viennese Jewish atheist, self-educated, short, and homely. Freud the mentor could, literally and figuratively, look up to Jung. He could respect and even love Rank, but it was a decidedly more paternal or elder brother relationship; Rank did all the looking up. He was devoted, but not blinded with devotion. He listened acutely to the others in the little society, but he also spoke his mind. The Professor did not hold his Viennese circle in high esteem. It would have been his way to tell Rank just what he thought of the others. In any case, Rank had eyes and ears, and a curious and discerning mind. He was bound to Freud, but not necessarily to his theoretical system. Emotionally sheltered at last, Otto Rank could be flexible in mind while loyal in spirit, incorporating whatever made sense and felt right.

RANK AND THE HERO

Rank's second published book, *The Myth of the Birth of the Hero*, was written between 1907 and 1908.[35] Freud contributed several paragraphs on the "family romance": This is the idea that children, in protest against their parents, often fantasize a more elegant or heroic lineage.

For this project, Rank spread out a sheet of heavy paper about one meter across and half that high. He ruled it vertically into eight columns; in the left margin he listed the names of twenty-six hero figures, starting with Sargon and ending with Karna and Semiramis, and including Oedipus, Moses, and Jesus. Each example was analyzed according to five headings, as in the following example:

OEDIPUS
  I. *Parents:* King/Queen
 II. *Prehistory:* Mother's dream
III. *Course*
    a. *Type:* Exposure, mountain (water)
    b. *By:* King-Father
IV. *Rescue:*
    Man—Double-shepherd ⎫ Royal foster parents
    Woman ⎱ Sphinx
    Animal ⎰
 V. *Return—Victory/Revenge:* Victory = Revenge

Rank discussed only about half the heroes in the book itself, which is relatively short and reads in large part like an encyclopedia of myths. Unfortunately he did not present the chart, which would have helped the reader grasp his organizing principle.

Rank's own heroes were philosophers, writers, composers, and actors, and perhaps Napoleon. The hero, from antiquity, stands somewhere between god and man, a superhuman, but vulnerable, symbol of greatness. Heroes connect us with heavenly or Olympian origins, with great achievements and noble endings. They help us forget that we were expelled from the womb helpless and bloody; yet their stories immerse us in the primordial sea where Darwin found our ancestors.

In his introduction, Rank notes that in *The Artist* he spoke of myth as the collective dream of a people, *Massentraum*. He used the phrase *seelischer Gebilde,* "structures of the soul," acknowledging the thesis of Adolph Bauer (1882) that the similarity of myths across cultures results from general traits of the mind (the *Seelenleben* or inner life) rather than from the existence of a primeval community or migration.[36] This foreshadows Jung's ideas of the archetype and the collective unconscious.

Rank uses psychoanalytic theory to develop "on a large scale for the first time" a psychological approach to the interpretation of myths. Rank, 24 and just starting University, was precocious by any standard and audacious in staking such a claim in an area embracing psychoanalysis, anthropology, and literature. Freud was 21 when his first scientific paper appeared, 35 when he published his book on aphasia (1891).

Rank presents some fifteen hero myths, the longest being Cyrus. The catalog becomes tedious, although the similarities are compelling. He adds a coda to Oedipus with a series of Christian myths with similar features, of which Judas is a paradigm. He unknowingly killed his father in a fight and married the widow, his mother. When the crime is revealed, he repents through Jesus.

In the last part of his book Rank compares the "standard" myth with a human skeleton seen on X-ray: The skeleton as a constant element supporting diverse body types is like the standard saga underpinning varied myths. (Roentgen discovered the X-ray in 1895, about the same time Freud discovered psychoanalysis.) Here, in Rank's words, is the "skeleton" myth:

The hero is the child of most distinguished parents, usually the

son of a king. His origin is preceded by difficulties, such as conti-
nence, or prolonged barrenness, or secret intercourse of the parents
due to external prohibition or obstacles. During or before the pregnancy there is a prophecy, in the form of a dream or oracle, caution-
ing against his birth, and usually threatening danger to the father
(or his representative). As a rule, he is surrendered to the water,
in a box. He is then saved by animals, or by lowly people (shepherds),
and is suckled by a female animal or by a humble woman. After
he has grown up, he finds his distinguished parents, in a highly
versatile fashion. He takes his revenge on his father, on the one
hand, and is acknowledged, on the other. Finally he achieves rank
and honors.[37]

In discussing why the hero must sever relations with his parents, Rank points to the individual imagination, tracing it back
to the imaginative life of the child. Freud's discovery that neurotics preserve the emotions of childhood points to such residuals
in normal adults. Rank here anticipates and paves the way for
child analysis. He also emphasizes the victim role of the son,
placed in jeopardy by the father. "Revenge" describes the de-
nouement, whereas Freud postulated an innate patricidal wish
in every boy.

The ego of the child acts like the hero of the myth; "indeed
the hero is only to be understood as a collective ego (*Kollektiv-
Ich*)."[38] The hero myth, with royal and humble parents, is the
family romance played backwards. Instead of being cut off from
good parents and brought up by bad ones, the hero is cruelly
exposed at birth and then rescued by good, though lowly, surro-
gates. In dream symbolism, the box (womb) set adrift represents
birth, as does exposure of the chosen/cursed infant (though it
appears to be a putting to death). Myths of floods are widely
distributed, and may be regarded as placing the community
in the hero role, with God as the wrathful father.

This book, the first by Rank to be translated into English
(1914), has probably been in print in the United States longer
than any other of his works. The presentation is a blend of
Freud's new psychology and Rank's encyclopedic grasp of mythology. As with dreams, myth elements can be transposed by
the interpreter. To Freud, the hero birth story is an elaborate
projection, whereby the boy's patricidal anger becomes the father's wish to get rid of the son. Not only does the projection
avoid guilt on the boy's part for what happens (patricide), but

it justifies whatever hostility he may actually feel. This juggling of elements does violence to the myth in denying significance to the themes of infanticide and separation/alienation from the family of origin. Oedipus would not knowingly have killed his father; the deed evolved from an infanticidal act which alienated the innocent child from his biological family. Already in this work, Rank takes into account the ambivalence of parenthood. Later he concluded that, by accepting paternity, men recognize their mortality; the father perceives and accepts the child as his replacement and as a sign of inevitable death.

In this early work, Rank's struggle with birth and will contains post-Freudian elements. Noting parental hostility toward their offspring, Rank writes: "In the myth the parents refuse to let the child be born, which is precisely the reason of the hero's lament; moreover, the myth plainly reveals the desire to enforce his materialization even against the will of the parents." Rank later taught that will first shows itself as counter-will, expressed by the individual's heroic, though embryonic, determination to live his own life. Ambivalence appears forthwith, since living entails dying. "The vital peril, thus concealed in the representation of birth through exposure, actually exists in the process of birth itself." Rank offers two interpretations: one, that the hero in being born has triumphed against opposition; two, that in sensing his bitter destiny, the hero deplores his birth. Indeed, the hero accuses his parents for "having exposed him to the struggle of life."[39]

The revised Ten Commandments in Rank's adolescent diary state, "Thou shalt not give birth reluctantly." Such reluctance exists even where the parents, like Laius and Jocasta, are well endowed. Their reluctance is projected onto the oracle, who predicts the double crime of patricide and incest. The couple's conscious wish is to have a child, to overcome barrenness. Laius, father of Oedipus, has in common with Hjalmar, father of Hedvig in *Wild Duck*, a desperate selfishness which allows him to sacrifice his child to save his own life.

As the less-favored child in the Rosenfeld family, which in his view was ill-equipped to raise children at all, Otto's own existence might be compared to that of the hero. Initially he saw himself as victim, propelled willy-nilly into a psychologically hostile environment. This exposure should have killed his spirit, but he—and it—survived. He watched himself choose life by

edging close to suicide. Psychologically Rank annihilated his father, then partially reclaimed him as the source of worthwhile
traits. Like Weininger, but only temporarily, he resisted sexual
feeling—a symbol of life and of mortality—by consigning women
to untouchable whoredom. In Rank's family, as in that of Ekdal,
a harsh, immature father tyrannized a mother and child who
were courageous, honest, feeling people. From helpless castaway
bemoaning his fate Rank became an intrepid explorer and culti-
vator of the no man's land in which he found himself.

Freud, by contrast, was born to a princely estate. His struggles
had other causes, so it follows that some of Rank's major themes
do not preoccupy his mentor. Will and existential despair emerge
in the *Hero* book as themes that absorbed the young philosopher-
therapist thereafter. Even a link to the trauma of birth appears
when Rank cites Lucretius: "Behold the infant: Like a ship-
wrecked sailor cast ashore by the fury of the billows . . . after
Nature has dragged him in pain from his mother's womb."[40]

The incredibly rich and compact Oedipus myth draws two
paradoxical strands together in what is stated and what is only
implied. The child, feared and cursed by his parents as the har-
binger of mortality, curses them for *his* mortality—for life limited by death, and the consciousness thereof. The family both
protects and exposes the child. To have needs met affirms one's
vulnerability at the same time that it proves love. The price
of love—consciousness of vulnerability—like the price of life—
consciousness of death—is high but need not be prohibitive. Self-
conscious people can transcend nihilism *if they will*. Rank himself did so, as a poet who increasingly engaged with the actors
and scenery of the real world, a world which at first he despised,
then studied, and finally loved.

Rank reminds us that the heroes of old did not write their
own stories. The myths by which we know them are produced
by poets and storytellers, an oral history passed through generations of rapt listeners. Myth-makers please the public by giving
the hero a heroic childhood, "a wonderful infancy" to accompany
his extraordinary life. That romantic vision of childhood derives,
of course, from the poet's consciousness of his own birth and
development, artistically elaborated. So poet and audience identify themselves with the hero in creating a shared origin. "The
true hero of the romance is, therefore, the ego, which finds
itself in the hero."

The myth allows ordinary people to experience vicariously the expression of two conflicting motives: loving gratitude toward the parents, and revolt against them. As in the Oedipus story, parents may be symbolized by two images (rejecting birth-parents, loving adoptive parents). They may appear as animals: the wolf with Romulus, the swan with Lohengrin.

Along with the frequently appearing box or basket in the water, these symbols *unsex* the birth process. Rank argues that concealment of the sexual aspects of the birth process poses an enigma for children, who may resolve their ignorance and discomfort in several ways, all of which appear in hero myths. They may play the fool and accept the "stork" explanation, or twit the mother in effect by taking suck from nursing animals, whose sexuality is plain and not denied. They may follow the prohibition, as in Lohengrin, against asking where the hero came from or, contrarily, the Oedipal imperative to solve the riddle and then investigate the sexual family secret to its shocking, blinding end.

Ideas tumble over one another in Rank's writing like charms on a heavy bracelet. In some places they obscure the connecting chain. The linking argument is strong, but the material is dense and the connections may be lost to the untrained eye. By contrast to this jeweler-artisan writing, Freud's texts are those of a forester-scientist who guides the reader along a path so clearly marked that one cannot fail to see; one can refuse to follow, but there is little danger of getting lost.

In concluding his book, Rank briefly deals with mental illness and social psychopathology. A fantasy repressed by the hysteric is experienced—lived out—by the pervert. The paranoid's delusion corrects the inner world, but the criminal changes the outer world to suit his mind. The anarchist, along with the hero, is a typical rebel, renovator, revolutionary. The paranoid identifies with the fearful father, but the anarchist, like the hero, assassinates the king.

As Rank was writing this book, Adolf Hitler, a disgruntled adolescent from Linz, arrived in Vienna. Five years Rank's junior, he drew and painted and considered himself an artist. He took odd jobs around Vienna, unfortunately failing to be accepted in an art academy. His dislike for human diversity was fueled in the multilingual political and cultural kaleidoscope of the city. In him grew a more virulent anti-Semitism than that of Otto Weininger and Mayor Karl Lueger, whose effective demagoguery he admired. Between 1907 and 1913 Hitler painted signs, carried suitcases, and shoveled snow in Vienna, staying in dismal flophouses and nourishing his hatred of the decadent Habsburg Empire, its curse-of-Babel parliament, and the ultimate symbols of difference, its Jewish, Slavic, and gypsy minorities.

CHAPTER 5

The Psychoanalytic Movement

*After all, our Aryan comrades are quite indispensable to us;
otherwise psychoanalysis would fall a victim to anti-Semitism.*
—Sigmund Freud, 1908[1]

Freud was a man of action as well as ideas. Unlike most scientists, content to scatter their ideas like seeds on stony ground, Freud envisioned a movement to nurture and disseminate his radical truth. When he hired Rank as Secretary of the Wednesday Psychological Society, he formalized the first psychoanalytic organization. But, the Viennese Society disappointed its founder and leader; Freud did not care for most of his Viennese admirers. Only Rank showed real promise, and he was just preparing to enter the University.

Many supportive letters and several important visitors from outside Austria fueled Freud's hopes and his ambition to create an international movement. As a scientist he did not want to lead the movement, but as conquistador—a term he once applied to himself—he wanted to see it grow. Carl Jung, the first important non-Jew to embrace Freud, personified the movement and quickly assumed the leadership role in seeking to fulfill their shared vision of international triumph and scientific immortality. In the first major psychoanalytic schism, Jung's rise in the fledgling movement between 1907 and 1911 coincided with the purge of Alfred Adler. Rank appears to have been an onlooker, simply keeping the minutes and pursuing his academic work and writing; as befit his status, he did not take sides in political and personal conflicts. The minutes and the Freud-Jung correspondence give some indication of Rank's development during this time, but we know nothing of his personal relationship with Jung.

THE BEGINNING OF PSYCHOANALYTIC POLITICS

In the fall of 1907, Freud dissolved the "little society" in order to establish a more formal arrangement. Members were now expected to pay dues to cover expenses, the largest portion going toward the salary of Rank as Secretary for a second year. Membership grew to twenty-one, newcomers more than replacing resignations.

Despite the new structure, Society meetings became increasingly personal. Members' presentations were sometimes frankly autobiographical; at other times they were suspected to be. For example, a discussion on sleep was led by an insomniac. When a new non-Jewish member presented a talk on his premarital sex life, the group discussed the difference between Aryan and Semitic upbringing, and whether the speaker was healthy or neurotic. Sessions often degenerated into a new form of *ad hominem* attack: psychoanalytic character assassination. For example, Hitschmann said that Wittels was interested in the topics of pregnancy, chaste female medical students, and syphilis because he was sexually thwarted by all three. Objections were raised to "outbursts of rage and indignation," which, understandably, occurred even more often.[2]

As a result, in February 1908, new rules were adopted. It was decided to devote some sessions to book and journal reviews. Rank, as Secretary, was given the responsibility of organizing these, with Hitschmann to advise him. Each member was to give one major presentation annually. To control the unruliness, Freud reluctantly agreed to intervene as chairman if a speaker was being interrupted or distracted. Freud said he found it painful to reprimand anyone and threatened to end the meetings if the members could not have civil, honest exchanges of scientific opinion. He hoped that "deeper psychological understanding would overcome the difficulties in personal contacts." On the matter of intellectual private property versus "intellectual communism," it was decided that ideas could be freely used by others unless a claim of ownership was invoked by its author.[3]

As a scientific observer of his patients and himself, Freud put great stock in perseverance and analytical logic. While he opposed the intuitive, artistic side of himself, he welcomed confirmation of his insights from literature. Thus he was delighted when Rank discovered a passage from Friedrich Schiller illustrating Freud's concept of free association. The passage, which Rank shared with the Society, appears in a letter of 1788 in which the poet-philosopher counsels a friend who complained about a lack of productivity. Among other things the passage expresses Rank's concern that too strong an intellect interferes with creativity.

> The basis for your complaint seems to me to lie in the oppression of your imagination by your intellect. I must express an idea here with a comparison. It seems a hindrance to the creative work of the soul if the intellect examines too closely the ideas that press in, as it were, upon the gates. Taken by itself an idea may seem very odd and very trivial, but perhaps will become important through another which follows; combined with others which may seem equally absurd or unappetizing, it may form a very potent link: this the intellect cannot judge unless it holds the idea long enough to view it in connection with the others. With a creative person, methinks, the intellect has withdrawn its guard from the gates; ideas rush in pell-mell and only then does it survey and study the great mass of them. You Gentleman Critics, or however you call yourselves, are ashamed or frightened of the momentary, passing madness found in every true creator, the longer or shorter duration of which distinguishes the thinking artist from the dreamer. You complain of your unfruitfulness because you spurn too soon and sift too fine.[4]

Freud excitedly wrote Jung, suggesting the quotation be read at the first psychoanalytic Congress:

> *Our secretary Otto Rank has found a delightful passage in justification of our psychoanalytic technique. It would take Rank only a few minutes to read it and it would close our morning on a suitable note. Rank, who is coming with us, is a nice, intelligent youngster. He graduated trade school as a machinist, and now is studying Latin and Greek to pass his*

Matura *examination to get into the University. He is 23 years old; he must have sent you his somewhat impenetrable book* The Artist, *which, however, contains the best explanation of my complicated theories to have reached me thus far. I expect a lot from him once he has finished school.*[5]

Just a year earlier, when Jung had criticized Rank's *Artist* as being difficult to understand and too much an echo of Freud, Freud had replied:

Clearly Rank will not have much success. His writing is positively autoerotic; he lacks any regard for pedagogic considerations. Moreover, as you notice, he has not overcome the influence of his previous intellectual fare and wallows in abstractions that I cannot get a firm hold on. But his independence of me is greater than appears; very young, he has a good head and is thoroughly honest and open, which is especially commendable in such a youngster. Of course, from your way of presenting the material we expect a great deal more.[6]

During the intervening year, it is clear, Rank had climbed in Freud's esteem. Jung responded well to Freud's enthusiasm and was much more supportive of Rank's work.

The pious exordium by Rank suits me very well. I've read Rank's book, half understood it, and am distinctly impressed by his intelligence. This man is certainly a good find. The only thing lacking is the empirical "contact with reality." I have seen from his book that in theory he has felt his way into your thinking very deeply, more deeply than I have. But then, he had the privilege of your personal stimulation, which has given him a thousand shortcuts to knowledge.[7]

Freud used the Schiller quotation, with acknowledgment to Otto Rank, in the second edition of *Interpretation of Dreams* (1909).

In the same session in which Rank recited the quotation, he offered a case report on Schiller in which he argued that eye problems led the poet to write his William Tell drama, which portrays a blind archer. Having employed Adler's theory, Rank was roundly attacked by Stekel ("painful"), Hitschmann ("paradoxical and forced, and inferiority dragged in by the hair"), Graf, and Federn. Adler defended the inferiority thesis, saying there cannot be a playwright without poor eyes. Freud, standoffish in the past toward Adler's idea, this time said, "Rank's interpretation is a particularly beautiful mythological confirmation of Adler's principle and secure as are few interpretations."[8]

FREUD AND HIS SOURCES

At the Society meeting of April 1 Hitschmann presented a talk on Nietzsche's *Genealogy of Morals.* This session was particularly interesting both because of Freud's denial of Nietzsche's influence on his work and on account of the others' reactions, especially Rank's.

In his presentation, Hitschmann said that Nietzsche combined a love of language and art with an inclination to strong (homosexual) friendship. The German philosopher's joyous, spirited writing contrasted with his gloomy life. Adler felt Nietzsche was "closest to our way of thinking" of all philosophers and placed him on a line from Schopenhauer through Marx and Mach to Freud. "In Nietzsche's work one finds almost on every page observations reminiscent of those we make in therapy when the patient has come rather a long way and is capable of analyzing the undercurrents in his mind." Graf saw Nietzsche's works as a "self-cure," by which Nietzsche "came from his weak nature to his strong ideas. . . . his development does not follow a straight line as does that of many other thinkers and explorers. . . . his later philosophy is rooted in his struggle against his illness by means of self-analysis."

Federn asked if there was any aspect of psychoanalysis Nietzsche had *not* anticipated. "He intuitively knew a number of Freud's discoveries; he was the first to discover the significance of abreaction, of repression, of flight into illness, of the instincts— the normal sexual as well as the sadistic ones. . . . It is worth mentioning that Otto Weininger also had to struggle with the suppression of sadism (ideas of lustful murder); his book shows him to be a highly ethical individual.

"Although Nietzsche discovered the conditions of mankind's childhood," Federn continued, "he never recognized the conditions of his own childhood." In this epigrammatic distinction, preserved in Secretary Rank's faithful hand, Paul Federn elegantly set off Freud's discovery from the insights of intuitive geniuses before him.

Rank summed up his own view of Nietzsche: "That he explored not the external world, as did other philosophers, but *himself* reveals a development reversing the earlier transfer from within onto the external world."[9]

Freud's reaction to the discussion of Nietzsche sheds light on his strong ambivalence toward philosophy, his attitude toward intellectual influence, and some of his differences with Rank.

Freud spoke candidly to the group of his peculiar relationship to philosophy: "Its abstract nature is so unpleasant to me that I will not study it. I do not know Nietzsche's work; occasional attempts at reading it were *smothered by an excess of interest* [emphasis added]. Despite the similarities which many people have pointed out, I can assure you that Nietzsche's ideas have had no influence whatsoever on my own work."[10]

Historians have said it is highly unlikely that someone growing up in Freud's milieu would not have been exposed to Nietzsche's influence. Indeed, as a university student, Freud participated in a reading society for five years; the group not only studied Schopenhauer, Wagner, and Nietzsche but actually corresponded with Nietzsche.

In all probability, Freud's startling denial of Nietzsche's influence on his work did not convince anyone. It did, coupled with what followed in that session, illustrate Freud's ambivalent relationship to the past. He tried to master it. His penchant for objective truth cloaked his subjective distortions in the garb of modern science, whether in relationship to Oedipus, Nietzsche, or Josef Breuer. Freud handled the matter of intellectual influence or indebtedness variously: He brusquely denied Nietzsche and Fliess; he was ambivalent toward Breuer and Charcot; but he praised Brücke and Meynert, the great laboratory scientists who had nothing to do with psychoanalysis itself.

Having flatly denied Nietzsche's influence, Freud went on to tell the group that his sexual theory of the neuroses actually derived from an idea expressed to him at different times by three great physicians, Breuer, Charcot, and Chrobak. In suggesting this origin of his theory, Freud—as he often did—tried to convert café chaff into scientific gold. In certain remarks never intended for public discussion, Freud found deep truths. But he used the remarks to justify himself at the expense of these unwitting mentors. Freud's capacity to forget priority, as with Fliess, is here matched by his assigning priority where none really existed.

Freud explained that he had long forgotten the doctors' seminal remarks, only to recall them when "faced with repudiation of this concept, I attempted to justify myself." In brief, the humble sources of Freud's sexual theory were ribald comments by three reputable men. Hysteria is a problem, they said at various times: of the boudoir (Breuer); of the genitals (Charcot); curable by repeated doses of a normal penis (Chrobak, eminent Viennese gynecologist, whose bawdy prescription was told to Freud in Latin).

These crude "theories" had stimulated Freud's interest in the patient's current sex life and childhood sexual history, he said. Freud claimed simply to be the first who was not afraid to address scientifically what the others "knew" but would not talk about openly. On reflection, he concluded that these men did not really know what message they had imparted. Freud became wedded, one might say, to an idea with which they only flirted. The ideas were much more tawdry than the sexual theory, but because of their distinguished sources, they lent Freud a cloak of respectability. The physicians were distinguished, but their remarks—especially Chrobak's—were casual or cynical asides, not to be cited publicly. In one of the strangest cases of handling credits for a scientific discovery, Freud reminded the two Viennese physicians of what they had said, and both denied it! (Freud says that Charcot would have denied it too.) That did not stop Freud from invoking them as unwitting precedents. He thus made them his supporters over their objections.[11]

This detail illustrates Freud's extraordinary manipulation of influence—his indebtedness to, and independence from, mentors. Unable to accept Nietzsche's gifts outright, he concocted an influence from three physicians whose status was important. In order to break out of his scientific isolation, Freud "remembered" these sources and readily confessed a lack of originality. His intellectual modesty was more than compensated for by the cloak of respectability which he borrowed or purloined from his mentors. Though keenly attuned to scientific priority, Freud displayed amazing lapses of memory and conduct in regard to Fliess and Nietzsche. Was his memory selective again in the case of the demurring doctors? Freud probably heard such sexual remarks from dozens of lesser men than these. Even if his memory was right, using his sources' names in such fashion was not. To defend an unpopular idea is difficult, but Freud ought to have done it alone, not with the disavowed words of other authorities. If they did express those thoughts informally they were entitled to their privacy; they neither sought nor wanted credit for such insights. Freud's self-justification ends deviously: "I have certainly not disclosed the illustrious parentage of this scandalous idea in order to saddle others with the responsibility for it."

Freud complained of being isolated from colleagues because of his ideas, but this episode shows how the isolation might have resulted from his insensitive and self-serving conduct. Breuer and Chrobak vehemently denied paternity of Freud's "bastard" theory. Freud's need to share "credit" led him to dismiss their denials as just one more example of repression. A serious vocational hazard of psychoanalysis, exemplified first by its creator, is the assumption that truth is in the ear of the Freudian listener; he knows better than the speaker what can be taken at face value. As Rank eventually realized, that is another form of subjectivity, though couched in terms of objective science. Its effect is to put "truth" before relationships, even before reality. (Charcot and Chrobak were dead before Freud published his history in 1914, but not Breuer, about whom Freud no longer cared.)

Freud's theory, in keeping with its ribald origins, contained at this stage the sense that a good roll in the hay keeps the analyst away: Freud might well have said it in this fashion. He saw danger in masturbation and coitus interruptus, while the sexual element in neurosis provided a biological anchor to his theory. "I am rather annoyed with Bleuler," he wrote to Jung, "for his willingness to accept a psychology without sexuality, which leaves everything hanging in midair. In the sexual processes we have the indispensable 'organic foundation' without which a medical man can only feel ill at ease in the life of the psyche."[12] In Breuer, Charcot, and Chrobak Freud found sources of support by stretching a point, while simultaneously stretching to evade the "mid-air" psychology of a Friedrich Nietzsche, who lacked the "indispensable organic foundation."

THE SALZBURG CONGRESS

On Easter Sunday, 1908, forty-two people met in Salzburg for what came to be known as the First International Psychoanalytic Congress. Over half were Austrian, most of them from Vienna, a six-hour train ride away. Most were doctors or professors; there were only two women. A. A. Brill, the Hungarian-American psychiatrist who first translated Freud into English, represented the United States. Besides Otto Rank, three of Freud's future inner circle were there: Karl Abraham from Berlin, Sandor Ferenczi from Budapest, and Ernest Jones from London's medically fashionable Harley Street.[13]

The Congress was loosely organized; there was no chairman or secretary. But there was an agenda. As first speaker on Monday morning at eight, Freud presented his analysis of an obsessive-compulsive young lawyer, the "Rat Man," a case already known to the Viennese group. Listeners lined both sides of a long table, at the head of which sat the Professor. His soft-spoken oratory was spellbinding. At eleven o'clock he suggested ending, but he was pressed to go on, which he did until almost one in the afternoon. Speaking without notes, he enthralled the audience for almost five hours. "Perfection itself," said Jung.[14] The other presentations were overshadowed by that of Freud—for which, in any case, most of the attendees had come. Rank was introduced through his Schiller discovery. And Abraham gave a paper which provoked Jung because it failed to give him due credit for a particular idea.

Freud was elated by the international character of the successful meeting, but the other Viennese were unhappy. Freud and Jung had no concern for democratic process or even for diplomatic tact, and simply left the Viennese out of their plans to launch a psychoanalytic periodical, the *Jahrbuch* [*Yearbook*], to be edited by Jung. The Viennese sensed that Jung could not be trusted, but Freud scolded them for what he considered petty jealousy and reminded them of the importance of cultivating well-connected non-Jewish adherents. Freud had to remonstrate with Abraham, too, because of his failure to properly credit Jung. Freud said Jung was special, since "a Christian and a pastor's son finds his way to me only against great inner resistances. His association with us is the more valuable for that. I nearly said that it was only by his appearance on the scene that psychoanalysis escaped the danger of becoming a Jewish national affair."[15]

After the Salzburg Congress, Freud corresponded actively with Jung in Zurich and with Abraham, who had started a psychoanalytic society in Berlin. Freud tried to keep peace between his two strongest non-Viennese supporters, who disliked one another. "I get on most easily with you (and Ferenczi)," Freud wrote Abraham, attributing that ease to their Jewishness, a "racial preference." Freud asked Abraham to make the extra effort necessary to include "the more alien Aryan," Jung. The published letters of these three men are a rich source of information about the ideas and personalities of the movement, including Rank. For instance, Freud proposed to Jung that "little Rank" be the reporter from Vienna for the *Yearbook*: "You know from his *Artist* how well he can formulate my ideas."[16] For the next fifteen years, Freud's references to Rank were virtually all positive.

GROWING PAINS: FREUD AND JUNG

Two episodes in Jung's analytic practice during this period illustrate the growing pains of psychoanalytic theory and practice. They also shed light on the intense private relationship between Freud and his Swiss disciple. Otto Rank probably knew something about these episodes, if not the details. He certainly participated in discussions of similar cases in the Vienna Psychoanalytic Society (as the Wednesday group was now called) and privately with Freud.

The first episode involved a brilliant Viennese physician, Otto Gross, who was addicted to opium and whom Jung agreed to treat during the withdrawal period. Freud expressed relief about referring Gross to Zurich because, he wrote, "the dividing line between our respective property rights in creative ideas would inevitably have been effaced . . . Since I treated the philosopher Swoboda I have had a horror of such difficult situations." Freud remembered the priority conflict with Fliess and shied away from the temptation and the hazards of too much intellectual stimulation (as he had also with Nietzsche). Jung analyzed Gross for hours at a time and wrote, "Whenever I got stuck, he analyzed me. In this way my own mental health has benefited." Jung found in Gross a fascinating colleague and companion, even a twin brother, except that Gross suffered from dementia praecox ("early dementia," a term for which Bleuler substituted "schizophrenia" in 1911). "He is one of those whom life is *bound* to reject," Jung prophesied, and correctly.[17] Jung's frank acknowledgment of the impact of patient upon therapist is remarkable; his enthusiasm, openness, and compassion are refreshingly unorthodox. Freud approved of Jung's efforts, with gratitude.

A young woman patient, Sabina Spielrein, had a deeper involvement with Jung. He began his analysis with her when she was hospitalized in 1904 as an 18-year-old hysteric; with Jung's encouragement she went on to study medicine and become a psychiatrist. At some point they had begun an affair. In 1909 someone, probably Jung's wife, informed Sabina's mother of the situation. She in turn accused Jung, who replied that because he charged no fee he could act with Sabina as a man rather than a doctor; for ten francs an hour, Jung said, he would resume his professional role. Meanwhile Spielrein wrote Freud, asking for his help to free her from Jung so that she could love someone else; she felt she had to either forgive Jung or murder him. Freud defended Jung to Spielrein and then wrote Jung, "To be slandered and scorched by the love with which we operate—such are the perils of our trade." At last ashamed, Jung confessed the truth to Freud, admitting that his response to her mother was "a piece of knavery."[18]

Jung had feared Freud's anger, but he received a magnanimous reply.

> *Such experiences, though painful, are necessary and hard to avoid. Without them we cannot really know life and what we are dealing with. I myself have never been taken in quite so badly, but I have come very close to it a number of times and had a narrow escape. I believe that only grim necessities weighing on my work, and the fact that I was ten years older than you when I came to psychoanalysis, saved me from similar experiences. But no lasting harm is done. They help us develop the thick skin we need and to dominate 'counter-transference,' which is after all a permanent problem for us.*[19]

The matter ended well, and in 1911 Dr. Spielrein became one of the first women to join the Vienna Psychoanalytic Society.

Freud had more trouble with Jung's occultism than with his sexual indiscretion. On Jung's belief in precognition, the ability to foretell events, Freud reflected: "Keep a cool head, for it is better not to understand something than make such great sacrifices to understanding." But by then (1909), Freud was calling Jung "my successor and crown prince" and saying, "If I am

Moses, then you are Joshua and will take possession of the promised land of psychiatry." A year earlier Jung had asked to be
treated like a son, but now he said he was glad to be free from
"the oppressive sense of your paternal authority." When Jung
complained of difficulties that followed his first successes in psychoanalytic practice, Freud advised: "Just give up wanting to
cure; learn and make money, those are the most plausible conscious aims."[20]

THE VIENNESE CONTEXT

As psychoanalysis gained admirers it also created enemies. Freud
finished the second edition of *Interpretation of Dreams* in the
summer of 1908. In its preface he expressed bitterness toward
psychiatrists and philosophers for rejecting him, and gratitude
to his small circle of co-workers and a larger audience of appreciative laymen. The sociopolitical context of the new movement—
and of Rank's young adulthood—provides a perspective.

Some critics felt psychoanalysis represented a regression to
prescientific or "old wives' " psychiatry, and some argued that
its success was a phenomenon of *genius loci*, the spirit of a
place.[21] According to this argument Vienna was fertile ground,
prepared by the success of Krafft-Ebing's *Psychopathia Sexualis*
(1886) and Weininger's *Sex and Character* (1903), not to mention
the sexual intrigue of Schnitzler's plays. Freud's lay audience
was at least as psychologically sophisticated—and more eager—
than the medical profession. Later this *genius loci* argument
was misunderstood to imply that Vienna was debauched. Beneath the glittering surface and behind various doors abounded
carnal mischief, corruption, and hypocrisy, but no more than
in many other cities of that era.

Vienna was unique in other respects. The last bastion of a
fading old empire, the city had as its mayor a popular demagogue
named Karl Lueger (1844–1910). A polished orator, Lueger had
moved away from his earlier liberalism to an opportunistic mixture of progressive municipal socialism, traditional conservatism,
and selective anti-Semitism. Between 1897 and his death in 1910,
Lueger lit the streets and ran streetcars with electricity, created
parks and schools for the lower class, and provided flood control
on the Danube, housing, and social security. He became almost

as popular as Emperor Franz Josef, who so opposed Lueger's anti-Semitism that he refused to let him serve as Mayor until Lueger was elected for the fifth time.[22]

Once the seat of the Holy Roman Empire, Vienna had a population about 90 percent Catholic. After thirty years of large-scale immigration from points east, Jews numbered 150,000, almost 10 percent of the population, at the turn of the century.[23] Otto Rank was one of a substantial number of Jews who registered as "unaffiliated." Conversion, usually to Catholicism, was relatively common; conflicts arose between the more assimilated Jewish population and newcomers. But hoped-for gains in the liberal tradition did not materialize, and although Jews were overrepresented proportionally in the professions, they were discriminated against economically and politically. Still, this was a far cry from the pogroms to the east.

A world capital of music, medicine, and psychoanalysis, Vienna enjoyed an intellectual ferment in philosophy, literature, and science. Hugo von Hofmannsthal (1874–1929) was part of *Jung Wien* (Young Vienna), a writers group which flourished in the 1890s. It included Hermann Bahr, Arthur Schnitzler, Theodor Herzl, Richard Beer-Hofmann, and Stefan Zweig, "a circle of patricians, dandies, thinkers, and scoffers" who dominated literary Vienna. Solomon Liptzin describes this group eloquently in a way which shows the ferment and conflict that characterized and finally ruptured the mentorship of Freud and Rank. Referring to the "aesthetes" of *Jung Wien,* Liptzin says:

> As thinkers they were determinists, but as poets they were believers in free will. They held that eternal laws rule the rippling of waves, the growth of grass, the flight of birds, the streaming of thoughts within the mind of man. They recognized, however, that acceptance of pure determinism means abandoning all our ethical concepts of guilt and atonement, sin and virtue, and even such distinctions as important and unimportant. . . . [yet] They preferred clarity to profundity and the honest weapons of logic to the poisonous arrows of mysticism.[24]

GROWING PAINS AND PLEASURES: OTTO RANK

At the age of 24, Otto Rank was too old for high school and too young to be a psychoanalyst. Dividing himself between the classroom and the Freudians was itself a psychological feat, since his identity could not be based on full membership in either context. In the summer of 1908 Rank graduated from Gymnasium, and that fall he entered the University of Vienna to pursue his doctorate with a major in philosophy and a minor in German. At last he was in an academic setting that provided some peers in age and ability.

At this time, Rank formalized his adopted name and, in order to do so, converted to Catholicism. Although registered as "unaffiliated," Rank had to go a step further to justify changing his name from Rosenfeld; an earlier application to legalize "Rank" as a pen name had been turned down. As a nominal Catholic he applied again, and was successful. Rank's temporary foray into Catholicism—he converted back to Judaism before his marriage—was a secret that has only recently come to light.[25] (Even his daughter did not know of it.) Given the antireligious sentiment of his diary, and the atheistic milieu of psychoanalysis, we can conclude that Rank's motive for converting was expediency. He never denied his Jewish roots, but his change of name clearly represented a separation from his family of origin and a self-redefinition.

Rank's identity included something of an actor, which he once hoped to be. To some extent he created a role for himself and developed a personality to fit. Living in two different milieus—partially at home in both but not wholly in either—taught Rank how to be flexible in external roles while forming a consistent internal sense of himself. (In his diary he noted his marvelous capacity for accommodation.) Active, creative identity formation is consistent with Rank's philosophy of knowledge and experience. His view of truth as a subjective creation set him apart from Freud, who viewed it as something to be investigated rather than invented, objectively proven rather than subjectively lived.

In the Vienna Psychoanalytic Society, Rank dutifully performed his secretarial chores. Yet in the minutes the development of his independent ideas was increasingly evident. He spoke up at times with remarkable boldness. In the minutes of 1908–1909, Rank's development can be traced through another encounter with Nietzsche, and a challenge to Freud, illuminating a new self-definition.

The presentation on Nietzsche concerned his posthumously

published *Ecce Homo* (1908), an autobiographical work. Some of the points made in Rank's minutes highlight his own identity issues.[26] For Nietzsche the essence of illness was the will not to recover; he regarded illness as an excessive sensitivity to life, necessary for spiritual development. Nietzsche felt the Dionysian in himself, a high regard for passion and the drive to give form and expression to it, "to spend oneself in one's work." He had a tendency to dramatize, to "try himself out in ever new forms . . . forever discovering himself in a superior being." A tender, sensitive, affectionate soul, he recreated himself as the instinct-driven Dionysus.

Rank disputed those who said Nietzsche was neurotic. He asserted that what appears to be neurosis can be found in all unusual men and also in the normal human being. Freud defended Nietzsche against psychiatrists who put him down as a syphilitic. The paresis was crucial in this enigmatic man, Freud said, because it loosened his mind to see through all the layers to the base instincts. According to Freud, *Ecce Homo* showed a mastery of form that supported its validity. "The fact that Nietzsche was at first the victim of a conspiracy of silence, and then later became a fashionable idol, is almost comical," said Freud, who might have been speaking of himself.

Freud's remarks probably reflect Rank's influence. Freud continued: "The degree of introspection achieved by Nietzsche had never been achieved by anyone, nor is it likely ever to be reached again. What disturbs us is that Nietzsche transformed 'is' into 'ought,' which is alien to science. In this he has remained, after all, the moralist; he could not free himself of the theologian." Freud again stressed his inability to study Nietzsche, "partly because of the resemblance of Nietzsche's intuitive insights to our laborious investigations, and partly because of the wealth of ideas, which has always prevented me from getting beyond the first half-page whenever I tried to read him."[27]

It could not be by chance that Rank selected "Cursed to Stand" from the Grimm Brothers for presentation in February 1909. The tale concerns a boy who did not immediately obey his father's command. Angered by his son's defiance, the father cursed him to remain fixed to the spot forever. After some years, the boy died. Rank concluded his analysis: "In this case of hysterical paralysis, the motivation—that is, the stubborn boy's resistance to his father's order—is very clearly expressed." Rank, the "son" of the Little Society, was the only one who took orders. No one commented on the aptness of his choice of theme. Stekel observed that the story symbolizes priapism. Freud commented that it is the prototype of passive resistance. He may have sensed Rank's identification with the quietly defiant son.

By this time Rank could hold his own in debating clinical matters, if not from experience, at least out of a strong sense of the patient's need. Rank applied intelligence and sensitivity to form clinical judgments that were often better than those expressed by his elders in the Society. For example, he rebutted the claim that one could psychoanalyze a patient without comprehensive knowledge of that person's language. A speaker had argued that facial expression and behavioral factors would provide adequate clues for analysis. Rank argued that "the language of psychoanalysis is very difficult to understand, by contrast with the language of love, which is international. The psychoanalyst needs an adequate knowledge of his patient's language, down to its most subtle possibilities for expression, and the nuances of dialect, in order not to throw into question the prospects for a cure."[28] In later years the mature Rank, who practiced analysis in his second language, warned therapists not to impose either idiom or ideology upon their patients.

While Rank made forays into clinical discussions, he never let go of his primary concern: the artist first, and creativity in general. Even a discussion of Karl Marx by Alfred Adler had a bearing on the subject: How does increasing consciousness of man's own inner workings affect society? Freud was receptive to the lecture, which Adler hoped would demonstrate that "the theory of class struggle is clearly in harmony with the results of our teachings on instincts." In response Freud outlined a theory of human progress: "The enlargement of consciousness is what enables mankind to cope with life in the face of the steady process of repression." And vice versa; each process is a condition for the other. Freud praised Rank, citing "The Incest Motif" for examples of how poetry reflects the ongoing repression, and calling *The Artist* "the first introduction of psychology into historical studies."[29] (Freud's own venture into this area came with *Totem and Taboo*, in 1913.)

Adler concluded the session dramatically: "Marx's entire work culminates in the demand to make history *consciously.*" Adler's creative optimism and its accompanying responsibility characterize Rank more than Freud, whose outlook was pessimistic and deterministic. Incidentally, Freud's Viennese followers represented diverse political leanings as well as occupations. Freud was an apolitical moderate, Sadger quite conservative, Adler an outspoken socialist and feminist. Rank's political views were unstated, though he became rather liberal. Adler's idealism is later echoed in Rank's will theory: The artist consciously creates his or her personality.

The theme of consciousness, its growth and consequences, continued to be central for Rank, and it came up again in a discussion of poets and psychology. Summing up his *Artist*, in late March, he restated his conviction (in agreement with Freud) that "when the unconscious is made conscious, art ceases to exist." Rank saw this process as "an inescapable sign of the development of our times, which documents the deterioration of art as consciousness advances (Hofmannsthal, Wedekind, etc.). The poet can cope with his personal conflicts only if he brings them to consciousness as far as possible, but then he is not in a position to analyze them in universally valid human terms; they remain all too subjective, and it is understandable that the public must reject them." Freud ended the evening with highest praise for Ibsen, who "showed us the summit of modern art." That great writer, he said, not only unified and simplified problems, but concealed and contained himself. Like Rank, Freud felt that historical development led to the decline of such art.[30]

The seemingly abstract discussion of art and the advance of civilization lay closer to the feelings of Rank and Freud than might be suspected. At the core of the issue was the conflict between the expression of truth by the artist and by the new science of psychoanalysis. This conflict arose the very next session, when Rank spoke on "The Psychology of Lying."[31] The discussion can be viewed as a caricature of the differences between art and science, and thus between Rank and Freud. Rank said he based his presentation "predominantly on the observation of several persons," not on a review of literature. Clearly he wanted to get away from books and philosophy into clinical observation and scientific demonstration. He was ready to impress the group with his grasp of their terms and techniques without sacrificing his artistic soul.

Rank did not say whom he observed. Presumably they were classmates, acquaintances, and family, especially his father. Could Freud and other analysts have been Rank's subjects? Definitely. But in that case Rank's audacity would have been balanced by consideration for his audience—and himself. He would hardly confront Freud in the Society meeting as a type of liar, yet many of the points he made fit Freud very well. Either Rank was a masterful actor of an "innocent" role, or he was unaware of the coincidental resemblance of Freud to his subject.

Rank linked pathological lying—that which is both compulsive and clumsy—to a sexual secret. The matter imperfectly hidden by the lie relates to sex, specifically masturbation. Correspondingly, a compulsion to tell the truth derives from a self-controlling prohibition of masturbation. Rank proposed a "masturbatory character" akin to the anal character, listing cleanliness, defiance, avarice (including frugality and the passion to collect), punctuality, secrecy, shyness, adolescent suicide attempts, and kleptomania, as associated characteristics.

The thesis found modest support from Stekel, who added, "Lying is the first stirring of creative power." But Freud reacted strongly against the paper, saying he did not wish it to be submitted for publication. Rank's "speculations," he said, "are for us without value. There is no merit in having bright ideas; those are easy to come by." Then Freud tempered his harshness, saying "the speaker touched very intelligently upon a series of the most interesting problems"—i.e., the consequences of infantile masturbation, why it stirs up guilt, and what happens to the character when it is overcome. Freud considered Emile Zola a "truth fanatic," fitting Rank's characterization, although he was not sure of the mechanism. Adler and Federn were mildly critical, and Sadger defended Rank's ideas but said that he lacked a gift for popular presentation.

Rank closed the meeting by saying, "Actually, my ideas have not undergone any direct or factual refutation. Rather, I believe the validity of my findings and assumptions has been confirmed by the fact that some of the gentlemen (Stekel, Sadger, Hitschmann) agreed with my views, their concurrence being in part quite open and in part concealed by misunderstandings. I was particularly gratified by Professor Freud's affirmation of my main point—the fanaticism for truth. Now that some misunderstandings have been cleared up and several controversial points set right, I want to express my appreciation for the active interest in my paper and in the discussion."[32]

Unfazed by the criticism, Rank bounced back like a rubber ball. The group had refrained from *ad hominem* speculation regarding his interest in the subject; naturally they would have wondered about its relation to Rank's sexual development. It would not have occurred to them—except possibly to Stekel— that Freud himself was one of Rank's subjects. Freud fits the description in many ways. He was both a collector (of books, archeological artifacts, mushrooms) and a "truth fanatic," the latter evidenced by his compulsion to analyze and confess his faults, his need to place honesty ahead of diplomacy, his identification with Oedipus, and the very invention of psychoanalysis. Freud also had lied clumsily, if not pathologically, in the Fliess-Weininger affair, the embarrassing exposure of which occurred in 1906. Regarding masturbation, Freud supported the old medical prohibitions in principle, if not in method. He thought it damaging, and did not share the enlightened position of Havelock Ellis and other reformers of the time. Freud was punctual and in some matters secretive. Nothing is known of any adolescent suicide attempt, for example, because unlike Rank Freud destroyed his adolescent diaries.

That Rank had the audacity to analyze Freud we know from his readiness to challenge the analysis of one of Freud's own dreams (in the diary). Later evidence indicates that he analyzed Freud's dreams from time to time over the years, to Freud's great delight. In an earlier session of the Society, during a discussion of *Wild Duck*, Rank took the position that Ibsen's Hjalmar Ekdal, a caricature of Simon Rosenfeld, could neither be helped nor hurt by insight or interpretation; such a man is impervious. Freud, too, was impervious to insights not of his own making and chose to avoid certain ideas—for example, from Nietzsche and Otto Gross. Perhaps Rank was playing Oedipus to Freud's Sphinx, analyzing the "riddle" of Freud's psyche. Freud's immediate flurry of protest would lead a traditional analyst (if not Freud himself) to say that Rank came too close to the quick for his mentor's comfort.

By the spring of 1909, at age 25, Otto Rank jousted with the best minds in the elite company of psychoanalysts. He combined a successful academic career with a solid apprenticeship to the increasingly famous Sigmund Freud. The homely, bookish youth had developed good clinical acumen and a desire to understand and help suffering human beings. With his second book underway, Rank was living up to Freud's high expectations.

FIRST VISIT TO AMERICA

Of all Freud's Viennese disciples, Otto Rank was to have the most impact on the American psychoanalytic movement, although he did not visit the United States until 1924. For several years prior he had analyzed and taught American visitors to Vienna, and his important role in the movement was increasingly recognized from his publications. (In those days, German was the dominant international language of science.) Freud, elated at an invitation to America, became harshly critical of the United States after his first and only visit there. He even blamed America for turning the heads of some important disciples: Jung, Rank, and Ferenczi.

In 1909, Freud was invited by G. Stanley Hall, a psychologist and the president of Clark University in Worcester, Massachusetts, to commemorate the twentieth anniversary of the founding of the school by delivering a series of lectures. Freud was amused at the idea of celebrating a mere two decades; the University of Vienna, the school of Freud and Rank, had been founded in 1365. Nevertheless Freud was thrilled, because this was the first such honor for a man who felt unappreciated at home. He was yet more pleased when Jung and Ferenczi were invited also. The three sailed together.[33]

In September Freud gave five lectures at Clark, before an audience including William James, James Jackson Putnam, Adolf Meyer, Ernest Jones, and A. A. Brill. Given in German with Freud's extemporaneous clarity and forcefulness, the lectures were published in English the following year and became a standard introduction to psychoanalysis for the next decade.

Freud instructed and charmed his audience by following Schopenhauer's advice: "Say extraordinary things by using ordinary words." He welcomed the nonmedical majority in the audience. He gave interviews to the press. He brought hope to a public accustomed only to asylum psychiatry, useless neurology, and dangerous quackery. Physicians responded eagerly to the prospect of a scientifically supported therapy for the neuroses.

The Clark lectures revealed Freud at a peak of optimism about the power of psychoanalysis. Recognition of the sexual underpinnings of the mind would lead not to debauchery, he said, but to sublimation and freer choice. "Our hysterical patients suffer from reminiscences." He spoke of resistance and repression, sublimation, dreams as wish fulfillment, slips and forgetting, infantile sexuality, the Oedipus complex, and, in the last lecture, transference. Every neurotic in treatment "applies to the person of the physician a great amount of tender emotion, often mixed with enmity, which has no foundation in any real relation, and must be derived in every respect from the old wish-fancies of the patient which have become unconscious." Freud ended with a compassionate plea for recognition of our sexual nature, part of which "has a right to direct satisfaction and ought to find it in life." Sublimation into higher cultural pursuits is fine, but it cannot be pushed too far, and "the happiness of individuals cannot be dispensed with as one of the aims of our culture."[34]

The response was mostly favorable. One listener who had mixed feelings was William James (1842–1910). A graduate of medical school, James taught psychology and philosophy at Harvard. As an author he was respected in Europe, where he had spent some childhood years. Freud called him "a great man, the only American genius; he spoke German better than I! He thought I was crazy." James did not care for Freud's scientific pretensions, but thought that his work would add to our understanding of human nature.[35]

The most important American to champion Freud was Dr. James Jackson Putnam (1846–1918). A pedigreed Bostonian, a distinguished Harvard neurologist who had studied with Charcot and Meynert, and an eloquent spokesman for moral principle, Putnam challenged Freud's strict determinism and pessimism about human nature. Nevertheless he became Freud's chief supporter in America. With Hall, James, Meyer and Putnam involved, Freud could rest assured that psychoanalysis would not be a "Jewish national affair" in America.[36]

Besides establishing good professional contacts and obtaining his first and only honorary degree, Freud toured enough to see the Adirondacks, Niagara Falls, Coney Island, the Metropolitan Museum of Art, and his first movie. Yet he returned to Vienna with a literal and figurative bellyache. American food did not agree with him and toilet facilities were sparse, especially for a man with prostate trouble and accustomed to European conveniences. A tour guide had injured Freud's vanity at age 53 by saying, "Let the old fellow go first." A misguided hostess decorated a cabin at Putnam's retreat with the colors of Imperial Germany to honor her eminent German-speaking guests from

Austria, Switzerland, and Hungary. Freud later said that America was "a gigantic mistake" and, in a whimsical prediction that the black race would eventually supplant the white, joked: "America is already threatened by the black race. And it serves her right. A country without even wild strawberries!"[37]

Freud, Jung, and Ferenczi sailed back together, making plans for the future of psychoanalysis, discussing theory, and analyzing each other's dreams. Back at work in October, Freud wrote, "Quite against my will I must live like an American: no time for the libido." Jung's reply, partly based on his treatment of an American doctor, scorned the new country: "In America the mother is decidedly the dominant member of the family. American culture really is a bottomless abyss; the men have become a flock of sheep and the women play the ravening wolves— within the family circle, of course." He doubted such conditions had ever existed in the world before.[38]

BACK IN VIENNA: SEEDS OF RANKIAN PSYCHOLOGY

The eighth year of the Vienna Psychoanalytic Society and Rank's fourth as Secretary began in October with Freud's return. There were several new members, one of whom must be mentioned. Dr. Victor Tausk, formerly a lawyer and judge in Croatia, then a stage director in Germany, came to study medicine in Vienna thanks to financial help from members of the Society: a parallel with Rank. Tausk, 30, became a brilliant and controversial analyst whose career ended in an early suicide.

Though Rank spoke rarely—at least for the record—in these meetings, two of the themes taken up anticipate developments in therapy and theory for which he became famous. The first is what came to be called active therapy; the second concerns the earliest source of anxiety.

With respect to the first, Freud spoke of using the transference actively with patients who had experienced little pain: "One must try to play fate in their lives." After a strong transference has been established, the analyst tells the patient he is leaving for vacation or suggests termination. Threatened with loss of love, the patient experiences "outbursts of affect." This was the first mention of setting an ending to analysis, about which Freud wrote in 1918 and Rank thereafter. Freud later disavowed this technique as an American-style short-cut.[39]

Perhaps it is surprising that no one made more of this point before Rank. Using termination to provoke affect appeared in the Society's discussions long before it appeared in print; since the minutes were published only recently, Freud's initiative in the matter is scarcely known.

The second issue was raised in a session entitled "What Can Pediatrics Expect from Psychoanalytic Research?" Freud said: "In reference to anxiety, one must keep in mind that the child first feels anxiety as a consequence of the act of birth." Having pointed out that every affect is first manifested as an attack of hysteria and that the affect is simply the reminiscence of an experience, Freud called upon the pediatrician to help study the origin of affects. "Most children have one trauma from which point on they behave like hysterics," Freud noted: "being weaned from the mother's breast; it is a trauma of psychological significance in relation to the pleasure taken in nourishment. From here repression begins." Thus Freud conceived what Rank carried and finally delivered, in somewhat modified form, in 1923: the birth trauma theory. Freud's role in this idea has been recognized because he added this footnote to *Interpretation of Dreams* (1909): *"Moreover the act of birth is the first experience of anxiety, and thus the source and prototype of the affect of anxiety."*[40]

At this time Rank was not a controversial figure for Freud and Jung, unlike Abraham, Adler, Bleuler, Stekel, or even Eitingon. To Jung, who disliked Stekel, Freud made a limited defense of his most provocative follower: "Unfortunately, he has the best tracking nose of any of us for the sense of the unconscious. For he is an absolute swine, and we are truly decent people who only reluctantly yield to the evidence. I have often contradicted his interpretations and later realized that he was right. So we must hold onto him and, with mistrust, learn from him." In the same letter Freud told Jung that Eitingon was the only one in Vienna he could talk to; they took evening walks, and "I analyze him just in passing." Jung's reply matched Freud's occasional tactlessness: Eitingon "cannot be counted among the highest joys. His vapid intellectualism has something exasperating about it."[41] Jung was jealous of Freud's warmth for another man, and very competitive.

The correspondence between Freud and Jung sheds light as well on analyzing one's own family members. Jung reported an outbreak of jealousy on the part of his wife, Emma. Unlike the episode with Sabina Spielrein, this time her worries were groundless, and so Jung tried to analyze her. He concluded, "Analysis of one's spouse is one of the more difficult things unless mutual freedom is assured. The prerequisite for a good marriage, it seems to me, is the licence to be unfaithful." And Emma was pregnant again! Jung's narrow escape with Sabina Spielrein left him chastised but not chastened. In answer, Freud simply remarked that he would have thought it impossible to analyze one's wife. But the father of little Hans [Max Graf] "proved to me that it can be done." Freud went on: "The technical precept which impresses me lately, 'overcoming the counter-transference,' would in this instance surely be too hard." Later Freud analyzed his daughter, Anna.[42] And as a last resort to forestall their break in 1925, he tried to analyze Otto Rank.

As the year ended, creativity, philosophy, and biography were topics of discussion. One of Tausk's phrases foreshadows Rank's later work: "The most perfect adaptation is that which we find in the genius, in that he himself creates his own milieu." On December 1, Freud presented his first psychobiography of genius, on Leonardo da Vinci. The members raved about it. Freud called Leonardo one of the freest human beings, and Rank said that this derived from the artist's relationship to his parents: "All along he endeavors to free himself from old age (father) and return to Mother Nature." Rank moved the focus not only from father to mother, but from elitist to democratic: "One must consider whether, for mankind as a whole, it would not be more advantageous overall for there to be fewer neurotics" even at the cost of some geniuses, "and instead to have an average type of greater merit."[43]

The first mention in the minutes of Rank's involvement in clinical psychoanalysis comes in January 1910, when he speaks of analyzing a young girl's dream. It is also the first indication of Rank's real involvement with a woman. Described as a lady friend, not a neurotic, she had left an unhappy home and supported herself for a few years as a governess, but was unemployed at the time of the dream, which she asked Rank to analyze.

Rank's essay, really a monograph, was published as "A Dream That Interprets Itself." The dream takes two pages, the analysis seventy-five. Rank emphasized the sexual material as well as the wish-fulfillment aspects of the dream, and this emphasis found its way into the third edition of Freud's *Interpretation of Dreams* (1911). Freud called Rank's paper "perhaps the best example of a dream interpretation" and said that it would take a whole course of lectures to encompass the entire work. Similar praise came from Leonard Blumgart, an American analyst who summarized the essay in English.[44]

The fact that Rank began his clinical research with a normal subject befits his nonmedical orientation and his lifetime preoccupation with wholeness and creativity rather than pathology. His involvement with this woman, about whom we know nothing more, raises the issue of attachment to the patient by the therapist, i.e., the counterpart of transference. "This counter-transference," Freud said in 1910, "must be completely overcome by the analyst; only this will make him the master of the psychoanalytic situation; it makes him the perfectly cool object whom the other person must lovingly woo."[45] Freud had spoken of psychoanalysis as a "love" treatment, and took some pains to address the problem of the analyst's emotional involvement, which must be strictly controlled. The concept of counter-transference was introduced to explain untoward love or other emotion on the analyst's part.

Although Freud concluded that the analyst must have the objectivity and demeanor of a surgeon, he saw no need for all psychoanalysts to be physicians. Otto Rank, the first nonmedical analyst, fought alongside Freud against those who wished to limit psychoanalysis to medical practitioners, or to have it dominated by psychiatry.

TUMULT: JUNG FOR PRESIDENT

The second Congress of the International Psychoanalytic Association (IPA) took place on March 30, 1910, in Nuremberg, Germany. A week earlier Freud had written Abraham that he no longer got any pleasure from the Vienna group, calling Stekel, Adler, and Sadger the "older generation" and "a cross to bear." At the Congress, in a move obviously orchestrated by the three who had visited America together, Ferenczi proposed that Jung be made lifetime President of the IPA. This would remove the center of psychoanalytic activity from Vienna to Zurich; it also would give Jung dictatorial control over publications.

The Viennese—about twenty out of some sixty registrants—

rose in protest and met in a private caucus called by Stekel. Suddenly Freud appeared, terribly distraught, to defend the crowning of Carl Jung: "An official psychiatrist and a Gentile must be the leader of the movement," he pleaded. After long debate Freud suggested that the President be elected for only two years, and not have censorship power. Stekel wrote, "We accepted the compromise advocated by our adored master."[46]

This episode reveals, as Jones put it, "that Freud, despite his extraordinary genius in penetrating the deepest layers of the mind, was not a connoisseur of men."[47] Freud squandered his trust in Carl Jung, and the Viennese knew it. Their great respect and love for Freud made his slights of them especially painful. His hope that they would sacrifice their pride for the sake of the movement—largely to assuage his fear of anti-Semitism—foundered at Nuremberg. If Freud was a prophet without honor in his own country, his motley crew of Viennese followers lacked honor in the eyes of their own prophet.

Freud had crusaded for Jung to be President of the IPA despite serious differences that had developed between the two men. For example, Freud suggested linking the fledgling IPA with an International Fraternity for Ethics and Culture involving the liberal Swiss psychiatrist Auguste Forel. Jung recoiled from the idea: A secular affiliation would not help. Instead Jung fervently espoused a charismatic psychoanalytic movement strong enough to overturn two thousand years of repressive Christianity. Jung's goal was, via symbol and myth, to "absorb those ecstatic instinctual forces of Christianity for the *one* purpose of making the cult and the sacred myth what they once were—a drunken feast of joy where man regained the ethos and holiness of an animal." To achieve this goal a myth-supported movement would be needed: "Religion can only be replaced by religion." (Jung's words foreshadow the openness he would express after 1933 to the charismatic substitute religion of Adolf Hitler.) But Freud flatly declined the role of founder of a religion, and said that the need for a substitute religion must be sublimated.[48] But in order to transplant the seedling of psychoanalysis from the inhospitable soil of Vienna, Freud compromised a great deal and settled on Jung.

Back from the Congress, Freud led a sad and difficult meeting of the Vienna Psychoanalytic Society. He stepped down as Chairman and called for a new leader of the group, which had become too large and formal to be guests in his home. In the end Freud accepted a new role as scientific chairman. Alfred Adler became President (Chairman), to assuage him for the elevation of Jung to President of the IPA. Adler appointed an executive committee consisting of Federn, Hitschmann, Rank, Steiner, Stekel, and Sadger. A new periodical, the *Zentralblatt,* was created to supplement Jung's *Yearbook.* It was co-edited by Freud, Stekel, and Adler. Freud reminded the group that "reconstituting the society should not cause any shifts in our Secretary's [Rank's] position, and that he should be considered for the Secretaryship of the *Zentralblatt.*"[49]

Both Adler and Rank suggested that a café be the future meeting place for the Society, but the majority favored a more austere location. A room was rented for Wednesday evenings from the College of Physicians. Dues were raised from an unspecified sum to sixty Kronen (about fifteen dollars) for psychoanalysts and half that amount for laymen. A supporting fund was announced, the first contribution to which (probably from Freud or a wealthy patient) was 200 Kronen: this supplement to dues was necessary to pay Rank's salary as well as the rent and other expenses, including the purchase of a typewriter. Rank's annual salary was set at 800 Kronen, about $200.[50]

After Nuremberg and his consolation of Adler, Freud smugly wrote Jung, "I am satisfied with the outcome of my statesmanship. Fair competition between Vienna and Zurich can only benefit the cause. The Viennese have no manners, but they know a good deal and can still do good work for the movement." Jung, now President of the International, concerned himself less with the Viennese than with divisions at home in Zurich, especially the ambivalence of Bleuler, his chief. (Bleuler introduced the term "ambivalence" into psychiatry—which, in view of his personal vacillating, made him a target for analytic sarcasm.) Freud advised Jung to stand firm, not to downplay differences. "Psychoanalytic candor!" wrote Freud: "There will be an opportunity for revenge, which tastes very good cold. For the present you will be paying the price for the help you once received from Bleuler; it could not have been had for nothing any more than the help I received from Breuer." Later Freud became angry about Jung's placating style, saying, "In your place I should never have given in."[51]

In the fall, Jung's group became caught up in conflict over

whether to admit nonphysicians. Freud mentioned Rank in support of a liberal policy: In Vienna a restriction would be "impossible, if only because we should then have to exclude our Secretary
of many years." Freud also had several promising student members and valued young over old. The only automatic exclusion
in Vienna applied to current patients.[52]

CHANGES IN THE VIENNA PSYCHOANALYTIC SOCIETY

The fall of 1910 marked the expansion of the Vienna Psychoanalytic Society. Some two dozen regularly attended, twice as many
as before, usually including at least one woman (physicians Margarete Hilferding and Sabina Spielrein were both members).
There was considerable turnover; for example, musicologists
Graf and Bach withdrew informally, and Wittels had resigned.

For Rank the picture had changed radically in just four years.
Rescued from obscurity by Adler and Freud, brought into a
respectable and stimulating Society, Otto Rank had applied his
intelligence and scholarship while developing some confidence
and charm. His short, slender stature, beady eyes, prominent
ears, and upright crown of hair made him look like a startled
bird. By profession a locksmith and lacking a high school diploma,
he had yet become one of Freud's closest associates. Rank was
welcomed into this elite group for several reasons. Young Otto
was no threat to anyone, just a precocious post-adolescent whose
deference, devotion, and great capacity for work endeared him
to everyone. He took a goodly share of the Professor's criticism,
yet also asserted and defended independent ideas. After four
years as Secretary he had finished half the requirements for
his doctoral degree at the University of Vienna. By 1910, Rank
had published monographs on the artist and on mythology. As
a matter of fact, after Freud, he had become the leading psychoanalytic writer in both quantity and quality, though perhaps
not widely recognized as such. Freud would have expressed such
appreciation to his young protégé in private, to protect him
from the others' jealousy.

In the enlarged Vienna Psychoanalytic Society Otto Rank,
26, was not only a peer in terms of contributions, but at last
had fellow members in his age group. Eight new members were
between 23 and 30. The majority still were, like Adler (40),

somewhere between Rank and the Professor, who was 54. Yet Rank began to stay more in the background, refraining from major presentations and making fewer comments as well. Rank had enough to do with his studies, his small but steady output of psychoanalytic papers, and the collection and development of new material for the upcoming third edition of Freud's *Interpretation of Dreams*. Besides all that he had good reason to stay clear of the ominous political tensions in the movement.

Of the new members, Hanns Sachs (1881–1947) became very important to Rank personally and to the psychoanalytic movement. Along with Rank, Abraham, Ferenczi, Jones, and Eitingon he joined the inner circle around Freud. Vienna-born, trained in law, a modest man with a good sense of humor, Sachs was deeply interested in literature and the arts. He had attended and been captivated by Freud's Saturday lectures. To a private meeting with Freud Sachs brought a copy of his own newly published German translation of Kipling poems. The two men enjoyed talking and Sachs soon joined the Society. Within the year Sachs established himself in an informal leadership position, eventually joining Rank at Freud's dinner table once a week and making a threesome for a long walk through Vienna on Wednesday nights after the Society meeting. Sachs remarked that his friendship with Rank came "as near to mutual intimacy as it is possible with a person of such extreme reticence in all personal matters as he was." Sachs reminisced further: "Freud probably thought it would be a good thing to have at least two men near him who were willing to team together without jealousies and animosities."[53] Hanns, the same age as Otto's brother Paul, was the only other nonphysician in Freud's inner circle.

ADLER: A DISSENTER CAST OUT

As time went on, Freud became less and less tolerant of Adler and Stekel. By late November he was grumbling about them both, wishing he could get rid of them but not seeing how. Adler reminded him of Fliess: "the same paranoia."[54]

Freud wished to avoid the appearance of despotism, but he feared that Adler's deviations would come to be regarded as an alternative psychoanalytic position, one which both contradicted Freud and was more palatable and popular. In letters to

Jung, Freud confided his dismay at the way Adler's theory minimized the sexual drive.[55] This modification left out what Freud
considered to be the essence of his discovery. Ironically Carl
Jung, who disliked Adler, not long after made similarly fundamental modifications of Freud's sexual theory. Soon Freud found
himself in full command of his theory but with a smaller company
of supporters.

With Freud's approval the loyal Hitschmann called for an
airing of Adler's theories to decide whether they could be sub-
sumed within Freud's doctrine. In January and February, 1911,
Adler held forth. He challenged the libido (sexual drive) as the
prime mover in neurosis, questioned the universality of wish
fulfillment in dreams, and denied that incest fantasies—the Oedipus complex—constituted the core of neurosis. In addition, he
claimed that transference promoted recovery by providing the
basis for a rebellion against the analyst. For Freud, the transference was primarily a love feeling that kept the patient at work
in treatment.

Adler praised Freud and denied that these ideas were incompatible with psychoanalysis. But he did not hesitate to elaborate
a distinctive theory of organ inferiority and masculine protest,
culminating with the statement, "There is no principle more
generally valid for all human relationships than 'on top of' and
'underneath.'" This differed so much from Freud that it is no
wonder the Society could not contain both men. Adler and his
friends were willing to stay, but Freud and his supporters would
not have them. Federn was the first to say so, calling Adler's
views a danger, a sign of retrogression, and a help to the opponents of Freud's teachings. Others disagreed, especially the ve-
hement Stekel, who spoke out on Adler's behalf. Still others,
like Furtmüller, tried to bridge the gap.

Adler anticipated Rank's later idea of an inevitable struggle
of wills between therapist and patient. Some of the comments
by Adler suggest elements of Rank's later definition of will. (The
"ego instinct" was Freud's original category for life-preserving,
as opposed to sexual, drive.)

> The ego instinct has become a concept without content. If, how-
> ever, it is considered, not as something that has become rigid, but
> as the sum total of all exertions, as a posture directed against the
> outside world, as a wanting to be important, as a striving for power,
> for dominance, for being "on top"—then it becomes evident that

this wanting to be important must have (1) an inhibiting, repressing, modifying influence on certain instincts, but (2) also, and above all, an intensifying effect.[56]

Freud expressed grave disagreement. He complimented Adler on his capable intellect and gift of presentation, but faulted him for a "reactionary tendency" which offers more "pleasure premiums" to attract those who cannot face the harder, deeper truths of psychoanalysis. "But therein also lies the real value of his writings," Freud went on, "insofar as they do offer an acutely observed ego psychology." In those days, however, "ego psychology" was a pejorative term. Freud thus labeled Adler's thinking useful but superficial, overly influenced by both biology and social concerns. In Freud's view the ego strives to deny the unconscious. Adler's theory did just that, like a cowardly ego. But there was nothing cowardly about Adler's confrontation with Freud. It may have been an inevitable expression of his own masculine protest, a force which for him took precedence over libido. That force might take on the guise of sexuality, but actually stood behind it as primary. "The 'purely' sexual is nothing primary," Adler declared in defiance of Freud, assuming that a scientific society could tolerate such differences, if not welcome them.

But Freud felt that the movement and his leadership were at stake, and his final argument brooked no rebuttal. "I consider Adler's doctrines to be wrong and, as far as the development of psychoanalysis is concerned, dangerous. But these are scientific errors, brought on by the use of wrong methods (by drawing in social and biological viewpoints); and they are errors which do great credit to their creator."[57] Adler was damned by the faint praise as well as by Freud's pontifical criticism.

As Freud had found fault with the scientific validity of Adler's work, he could argue that the Society had operated with strict objectivity. Adler attended the next meeting, although he had already submitted his resignation as Chairman because of the "incompatibility between his scientific position and his position in the Society." Freud was then elected Chairman by acclamation. Over Freud's objection, Furtmüller got a majority to resolve that they did *not* find any incompatibility of beliefs with Adler. Freud argued that Furtmüllers's resolution was "a criticism we could spare Adler and an overture we could spare ourselves."

Furtmüller was Adler's friend, and obviously Freud wanted to get Adler out, not spare him.[58]

In a letter to Jung that night Freud referred to Hitschmann approvingly as "quite orthodox," noting that the older members generally opposed Adler while the younger ones had sympathy for him. "I must avenge the offended goddess Libido," Freud went on, promising to see "that heresy does not occupy too much space in the *Zentralblatt.*" This remarkably ideological letter continues: "I would never have expected a psychoanalyst to be so taken in by the ego. In reality the ego is like the clown in the circus, who is always putting in his oar to make the audience think that whatever happens is his doing."[59]

If Rank had any leanings toward Adler at the time, he did not offend Freud by showing them. Two weeks later Freud confided to Jung his disdain for all but one of his local followers: "None of these Viennese will ever amount to anything; the only one with a future is little Rank, who is both intelligent and decent."[60]

Freud was increasingly eager to get rid of Adler as summer approached, and by mid-June the purge was accomplished. Freud had written the publisher of the *Zentralblatt* that he could no longer serve as coeditor with Adler. The publisher took it up with Adler who resigned forthwith from that and the Vienna Psychoanalytic Society as well. Freud predicted that "a few rather useless members" would follow Adler out. After the summer break, Freud forced a choice within the Society between himself and Adler's circle on the grounds that "its activities bear the character of hostile competition."[61] The vote, after strenuous debate, was eleven to five for separation, with five not voting. Furtmüller, Hilferding, and four other Adlerians then resigned.

In his memoir of Adler, Furtmüller described Freud as cosmopolitan, careful in dress, prestige-conscious, and an elegant speaker, while Adler was the common man, somewhat sloppy, indifferent to prestige, and artless in speech, although he knew how to make a point. Both men were domineering, not to say stubborn. Freud's use of the couch made the doctor superior; Adler talked with his patients face to face, conversationally. Furtmüller characterized the Secretary as "Freud's son Benjamin, or beloved disciple John," suggesting that Rank's eventual defection, following Adler, Stekel, and Jung, was Freud's most poignant loss.⁶² At any rate, Freud's separation from Adler marked a new phase in the psychoanalytic movement, since his breaks with Breuer and Fliess preceded the movement. From 1911 on, intellectual independence in Freud's circle had to be subordinate to orthodoxy. From that time on, Rank once said, most of Freud's writing was a reaction to his critics.

Alfred Adler, who called his independent school "Individual Psychology," moved from Vienna's Leopoldstadt to the center city and gave up his general medical practice to specialize in psychiatry. His interest in education led to consultations with the Vienna school system, where he developed child guidance clinics after World War I; there were more than thirty when the fascists closed them down in 1934. In that year the Adlers left Vienna permanently to settle in New York. He had made his first lecture tour in the United States in 1926 and was well received by American audiences from that time on. Ironically, Adler, like Freud, later purged his circle of followers who became too independent; he became a rather conservative, exhortative pedagogue.

Freud's hostility—hatred is not too strong a word—never abated. Through the years he was bitterly critical of his early supporter. In 1937, when Adler died suddenly in Scotland at 67, Freud, then 82, wrote to Arnold Zweig: "I don't understand your sympathy for Adler. For a Jew boy out of a Viennese suburb a death in Aberdeen is an unheard-of career in itself and a proof of how far he had got on. The world really rewarded him richly for his service in having contradicted psychoanalysis."⁶³

RANK'S NARROW LINE

Just before his twenty-seventh birthday, Rank asked, and was granted, three weeks leave to travel to Greece with a group from the University of Vienna. Freud wrote Jung about Rank's trip at the end of April:

Yesterday little Rank returned from the University tour of Greece in a state of bliss. I had given him the money for it in return for the work he had done on the third edition of Interpretation of Dreams. *It was hard-earned money, but that didn't prevent the poor boy from bringing me two—and not at all cheap—Greek vases in token of his gratitude. He is a fine man. He has just given me a splendid paper on the Lohengrin theme.*[64]

Shortly after this warm exchange, Rank had to maneuver deftly at a meeting to placate Freud without retracting his own ideas (May 3, 1911: before Adler left). Federn, perhaps referring to *The Artist*, had spoken of libido in a broad sense, "as Rank has done," not just as a sexual force, but as something leading to excitation of various organs. Freud then clarified his own definition as "only the urging of the sexual instincts," objecting to Jung's application of the term to "every kind of psychic tension." Freud criticized Jung but not Rank. Someone sympathetic to Adler then referred provocatively to *Rank's* broader conception.

Since Adler had been roundly criticized for his differences with Freud, his sympathizers did not want to let Rank off easily. When his turn to speak came, Rank acknowledged that "it is true that I took the concept of libido in its broad range, but I did consider the things onto which I extended this concept as being sexual. One could therefore regard my statement as being an unjustified extension of Freud's concept just as much as being an enrichment of it."[65]

Rank knew how to be diplomatic, giving something to each side in the conflict and letting Freud determine the extent of the error or enhancement, if any. Loyalty to Freud took precedence over innovation—Rank had a great capacity to adapt— but there was a hint of a dare in Rank's position. He said, in effect: "I made a conscientious effort with your encouragement; my creative work goes beyond your standpoint. I rest my case: Call it enrichment or call it error." Freud said that his own broad concept of sexuality only recaptured the earlier meaning of the term, which included love as well as eroticism.

Adler and Rank had little or no contact after 1911. Alexandra and Kurt Adler cannot recall their father ever mentioning Rank. Clarence Oberndorf, a leading American analyst, relates a curious episode during Adler's first visit to the United States in 1926, when he told Adler of Freud's recent break with Rank. "That is the will of God," Adler exclaimed; "the little fellow always tried to set the old gentleman against me!" The minutes (which Furtmüller called "careful and adequate") do not bear out Adler's claim. He may have been jealous of Rank's special status with Freud, and upset that the protégé he discovered could not heal the breach between the two older men.

Seeing Adler purged must not have been easy for Otto Rank, who was once Adler's patient and "discovery." Rank was to witness more strife and bitterness in the next two years before his place was assured in a unified movement.

CHAPTER 6

War and Marriage

We mustn't quarrel when we are besieging Troy . . . [1]
—Freud to Jung, 1908

Freud, Adler, Jung, and Rank, the four founders of depth psychology, never met together again after the Nuremberg Congress of 1910. In September 1911, without the Adlerians, the Third International Congress of Psychoanalysis at Weimar, Germany, took place in an atmosphere of optimism and collegiality. The movement was growing, with several new national associations, including two in the United States: The New York Psychoanalytic Society led by A. A. Brill, and the American Psychoanalytic Association led by James Jackson Putnam. Putnam gave a major address at Weimar on psychoanalysis and philosophy. Too idealistic for Freud, Putnam played an important role because of his prominence in America. (Rank translated one of Putnam's articles for publication in German.) Rank, now sporting a mustache, gave a very well received paper on "Nakedness in Poetry and Legend." A Weimar newspaper summed up the Congress by saying that "interesting papers were read on nudity and other current topics." After this, journalists were not welcome at psychoanalytic Congresses.[2]

THE RANK—JONES RIVALRY

Ernest Jones (1879–1958) returned from North America to London in 1911 to become the leader of psychoanalysis in the English-speaking world, and Rank's colleague and rival for the next fifteen years. At five feet five inches tall, Jones was two inches shorter than Freud, and an inch taller than Rank. Jones's "vitality and flow of quick, precise talk, his very alive eyes and gestures, marked him out in most company." As early as 1909, Jones expressed both leadership ambition and loyalty to the cause, apologizing to Freud for some transient rebelliousness that arose from "an absurd jealous egotism" and "a strong Father complex." Perhaps recognizing the Welshman's ability to recover from professional difficulties, Freud saluted Jones for his diplomatic skills and remarked upon his interest in cultural psychology and in the normal rather than the pathological—also Rank's primary area of interest.[3]

Jones is probably best known for his monumental biography of Freud, long recognized as definitive. Much recent information from previously unpublished letters and other sources, however, points to important omissions and biases in Jones's reporting. Yet it remains very difficult to check facts because much of the material Jones had at his disposal—notably, Freud's voluminous correspondence with Ferenczi and Rank's wartime correspondence with Freud—is still not available to scholars.

Ernest Jones had an unusual love life. For seven years he lived with Loe Kann, who was analyzed by Freud before the war, but Jones took up with a friend of hers intermittently. Finally he married yet another woman he had known only briefly, and she died two years after they were married. The following year, 1919, while visiting Freud, Jones met and fell in love with Katharina Jokl of Vienna. They were engaged in three days, and, with Rank's brother, Paul, untangling legal red tape, the marriage ceremony took place within three weeks. Like Jung, Jones needed Freud's help with a woman patient and colleague who claimed to be his lover. Mrs. Joan Riviere, who first translated some of Freud's works into English, went to Vienna after the war and figured in a major conflict between Jones and Freud. In speaking of that time Jones only belabors his grievances with Otto Rank who—even Freud believed—was a scapegoat for Jones's anger at the untouchable father figure.[4]

In his Freud biography, Jones discussed Rank at length. The later enmity between Freud's two most powerful disciples dictates caution on the reader's part; unfortunately, Rank never told his side of the story. Although he once spoke of being the only one who could write a full history of the psychoanalytic movement, Rank never did so. Freud set the stage for sibling rivalry by telling Jones that, despite the impressive work of Federn and Hitschmann, only "little Rank" showed real scientific promise among those in Vienna.[5]

Although he could argue forcefully, Rank was unusually restrained in discussing the personalities and politics of psychoanalysis. In his writings he boldly took issue with colleagues and with Freud, but even in private conversation and letters he eschewed gossip or backbiting. In this respect Rank differed from many others, including Freud, Jung, and especially Jones.

Even Freud mistrusted and disliked Jones from early on: "I saw him as a fanatic who smiles at my faint-heartedness . . . I tend to think he lies to the others, not to us." Freud compared Jones to "the lean and hungry Cassius," and said, "He denies all heredity; to his mind even I am a reactionary."[6] Freud's reference to "lies" is unclear, but Jones had been accused in three incidents of indecent behavior with children, resulting in a loss of position and prospects for a career in England. He traveled with his mistress, Loe Kann, representing her as his wife. Again in Toronto, Jones found himself in trouble several times; in 1911 he paid a woman patient $500 to prevent a scandal.[7]

Freud's deep-seated need for non-Jewish support undoubtedly helped Jones. Freud thought that being Jewish made understanding psychoanalysis much easier. Jung, the Swiss pastor's son, came to it, he felt, with more difficulty. In a curious remark to Jung, Freud erased the difference between himself and Jung by making a comparison with Jones: "I find the racial mixture in our group most interesting; he is a Celt and consequently not quite accessible to us, the Teuton and the Mediterranean man."[8] Submerging his own ancestry in the "Mediterranean," Freud tempered his Semitic genes with the Roman and Greek elements he—and Jung—admired.

In his Freud biography, Jones described Rank as timid and deferential, qualities he attributed to Rank's humble social origins—decidedly lower than those of the other principals in the early psychoanalytic movement. Thanks to his training in technical school, Jones observed, Rank "could handle any tool expertly."[9] Jones marveled at Rank's ability to eke out a living; Freud repeatedly told the Committee that if any of them ever became rich, that person's first duty would be to take care of

Rank. Freud also said that "in the Middle Ages a clever boy like Rank would have found a patron," but "it might not have been easy since he is so ugly."[10] Jones noted modestly that none of the inner circle was favored with good looks. Freud, who was greatly concerned with looks and money, accepted in Rank a man endowed with neither. Jones explains why:

> Rank would have made an ideal private secretary, and indeed he functioned in this way to Freud in many respects. He was always willing, never complained of any burden put upon him, was a man of all work for turning himself to any task, and he was extraordinarily resourceful. He was highly intelligent and quick-witted. He had a special analytic flair for interpreting dreams, myths and legends. His great work on incest myths, which is not read enough nowadays, is a tribute to his truly vast erudition; it was quite mysterious how he found the time to read all that he did. One of the compliments I treasure in my life was when he asked me wherever I had found all that material in one of my nonmedical essays; that the omniscient Rank should be impressed signified much. Rank also had a keen eye for practical affairs and would assuredly have been very successful had he entered the world of finance. . . . For years Rank had close, almost day-to-day contact with Freud, and yet the two men never really came near to each other. Rank lacked the charm, among other things, which seemed to mean much to Freud.[11]

Because of their rivalry, Jones's praise carries much more weight than his criticism of Rank. Contrary evidence about Rank's personal charm comes from Freud himself: "Why is it there cannot be six such charming men in our group instead of only one?"[12] And for Jones to say that Freud and Rank never became close indicates blind envy. Rank was virtually adopted into Freud's family; he was constantly involved with his mentor (as Sachs and Wittels pointed out); he and Freud analyzed one another's dreams; and Rank wrote letters on behalf of Freud and himself for years. The loss of Rank was much harder on Freud than that of any other friend or disciple, and Jones had a major role in bringing about that schism.

RANK AS A DOCTORAL CANDIDATE

Although he kept himself in the background, Rank continued to keep minutes and absorb ideas from the Vienna Psychoanalytic Society in 1911–12. Dr. Sabina Spielrein had come to Vienna at about the age of 25, and was a new member whose intimate relationship with Jung—resolved with the help of Freud—expressed itself in her persistent attempts to keep those two men together. Theodor Reik, 23, like Rank a doctoral candidate, was voted in as a member on the strength of his paper "On Death and Sexuality." He remarked that both Weininger and Swoboda regarded intercourse as partial dying, and quoted Fliess: "All fear is fear of death." Freud contradicted Fliess, saying that "any anxiety is fear of oneself, of one's libido."[13] We can see in this debate the precursor of Rank's theory of life fear and death fear.

Rank emerged from a prolonged silence at meetings to lead one of the many discussions on masturbation. This time he emphasized the feeling of guilt, which, he argued, had an internal source and was not simply the result of social disapproval. Subsequently Freud said that more attention should be paid to the sense of guilt and praised Rank for "the most correct statements about it up to now." At this time Rank opposed Stekel (as Freud often did) by insisting on the origin of guilt within oneself: Anxiety "takes on the disguise of a feeling of guilt and becomes capable of attracting other feelings of guilt"; hence masturbation becomes a kind of guilt reservoir. Tausk pointed out that Rank had elaborated on a casual remark by Freud that "the sense of guilt is anxiety that has been bound." The discussions on masturbation in the Vienna Psychoanalytic Society were edited and published in 1912, including a paper by Rank.[14] His interest in the problem of guilt from within continued throughout his life and surfaced in a chapter on sexual learning in *Modern Education* two decades later.

Besides the publications already mentioned, Rank contributed a number of shorter papers, book reviews, and translations to the *Yearbook*, and one monograph, *Die Lohengrinsage* [*The Lohengrin Legend*], all in 1910–11. Most have never been translated from the German; a listing of titles demonstrates the scope of Rank's interests and the amount of energy he had. "An Example of the Poetic Utilization of a Slip of the Tongue" was based on Shakespeare. "Schopenhauer on Insanity," "Baudelaire's Incest Complex," "A Disguised Oedipus Dream," "A Contribution on Narcissism," "Some Evidence of Rescue Fantasies," "On Delayed Obedience," "Rosegger on Maternal Love," "A Self-Confession of Wilhelm Busch," "Toothache Dreams," and "Losing as a Symptomatic Act" were shorter papers. Rank also published reports of the Congresses at Nuremberg and Weimar, translated papers by Brill and Putnam from English into German, and wrote reviews of works by Adler, Brill, Ferenczi, Jones, Stekel, Tausk, and five others.

Rank's paper on narcissism was recognized by Havelock Ellis (who originated the concept in 1898) as a seminal work: "Rank's study evidently impressed Freud who in 1914 accepted and emphasized Rank's view, stating positively that there is a primary Narcissism in every individual, the libidinal complement to the egoism of the instinct of self-preservation."[15] Recent writing on narcissism characteristically overlooks this key example of Rank's influence upon Freud.

Rank's main task at this time was completing his studies at the University of Vienna. *The Lohengrin Legend,* his doctoral thesis (181 pages), was published in 1911 by Deuticke. A medieval German myth about a hero who arrives by swan-boat to champion a fair lady against her persecutors, *Lohengrin* became familiar to the world through Wagner's operatic masterpiece, first produced in 1850. The mysterious hero disappears after the lady breaks a vow and asks his name (a theme found in Eros and Psyche and other legends).

For the first time in psychoanalytic literature, Rank dealt with death symbolism on a par with birth symbolism, and related the two. Stekel, who made use of the theme in a book published the same year, praised Rank for his research, which found in legend "unshakeable proof" for the tenets of individual psychology. Rank's book was accepted by Professor Hans Much as the first doctoral thesis on a psychoanalytic theme.[16] The work has never been translated; it has had some influence on the study of folk literature and symbolism. Surprisingly, Lohengrin was never mentioned in the minutes of the Vienna Psychoanalytic Society.

Rank's penchant for privacy allows us only to speculate on his love life during this period. Freud tells an amusing episode, acknowledged to be Rank's contribution, in a 1912 addition to *The Psychopathology of Everyday Life.* The story concerns a young man (surely Rank) who misspoke in addressing a young lady in the street. Intending to say, "May I accompany [*begleiten*] you?" he uttered the non-word *begleitdigen,* a hybrid of "accompany" and "insult" [*beleidigen*]. Freud interprets the slip of the tongue as showing both Rank's fear that she would be insulted and its justification in the impure intentions lurking in his offer. Freud liked the example so much that he used it in his lectures, where he added that the young man in question "was certainly a timid character" and had little chance of success with the lady.[17]

We know little of Rank's associates at the University, though given his duties at Freud's side and his prolific output, he had little time for extracurricular activities. He belonged to a Jewish non-dueling fraternity with his friend Max Praeger (later a publisher), who, like most of Rank's classmates, was five years younger than Otto.[18] Theodor Reik (1888–1969) also received his Ph.D. from the University in 1912. A prolific writer for lay audiences, Reik became part of what was called the "psychoanalytic triad" around Freud with two other nonphysicians, Rank and Sachs. Reik had older brothers with the same names as his co-workers, Otto and Hans; his sibling rivalry came out in collegial struggles, and Freud reproved him for being tactless, as well as for a lack of scholarly focus.

Reminiscing years later, Reik said Rank was talented, "the best of us." Reik knew Rank's brother, Paul, and his mother. He saw Rank as very ambitious, one who would have the skill and drive to go from clerk to president of a department store. Reik recalled that at the time he joined the Vienna Psychoanalytic Society, the veteran member Hitschmann wanted only physicians to present papers; Freud overruled that idea on behalf of the nonmedical trio. Reik, like Rank, received financial help from Freud as a student, and support as a lay analyst later on.[19]

In August 1912, Freud wrote to Rank from Karlsbad, inviting him to England, where Freud, Ferenczi and he would stay with Ernest Jones for ten days. Freud asked Rank to be his guest for the journey, "as my thanks for your latest, excellent book (*The Incest Motif*)." Rank accepted with profuse gratitude, and Freud replied, "Warm regards, and I hope you will not flunk in the autumn as a result of your very wise decision favoring the pleasure principle." (Rank received his doctorate in November 1912; the *Incest* book appeared earlier in the year.)

Since Freud and Rank were rarely separated, correspondence between them is relatively scarce. The letter cited reveals the confidence Freud had in his young colleague, now 28 and close to his doctoral examination. "What is most regrettable about the changes in Zurich is the certainty that I did not succeed in bringing together Jews and anti-Semites, whom I hoped to unite on psychoanalytic ground." Freud's disappointment with regard to the increasing strain with Jung was mitigated, he wrote, by his confidence that it would not come to the kind of split he had with Adler. "But who knows? In any event it is now time that we bring ourselves closer together, to which end the London trip should contribute."[20] The togetherness Freud had in mind was the formation of a Committee, or "Old Guard," suggested by Jones in response to the growing tensions with both Jung and Stekel (Freud's conflict with Stekel had erupted in May). Unfortunately, the trip to England had to be canceled owing to the illness of Freud's eldest daughter.

Rank had first presented on the "Incest Motif" back in 1906, when he began as Secretary of the Wednesday Psychological Society. In the book, which was finally published in 1912, Rank attributed the delay to his own hesitation rather than to external factors. An excerpt from the introduction conveys his thinking on the study of creativity through biography ("psychographs") and the prospects for life and art in the post-psychoanalytic world.

> A Freudian probe into the depths of the unconscious and the in-stinctual drives, and its disclosure of the primordial roots of human thought and action, is not likely to bolster widely held notions of the sublimity of human nature or the artist's divine calling. Schiller's apt phrase that hunger and love, in their widest sense, rule the world appears to be no less valid for the poet himself. Indeed, we find that erotic and egotistic [self-preserving] drives take part in the genesis and shaping of a work of art not only incidentally but in a determining and decisive way. This realization may in-crease our awe of the forces of nature thus capable of unfolding such blossoms of sublime poetry, valuable for all humanity, from such primitive instinctual roots. . . .
>
> Finally, the most serious reproach that may be raised against our undertaking touches the "abuse" of the poets and their works when employed for such analytical purposes. The question may be raised: Why throw a glaring light into the most secret recesses of the poet's soul when the biographer has already delved into the most hidden and intimate details of the careers of these helpless subjects? Even if the possible theoretical value of such psychographs should be admitted, one must acknowledge the damage to, even canceling of, aesthetic enjoyment of these works by such disclosure of the ultimate roots of poetic production.

With regard to the first objection, we may point to the broadened insight into the nature of the work of art and of artistic production that such an approach would open up. This alone would fully justify such an attempt. But the full import of our endeavors goes beyond this disclosure of the hitherto puzzling processes of poetic creation. Ultimately our effort aims to fathom the universal human soul. And is not this, even more than nature study as a whole, both worthy and in need of investigation, for so long denied to it? Exploration of the normal psyche and its laws is evidently possible only with psychologically abnormal subjects, both the inferior and superior. For the normal we lack the approach and, especially, the motivation for penetrating the depths of the psyche. We do have incentive with regard to the psychoneurotic, who because of his undeveloped emotional life, fails to adapt to civilization, and with the artist, to whom God grants the gift to impart his sufferings through creative work. From knowledge of these somewhat extreme life-styles we are able to construct a picture of normal psychological development and the average human soul. . . .

Our entire psychological and therefore cultural development obviously rests upon progressive widening of consciousness, which is tantamount to an ever-increasing mastery of unconscious drives and affects. This process is linked with the biologically fixed repression of culturally unusable drives, heightened by the demands of civilization. This state of affairs would soon lead to a general neurosis were it not for the fact that the concomitant and progressive improvement of instinctual life and the enlargement of consciousness balance one another. . . .

[Ludwig] Klages posed the question: "Do we perceive in our art the twilight gleam of humanity on its way to extinction? Is reason an enemy force capable of extinguishing the fire of the will? Might the passions at last become extinct in a fanaticism of knowing which itself ends in apathetic omniscience?" Whoever is disconcerted by such prophecy of an insipid future should keep in mind that this does not mean the sudden elimination of all artistic activity from modern civilization, but the gradual replacement of certain artistic aspirations and interests by other intellectual and emotional activities equally elevating and satisfying to the bearers of a future culture.[21]

Rank dedicated this magnum opus "To my revered teacher, Professor Dr. Sigmund Freud, in gratitude."

Wilhelm Stekel, whom Freud called "a case of moral insanity," resigned from the Society in November but kept control of the *Zentralblatt.*[22] The Freudian loyalists started a competing journal, the *Zeitschrift*, edited by Ferenczi and Rank. Meanwhile, Rank and Sachs had started a new journal, *Imago*, for papers on psychoanalysis in relation to the arts and society. Thus Rank, on the eve of receiving his doctorate, became coeditor of two psychoanalytic journals and the author of a fourth—and this time monumental—book.

Sachs, having become librarian of the Society, described Otto as "Lord Everything Else": Rank, as Secretary, took care of everything except presiding at meetings and keeping the accounts. Sachs's elevation to the executive committee meant that he sat next to Otto, who sat at Freud's left. After the Wednesday night meetings (which, in the rented hall, began at 9:00 P.M.) the two younger men accompanied the Professor on his vigorous walk through the deserted streets—most of Vienna went to sleep before eleven—discussing the events of the evening and Freud's newest ideas. "Behind every discovery he showed us a long row of new question marks. We learned how it happened that he was progressing restlessly, never coming to a standstill."[23]

THE SCHISM WITH JUNG

At this point, Rank emerged as Jung's full-fledged competitor for Freud's highest esteem. Intellectually the two were a good match, but whereas Jung could be brash to the point of nastiness, Rank was usually mild, if not timid. The physical contrast between the tall, commanding Aryan and the homely little youth from Vienna's Jewish quarter could hardly be greater. Though most people, including Freud, found Jung more attractive and exciting, Rank proved to be more likable and dependable and undoubtedly less threatening.

To Freud, Jung had moved toward religious mysticism while Rank upheld Freudian doctrine and developed it creatively in acceptable ways. Jung yielded the high ground on which Freud placed him, while Rank had plugged away at his manifold tasks: a hare and tortoise race for Freud's respect. Rank proved himself with unfailing devotion and effectiveness, first as Secretary and researcher, then as editor and executive.

In 1912 Jung struggled with Freud over both theoretical and administrative differences, leading to mutual recrimination sometimes mixed with what might generously be called psychoanalytic understanding. Jung received Rank's book about the first of August and wrote Freud, "It is a very distinguished piece of work and will make a big impression." But since Jung had reversed the Freudian derivation of anxiety from the incest prohibition, he disagreed with Rank's premise while praising his "splendid material."[24] Jung, furthermore, saw in the new *Imago* a rival to his own *Yearbook*. But Jung had few grounds for complaint, since (as he put it) all his libido went into his own work. To Freud's dismay Jung neglected his Presidential duties: He took little interest in guiding the emerging national psychoanalytic societies and in planning the next Congress.

A pivotal figure who consoled Freud in the controversy with Jung and who points up the difference between Jung and Rank was Frau Lou Andreas-Salomé, who attended the Society meetings in 1912–13 and kept a diary. She came to Vienna at 51 after having met Freud, Jung, and Rank the previous year at Weimar. Partner in a sexless marriage, Lou, as she was called, had many lovers, including poet Rainer Maria Rilke and analysts Poul Bjerre and Victor Tausk. As a young woman Lou had been close to, if not intimate with, Friedrich Nietzsche. She knew many of the creative geniuses of Vienna, including Martin Buber, von Hofmannsthal, Beer-Hofmann, and Schnitzler. Freud once wrote to her of "your superiority over all of us—in accord with the heights from which you descended to us."[25] She was, like Ludwig Binswanger, Oskar Pfister, and James Jackson Putnam, someone Freud admired despite major philosophical differences. Probably their way of handling differences, coupled with the respect accorded him and his ideas by these distinguished non-Jews, kept the four in Freud's good graces. An independent spirit, Lou met with Adlerians in Vienna as well as with the Freudians. Freud tolerated this behavior in her case, requesting only that she not discuss either side with the other.

Lou's arrival as a guest at the meetings in the fall of 1912 coincided with Stekel's departure. Stekel interrogated Lou about Freud at a meeting of Adler's group and insisted that he himself was not an Adlerian. Lou decided the crossfire was too unpleasant and stopped attending Adler's meetings.

But Lou could not stay clear of the conflict with Jung, which had been worsening. Jung had just returned from America, where he had presented his own revisions of psychoanalytic theory, much to Freud's consternation. Jung thought he was making psychoanalysis more widely acceptable, but Freud wanted none of that kind of acceptance. Jung was furious and told Freud: "I have done more to promote psychoanalysis than Rank, Stekel, Adler, etc., put together."[26] Freud became cold: His letters opened with "Dear Dr. Jung" instead of "Dear Friend." The two men finally met in Munich and patched things up superficially, only to have a final explosion occur in January.

Jung, denying any neurosis whatsoever in himself, accused Freud of treating his pupils like patients: "In that way you produce either slavish sons or impudent puppies. . . . Meanwhile you remain on top as the father, sitting pretty. For sheer obsequiousness nobody dares to pluck the prophet by the beard."[27] Jung promised to stand by Freud publicly, but privately he would tell him what he really thought of him. To Jung, of course, Rank was the prime example of a slavish son.

On January 3, 1913 Freud contradicted Jung, saying that in Vienna he was criticized for allowing his followers *so much* latitude. Then, with an almost surgical aloofness, he cut the bond with his erstwhile crown prince: "It is a convention among us analysts that none of us need feel ashamed of his own bit of neurosis. But one who while behaving abnormally keeps shouting that he is normal gives ground for the suspicion that he lacks insight into his illness. Accordingly, I propose that we abandon our personal relations entirely. I shall lose nothing by it, for my only emotional tie with you has long been a thin thread."[28]

Lou recognized great distress on Freud's part in February, in regard to Tausk—another brilliant but troublesome follower—as well as Jung. Talking with Freud at dinner and afterwards, until he took her home at half past one, she concluded that he was drained from these disputes with his more aggressive, independent followers and longed to pursue ideas in the peace that had existed before the psychoanalytic movement began. Musing about this, she wrote in her diary:

> So I understand very well indeed that men of intelligence and ability like Otto Rank, who is a son and nothing but a son, represent for Freud something far more to be desired. He says of Rank: "Why is it that there can't be six such charming men in our group instead of only one?" Even in his wish for a half-dozen the individuality of the man referred to is put in some doubt. And yet just this [doubt] serves to reassure Freud in the face of threatening "ambivalence." During one evening's discussion, when Rank lectured on regicide, Freud wrote the following note to me on a piece of paper:

"R disposes of the negative aspect of his filial love by means of this interest in the psychology of regicide; that is why he is so devoted."[29]

In September 1913, the Fourth Congress of the International Psychoanalytic Association took place in Munich. The Viennese analysts stayed at the same hotel with the Swiss; Freud hoped to avoid a public display of the smoldering tensions. Jung, finishing his first two-year term as President of the IPA, stood for election again—an affront in itself, considering both his disavowal of psychoanalytic theory in lectures and papers, and his personal split with Freud. Jung even endorsed some of Adler's ideas, a twist of the knife in view of his tremendous contempt for the man long before Freud purged him. Meanwhile Ferenczi was disturbed by a comment of Maeder, Jung's associate, that scientific differences between the Swiss and Viennese reflected differences between Aryans and Jews. Freud counseled a strong reply: There can be no Aryan or Jewish science, notwithstanding differences in outlook on life.[30] Apparently still hoping to unite Jews and anti-Semites in the cause of psychoanalysis, Freud went into the Congress supporting Jung's reelection. But Jung's high-handedness in the role of Chairman so offended Freud's admirers that they protested with blank ballots. Jung won reelection with 52 votes and 22 abstentions. Afterwards, Jones reports, Jung came up to him and said sourly, "I thought you were a Christian," or words to that effect.[31]

The break with Jung aroused the kind of feeling Freud had had toward Fliess. Freud's passionate attachment to Jung resembled that which he enjoyed with Fliess, although with Jung, nineteen years younger, Freud was the mentor. Freud used the same word, "brutal," to describe both Fliess and Jung after the respective partings. The record shows that Fliess was wronged by Freud, but that Freud in turn was wronged by Jung. The Swiss knight was inspired by Freud in 1906, was rescued from his own folly with Sabina Spielrein by his wiser mentor, and then gained power in the movement. Jung eagerly picked up the ball, agreed to lead, but then decided the game should be played his own way. His disdain for teammates makes Freud look like a model of tolerance. He abused Freud's excessive trust, taking the limelight for his own revisionist crusade, notably in the United States.

In this context we are considering psychoanalysis less as a science than as a movement that engaged Freud and Jung in a shared hope and strategy of intellectual and, for each in his own way, emotional world conquest. Science allows for diversity, invites challenge, and brooks no orthodoxy. But the organization of science does require agreements, contracts, and compromise and engages all of the strengths and foibles of human relationships. Freud might have chosen to carry on his rather successful practice, write books, give lectures, and leave the wider acceptance of psychoanalysis to the usual process of dissemination. He chose instead to act as missionary, or rather, to find a missionary to act for him while he continued as teacher and prophet. Lou thought he wanted peace and quiet to think and write, not a crusade to lead, but inside Freud there was a crusader elbowing the thinker. While Freud can be faulted for promoting Jung too hastily, he survived that mistake with flying, if slightly tattered, colors.

Freud acknowledged his own poor judgment in trusting Jung so much, and accepted political advice from the Committee. Together they succeeded in getting Jung to resign, first as editor of the *Yearbook*, then as President of the IPA; and by 1914 there were three schools: psychoanalysis, individual psychology (Adler), and analytical psychology (Jung). Abraham would be the interim President until the next Congress. Scheduled for Dresden in the fall, it was to be canceled by the outbreak of war.

FREUD'S SECRET COMMITTEE

Jones had first proposed the idea of a secret inner circle in the summer of 1912 to Ferenczi, who felt it was an excellent idea. The two then presented it to Rank, who also agreed. Jones recounts:

> Rank, who for years was Freud's man of all work, was devoted to him. As for Ferenczi, he was the staunchest and most enthusiastic colleague anyone could ask for, and Freud would, I feel sure, have placed no one above him in his estimation. Well, when I introduced Rank to him as the latest recruit to our little group, Ferenczi eyed him keenly and put the question to him: "I suppose you will always be loyal to psychoanalysis?" I felt myself it was almost an insulting

way to greet a new adherent, and Rank was distinctly embarrassed when he answered: "Assuredly."[32]

Jones ranked the group from most to least in Freud's affections: Ferenczi (age 40), "easily first"; Abraham (36), Jones (34), Rank (29), and Sachs (32). Jones compared the Committee to Breuer, Fliess, and Jung—all of whom parted ways in bitter conflict with Freud. (On the occasion of Ferenczi's fortieth birthday, Freud recalled his own, in 1896, as the "peak of loneliness," when he had "lost all my old friends and hadn't acquired any new ones."[33] This is a surprising lapse: Fliess was Freud's intimate friend then, but his name is blotted by Freud from the record!) In the summer of 1913 Freud presented each member with an antique Greek intaglio, which each had mounted in a gold ring; hence the "Ring" group.

Jones commented on the sensitivity of Committee members to the faintest evidence of anti-Semitism. He thought Ferenczi and Sachs were most sensitive, then Freud; Abraham and Rank were less so. (Jones's insensitivity can be seen in his "astonishment" at the sensitivity of Jews in this regard, and in his 1945 article on the Jewish Question.) Jones had a considerable language adjustment to make, aside from the ethnic difference. While he understood German well, he would sometimes write in English to Committee members. All the members had a good sense of humor. Freud quipped that a real sign of the acceptance of psychoanalysis in Vienna would be when shops advertised "gifts for all stages of the transference."[34]

Freud's letters to Karl Abraham in Berlin reveal his attitudes leading up to the formation of the Committee. After Freud "completed the purge" of Adler and his followers, he minimized the loss but complained, "With the single exception of Rank, I have no one here in whom I can take complete pleasure." Glad that Abraham was corresponding with Rank, Freud wrote: "Politically I am crippled and see all hope for psychoanalysis in the unity of the four or five who are closest to me." And in June 1913, after his personal break with the man Abraham had mistrusted for five years: "Jung is crazy, but I have no desire for a separation and should like to let him wreck himself first."[35]

For the story of the Committee's formation we must rely on Jones's biography of Freud. As Jones was the only one to have had access to the correspondence between Freud and

Ferenczi and to other material, we have to accept his account of the relationships among Committee members. It is important to bear in mind, however, that Jones was an actor in this group and had his own political and personal viewpoints. His descriptions are thus biased and limited although important nonetheless.

"Freud had all through his life many non-analytical friends, all of whom, so far as I know, remained faithful to him. He had three intimate friends who shared his scientific work, Breuer, Fliess and Jung, who had all parted from him. We [The Committee] were the last he was ever to make." Jones omits other intimate colleagues who came into Freud's life beginning in 1912, especially women like Lou Andreas-Salomé, Beata Rank, Helene Deutsch, and Marie Bonaparte. Jones hardly mentions Sabina Spielrein, the first woman analytic colleague, who influenced Freud's later theory of the death instinct. Of all of these, only she and Deutsch had a medical—or any—degree. Lou, Anna Freud, Marie Bonaparte, and Jones's Viennese wife, Katharine, even received the symbolic Committee rings.[36] But Jones slighted these people, and even Anna Freud, in overstating the importance of the Committee.

Jones also omits mention of nonanalyst friends who left Freud, especially Max Graf, musicologist and father of Freud's patient "Little Hans" Graf, whose memoir Jones ignored, met Freud in 1900, became a regular at the Wednesday meetings, and used Freud's ideas in musical biography and interpretation. His attendance subsequently became sporadic, and he finally left in 1913. Graf regarded Freud as a great investigator and discoverer who had the imagination of an artist. Both a rationalist and a romantic, a cultivated intellect and brilliant speaker, Freud, as a positivist, had little tolerance for metaphysics; he was surprised when Graf showed him passages in Kant and Leibnitz on the unconscious. Graf was disturbed that Freud could not accept Adler's admittedly deviant views. "Good-hearted and considerate though he was in private life, Freud was hard and relentless in the presentation of his own ideas. When the question of his science came up, he would break with his most intimate and reliable friends." Graf felt there was the atmosphere of a new religion in the Society, with Freud as the prophet and the students, "all inspired and convinced," as his apostles. In his reminiscence, Graf recalls Freud's beautiful eyes, which seemed to look at man from the depths, but contained something distrustful and, later, bitter.[37]

Graf did not write about Rank, but others of this period did leave a record. Sandor Rado (1890–1972) came to Vienna from Hungary about 1913. To him Freud had the bearing of a *Geheimrat* or privy councillor, with fur-lined great coat and ivory-handled cane. With Freud was "a young, poorly dressed boy who was agitated, fidgety, and talked to him all the time." Otto Rank, then almost 30, looked younger than his years. Rado described Freud's lectures as "stunning" and of great emotional appeal; and "his sentences were dictated for the typesetter." (Nonetheless, Rado caught three slips of the tongue in the two-hour presentation!)[38]

Another observer of those crucial years was Edoardo Weiss (1889–1970), founder of the Italian Psychoanalytic Society and a medical classmate of Tausk in Vienna. He began attending the Wednesday meetings in May 1913 and would go to the Café Bauer afterwards. "At these informal meetings, I remember, Otto Rank always sat close to Freud, showing him the greatest attention. Freud talked about things that he never mentioned in the Society meetings and revealed that his interests extended far beyond what he wrote about." Those interests included parapsychology: telepathy, extrasensory perception, clairvoyance. "In my opinion," Weiss concluded about the mentor and his protégé, "Freud must have grossly misjudged Otto Rank for many years." Weiss thought that Rank expected to become Freud's legitimate successor, but that he eventually deviated even more than Adler and Jung.[39]

BEFORE THE WAR

Rank's graduation on November 22, 1912 received no notice in his minutes, but he became more active in Society discussions on death, incest, marriage, narcissism, and feminism.[40] A brief overview of sessions of The Vienna Society during 1913 will bring into focus Rank's role in the ongoing development of psychoanalytic thought. Significantly, and perhaps surprisingly, Freud and Rank supported each other in denying a biological basis for the incest taboo. "The destructive effect of incest on the race is by no means proven," said Rank.[41]

In April 1913, just before his twenty-ninth birthday, Rank joined in a discussion of celibacy and neurosis. In a cryptic comment that may bear on his own preoccupations, Rank confirmed that a purely erotic motive could play a part in the decision to marry: "For many persons, marriage is the only possible form of love life because their rejection of sexuality—the normal part of which we call fidelity—prevents them from practicing polygamy." Freud said that the quality of the parental marriage has the greatest influence on one's decision whether or not to marry. "Matrimony is a difficult cultural task," he said, "and one has to be healthy to fulfill it."[42]

There was a lively interest in narcissism, the libidinal attachment to one's own ego. Rank criticized what he considered sloppy definitions and explanations. In a session attended by only eight (none of them women), Rank took Sadger (the antifeminist) to task: "The derivation of narcissism in girls from the lack of a penis and from the wish to make up for that defect is quite reminiscent of Adler's 'masculine protest'; it is, however, just as untenable, since there are a good many girls and women who are proud of *purely feminine* (real or imagined) merits."[43]

As co-editor of two journals, Rank spent much of July traveling. Freud wrote: "Dear Doctor, . . . I congratulate you on being in Paris. Too bad, that you should be lonesome in a city of millions." Freud assigned Rank a few tasks—seeing people, prodding a procrastinator, visiting the publisher Deuticke (Leipzig)—and wished him "the finest of vacations, interrupted by the tidings you will send."

Back at the Vienna Society in the fall after the Munich Congress Rank joined in a discussion about explosive anger: Since the affects expressed thereby usually have another source, "rage is often directed toward entirely indifferent persons or occasions; indeed, one might regard this precisely as a characteristic of rage." He opposed the idea that it takes a loved or hated person to evoke rage. Furthermore, "Just like the beasts, man can be observed to fly into a rage easily if difficulties get into the way of his desire for love." And, with what must have included a silent nod to his own father, Rank agreed with another speaker's contention that alcohol plays an important role in such outbursts.[44]

Otto Rank and Hanns Sachs, co-editors of *Imago*, wrote a monograph on applications of psychoanalysis in the sciences and humanities (1913); its translation into English brought Rank's name forward again in the United States just after his *Myth of the Birth of the Hero* appeared. According to Sachs, he and Rank shared "all our plans and ideas, so that every product of this period bears some marks of our discussions." Sachs continues: "During our friendship we not only worked well and smoothly together, but had also a great deal of fun . . ."[45]

In these years (from 1912 to 1914), besides the two books, Rank published such essays as "Actual Sexual Excitements as Cause of the Dream," "On Hearing Colors," "A Contribution to Infantile Sexuality," "Contributions to Symbolism in Poetry," "Shaw and Multatuli on Sexual Repression," "Diderot on Women," "The Family Complex," "Slips in Everyday Life," "The Fish as a Sexual Symbol in Modern Art," "The Birth-rescue Fantasy in Dream and Poetry," "E.T.A. Hoffman on Insanity," "Homosexuality and Paranoia," "The Incest Complex: Quotes from the Daily Press," "A Catatonic Episode," "Masturbation and Character Formation" (32 pages), *"The Woman of Ephesus:* Interpretation of the Faithless Widow," "Multatuli on Hysteria and Curiosity," "Mythology and Psychoanalysis," "Myth and Fairy Tale," "Nakedness in Legend and Poetry" (90 pages), "Multiple Meanings of Dreams During Awakening and Their Occurrence in Mythological Thinking" (65 pages), "Folk Psychology Parallels to Children's Sex Theories," and a number of notes and reviews. None of these have been translated, although abstracts of some appeared in English.

The fourth edition of Freud's *Interpretation of Dreams* appeared in 1914. Not only did Rank help with the editing, but he contributed two chapters to the book: "Dreams and Creative Writing" and "Dreams and Myths." Freud had hoped to write another book on dreams, using material from patients that could be analyzed more fully than he was willing to do with his own dreams. Rank was to coauthor or contribute to that book, one that Freud never brought to fruition; instead, the chapters by Rank were incorporated in the next four editions of Freud's masterwork, with his name appearing below Freud's on the title page. This collaboration remains unique in the history of psychoanalysis, testifying to Rank's unchallenged position of esteem with his mentor.

The most prolific psychoanalytic writer, Rank published five books and many articles and reviews totalling more than one thousand pages before he was thirty. That he was not honored more for this achievement may be due to the fact that Freud's disciples considered each other's publications of no account and seldom read or quoted them, recognizing only the authority of the Professor.[46]

At the same time Rank became enamored of the newest art form, the motion picture. He saw H. H. Ewers's Faustian film, *The Student of Prague*, soon after it debuted. Drawing on E. T. A. Hoffman and Edgar Allan Poe, the story concerns a youth who trades his reflection in the mirror to the devil for a promise of love and fortune. The youth's mirror image then enters the story with a diabolical will of its own. The conflict in the frantic student's divided soul ends only when he shoots his reflection in the mirror and falls dead. Rank took this story as the starting point for his long essay on "The Double" (1914), a seminal work on the relation of shadow, reflection, ghost, and twin to the idea of soul and immortality. This theme fascinated Rank up to his last days, and *The Double* [*Der Doppelgänger*] has appeared in several editions and translations.

Deserving mention for its ironic timeliness is a paper on "The Family Romance in the Psychology of the Assassin" (1913). Rank incorporated the material in the updated English translation of the *Hero*. It is the regicide theme that Freud and Lou talked about as the safety valve for Rank's father complex. Rank wrote that certain fantasies are handled differently by different types: The neurotic represses, the "pervert" expresses. Thus a paranoid's delusion corrects the inner world, while a criminal's act changes the outer world. The paranoid identifies with the father, but the anarchist kills the king. In effect Rank wrote a kind of insanity defense for the assassin, whose patricidal urge is quite unconscious and whose apparent political motive only screens the wish to kill a different person. This paper appeared, coincidentally, the year Adolf Hitler left the Vienna he despised for Germany, where he distinguished himself fighting for the Central Powers.

RANK AND FREUD DURING THE WAR

After a series of military conflicts in the Balkan–Asia Minor region, fueled by both rising nationalism and imbalance among the European powers, came the assassination. In late June, 1914, a Bosnian student shot Archduke Ferdinand, heir to the Austro-Hungarian throne. Emperor Franz Josef declared war; he was soon to be joined by Germany and Turkey. These Central Powers were opposed by an increasing number of Allies, including Russia, France, Belgium, England, Italy, and eventually the United States. The last European experience of war dated back to 1870; what most parties expected to be a brief conflict became the World War and set a new standard for destructiveness. Airplanes, submarines, machine guns, and gas weapons were some of the fruits of technology turned monstrous. The carnage took the lives of 20 million and wounded many more. Afterwards the map of Europe was redrawn, with new countries called Czecho-slovakia and Yugoslavia carved out of the Habsburg Empire and Austria and Hungary finally separated.

The war brought hunger, cold, and fear to many cities, including Vienna, where initial optimism about the outcome gradually faded. Communications were lost or interrupted. Freud, whose three sons entered military service, noted wryly that Jones was now "the enemy." In August and September, 1914, while Freud cataloged his collection of antiquities, Rank arranged and cataloged Freud's library; the two spent a great deal of time together, and Freud remarked gratefully that Rank was "as cheerful as ever."[47] Abraham and Ferenczi served as army doctors; Sachs was excused for health reasons and remained near Freud. Otto Rank was happy to be temporarily rejected by the army; he was "fighting like a lion against his Fatherland," Freud wrote in December to Ferenczi.[48] The Vienna Psychoanalytic Society met about every three weeks, but only the roster was kept, no minutes. The *Zeitschrift* and *Imago* kept going at half-speed, but the *Yearbook* ceased publication. Rank was making "fine progress," Freud wrote, on the problem of the epic, which would be his topic for a thesis to be submitted for admission to the University faculty. Evidently nothing came of it, despite Freud's opinion: "Rank has brilliantly solved the problem of Homer."[49]

By June 1915, Italy had declared war on Austria-Hungary, and in a new call-up Rank was taken into the Austrian army. Freud bemoaned the absence of friends and helpers, and in early July remarked that even Rank, who was stationed in Vienna, had not come by. Rank was serving with the heavy artillery section, appropriate for a man of frail physique, high intelligence, and machinist's training. Rank was around long enough to persuade Freud to prepare his forthcoming lectures—usually extemporaneous—for publication; in the winter semester (October to March) of 1915–16 and 1916–17 Freud addressed a large mixed audience at the University in twenty-eight talks, his last such series. The resulting *Introductory Lectures on Psychoanalysis* became his most widely disseminated work, appearing in at least sixteen languages, including Chinese, Hebrew, and Arabic, mostly during Freud's lifetime.[50]

In January 1916 Rank was transferred to Krakow, then at the easternmost tip of the tottering Habsburg Empire, where he served for three years as editor of the *Krakauer Zeitung [Krakow Times]*, an Army and general newspaper. This was a sensible post for a prolific writer-editor. (The celebrated Austrian novelist Robert Musil, Rank's contemporary, held a similar post, and poet Rainer Maria Rilke met with Freud, and possibly Rank, during a military stint in Vienna before Rank's departure.)

Freud suffered in Rank's absence, but Hanns Sachs filled in manfully to keep the two journals—all that was left of the international psychoanalytic movement—going. Rank was able to get away from Krakow to Constantinople for the month of August 1916; he made a couple of brief visits to Freud and saw some of Warsaw.[51] The *Krakow Times* was apparently the only German daily in Galicia (8 million inhabitants); it stressed literary, artistic, and scientific topics as well as news and provided many book reviews. Rank solicited advertisements for books and requested that review copies be sent to the paper. As a journalist, Rank excelled in abusing British Prime Minister David Lloyd George. Notes and clippings among Rank's papers reflect an interest in the contemporary writer Grete v. Urbanitzke. At times he turned again to writing poetry, some of which is melancholic in tone, some lighter.

In 1917, the essay on Homer and the folk epic, so highly praised by Freud, appeared in *Imago* (57 pages). In September Rank finished revising his first book, *The Artist*, a decade after its original publication. The first edition had been out of print for two years, prompting Rank to revise it. In the new preface, despite Brobdingnagian sentences, Rank reflects with feeling on his development and outlook in that bleak time, and on the evolution of Freudian psychology as well.

There is always something awkward in observing oneself in the mirror of one's own past, especially when no inner necessity but

1

2

3

Born Otto Rosenfeld in 1884,
Rank (1) had one brother
three years older. Their
parents, Simon and Karoline
(2), had moved to Vienna
amidst large scale Jewish
migration. Simon, an artisan
jeweler, had a drinking
problem, tyrannized the
family, and eventually left:
not even a picture remains.
Paul Rosenfeld (3, rt.) got an
academic education and
became a lawyer. Having no
choice, Otto went to trade
school and became a
locksmith.

4

The Rosenfeld apartment, at the extreme right (4), stood beside a tavern in the working-class Jewish quarter called Leopoldstadt.

Handicapped from youth by rheumatic fever, Otto was exhausted by long days in the machine shop. At night, from age 15 to 19—partly to escape his unhappy home—Otto immersed himself in books and in the glory of Viennese culture, especially plays, concerts, and opera. He recorded his ideas and feelings in an important unpublished diary, begun when he was 18. The title page (5) reads, "Judgments and Thoughts about People and Issues." At age 19 he used both family and pen names, a sign of his newly emerging, self-created identity.

5

Urtheile und Gedanken über Menschen und Dinge

in Form eines Tagebuches

von

Otto Rank [Rosenfeld].

Begonnen am 1. Januar 1913 in Wien

Wien.

1. *Januar.*

—1

> Vienna 1 Jan [1903]
>
> "I begin this book for my own enlightenment. Above all, I want to make progress in psychology. By that I understand not the professional definition and explanation of certain technical terms established by a few professors, but the comprehensive knowledge of mankind that explains the riddles of our thinking, acting and speaking, and leads back to the underlying fundamentals. To approach this ideal, which only a few have attempted, self-observation is a prime requisite and to that end I make these notes. In them I try to fix passing moods, impressions, and feelings, to preserve the stripped-off layers that I have outgrown and in this way to keep a picture of my abandoned way of life ..."

6

The self-educated youth had interests in psychology, acting, and writing when he came upon the works of Sigmund Freud. Applying psychoanalytic ideas he wrote an essay—"The Artist"—which so impressed Freud that he hired Rank as his Secretary. This enabled the brilliant young man to complete high school and attend the University of Vienna (7), where he obtained his Ph.D. in 1912. By then, at age 28, Rank had published four books: *The Artist, The Myth of the Birth of the Hero, The Lohengrin Saga,* and *The Incest Motif in Literature and Legend.*

7

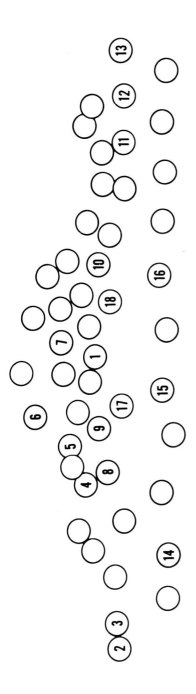

1. Sigmund Freud; 2. Otto Rank;
3. Ludwig Bunswanger; 4.
Ludwig Jekels; 5. Abraham A.
Brill; 6. Edward Hirschmann; 7.
Paul Federn; 8. Oskar Pfister; 9.
Max Eitingon; 10. Karl
Abraham; 11. James J. Putnam;
12. Ernest Jones; 13. Wilhelm
Stekel; 14. Eugen Bleuler; 15.
Lou Andreas-Salome; 16. Emma
Jung (C. G. Jungs Frau); 17.
Sandor Ferenczi; 18. C. G. Jung.

The 1911 Psychoanalytic Congress at Weimar. All the important pioneers appear here except Alfred Adler, who had just been forced out of the psychoanalytic movement because of differences with Freud. Carl Jung, Freud's greatest hope, towered over his mentor in real life, but not in this picture. Rank stood modestly at the edge of the group, but he was already Freud's favorite colleague in Vienna. About two years later Jung split with Freud, leaving Rank in an unrivalled position.

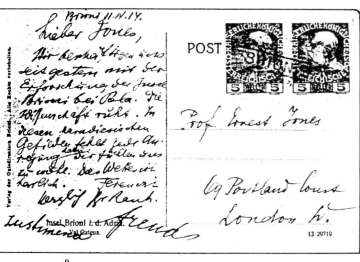

9

10

From their holiday in Brioni in 1914 Ferenczi, Rank, and Freud wrote to Jones in England (9): "Science is resting. In these heavenly fields there is no stimulation; we are feeling too well for that." World War I soon changed the atmosphere.

A reluctant soldier (10), the frail Rank was called up in 1915 and served as editor of a wartime newspaper in Krakow, at the eastern edge of the tottering Austro-Hungarian Empire.

In 1920 psychoanalysts met at The Hague, probably the first international scientific group to convene after the war's devastation. Rank accompanied Freud and his daughter, Anna (11). In a group picture (detail, 12) Rank stood in the position of honor behind the Professor.

11

12

Rank returned from Krakow with Beata, his Polish bride, to be Freud's right-hand man as editor, teacher, analyst, and executive. The birth of Helene in 1919 brought Otto Rank to a new awareness of the mother-child bond and the fundamental issues of separation, ego development, and will. A photograph of Freud, who encouraged Beata to become a lay analyst, can be seen in the background (13). The Rank family lived in central Vienna, in the building which housed the office of the Verlag (Publishing House) (14) which Rank directed.

13

14

Freud's inner circle, the secret "Ring" Committee (15), ran the International Psychoanalytic Association after Jung's defection. Sitting: Freud, Ferenczi, Sachs; standing: Rank, Abraham, Eitingon, Jones. Rank and Sachs were the only nonphysicians; Jones was the only non-Jew.

Rank broke with Freud in 1926, two years after his *Trauma of Birth* appeared; it impressed and then split the Committee. In this detail (16) of a Congress photograph in 1925, Rank (right) stands apart from the Committee—Jones, Abraham, Eitingon, and Ferenczi—seated at the center of the group.

some outward push compels review and meditation. It is no pleasure to be reminded that one has grown older; but it is yet more painful to have to see *how* young one used to be. If there are drawbacks in having to review and judge anew a youthful work twelve years after writing it, the difficulties increase considerably where the topic is *psychoanalysis,* a young science whose rapid progress can be followed only with seven league boots suited to its many-dimensional kingdom, not as the author did, who for the past three years had to exchange his for clodhoppers. . . .

What to start with gives this work a general base and scientific support is the fact that it rests on the secure foundation of Freudian psychology and moreover is obliged to those direct philosophical forerunners of psychoanalysis, Schopenhauer and Nietzsche, for many ideas, if also the tendency to speculate and overreach to grasp the whole, which may be excused by the author's youthfulness. How deeply the process of conception and observation is rooted in the fruitful soil of psychoanalysis can be seen clearly only now, with Freud's teaching a complete and finished science, which to be sure has proved much of the author's position—drawn from an immense craving for knowledge—premature, but has fully confirmed the general conception and many specific trains of thought. . . .

Since Freud's insight that everything which appears today as inner conflict, however senseless it seems, was once in the history of our development an outward reaction serving some good purpose, there have been individually successful attempts to reconstruct this actual pre-historic development from the ontogenetic psychology known through analysis. The real although unavowed aim of this book is to show the psychological impetus progressing from outside inward and constantly mounting, making the artist both possible and necessary in cultural development. The principle of development Nietzsche applied to the genesis of moral ideas is used automatically. Later this became very important in psychoanalysis, and already has contributed greatly to the solution of problems in other fields of knowledge. Applying this principle to the problem of the artist, at that time with inadequate means, above all rescued him from the customary aesthetic-philosophical approach and assigned him a place as an essential broker and bearer of culture. For the artist represents the highest stage of development on the way from material civilization to inner culture, from which man seeks, by inner enrichment, to replace those fragments of reality abandoned under external duress. According to Freud, the artist is able to restore via a special detour this originally pleasurable relationship to the outer world which mankind lost in attaining civilization. . . .

The passing slice of time has enriched the author in years and experience, but also led mankind to the brink of monstrous cultural catastrophe, in the face of which all the understanding and expectations drawn from regular developmental potential must seem to us weak and empty.[52]

Written from a small Moravian spa, these words convey Rank's many sides: devoted follower; half-modest, half-proud innovator; an enthusiast for living and understanding, stunned by the monumental destruction of modern war.

Rank visited Vienna at Christmas, and Freud wrote to Abraham: "He is now a prisoner of the editorial department of the *Krakauer Zeitung* and is in very low spirits." Jones makes the point repeatedly that Rank suffered two or three severe depressive episodes during the war, followed by a manic rebound later. This letter of Freud's, however, is the only evidence cited.[53]

Rank's revised *Artist* did not appear until later in 1918; a shortage of paper caused the delay and apparently led Rank to make additional changes. The book bears the designation "Enlarged second and third edition," which probably resulted from announcements of a second edition being followed by a delay, orders coming in, and then new revisions.

In September a large group of psychoanalysts assembled in Budapest, all from the Central Powers except two from neutral Holland. Considering the imminent end of the war and of the Austro-Hungarian Empire, the participants at the Fifth International Psychoanalytic Congress were riding high. Government officials announced a psychoanalytic clinic, major private money was in the offing, and Ferenczi won a university appointment. He was elected President of the IPA at this Congress, the only one attended by Freud's wife, Martha, and the only one at which Freud read a paper instead of speaking in his accustomed free form. At this Congress Herman Nunberg, who had first attended the Vienna Society in 1914, proposed a new requirement that every analyst be analyzed. Victor Tausk and Otto Rank, both officers of the Austrian Army, energetically opposed the motion, and it failed to pass.[54] (Not until 1926 was the requirement established.) Freud did not think it necessary; he had analyzed Ferenczi, who had in turn analyzed Jones, but these were personal choices, not a requirement. Rank and Tausk could not be expected to have anyone but Freud as their analyst. Eventually each did, in his own unhappy way, attempt to become Freud's patient.

During the war, Rank's personal and professional life began to change. There were a number of reasons for the shift. With the departure of Adler and Jung, Rank became first among Freud's followers. He had obtained his doctorate, but his bright future was clouded by the onset of war: He became a reluctant soldier. Yet the war forced him to become more independent, both in his career and in his personal life. He was to return to Vienna a changed man.

STARTING A FAMILY

From 1916–1918 Otto Rank spent his tour of duty in Krakow, Poland's capital for centuries and a cosmopolitan center of culture and learning. By the late nineteenth century, the city boasted six museums; the arts, sciences, and industry thrived there and offered a stimulating post for Lieutenant Rank.

During his hitch, Rank attended concerts in the role of music critic for his paper. At one of these he was introduced to a very attractive young woman, Beata Mincer, a student of psychology and lover of music. Beata knew of Rank through an aunt who had studied in Vienna with him and told her niece about his book *The Artist*. The duration of their courtship is not known, but probably the couple met early in Rank's tour of duty. Otto and Beata were married by a rabbi in a military ceremony on November 7, 1918. Since he had become Catholic to legalize his name change, Rank reconverted to Judaism in October in order to have a Jewish wedding.[55]

The armistice came four days after the wedding. Soon the bride, 23, and groom, 34, returned to Vienna. They met the Freuds soon after their return. Beata, called "Tola" by her friends, was beautiful, intelligent, and charming and immediately endeared herself to the Professor. Paul Roazen, who interviewed many Freudians, wrote: "Whereas Tola Rank was beautiful, with more than a touch of elegance, her husband was almost an ugly man. But they made an admirable couple, and she deferred to him with nineteenth-century femininity."[56] A student of psychology, Tola had helped Otto with his extracurricular work on *Imago* in Krakow, but in Vienna she was not involved at first in her husband's professional life.

The post-war period was grim. Freud and his family did receive some financial help from friends and former patients, notably Anton von Freund. A wealthy and well-educated brewer, von Freund was treated by Freud and decided to establish the first psychoanalytic clinic in Budapest. He had received one of the signet rings of the Committee when he was stricken with cancer. His philanthropy supported plans to establish an international psychoanalytic publishing house (Verlag), since Freud preferred autonomy to dealing with established houses like Deuticke and Heller.

Just weeks after the Armistice, Rank was to go to Budapest to see von Freund. The trains were dilapidated and Tola expected to stay in Vienna. But Otto changed his mind and came back from the station to fetch her, and they went together to see the benefactor. There, in his elegant house, Tola's professional education began in earnest. "They spoke about nothing but psychoanalysis . . . I had some notion, but I really felt as if I were out of the conversation. So I went to Toni Freund and told him that I'd like to learn something about psychoanalysis. I told him that everyone talked so animatedly and I sat like a little mouse." She read some of Freud's essays about dreams and discussed them with Toni and Otto and began to clarify her thinking.[57]

For a time it appeared that the Verlag would be located in Budapest, and Rank spent considerable time there working on it. Pressure from Freud and political events moved the site to Vienna and ended the grim possibility that Rank and Freud would be separated permanently. Instead, Rank was made Managing Director of the Internationaler Psychoanalytischer Verlag at its founding in January, 1919.

Before the war Rank had little or no clinical practice. The new publishing venture, with its large subsidy, offered Rank a guaranteed salary, with which he could support a family and also provided an office and living quarters at 5 and 3 Grünangergasse, a handsome building in the center city. Unfortunately, the $500,000 provided by von Freund did not secure the project for long. Only one-fourth of the money could be brought out of Hungary; once converted to Austrian currency, it was especially vulnerable to the post-war inflation that cut fortunes into confetti. There were some additional donors, and Freud sent Rank some patients, so life could go on.[58] The new husband worked as analyst, editor, publisher, and training director for would-be analysts coming to Vienna, mostly from the United States.

In March Rank went to Switzerland for three weeks to help organize a branch of the IPA and work on publishing arrangements. Tola, already four months pregnant, accompanied him. Jones came in from London to see Rank for the first time in five years. To Jones, Rank seemed to have undergone a remarkable transformation. He said Rank "presented two quite different personalities before and after the Great War; I never knew anyone change so much. His personal experiences during the war brought out a vigor and other manifestations of his personality we had never suspected." For Jones this was the dividing line between Rank's sane and purportedly disturbed behavior.

> I was very astonished at the remarkable change the war years had wrought in Rank. I had last seen him a weedy youth, timid and deferential, much given to clicking of heels and bowing. Now in stalked a wiry, tough man with a masterful air whose first act was to deposit on the table a huge revolver. I asked him what he wanted with it, and he nonchalantly replied: *"Für alle Fälle"* (for any eventuality). How had he got it through the frontier examination? When the official pointed to his bulging pocket Rank had calmly answered, "bread." The change had coincided with his resuming his work in Vienna after the war years in Krakow. At the time his Viennese friends connected it with some response to his recent marriage, but later on it became plain that it must have been a hypomanic reaction to the three severe attacks of melancholia he had suffered while in Krakow.[59]

Jones's description and his diagnosis seem to be far-fetched. It is hard to imagine that Rank would risk job and family, even life and limb, in such a prankish feat. Nothing else about his behavior at that time evoked such criticism; indeed, Jones indicates that the two got on very well in all personal meetings, and that Rank's work was commendable in quality and astonishing in volume. An alternative explanation of the episode is that Rank had the gun (perhaps a disabled war souvenir) legitimately, and that he was pulling Jones's leg.

It is also possible that Jones confused Rank with Tausk. Victor Tausk, whom Jones saw as one of the more troublesome members of the Vienna Psychoanalytic Society, shot himself with his army pistol July 3, 1919 at age 42. The suicide, three months after Jones met Rank in Switzerland, stunned the psychoanalytic community, but the background details have only recently emerged. Jones omits the tragic story from his biography.

It appears that Freud had refused Tausk's request for analysis

and instead referred him to Helene Deutsch (1884–1982),
Tausk's junior by seven years and a social friend. She analyzed
him for the first three months of 1919, while herself in analysis
with Freud. At the end of March, Freud insisted that she break
off the analysis with Tausk, who had become an overly prominent
subject in Deutsch's own analytic sessions with the Professor.
After Tausk's suicide, Freud expressed his dislike for the man
to Frau Lou, Tausk's sometime lover: "I confess that I do not
really miss him; I had long realized that he could be of no further
service, indeed that he constituted a threat to the future. . . .
I would have dropped him long ago if *you* hadn't raised him
so in my estimation."[60] Freud's handling of the case raises questions about his own intellectual and sexual jealousy. Jones's total
omission of the story raises questions about his possible confusion
of Tausk with Rank in the gun episode.

In August the Ranks' first and only child, a daughter, Helene,
was born. At the time of her birth, the Ranks lived in a four-
room apartment adjoining the Verlag office. Upstairs lived Rank's
mother and his brother, Paul Rosenfeld, who was then practicing
law. Rank's father and mother had been divorced; Beata met
her father-in-law only once, by chance. (Helene never knew
him.)

Tola became Freud's hostess for social events, entertaining
in her spacious apartment for such visitors as Lou Andreas-
Salomé; one Christmas they had a party for Freud's foreign
patients. Since Freud had only grandsons so far, Helene was a
surrogate granddaughter. Born in 1896, Tola was a few months
younger than Anna Freud, and the two worked together in the
office. Tola won Freud's intellectual respect and is cited in a
footnote to a paper he wrote in 1919. Such acknowledgment
was no small thanks, and everyone knew she stood well with
the Professor.[61]

Jones and his publications assistant, Eric Hiller, made their
way to Vienna in late September, the first foreign civilians in
the forlorn postwar capital. Enroute they were stunned by the
sight of ragged, starved Austrian officials and even emaciated
dogs too weak to go get scraps of food. In this context Jones
was pleased to host the Freud family and the Ranks at a fine
dinner: "It was moving to see what an experience a proper meal
seemed to mean to them." Jones spent most of a week working
closely with Rank on publishing plans in Vienna and London.

"Rank struggled heroically with the endless problems," Jones recalled, "and accomplished super-human feats in coping with them almost single-handed."[62]

Meanwhile the political situation in Hungary suddenly changed, and was no longer supportive of psychoanalysis. Ferenczi lost his professorship. Max Eitingon was invited to join the Committee in place of the fatally ill von Freund. At Freud's urging, the affable Ferenczi gave up the Presidency of the IPA to Jones.

At the end of the year, Freud and the Committee were energetically planning the Sixth International Psychoanalytic Congress. If Freud could not unite Jews and Anti-Semites on psychoanalytic ground, he did bring together scientists and therapists from opposing sides of the bloodiest war in history. Emperor Franz Joseph, who had reigned from 1848, died in 1916 before the Empire was broken up. In that year Freud turned sixty; his lingering numerological superstition, based on the Fleissian theory of periodicity, led him to expect his own death in 1918. He lived to see and create a great deal more, and to be better known in the annals of human progress than his Emperor. To the great credit of Freud and Rank, the psychoanalytic movement rose out of the ashes of war ahead of most if not all other international associations.

Otto Rank, now a mature analyst, embarked on a career that included treating patients, training physicians from abroad, writing, editing, and administering the affairs of the postwar movement, at Freud's side and in a bleak city that was a mere shadow of the old, imperial Vienna.

CHAPTER 7

The Committee

From 1848 to 1914, Vienna produced a culture of facades, decors, and costumes, illuminated by a few thinkers of astonishing penetration. . . . Their way of unmasking layer after layer of illusion in quest of a kernel at the center has become a paradigm for cultural critics, social scientists, and writers everywhere. If we today see sham all about us while positing a genuine order at the core, we are reviving a vision of reality that the Viennese modernists pioneered. . . . This combination of ultimate optimism with short-run pessimism is but another of the paradoxes of Viennese culture.
—William M. Johnston, *Vienna, Vienna*

Following the war, Vienna suffered from inflation that virtually destroyed the middle class. The glittering prewar capital of the last European dynasty, left with only one of eleven national provinces, lost much of its sustenance as well as its pride. People were starving, and refugees flooded the city from all over the dismembered empire.

The war had slowed, but it did not stop, the progress of psychoanalysis. Freud, Sachs, Rank, and Ferenczi kept *Imago* and the *Zeitschrift* going at half speed. Ferenczi analyzed his commanding officer while both were on horseback and claimed the first "hippic psychoanalysis."[1] Budapest became a rallying place for the movement. Psychoanalytic ideas influenced the treatment of shell shock and other war neuroses, enhancing Freud's reputation in psychiatry.

During the war years, Rank did not publish as much but he did make some important contributions. In 1915 he published relatively short articles: "A Case of Determination to Find," "Parapraxis and Dream," "A Dream Poetized," "The Play within *Hamlet*," "The Costly Misprint," and "Unconscious Self-betrayal." In the next years he published less: one book review in 1916, then the big papers on Homer and the folk epic (50 pages) in 1917. The revised *Artist* finally appeared in 1918. In 1919 came "Daphnis and Chloe," "Strindberg on the Meaning of Psychotic Symptoms," and *Psychoanalytic Contributions to Research on Myth,* which anthologized thirteen of Rank's prewar papers, including "The Double" and "Nakedness." This last prompted Freud to say, "His achievements are truly amazing."[2]

At 35, when he was just over half Freud's age, Rank became Freud's virtual partner. He was a publisher as well as an editor, began analytic practice in Vienna and set up a training program for foreign visitors, and traveled as Freud's emissary. He usually wrote to the other "Ring" or Committee members on behalf of himself and Freud, and among his papers he kept a file of 327 *Rundbriefe,* or circular letters, sent and received by Committee members over the next five years. (These important documents in the history of psychoanalysis have yet to be published.) Rank and Freud formed a strong team at the center of the Ring, but changes in the two men, abetted by maneuvering among the others, brought the partnership to a difficult end.

ART, SCIENCE, AND RELIGION ACCORDING TO FREUD

In an essay on psychoanalysis he wrote during the war, Havelock Ellis complimented Freud's artistic qualities. Freud attacked the compliment as "the most refined and amiable form of resistance, calling me a great artist in order to injure the validity of our scientific claims." With his special mixture of humility and pride, pessimism and optimism, Freud added, "This is all wrong. I am sure in a few decades my name will be wiped away and our results will last."[3]

This was false modesty. From the time he fancied his bust in the University courtyard, Freud had a grand wish for immortality as a scientist. In 1917 Freud savored the news that someone had proposed his name for the Nobel prize. Characteristically he downplayed both his hope and the award itself, which he coveted and never won.[4] In a paper, "A Difficulty in the Path of Psychoanalysis" (1917), Freud placed himself in succession to Copernicus and Darwin. He listed three scientific blows to man's collective ego: first our planet was displaced from the center of the universe, then divine creation was challenged by the theory of evolution, and finally psychoanalysis upset the assumption that we control our own minds.

Freud's immortality was linked to his self-image as a scientific explorer who discovers a truth which conquers the world after being initially rejected. This image combined science with social movement, in precisely the form taken by psychoanalysis. In pursuing that goal Freud rejected the identity of the artist, which was precisely the role most important to Otto Rank.

The artist's genius sets him apart, then gradually makes him admirable and creates a following. In art, as Kant said, genius makes its own rules. Freud admired artists, known and unknown; his writings and his collection of ancient figurines attest to this. He credited writers from Sophocles to Schnitzler with knowing intuitively and expressing creatively what he laboriously reduced (or elevated) to a science. But as a strict scientist Freud viewed artistic creativity with misgivings, as relying on intuition rather than discipline. (When courting Martha, remember, Freud envied her cousin the artist's facility with women.) Freud both applauded and put down artistic gifts. He awaited the muse in himself but also distrusted it. Art favors beauty over truth; it expresses truth as beauty. Science subordinates or reduces beauty to truth. Although many great scientists were not ashamed of aesthetic feeling, Freud consciously spurned art and philosophy in his eagerness to transcend them with science.

As Rank indicated in *The Artist*, Freud was the first hero of the new psychological era: a physician of the soul. Historically he followed and supplanted mankind's religious and national and artistic heroes as scientific healer of the cultural or collective soul. The disturbing self-consciousness of the nineteenth century, which shook the rational, romantic, and religious foundations of society, could also be used to heal the afflicted psyche, the suffering neurotic. Beginning with himself, like Nietzsche, Freud brought this outcast patient into the light of a new psychology; indeed, he invented the light that revealed the problem in a new way, to create a new psychology. Freud brought under medical control that Nietzschean self-consciousness which threatened man's sanity. Almost single-handedly, Freud turned a monster into a helper, a nightmare into a comprehensible dream. To many, it was still ugly, dangerous, and frightening, but Freud simultaneously challenged and comforted his listeners. He performed a kind of magic but reassured them it was science. He dared to tamper with the soul, but with the attitude of a careful surgeon. Yet in Kant's sense it was as a creative artist that he made new working rules for the psychological era.

Freud created the scientific healing of souls, making systematic what great writers knew by intuition. He wanted to perfect their insights with his research. His therapy challenged traditional psychiatry as well as quacks and faith healers. He was not content to practice, write, and teach; he wanted to lead, to establish a movement. Although he scorned religion, as leader of a movement he brought about discipleship and orthodoxy: Adler's excommunication and Jung's apostasy created sects, a phenomenon alien to scientific ideals. Freud could express himself dramatically as a conquerer, a messiah, or a martyr. He solved riddles of the soul cognitively, like Oedipus; then, like Moses, he led the exodus from ignorance to a scientific promised land; and then he took the martyr's role, as a man of truth betrayed by unbelievers. All the while he kept his Jewish identity—but not his faith—with mixed feelings of pride, fear, and resignation.

This paradox in Freud's attitude about religion is well illustrated in an exchange Freud had with the Swiss pastor Oskar Pfister on the question of religion and Jewish identity. Freud wrote:

> From a therapeutic point of view I can only envy your opportunity of bringing about sublimation into religion. But the beauty of religion assuredly has no place in psychoanalysis. Naturally our paths in therapy diverge here, and it can stay at that. Quite by the way, how comes it that none of the godly ever devised psychoanalysis and it had to wait for a godless Jew?

The pastor boldly answered:

> Well, because piety is not the same as the genius for discovering, and because the godly were for a great part not worthy to bring

> *such an achievement to fruition. Moreover, in the first place*
> *you are not a Jew, which my boundless admiration for Amos,*
> *Isaiah, the author of Job and the Prophets makes me greatly*
> *regret, and in the second place you are not so godless, since*
> *he who lives for truth lives in God, and he who fights for the*
> *freeing of love "dwelleth in God." If you were to become aware*
> *of and experience your interpolation in the great universals*
> *which for me are as inevitable as the synthesis of the notes of*
> *a Beethoven symphony are to a musician I should say of you*
> *"There never was a better Christian."*

Pfister made a good match for Freud, and it is no surprise that
the two respected each other. Binswanger, also, was immune
to both Freudian discipleship and ambition. He once asked
Freud why his talented disciples Adler and Jung had defected
and was told, "Precisely because they too wanted to be Popes."[5]

THE SEVEN RINGS

Historians have tended to dramatize the Committee as either
sinister or romantic. Most likely it was neither. Sometimes Freud
was not a good judge of character, a fact which he admitted
after his falling out with Jung. He had had many personal difficulties—with mentors, with peers, and with disciples. It seemed
necessary to have a group of trusted intimates to guide the movement, if there was to be one, and Carl Jung's two-phase departure
called for a stabilizing move. Formed in 1913, the Committee
did not begin to work in earnest until after the war. Keeping
it secret and creating a bond with symbolic rings seemed to
Jones a throwback to Charlemagne or King Arthur, but that
hardly mattered. No one outside seemed to care that election
of officers of the IPA was merely a ratification of what Freud
wanted, not a democratic exercise.

To replace Jung, Freud had five surrogate sons, Rank being
the youngest. Freud gave each a ring in May 1913, the same
year he published *Totem and Taboo,* which deals in part with
myths of overthrow of a patriarch by his sons. In 1919 the group
added Max Eitingon; it now comprised seven men in four cities:
two in Vienna, three in Berlin, one each in London and Budapest. They wrote *Rundbriefe,* about every ten days. In 1919
Rank turned 35, Freud 63. The others may be reviewed briefly.[6]

Ernest Jones, 40, was born in Wales and practiced in London after a few rather tumultuous years in Canada. The only non-Jew in the group, he founded the *International Journal of Psychoanalysis* in 1920, wrote many papers, and was President of the IPA from 1920 to 1924 and from 1932 to 1949, a total of twenty-one years. He helped to rescue the Freuds from Nazi Austria in 1938 and wrote the authorized Freud biography. He also wrote an autobiography. His correspondence has not been published, but a new biography appeared in 1983, revealing professional problems in his early career, a stormy love life, and extreme conservatism. Jones admitted to being excessively critical. He had two serious hobbies, postal chess and figure skating.

Karl Abraham, 42, the first German psychoanalyst, carried on a major correspondence with Freud which has been published in an abridged edition. Abraham studied psychiatry with Jung and tried to warn Freud about what he saw as the dangerous parts of Jung's personality. Gifted in languages, he shared Rank's interest in myth, wrote some important papers, and set up the first psychoanalytic training institute; his analysands included Edward and James Glover, Ella Sharpe, Melanie Klein, Helene Deutsch, and Sandor Rado. Although deeply loyal, he was also able to argue with Freud. Abraham shared Jones's conservatism and, later, warned the Committee against Rank's apparent deviation. Along with Sachs and Eitingon, he had a training program that rivaled Vienna's.

Hanns Sachs, 38, a Viennese lawyer versed in literature, a good lecturer and raconteur, was at Freud's side throughout the war. For years he considered Rank, the other nonphysician member, his closest friend. With Abraham and Eitingon, Sachs settled in Berlin, where he analyzed many notables, including the brilliant Franz Alexander. Both a scholar and *Lebenskünstler* ("life artist" or *bon vivant*), Sachs emigrated to Boston in 1932. His memoir of 1944 first revealed the secret of the group of seven rings.

Max Eitingon, 38, emigrated to Leipzig from Russia as a young man, met Freud while studying in Zurich, and settled in Berlin with Abraham. The only wealthy man among the psychoanalysts in those days, he financially supported a number of projects. A shy man who stuttered, Eitingon was less well known than the others. Freud viewed him as a devoted son, calling him Max at the younger man's request. Eitingon advocated mandatory training analysis. He headed the International Training Commission from 1925 to 1943 and the IPA from 1925 to 1932, and organized the Palestinian Psychoanalytic Society after emigrating to Jerusalem.

Sandor Ferenczi (born Fraenkel), 46, was the most beloved of the group. A warm and romantic soul, he called himself a wise baby, and to some he was an *enfant terrible*. His father migrated from Krakow to Hungary, where he ran a large bookstore which indulged Sandor's reading passion. Musical and poetic, Ferenczi studied medicine in Vienna, becoming very close to Freud, who analyzed him. He in turn analyzed Jones, Michael Balint, and Clara Thompson. Though a psychiatrist, he supported lay analysis and opposed medical domination of the profession. His important correspondence with Freud (over 2,000 letters) has yet to be published.

VERLAG AND OTHER MATTERS

On November 19, Rank left Vienna to work out plans for the next IPA Congress. He traveled with Oskar Pfister and British physician David Forsyth. They went to Holland first and then to England. (Funds for the trip came from Toni von Freund.) The Hague was selected over Berlin as the next Congress site, since Holland had been neutral during the war and would attract the most participants from all sides. After six weeks away from Tola and Helene, Otto returned on New Year's Eve, laden with provisions one could not obtain in postwar Austria.

Helene was less than six months old when her father's extensive trip took place. Tola did not lack for company and spent much time with the Deutsches and Anna Freud. Back in Vienna, Otto had a very busy but not consistent schedule. He had begun his psychoanalytic practice with two or three patients—referrals from the Professor (they never spoke of Freud by name). Rank spent every Wednesday evening with Freud from dinner on; the Vienna Psychoanalytic Society met on alternate weeks.

January 1920 brought double tragedy. Anton von Freund succumbed to cancer at age 39. (Rank and Freud wrote an obituary.) Then, totally unexpectedly, Sophie Freud Halberstadt, 26, fell ill and died of influenza, leaving her husband and two small children. She was the second youngest of the six Freud children.

Martha and Sigmund did not make the long trip to Hamburg
for her funeral. Freud stoically controlled his grief: "As a confirmed unbeliever I have no one to accuse. . . . Deep down I
sense a bitter, irreparable narcissistic injury. My wife and Annerl
[Anna] are profoundly affected in a more human way." Although
she lived in Vienna, Freud's aged mother received the sad news
from him by letter: "I hope you will take it calmly; tragedy
after all has to be accepted. But to mourn this splendid, vital
girl who was so happy with her husband and children is of course
permissible."[7]

Letters between Jones and Hiller, both in London, and Rank
bear witness to the pressures of the time. Jones wrote in English;
Rank wrote in German to him, in amusingly faulty English to
Eric Hiller.

> *26 July 1920*
>
> *Dear Hiller!*
>   *Today I had the visit from Mr. H——who came with your*
> *introducing letter and the strict wish to be analysed only by*
> *Dr. Rank. I told him that in this circumstances—although I*
> *make analyses, what is true—I take it to be my duty to send*
> *him to Federn to whom he has been advised by Dr. Jones (it*
> *is not right English I feel!). He is going today to Federn but*
> *decided before that he will not be analysed by him. As I know*
> *that Federn is going in the next days on the country—and*
> *Hitschmann also—I will take him for analysis when he comes*
> *back from Federn to me and I have written today in the same*
> *sense to Dr. Jones. He seems to be a quite sympathic fellow*
> *and I will help him as I can, also to get a flat, etc.*
>
> *Rank*

Since Rank and Jones had spent much time together and
used the *Du* (intimate) form of address between them, it is surprising that they had not discussed Rank's clinical work. Jones
had told the patient that Rank did not conduct analyses. Rank
clarified the matter, telling Jones that he was analyzing patients
sent by Freud, including difficult cases. H——was ideal, since
he knew some German and was an artist. If the man paid two
pounds weekly, that would bring in twice what Rank was earning
on an hourly basis at the Verlag. He asked Jones to refer cases
to him, since he needed the work to live.[8]

The year was difficult. Rank had been ill for a time in the

spring. He felt the frustration of having to set aside his scientific work. The English patient turned out to be a real challenge. In July he wrote, "I am so tired."[9] Helene, who "grows very quick," celebrated her first birthday on August 23.

The Sixth Congress of the IPA, which met at the Hague in September, lasted four days. For the first time since the war, professionals came together from opposing sides in a demonstration of international amity. The psychoanalytic movement, which always had difficulty keeping peace within its own house, made a signal demonstration of scientific cooperation transcending national hostilities. There were sixty-two members, including newcomers Georg Groddeck and Melanie Klein, and fifty-seven guests. The latter included Anna Freud and Beata Rank, who traveled with the Professor and Otto. Freud was in good spirits and said of Frau Rank, "She is like a daughter, not just a student."[10]

But soon Freud's spirits plummeted again. When Oskar Pfister wrote to congratulate him on the progress of psychoanalysis, Freud replied that although he was happy many had joined, his own pleasure had been greatest when he was alone. "The way in which people accept and digest it has brought me no other opinion of them than their previous behavior when they uncomprehendingly rejected it."[11] Freud wanted a movement, and he got his wish. But fulfilled wishes do not always bring happiness, as Freud himself remarked more than once. For example, during the war he had all the leisure he ever wished for and could do little with it. The "more human" grief that Martha and Anna showed for Sophie was probably more alive in him than he could admit.

The directors of the publishing house (Verlag) now included Freud, Ferenczi, Rank, Jones, and Eitingon, a sub-Committee. "What is certain," Jones recalled, "is that the Verlag could not have come into existence at all, or survived for a day, without the truly astounding capacity and energy, both editorial and managerial, with which Rank threw himself into the task. It was four years before he ever got away from Vienna on any sort of holiday, taking with him even then a mass of material to deal with." Shortages were plentiful in Vienna; paper and printer's type had to be scrounged. Labor disputes and poor communications facilities added to the chaos. Rank bought his own string, wrapped book parcels, and carried them to the post office. "Rank struggled heroically with the endless problems," wrote Jones, "and accomplished super-human feats in coping with them almost single-handed."[12]

The publishing picture was grim. Many excellent articles had been published in German, but there were few good translators. Jones, in establishing relationships with people in the United States, invited and accepted papers in English that Freud and Rank would have rejected. "Professor told me yesterday," Rank wrote, "that in his opinion the Journal should stress more the translation of good German papers than the publication of bad American ones." Economic conditions were such that new books were listed by publishers without prices, because it was impossible to gauge inflation week to week, let alone months ahead. Rank yearned to get away from what he called a disgusting situation, but he carried on with barracks humor: "I reminded the printer by telegram and threatened that England would seize his shop unless he delivered the work on time!"[13]

The *Rundbriefe*—circular letters sent by members of the Ring—began after the Hague Congress. They were filled with editorial, organizational, and business concerns. Each sender mailed out three identical letters simultaneously; personal correspondence could be added to the appropriate envelope. Rank held a special position, since he usually wrote on behalf of the Professor and himself; Freud cosigned his letters. Steps were advised to keep the Ring secret from Theodor Reik, then Rank's assistant. Rank recommended the familiar *Du* form of address, which was already in effect between Rank and Ferenczi, Jones, and Sachs.[14] The custom of using surnames continued a while longer.

At the end of the year, Hiller came from London to help Rank with English-language matters. Meanwhile the hardships of the postwar chaos plus one big mistake—the only financial misjudgment Rank ever made, in Jones's opinion—began to weigh heavily on the new enterprise. It seems that the von Freund fund could have been put into Czech or Austrian currency. The latter was chosen with the reasonable expectation that it would be more stable than that of a new and untried nation, Czechoslovakia. But the reverse proved true. Then Rank ran afoul of Pfister, who wanted to hold the Verlag to a currency stipulation. Freud came to Rank's defense, urging the Swiss to consider the quintupling of expenses and not to "exploit the dreadful weakness of our currency."[15] Pfister and Rank made up nicely, only to face another issue, this time a question of editorial judgment.

The publication of the controversial novel *Der Seelensucher* (*The Soul Seeker*) by Georg Groddeck, M.D. (1866–1934), who ran a sanitarium in Baden-Baden, provoked the Swiss Society to question the editorial judgment of the Verlag. Rank and Freud cosigned a ten-page typed letter defending the book, which Freud put on a par with Rabelais. At the Hague Congress, Groddeck had called himself a "wild analyst," to the dismay of many in the audience; that label stuck. His vital personality appealed to Freud and the more liberal members of the Ring group, Rank and Ferenczi.

From the "wild analyst" Freud took the concept of the "It" (*Das Es*), which Groddeck had borrowed from Nietzsche. In English the word seemed too mystical and was translated to the Latin "id." Freud's notion of the ego as passive and dominated by the unconscious seemed to fit Groddeck's doctrine, that we are lived by the "It" and must learn to yield ourselves to that force. (Groddeck later said that Freud took over the term but not his meaning.) In the period 1920–23 Freud revised his topographic theory (consisting of unconscious, preconscious, and conscious), introducing id and super-ego as the forces with which the ego contends, but which it also draws upon. Whereas neurosis had earlier been attributed to conflict between sexual and ego (self-preserving) instincts, the new theory held that the defenses operate not against the unconscious per se, but against an instinctual id, the reservoir of libido. In the redesigned topography, the ego derives its energy, mostly desexualized and sublimated, from the id. But Freud introduced a new dualism in *Beyond the Pleasure Principle* (1920): a life instinct versus a death instinct. The latter, a regressive, destructive force, leads back to primordial simplicity, an inorganic wasteland. The life instinct, a binding and unifying force that fosters complexity, brings the formerly demonic sexual instinct into a constructive role.

The plasticity of Freud's thought was remarkable. He adopted changes—in his own good time—that profoundly altered his basic theory. Unmovable in the face of certain opposing ideas, he could then leap ahead, abandoning his old position, when ready. His "predictable unpredictability" played havoc with the

Committee as Rank and Ferenczi began to develop new ideas. For example, their appreciation of Groddeck was shared by Freud but not by Jones.

Groddeck, like Stekel, had a flair for exploring the unconscious, but handled it with more grace and dignity. In 1917, during the war, Freud first embraced Groddeck as a talented psychoanalyst, warning him not to get involved in priority struggles "because experience has shown that a man with unbridled ambition is bound at some time to break away and, to the loss of science and his own development, become a crank." In an effusion reminiscent of his early letters to Jung, Freud wrote, "I must lay claim to you, must insist that you are an analyst of the first order" and "I do not think I could easily get along without you." When other publishers would not accept *The Soul Seeker,* Freud and Rank took it: "We will ask you to allow us this heretical work for publication because I myself am a heretic who has not yet turned into a fanatic."[16]

Some of Groddeck's ideas are recognizable in the work of Rank, and vice versa. Lawrence Durrell paraphrased him vividly:

> The It is ambivalent, making mysterious but deep-meaning play with will and counter-will, with wish and counter-wish, driving the sick man into a dual relation with his doctor so that he loves him as his best friend and helper, yet sees in him a menace to that artistic effort, his illness.
>
> The illness, then, bears the same relation to the patient as does his handwriting, his ability to write poetry, his ability to make money; creation, whether in a poem or a cancer, was still creation, for Groddeck . . . The cure is always a result of having influenced the It, of having taught it a less painful mode of self-expression. The doctor's role is that of a catalyst, and more often than not his successful intervention is an accident.[17]

Groddeck wrote of every man's envy of mothers. "His big belly expresses his wish for a child; or man wants a brain-child like Pallas Athene, who was born from the head of her father, Zeus. . . . Man can never cease longing to return to the womb of his mother. . . . Every sick man is a child. Everyone who cares for a sick child becomes a mother." According to Martin Grotjahn, Groddeck taught people "how to endure creative anxiety."[18] Ferenczi regularly enjoyed and talked about analytic holidays that he and some of his patients spent with the effervescent Groddeck, who was also sought out by Karen Horney and Frieda Fromm-Reichmann.

"ACTIVE" THERAPY AND NEW TENSIONS IN THE RING

Ferenczi had presented a paper at the Hague on his method of "active therapy," and he and Rank shared an interest in the development of therapeutic technique which was no secret from Freud. In 1921, Rank began to separate theory from therapy: "I allowed the patient a much more active part not only in the analytic situation but also in life, by putting the whole emphasis of the process on an emotional, instead of an intellectual experience." Active therapy meant that the analyst made suggestions, emphasized the time limit, and otherwise used reality factors to increase tension therapeutically while also giving support.[19]

The new interest in the technique of analysis reflected two separate elements. The first was the need to establish psychoanalysis as a therapeutic technique designed to help patients, and not only as theoretically important in understanding everything from myth to social movements. The second was the need to document what happened between analyst and patient in the analytic session. Not since 1912 had Freud expressed himself on technique, and at that time he urged a surgically sterile approach to the patient's emotional life. Considering his own close call, Jung's affair with Sabina Spielrein, and similar allegations against other analysts—especially Jones—Freud had cause for concern. Could a therapist maintain professional decorum in the presence of emotional nakedness and sexual attraction? Did not Freud himself call psychoanalysis a "love" treatment, in which positive transference is necessary for the work? Given the fact that Freud himself did not act toward most patients with the aloofness he wrote about, it is not surprising that Ferenczi and Rank began exploring the analyst's role as an active participant, one who directs and limits as well as listens and interprets.

Although only two Americans attended the Hague Congress, several had been to Vienna for analysis beginning in 1919, and by 1921 Freud was swamped with success. He could not handle all the people who wanted to be analyzed by him. Thus in March he agreed to accept a woman doctor referred by Pfister, if she could pay the current fee of forty francs an hour and remain for four to six months; in those days that was sufficient. In October he was sure he could take her, but in November he wrote, "Fraulein E. is not with me, but with Rank, who praises her highly. I could not take her, as British and American doctors have been taking up all my time. So I now work for dollars and cannot manage anything else."[20]

Putnam had died, but other respected physicians supported psychoanalysis in the United States, including Drs. Smith Ely Jelliffe and William Alanson White. They edited the *Psychoanalytic Review* and put out a series of monographs, which included translations of Rank's *Myth of the Birth of the Hero* and the Rank and Sachs monograph *Significance of Psychoanalysis for the Social Sciences and Humanities*. The *Review* published English-language abstracts of papers from *Imago* and the *Zeitschrift*, so Rank's name was well known in the United States, along with those of Freud, Jung, Ferenczi, and Jones.

The New York psychiatrists who came to Vienna in 1921 were Monroe Meyer, H. W. Frink, Leonard Blumgart, Albert Polon, Abram Kardiner, and Clarence Oberndorf. When the six arrived in September, each had an introductory interview with Freud. Near the end Freud apologized for a miscalculation: He had time for only five of the six (plus four other patients, making nine analytic hours every day except Sunday). Each man was asked if he would mind being analyzed instead by Dr. Otto Rank, with the inducement that it would cost half as much. All six refused, and they spent an anxious night before convening with Freud the next afternoon at 3:00. Would he draw lots? Send someone away? Elated, Freud revealed a discovery made by Anna, a "mathematical genius": Just as five times six is thirty, so also six times five is thirty. If each of the gentlemen would give up one hour per week, all six could be analyzed by Freud. They did, and the five-hour week was born.[21]

Freud felt his time and effort were best directed toward working with those who would influence the English-speaking world. There was no American in the Ring group, but a number of current and future leaders of psychoanalysis in the United States came to Vienna. Two of the most important Americans kept their distance from Freud. Dr. White was a fiercely independent hospital superintendent who said, "The time has come to free

American psychiatry from the domination of the Pope at Vienna."[22] The Swiss-American professor Adolf Meyer also kept aloof from psychoanalysis.

The Vienna Psychoanalytic Society continued to meet on alternate Wednesday evenings, when the foreigners met with the Viennese pioneers, including Rank, who had become Vice-Chairman. Freud and Rank, both extremely busy, set aside time for each other. Rank dined weekly with the Professor; they exchanged ideas, worked on plans, and wrote *Rundbriefe*. Freud's *Group [Mass] Psychology and the Analysis of the Ego* was his only major work of the year. Rank's involvement with the work is evidenced by the gift of the manuscript that Freud made to him.

In early fall the whole Committee met with Freud in Berlin and took a ten-day trip, guided by Abraham. There was a good deal of vigorous walking, and Freud tested their fear of heights. When asked if he himself ever suffered from acrophobia, he said yes, but that he had overcome it through will power. Jones remarked that that was "not a very analytic way of dealing with it." The group drew closer on this occasion, marred only by colds, which afflicted everyone. Freud read two papers to the group, one on telepathy, which brought mixed reactions and was not published during his lifetime. Ferenczi heartily approved it, Jones disliked it, and the others fell somewhere in between.[23] Jones also disliked lay (nonmedical) analysis.

Needless to say, Rank was the prime lay analyst. In the circular letters Jones accused Rank of beating a dead horse on the subject of lay analysis after Jones had assented to Freud's liberal view. Rank did not trust Jones's gesture. The *Rundbriefe* show that differences appeared consistently between liberal and conservative Ring members, starting with the issue of Groddeck's ribald book, and then on whether telepathy was a fit subject for discussion at psychoanalytic meetings. Ferenczi and Rank generally lined up to Freud's left, Abraham and Jones on the right.[24]

Homosexuality proved divisive for the Committee—a significant issue which Jones omitted in his Freud biography. Rank stood with Freud against the others in saying that homosexuals could be members of psychoanalytic societies. "To the world," Jones warned, "homosexuality is an abhorrent crime the committal of which by one of our members would discredit us seriously."

Even Ferenczi said, "These people are too abnormal." Rank and Freud disagreed: "In effect we cannot exclude such persons without other sufficient reasons, just as we cannot agree with prosecuting them legally." The decision should be based on the general qualifications of the individual, Freud and Rank argued.[25] It was a dissenting position at the time, and many psychoanalysts still do not accept it.

Freud was considerably more flexible than many of his "orthodox" followers and broke his own rules sometimes, as in changing to the five-hour week. When Oberndorf brought a supply of Havana cigars to 19 Berggasse, Freud willingly made an exception to his long-standing rule against accepting gifts from patients. And there was a blurring of lines between what we now call training and personal analysis. Freud, who was not always scrupulously discreet, shared some impressions of the American analysands with Rank, who commented thereupon to the Committee in utmost confidence: "They are all very modestly accomplished analytically, and as personalities do not stand above the average. The Professor expects something soonest from Blumgart, while he remains disappointed with Oberndorf, who lacks a pleasing personality besides."[26]

Oberndorf, later four times Secretary and twice President of the American Psychoanalytic Association, was acutely aware of the competition among the Americans in Vienna at the time. These men also compared notes: Freud was more active with some analysands than others. For example, he might advise sexual abstinence to increase anxiety. One man with a fear of the dead was told to go to a cemetery at midnight. Freud could be harshly critical of a patient for lack of effort in the analysis or for his behavior outside. Oberndorf once inadvertently aroused Freud's anxiety and displeasure by going out to see what had happened during riots among Vienna's poor. It was a cold day in December, and there was great anger at President Wilson's policies and at Americans in general. "What?" exclaimed Freud, "You went out that night alone?" Freud had no patience for behavior he considered foolhardy or stupid.

One of the Americans, Abram Kardiner, recalled his training in Vienna, which ended the next April, with mixed emotions. According to him, Freud was not interested in the "Jewish boys from New York," whom he kept in analysis only four to seven months; he kept the Britishers two years. "Freud talked to me—

I had a way of engaging him."[27] Except for Blumgart, the others said Freud did not talk much.

To Kardiner Freud expressed hatred of Adler, disrespect for Stekel, and reverence for Rank. Kardiner thought Rank was "phony" but Freud insisted otherwise, predicting, "You'll see!" To Kardiner Rank had a disorganized mind and looked like a monkey, but Freud lauded his careful, accurate, and brilliant thinking and his elegant analytic work. This high praise impressed Kardiner because Freud gave it so rarely. Rank got most of Freud's patient overflow: Freud had economic power, Kardiner noted (explaining the return to Freud of Wittels and Sadger from Adler's group). A younger analyst, Paul Schilder, once defended his being unanalyzed by pointing to Rank as another example who turned out well.

In Vienna, rife inflation had brought the value of 9,000 Kronen down to merely three dollars. Kardiner recalled that a meal was 75 cents, an orchestra seat 16 cents. Rank, who was envied and hated by the psychoanalytic fraternity in Vienna, not only got the choice of cases referred by Freud but commanded a fee of five dollars an hour, which Kardiner called "a fortune."

The year 1922 began with a visiting lecture series, which included Ferenczi, Abraham, and internist Felix Deutsch, Helene's husband. Vienna was full of eager listeners. The Verlag had bought the rights to psychoanalytic books that had been published by Heller, and Rank promptly brought out a second, enlarged edition of *Myth of the Birth of the Hero* (only the first edition has been translated into English). He also published, in *Imago,* a long essay on *Don Juan* and edited a revised collection of his papers on mythology and psychoanalysis.

By March, Rank felt overburdened by the *Rundbriefe*—those from Vienna were usually the longest, as much as eight double-spaced typed pages—and agreed to Jones's suggestion that the frequency of writing be reduced to twice a month. Alone in Budapest, Ferenczi had become so dependent on the letters that he developed "withdrawal symptoms." But he and Rank arranged to get together to do some writing on therapeutic technique before the next IPA Congress, to be held in Berlin.[28]

Planning for the forthcoming Congress consumed time and energy. Jones was to preside. Tensions between Vienna and London began to mount. Rank criticized Jones on the editing of the *Journal*. Freud and Rank rejected "trans-Atlantic rubbish"—inferior American papers—that Jones favored. Vienna was irked when the London Psychoanalytic Society barred laymen from the practice of psychoanalysis. An American suggestion that authors' degrees be printed with their names was rejected by Vienna: The idea was seen as an attempt to boost medical analysts at the expense of the nonmedical.[29]

As early as January, 1922, Freud had remonstrated with Jones for endangering the atmosphere of the Committee. In March Freud pressed Jones about delays in publishing and urged him to streamline the process, which was holding up two of his own books. "Pardon my meddling with your affairs," Freud wrote, "but they are ours and mine too and Rank is too meek to oppose you in these quarters." The reference to Rank brought a "mirthless laugh" from Jones, who was then sure that Freud did not know about Rank's frequently overbearing missives to London. Jones countered, defending himself to Freud with some success, but relations with Rank deteriorated further. Although Jones was President, and Abraham Secretary, of the International Psychoanalytic Association, Rank made and implemented certain decisions about the Congress without consulting the officers. Abraham vented his spleen about it in July.

Freud and Rank were away from Vienna at separate vacation spots, and a letter remarkable for its warmth and support came from the Professor to Rank.

> *Bad Gastein, 8 July 22*
>
> Dear Doctor,
>
> It is a pity that I should pull the rope (not such a long one at that) which ties you to your profession when you have scarcely begun your holiday. I must thank you for all you sent, for the official and private letter. At the same time I feel I must ask your forgiveness for the small unpleasantnesses of Abraham and Jones, since they are in truth reactions that belong upon me and are displaced to you. In themselves they seem to me quite unjustified; I have in memory everything that you have written, and after something like 15 years collaboration I can bear witness for you that you are not among those who have to vent their moods towards their friends.
>
> I am doing just that which you regarded as impossible, writing one article after the other, since to write them simulta-

*neously isn't possible. The first two, "Interpretation of Dreams"
and "Neurotic Mechanisms," are already assembled, the first
already half written. I have only one fear, that the holiday
time will not suffice for all the plans. The time goes so fast,
one week is already over. It is a pity for every day gone, the
days are so preciously quiet, free and gay. Add thereto the heavenly air, the water, the Dutch cigars and the good eating, all
as like an idyll as one can possibly have in middle-European
hell.*

*When this letter is ended, I go to the square for a large
envelope in which I can enclose a consignment intended only
for you, including the short postscript to "Little Hans" that
you need. Then, I interrupt my productive work in order to
write the supplement to Lowtzky's paper and to read your
manuscript. The latter will, I hope, lift from me an old burden.
I am never quite sure whether, at the crucial time, I did right
in keeping you from the study of medicine. I believe, on the
whole, I was right; when I reflect upon my own tedium during
my medical studies I become more certain, but when I see you
move fully and rightly into the saddle of the analyst, then
the necessity to justify my own action drops away. . . .*

*Give my warm regards to the entire colony, especially to
your wife and daughter. And you, enjoy the agreed-upon vacation and freedom from work.*

> *Cordially your*
> *Freud*

In a subsequent letter (20 July) Freud said that Abraham
was superior to Jones, whose irritability wasn't of consequence.
Again Freud expressed his sense of injustice on Rank's behalf
and suggested that Ferenczi could help: "His obvious lovableness
intends him for the role of mediator. Also, he has the most influence with Jones because of the analysis." (Ferenczi had analyzed
Jones.)

The manuscript Freud was to read came from the monograph
Rank was writing with Ferenczi on therapy; hence Freud's reference to medical school and Rank's work as an analyst. Freud
considered the paper to be a valuable piece of work, but too
complex to be easily absorbed as a Congress lecture. "I therefore
suggest that you rewrite the paper with much more breadth
and didactic ease and that you throw an easier fragment to the
Congress. I do not need to say that such a work written by

anyone else I would simply have judged to be very good and valuable."[30]

Ferenczi stayed with Rank in Seefeld, a beautiful mountain resort near Innsbruck, where both Sachs and Abraham paid them a visit. All used the *Du* form of address then except Freud. He used the intimate form only with family and a few friends from childhood.

Freud had given Rank a note to insert in the *Rundbrief* duly mailed in August: "I found the friendly attack against Rank very amusing." Then Freud challenged Abraham, the attacker. Freud did not sense any insurmountable threat to the Committee, and Rank was riding high. The Ring members could be angry with one another but not with the Professor. Freud understood this, and he tried to point out the displacement of hostility from himself to Rank. Hence Freud's levity: What was amusing was the displacement, and he, as premier analyst, could still teach the younger men something about themselves. But Abraham and Jones did not like having their policy judgments reduced to an issue of transference, even by Sigmund Freud himself. He insisted that he had read all the letters written by Rank, something which Jones and Abraham openly doubted. Jones felt Rank was lobbying against him with Freud, lying to get his way. But Freud studied all the *Rundbriefe*, replying in detail with full knowledge of all the charges and counter-charges.

Freud's private letters to Rank in the summer show that the relationship of the two men was at its peak. Unfortunately we do not have Rank's replies. Writing to each other was unusual for them, and it afforded Freud an occasion to express things that probably had been felt but not said before.

Pension Moritz, Salzburg, Berchtesgaden 4 Aug. 22

Dear Doctor,

> I am writing you from a charming work room with a view of apple trees, green meadows, and dark spruces, out of a precious quietness. Eitingon, who was here last year, bound the innkeeper to make it specially pleasant for us here, and it seems to have been successful. Since you inquire about my health, I shall first thank you for describing it to the others, in the circular letter, as satisfactory, and then confess to you alone that it is not so. The appearance of stomach trouble in Gastein (incidentally, recurrent every year) made it necessary for me to combine

the bathing cure with the Karlsbad drinking cure, and under the combined action of their healing powers a strange bodily tiredness set in. The stomach disturbance (attributed by the wise to the radioactive drinking water of Gastein) seemed almost to vanish upon leaving the place but yesterday appeared again and leaves me not exactly happy.

All conjectures, pessimistic as well as optimistic, appear still to be in free play. In practice we shall follow the latter. It will not have escaped you that for some time now I have not felt sure of my health. I speak of it to no one else because one gets to hear nothing but the usual insincerities. You are still the youngest and freshest among us, while one knows that age so near 70 is quite a serious matter.

I dislike occupying your imagination with such acknowledgments, which begin to sound hypochondriacal, and, on that account, I add that I am clear in spirit and eager for work. Just now I am working on a paper that I call "The Ego and the Id." It stands under Groddeck's patronage and will become either an article or a small pamphlet like the "Beyond [the Pleasure Principle]," of which it is really a continuation. It has progressed quite far as a rough draft, awaiting ideas and moods without which it cannot be finished.

In the interest of rest and in order to be at liberty to work, I have foregone several possibilities of earning money, possibilities which impressed me and should impress you, too. In Gastein I refused the wife of a copper king, who most certainly would have covered the expenses of my stay here. Here at Salzburg another American woman wrestled for treatment who would surely have paid $50 a day since she was accustomed to paying Brill in New York $20 for half an hour. (By the way, a new proof of Brill's decline under the control of the American dollar.) But she will get nothing, I do not sell my time here. I am thinking of bestowing her on Frink, who, with his future wife, a very fine woman, visited me in Gastein for six days and will come to Berchtesgaden, also not without thoughts of analysis back of it, for as yet by no means is he completely well. But neither will I allow him to come up to the mountain.

I sent by registered mail from Gastein the manuscript intended for your lecture. I am very glad to hear that you have now decided upon rewriting on another, more limited subject [Perversion and Neurosis]. I think perhaps you did not fully value the motive of my recently expressed regrets that I had not permitted you to study medicine. I thought under those circumstances I would have no doubt as to whom I would leave the leading role in the psychoanalytic movement. As it now

*stands I can't help but wish that Abraham's clarity and accuracy
could be merged with Ferenczi's endowments and to it be given
Jones's untiring fountain pen. . . .*

The letter indicates that Rank was blocked from the leadership role by his lack of a medical degree, despite Freud's own
support for lay analysis. In closing Freud mentioned Minna, who
"thanks you sincerely and will certainly write you herself."
Minna Bernays, Martha's unmarried sister, lived with the Freuds
and sometimes accompanied Sigmund alone on extended summer absences. He is said to have enjoyed an intellectual compan-
ionship with her that was missing in his marriage. Despite the
common assumption of Freud's probity and marital fidelity,
there is plausible speculation that he had an affair with Minna.

The career of Dr. Frink, Freud's favorite among the Americans, fell short of expectations. He developed a psychosis during
treatment, improved, then fell in love with a woman patient
(who was also seen by Freud for a time). The woman's husband
protested vehemently, then died. Freud, more tolerant than
many Freudians, did not oppose the marriage of therapist and
former patient. But it soon failed; Frink had another breakdown
and spent his last years in a mental hospital. The American establishment took a dim view of Frink's behavior, and the events
did not help Freud's reputation in the United States as diagnosti-
cian, therapist, or judge of character.

In connection with Frink, Beata recalled a remarkable anec-
dote about Freud's attitude toward money and women. In 1922
Freud was with Dr. Frink and his future wife. The woman was
wealthy and went out and bought a piece of jewelry which cost
two thousand dollars. Having seen the piece, Freud said to Tola,
"If a woman has so much money, spends so much for a piece
of jewelry, what do you think she would give for the Verlag?"
Tola wondered where he got that fantasy! She laughed in retro-
spect: "Although I wasn't so wise, I thought to myself: One had
nothing to do with the other!" In any case, Freud's hope for
"millions" for the Verlag from Mrs. Frink came to naught.[31]

AT A BOIL

At Berlin in late September, the Committee met in productive,
harmonious discussions and posed for an idyllic photograph. The

seventh Congress drew 256 participants, about half of them members of the IPA. Eleven Americans were there. The level of scientific expertise was high, and there were many new faces, some to become well known. It was the last Congress attended by Sigmund Freud. He was sufficiently impressed with the work of Rank and Ferenczi, even though they downplayed the castration complex, that he proposed a prize to encourage more papers on the mutual influence of theory and therapy.

Things were bad in Vienna. After the hunger riots, the Relief Commissioner estimated that there were 400,000 homeless derelicts in the city. The capital of the grand dual monarchy had been reduced after the war to a head without a body, a splendid cultural center without a hinterland to help it live. Each piece of the patchwork empire went its own way, so that figuratively, and sometimes literally, communication and transportation broke off at some newly established frontier. Self-determination for the Slavs and other minorities was long overdue, but the timing and manner of its coming hurt Austria terribly.

In the summer of 1922, Freud was thinking not only of moving the Verlag to Berlin, but of leaving Austria himself. For a time it appeared doubtful whether, under such terrible conditions, anyone would come from abroad to study in Vienna. But the crisis passed, and the few who knew that Freud thought of emigrating kept it to themselves.[32]

All too soon after the Congress, the correspondence among the Committee members indicated trouble brewing, prompting Abraham to remark that the Committee was the opposite of a neurotic family: "Those people fight as soon as they are together and are full of love as soon as they are separated."[33] Again in November, Freud had to assert to the Committee that he had read—in fact coauthored—the two previous letters cosigned with Rank. These had aroused Abraham's ire; he and Jones could not believe that Freud knew and approved what Rank wrote. They did not accept Freud's word. In a private letter to Rank, Freud said: "Jones has shown himself to be very incompetent."[34] This reflected Freud's detailed knowledge of the personal and business aspects of the Verlag and the English Press. Freud evoked protests from London and Berlin when he wrote: "I cannot support any tendency whatsoever to produce affects against Rank which are really directed against me. . . . I have no doubt that I am the main participant and that Rank, rather innocent himself, is in the position of a screen which has to catch the negative part of an ambivalent affect." Freud's *Rundbrief* went on for six pages of strenuous, tough diplomacy.

> *For some months I find myself in the painful but inevitable position of having to criticize our friend Jones, to express my dissatisfaction with his actions against different persons, to attack his activities as director of the Press and things of this kind. I do it with my usual candor, without any bitterness and without giving the impression that I had therefore forgotten Jones's value and merits. I wish I were really infallible and that you all would know it: Then it would be easier for you to take a stand and to make decisions. But as this wish certainly cannot be fulfilled, I cannot do anything but present the situation to you frankly. If one or the other of you thinks I am wrong, I count on the tolerance in you which I myself am willing to use towards you. Probably on neither side will anything really bad and unforgivable be discovered. Differences cannot be avoided, not even in a family, but behind them stands the certainty that one cannot get away from one another, and that he does not even want to get away.*

At this point, Freud declared that he would not attend the next Committee meeting: He wanted to let the group thrash things out themselves. Then diplomacy failed him, and he wrote: "Jones should complete the short analysis he had with Ferenczi." That probably undid all the good intentions of paterfamilias Freud. That Jones would prostrate himself before a rival brother would have been unthinkable; that Freud suggested it makes him seem either naive, or intoxicated with his own power and influence. He did have a tendency to express whatever came into his mind. Rank, though not always diplomatic, would surely have considered the idea futile and provocative. Freud's letter ends: "I find no reason to reproach Rank in anything, he who now, as always, has given his best."[35]

The response to Freud was stubborn, if still polite. Abraham (who usually wrote for Eitingon and Sachs) sent a long *Rundbrief,* an open letter to the Professor complaining of Rank's unnecessary harshness and noting that his last two letters were not signed by Freud. Abraham concluded, wrongly, that Freud had not seen those letters and would not support them. Jones, of course, rejected Freud's diagnosis of neurotic displacement of hostility onto an innocent Rank. He suggested that Rank could use some analysis. Even Ferenczi thought Rank had exhibited some lack of diplomacy.

Freud's remarkable reply (15 December), four large pages filled with his dense Gothic script, begins, "Let me saddle up the hippogriff once more before I retreat into my dotage." Freud showed his grasp of the administrative, financial, and public relations issues surrounding the publications business. He blamed much of the failure on Jones's inability to find anyone more suitable than Eric Hiller to work inVienna. (Jones argued that Hiller quitbecause Rank was impossible.) Then Freud struck a blow: "In 15 years of consistently intimate working relationship with Rank the idea scarcely occurred to me, that *he* needed an analysis. And with that let me shut up."

With this rebuke—almost a dare—Freud not only vouched for Rank, but implied there was much more to be said against Jones. Aside from his personal contact with the Englishman, Freud knew a great deal from having analyzed Jones's mistress (Loe Kann) and some of his former patients and colleagues (like Joan Riviere), and from talking with Ferenczi. Freud's *Rundbrief* went on:

> *I can only say the following: if an unlikely incident would for the third time throw additional money into my lap for the support of psychoanalytic literature, I could not decide to risk this money for an independent press in London. Because I do not see there one personality to whom a businesslike enterprise could be entrusted. (Jones declares rightly that he can only be an editor. Riviere—very efficient—is only a translator. Hitschmann is untried, perhaps only interested in legal formalities.) We are spoiled here in Vienna. Rank has not only shown merits as an editor but also developed himself into an efficient businessman—he has sacrificed years for that. We were lucky enough to find a location in most difficult times and to find in Storfer, who will remain with us, an excellent producer well experienced in business. But only the productive person has lasting good luck.* [36]

Rank wrote an independent *Rundbrief,* angry and autocratic, as an appendix to Freud's.

> *This would be much harder for me than you may believe, if the Professor out of his kindness and fair judgment had not interposed his letter, which eases my personal stand and at the same time spares me from the need to express the bitter feelings that force themselves upon me. If I feel nevertheless the need to say a few words for myself concerning the personal side before going over the facts, I do it as an appeal to you to keep in mind how difficult*

*and responsible my position is, as I feel it day after day and hour
after hour. If you can do this, it will certainly deter you from
concentrating on reproaches and raising obstacles about petty
things. For years I have been devoting myself to fighting against
enormous external difficulties in the interest of the psychoanalytic
movement. I may say I have been fighting successfully, albeit often
in despair, realizing the size of the task and my own feeble powers—
and not without paralyzing lassitude and fatigue. I wished in these
moments and in these situations that you might have helped me
with your friendship instead of looking at each of my remarks
through a magnifying glass to tell me that it was my fault when
everything did not go smoothly. I think we should be glad that
so much went well and give each other mutual assistance where
there are difficulties and mistakes. I hardly need say that you will
find in me the old friend and helper as before, if only, I pray,
you will not hold me responsible for all and everything that is
going on inside the psychoanalytic movement. It is not pleasant
to be regarded as the symbol of a thing if one cannot enjoy also
the advantages of the symbol, namely to be the surrogate for the
whole thing instead of being used in this way only from time to
time when it is unpleasant.* [37]

Rank went on in this long letter, which took him a whole
afternoon to write, to clarify the situation with regard to relations—fiscal, legal, and attitudinal—between the English Press
and the German Verlag. He thought it time for the Press to
stand on its own. It was impossible to run a business, he argued,
when everyone who contributed some money or effort felt free
to complain about the paper, or the type, or the content, or
the editors.

> One *will* and one *hand* has to direct everything in an enterprise,
> which may then turn out good or bad, but otherwise it comes to
> nothing. Perhaps you will see in this another indication of my
> autocratic trends, but I cannot help it, that's how it is when you
> have to deal with different people, and the more people there are,
> the more energetically you have to carry out your will (of course,
> not against reason but against the divergent opinions).

Rank's letter ends with new developments. Interest in psychoanalysis in Russia had grown to the point where a Moscow
group asked to affiliate. Rank and Freud favored it, pointing
to the example of the Americans: "I do not think that the Moscow
people represent, humanly or analytically, poorer material than

the New York group did when it was admitted and where we succeeded through their admission in gaining good influence in the long run." Eitingon had made a foray into France, and a group was beginning to meet in Paris. The letter ended "With cordial regards and greetings for Christmas and the New Year, in old friendship for the New Year."

Committee correspondence slowed somewhat in the new year (1923). A serious but also amusing discussion concerned a Chinese version of psychoanalytic texts. Abraham reported that a professor from Peking planned to translate Freud's works, which he knew in both German and English versions, but would have to invent some new ideographs. For example, the Chinese symbols for "heart" and "power" would be combined to translate "the unconscious." Ernest Jones responded enthusiastically: "From what we hear here of the Renaissance of thought in modern China I should judge it a country in which Psa [psychoanalysis] would spread widely and rapidly; the Verlag must be awake to the possibilities, though we can hardly expect Rank to add a Chinese section to his other burdens at present! By the way, does not *Herz-Kraft* ("heart power") correspond rather to Libido than to Unconscious?"[38]

Rank reported, among other things, on the difficulty of setting up analytic practice in Vienna. Sabina Spielrein had gone to Geneva (where she analyzed Jean Piaget) but could no longer make a go of it, and considered relocating to Berlin. (She eventually returned to Russia and disappeared before World War II.) Rank had seen the new *Encyclopedia Britannica,* which reported on events between 1914 and 1923 and included three chapters making extensive reference to psychoanalysis. He noted a spate of new novels in English, German, and French touching on psychoanalytic themes, and hoped to find time to explore the influence of psychoanalysis on literature, so as to test his prophecy in *The Artist.*[39]

Jones reported on a "detailed criticism" of active therapy at the London Society by Edward Glover, a protégé of Karl Abraham. Ferenczi expressed his hurt feelings, to which Jones replied that he meant "critical overview," not adverse criticism: "I do not identify myself with any criticism of active therapy beyond what you yourself have emphasized, e.g., caution for beginners, etc." This is reminiscent of the lip service Jones gave to lay analysis. Later in the year he came to verbal blows with Ferenczi over his failure to credit the Hungarian with priority in a paper on auto-suggestion and hypnosis. Jones's insistence that Ferenczi's discovery was a truism (and therefore not citable) severely strained relations in the Committee.[40]

FREUD'S ILLNESS

On April 20, Freud underwent surgery for a growth affecting the right upper jaw and palate. For two months he had noticed a "tissue rebellion" in his mouth, which he attributed to smoking but assumed was benign. On April 25, Freud informed Jones that he was not yet working and could not swallow.[41] Rank told the group on May 1, in a paragraph sandwiched between other items:

> *The Professor himself unfortunately had to undergo a small operation last week; it was a leukoplakia of the oral mucosa (inside left cheek), caused by heavy smoking, which had to be removed because it annoyed him. The Professor had to interrupt his work a few days, having difficulty eating and speaking, but he finds himself well again and working for a few days.*

Rank omitted the date of surgery, which was ten days earlier, not "last week." He evidently wanted to minimize the whole thing (as did Freud) and waited so he could report a happy ending. But he also put the lesion on the wrong side and in the wrong place (it was on the right palate and jaw, not the left cheek). Very likely he got his information piecemeal; Freud hid the initial surgery even from his family. Felix Deutsch had seen the lesion and judged it malignant, not letting on to Freud. The Ranks and the Deutsches were close; sooner or later the news passed from Felix to Otto.[42]

In June another tragedy struck the Freud family. Heinerle (Heinz) Halberstadt, younger son of Freud's daughter, Sophie, who had died the year before, was spending a few months in Vienna with Freud's eldest, Mathilde, and her husband. A frail boy of four, he was loved by his grandfather, who considered him the most intelligent child he had ever known. After a tonsillectomy, which coincided with Freud's operation, Heinerle succumbed to tuberculosis. While other losses had caused pain,

Freud said this one killed something in him for good; it was the only time anyone saw Freud as an adult in tears. That summer Freud said he was suffering from the first depression of his life. Although he had written that the death of a man's father is the most poignant loss, Freud himself felt the pain of his little grandson's death much more. He had resisted depression amazingly, having lost his father, his half-brother Emanuel, Sophie, and a nephew and niece before this greatest tragedy.[43]

Freud was to be allowed to go on his summer holiday, which would include two weeks in Rome with Anna. Meanwhile, Rank and Ferenczi met in the Tyrol mountains to complete their book on active therapy. They discussed the conflicts within the Ring; according to one report, Rank wanted to get Jones out of the Committee then, but Ferenczi restrained him.[44]

Visiting Freud in Lavarone, Dr. Felix Deutsch examined his mouth and saw a malignant growth: It would require more extensive surgery. Fearing Freud's refusal to consent—even his suicide—and in view of the planned trip to Rome, Deutsch withheld the truth. In late August, Deutsch, Anna, and the Committee considered the alternatives together. Rank already knew about the diagnosis of cancer, which the others now learned. Later, at dinner, Jones recalled, Freud's name was mentioned, "whereupon to our amazement Rank broke out in a fit of uncontrollable hysterical laughter." Later the Committee considered how to persuade Freud to accept another, more serious operation. "Sachs suggested this would be the thought of Anna, and Rank, striking to a deeper level, suggested Freud's old mother." Jones and the other physicians felt they had no right to take the decision out of Freud's hands, but still he was not told the truth. Ironically, in Rome Freud received a newspaper clipping from Chicago which said that he was dying and was transferring his pupils to Otto Rank.[45]

What happened at the meeting of the Committee at San Cristoforo can only be fleshed out now, sixty years later, with the publication of *Ernest Jones: Freud's Alter Ego* by Vincent Brome. There, in a previously unpublished letter from Jones to his wife, we learn that August 26, 1923, was spent "thrashing out the Rank-Jones affair." Although Rank and Ferenczi were angry already, the last straw was an offensive remark by Jones about Rank. In his Freud biography Jones wrote, "It appears that I had made some critical remarks about Rank—I cannot

remember now to whom—and he at once brought up this un-
friendliness on my part." In his earlier book, *Freud and his Early
Circle,* Brome could not pinpoint the "casual remark" which
hit the Committee "like a bombshell." After Jones's death he
found the letter, which clarifies the matter a great deal. "Very
painful," Jones wrote to Katharine about the fight in San Cristoforo, "but I hope our relations will now be better and believe
so, but on the other hand expect Ferenczi will hardly speak to
me, for Brill has just been there and told him I had said Rank
was a swindling Jew (gross exaggeration)."[46]

Whatever Jones actually said, he apologized to Rank for hurting his feelings, claiming, however, that the insult had been
unintentional. Rank would not accept the guarded apology,
which only angered him further so that he called for Jones's
expulsion from the Committee. The letter to Katharine from
Ernest identifies the intermediary (Brill) and reveals the tenor
if not the substance of an offensive remark: It was an ethnic
slur, which, exaggerated, became "swindling Jew." Jones's brashness has been commented on here, but not his anti-Semitism.
The only non-Jew on the Committee, he was sensitive to the
issue, but assumed too easily that integration was achieved because all of them were nonbelievers. His hazy recollection of
Jung's anti-Semitic leanings also suggests insensitivity on Jones's
part. The *Rundbriefe* show that Jones could prey like a wolf,
but when strongly challenged (on lay analysis, or active therapy)
he suddenly claimed innocence and joined the others, lest
Freud's ire be aroused. At San Cristoforo Jones apologized to
Rank only for an "unintentional" hurt. Granted, he did not in-
tend his insult to pass Brill's lips, nor did he want it exaggerated.
That hardly excuses the double affront represented by half an
apology.

Abraham defended Jones, and somehow the group restored
peace, if not harmony; afterwards Freud received them. Writing
a year after the meeting at San Cristoforo, Jones said, "Finding
myself, largely because of Rank's skillful maneuvering, faced
with unanimous opposition and condemnation, I saw how hopeless it would be for me to take a firm stand that would be tantamount to denunciation of Rank; this was the chief, though of
course not the only, reason for my state of inhibition then."[47]
Jones denied fault altogether. But if the Committee—including
Abraham—had unanimously condemned Jones (as he says), the
reason must have been his behavior, not Rank's cleverness.

Freud underwent two operations in the fall, after which he needed a prosthesis for the upper right palate in order to eat and speak. Even so, his speech sounded nasal and thick, akin to that of a cleft palate victim, which he had virtually become. The prosthesis was difficult to remove and replace, which was necessary for occasional cleaning. Freud would not allow anyone to nurse him except Anna, with whom he made a pact: She would show no emotion, handling everything with the objectivity of a surgeon. This she adhered to despite gruesome ordeals over the next sixteen years, which included dozens of minor but agonizing operations.[48]

Jones wrote of "our beloved and revered Chief" in response to news of the first surgery, trying to be optimistic toward the Committee. "Of the difficult days we spent in S. Cristoforo I will here only point to the bright fact that no others than psychoanalysts could have succeeded in such circumstances to the extent we did, one more reason for being grateful to our science." No doubt there had been a great deal of discussion among the members of the Ring over what they would do if Freud became incapacitated or weakened. Freud himself had treated the theme of the brother-horde and their wishes to protect or supplant the father in *Totem and Taboo.*

Although Freud called several of the Ring his sons, only one, Otto Rank, really faced the loss of a surrogate father. Max Schur, later Freud's physician, expressed the now standard interpretation that Rank reacted to Freud's illness with revolt and defection. Freud himself pointed out "the parallel that existed between the sons of the primal horde and some of his own followers who were awaiting the death of the 'primal father.'" The question remains: How did the youngest and freshest Ring member, the charming, devoted, brilliant, and industrious Otto Rank—to use Freud's adjectives—become a defector, a renegade from psychoanalysis?

CHAPTER 8

Active Therapy and
The Trauma of Birth

Indeed it is these ego forces which finally bring about the process of cure, the further transference of the libido from the analyst to "more real objects" in life, or which makes it possible to stand unsatisfied free-floating libido . . . The problem is to get the patient, with the help of the love for the analyst, to give up this love. This would be a contradiction in terms and quite impossible if the intelligence of the patient did not assist . . . It is remarkable with what haste the libido, as it frees itself from the cure, seeks out new interests in life. We see the process of sublimation, which in ordinary life requires years of education, take place before our eyes . . .
—Otto Rank and Sandor Ferenczi, 1923[1]

By far Freud's favorites among the Ring members, Ferenczi and Rank enjoyed the Professor's critical support for their book on active therapy, despite its strong pull toward what we now call ego psychology and existential therapy. The authors, closest of friends, placed a new emphasis on experience in the present to balance interpretation of the past, on therapeutic intervention rather than passivity, on intelligence and love rather than impulse and sex. These factors soon proved to be too radical for the conservative mold into which psychoanalysis rigidified. Ferenczi and Rank not only professed their loyalty—"We therefore believe that we are in no way differing from Freud"[2]—but developed their ideas as an extension of psychoanalytic technique which met his approval over a period of years.

193

After getting his way at the time—quashing active therapy, seeing Rank depart and Ferenczi retreat—Ernest Jones later rewrote the history of the events. Long after his two colleagues were dead, Jones simply lied: "Without discussing it with us, or even informing us about it they wrote and published a book which, to the rest of us, revealed at once the seeds of serious divergent tendencies."[3] That Ferenczi and Rank were collaborating on a book was no secret, as the *Rundbriefe* indicate. That their ideas were divergent from those of Jones and Abraham is certainly true, but Freud had been favorably impressed. That the Committee had a rule about collective approval before publishing seems to have been invented by Jones after the fact. Since Freud knew all about the work of his two favorites, a call for Committee approval would have insulted him. But most telling is the fact that this book, like Rank's *Trauma of Birth*, was discussed in London and Berlin with considerable interest, if not complete approval, before Jones and Abraham mounted their attack on Ferenczi and Rank, which included the false charge of revolutionary conspiracy against Freudian doctrine. For his part, Freud welcomed the divergence, saying to Ferenczi, "That you or Rank should in your independent flights ever leave the ground of psychoanalysis seems to me out of the question."[4]

Jones traced the beginning of Rank's heresy back to 1919, when Otto and Tola, then four months pregnant, traveled to meet him in Switzerland. Jones recalled many years later that Rank "astonished me by remarking in a dismal tone that men were of no importance in life; the essence of life was the relation between mother and child."[5]

Jones's astonishment underscores his devotion to the patriarchal psychoanalytic view of the family. Although the mother-child relationship has long since claimed developmental primacy even in psychoanalysis, in those early days the father-child relationship was seen as holding the key to understanding and therapy. The core complex was Oedipal in origin, and the menacing father blocked the incest wish by evoking an even more powerful castration fear. "Penis envy" was established as a psychoanalytic concept by 1914; Rank expressed to Jones what might be called "womb and breast envy." Be that as it may, Rank seems to have anticipated subsequent psychoanalytic thinking about the human condition. Rank's views of that time are now taken for granted, usually without due credit being given to him.

Obviously Tola's pregnancy moved Rank both emotionally and ideologically. Even in adolescence Otto was a keen observer of parenthood, its difficulties and possibilities. The fact that his psychological theory was influenced by his own experience of family life follows naturally: He always tried to integrate experience and understanding. In 1921 he presented a paper on marriage that again disturbed Ernest Jones.[6] Rank argued there that the relation between married partners inevitably repeated, on each side alternately, that between mother and child. Again, Rank's prescient idea eventually found its way into the accepted wisdom on marital dynamics.

The year 1923 brought a whole constellation of changes: the publication of Rank's *Trauma of Birth*, the development of Freud's cancer, completion of *The Development of Psychoanalysis* by Ferenczi and Rank, and the near breakup of the Committee. Following his second operation, Freud was not inclined to meet with the Vienna Psychoanalytic Society, and Rank led many of the sessions without him. Foreign visitors demanded more and more analytic hours and also required more lectures.

Rank, meanwhile, had proved himself an able secretary, theoretician, clinician, editor, executive, and family man. In the summer, an important paper appeared in English which deserves attention as an example of Rank's achievement, approved by Freud, which also anticipates later developments.

"PERVERSION AND NEUROSIS"

By the early 1920s, psychoanalysis had matured to the point where its pioneers could distinguish between good and bad practice. They winced at some of the would-be analysts who came from abroad, having swallowed but only half-digested Freud's teachings. These well-meaning men (rarely a woman) were treating cases with often poor results, and sometimes wreaking havoc. Freud and his Committee analyzed this second generation, lectured to them, evaluated their personalities and their thinking, and so addressed the problem of training.

How Rank handled psychoanalytic theory on the eve of his independence can best be seen in his presentation at the Berlin Congress. "Perversion and Neurosis" appeared soon after in the *Zeitschrift* and the following summer (1923) in the *International Journal of Psycho-Analysis.* Expanded in print to some 12,000 words, the paper bridges theory with clinical and social psychology. Rank builds on Freudian concepts, but his conception shows an early emphasis on ego psychology and foreshadows some philosophical differences with his mentor. It also shows that Rank had become a stimulating teacher.

At this time, the term "perversion" embraced homosexuality, masochism, sadism, exhibitionism, fetishism, kleptomania, and some forms of masturbation. These very terms were subject to sloppy use, Rank claimed. Although pre-Freudian descriptive psychiatry was static and therapeutically helpless, many Freudians, according to Rank, exaggerated the role of the dynamic unconscious by ignoring manifest behavior. For example, a pathologically prudish woman would be called an exhibitionist because of her presumed underlying reaction formation. A man could be labeled homosexual because in analysis he revealed a passive-feminine attitude toward the father. Rank urged that the terms associated with perversion be used "to designate only what they formerly meant, namely, the manifest expression of the perversions in question."

Rank opposed the Freudian tendency to view appearances only as masks, and the unseen as a deeper and truer reality. Relationship, the heart of Rankian therapy, was the guiding principle in Rank's approach to terminology. He saw the exaggerated use of Freudian psychodynamics as dehumanizing. To relate in human terms is to respond to what another says and does, to take seriously what is manifest. To second-guess, assuming that one "knows better," reduces the other person if not to a specimen, then at least to a subordinate partner. In diagnosis, as later in his therapy, Rank insisted on the validity of what was conscious, without denying the unconscious. He maintained his humility in the role of therapist, recognizing that psychoanalysis did not make its practitioners omniscient. Analysts never lose their subjectivity, he argued, and their science is weakened when they pretend otherwise.

In his paper, Rank summarized the Freudian view of neurosis as lying on a scale between normality and perversion. Like perversion, neurosis represents an infantile fixation—an attachment to an early stage of development. But neurosis, unlike perversion, includes some dominant inhibition. One could ask if psychoanalysis might only release the inhibition, resulting, say, in overt homosexuality? Rank acknowledged this possibility, but stated that ideally, analysis should uncover the causative fixation behind both the neurosis and the perversion, thus curing the patient.

Moving adroitly between the teachings of biology and sociology, Rank addressed the paradoxical situation of the child. Appearing on earth as a byproduct of the sexual union, the child is molded by social forces that reflect a certain hypocrisy. Rank says children are normally perverse; the healthy child fixates only in transit to the next developmental stage. But what is the final stage or goal of libidinal gratification? According to society, Rank says, it is having children. Parents transmit this acceptable goal of human sexuality to their children, who then view the capacity to reproduce as the crucial difference between themselves and adults. Rank goes on to say:

> Soon after it has become freed through the act of birth from the microcosmic biologic system of things and has learned to direct its instincts towards self-maintenance, the child is again immediately forced into the larger biologic system of things—in that it prematurely, by the mechanism of identification, adopts into its immature sexual system the adult's sexual goal, which, however, also serves the process of self-development. To get a child from the father like the mother, to identify itself with the mother, so as to participate in the much desired exclusive love of the father, is actually the sexual goal of children of both sexes, though often only shyly admitted and always soon deeply repressed. . . .
>
> This "dangerous age" in children can perhaps be most simply characterized by describing it biologically as the point of contact between individual and generative tendencies, and psychologically as the first conscription of libido into the service of the idea of propagation. Propagation itself is certainly a biologic fact; strictly viewed it is actually biology itself. This, however, should not prevent us from recognizing that in the exaggerated emphasis which our culture lays upon it it is actually *the scientific formulation of an infantile theory of sex.* For the adult neither the child nor propagation is usually the conscious sexual aim, but rather the sexual act proper which consists in the union of the two sexes, and itself in turn serves only a deeper narcissistic libido satisfaction.[7]

The essay shows Rank's vital interest in contemporary biology and sociology; he has broadened his scope from art and philosophy, so that no area concerning human life now remains outside his grasp. He pioneered in what later was called "systems analysis." Now he points to a conflict between personal and societal goals with respect to sex; later he follows it into the realm of individual will versus subordination to community life.

Most importantly, this paper has a thrust independent of Freud's thinking, although Rank intended only a complementary extension, as in his work with Ferenczi on active therapy. Freud's approval reflects his capacity to tolerate difference in one he liked and trusted. But, as we will see, he was unable to withstand what he felt was disloyalty to himself and to the cause of psychoanalysis.

In the paper, Rank goes on to show that the child's wish for a baby is the naive and permissible substitute for the unacknowledged sex act. The birth of a baby at once gratifies and burdens its parents. This "conflict between individuation and generation" is a theme prominent in Rank's later work. The wish for a baby is intensified by the fact that the goal cannot be attained, which blocks the child's identification with the parents and "forces him instead towards development of the ego in the period up to maturity." Ego development is undermined, often to the point of neurosis, by clinging (fixation) to the repressed wish for a child. Rank speculates here that the displacement of the wish for a child is the source of a characteristic of *homo sapiens*—namely, a libido that cannot be fully satisfied. (Later, Rank would attribute this dilemma of dissatisfaction to the awareness of death and the striving for immortality.) Although Rank discusses the Oedipus complex, his focus on the wish for a child (not intercourse with the opposite-sex parent) strikes a new note. "As in all infantile sexual theories," he said, "there is also in this one (according to which libido is merely a means of getting children) a kernel of truth, which however is only too readily put forward by the adult as the whole exclusive truth, contrary to biologic and still more to psychologic evidence."

The normal individual substitutes the ego ideal of manhood or womanhood for the infantile wish for a child. The "pervert" eliminates that wish, avoiding the sex act while gratifying component instincts. The neurotic clings to the wish unconsciously but inhibits the masturbatory gratification that is open to the pervert and the child. Rank sums up masturbation (so much discussed in the Vienna Psychoanalytic Society) as "the representative of the whole infantile libido. . . . a narcissistic satisfaction, for the child himself plays the part of two objects libidinally."

In a passage which links early Freud to modern ego psychology, Rank wrote:

> One may say that in the successive outbreaks of periods of masturbation, often well into the years of puberty, the conflict kindled in early childhood between auto-eroticism and object-libido, between the ego instincts and the sexual instincts, between individuation and generation is continually breaking forth anew and more violently. (The obstinate denial of the reproductive libido which undoubtedly lies behind masturbation has found justifiable expression in the apparently misleading designation of this kind of libido satisfaction as onanism, since the biblical Onan represents a man who neglects the human obligation to propagate.) In masturbation itself there lies besides regression to an infantile auto-eroticism an important psychobiologic advance in the direction of permitting or affirming sensuality, which in consideration of the special tendency of neurotics to repress the sensual bodily components we may designate as "healthy."[8]

Bringing the sin of Onan into perspective, and affirming a positive element in masturbation, Rank goes on to pinpoint "that factor which determines the final fate of onanism and with it that of the whole infantile libido. It is the *sense of guilt,* which, of uncertain origin, proceeding out of the deepest and most tangled roots of the ego and the sexual instincts," moderates claims of the ego by pressing toward reproduction, and at the same time rejects displacements of the reproductive tendency that might impair ego development. Rank is not speaking of Oedipal guilt or castration fear. The guilt is profound, of mixed and uncertain origin; in psychoanalytic parlance it is pre-Oedipal. We might call it innate or existential.

> Normally this sense of guilt, which might be subdivided as biologic or sociologic, according to circumstances, is elaborated into ethical, social, and probably also aesthetic inhibitions, or alternatively, standards of value, thus making it possible for so many egos to live together and also for sublimation to arise. In the neuroses, however, we have before our eyes the unsuccessful cases, the "flaws," which are characterized perhaps by a surplus of instinctual desire and certainly by a great deal too much free-floating sense of guilt. One may safely say that the nature and degree of the sense of guilt determine the nature and degree of mental health or sickness; in the latter case, they also determine the nature and degree to which the patient is open to influence, that is, his chances of being cured.[9]

The chief element provided by psychoanalysis for therapy, Rank finds, is alleviation of guilt, or "freedom from too much of that sense of guilt under the normal pressure of which we all in modern cultural society live." This requires an "analysis of the structure of the ego out of which the sense of guilt seems ultimately to spring." Guilt operates against the useless or perverse instinct components, but in neurotics the protection is so strong that it prevents development and inflicts punishment via symptoms. The pervert lacks this inhibition, but even in those cases deep analysis will ultimately uncover guilt. Guilt impinges on the pervert from outside in the form of social condemnation.

In closing, Rank makes an almost poetic summary of the perversions, exhibited as a narcissistic arrest in development in those who

> convert into reality the infantile theory of conception and birth to which neurotics cling in their unconscious, but with the decisive modification that they do *not get* children but rather wish *to be* children, or more accurately, *are* children themselves. The homosexual shows his childishness by ignoring the difference of sex; the masochist by letting himself be beaten like a child; the exhibitionist by exposing himself with pleasurable infantile shamelessness . . .
>
> Now, the homosexual protests against the *object*, by turning it into its opposite; the exhibitionist against the sexual *organ*, by denying the differentiation; the masochist against the *act*, by degrading it to punishment; the sadist protests against the *libido* itself, by expressing it in the form of hatred and cruelty.[10]

This paper, long since ignored, stimulated considerable discussion in the 1920s, and it marked the beginning of Rank's gradual but steady move away from the instinct-dominated, ego-minimizing Freudian psychology. While here he speaks of the neurotic's "surplus of instinctual desire" and free-floating guilt, later Rank developed the notion that the neurotic suffers because of a strong but inhibited will. Rank's interest in creation and birth appeared in his first writings on the artist and the hero. As the father of a three-year-old, he examined the impact of societal myths about procreation on children's mental development. Rank saw much more in his daughter's development than could be explained by the Freudian version of Oedipus.

THE TRAUMA OF BIRTH

In August 1923, Helene celebrated her fourth birthday. In Freudian terms she was in the midst of the Oedipal phase. Rank was preoccupied that spring with a pre-Oedipal thesis, dictating the manuscript of *The Trauma of Birth*. In that monograph Rank concluded that anxiety, neurotic and normal, derived from birth—from primal separation from the haven of the mother's womb. After that came the trauma of weaning, and only thereafter the fear of castration.

The book was dictated without notes, "off the top of his head," as his typist, Editha Sterba recalled. She sat at a desk outside his office in the hallway, where he paced up and down, speaking rapidly but allowing her time to catch up when she needed to. In training to become a lay analyst, Sterba registered surprise at some of Rank's material. In good humor, Rank said, "They will all be surprised."[11]

The book had been in preparation well before Freud's first operation. Rank presented Freud with the manuscript on his birthday, May 6, with a flowery dedication. The timing is important, since it proves the work was not a reaction to Freud's illness, nor was it kept secret from him. Rank intended to honor Freud, not forsake him, despite the surprises he knew were to be found in the book.

Many years later Beata spoke of Otto's life in that period, praising his intellect and his extraordinary tenacity in work. "He worked with extreme ease and nothing really interfered"; she or little Halusia (Helene) could come in the room and speak to him and he would respond to a question, pleasantly if not always cogently, and go on working. He typed well and liked to do his own work; the secretary (sometimes Tola) would usually work on less personal projects. "He was a very tender person, an extremely devoted one. I think of people who are devoted to their careers; he was certainly one of the nicest." She had only a vague recollection of his relationship to his colleagues, "his brother figures; he was very fond of Ferenczi and Hanns Sachs. And he was always wrapped up in his deep feelings." Tola, almost twelve years younger than Otto, felt she was too young to understand these depths in 1923, when she emerged from spousal shadow into junior colleagueship. "He was close to Professor and his family . . . very appreciative of Mrs. Freud, and, I think Anna was very close to him."[12]

Anna Freud, who never married, was rumored to be a potential match for a number of the eligible bachelors around Freud, especially Otto Rank. She was only ten when Rank established his filial tie with Freud; Otto's relationship with Anna was probably fraternal, and his courtship and romance took place away from the Freud family and Vienna. Paula Fichtl, the Freuds' maid, said that Anna was attracted to older men, but when she was ready to marry, they were no longer available. Perhaps Rank was one such. A rare letter between the two began "Dear Dr. Rank" and closed "Your Anna Freud."[13]

Tola followed her friend Anna Freud into the sanctum of the Vienna Psychoanalytic Society in May, having accepted an assignment from the Professor to give a paper. She had attended meetings regularly, but Freud said there could be no permanent guests. Tola's paper, on the merits of which she was elected to the Society, concerned "The Role of Women in the Evolution of Human Society."[14] Her work on this topic thus coincided with Otto's preparation of *The Trauma of Birth*.

Rank dedicated his book *The Trauma of Birth and Its Meaning for Psychoanalysis* thus:

SIGM. FREUD

Presented to the Explorer of the Unconscious

Creator of Psychoanalysis

6 May 1923

On receipt of the newly published book, Freud replied: "I gladly accept your dedication with the assurance of my most cordial thanks. If you could put it more modestly, it would be all right with me. Handicapped as I am, I enjoy enormously your admirable productivity. That means for me too: 'Non omnis moriar.' "[15] The quotation, from Horace, means "I shall not completely die."

The standard histories of psychoanalysis emphasize the surprise impact of *The Trauma of Birth*. Freud knew of it long before the other Ring members, of course. On first reading it, Jones praised and quoted from the book; only later did he raise the issue of surprise as a breach of promise and call it surreptitious and "regressive," the product of a disturbed mind. Initially, Freud accepted the filial gift enthusiastically; but later, swayed by Rank's rivals, he was to condemn Rank for its publication. In July Rank and Ferenczi worked on their book in the Tyrol Mountains. In late August the Committee met at San Cristoforo where, as recounted, Jones survived Rank's move to expel him because of an anti-Semitic insult.

DAVID AND GOLIATH: FREUD'S DREAM OF RANK

In his letters from Vienna, Rank followed the Professor's instructions and gave the Ring a minimum of information about Freud's illness. Freud's major surgery had been done on October 12, 1923, by Dr. Hans Pichler, a leading expert in the field (unlike the first surgeon who operated in April). After two weeks Freud was allowed to go home. But cancerous tissue was found again, and another operation was performed on November 12. Freud took almost two months to recover and did not resume his practice until after the New Year.[16]

Rank informed the Committee of a new interest in psychoanalysis in Paris not unimportant for his own future. His letter ended with a reproach to "dear Ernest" about his handling of a scientific priority conflict with Sandor Ferenczi. Abraham assumed the role of umpire in this dispute, reminding Jones of talks "under the big willow tree" in August wherein sibling rivalry had been the topic: Ferenczi was the oldest, Rank the favored youngest son. Jones apologized for (again) causing pain to his old friend Sandor, pleading that he had no evil intention and justifying the lapse. Like Otto at San Cristoforo, Sandor could not accept the apology, and the conflict dragged on.[17] So did Freud's slow recuperation. Rank also took sick toward the end of the year, adding to the dismal tenor of the *Rundbriefe*.

Freud's operations made it painful and difficult for him to speak. There was an exchange of letters between him and Rank in late 1923; the two men discussed demands from Jones for assignment of all English translation rights to his Press. Freud saw Jones's request as a "threat" and angrily criticized him. Bitterly, he also said Jones was insincere in his wish for Freud's recuperation: "The quality of my condition is in remarkable contrast to the praises of it which Jones sends." [18] Freud was willing, however, to give the Press another chance, feeling he could not afford to be blamed for letting it die. Rank replied, his patience at an end:

Not only does the Press want to live, but also the Verlag, and the movement, and up to now the Press has only hampered

*the Verlag and the movement . . . As an author I feel that I
have been sufficiently harmed by the Press, especially by Jones,
who has stood in the way of my American translations, without
producing them at all in English. (By the way, The Artist is
translated now and I have two offers for translation of the Incest
Motif) . . . It depends only on you to decide if you want to
give the Press one more chance. The Verlag and I will not any
longer.*

But the Press lived on, and neither of Rank's books was published
in English.

On November 20, eight days after Pichler operated the second time, Rank visited Freud. On returning home he wrote a
letter which, with Freud's reply, illuminates their relationship
at a time of stress and change. During the time of Freud's illness,
he and Rank appear to have been very close.

The letter that Rank wrote concerned a dream that Freud
had had. Unfortunately, we do not have a transcript of the
dream. Yet the letters are nonetheless revealing.

*This evening an interpretation of the witty dream you told me
today occurred to me, which is too apt to be withheld from
you and which, I hope, will amuse you. If, by this, I should
possibly slip into the error of psychoanalytic accusation which
you disapprove of, I try to comfort myself that you do it yourself
too by identifying yourself with L. G. (who in the dream discusses the ego and the id).* [L. G. must be David Lloyd George.
Like Ernest Jones, Lloyd George, British Prime Minister at the
end of World War I, was of Welsh background, and to his detrac-
tors was known as "The liar from Wales." Rank was well-in-
formed about L. G., having specialized in attacking him when
he (Rank) was wartime editor of the *Krakauer Zeitung.*]
*You tell yourself—the night before going home—that you
have remained silent long enough and that you will return to
public life and work, for instance, to speak—and in English
at that (analysis) which is much more difficult not only for
us Germans but more difficult in general. You can do it as
well as that great English orator, you even make English jokes
and puns. That means that in the dream he does it in your
place, transgressing, in addition, one of your basic laws by mis-
using analysis in the service of politics. That must mean: It is
high time that I return to work, the others do not understand
me, do not know how to "translate" me (the ego and the id)*

and misuse psychoanalysis for their personal interests; they understand nothing [nichts] *or less than nothing* [übernichts]. *It reminds one of the well-known comparisons:* nix-nix-aber schon gar nix (*nothing, nothing, but absolutely nothing*).

Of course, that is only one of the actual meanings of the dream, which fulfills your "ego" and relatively your "super-ego." It is probably difficult to find what the "ego" has to say to this, the dream having the character of a thought process. But this interpretation may provoke you—I mean "provoke" in both senses—also meaning to provoke you to complete this interpretation, whereby I hope that the deepest strata reveal as decisive a will for recovery as this first one.

And Freud's reply:

Vienna, 26 Nov. 1923

Dear Dr. Rank,

It has been a long time since you have tried to interpret one of my dreams in such a powerful analytical way. Since then much has changed. You have grown enormously and you know so much more about me and the result is different. Your work gives me the opportunity to test out where your assumption joins one of my own associations and also to examine finally the interesting problems of the relation of the super-ego in this dream. . . .

Now comes the question: Against whom is the dream directed, is it in any way directed against a certain person? The association refuses to answer, it says only: Bonar Law [Prime Minister after L. G.; died a few weeks before the dream]. *But instead we have the fact that the dream was told to certain persons, to Anna and to Dr. [Felix] Deutsch. It must, therefore, have a meaning for these persons. The report I had read in the newspaper had said that L. G. was accompanied by his wife and daughter. This point was decisive for the construction of the dream for these were evidently my nurses, without whom I would not have survived these difficult days. Hence, this is evidently a dream of loving recognition of my ladies [Anna, Martha, Minna]. The animosity, therefore, must be directed against males. I had relied in feeling indeed on Professor Pichler, but with the second operation disappointment set in, loosening of the homosexual tie. Back to the women. Dr. Deutsch is very little involved personally. Why should I have told the dream to him—and that for unfriendly reasons? Assumption*

*tells us because it was a familiar way to tell the dream to you.
Maybe. More evident to me is the criticism of Jelgersma [Dutch
analyst]. You will remember that his merit was the recognition
of the dream, and how much misunderstanding and overbearing was connected with it; he is now to be rewarded by a special
issue in his honor of the poor* Zeitschrift, *manhandled by you
and Storfer, the* Zeitschriften *which now almost take the wom-
en's place. Hence, the affect I showed later on in the conversation
with you makes it very probable that you too as well as Storfer
are hidden behind the figure covered by Bonar Law. And the
question about the super-ego? Does it also act so forcibly, does
it show such a brutal will to recovery? In no way, that would
not be like it. There is only one association to L. G., "Liar from
Wales." The super-ego merely says to the dream: All right, you
old jester and boaster. This is not true at all!*

*And now comes a second surprising association, which
leaves no doubt about the attitude of the super-ego. L. G.'s
name is David, and now a sudden inspiration tells me that
Lou always called her [husband] Herbert "Davy" because she
wants to have in him a father substitute (his father's name
was really David), which means: Attention here, the old one
and the young one are interchanged, you [Freud] are not David,
you are the boasting giant Goliath whom another one, the young
David, will slay. And now everything falls into place around
this point, that you [Rank] are the dreaded David who with
his trauma of birth succeeds in depreciating my work.*

*After having changed David back into Goliath, the super-
ego has no further objections against the identification of
L. G. and can remain silent. Thus can I continue your interpretation. I hope to see you soon, I was not operated on again, I
am free of pain and medicines.*

> *Cordially, your*
> *Freud*[19]

Freud's response combines stern interpretation with loving
forbearance toward Rank. The dream reveals Freud's ambivalence toward his maturing protégé in the face of his own cancer-
confirmed mortality. Freud's concern with the theme of dethroning, or patricide, had been expressed earlier with Jung and
Adler, and Freud once (with humor, to Lou) diagnosed Rank's
interest in regicide as a sublimation of Oedipal aggression, "the
negative aspect of his filial love." The immortality Freud saw

for himself in Rank's new work changed to a feeling of being depreciated, akin to Laius sensing his own overthrow in the advent of a son. Within a week Freud received the first copy of Rank's book and responded "Non omnis moriar."

At Christmastime Hanns Sachs visited Vienna. Freud shared some misgivings about Rank's new book, fueling the engines of criticism in Berlin. Sachs later professed shock at Otto's behavior: "He did not say a word about his new ideas to me until he presented me with a printed copy, although we had stayed at the same summer resort and had seen each other daily while he was writing the book." [20]

RELATIONSHIP THERAPY: *THE DEVELOPMENT OF PSYCHOANALYSIS*

Freud's return to work at the beginning of 1924 was announced to the Ring with pleasure by Rank. Freud even chaired a meeting of the Vienna Psychoanalytic Society, at which Ferenczi spoke on the work he coauthored with Rank and just published, *The Development of Psychoanalysis.* Three Berliners attended as well.

The first biography of Freud, written by Fritz Wittels, had also just appeared. Rank found it tasteless and tactless, but Freud, expecting little, was more tolerant and sent the author a list of corrections. Wittels, who had been allied with the exiled Stekel, offered a colorful, admiring, but partly critical portrait of Freud. "A self-appointed seer," Wittels wrote, comparing Freud to Charcot; "the gift resides in the will to accept one's own visions." The book correctly treats the Fliess episode as Freud's fault, which brought a strong protest from Freud. Rank— who must have found this offensive—is described as Freud's Eckermann (who was to Goethe as Boswell was to Johnson), and Wittels expressed the hope that Rank had kept "careful notes" on his private conversations with Freud.[21]

Wittels reports favorably on active therapy, praising Stekel for completing analyses in three to six months. If it took longer Stekel would "outwit the transference" by exchanging patients with other analysts! [22] This must have made Rank cringe.

Conflict between Vienna and Berlin intensified when a Rank analysand, Cavendish Moxon, returned from Institute lectures in Berlin bearing tales of intrigue: He had been questioned at length about Rank's "active" technique, casting aspersions at Vienna. Rank took offense at what he felt was an effort to undermine his work with someone just out of analysis. Rank declared that he would not send students to Berlin anymore. Ferenczi sided with him, welcoming objective criticism but not devious attacks. (Moxon became a lay analyst in California and published a number of psychoanalytic papers, some interpreting Rank's ideas.)

By January 15, copies of *The Trauma of Birth* and *The Development of Psychoanalysis* had arrived in England. That day Ernest wrote the Committee thanking Otto warmly for sending his book: "Without pretending to have assimilated all its contents as yet, I am sure that we could all corroborate many of his views at once, e.g., the close connection between psa treatment and repetition of pregnancy and birth." At this point, Jones made no complaint about the question of sudden, secret publication; that issue arose later. It appears that Jones's delayed complaint about the treacherous surprise was based on a rule he invented after the fact, perhaps with the aid of Hanns Sachs, who felt slighted by Rank (who had grown closer to Ferenczi).

On January 20, Rank sent a bitter critique of Jones as editor and colleague to Berlin and Budapest only, explaining that the Professor had suggested "against my own inclination" that Jones not be included in the correspondence. Jones had again made some hostile remarks about Rank in correspondence with Brill, who relayed the matter to Vienna. Instead of correcting the statements, Jones reproached Brill for disclosing them: an echo of San Cristoforo! By laying the matter before the others and excluding Jones, Rank opened himself to attack on procedural grounds. Perhaps Freud, who suggested the move, hoped to isolate Jones as a troublemaker. It seems, however, that Jones was, along with three strong allies in Berlin, himself working to isolate Rank and Ferenczi. Later evidence shows that Jones was ready to dismiss Freud himself in order to further his own view of psychoanalysis and enhance his control of the movement.

Word came to Freud that the recent books on birth trauma and active therapy had created an unpleasant stir in Berlin. In a long letter Freud responded that although he had shared some misgivings with Sachs, he did not condemn *The Trauma of Birth*, "a very important book" the dedication of which he had gladly accepted. Defending scientific freedom, Freud reminded the Committee of his tendency to absorb new ideas slowly. He said that to wait for his approval to publish would risk an idea's growing old. Freud thought the book on technique was sketchy, but valued it as a refreshing challenge to established analytic habits. Its emphasis on experiencing Freud took as a corrective to his own stance. He doubted that a shorter time limit for analysis, four or five months, would be enough to delve deep and make lasting changes (though not so long before, Freud's analyses had been short, too). Also, his practice consisted chiefly of teaching analyses, which "cannot be conducted exactly like therapeutic analyses." [23]

On this point Ferenczi and Rank differed with Freud: "The correct didactic analysis is one that does not in the least differ from the curative treatment. How, indeed, shall the future analyst learn the technique if he does not experience it just exactly as he is to apply it later?" Some excerpts from their little book, eclipsed for fifty years along with its authors, will show why it again is drawing the attention of analysts and psychotherapists.

Ferenczi and Rank taught that remembering, while important, is not the only therapeutic element. Repetition of living and feeling patterns, which Freud considered forms of resistance, were taken by Ferenczi and Rank to be inevitable and essential. These patterns must be understood and utilized as expressions of the unconscious, a "language of gesture." "Thus we finally come to the point of attributing *the chief role in analytic technique to repetition instead of to remembering.*" [24] In the analytic situation, developmental stages are replicated in the present. Some important things cannot be remembered at all; they must be experienced first because they never were conscious! The analyst might suggest abstinence, or approaching a phobic stimulus—"active therapy"—in order to elicit relevant feeling. The analytic situation places the patient in the relation of infant to parent. The ego resists what the libido would express in the transference, but the resistance is to be valued, is like a mainspring which regulates the unwinding of the libido. Resistance must be valued also for its content, which reveals where the ego fixations took place. One does not have to repeat the individual's whole development, just those phases in which neurotic fixations exist.

At the beginning of the analysis the ego learns to accept

libidinal expressions which earlier were forbidden and repressed. Then, after transference has developed positively, the libido can be experienced in the present relationship with the therapist. In the weaning (ending) phase, the ego adjusts the freed libido, "the newly awakened desires," to reality. "Naturally these ego forces do not need to be thrust upon the patient by any sort of moral talk or by giving him anagogic goals [a critique of Jungian exhortation], for they exist from the first in every patient who is not insane, just as much as the desire for transference." [25]

This passage continues with the quotation which begins this chapter. It celebrates life newly entered into by the neurotic, with the analyst as midwife and love object. Freud was never this optimistic a therapist. Ferenczi and Rank had developed in ways quite unlike their colleagues in London and Berlin, whose responses to this kind of enthusiasm were chilling. Jones praised the book in part, but found in it a dangerous similarity to Jung's tendency for "replacing analysis of childhood by discussions of current situations only." Freud expressed concern that tyros or overly zealous therapists might misuse the ideas, but expressed no fears about the authors themselves. In Berlin, Abraham and Rado were less sanguine even about that.[26]

Ferenczi and Rank, speaking from experience, warned against the excesses of intellect over emotion in the analytic process. They felt it was a mistake to impart theoretical knowledge to the patient; it was also wrong to interpret everything in terms of the past. Some emotions are provoked in the present and belong to it. The analyst must be able to distinguish between what is infantile and what is justified by the here and now, and "to understand and get the patient to realize what is common to both." Analysis of the ego was heretofore neglected, they point out, though Freud recently had given "valuable hints" about it. The book ends with a messianic vision in which the fragmented, overspecialized medical profession is reunified under psychoanalytic influence.

Meanwhile Freud said he found Rank's own book (*The Trauma of Birth*) "incomparably more interesting" than the joint one. However, Freud insisted on keeping the father in place as the enforcer of the incest ban, while Rank attributed the incest horror to an ambivalent wish to return to the womb, which revived the birth anxiety. Freud regarded this difference neither as a revolution nor as a contradiction of psychoanalytic knowledge.[27]

Jones responded favorably to Freud's defense of the controversial books, saying he had read them but needed time to assimilate their ideas before making a final judgment. Like Freud, he criticized the book on therapy because it lent itself to misuse by "ambitious or reactionary readers" and because it was too "dogmatic and even dictatorial." (Jones's "reactionary" can be defined as one who denies the primary role of infantile (Oedipal) sexuality.) Then he praised *The Trauma of Birth:* "I agree with [anthropologist Geza] Roheim that there is a vast support for Rank's theory to be obtained from anthropological data." Jones complained that the therapy book would have benefited from prepublication critiques by Committee members, but made no such argument—yet—about Rank's own opus.[28]

Abraham responded to Freud in private letters, deferential in tone, defiant in content. He expressed concern about "ominous" developments arising from ideas not "obtained in a legitimate analytic manner." He denied "hunting heretics," but felt he had to give a warning. In both new books he saw "manifestations of a regression in the scientific field, the symptoms of which agree in every small detail with those of Jung's secession from psychoanalysis." He hastened to note the great difference between the "pleasant qualities" of Ferenczi and Rank and the "deceitfulness and brutality" of Jung. He justified his intervention "to protect you from worse to come," and he claimed credit for having kept the Committee from falling apart at San Cristoforo.[29]

THE COMMITTEE: COMING APART

There were many reasons for the divisiveness, tension, and sometimes nasty clashes among members of the Ring at this time. First, they often honestly disagreed on matters of technique and theory. Alliances were formed in part on the basis of their own particular interpretations of Freudian psychoanalytic theory—as with Rank and Ferenczi.

Second, various Ring members sought to control the direction of the movement in their own way. Jones, for example, wanted to control publications of the group in English. Rank and Ferenczi were closest to Freud personally, geographically, and, at times, philosophically.

Jones and Abraham took on the role of jealous brothers, faulting the father for his special love of the youngest. Like the older sons of the biblical Jacob, they would have gladly sold Rank, the audacious dream interpreter, into slavery. To put it another way, Rank was to Freud as Cordelia to King Lear; Jones and Abraham stand as the jealous and devious siblings. (On January 1, 1923, just after Freud, from his hippogriff, snorted at the very suggestion that Rank needed analysis, Jones said in a private letter to Abraham: "I have renounced the hope of leading the Professor to any sort of objectivity where Rank is concerned. One must recognize with regret that even Freud has his human frailties and that age is bringing with it one-sidedness of vision and diminution of critical power.")[30]

The psychoanalytic movement had also truly grown; there were societies in many countries. Different factions within the Ring wanted to make sure that the stewardship of the movement would remain within their own sphere of influence. And finally, no matter how well Rank hid Freud's illness from other members, it was clear he was quite ill. If he died—or became incapacitated—who would take over? This uncertainty intensified the battle for ascendancy among the members of the Ring.

Why did Freud's efforts fail to unite them? His appeal to tolerance, objectivity, and fellowship might have healed the breach if the members of the Ring respected and needed him as before. Freud did not like to rule with a heavy hand, as he had said years before to the Vienna Society. Freud's power derived rather from his use of words, and from his access to funds and important people. And owing to the cancer he would no longer eat or speak in public, and it seemed he was facing the end of his life. Crippled in speech and dogged by pain, Freud tried to heal the Committee, itself crippled and racked with conflict. The quarreling sons sought his approval but, except for Ferenczi, did not change their positions.

The Ring group controlled the psychoanalytic movement: They were the officers, editors, and publishers. Jones, president of the IPA after Ferenczi, transferred the leadership to Abraham in 1924. The societies in Berlin and London had grown larger than Vienna's; New York was gaining fast. Freud had time for only a few cases, and Rank was limited by his role as editor and publisher. The loyal old guard, like Federn and Hitschmann, were outshone by Helene Deutsch, Wilhelm Reich, Herman Nunberg, and nonphysicians like Siegfried Bernfeld, Theodor

Reik, and eventually Anna Freud. Ferenczi remained rather isolated in Hungary; Sandor Rado left Budapest for Berlin, as did Franz Alexander and Melanie Klein.

Thus London and Berlin became power centers beside which Vienna grew humble, merely a precious part of history. Like his late old emperor Franz Josef, Freud was an increasingly impotent monarch of a divided kingdom. Rank, once dubbed "Lord Everything Else," held the equivalent of several cabinet positions, but psychoanalysis had become bigger than Freud and Rank could manage. After exhausting von Freund's bequest, the movement needed income from publications, patients, dues-paying members, and other philanthropists. (The fight for scarce resources had increased friction within the Ring even before Freud's illness.)

At the same time, between the end of the war and 1924, psychoanalysis was maturing as theory and therapy. Freud had invoked a death instinct; Ferenczi and Rank were moving into ego psychology and relationship therapy; and Rank had asserted the primacy of the maternal tie and discovered in its loss the key to human anxiety. These developments might have contained errors, but Freud was amazingly open to new ideas, more so than his most orthodox followers. Among these were the newly emerging powers Abraham and Jones, who were more concerned with recruitment, training, and organization than with scientific or clinical creativity. Sachs and Eitingon were soft-spoken or allowed Abraham to speak for them, and were less concerned with the politics of the movement.

On February 15, 1924, Rank wrote Freud an unusually forceful letter. He expressed his gratitude for the Professor's support, but told him he needed to be fully understood. Deferential but no longer docile, Rank charged Freud with missing the point of his theory and his clinical work.

> *As I am deeply concerned that you not misunderstand me—much more than I need recognition by my psychoanalytic colleagues, from most of whom I have never expected much understanding of my work—allow me to express candidly wherein I believe I was misunderstood.*
>
> *In your endeavor to help our colleagues arrive at an understanding and acceptance, you point out at once the well-known womb fantasy, to which I assign only a special position. But*

*the essential basis of my viewpoint is, if I may say so, the very
reality of the womb. Following this misunderstanding you speak
about the return to the womb in fantasy, while according to
my position, in neurotic symptoms as well as in the sex act,
we have to deal with much more than fantasy, namely, a real
though partial return. . . .*

*I would prefer to discuss the problem of the inhibition of
the incest drive (back to the mother) with reference to practical
experience rather than to drive theory, which is still in a state
of uncertainty and really has yet to be created. To me each
simple case of impotence has shown that the essential factor
is the unconquered anxiety before the maternal genital and
not the paternal prohibition. . . .*

*I hope you will not think that I want to present my work
as something totally new and independent. On the contrary,
I would like to stress that I can boast of a more extensive concordance with your views and an even stronger connection with
them. The concept of anxiety at birth takes the first place. As
I have said, not only do I find no contradiction, but rather
the most perfect harmony with your theory of drives. . . .*

*Also in therapy, where it seems you are less able to go along
with me, I start from the practice of setting an ending in advance, in order finally to make a connection with your result
in the history of an infantile neurosis* [1918, the "Wolf Man"
case, where Freud set an ending]. *On the basis of the rebirth
experiences of the patient in the end phase of analysis, as is
well known, you arrived at a series of questions which up to
now have resisted any solution, but which, through my viewpoint (may I say without presumption) have become comprehensible and soluble without contradicting your assumptions. At
the same time I see in this case an unambiguous proof that
the birth experience has appeared spontaneously at the end
of the treatment with your cases as well as with mine. I have
been forced by analytic experience only, not by speculation,
to understand this as a general analytic—and hence a common
human—experience. I believe I have made progress too, insofar
as we understand something now that we did not recognize
before and which we can now use therapeutically. I do not
hold the shortening of analysis to be as important as it may
appear. This came about as a very welcome gain from the new
insight. Finally the parable you use* [see below] *gives me the
best opportunity to demonstrate the difference in our improved
technique. We do not ignore the enormous importance of the
analysis as a means of research. What we criticized in our joint*

*book was only that any or every analytic therapist could, in
the name of research, lengthen analyses without limit and let
them run dry therapeutically.*[31]

Freud was more of an investigator than a therapist. He
thought the need to help was a liability in analytic work. Later
he reproached Rank for shortening analysis to accommodate
the American values of speed and greed. But Rank's short-term
therapy evolved from his clinical work in Vienna (praised by
Freud) and expressed concern for the patient, who too often
was not helped by analysis. Rank dared to identify an ethical
problem in which the analyst's need for data conflicts with the
patient's need for help.

The parable to which Rank referred in his letter was Freud's
remark that it took six weeks for his beard to regrow after the
operation, and that three months later he was still suffering from
changes in the scar tissue. "So," he concluded, "I find it rather
hard to believe that it is possible in a slightly longer time, four
or five months, to penetrate into the deep layers of the unconscious and bring about lasting changes in mental life." [32] Fully
aware of the sensitivity of the surgical metaphor, Rank continued
his argument.

*I believe that therapeutic analysis is not a process of healing
or regeneration, as you hint in your parable, but an operation
which can and even must be performed in a much shorter time,
so that the patient does not die from the operation. It is true
that this surgical incision is only possible if one knows beforehand or can state quickly where the seat of the evil is located.
It does not make much difference for it remains only a technical
problem, at what depth the evil is rooted. I believe you will
agree that the trauma of birth, the earliest attachment to the
mother up to the trauma of weaning and sexuality, belongs
to the deepest strata which we can ever penetrate. And I can
assure you that in every analysis this is possible within the
first months and it can be done not only without the slightest
damage to the patient, but also will make the solution of the
conflicts, neurotic as well as actual, easier or at least faster.*

Rank ended with a reference to Ferenczi's recent lecture
in Vienna, which showed that the new therapeutic approach
was not at all sterile from the standpoint of science. The letter

ended, "With my warmest greetings and my gratitude, as always."

FREUD AND RANK: STRAINED RELATIONS

More conflict over personalities and procedures erupted in February when Rank and Ferenczi angrily declined to be part of the program at the forthcoming Salzburg Congress in April. Jones had invited them as discussion leaders, not featured speakers.

In late February, while Abraham was accusing him of Jungian apostasy, Rank was stricken with a severe sore throat and confined to bed. Freud did not see or talk to him for over two weeks. Jones consoled him but in the next paragraph of his letter charged Rank with inventing a pretext for complaining about the Salzburg arrangements. Jones still hoped Ferenczi and Rank would participate in the Congress discussions.[33] The hostility in the Ring must have hurt Freud more than it did the other members, who by then had developed thick skins and low expectations. The Ring was not behaving like the primal horde discussed in Freud's *Group Psychology,* in which things were kept under control by the powerful and dreaded primal father. Instead we see a parody of the barbarian kings described in *Totem and Taboo,* Freud's prewar study: Social taboos immortalize and protect the king, but also bind and burden him, making him powerless and miserable.

Freud rebutted Abraham's dire prediction warning about Rankian heresy in a private letter.

> *Let me assure you that an apprehension of the kind that you expressed is not so far from my mind. When Rank first told me about his findings, I said jokingly: "With an idea like that anyone else would set up on his own." I think that the accent is on the "anyone else," as you yourself admit. When Jung used his first independent experiences to shake himself free of analysis, we both knew that he had strong neurotic and selfish motives that took advantage of this discovery. I was then able to say with justification that his twisted character did not compensate me for his lopsided theories. . . .*
>
> *In the case of our two friends the situation is different. We are both confident that they have no evil motives other*

than those secondary concomitants of scientific work, the ambi-
tion to make new and astonishing discoveries. The only danger
arising out of this is of falling into error, which is hard to
avoid in science. Let us assume the most extreme case, and
suppose that Ferenczi and Rank came right out with the
view that we were wrong to stop at the Oedipus complex, and
that the really decisive factor was the birth trauma, and that
those who did not overcome this would later break down also
on the Oedipus complex. Then, instead of our sexual etiology
of neurosis, we should have an etiology determined by physio-
logical chance, because those who became neurotic would ei-
ther have experienced an unusually severe birth trauma or
would bring an unusually "sensitive" organization to that
trauma. [34]

Freud, and presumably the others, did not see the birth
trauma in terms of psychology. Freud went on to say that years
of observation would tell which thesis was exaggerated and
which underrated. Meanwhile both could exist happily under
the same roof; he saw no evil in such a plan. In closing he said,
"I really am no longer the beast of burden that I used to be."
Freud said he would neither read a paper nor attend the Congress dinner at Salzburg; the "injured functions" of speaking
and eating would not be exhibited.

Ferenczi sent a letter to Freud on March 18 with a copy
to "Dear Otto." In this letter Ferenczi attacks Abraham's ambition and jealousy, denouncing him for suggesting (privately) to
Freud that the two new books smacked of desertion from psychoanalysis. He blamed Abraham for destroying the Committee,
calling into question both his hostility toward Rank and his failure
to see that Jones's anti-Semitism was incompatible with membership on the Committee.

Ferenczi then said he opposed Abraham as next President
of the IPA, suggesting Eitingon as the one impartial candidate
besides Freud. Ferenczi promised to stay in contact with Abraham for the sake of the movement "and always to reciprocate
his politeness, now all the more a cover, with politeness." In
closing he wrote: "You will soon convince yourself that I have
not in the least deviated, either personally or scientifically, from
you and your teaching (which you would not have believed,
anyway)." [35]

Freud had more tolerance for differences than for poor judgment or lack of finesse. Ferenczi's pledge of allegiance was more than Freud needed or wanted. But Rank's brashness bothered him, and he hoped Ferenczi could mediate. A copy of his sad, eloquent reply to Ferenczi also went to Rank, probably from Sandor.

> *My confidence in you and Rank is unconditional. It would be sad, if one could find oneself deceived after a 15- to 17-year relationship. But you stress too much that I should agree with you in every detail, and Rank is terribly blunt, he stirs people up against him, does not make use of the assured superiority which would fit him so well as the person nearest to me in so many respects. His work has been invaluable, his person would be irreplaceable. Now when he is preparing to go to America for half a year—certainly no secret to you—I am afraid that his health will not be up to the strains awaiting him there. On the other hand, I am not sure of seeing him again when he returns in the fall.*
>
> *I do not doubt that the other members of the former Committee also feel respect and attachment for me, and yet it happens that I am deserted just when I am an invalid with decreased working strength and depressed mood, one who defends himself against extra work and does not feel equal to any trouble. I will not try with this complaint to influence you to take a single step to preserve the lost Committee; I know that what is lost is lost: I have survived the Committee that was to have succeeded me, perhaps I shall yet survive the International Association. I only hope that psychoanalysis will survive me. But taken all together it makes a sad ending to life.*[36]

Freud declared his continuing support for Abraham as IPA President, with Rank as Secretary. Abraham expected the top position after having served as Secretary himself. By the same token, Freud hoped to see Rank take the Presidency next. But Rank would never be able to work with Abraham.

After a long discussion with Rank in March, Freud decided to withhold his forthcoming paper, "On the Passing of the Oedipus Complex," which criticized the birth trauma theory. But Freud told Ferenczi that Rank's monomaniacal enthusiasm did not make friends. Moreover, he said, the purported shortening of treatment implied sacrificing the analysis to suggestion (akin to hypnosis), and gave adversaries ammunition for their attacks on the innovators, even if not justified. Freud could even see a slight similarity between Jung and Rank, in that both were blinded by their own experiences when relatively new in analytic practice. "Otherwise I do not want to compare either the persons or the discoveries. Jung was a bad fellow." [37]

Rank also wrote Ferenczi about his long discussion with Freud. Rank thought Freud's adamant support of Abraham might break up the IPA; evidently Freud also saw the danger. But Eitingon, a compromise choice, was away, and was possibly in bad health. Freud's draft paper did constitute a withdrawal of support. But Rank was most astonished and offended when Freud admitted having read only half the book (and not very well, Rank thought)! Adding insult to injury, Freud credited Rank neither for stimulating his new paper, nor for discussing why the Oedipus complex was destined to decline—the principal thesis of *Trauma*. Rank was thus embroiled in a priority fight with Freud. The letter sputters to an end:

> *The Professor is testing out my point of view in technique, according to his own words, by giving all of his present patients, of whom most have been in analysis for two years, my book to read and asking them to give their impressions. Even as I write this, I still cannot believe that such a thing is possible (but there can be no doubt about it).* [38]

Such "testing" flew in the face of Freud's own precepts, and could demonstrate nothing except how *not* to do therapy or research.

Rank's disappointment and anger over *The Trauma of Birth* followed Freud's retreat from saying that it was "the greatest advance since the discovery of psychoanalysis, even if only 33% or 66% is true." By the end of March, Freud admitted to Ferenczi that he had liked the book better in the beginning, and was moving from the 66% to the 33%. [39]

Freud's ambivalence kept him stirred up. He bristled both at Rank's assertiveness and at Ferenczi's fawning deference. Although he denied any bitterness, Freud observed to Rank that his critical remarks on the birth trauma seemed to have had little impact. Freud proposed to let the matter rest, saying that the two (or three) of them could be "for once, of different opinions." [40] In the same letter Freud said he was determined to transfer the Presidency of the Vienna Psychoanalytic Society from himself to Rank, preferably before the Salzburg Congress, so as to enhance Rank's status there. Rank was cool to the idea, predicting that the Viennese would try to dissuade Freud from stepping down. Besides, his six month absence in America would interfere with that responsibility.

By return post, Rank replied to Freud with a mixture of reverence and anger:

> *I believe that you underrate—apart from my personal feelings for you—the high respect I have for you as the founder of psychoanalysis and as my teacher, when you are so sure that your criticism has impressed me so little. If it seemed this way, it may stem from the fact that I have several times gained the impression that your criticism—quite apart from factual points of view—was not exactly friendly from the start. Otherwise you would not have failed even to suggest wherein you saw the frequently stressed value of the book, while you expressed, without leaving any doubt, what you saw as its weaknesses.*

Rank went on to complain about two slights. Freud, in his draft paper, failed to deal with Rank's new approach to the Oedipus complex, or even give him credit. Furthermore, Freud had made a slip of the tongue, saying Rank put down the Oedipus complex when he had meant to say the castration complex.[41] With hindsight we can say that Freud's slip was prescient, for Rank did forswear the Oedipus complex in time. But at that moment Rank insisted he was engaged in helping, not hurting, Freudian psychoanalysis, and he wanted Freud to be cognizant of that even if he could not be wholly supportive.

Everyone wondered how long Freud might live, or, living, how his incapacitation would affect his authority. Each of the favored circle had a personal agenda, a stake to defend, and there were at least two divergent views of psychoanalysis among them. Having recovered from the mistake of naming Jung the leader, Freud chose to form a secret group of paladins. The chores and the rewards of psychoanalysis would be theirs but they had to live in Freud's shadow peacefully and productively while awaiting their day in the sun.

Despite Freud's awareness of Jones's anti-Semitism, he decided that the Englishman was indispensable and pacified the Committee at San Cristoforo. Freud must have heard about

Rank's angry explosion there from several sources. Brill also tat-
tled on Jones more than once. But Freud was able to overlook
Jones's anti-Semitism because of his importance to the cause.
Freud felt that anti-Semitism was inevitable in non-Jews and
believed in the psychoanalytic principle that it is better to have
it on the surface, the better to control it. He bore the insult—
or, rather, he required Rank and the others to bear it for the
sake of the survival of the movement. Supposedly, after the Jung
episode Freud never completely trusted a non-Jew. There was
little temptation to trust Jones: His lack of sensitivity and truth-
fulness mitigated against that. He worked indefatigably and effectively, however, making himself indestructible if not
indispensable.

Rank and Ferenczi were left feeling Freud had let the bigot
get his way. Almost a century before, Sigmund Freud had
watched his father meekly pick up his cap and walk on rather
than quarrel with anti-Semites in the village street. The young
Sigmund disapproved of his father's passivity. But an older, less
idealistic Sigmund compromised himself rather than fight the
same evil in milder but still vicious form. Freud always feared
that psychoanalysis would be put down as a Jewish science, despite his claim that it took a godless Jew to discover it. He had
pleaded with his Jewish followers to bear with Jung at Salzburg
in 1908: The Gentile was needed to save Freud's creation. Jones,
who manifestly was tainted by prejudice, could be considered
genuine and useful, if not likeable.

But Freud's actions backfired. Rank and Ferenczi simply
could not have been expected to cooperate with Jones; it was
as unrealistic as expecting Jones to continue his analysis with
Ferenczi. The end—psychoanalysis—could not justify the means,
even to appease Sigmund Freud.

OTTO RANK'S BIRTH TRAUMA

The real importance of *The Trauma of Birth* emerged later,
after the theory itself was beyond salvage. (Although he referred
to it in some of his later work, toward the end of his life Rank
told a friend he wished he had never written the book.) [42] Rank's
theory established the first separation as a prototype for all anxiety: Birth precedes weaning, weaning precedes walking, walking

precedes the Oedipus conflict. He identified the mother as the original locus both of comfort (the womb) and of distress (birth). Adult conflict about the sex act was ascribed to anxiety centered in and symbolized by the female genitals.

Since birth was not part of conscious memory (unlike some Oedipal wishes, fantasies, and experiences), working through neurotic conflict in analysis meant experiencing some feelings for the first time, notably primal separation anxiety. All this provided plenty of grist for psychoanalytic mills. But Rank's great emotional discovery behind the new theory was the analyst's identity as mother in the transference, as much or more than as father. Rank's idea shook the patriarch in theory and in real life: Freud's was a masculine perspective, though clearly not as extreme as that of Jones.

Rank was now experiencing his own psychological trauma of birth. He was about to leave Vienna—his wife and child, his mother and brother, his foster father—to make his way to New York for six months. Perhaps it was easier to go if "father" was angry: Rank had spared Freud some of the Committee's wrangling, but not all that he could have, and he made some of it worse. On the other hand, Freud had lent his protégé full support, only to withdraw it increasingly under pressure from Rank's enemies.

A mellower time came in April. Freud decided not to go to the Salzburg Congress at all; the ostensible reason was his prosthesis, yet he also wanted to spare himself the spectacle of his Committee in conflict. Rank was taken aback, but supported the decision. Although suffering a third bout of illness, he agreed to assume the Presidency of the Vienna Society, which he had been chairing most of the year anyway. He was gratified by the Professor's encouragement of his trip to America. Rank and Ferenczi also agreed not to oppose Abraham as President of the IPA, having worked out an arrangement by which Max Eitingon would become Secretary.[43]

On April 6, two weeks before the Congress, Ferenczi wrote a letter announcing the end of the Committee, but said he hoped "that everything possible will be done which the common interest requires." Abraham, whom Freud had called "unfriendly" toward Rank and Ferenczi,[44] received a remarkable private letter from Jones.

April 8, 1924

Dear Karl:

*Events are moving with startling rapidity, and we must
be prepared for everything. I enclose a copy of Prof's letter to
me today and await with impatience the one he sent to you.
You have my understanding sympathy in having also to undergo my experience of being unfairly treated by one's best-
loved friend, but I am sure you will deal successfully with the
situation. It is not hard to make every allowance for him when
one considers all the factors, age, illness, and the insidious propaganda nearer home; the deepest reason of all I will indicate
in a moment. At all events it shows the imperfection of his
objectivity, for no one could possibly have displayed a purer
and more loyal attitude than you have done in this difficult
year.*

*The Glovers [Edward and James, British psychiatrists] gave
a pitiless analysis of the* Gerburtstrauma *[birth trauma] at our
last meeting, revealing the* Vaterablehnung *[father rejection]
and flight from the Oedipus complex as its essential motive.
That Otto conceals this from Prof and displaces it on to us is
indicated by the way in which the book was secretly published,
by his ignoring of our letters and questions for weeks (with
the final cessation of his* Rundbriefen*), his abnormal outburst
over the Symposium, his Jung-like decision to go to America
without letting any of us know, and a dozen other signs. I
shall not be surprised if he does not come to Salzburg after
all. If he does I shall make every effort to regain relationships
with him if he shows the slightest wish for it, but I dare not
build too many hopes on this in view of his psychological situation, which daily becomes plainer. There is for me, however,
and I trust also for you, one unalterable condition: I will not
sacrifice my intellectual convictions for friendship with any
man on earth, not even Prof himself. It would be a strange
irony if we lost some of Prof's intimate friendship through too
great loyalty to his work, but it may possibly prove to be so.
We may have to choose between Psa and personal considerations, in which case you may be sure I for one shall have no
doubt.*

*The real tragedy is this. I fear that Prof, with his clear
mind, cannot be altogether blind to the unconscious tendency
in Otto. Ten years ago he would surely have put his work before
all else; but now, old, ill, and tied by the strongest claims of
affection (which Otto has so fully justified in the past), he can*

*hardly face the possibility of having once more to go through
the Jung situation and this time much nearer home, with someone who perhaps means more to him than his own sons. This
thought must call for our deepest sympathy. It is probably the
real reason why he will not come to the Congress, either to
the Committee meeting or the Symposium, where there is the
risk of his unconscious fears being exposed; and also the reason
why he must project his accusations of disruption to a distance
to Berlin or London.*

*You may show this letter to Hanns. Many thanks for the
programme, which looks well.*

*yours always loyally
Ernest*[45]

This previously unpublished letter starkly tells the difference
between north and south in the conflict around Freud. Jones,
who became famous as Freud's ardent, eloquent defender, put
intellectual conviction ahead of his relationship with the aging
Professor. He would have abandoned Freud if his own ideology
could not overcome Rank's with their mutual mentor. Rank and
Ferenczi had quite another notion of loyalty to Freud personally
and to his work. They put a higher value on relationship—as
therapists, theorists, and colleagues. Their feeling for Freud and
each other was nourished by more extensive personal contact,
both intellectual and emotional.

Jones was like Freud in his ability to cut off a disliked opponent. In this case, like Jung, he was ready to cut off Freud himself.
But Rank identified more with Freud's imaginative power, his
encouragement of creative work, and his warmth. In the ideological crisis, the northern contingent of the Ring fought on conservative lines. It held a base of power in numbers and influence,
with many trainees and the English Press in its camp. The south-
ern group ran the German language publications, and fought
along liberal lines to humanize psychoanalysis and make it more
effective. Both sides could be autocratic and angry. Neither had
much use for the other, except as organizational need and the
Professor's wishes dictated. Sachs and Eitingon in Berlin had
some moderating effect, but they were not strong figures. The
cutting of the vital tie to Freud that Jones—of all people—was
prepared to do in April could not be done so easily by Rank.

His birth trauma theory was a pre-Oedipal extension of what

Rank had learned at the Professor's side. Not a rebellion, the new work was a tribute, accepted by Freud as the greatest progress since the beginning of psychoanalysis. Freud's gradual withdrawal of support forced Rank to either recant or fight back, perhaps for the first time in his life. In the year to come he was to do both. Rank turned forty on April 22. Helene Deutsch gave a party for him, at which he was heard to say that it was time for a change in his life.[46] Five days later he hastily left the Salzburg Congress for New York.

CHAPTER 9

Breaking with Freud

*To wish and to will. Our worst faults are the consequences of
confusing the two things.*

—Henrik Ibsen[1]

His first trans-Atlantic crossing gave Rank an opportunity to
orient himself at a critical time. Just forty years old, the closest
and youngest of Freud's intimate colleagues, Rank enjoyed something of an international reputation in his own right, and he
had analyzed and taught a number of the prominent analysts
who awaited him in New York. His European base, on the other
hand, was steadily eroding. Freud, his major support for almost
twenty years, was 68 and ill. The strife-ridden Committee had
become inhospitable to Rank and was already having an effect
on Freud's support of Rank. And a number of young disciples
surrounding Freud in Vienna were displaying the loyalty, energy, and even the talent that Rank had shown over the years.
People like Helene Deutsch, Siegfried Bernfeld, and Wilhelm
Reich made the Vienna Psychoanalytic Society stronger than
ever. Rank had now to consider his own future in a small but
increasingly competitive arena. By 1924 there were 263 IPA
members—all the recognized psychoanalysts in the world. Now
middle-aged, Rank was one of only nine pioneers present for
the eighth Congress in Salzburg who had attended the first
Congress there in 1908. The others were Abraham, Eitingon,

Federn, Ferenczi, Hitschmann, Jekels, Jones, and Sadger.[2]

Rank received assistance with lodgings in New York from Edward Bernays, Freud's American nephew. A few years younger than Rank, he was a pioneer in the field of public relations and had helped arrange for the publication in the United States of some of Freud's writings. Due to a misunderstanding or insensitivity on Rank's part the two men—who had corresponded—never met. Rank expressed to Freud his bewilderment at Bernays's irritation over the matter, and Freud advised him not to worry. Both Bernays and Freud disliked the way Jones was handling the English and American translation rights to Freud's books. Freud, exasperated, wrote to Rank: "It [Jones's proposal] is so insincere and so involved that I am doubly glad to have unloaded the whole matter on you."[3]

In a sense, Freud himself had more influence in the United States than he did with his intimate circle of sibling rivals. He could have named his price to sit as an expert witness at the Leopold and Loeb trial in Chicago, to make a movie for Samuel Goldwyn, or to write articles for American magazines. But Freud's only visit to America fifteen years earlier (at age 53) was not, for him, a happy memory. To charge a good fee for analyses there, he told Rank, was the only reasonable way to bear a "sojourn among such savages: to sell one's life as dearly as possible." Rank's clients were mostly psychiatrists, men who had been to see Freud in Vienna but who wanted and needed more treatment. "Nice that you now have nearly all of my former analysands," Freud wrote, "whose analyses I recall without any satisfaction. It often seemed to me that analysis fits the American as a white shirt the raven."[4]

Calvin Coolidge was president when Rank arrived in 1924, having succeeded Warren Harding, who died in office the year before. Mussolini's Fascist government was in power in Italy. Adolf Hitler, just sentenced to five years' imprisonment following the Munich coup, was released before the end of the year. Woodrow Wilson, born the same year as Freud (1856), had died in February at age 67, just two weeks after Lenin. The year's notable music included Gershwin's *Rhapsody in Blue* and *Turandot* by Puccini, who died later in the year. The Olympic Games in Paris brought to world fame a tall American swimmer named John Weismuller, while Yale student Benjamin Spock rowed on the U.S. crew.

The age of electric appliances and combustion engines, of mass production and mass communication, had arrived. In a land of about 110 million people there were 20 million automobiles, which were fast changing the cities and countryside. Radio brought news, sports, music, and other entertainment in one language across a great continent, an amazing phenomenon to a European who was used to finding language barriers every few hundred kilometers. Telephones, movies, even airplanes, were commonplace.

In Europe, the Great War, which had decimated the old Austro-Hungarian Empire and humbled proud Vienna, had— at the cost of machine guns, air and submarine warfare, poison gas, and unprecedented carnage—offered a promise of lasting peace. And on both continents Einstein, Marx, and Freud had become household names, as confidence in human accomplishment collided with new uncertainties about how the universe, the nation-state, and the human mind were governed.

RANK AS LECTURER

Just after his arrival in New York, Rank delivered a lecture at the Academy of Medicine. Sponsored by the New York Neurological Society, the event drew an audience of 150. Among those taking part in the discussion were many who had known Rank in Europe, including rival A. A. Brill, a European emigré who first translated Freud into English; Smith Ely Jelliffe, influential psychiatrist and editor; Thaddeus Ames, sometime Jungian, ex-President of the New York Society, and the man who had invited Rank to America; and Drs. Oberndorf, Stern, Meyer, and Polon, pioneers who had been analyzed by Freud in Vienna, but evidently not to their full satisfaction. Brill had first met Rank in 1908, the others after the war. The ambitious and temperamental Brill experienced Rank's arrival as competition but acceded to Freud's wishes.

Rank's first lecture in America, "Psychoanalysis of Organic Conditions," was soon published; it offers a glowing forecast of the prospects of psychoanalytic therapy for conditions such as asthma, migraine, convulsions, and chorea. He scarcely mentioned Freud. Rather than present himself as Freud's representative, Rank offered "a new viewpoint, introduced by me." His new theory involved the "embryonal unconscious," which he defined as that nucleus that was never repressed because it was never conscious. This stage occurs during the intrauterine period, a blissful state which ends in the trauma of birth. Rank based his discovery, "the most recent analytical understanding of the unconscious," not on mere speculation but on "the results of long years of analytical experience of the neuroses." He then proceeded to sketch his new birth trauma theory, claiming that the embryonic "memory of Paradise" constituted the "physiological nucleus of the unconscious." He concluded that hysteria, other neurotic symptoms, and even organic conditions can all be traced to the expulsion from that paradise and the terrible unconscious conflict about whether and how to return.[5]

Rank thought the birth trauma theory was a radical improvement, but not a violation, of Freud's instinct theory. Freud had, through sex, united the physical and the mental, the body and the soul. Rank located the union at a much earlier stage, in the womb. He went on to link hysterical paralyses with the fetal position, asthmatic breathing and headaches with being squeezed through the birth canal. If Freud's explanatory metaphor was the Oedipus myth, Rank's was the expulsion from Paradise. With his imaginative leap Rank outdid Freud's scientific-materialistic bent in trying to pin down the physical basis of mind.

Rank's need to make the psyche cellular, as it were, stemmed partly from his overzealous imitation of Freud, partly from his awareness of the medical domination of psychoanalysis in America. Freud's support of "lay"—nonmedical—analysis helped Rank, of course, but in New York Rank emphasized the biological underpinnings of his theory. What the Americans did not yet know was that Freud, after initially applauding it, now had grave doubts about Rank's new theory, and that Jones and Abraham saw Rank moving close to Jung-like apostasy.

A week later Rank spoke on "Psychoanalysis and Psychiatry" for an audience of some 200. Then, before a group at Columbia University invited by sociologist William Ogburn, Rank discussed a theme he had first developed as an adolescent steeped in Nietzsche, Ibsen, and Freud: psychoanalysis as a cultural factor. He gave the same talk at the New School for Social Research. Rank was the guest of honor at dinner parties hosted by Smith Ely Jelliffe and Adolph Stern; the latter was President of the New

York Society and Secretary of the American. On May 27 Rank read a paper called "The Essence of the Psychoanalytic Therapy" to the New York Society. The title and text show some Germanisms, but considering its complexity, Rank probably had some help with the translation. By June, Rank had settled into quarters at 117 West 58th Street and was using a printed letterhead with that address.

RANK AS THEORIST AND THERAPIST

Otto Rank was elected an honorary member of the American Psychoanalytic Association on June 3, 1924. At the same meeting, held at the Hotel Traymore in Atlantic City, newly inducted regular members included Karl Menninger of Topeka, Martin Peck of Boston, and Harry Stack Sullivan of Baltimore, all of them to become formidable figures in American psychiatry. The minutes of this fateful meeting record a paper on urethral eroticism by Dr. Isidor Coriat and one on spontaneous cures by Dr. Stern. The minutes went on to read: "The members and guests then had the rare pleasure to listen to a paper by our distinguished guest, Dr. Otto Rank, of Vienna, on 'The Trauma of Birth, in its importance for Psychoanalytic Therapy.' " Psychiatrists present besides those mentioned included Brill, White, Jelliffe, and Trigant Burrow.[6]

> I do not remember how I got to the meeting nor what was said there, but I still retain a vivid impression regarding the quality of the several speakers. With one exception all seemed to me unimpressive, if not actually dull, until the slight, boyish figure of Rank appeared beside the speaker's desk. He was the very image of my idea of the scholarly German student and he spoke so quietly, so directly and simply, without circumlocution or apology, that despite the strong German accent I was able to follow his argument and I thought to myself, "Here is a man one could trust."[7]

Jessie Taft (1882–1960) was one of the few women to obtain her doctorate at the University of Chicago before the war, going on to a distinguished career in mental hygiene and social work education. She was first Rank's patient, then his student, his colleague, and, finally, his biographer. She wrote of him, "For the second time in my life I had met genius" (the first was proba-

bly George Herbert Mead). Taft had no idea of any conflict between Rank and Freud or Rank and his "brothers" in the Committee until much later.

Rank's birth trauma lecture, a brilliant condensation in English of a complicated theory, appeared in July 1924 in *Psychoanalytic Review*, just one month after its delivery to the APA.
In the paper, Rank credits Freud with two seminal ideas: the
primacy of birth anxiety, and the usefulness of setting a termination date in analysis. Freud had done so, and particularly recommended it with obsessive-compulsive patients like his "Wolf
Man." Rank discovered that once an end date was set, the patient
experienced reactions "which could be conceived only as a reproduction of the separation from the first original libido object,
namely, the mother. That is, the patient attempts to repeat in
a quite obtrusive way the process of birth." The birth trauma,
Rank said, was not recognized earlier "because it apparently
suffered a much stronger repression even, than the manifestations of infantile sexuality." The parallels to Freud's style of presentation are unusually marked in this paper: Rank was clear
and concrete, and combined boldness with humility.

The impact of Rank's "bombshell," as one person called the
lecture, was based on the impression that he was Freud's emissary. Even after his break with Rank, Freud said that Rank,
unlike Adler, based his new theory on psychoanalysis and attempted to solve analytic problems legitimately. However surprised they may have been, Rank's American audience would
not have had reason to question the authority of Rank's pre-
Oedipal discovery. Even those who recalled how Carl Jung had
used Freud's mantle while purveying his own ideas in America
could distinguish between the charismatic, arrogant Swiss psychiatrist and the assertive but soft-spoken Viennese psychologist.
What they heard in Atlantic City was a new thesis expressed
confidently by a protégé of Freud's with his own independent
ideas, yet still loyal to Freud.

According to Rank, successful therapy consisted of, or at least
resembled, a psychological rebirth. One gives birth to a new
self, with the analyst as midwife. Rank's grounding in philosophy
and history appears in *The Trauma of Birth*, where he traced
the psychological midwife back to ancient Greece. The passage
reveals not only his interest in mentor relationships, but in the
mother as mentor. (The original Mentor, to whom Odysseus en-

trusted his son, was sometimes inhabited by Athena; the classic advisor was therefore both male and female.)

> Nietzsche saw in Socrates "the type of *theoretical human being*" who, in unshakable optimism, believes "that thought, following the clues of causality, reaches even into the deepest abyss of Being, and that thought is able not only to recognize Being but also even to *correct* it." Socrates, as is well known, left no literary work, but was content to influence his pupils and disciples through "mere speech." In this technique, in its aim at self-knowledge, in its intuition that insight leads to virtue, and not least in its whole therapeutic effect, one ought indeed to designate him as the primal father of the analytic technique, which found in Plato its worthy theorist. This comparison contains deep justification, when we remember that Socrates himself likened his dialectic therapy of drawing forth thoughts to the *practice of midwifery*, as he practices it in imitation of his mother, who was a midwife.[8]

Rank's therapeutic optimism contrasted with Freud's increasing pessimism: "Only a few patients are worth the trouble we spend on them," wrote Freud, "so that we are not allowed to have a therapeutic attitude, but we must be glad to have learned something in every case."[9] Like Rank, however, the Americans were not content with mere academic progress, and the therapeutic results of their own analyses and those with their patients left much to be desired. Many analysts wanted to help people. This was pragmatic idealism, since neither doctors nor patients could afford to engage in psychoanalysis unless it worked. To the Americans, Rank seemed a dream come true. With Ferenczi he had developed a brief, active, intensive form of therapy. It emphasized present relationships rather than the past, and actual emotion in addition to intellectual understanding. The focus on the mother, separation, and individuation offset the Freudian emphasis on historical, Oedipal, and instinctual factors. And Rank's method bore Freud's imprimatur despite bitter opposition from Jones and Abraham.

Critics could and did fault Rank's theory by focusing on the physical aspect of birth trauma. For instance, Clarence Oberndorf, President of the American Psychoanalytic Association, disputed the theory because his own birth was so traumatic obstetrically: Forceps crushed his skull, and he lingered near death for months. "Here was a most severe birth trauma, and yet the anxieties that I have experienced since childhood seem to have been less than the average." He recommended follow-up studies of children born after difficult labor. Even Freud eventually suggested collecting obstetrical data—the only time he ever recommended a statistical test of a psychological hypothesis.[10] Efforts at the time to relate brain injury to difficult birth gave Rank some fleeting credibility, but eventually created more problems. His theory boosted humane delivery procedures but also led some zealots to promote Caesarian sections as preventive medicine.

This exaggeration of the physical aspect of birth trauma did not destroy Rank's theory, nor should it have. After these attacks began, Rank clearly emphasized the *psychological* trauma of separation from the mother. This was not as great a change as that made by Freud in his sexual theory of neurosis. At first Freud believed that his patients' stories of childhood sexual trauma related to actual events. Later, he came to the conclusion that the patients were expressing fantasies based on unconscious wishes. Similarly, Rank shifted his focus away from the physical aspect to the psychological, which had been his goal from the start. Skeptics carped at Rank's biological assumptions, while supporters valued his psychodynamic theory and philosophy, which came without any medical trappings.

The leading New York analysts soon came to Rank for analysis or supervision; he had six calls within ten days. Psychiatrist Abram Kardiner, who had met Rank in Vienna while in analysis with Freud, recalled, "He had a method to cut down neurosis at the main trunk instead of picking at leaves and twigs. We all flocked to him." There was jealousy toward the new celebrity, too. "For a fellow who wore patches on his pants in Vienna he was charging $20 a visit." The New York doctors charged two to five dollars. Rank's phone was ringing not only from patients' calls, but from the stockbroker's.

Rank "got Americanized fast," according to Kardiner, although some of the stories Kardiner told were not accurate. For example, he said that Mrs. Rank was soon riding in a Rolls Royce, and that Freud did not know in advance about the publication of *The Trauma of Birth*. Erroneous statements like these became grist for the rumor mills of the time and thereafter. (Rank did have a Chrysler later, in Paris, and all the Committee members *except* Freud and Ferenczi were unprepared for the new book.)

Though he envied Rank's earning power, Kardiner said that

Rank was "not a swindler" (thus literally rebutting the accusation attributed by Brill to Jones). Kardiner believed that Freud did not want to "excommunicate" Rank, but that Rank "had bigger fish to fry, and no longer cared about Freud." Rank did care, as the unfolding events from 1924 to 1926 (when the final break occurred) make clear, but not enough to stop his own development. Despite his misgivings, Kardiner considered Rank "the most extraordinary catalytic agent that ever hit the psychoanalytic movement."[11]

Meanwhile, Rank taught the Americans much of what is now accepted in psychodynamic psychotherapy if not in psychoanalysis itself. He regarded the mother as the central figure in child rearing, rescuing Jocasta from the narrow role of Oedipal sex object. *"Im gegenteil, die Mutter! On ze contrary, ze mozer!"* Rank the supervisor said, mixing his native German and foreign English. He was countering the Freudian father emphasis. (In the Freud concordance, "father" appears some 4,000 times, "mother" only 3,000.) Along with much of his work, Rank's feminist perspective in psychoanalysis has been submerged, kept out of the mainstream of psychoanalysis, for over half a century.

> It has been noticed, especially in recent times, that our whole mental outlook has given predominance to the man's point of view and has almost entirely neglected the woman's. The clearest example of this one-sidedness both of social and scientific thought is possibly the fact that long and important periods of the development of human culture stood under the sway of the so-called mother right ("discovered" by Bachofen). These periods were under the rule of the woman, and obviously special efforts in overcoming resistances had first to be made in order to accept as facts these periods which had been "repressed" even from the traditions themselves. How far this attitude survives even in psychoanalysts is shown in the fact that, as a rule, we tacitly represent sexual relations only from the man's point of view, ostensibly on account of its simplicity, but if we are more honest, from an insufficient understanding of the woman's sexual life. I hardly think that this attitude is the consequence of a social underestimation of woman, as Alfred Adler thinks, but the reverse. Both are the expression of that primal repression which tries to degrade and to deny woman both socially and intellectually on account of her original connection with the birth trauma.[12]

Rank went far beyond the literal interpretation of the birth trauma theory, out of which traditional psychoanalysts tried to fashion his tombstone. Rank's early emancipation from the masculine dogmatism of psychoanalysis remains more significant today than his overly fanciful explanation of its cause and cure. He wanted to "reinstate the high estimation of woman" that was repressed along with the primal memory of the birth trauma, "and we can do this by freeing her from the weight of the curse on her genitals." Oedipal castration, the primal Freudian menace, was every little boy's cautionary tale, which ended unhappily as the female genital! Rank did not stop at liberating women from their curse; he pointed out "a valid, although intensely repressed, masculine counterpart to the girl's envy of the penis . . . the boy's unconscious wish to be able to bear children through the anus."[13] Eventually Rank found a better way to express himself on male-female differences in creativity.

Since Rank left very little written case material, we must rely on reports of his former patients and students for the details, color, and feeling of his therapeutic approach. Fortunately there are enough such reports, varied in content and circumstance, to construct a balanced, realistic portrait. Dr. Clara Thompson (1893–1958), an independent psychoanalyst and a teacher and writer, was the American closest to Sandor Ferenczi. She experienced and explicated the technique developed by Ferenczi and Rank after 1920. At that time most analysts rigidly followed Freudian ideas, delving deeply into the patient's past to explain a feeling or symptom. With this approach, here-and-now feelings toward the analyst were studied purely as transference manifestations. It was as if the driver of an automobile focused mostly on the rear-view mirror. Analysis was geared to time past, the road already traveled; insight meant finding historical connections, which then gained scientific status as causal explanation. Despite wondrous achievements in explaining dreams and other expressions of the unconscious, analysts and their patients remained rather unhappy with the results. Insight was not enough.

Based on Rank's concept of analysis—and giving due credit to him—Clara Thompson put forth the reason for frequent analytic failure, stating it perhaps more vividly than Rank ever did in print. Having discussed the tendency to refer any statement about the analyst back to the patient's father, or another childhood figure, she noted that this drew the attention of both partners in the dialogue away from their actual relationship.

Rank was the first to point out that in doing this the patient was led away from the living present, the area of real feeling. As he put it, it is always easier to talk about the past because it is not present. He and Ferenczi stressed, for the first time, that not every attitude toward the analyst is transferred from the past, that there is some reaction to the analyst in his own right, and that it is actually anxiety-relieving and, therefore, stops the progress of analysis, to point out to the patient, "You do not really feel this way about me but about your father, etc." Thus, if the patient finally gets the courage to tell the analyst he looks like a pig, the whole issue may be conveniently buried by referring it to the past, saying, "That must be what you thought of your father." Two things may happen as a result—the analyst does not have to face the fact that he does look like a pig and the patient feels, "I got safely out of that one," but he does not feel more secure thereby because he knows he really meant the analyst and not his father. From that day on he is likely to assume that the analyst's feelings have to be protected. Realizing this, Rank and Ferenczi discovered the importance of the picture of the analyst in his own right—thus transference became more precisely defined as only the irrational attitudes felt and expressed toward the analyst.[14]

Thus Rank and Ferenczi were forerunners of the interpersonal psychiatry developed by Harry Stack Sullivan, whom Thompson analyzed while she was working with Ferenczi. Unfortunately, Ferenczi broke with Rank in order to stay with Freud, from whom he ultimately separated anyway over differences of technique. Freud concluded that Ferenczi had inordinate therapeutic zeal. And Jones consigned him with Rank to the psychotic category.

Clara Thompson's example of the analyst repulsing the patient expresses the negative side of the transference problem. Positive transference is a more common occurrence, and no less difficult. It goes back historically to Anna O. and her wish to have a baby with Dr. Breuer. Freud recognized this love as an artifact of the therapy situation, a sexualized wish for the father, and thus was not alarmed as was Breuer by Anna O's desire. Freud's theory of transference allowed him to accept the love without seeing it as personal. He saw Anna O's wish as a motivating factor that provided the key to analytic study. Without detracting from Freud's contribution, we may say that he was not the first to observe the feelings that he explained as transference. The great English physician Thomas Sydenham

(1624–1689), probably the first to define hysteria as a mental disorder, observed that men as well as women could be afflicted. "All is caprice," he wrote; "they love without measure those whom they will soon hate without reason."

Freud made sense of that caprice with his discovery of transference. Then Rank took both theory and therapy a step further. He argued that there is more to be done with transference than explaining the past. He believed that the transference should be encountered and lived out in the therapeutic relationship, not always displaced somewhere else. To some extent the love and hate must be taken personally by the therapist. In so doing, therapists confront their own needs and wishes (not to mention their wills—Rank comes to that later). Therapists have to reckon with strong affect, not deny its pertinence, its validity in the present, and its effect upon them as human beings. And according to Rank that is possible and necessary to do (though there is no precise formula) within the bounds of professional demeanor.

FREUD AND RANK: GROWING APART

Early in May, Freud had written Abraham that he was moving away from Rank's birth trauma theory. "I believe it will *fall flat* if it is not criticized too sharply, and Rank, whom I value because of his gifts, his great service to our cause, and also for personal reasons, will have learned a valuable lesson."[15] Thus Freud gave his blessing to Rank's trans-Atlantic voyage, a mission on behalf of psychoanalysis which satisfied both men, though not most of the Committee. Furthermore, Freud feared he might die before his foster son returned. As with Jung fifteen years before, Freud depended heavily on frequent letters from the traveler. They were, it turned out, too few to suit the older man.

Sandor Ferenczi wrote to Otto to inform his friend about developments since the Salzburg Congress. "Everyone, including the Viennese, seemed offended because you left before the end of the Congress. At the gala dinner the sarcastic Hitschmann took the liberty of making some satirical remarks in a humorous speech about the 'hero' Otto who, he hopes, will now be rescued from the waters and so get over the trauma of birth." Ferenczi considered Jones's presidental address to be a virtual "funeral oration for the Professor, very tactless." In closing, Jones praised Freud and Abraham together, whereupon Abraham, the new President, toasted Freud and Jones. "Very well pre-arranged," Sandor told Otto, who could not have agreed more. Abraham extended the olive branch to Ferenczi, but pointed to errors of form and fact in Rank's latest book; he also tried to exert influence on the journals which Rank co-edited with Ferenczi and Sachs.[16]

Otto's first letter to Sandor delighted the Hungarian with an invitation to come to New York. Rank's success was overwhelming, and he had clients to spare. Ferenczi began to shut down his practice in anticipation of a fall departure from Budapest with his wife. He asked Rank for help with visas and travel plans. Rank was due back in Vienna in October, so perhaps the plan was a tandem arrangement for the two Europeans.

Meanwhile, Trigant Burrow (1875–1950), a prominent American psychiatrist, wrote to Freud in July with strong misgivings about certain ideas, "particularly coming from a psychoanalyst of Dr. Rank's reputation and experience." Surprised at Rank's suggesting a defined ending to analysis, Burrow had asked him about Freud's attitude toward the practice. Rank had indicated that Freud was not opposed to it and intended to try it himself. The incredulous Burrow wanted to confirm this. To Burrow the innovation by "Dr. Rank and his school" was "just another feature of an increasing program for trimming the method of psychoanalysis to the public whim."[17]

Freud promptly answered Burrow's four-page letter with little more than a paragraph.

> *I have read your letter with interest, and I believe you have developed concerns which fortunately are not justified. One cannot speak of the new method of psychoanalysis developed by Dr. Rank, and of his school. There is no similarity between this occurrence and the action of Dr. Jung. There is merely a modification in technique which can certainly be tried out. It promises a shortening of the analysis. Whether this will be the case, experience will show. I am not taking part in this modification, but am not inimical toward it. But I shall wait and see what the experience will teach us. Dr. Rank stands too close to me for me to expect that he would go the way of others before him.*[18]

This moderate reply was confirmed in Freud's next letter to Rank. He put Burrow down as a sometime Jungian and an "incurable fool":

> *But the episode in itself has moved me deeply. In the months since our separation I am even further from agreeing with your innovations, I have seen nothing in two of my cases that have been completed that confirms your views and generally nothing that I did not know before; the final birth fantasy seems to me still to be the child that one gives, analytically, to the father. I am often much concerned about you. The exclusion of the father in your theory seems to reveal too much the result of personal influences in your life which I think I recognize, and my suspicion grows that you would not have written this book had you gone through an analysis yourself. Therefore I beg of you not to become fixed but to leave open a way back.*[19]

Of course, Freud was referring to Rank's unhappy childhood with the father he virtually disowned. The letter ominously recommends analysis for Rank, a suggestion Freud had angrily opposed when Jones brought it up less than two years earlier. Rank pondered and rewrote his reply three times; four versions of his letter were found among his papers. It crackles with indignation but is not without good will. Having hoped to wait until they could talk in person, Rank now saw a need to confront the issues without delay.

> *The fact is that I have undergone the same experiences as you: I have found in all my work here, which is many-sided and intensive, day by day and hour by hour, nothing but confirmations and even additions to my point of view, which, moreover, has been confirmed here too from different sides. By chance I have had an opportunity to see again in just these last few days how the fantasy of giving a child to the father cannot be resolved analytically and put to use therapeutically except by leading back to the mother and one's own birth.*
>
> *For the rest I cannot understand why you lay so much emphasis on the final birth theory, which therapeutically and theoretically is not nearly so important as the basic concept that the transference libido is a purely maternal one and that the anxiety basic to all symptoms was originally tied to the maternal genital and was transferred to the father only secondarily. If you interpret the phenomenon of transference starting from the father, in analysis with men you get homosexual fixa-*

tion, with women heterosexual fixation; that is really the case with all the patients who come to me from other analysts. The analysts who are among these patients feel this subjectively and objectively; subjectively since they lost nothing of their neuroses, objectively since with this technique they could not cure their own patients. And that is not the fault of the analysts here, who are no better or worse than Europeans, but the fault is in method and technique. When analysts saw they could work more easily with my modifications and get better results—with their patients as well as in their own analyses—they praised me like a savior. I am not so blind as not to subtract a good part of these successes as complex-conditioned, but what remains is a bit of truth and reality which one cannot remove from this world by closing one's eyes.

I have the strong impression that you will not or cannot see certain things, because sometimes your objections sound as if you had not read or heard what I really said. (I remind you that I corrected an imputation by you to me and Ferenczi of something we never said; it was just the opposite.) Again now you say that I have excluded the father; of course that is not the case, and cannot be; it would be nonsense. I simply tried to give him the correct place. You appear to bring in the personal relation between us, where it does not belong. In this connection it gave me the distinct impression that you were saying I would never have taken this viewpoint had I been analyzed. This may be true. The only question is, whether that would not have been very regrettable. After all that I have seen of analyzed analysts, I can only call it fortunate. For the rest, you know as well as I do, first, the accusation that an insight is derived from a complex means very little in general, and second, it says nothing of the value or truth of the insight. All the less, since psychoanalysis has shown that the greatest achievements themselves result from complexes and their overcoming.

While writing this I feel painfully that through scientific difference, which one would think could be discussed seriously, dissonance has come into our personal relationship. To some degree it may be inevitable in all human relationships. Again I gather from your letter that your personal feelings toward me could still be the same old ones. All the more deeply do I regret that objectively you do me so little justice. For instance, I am convinced that you have an absolutely wrong idea about how I use psychoanalytic technique. Actually I have taken nothing away from it, I have only added something which I truly

think is very important, and which others already consider es-
sential for the understanding of their cases and their therapeutic
handling. I don't know how far I can still hope to show you
what I can do with cases. At any rate, it is more and better
than when you spoke very highly of my therapeutic achieve-
ments.

I don't know either how much your judgment or prejudice
against my position has been influenced by noisy ranters who
from time to time feel the irresistible urge to set themselves
up as saviors of the psychoanalytic movement or your person,
without seeing that they only give full rein to their childish
jealousy. In the same way the Berlin plans and plots I hear
about seem so foolish and so unworthy of a scientific movement
that I hope you likewise will have little use for them. I wonder
what is to be gained by it in the end. If they want to remove
me from my official positions, to which, until now, I have been
tied not by ambition but by duty, care, and toil, they can do
so without any backstairs politics, should you think it desirable.
If they want to refute my point of view, again there is no need
for plotting of intrigues. The more light is thrown on them
the more agreeable to me, for the more obvious will be the
abysmal ignorance of people like Abraham. Do you really be-
lieve, Dear Professor, that an argument by a man like Abraham
will impress me, when I am in doubt of your judgment in this
matter?

But I think that for these people intrigue itself is more
important than reaching certain goals. This is exactly the point
where I leave the game if the cards are not put on the table
on both sides. One cannot expect me to let myself in for a
repeat of concessions and compromises after my experience with
the ex-Committee, allegedly in the interest of the psychoanalytic
movement, really in the personal interest of the participants,
who know very well how easily you can burn your fingers at
the pleasant spectacle of an auto-da-fé. Perhaps you will tell
me that I am mistaken, that on the contrary Abraham is ready
for peace. That is just the hypocrisy against which I defend
myself, that one allegedly makes sacrifices that serve no one,
but that ruin the movement for which they have allegedly been
made. Let us not forget that the psychoanalytic movement as
such is a fiction but men who make a movement are no fiction,
and for those who are now eager to work at a psychoanalytic
movement I confess, I have no liking. [20]

The letter ends with the recognition that it represents a "last
hope" in a personally painful situation. Rank sends best wishes

for Freud's health, regards to the family, and signs "Your devoted Rank." In light of the available letters of Jones, Abraham, and Freud, Rank seems to have grasped the situation accurately and responded with an eloquent mixture of emotion and restraint.

Rank's letter crossed in the mail with one from Freud urging resolution of their differences and patience with colleagues, and containing the assurance that even Rank's critics were impressed and stimulated by his ideas. "I know you are not lacking acclaim for your innovation, but consider how few are able to judge and how strong the desire is in most of them to get away from the Oedipus wherever a path seems to open."[21] Not only had Rank lived with the Oedipus theory for nearly two decades, but he was Freud's in-house expert on mythology and had authored the grandest survey ever made of the incest theme in literature and myth; he could only have felt patronized by Freud's warning.

Furthermore, Freud neglected an important theme in the Oedipus story: Laius, father of Oedipus, set out to kill his infant son because the oracle foretold the double crime of patricide and incest. The infant was guiltless, the father selfish. As Rank and others have pointed out, the story illustrates the problem of hostility toward the young on the part of parents, who see their own displacement and mortality in the consciousness of creating the next generation. This very issue now faced Freud: Could he allow his spiritual son to live, or did he fear the death of his own work? Freud so identified himself with Oedipus that Rank's elevation of the mother to the primary family role seemed to abolish (in Freudian terms, castrate) the father.

Two days later Freud received Rank's angry, anguished letter and immediately replied. He wondered whether Rank meant "to break with us and our cause after an intimacy and collaboration of more than 15 years and to justify thus the calumny which infuriated you so much." Freud patiently argued again the differences in theory, allowing room for disagreement. If Rank could not accept his primordial horde idea, or his recent separation of ego and id, Freud said, "Do you really believe I would not have invited you for meals or would have excluded you from my circle? True, you were always very reserved in taking a critical stand, probably too much so. And now you seem shattered and offended that I refuse your trauma of birth." Freud reproached Rank for insulting Abraham and continued, "An evil demon makes you say: This psychoanalytic movement is a fiction, and puts in your mouth the very words of the enemy. An abstract thing can be real too."[22]

In Ibsen's play *The Wild Duck,* a narcissistic father allows his young daughter to sacrifice herself for him. Now Freud gave Rank cause to feel again the adolescent indignation aroused by that play. Freud would sooner sacrifice Rank than find any fault with himself.

> *Had my illness progressed further it would have saved you a decision, certainly not an easy one. Since it seems I have to be prepared to go on living, I am faced with a situation which a short time ago I would have rejected as unthinkable. Especially painful, because I find the reason for this loss so insufficient; hardly a comfort that I cannot discover my own share of the guilt. My feelings toward you have not been shaken by anything. I cannot, as yet, give up hope that you will return to a better knowledge of yourself.*[23]

In this paragraph Freud reveals sadness, love, anger, and self-pity. But his love depended on Rank's changing. Freud could not be a parent who allowed a child full independence. He could not trust years of paternal guidance to set a course without having to control it forever. It must have hurt Rank deeply to read that Freud found "insufficient reason" for the difficult situation. In so saying, Freud denied Rank's individuality and reduced their difference to a transference neurosis. Freud turned away coldly now from Rank's painfully articulated argument after having celebrated its creation—Rank's psychological birth—only months before. To this injury Freud added insult by saying he found no fault on his own side. Pleading innocent, he left Rank very little room to maneuver.

In 1924, these two great psychologists and confidants struggled to find a relationship of mutual respect with equality where before there had been fealty. Both men were sad, stubborn, and hurt. At the same time, Rank had bad news for Ferenczi, his best friend: Prospects in New York were no longer good. Patients who, someone joked, had lined up on Broadway in droves had virtually disappeared. Analysts were competing with each other. Rank warned Ferenczi, "You would be dependent on the others who are themselves hungry fish and live off the scraps of the big neurologists and psychiatrists." Rank viewed his own success as unique, not to be repeated even by himself. The analysts, his main clientele, made sacrifices to come to him.

"Naturally, they would also like to get rid of me soon, after they have learned all they can, and that leaves little hope that they would eagerly receive another stranger." Brill expressed outright jealousy at the prospect of Ferenczi's coming, Rank told his friend. He went on:

Actually, I have saved psychoanalysis here, perhaps the life of the whole international movement. The analysts here were for the most part uncured and dissatisfied with Professor's analysis; as they themselves and the whole world said, they came back even worse. Most of the important psychiatrists were more favorable toward psychoanalysis than is the case anywhere in Europe, but they saw these analysts with their fixation on Freud in love and hate, and no longer sent them patients because they could not see a single success. That was not the fault of the analysts, who simply repeated what Freud had done with them, namely, to understand in the transference a manifestation of libido toward the father, whereby resulted a homosexual fixation on the analyst in male patients, a heterosexual fixation in female patients. Just as they say there are no virgins in Paris, so in New York there are no patients (analyst or not) without a previous analysis or several. . . .

I have restored their confidence in themselves and in analysis, by analyzing them and showing them how one should analyze. They are highly satisfied with both, so satisfied that they believe they do not need me any more. . . . One has to wait and see what fruits my work here will bear, and it is not impossible that later on one or both of us can return.

In the meantime . . . by chance I heard that they have various plans in Berlin to neutralize both of us. The leader of the movement is, of course, A., who will come to see Professor this month, and your old enemy Rado, who seemingly has taken over the part of your antagonist. I don't know whether you are aware of these intrigues and keep them secret in order not to disturb me. I can only tell you that all this leaves me cold and that I have been prepared for a long time to use the formula of the Saxon King, which Professor suggested to me: Finish your dirty business by yourselves. In any case I shall not participate in politics any more but neither will I suffer them to play politics with me; I am really tired of the whole thing and find it repulsive. [24]

Meanwhile Freud had remonstrated with Ferenczi for having gotten so involved with Rank's rebelliousness. Writing to Ferenczi, Freud compared Rank to Adler but forecast a less successful outcome for Rank if he made himself independent, "since his theory contravenes the common sense of the laity, who had been flattered by Adler's striving for power." By September Freud had received another chilly letter from Rank which led him to accuse his former protégé of playing a role for years in order to embezzle from those who trust him. "I still find it hard to believe that Jones's suspicions of him should have been so right."[25] In late September Ferenczi renounced Rank, under pressure from Freud and persuaded by Rank's intemperate stance.

AMBIVALENCE

When Rank returned to Vienna in October, he had a long conference with Freud, in which he told him that his behavior resulted from Abraham's provocations. Rank seemed confused (Freud informed Eitingon); he thought Freud wanted to drop him and explained that he felt he had to think of supporting himself elsewhere. Rank announced his intention to return to America for another six months, a plan which was incompatible with his role as editor and publisher in Vienna.

Freud asked Rank to meet on November 1 with him, Ferenczi, and Eitingon. That meeting went badly. "As you see," Freud wrote Jones, "an open break has been averted. Rank himself had not intended one, and a scandal would not be in our interest either. But all intimate relations with him are at an end. . . . Not only I, but the two others present at the interview found it very hard to regard him as honest and to believe his statements."[26]

On November 19, Rank came to say good-bye to Freud for perhaps the last time. Freud attributed his own calmness to age, to his feeling that the relationship had been "amortized" over fifteen years, and because he found himself blameless in the matter.[27]

Lou Andreas-Salomé heard about the situation from Eitingon and wrote Freud about Rank: "What on earth has come over this bird of ill omen that he has given up what was the most precious thing in his life, namely, your trust in him? How can he imagine that he can replace that basis of his existence with his 'idea,' even if there had been ten ideas instead of one? Where can one find a fibre of his being whose roots did not draw their sustenance from you and whose deepest ramifications do not lie within you?"[28]

The answers to her questions are contained in the mixture of enthusiasm and pain expressed in Rank's own words to Freud and Ferenczi. Rank chose not to dismiss Freud but to grow beyond the limits of the dependency which he had admittedly needed and enjoyed, but also paid for, up to this time.

Freud promptly offered his interpretation of Rank's actions to Lou: Rank felt his livelihood was threatened by Freud's illness and thought of America as a place to get started on his own. "It is really a case of the rat leaving the sinking ship. As his behavior shows, it cannot have been easy for him. He goes around with a terribly bad conscience, makes a hangdog impression, and looks extremely unhappy." Freud analyzed the problem as a father complex, finally putting Rank down as yielding to the "temptation to make analytic discoveries, to which every non-analyzed beginner—and that is what he was—is exposed." Freud, who had so highly praised Rank as therapist and theorist, now brutally dismissed him. "He cannot yet feel secure himself, for he did his best not to break off his contacts here. . . . But in this he did not succeed."[29]

When he returned from America Rank had told Beata that he planned to go back in a month or so. Beata was aware of some of the problems of the Committee and had even had some conversations with Freud in the hope that she could ease the conflict. She was not happy about Otto's plan, having seen him so little since April, but dutifully took him to the train station when the time came. To her amazement, he appeared back at home shortly, having changed his mind! Then, after another month or so, Rank departed once again; this time—in late November—he reached Paris, only to turn back again. Talking about this crisis in her husband's life thirty years later, Beata Rank became quite upset when asked whether Otto had had a depression: "I couldn't tell you now! I hate to speak about it. I really don't know. Oh, certainly he was in conflict. I saw he couldn't make himself go away. He wanted to and he couldn't. That's probably as close as I can bring it out. That he couldn't make himself go. And this was the time he went to the Professor and told him about his conflict. And the Professor saw him." Mrs. Rank's interviewer (Dr. Kurt Eissler) tried to determine whether Otto experienced more difficulty from leaving her or Freud. Distressed, she could only reply, "From both, probably."[30]

There are many rumors as to what happened to Rank in Paris. Ernest Jones claims that Rank suffered a severe depression; he felt Rank had nonetheless retained clear insight into his condition. Back in Vienna, Rank began seeing Freud on a daily basis beginning the second week in December. Freud, who suited himself when it came to keeping confidences, discussed Rank's case in letters to Abraham, Jones, Eitingon, Ferenczi, Joan Riviere, Marie Bonaparte, and probably others. Freud's message was that Rank had acted out the birth trauma neurosis. Rank had revealed to him an unconscious wish to be born full-grown from the head of his father, like Athena from Zeus. According to Rank (wrote Freud), Freud's cancer had proved to be too much to bear for the prodigal son. Obsessed with financial worries, Rank moved so hastily toward an independent career that he stumbled off the path of psychoanalytic discipline. Finally contrite, Rank wanted to go back to America to undo the damage he had caused. Freud thought that would be difficult, but his mistrust of Rank had disappeared. Freud decided that Rank had achieved a cure through living, which only needed confirmation in a few analytic sessions.[31]

Would the others accept it? Rank wrote the Committee brothers as if on bended knee.

> *Vienna, 20 December 1924*
>
> *Dear Friends!*
>
> *After what lately has happened to me and because of me, I feel the need to report to you, direct or indirect participants, a change which has taken place in me and to me and which—I hope—justifies my addressing you in the old form, as former mutual friends and colleagues, with the intention first to explain my conduct and, insofar as one or another of you was personally vexed by it, to apologize and finally make amends.*
>
> *Not until recent events in Vienna, which you likely know about, has my attitude and conduct toward Professor become clear to me. Certain things evidently had to happen first for me to realize that my emotional reactions against Professor and you, in that you represented brothers close to him, stemmed from unconscious conflicts, for which I can only now account to myself and to you, in this way having overcome them.*

 Suddenly I found myself again, leaving behind me a condition which I now understand as neurotic, and have come to recognize in Professor's life-threatening illness the trauma that precipitated the whole crisis and, furthermore, the type and mechanism of my reaction to it in terms of my personal childhood and family history—the Oedipus and brother complex. I thus had to work out conflicts in reality which I could probably have been spared had I been analyzed before, but which I think I have overcome through this painful life experience.

 From analytic interviews with Professor in which I could explain my reactions in detail from emotional attitudes, I gained the hope that I succeeded primarily in clearing up the personal relationship, since Professor found my explanations satisfactory and forgave me personally. Later there will be time for discussion, explanation and rapprochement in the scientific realm, where I can look at things more objectively, having removed my emotional resistance, and so make up for everything as much as possible.

 But even before this can happen I would like to ask each one of you to understand my emotional statements against him to have been caused by that condition and to pardon them as reactions not meant personally. Let me emphasize as a mitigating factor that I never uttered these things beyond our intimate circle, but only in Committee letters and meetings and in two letters to Professor from America last summer.

 Mainly I feel obliged to satisfy Abraham, whose critical remarks I have doubtless on occasion taken willingly as causes for stronger reactions, and whose role with Professor as my accuser I reacted to violently, due to my brother complex. I can only hope, dear Abraham, that my painfully won insight into this whole matter and my sincere regret will make it possible for you to forgive and forget the wrong which came to you from my state of mind.

 As to Jones, I probably failed him likewise from the same attitude, but I believe he gave me more emotional cause. Nonetheless I also beg you, dear Jones, to excuse the personal wrong I have committed, and I can only hope that you can move enough beyond present resistance to recognize and appreciate the sincerity of my regret.

 With Sachs our old and intimate friendship, which after all goes back before the Committee was formed, fortunately prevented your being in the brother lineup too, dear Hanns. But if unintentionally you should have been hit anyway, it would be as a twin brother, by something aimed more at myself,

*just as perhaps this motive of self-punishment also affected the
older brothers.*

*To Ferenczi and Eitingon, who hold a special place for
me, I wrote separately for that reason, though in the same vein.
For to the very end they offered me their friendly support here
in Vienna, to rescue me, as it were, though I could not understand and accept it.*

*It would make me happy to learn that my explanations
have met with the same analytic understanding from you as
from Professor, and also that they give you satisfaction which—
I hope—can form the basis for resuming our working group
in a not too distant future.*[32]

The letter does not lack firmness of purpose, but the enthusiastic, confident, angry Rank of the New York period has changed
into a pleading miscreant. Did Rank suffer a breakdown? Could
he have feigned a collapse? Jessie Taft found it "inconceivable
to those of us who knew him in the years of his maturity" that
Rank could so humble himself to the Committee.[33] She did not
say whether she thought he could have dissembled. Such a gesture might well have won over the aging Freud, considering
his emotional investment and great need; furthermore, Rank
was moved not only by self-interest but also by real anguish
and guilt, if not quite to the degree he professed. Either Rank
yielded to fear, or he crafted a defense for himself.

Several things suggest that Rank's contrite submission was
at least partly an act. His attempt to maintain professional ties
in Vienna had apparently failed. Brill's recent letter about Rank's
apostasy in New York threatened his new base there. Anchored
for years in the business and politics of psychoanalysis, Rank
knew he faced ruin in that arena if he broke with Freud. But
his anger at Jones and Abraham—and also Freud—could not
easily be overcome. Ferenczi, when pressed, also cut him off,
so Rank faced personal as well as professional isolation if he
did not recant. Finally, the "insight" about his Oedipus and
brother complex sounds wholly out of character for the mature
Rank.

In other instances Rank, for the sake of expedience, could
be chameleonic. At age 25, to expedite the name change from
Rosenfeld to Rank, he became a Catholic; he converted back
to Judaism to be married at 34. Earlier, as a student, Rank once
applied—literally begged—for a state stipend, using the most

flowery, genuflecting prose that any official of Franz Josef's monarchy could ever hope to see. From his diaries we know that Rank had no more respect for the royal-imperial trappings of petty grandiosity than he did for the Catholic church; but he could act! He even considered an acting career in late adolescence while attending the theater almost nightly for four years. And he once wrote in the diary about his tremendous capacity to adapt.

Now in his own life crisis Rank was being asked to sacrifice his independent creativity in both his work and personality. The choice was a matter of psychological life or stillbirth. Freud, at first the proud grandfather who glimpsed his own immortality in *The Trauma of Birth,* had begun to grumble about blemishes and deeper imperfections in the offspring, which no longer resembled its purported ancestor. Rank then had to choose between infanticide and patricide: "Abandon the child or me!" Freud, the father, hailed his own innocence. Was it not the rebellious, unanalyzed son replaying the Oedipal theme? In the letter of apology Rank became puerile and slavish. Insofar as his letter was sincere, Rank seems to have tried to reverse the birth trauma and return to the Freudian womb whence he came. In one fell swoop Rank denied both his theory and his life experience—a sorry comment on "successful" analysis. For he would be the first to say—and did—that there was no going back, no matter how elaborately we want to (as reflected in wish or fantasy) or try (through neurosis).

One might argue that Rank fell prey to what he later called "life fear," and surrendered his will to remain secure even at the price of abject dependency. The episode, then, would have included real emotional stress if not total collapse. Freud's acceptance of Rank's breakdown suggests that it was genuine, but Freud had a blind spot, which Rank could well have taken advantage of. Freud had a long-standing death fear, which was exacerbated not only by the cancer, but also by the strongly felt manhood of his spiritual son. Rank's retreat from independence to submission met Freud's need to remain the invincible, if not immortal, father.

The drama with Rank evokes a powerful Oedipal metaphor which Freud overlooked in his theory (Rank emphasized it later): *The turnover of generations requires that the young supplant the old.* But as a result, children receive a burden of unearned hostility from their fathers (not from their mothers, whose creativity and immortality are more obviously assured through parenthood). Freud, like father Laius, would rather sacrifice the baby—his son or grandson—than face his own ultimate limit, death.

Rank found himself in the position of mother Jocasta; she sacrificed her child to save its father. No sign of amazement or compassion came from Sigmund Freud about this mother's grievous dilemma. Rank's dilemma also compares with that in his favorite play, *The Wild Duck,* where the teenage heroine is told to shoot the duck, her favorite thing, to prove her love for her father. Instead she shoots herself. Even that proved acceptable to her self-justifying father.

Whenever anyone departed from the Freudian version of the Oedipus complex he was accused of being unable to face the awful death wish toward the father, and the sexual wish toward the mother. With the birth trauma theory Otto Rank went back to the mother as the source of life and of anxiety— he saw her not as the primary sex object, but as the primal paradise from which we are expelled, to return only in death. Sex, with its anatomical union, its bliss, its orgastic *petit mort,* represents a partial return.

With all due respect to Freud, we cannot dismiss alternative interpretations of Oedipus as mere escapes by the faint-hearted, by cowards who want to deny infantile sexuality. There is a Rankian interpretation that has to be confronted, too. It was developed during twenty years with Freud; Rank lived it out, and then for a brief time it looked as though he would recant in order to become again the one Freud called "my closest confidant, and my every wish was his command."[34]

TAKING LEAVE

If Freud was ready to forgive and forget after what must be one of the shortest analyses on record, the others on the Committee were not. Letters to Rank from them (Ferenczi's is missing) reek with pungent doubt under a veneer of welcome. While the others skeptically asked for more details of the analysis and change of heart, Jones put his boot to Rank's backside: "But the reason, or one of them, why your hostile feelings were more directed against me than anyone else was mainly because I was the only member of the whole Committee who refused to accept the neurosis, i.e., would not agree to the conditions and inhibitions it wished to impose, and insisted on treating you as normal and responsible for everything."[35]

Rank answered on January 7, 1925, the day he left for America, to say that his apology was a first step and that proof would come in future actions. "In any case I would like to assure you that the friendly manner in which you have accommodated me has greatly helped me to continue on the course taken." Sardonic wit? Rehabilitation, Rank then announced, required another trip to New York to set things right, "to scientifically explain my own standpoint, take back, qualify, or modify what was premature, uncertain or dangerous . . ." With Freud's stamp of approval on Rank's passport, the brothers could only fret helplessly. Of course, they had asked that Rank publish nothing new during the probation period.

In response to some probing questions from Berlin, Rank said that the big change came over him after he left Vienna for Paris, necessitating a heart-to-heart talk with the Professor. This time he found it impossible to leave Freud "in the lurch—as I was able to do the first time, in a manic state, which was to spare me the regret of loss as a direct reaction to his illness." He alleged (quite plausibly) that guilt toward the Professor turned into depression and forced him to return. "When I wanted to go to New York late in November, after the Vienna connections were broken, I wanted to go because of the success I had had there." Rank maintained that he could have capitalized on that American success, but a heavy conscience held him back. He apologized for having to leave for New York so soon that he could not see them, and then raised a shield against more probes: "Spare me touching on details which even under normal conditions one cannot present to a circle of friends but, at best, only to one's analyst. Professor knows the matter in detail of course, and I believe that should completely satisfy you, too."[36]

Even if Rank's behavior was calculated in regard to the brethren, his conduct toward Freud surely reflected real concern for the sick, unhappy old man. Freud needed him, he needed Freud, and the accommodation pleased them both. Rank knew that he had a slim chance of survival in Vienna without Freud: Neither the old guard (Federn, Hitschmann) nor the young (Nunberg, Reich, Anna Freud) would want him in their way. Conversely, in Rank's absence, Freud had no suitable deputy at hand. Rank was head of the Verlag, journal editor, Secretary of the Vienna Psychoanalytic Society, and, until recently, training director. (During Rank's long absence, a wealthy woman had decided to build a training institute in Vienna, which Freud wanted Ferenczi to come and direct; the grant never came, and Helene Deutsch took over the Vienna Institute in October, 1924.)[37]

Amazingly, Freud gave his instant blessing to Rank's return trip and so shielded the youngest from the angry older brothers. How Rank managed this remains something of a mystery. If anyone knew Freud's soft spots, however, it was Rank, and although he could be angry and impatient, he probably never did anything before New York to strain the bond of trust with Freud. To Freud he was more dutiful than ambitious, more circumspect with confidences than Freud himself, and full of managerial ken as well as book learning. Freud, trusting and patient, simply informed Abraham that Rank "wants to go to America to make good the harm he has done there, and he has no illusions about how much greater his difficulties will be than on his first visit."[38]

Freud in fact disliked most Americans, including those he had analyzed. Not for the first time did he prove a poor judge of character when his choice for President of the American Psychoanalytic Association, Horace Frink, turned out badly. Freud vowed this would be his last attempt to save them—they were good only for bringing in money. Jones responded prophetically about the Americans: "In fifty years they will be the arbiters of the world so that it is impossible for us to ignore them."[39] So inadvertently Jones added weight to Rank's argument for returning. Brill, Rank's strongest antagonist, became President of the New York Society in 1925, to hold office for eleven years.

Among those Rank had met on his previous visit were Dr. and Mrs. William Alanson White. Both had brief analyses with him, and White had promptly published the "Birth Trauma" lecture in the *Psychoanalytic Review*. Rank wrote Dr. White, Superintendent of St. Elizabeth's Hospital in Washington, to announce his arrival in New York on January 21.[40] White wanted to bring out in English the Ferenczi-Rank monograph on technique; Caroline Newton, who was analyzed by Rank in Vienna, had done the translation, which was published before long as *The Development of Psychoanalysis*.

Within a month Rank led a series of six seminars for the

New York Society. Detailed minutes were kept of the discussions, which included brief case presentations, queries on Rank's differences with Freud, and theoretical discussion on psychoanalytic treatment of schizoid and borderline patients and narcissism. Among those presenting material or comments were some influential figures in American psychiatry: Glueck, Polon, Stern, Kardiner, Oberndorf, Asch, Blumgart, Feigenbaum, M. Meyer, and Brill. Rank taught with intelligence and vigor.

"The technique of every analyst is active to some extent. The degree of activity must depend upon the personality of the individual analyst. Every analyst must have, to some degree, an individual technique." There was extensive discussion of end setting—the termination of analysis. Again, it was a matter to be handled sensitively on an individual basis and constituted, according to Rank, a technical extension of observations made in classical analysis. Rank discovered its value in part by studying patients' reactions to unplanned breaks in analytic work when he became ill. Rank deemed cases workable if a strong transference could be formed, rather than according to the diagnosis.[41]

Challenges to Rank came mainly from Clarence Oberndorf, who wanted statistics on the results of the birth trauma theory, and from Brill. Rank handled them deftly, finding agreement where he could but not avoiding confrontation. He would point out now and then that his views were not so different from Freud's, but there was no self-effacing apology, no backing up or backing down. Clearly, the Rank who led those seminars totally differed from the seeming obsequious neurotic who had just left Vienna. He was hardly the apologetic wayward son who came to correct the errors of his previous visit. At that time only three (but three powerful) Americans opposed Rank's innovations: Brill, Frink, and Oberndorf. "The others say that one must have one's Father Complex analyzed by Freud and one's Mother Complex by Rank."[42]

The notion that causal knowledge was therapeutic came under attack by Rank. "Analysis is an emotional procedure based on the transference. We do not have to make the unconscious conscious, but we must open communications between the various psychic levels." He opposed the idea that only intellectuals could benefit from analysis.

> Borderline cases, schizoids, etc., present a new problem and require a special technique. Instead of withdrawing libido in these cases,

you give it without explanation. The process is really not psychoanalysis but the utilization of psychoanalytic knowledge in a way similar to the . . . education of the child . . . the transference libido is not analyzed . . . One may even call the process suggestion, but in any event the transference is used intelligently. In a pure psychoanalysis (transference neurosis) the analyst would finish the case and never see the patient again. With borderline cases, as with the child the opposite seems necessary . . . Perhaps "pure psychoanalysis" cannot be used at all. It is really a laboratory product . . . A certain taboo has prevented analysts in Europe from entertaining the idea that analysis might be applied to different cases in various ways. This is due to an identification with Freud. If one takes all sorts and types of cases one must modify the procedure.[43]

This hardly constituted a retraction of heresy. If any analysts present were very unhappy, however, they did not show it; even Brill and Oberndorf were rather tame. Much of what Rank discussed anticipated the work of Harry Stack Sullivan and Frieda Fromm-Reichmann with schizophrenics, Otto Kernberg and Heinz Kohut with borderline and narcissistic patients, and Erik Erikson, Melanie Klein, and Margaret Mahler with children— though Rank did not write about these issues and he saw few such patients.

Rank's initial impact on New York was phenomenal, although as we shall see it later was minimized by political machinations. Fifty years later another leading Freudian analyst, the late Heinz Kohut, introduced some new ideas which seemed to broaden and humanize the analytic process. A Viennese-American, Kohut, like Rank, emerged from orthodox practice perplexed by the return of well-analyzed analysts for more help. He found ways to render it, promulgated controversial new theory, developed a following, fired up the analytic community, and was seen as a heretic by some of the orthodox. Like most Freudians he knew little about Rank, although some Rankian influence might have passed to him via August Aichhorn.[44]

How long Rank intended to stay in the United States is not clear, but he left in mid-February, right after giving his last seminar. Later he told White that he had to leave suddenly because of his brother's death in Vienna. Paul Rosenfeld had surgery while Otto was in New York and died in February at age 43, a bachelor.[45] On the way home Rank lectured at the Sorbonne in Paris on February 22; the printed announcement suggests it had been arranged well in advance.

In early March Freud wrote Abraham: "Rank is back, relating that he did his best to repair the damage done and a letter from Brill confirms it fully. . . . Rank himself is pretty depleted, and hardly capable of scientific work. I have restored my full confidence in him and am glad to say the same on behalf of Ferenczi, who just saw him."[46] (How Rank temporarily assuaged Brill cannot be known until the Freud–Brill letters become available.) The last letter in Rank's files from Freud is a short paragraph written May 2. He regretted Rank's last letter [not available], expected to see him on his birthday (May 6), and reproached him: "You should not withdraw from your friends who so urgently wish your recovery. For my 69th birthday I want a cheerful communication from you announcing the happy end of the conflicts." But Rank was not among the celebrants.

He had recently been replaced as editor of the *Zeitschrift* by Sandor Rado, a psychiatrist critical of him and Ferenczi. Helene Deutsch, who had replaced Rank as Director of the Training Institute in Vienna, had begun her first classes in January. (Rado was working with the Berlin group, and Deutsch had also trained there for a time.) Rank was now listed only as Secretary of the Vienna Psychoanalytic Society along with Siegfried Bernfeld; apparently he never assumed the Presidency when Freud proposed it in 1924.

Despite these losses of official duties, Rank remained busy. He still co-edited *Imago* with Sachs, and at the Verlag he published a fine leather-bound collected works of Freud, who ultimately thought it extravagant: Too few copies were sold while the deficit grew. Although the Committee had asked Rank to publish nothing new of his own, he did not accede: He published his long articles on "Don Juan" and "The Double" as small books, along with a new monograph on the dreams from a young woman's analysis. Under Rank's direction the Verlag also brought out the fourth edition of his first book, *The Artist.* In its new preface, Rank claims priority over Jung in broadening Freud's concept of sexuality with the idea of a primal uniform energy (which later becomes the libido, whence the drives differentiate). The book is filled out with seven essays reprinted from journals and lists his bibliography to date: eight books, plus two with coauthors.

Freud reported that he and Rank were having fruitful analytic sessions together in June and that Rank had come out of his depression. Writing new material again, Rank presented a paper at the Ninth Congress of the IPA in Bad Homburg, Germany, in early September. Called "The Genesis of Genitality," the paper was read at terrific speed, like a Gatling machine gun, according to an American listener. Even Ferenczi could not follow it. Jones recalled that Rank talked excitedly of plans for the future, but was not friendly toward the Committee members. In contrast, Abraham, who presided at the Congress despite poor health, wrote Freud that "Rank tried in a commendable way to come closer to us and we, on our part, have—I believe— helped him in this." Abraham spoke to Rank at length and felt encouraged about their relationship but considered him mentally ill: His rapid speech, unscientific statements, euphoric mood, and imminent return to America meant "a new manic phase. . . . His trip to America is very unwelcome to the Americans and it would have been better for him not to go."[47] Abraham thus directly contradicted Freud's judgment in the matter.

In a Congress photograph Rank stands forward but at one side, appearing robust and confident. Afterwards he left, with Freud's approval, for his third trip to America. Apparently suffering from a lung abscess, Abraham got worse through the fall— as did his relations with Freud, now focused on the question of a movie being produced about psychoanalysis. Abraham's enthusiasm for it was met by coolness from Freud. On November 5, Freud chastised him: "You were certainly right about Jung, and not quite so right about Rank. That matter took a different course and would have passed over more easily if it had not been taken so very seriously in Berlin."[48] Abraham's health failed steadily, and he died on Christmas Day at age 48. In his eulogy, Freud said only one other had contributed as much as Abraham, leaving the curious to wonder which one.[49]

Meanwhile, in September Rank was ensconced in a hotel in Greenwich Village, New York, and was planning a trip to Chicago and Washington, where he would be the guest of Dr. and Mrs. White. He had also arranged to supervise Jelliffe in New York and was obviously on good terms with many Americans, though still not with Brill, who was the favorite of Jones and Abraham. Rank wrote friendly letters to Freud announcing his return to Vienna at Christmastime to resume major duties there.[50]

Return he did, but even with the death of Abraham, there could be no renunciation of his hard won individuality. Anxiety from the birth trauma, Rank taught, serves a purpose. "It prevents the child from going (completely) back to the mother. Were it not for anxiety the individual would perish." Suffice it to say that Rank could not go completely back to Freud. Ferenczi had retrenched to a more orthodox position with an article on the dangers of the active therapy he had promulgated, while Rank's interest grew in regard to theory and therapy as integrally related areas.[51] He began to write on these topics, but the works were not to be published until he left Vienna, and then by Deuticke. The last Rank book to come from his own Verlag was *Sexualität und Schuldgefühl [Sexuality and Guilt]* in 1926.

Beata Rank would not agree to move to America, but she was willing to compromise on Paris. Rank had some good contacts there too, where the French were setting up their own branch of the IPA. He knew Mme. Eugenie Sokolnicka, a member of the Vienna Psychoanalytic Society and André Gide's analyst. Like Rank a nonphysician, she nevertheless analyzed Dr. René Laforgue, the first Freudian psychiatrist in Paris. On the eve of his Sorbonne lecture (February, 1925) Rank had dined with Laforgue, a man ten years his junior, at the home of Princess Marie Bonaparte, a future analyst and financial angel for the psychoanalytic movement. Later Laforgue wrote Freud to refer the Princess for analysis and was surprised to find that Rank had not spoken about her.[52] Thus Rank let outsiders continue to think he was an open book to Freud, while developing and keeping separate compartments in his own life. Perhaps he had hoped to analyze the Princess himself.

On Monday, April 12, 1926, Otto Rank paid his farewell call on Sigmund Freud. Rank would be 42 in ten days, while Freud was nearing 70. They had met at the same address in 1905, when Rank was a precocious youth—a wise but nervous child looking for a father. In one of his better judgments of people, Freud had seen in him a helper with great potential. He cultivated Rank's genius and enjoyed his love. Rank repaid his mentor with ability, energy, and devotion. Now it was time to go. Rank's parting gift was a set of the recently published complete works of Nietzsche, twenty-three volumes bound in white leather.[53] Nietzsche, Rank's pre-Freudian mentor, was someone Freud could not read comfortably in his younger years because of an "excess of interest," as he put it, a denial of his own tendency to philosophize. Rank's gift said, in effect: Here is the mentor of us both! Probably it also expressed Rank's undying wish to be understood better by the most important man in his life.

Freud wrote to Ferenczi about that painful parting visit: "Two facts were unambiguous: that he was unwilling to renounce any part of the theory in which he had deposited his neurosis; and that he took not the slightest step to approach the Society here. I do not belong to those who demand that anyone should be chained and sell themselves forever out of 'gratitude.' He has been given a great deal and accomplished much in return. So quits! On his final visit I saw no occasion for expressing my special tenderness; I was honest and hard. But he is gone now and we have to bury him. Abraham has proved right."[54]

CHAPTER 10

Independence

*A deep conversion invariably involves deep emotional upset.
My feeling about Dr. Rank is that it is this emotional upheaval
that is responsible for his present confusion.*
—Dr. A. A. Brill, President, American Psychoanalytic Association[1]

For his swan song as head of the Verlag, Otto Rank published a collection of five of his papers, *Sexualität und Schuldgefühl* [*Sexuality and Guilt*]. Advertisements in the back of the book list twenty-one titles then available, including such new authors as Geza Roheim, Paul Schilder, Theodor Reik, and August Aichhorn (his *Wayward Youth*). Detailed descriptions of Rank's own books, with review excerpts, are included on several pages. At that time (Spring, 1926), seven of his books were available from the Verlag. The brief introduction to this last, self-produced title showed no sign of a break with Freud, who is complimented for his latest work on ego psychology.

Seemingly the combination of sexuality and guilt feeling belongs to the oldest soul property of mankind, perhaps it even characterizes psychologically the essence of human nature . . . the psychological core problem. Not only does the problem of fear, most important for the understanding of psychoneuroses, flow into it, also it contains the root of the ethical-religious concept of sin, the concept of legal guilt and punishment, in a word the essence of communal social life. . . . The central point into which the groping attempts merged were the (egoistic and narcissistic) *ego strivings* of the individual, who clearly gets into conflict with the supra-individual species bias exactly at the points of biologically preformed sexual development. In solving these unavoidable conflicts the individual has to lose, be it in the final adjustment to the normal sexual goal, reached only through partial waiver of sexual variety, or through attempts to pass the barriers of species and society in the failures we have come to know and understand analytically as perversion, neurosis, and crime.[2]

This passage recalls the argument of Rank's "Perversion and Neurosis" (which is reprinted in his book). But it anticipates a dualism which pervades the rest of his work: the inevitable conflict between individuality and conformity, psychology and biology, likeness and difference. Any implied pessimism is balanced by Rank's enthusiasm for psychological self-creation, what he later called the recognition and exercise of individual will. Here, though, Rank recognized the limits imposed by our physical endowment and our need for community, affirmation of which is the beginning of freedom.

The introduction ends with Rank saying he hopes to advance further toward a solution of these problems in forthcoming essays. He was already at work on two interlocking projects, which Deuticke published between 1926 and 1931. Each had three parts, so six monographs emerged in those years, along with articles, reviews, and two other books: the revised *Incest Motif* (1926) and *Seelenglaube* [*Soul-belief and Psychology*] (1930).

The two projects which unfolded over the next five years were the *Genetic Psychology* and the *Technique*. The latter follows up the work on therapy begun with Ferenczi. The last two of the three parts appeared in English under the title— Rank's choice— *Will Therapy* (1936). The other project was what we now call a genetic ego psychology. In contrast to the Freudian historical-analytic approach, this was a developmental-constructive theory. Only the last part—*Truth and Reality* (1936)—has appeared in English, which may account in part for the widespread ignorance of Rank's pioneering work in the post-Freudian world.

After the Ranks arrived in Paris (in April), they moved twice before finding a permanent residence and office. Their transient status led them to place Helene, seven years old in August, in a Swiss boarding school. In the summer of 1927 the family of three would settle at 9 Rue Louis Boilly (XVI), a beautiful three-story corner building across from the Marmottan Museum, near the Bois de Boulogne and some smaller gardens and parks.

Rank's arrival in Paris coincided with the founding of the French Psychoanalytic Society, with which he apparently had little connection. His name still appeared as co-editor of *Imago* in 1926, but that was the last year he had any official connection with psychoanalysis except for his honorary membership in the American Psychoanalytic Association (from which he was expelled in 1930). Hostile word travels fast; Jones and others spread the news of Rank's defection and "illness." Rank himself did not emphasize his separation from psychoanalysis. He mounted a large portrait of Freud in his Paris office, probably both for sentimental reasons and because it helped his practice. Several of the numerous Americans who came for analysis with him in Paris and New York assumed he was still a leading Freudian.

RANK ON FREUD ON RANK

In response to Rank's birth trauma theory of anxiety, Freud revised his own theory, in his last major theoretical book, *Inhibition, Symptom and Anxiety* (1926). Rank was quick to read and respond to it in the lead article in the January 1927 *Psychoanalytic Review*. Entitled "Psychoanalytic Problems," the essay is part of his work on genetic psychology and constitutes a forthright critique of psychoanalytic theory in relation to therapy. Rank does not hide his major differences with Freud, whose limitations are recognized and accepted along with his great achievements, and he faults analysts in general for their fixation on terminology, while making his own use of concepts refreshingly clear.

Rank redefined "complex" as "the sediment of a definite trauma." Rather than limiting trauma to pathological, accidental events, he used the term to denote "a biologically necessary step of development" which may or may not produce a residual problem. Here Rank anticipated the "critical period" of decades later, especially the epigenetic stages of Erik Erikson (who arrived in Vienna for training soon after Rank left). Rank also emphasized the ego and spoke of personality mechanisms, anticipating Anna Freud's important work.

He also criticized the overextended Oedipus model and castration complex, which Freud admitted had little relevance to women. Psychoanalysis by then had made death anxiety itself an offshoot of castration fear! But one cannot have a theory of neurosis which leaves out half of humanity. Rank again emphasized the mother tie: "Not all authoritative persons or figures . . . have a father significance, not even ultimately. For one patient the mother may have been the first authority, indeed perhaps she was for most human beings."

The prominent placement of Rank's essay in the *Psychoanalytic Review* suggests that Rank's trans-Atlantic connections were good—and also reflects William Alanson White's open-mindedness. He was to serve as President of the American Psychoanalytic Association in 1928, so his continuing endorsement of Rank was important. (A. A. Brill, hostile to Rank, became President of the New York Psychoanalytic Society in 1925 and held the office for eleven years.)

Freud's *Inhibition, Symptom and Anxiety* received an unusual double review—by a staunch Freudian and by Rank—in the American journal *Mental Hygiene.*[3] Adolph Stern, then President of the American Psychoanalytic Association, said the book proved that Freud had not lost any of his incisive powers and was still the best psychoanalytic writer.

Freud had originally considered anxiety a result of repressed libido, an overflow of excitation. His new theory assigns anxiety to the ego as a signal of danger associated with an earlier trauma and the need for defense. But while crediting Rank with good psychoanalytic ideas, Freud criticized his birth trauma emphasis.

No one who read Rank's long 1927 review could dismiss his approach as a simplistic biological theory. That many still did must be attributed to ignorance (Rank's book had not yet appeared in English) or narrow self-interest: The Rank-Freud schism was common knowledge by then, and psychoanalytic politics increasingly required practitioners to take sides.

In this, his only critical review of a book by Freud, Otto Rank debated his old mentor forcefully, if not happily: He preferred to develop ideas "out of the realm of controversy into more constructive fields." There was no disagreement about the source of the birth anxiety idea: It came from a "chance hint thrown out in a footnote" added to Freud's *Interpretation of Dreams* in 1909. Freud was referring to *physiological* anxiety, to which Rank linked "the separation from the mother as a trauma of great *psychological* importance." Although Freud credited Rank with a stimulating "reminder" which brought about this revision of psychoanalytic theory, Rank faulted him for slighting the psychological import of the mother-child separation. In this book, Freud for the first time "does not speak from his own analytic experiences but uses my experiences deductively and critically" to correct his own theory—inconsistently, Rank says.

So he severs "the great connection" which I have "discovered," in his assumption that birth is not experienced subjectively as separation from the mother, "since she is entirely unknown as an object to the completely narcissistic fetus."

. . . Freud rightly emphasizes the fact that in general we know too little about the newly born child and its sensations to be able to draw hard-and-fast conclusions with regard to it. But in spite of isolated child observations and even child analyses, the same thing is largely true for the child in general, in whom too much of the adult, especially adult sexuality, has probably been projected. Freud's warning. . . holds also for his own assertion that the mother does not represent an object for the newly born. We cannot make dogmatic statements as to that; rather, the whole matter amounts to nothing more than a quibble over words. For it is certain that the newborn child loses something as soon as it is born, indeed even as soon as birth begins . . . One might perhaps say that in parturition the ego first finds its object and then loses it again, which possibly explains many peculiarities of our psychical life . . . only on the theory of a reproduction of the birth severance can we explain why the child, when it misses the mother, reacts with anxiety, instead of merely longing for the lost object, as would the adult. . . .

To interpret the longing for the womb as a substitute for coitus, as Freud wishes to, is the very opposite of Ferenczi's theory, which, with its biological deepening of the Jungian concept and its linking on to mine, holds just the reverse—namely, that coitus is a (genital) substitute for the biological longing for the womb.

Freud . . . overlooks the fact that the first danger situation in birth involves a danger to life (death anxiety—birth anxiety), not the loss of the penis. My point was that this physiological anxiety in parturition (independent of the loss of object) undergoes a "psychical anchoring" in relation to the mother and the tendency to return to her. . . . I have merely attempted to place the first appearance of psychical anxiety—of which, even in Freud's opinion, the newborn is capable—in the birth act itself and not in early childhood, where it obviously arises at the loss of the mother, thus referring back to the first separation from her. . . . Analytic observations and experiences have brought me to the belief that in the case of patients under analysis, the libido (wish excitations) as it were covers anxiety—that is, anxiety temporarily disappears because the libido is gratified, not because a change of anxiety into libido has taken place. . . . I have never contended that anxiety in birth arises from the libido; I have maintained that anxiety is not produced from libido at all, although I am of the opinion that even in birth it is connected with loss of object—as I have said, is psychically anchored. . . .

It will be necessary perhaps to reinterpret the anxiety dream [e.g. nightmare], the Freudian explanation of which is based upon the old theory of the conversion of libido into anxiety. It is interesting that Freud does not mention the anxiety dream once in his whole discussion. In the anxiety dream there is certainly no question of an external danger, and yet the anxiety is quantitatively greater than is usually the case in reality. . . .

There are other contradictions in the book, obviously due to the resistances of Freud, who is following out my new line of thought to conclusions that necessitate a radical revision of his own views. . . . he has had to restrict the role of the most important mechanism of his ego psychology—repression—since it can no longer be held as the cause of anxiety, as he formerly assumed, but, on the contrary, is a consequence of anxiety. . . . he reinstates the old concept of defense . . . halfway, in his reluctance to give up his earlier concepts for new ones. For the mechanism of defense is again too general a concept. . . . [in referring to the] "procedure of making a thing as if it had not happened" he avoids using the simpler and more natural terms proposed by others. (For a long time I have used the term *Verleugnung*, "denial.")

If Freud finds it almost embarrassing that "after so much work we yet find difficulties in the concept of the most fundamental relations," is it not possible that this situation may be partly due to a resistance on his part of accepting any idea that originates from others? . . .

Whatever faults *The Trauma of Birth* may have, it certainly has not the fault that has been ascribed to it in analytic circles—that of being too radical. . . . When he states that my book stands on analytic—i.e., Freudian—ground, he is right, insofar as I was still endeavoring to bring my own experiences into harmony with his libido theory. His present change of position justifies this attempt, since he now wants to put my concept on psychoanalytic ground that he himself has already left in further pursuit of my views. In criticizing my presentation, [with its] attempt to save the libido theory, he has been compelled to give up this libido theory, a step that I did not yet trust myself enough to take completely in *The Trauma of Birth.*

Rank's essay has been overlooked not only by orthodox psychoanalysts but by more independent thinkers like John Bowlby, who have had to reinvent some Rankian wheels. Eventually Rank's rejoinder to Freud will take its place as a major document in the history of psychoanalytic psychology. Much of what Rank wrote is now widely accepted, with little if any credit being given him. Thus, few psychotherapists are aware that the idea of denial, one of the most important defense mechanisms, was introduced not by Sigmund or Anna Freud, but by Otto Rank.

The year 1926 brought Alfred Adler to the United States for the first time, and also Ferenczi. Ferenczi's alienation from Rank was complete, as evidenced both by his harsh review of the *Technique* and, even more hurtfully, by what happened when they met by chance in Pennsylvania Station. "He was my best friend," said Rank, "and he refused to speak to me."[4]

RANK AS VIEWED BY PATIENTS

Rank himself was back in New York, at the Hotel Holley on Washington Square, in October 1926. He analyzed patients and lectured weekly at the New York School of Social Work. Jessie Taft was one of those patients. A psychologist who was involved in testing children—a useful but not therapeutic skill—she felt her efforts to treat a few neurotic adults had failed, and they left her feeling guilty and fearful.

> When I finally came to my first hour with Rank, while consciously submissive, afraid, and fully aware of my ignorance of psychoanalysis, my underlying attitude was far from humble. I was, after all, a psychologist. I had some knowledge of myself and my problems. I had achieved a point of view, psychologically. If there was anything in my unconscious in terms of buried memories, I would have to be shown. And so the battle was joined; but I soon found that it was a battle with myself. I was deprived of a foe. It took only two weeks for me to yield to a new kind of relationship, in the experiencing of which the nature of my own therapeutic failures became suddenly clear. No verbal explanation was ever needed; my first experience of taking help for a need that had been denied was enough to give a basis for the years of learning to follow.[5]

Taft, two years older than Rank, was 44 at the time. Having no idea of his split with Freud and the Committee, she attended a Ferenczi seminar and spoke of it freely to Rank, learning of his distress only much later. With trepidation she invited him to Philadelphia, which was "still just discovering and disapproving of Freud." In January, writing from Paris, Rank agreed to come in the fall, since Taft had not only arranged lectures, but also had a sizeable group of analysands for him to see. Taft attended a study group in New York that winter and spring; a group of fifteen or twenty mostly younger psychiatrists gathered to discuss the *Genetic Psychology*, on which Rank had lectured in the fall.

One of those psychiatrists was Marion Kenworthy (1891– 1980). She had been analyzed by Rank and pioneered in the introduction of psychiatry in social work education. Kenworthy had invited Rank to lecture in New York, noting how much she had gained from her contact with him and what he had to offer students: "the broader point of view . . . the fine kind of idealism and the rich scientific and social understanding which you of all people in this field are equipped to give." A few days after writing this, Dr. Kenworthy received a letter from a young Boston psychiatrist, Martin Peck, asking her opinion of Rank. Peck wanted to be analyzed by Rank, but had heard that Ernest Jones considered him "hypomanic" and "discredited." Kenworthy, too, had heard such rumors, which she thought were unfounded. "I have tremendous appreciation of his ability as a sound teacher in analysis," she wrote, advising Peck to sign up without delay.[6] She made it clear that Rank was much in demand despite the efforts of Jones to undermine him.

Another noted American psychiatrist, Harry Stack Sullivan (1892–1949) was critical of Rank while confirming his popularity and importance. Sullivan considered Ferenczi "the genius of the psychoanalytic movement." Urging William Alanson White to invite Ferenczi to Washington, he wrote of "wild and rampant propaganda in New York at present. I am told that the word is all but shrieked from the housetops that 'unless ye shall have been analyzed by Rank ye have no pile of merits.'" Sullivan did not know that White had been briefly analyzed by Rank himself. In reply White observed, "I think these fellows from the other side [European analysts] are in this country to make money." He could not provide a stipend for any of them to travel to Washington.[7]

Drs. George Wilbur and Martin Peck, part of the early Boston psychoanalytic community, underwent analysis with Rank that fall in New York and in Paris in 1927. They and their wives saw Rank over several months, up to five hours weekly. Rank charged $15 per "sitting," the European fee. In those days Freud was charging $20, as Rank himself usually did in America. (He offered a reduced fee to social workers.)

Peck's wife, Wilda, kept a diary of her first thirty-one treatment sessions; this and similar patient reports uniquely illuminate Rank and his work.[8] Since he rarely presented any case material in his writing, they are our only access to the interior of the consulting room. Rank's conversational quality may strike readers as unconventional, but Freud's patients found him to be similarly forthcoming and philosophical.

Mrs. Peck was a reader of Havelock Ellis and was skeptical of the need for monogamy and even of the very emotion of jealousy. Rank told her that jealousy is deeply rooted, that free love risks an increase of syphilis. Evidently Mrs. Peck was an ardent feminist and freethinker; she said her husband was glad that Rank was "conventional" and Freud "such a model husband and father."

"Freud appears to be so," Rank replied. "That is the appearance." [This is the only remark I have encountered by Rank touching on Freud's private life.] When Mrs. Peck expressed a friend's opinion that sexual experimentation leads back to monogamy, Rank said: "Yes, but unfortunately most of us are doing the experimentation after marriage instead of before." She said that women like herself were not responsible under present circumstances because "temperament forced them to be pioneers of a new era." Rank said, "Yes, but don't forget the pioneers are also the victims."

Rank might well have been speaking for himself. According to Peck's diary, Rank told her that "the problem of human relationships is the most important in the world today." When she described being homesick for her daughter, Rank noted that this intimacy of motherhood is denied men—a view in keeping with what he allegedly told Jones during Beata's pregnancy. His summary of the aim of analysis was "freedom from the mother, adjustment to the environment, and discovering of abilities." Mrs. Peck had a hard time getting into the analysis. She brought in dreams. At one point she felt her mind was blank and Rank commented that for some people that is when the analysis really begins. "The patient must go on emotionally. Much of it can't be put in words. [It] can only be explained, if at all, afterwards."

In their twenty-second session Rank pointed out her fear: "fear of loving since it might involve losing." In her diary Mrs. Peck was effusive: "I had originally accepted P.'s [Martin Peck's] estimate of you as the rigid scientist that he was looking for and wanting, not the greater flexible, all-embracing mind. Every idea I have has been not only agreed with, but backed up, and reinforced by your knowledge and authority. Really an emotional experience." She recorded Rank's response: "You seem surprised at my views. I am not the so-called scientific person P. may think I am, but as you see me. . . . Science itself is emotional." Later that day she added this note: "Rank is like a tender watching mother. The thing I am to accept is love. All I haven't had, all I've wanted, flows through Rank, the medium, to me. I accept. I demand it. Like St. Barbara he sits in his tower dispensing heavenly love, and the suitors are converted. To accept love, one must accept risk of pain. . . . Not free love, but loving freely."

She read her "effusion" to Rank and he pointed out that she had a need to justify accepting what she wants; she still felt guilty. When she asked whether patients fall into groups, he said, "No. Each one works out his problem in his own individual fashion. All the analyst can do is watch him do it. It isn't possible to generalize or find types; it would be dangerous to try." Similarly, he said, "I cannot generalize about dreams. Everybody does it differently. Yours are logical because your mind works that way."

In answer to a question about homosexuality, he said it is "a vague term applied to many symptoms. So as to speak, it doesn't exist. It is love for one's self as seen in the persona of another like oneself whom one admires . . . strongly built up on narcissism. It is an ego symptom and not a sex symptom."

"It's a wonder to me with all our complexities that anyone ever achieves happiness," she said. "People like us don't," Rank replied, "We achieve it for a moment, and then we change and change again." They spoke about personality change and stability. According to Rank, mental qualities and needs remain unchanged, while the ego grows and develops, not just in relation to outside circumstances, but within the self. "Analysis attempts to harmonize and adjust this inner change." The person who clings to conventional life, home and family, may be compensating for inner instability with outer stability. And vice versa, she pointed out. "Yes," said Rank, "and an inner stability might need and demand change. It's very subtle."

Paris in the twenties attracted a host of writers and artists, such as Ernest Hemingway, Gertrude Stein, Sinclair Lewis, and Ludwig Lewisohn. George Gershwin arrived there along with Rank in 1926. So did an artist named Myron Chester Nutting (1890–1972). He sought an experience with analysis, not a cure for any problem, in 1927, and recalled it some forty years later in an unpublished memoir.

Rank was reluctant to take him initially, then agreed to a three-month analysis. Sessions were daily at first, then tapered off gradually to weekly, with a final visit some months after the last regular session. Nutting's recollection provides another good description of Rank's therapeutic manner.[9]

> Rank had a beautiful apartment that overlooked the Bois de Boulogne. It had a big window that looked out over the park. He had this huge couch, which was more or less what I expected, and he made me very comfortable there and we started the discussion. . . .
>
> He was a very interesting little man, and one of the most impressive things about him to me was the degree in which he kept himself out of the picture. I used to go into his waiting room, and then he opened the door and peeked around it. He wouldn't enter the waiting room. Then he'd smile and nod, and I'd go in and lie down on the couch. He'd sit just a little bit back of me, out of sight, and I'd look out at this beautiful view of the Bois de Boulogne.

Rank did not engage the client in free association around dreams, but responded immediately. In one dream Nutting kicked a man in a gray suit and said, "Do get the hell out of here!" Rank promptly reminded him that in the last session, on a hot day, Rank had worn a light gray suit for the first time! On the other hand, Rank would sometimes be baffled and admit it.

> Then he'd say, "Well, I t'ink that it means this and this." And he'd say something about it. Then he'd say, "Isn't it? Isn't it?" And sometimes I would be rather dubious because it didn't sound like a very convincing explanation to me; and at other times, it seemed to be extremely obvious and I wondered why I hadn't thought of it myself.

Once Nutting told a dream in which he was taking a walk on some farmland with two other men. In the dream he said, "When the 'tremens' expire, I become owner of this property." Awake, Nutting tried to analyze the strange word, but there was no connection—e.g., to delirium tremens. When Rank heard it he said, "Yes, yes. In three months. *Tres menses.* Three months, Latin!" It meant: When the analysis was over, Nutting would take possession of something important—more of himself.

> I really had great respect for Rank and already admired him for several reasons. One thing was his extraordinary memory; he kept no notes. He would say, "You remember last Wednesday when you told me this or that," and I couldn't. . . . But he would name the date and quote stuff that I had told him, verbatim. So, in many ways, besides being very pleasant to know, he was also one that excited quite a lot of admiration on my part. . . . He was very quiet, but he made these very sharp and penetrating observations.

At times Nutting felt stuck, that he was not getting anywhere. Then one day, coming to his session, he did something remarkable for a mild-mannered person. His little car was bullied out of a parking place by a limousine. Nutting stepped out and, not losing his temper, lectured the chauffeur on driving etiquette. Nutting felt better; ordinarily he let such provocations pass and felt badly. Having told Rank the story, Nutting wanted to know what caused the change. Rank recalled the aggression that emerged in Nutting's dream when he kicked the man (Rank) out.

> And so Rank said, "Well, I will tell you something that you may find rather comforting. I don't understand what happens." He said, "You don't understand, and neither do I." He just simply knew that from experience he could expect that certain things could happen if they were handled rightly and if the person's psyche and personality could be influenced for the better along certain lines. But he wouldn't pretend at all to try to give me a lecture on why it was happening because he said, "I don't know."

Nutting's memoir mentions two other Rank clients of that time, Ramon Guthrie, poet and professor of French at Dartmouth, and Thelma Lewisohn, wife of Ludwig, a man who later became Rank's friend and champion. Although a reasonably productive writer, Guthrie complained to Rank that he would like to have the discipline that his friend Sinclair Lewis had. Rank said, "Well, I will ask you a rhetorical question. I think it is a question you can often ask yourself very profitably—why the hell should you?"

Guthrie never spoke of Rank to friends, but made reference to him in a poem, "Yorick," which is a portrait of Myron Nutting.[10]

> [He] Read Freud, Jung, Adler. Learning that Otto Rank
> lived in Paris, signed up to take a quickie
> in ten sessions. One day halfway through,
> professed finding his faith begin to wane.
> "For instance, what's to keep me from *inventing*
> dreams to tell him? Say, something so absurd
> no one could dream it—like that I owned
> a white elephant that followed me everywhere
> I went . . . couldn't get rid of her because
> I couldn't bear to hurt her feelings?"
> Why not try it on him? I asked. "You mean it?
> He wouldn't see that I was spoofing?
> Well, I suppose I might."
> Next time we met I asked if he had told
> the analyst his dream. "What dream? Oh, that.
> No. When I tried to I found it was so crazy
> I couldn't even remember what it was about."

RANK THE VIRTUOSO

Jessie Taft's invitation to Philadelphia structured Rank's fall, 1927, calendar. It began an affiliation with the University of Pennsylvania School of Social Work that resulted in his most lasting influence and proved to be a continuing base for teaching his philosophy and his clinical approach.

Rank arrived in Philadelphia in mid-October and stayed at the Benjamin Franklin Hotel. He turned down an offer of lodging in Philadelphia from his translator and former patient, Caroline Newton, leaving the matter in Jessie Taft's hands. Taft, formerly his client, now became his colleague and friend. Her respect for Rank's genius was matched by her admiration for his ability to leave behind the doctor-patient relationship. "Never for a moment did he put me back into the role of patient, never did he utilize his knowledge of any innermost make-up to interpret even the most obvious aspects of my behavior . . . He gave freely the reality of what he had to give, but nothing more, even when he had to disappoint unrealistic expectations."[11]

Rank lectured at the Pennsylvania School of Social Work and carried on a busy practice. Two prominent Philadelphia psychiatrists were among those applying to him: Frederick Allen and Edward Strecker. Rank commuted to New York every week for a seminar, the focus of which was the second part of his *Genetic Psychology*: such topics as "Character and the Self," "The Significance of the Love Life," "Social Adaptation and Creativity," and "The Possibilities of Therapy." Taft also attended the New York seminar, where she observed that the members, mostly psychiatrists, "were no different from a group of social work students. They cared only for cases and chiefly their own. If there was ever any discussion of theory on the level of Rank's interests, I cannot remember it. Yet his patient and courteous consideration of every problem brought up in the seminar never failed. If he was bored with our lack of understanding, he did not show it, nor did he try to push the group beyond the level of its real concern."[12]

The seminar members constituted an impressive group of mental health professionals. Many were in leadership roles in child guidance or were active in the National Committee for Mental Hygiene (NCMH) and the American Orthopsychiatric Association; they contributed as adminstrators, teachers, and writer-editors as well as in treating patients. Mabel Moxon, a lay analyst who translated Rank's *Modern Education*, was another participant.[13]

Rank spent several weeks in Paris at Christmastime; in January 1928 he returned to New York. Adding to his exposure in the prestigious *Psychoanalytic Review*, Rank published several articles in *Mental Hygiene*, the journal of the NCMH. Four of these articles appeared in pamphlet form in 1927 as *The Practical Bearing of Psychoanalysis*. Although slightly dated—the papers were based on Rank's lectures of 1924—the booklet gave a boost to his reputation outside psychoanalytic circles. The NCMH, founded by Clifford Beers (*A Mind That Found Itself*, 1908), had as its medical director and journal editor Dr. Frankwood Williams, an enthusiastic Rankian in those years.

Ferenczi fared less well in America, at least according to Jelliffe, who, like White, felt that the Europeans were exploiting the Americans for money. Jelliffe remarked in October that

Rank's reputation was not helped by the fact that he traveled with his secretary—unlike Ferenczi, who brought his wife to America. Jelliffe's adult son had been Rank's patient in 1925.[14]

The identity of the "secretary" to whom Jelliffe refers can only be guessed. Jessie Taft accompanied Rank from Philadelphia to the New York seminar, but as a distinguished psychologist would have been known to Jelliffe. The same would hold for lay analyst Caroline Newton, whose father, A. E. Newton, was a prominent psychologist. Mabel Moxon's relationship with Rank as student and translator extended over several years. He had a secretary when he first came to New York in 1924, and his remarks to Wilda Peck about "experimentation after marriage" seemed to include himself. Rank was accompanied by Beata and Helene on only one of his numerous trans-Atlantic trips.

Jessie Taft and Virginia Robinson (1883–1977), Rank's closest American colleagues, undoubtedly loved him as friends, surely without romantic involvement. These remarkable women, nationally prominent in social work education, met in 1909 in their twenties. Years later, living together in Flourtown, near Philadelphia, they were persuaded to take on a foster child, a seven-year-old boy. This led to the adoption within a year of young Everett Taft, who was joined by a five-year-old girl, Hilda, a year later. Taft and Robinson were not the only female pair to adopt children in those days (the 1920s). Rank, as therapist to both women, knew the whole story and afterwards visited the family on several occasions. Robinson reflected after forty years:

> Good child-placing practice today would not have approved this placement of two children with two professional women but I think we survived this experience without harm to any of us. Grown up now, the boy with a good marriage and three children of his own, the girl with a responsible job as chief dietician in a big hospital, would not repudiate their unorthodox childhood experiences nor did we as adopting parents ever regret our experience in living with children we loved whose problems of growing up became our own to learn from, to help with as best we could.[15]

Beginning on January 14, 1928, Rank launched a series of six lectures on Monday evenings at the New York School of Social Work on East 22nd Street. Admission to the series (called "What is Truth?") was $10. The individual lecture titles resembled chapters from his writing on the two projects begun on leaving Vienna: Will and Coercion, Self and Ideal, Creation and

Guilt, etc. The flyer announces "Otto Rank of Vienna and Paris" and describes the series as "An attempt to present the essential problem of all Psychology and to explain why and where the last solution offered by Psychoanalysis in its various schools fell short." The roster of attendees includes almost 100 names, mostly women and presumably social workers, except for seven psychiatrists from the seminar. Rank had nothing to lose at this point by clarifying his differences with the Freudians; he seemed on his way to attract a following.

On April 19, just before returning to Paris, Rank gave a lecture entitled "Beyond Psychoanalysis" for a large audience at the Boston Society of Psychiatry and Neurology.[16] The paper became the lead article in the January 1929 issue of *Psychoanalytic Review,* reflecting the respect White and Jelliffe had for Rank despite continuing efforts of Jones, Brill, Sullivan, and others to discredit him. The Boston psychoanalytic society was being reestablished in 1928, and three members attending the New York seminar formed a strong Rankian wedge. As in the preceding lectures to predominantly social work audiences, Rank neither hid his criticism of psychoanalysis nor broke with the Freudians. Instead he built upon Freudian doctrine after citing its limitations. If Taft's statement about psychiatrists' limited interest in theory applied in Boston, then Rank's virtuoso presentation there was daring indeed. It is a tour de force, eleven pages of condensed psychology and philosophy. Over fifty years later, it is difficult but rewarding to read.

In it Rank attacked the biological basis of Freud's system, which, he claimed, could provide only a partial psychology. Anxiety, he felt, could not be wholly explained through biology— love even less so—despite Freud's effort to trace both back to the sexual impulse. Psychoanalysis confused genesis (origin) with causality, he argued, thus falling into the error of trying to reduce everything to the individual's past history. It paid too little heed to the present. Rank went on to say: "Freud's great merit was the overthrow of the medical superstition that the psychical is a matter of nerves, which indeed only represent the instrument on which the human emotional life is played. His error was that in place of the medical theory of nerves he wanted to put the biological sex theory, which was supposed to entirely explain everything."

Freud, while dethroning the old medical materialism, failed—Rank said—to establish his biological-causal solution.

That failure—Freud's "unspoken insight"—brought psychology into its own as an irreducible philosophical entity. Man's psychological makeup (in which Rank emphasizes the ethical component) must be seen independently of the biological. Indeed, the dynamic coexistence of psyche and soma is the basis of all human conflict. In Freud's struggle to derive the psyche from (and subordinate it to) biological drives, he misapplied biological concepts. Freud, Rank said, used myths to name his concepts, and thought he had explained the myths. But to "explain" the Oedipus myth as a product of the biological parent-child relationship is as unsatisfactory as "understanding" infantile development by giving it a mythical nomenclature. Psychological processes can be understood only in psychological—which includes mythical—terms. Freud himself, wrote Rank, "is a myth creator in the grandest style, in Plato's sense a real philosopher."

According to Rank, Freud's search for the biological basis of the psyche although called analysis was mainly *interpretation.* Where the psyche or soul is concerned, interpretation is almost everything; fact scarcely exists. Psychoanalysis gave us a new fact: the analytic situation. Freud interpreted that fact as chiefly a repetition of the Oedipus situation. Rank therefore labeled Freud's theory "an intellectualized flight from a fact [the new relationship] in which the interesting and valuable is just that which is new, that which lies beyond the 'transference.' " Rank's study of the analytic situation (his synonym for "transference") led him to synthesize new values. He found that the analytic situation presents love and teaches something about it: It is actual emotion, not just transference from the old child-parent relationship. "It is the origin, development and passing of this human relationship of sentiments which the analytic situation artificially produces and teaches us to understand." The analysis of this process as a joint task provides insight into the ego.

If the interpreted experience of love is ego psychology, Rank said, then the experience of relationship to another may be called Thou psychology. Rank called this relationship in a group of two (or more) the *ethical.* Just as Freud reduced love to instinct and slighted the ego, Rank said, so he externalized the ethical into an "Old Testament Jehovah who punishes and rewards." Hence the importance to Freud of the castration threat; it contrasts with Rank's ethical factor, which is derived from love, not fear.

Rank was acutely aware that the patient already knows or

soon learns the analyst's language and doctrine. Rank wanted
this doctrine to be analyzed as well; that is, the patient and
analyst must become aware of how they use the form or structure
of their relationship. The psychoanalytic doctrine and movement
had become the psychological problem, and a metapsychology
was required to deal with it: a new cognitive approach. Since
neuroses are less a medical problem than an interpersonal one,
Rank offered a theory that embraced the "ethical." So he confronted two problems beyond psychoanalysis: cognition and ethics, which he considered to be the main problems of philosophy
and of the human psyche. Rank's text is intriguing but not always
clear; one can imagine the difficulty his audience had confronting
these concepts and relations.

> Fundamentally they correspond to a single great problem, to the
> contrast between the ego and the Thou, between the Self and
> the world, between the inner and the outer. The theory of cognition
> attempts to determine the relationship between the inner and the
> outer, between appearance and Being, between phantasy and real-
> ity. Ethics tries to determine the more particular relationship of
> the ego to other similar egos, thus to the Thou.
>   . . . Anxiety originally relates to something external, an object
> or a situation; whereas guilt is, so to say, an inner anxiety, a being
> afraid of oneself. Anxiety is thus a biological concept, guilt is an
> ethical concept. So the great problem of the inner and the outer
> in a scientific sense could be formulated as the problem of biology
> versus ethics (or the reverse), in other words, as the great conflict
> between our biological and our purely human Self.

Therapy works, Rank says, by adjusting this ethical conflict,
by strengthing or weakening the inner or the outer. That is
the effective force in psychoanalysis, and also in art, religion,
and politics. Psychology tries to understand the inner, but uses
data of the external; it is "a *science of relations*, which easily
runs into the danger of overestimation of either the one or the
other factor in itself, instead of dealing with the relationship
between the two."

Deviation from the biological norm endangers life and survival. At the psychological level the tendency to deviate causes
anxiety: Some other ego will interfere with the development
of the Self. At a third level, the ethical, deviation causes guilt:
One's development may endanger another. Guilt unites one human being to another, while anxiety separates and isolates indi-

viduals. Sexuality is biological ego preservation or expansion, a counterbalance to death. Love is psychological ego expansion, a counterbalance to anxiety and guilt. "Hence we understand why in our love life the ethical is of importance equal to the biological." Understanding this, we are able to understand, and possibly treat, the problems and afflictions to which the human soul is heir. The neurotic is separated from others by anxiety and united to others by guilt. Neither his individuation nor his afflilation is healthy. The way to achieve wholeness, biologically and socially, is "through the positive love emotion. This I consider the real task of psychotherapy."

One familiar with Rank's later development can see in this paper the phenomenal workings of his mind. For Rank a problem solved was a problem dismissed, and he sacrificed linear, pedestrian logic for spiraling flights of conceptualization. In contrast to the density of his writing, Rank taught, treated patients, and supervised simply and clearly: People felt in this man the integration of theory and therapy. He was equally concerned with cognition and love. No academic philosopher, Rank wanted to make progress in psychology but not by sacrificing reality for scientific "truth," experience for intellectual understanding. He was willing, even glad, to tell a patient (like Nutting) that we don't know why change occurs.

Soon after that lecture Rank returned to Paris (he celebrated his forty-fourth birthday aboard ship), and he spent the rest of the year at home. He wrote extensively during this period: The third part of the genetic psychology, *Truth and Reality*, appeared as the philosophic accompaniment to Part 2 of the work on technique (later translated, with Part 3, as *Will Therapy*).

Rank's mother still lived in Vienna and he had many friends there, but apparently he seldom visited his birthplace after the move to Paris. Beata, however, returned often to Austria in those years and met several times with Freud. The relationship between Beata Rank and Freud ended bitterly with an afternoon visit to Freud's office sometime in 1928. Between the Professor and Otto there was no correspondence or contact, but Tola and Professor still enjoyed a cordial relationship until that day, when they talked of developments in France and more personal things.

As she was about to leave, Freud said, "When you go out now, you will see a man in the waiting room. He was formerly a patient of mine and now comes again. And this man gave your husband some money." To her exclamation of surprise he explained, "At the time Otto worked for his doctorate." Then Freud turned to her and said, "I think you should convey to your husband that he should return the money to this man, so that he can help other people, too." Tola, shocked and hurt, said she did not know what she would or could do. If Freud had written her in advance . . . but there had been no warning.

"It seemed as if I was supposed to encounter this man by design," Beata Rank recalled, still disturbed by the episode after twenty-five years. "But surely it could also have been by chance. What I mean is, the reaction was personal and I could not visit Professor Freud any more."[17]

Tola was understandably upset with Freud for embarrassing her so insensitively in the pursuit of his grievance with Otto. It was well known that she—like Jung's wife before her and Ferenczi's after—was in tears over her husband's break with Freud.[18] Freud knew not only that she had left Vienna unhappily, but that she sided with him generally in theoretical matters. Freud was callous in dealing with her. Always concerned with money, he was undoubtedly annoyed about Rank's continuing success in Paris and New York: He was, as we know, publishing articles, filling his treatment schedule and earning good fees, lecturing, and living in an elegant building. (Helene Deutsch described the Rank's Paris home as "a palatial residence . . . a luxurious salon frequented by many celebrated artists.") Freud did not hate Rank the way he did Adler, but he was angry, though he denied it: After the break he said "Now, after I have forgiven everything, I am through with him."[19]

But he hadn't forgiven and he wasn't through, as Tola now learned. Freud has been given much credit, deservedly so, for providing Rank the wherewithal for getting an education and starting a career. But Rank repaid him and the movement richly with two decades of assiduous work. Freud's partisans say that Rank owed everything to Freud, and his subsequent independence constituted an act of both ingratitude and folly. But Freud's failure to support Rank's development after his long apprenticeship and unstinting service was just as much a sign of folly or ingratitude. That Freud would pursue Rank for money is astonishing; that he would destroy the relationship with Tola by asking her is pathetic. But as we have seen, Freud more than once put the movement ahead of relationships.

THE NEUROTIC AS ARTIST

Back in the United States in January 1929, Rank again divided his time between New York and Philadelphia. As before, he left Tola and Helene, now nine, at home.

In 1929, *The Trauma of Birth* finally appeared in English, five years after its original publication. Martin Peck noted in his review that the work now seemed ancient history, only foreshadowing Rank's advances into ego psychology. Peck took pains to clarify that the trauma of birth was *not* to be evaluated obstetrically. Contrary to persistently misunderstanding critics, Rank never claimed that a minimum birth trauma is optimal, or that the tendency to neurosis varies with the severity of the birth experience. "Anxiety," Peck wrote, "is an essential stimulus to psychological growth at the same time that in other ways it is an obstacle. Therefore, too little as well as too much 'primal' anxiety may have undesirable effects."[20]

Rank spent the last day of February at Yale, at the invitation of Dr. Lloyd J. Thompson, to give an evening address, "The Psychological Approach to Personal Problems." He spent the afternoon touring the campus, concentrating on the famous primate laboratory.

> *The Chimpanzees with* whom *I spent two hours are simply lovely. They are making a thorough study of the psychologists around them and know already how to please them in their experiments. They don't know anything about time but are experts in regard to space because they spit right in the middle of your face from any distance. That's their way of lecturing.*[21]

Rank's humor, befitting a lover of Mark Twain, echoes his own metapsychology: Patients study their analysts and please them with their dreams and associations—which are not really "free."

Humor similarly lightened both Rank's lecture and the question period. The talk itself was recorded stenographically but never published in Rank's lifetime.

It was remarkable for its informality and ease of comprehension; it stands between the condensed formality of the Boston lecture and the conversational intimacy of the consulting room. Rank praised Freud for his pioneering work as both researcher and therapist, but argued that his psychology was biased; the patients were to adjust to certain ethical and social standards. The researcher was in this case altering the experiment by his presence. Rank came to feel that an objective psychology required the separation of research and therapy; he tried "to develop a therapy from a purely therapeutic standpoint, not with the idea of finding out new things about human behavior from a patient, but just helping to put him on his own feet." He continued his theoretical research separate from the pursuit of therapeutic results. In the consulting room he acted with disciplined spontaneity, engaging the patient in a role we now would call participant-observer.

> In this way I was able to work out both a psychology which I think is more objective and also a therapy which I think is more effective. Of course, I do not expect you to take my word for this, but in this short lecture I can only give you my personal attitude. This therapy of mine does not undertake to explain the individual to himself. In other words, in the course of psychoanalytic or therapeutic sessions I do not explain my psychology to the patient but rather I let him develop himself, express himself. The psychology I think can even interfere with the patient's development. This state of affairs is illustrated, for instance, in a certain neurotic type which we see nowadays, particularly here in this country. This type already suffers from too much introspection, and I do not think we can help these patients by making them more aware of their mechanisms. They need something else. They need an emotional experience.[22]

In this lecture, Rank outlined an idea which became the hallmark of his later work: The neurotic is not merely someone who failed to adjust to the world, but a potentially superior individual who fails at being creative. A good therapeutic result means that the patient adjusts himself and also, sometimes, the circumstances—which involves creativity. His task is "to create himself and then to go on and create externally." Rank contrasted his individual creative approach with the adjustment-oriented schools: the medical Freudian, the social Adlerian, and the normal (anagogic) Jungian. He boldly suggested that psychology had reached the point where scientific generalization was almost irrelevant: "I mean by this that in human psychology, each individual, as it were, has his own psychology." Rank the artist and philosopher was pointing out the limits of science. "In every case of psychotherapy of neurosis I now develop a kind of *ad hoc* technique. To each particular case I apply no general therapy or theory. I let the patient work out his own psychology, as it were."

Rank was not passive, of course, but he saw therapy as an occasion for encountering the patient in various modes of expression and experience. He was moving away from the demonstration and use of generalization to the development and affirmation of the new and the unique. "In other words, this psychology that I have arrived at is absolutely dynamic, there is nothing static at all. The static may exist, but if the individual is confronted with a new situation, in other words with life . . ." The last phrase is quintessential Rank: Life is always new.

Rank accepted the categories of Freud, Jung, and Adler—mechanisms, patterns, and types—but found them useful only up to a point, after which they impeded therapy and even theory. Rank saw the individual in therapy—his kind of therapy—"taking some of those mechanisms and building up something new to fit the present situation." To attempt to categorize everything is to deny the creativity, the uniqueness, of individual solutions to life. Psychology, he emphasized again, deals with interpretations more than with facts. People behave more according to their interpretations of themselves than according to what they are.

> In other words I consider psychology a science of relations and interrelations, or if you prefer a more modern term, a science of relativity. There is nothing fixed in the field of psychology: Everything changes; everything is different at different moments. It is constantly moving. One can only get cross-sections for this particular situation. For instance, a patient may tell something in one minute which he says he is sincere in telling, while an hour later he may say to another person something quite different, the opposite of what he said before, and this is again true in this particular situation with regard to this person. It is true; he is not lying; he is not lying in a psychological sense; he is true here to himself and true there to himself. In other words, again, it is all a matter of attitude.
>
> Now there is rather an interesting if not amusing aspect of this theory, of this attitude, in that it not only explains, as I think, the individual's reactions much better than any previous psychology, but it also explains the psychologists themselves. We have been wondering how it could be that here is Freud, here Jung, here Adler, yet they each interpret things in the same patient absolutely differently. I believe there have actually been tests made of dreams. I am thinking of the time when material was sent around to different analysts and how the material was interpreted differently by each. Each thinks he is right and the other wrong, but they all get results

or may get results therapeutically. How is that? It can only be explained, I think, from this point of view. The patient interprets himself in a certain way; if he is neurotic, you can give him something different in the way of interpretation, no matter what it is. It has to be *different* and he will accept it for the time being, and it may help him to look on himself in a different way.

Rank would be the first to say that neurotics are not fools, and therefore the interpretation he refers to must be thoughtful and germane, not insensitive or nonsensical. Nevertheless one can sense the discomfort that this kind of talk produced in both academic psychologists and clinicians. They were struggling to make use of, or modify, or even to disprove, psychoanalytic ideas. Then Rank came along to loosen their moorings. He was anchored and stable, but left most professionals adrift. He appealed more to intelligent laymen and nonconformist colleagues with his mixture of erudition and common sense, scientific sophistication and warmth.

Research on therapy after World War II found that one's theory matters less than one's way of relating to the client. Three qualities seem to characterize the best therapists: accurate empathy, nonpossessive warmth, and genuineness. This—and Rank's theory of relativity and his response to the new—explain why empathic, mature, vital personalities make good therapists even with relatively little training, and why lengthy training cannot make a good therapist of one who lacks these qualities.[23]

In the question period, Rank demonstrated his wry wit and delight in paradox. Asked for the criteria used to determine whether an individual was suitable for analysis, he began by saying the person should be analyzed first! Then he gave a case illustration, a woman with occasional anxiety symptoms who was rather well adjusted otherwise. He advised her to keep her symptom if she could; if we take away the symptoms there may be something worse underneath: Sometimes it is a question not of *can* we treat but *should* we treat! The seeming pessimism in this principle is offset by the implicit notion that changing the self is not to be taken lightly. With regard to taking away defenses, Rank's position was conservative. He would have liked George Fox's advice to fellow Quaker William Penn about the latter's ambivalent attitude to his sword: "Wear it as long as thou canst!"[24]

Inevitably there came a question about brief therapy. "I analyzed first according to Freud's technique and then gradually developed a shorter one, a technique that is getting shorter and shorter, so that I am almost afraid that soon I won't have to see the patient at all." Rank's Yale visit was one of his pleasantest memories in the United States. He promptly left for Paris amid indications that the political climate was shifting against him in professional circles.

Rank confided to Jessie Taft in midsummer his response to the difficulties facing him and his sense of rushing into the future ahead of the pack. He had finished a major new book by then and the exhilaration more than made up for the fate of his Yale talk, which, Rank wrote Taft, "shouldn't be published as it is and shouldn't be rewritten, probably shouldn't be published at all—It was just a talk!" He wished he could write poetry, or not write at all. "But I am afraid such a 'Samoan' life might be unreal—for me!" Dissent, scientific or political, must have entered the New York seminar.

> *The group's reaction and behavior does not surprise me. I have seen groups for twenty years and that's the reason why I don't want a group of my own or to be the "leader" of a group, although it is difficult to be all alone and all by yourself. On the other hand I may go so fast in order that no one can catch up with me—not only [even] myself.* [25]

Rank spent part of August in the south of France with his family, and wrote Jessie Taft on his return to Paris. He planned to return to New York in February (Beata was to accompany him on this trip), and to lecture in Chicago and at the First International Congress on Mental Hygiene in Washington. His mood combined the exhilaration and loneliness of genius; he was not embarrassed to cite a comparison of himself to Einstein. It would have taken an extraordinary mind and soul just to keep his life and work together: His books were published in German, he lived in France, and he conducted most of his analyses in English!

> *I congratulate you heartily [he wrote Taft] on your permanent teaching job because it is something one needs (we need). I wish I could do something of that kind, but I am afraid I never will. I am too much ahead of the current thought and—of my-*

*self. Or—as Dr. Williams in one of his recent letters put it
politely: I am a kind of Einstein in the field of psychology,
and therefore people don't understand me (of course with a
few rare exceptions!).*

*I was doing some analyses all the time—up to the end of
July. The book I finished within a few weeks and now it is in
print. The title is* Seelenglaube und Psychologie *[Soul-belief
and Psychology], showing how our scientific psychology grew
out of the belief in the Soul (Immortality) and still represents
for us the same although it denies the existence of the Soul.
In one word, psychology being our religion. This idea is carried
through all the stages of human development from the magic
world-view of the primitive to psychoanalysis and of course
to my own concepts.*[26]

Rank arrived in New York to a heavy schedule of analysis
and supervision, and resumed the seminar on February 5, 1930.
That, Taft recalls, was the first time she heard him use "will"
as the key term in therapy. She knew it was consistent with
his roots in German philosophy and his emphasis on the creative
drive of the individual. The seminar group quietly balked at
it. Taft overcame her surprise and initial resistance and felt "a
revelation that lit up my whole way of thinking and working."[27]

RANK THE PARIAH

Americans had first participated at the international level in
sizeable numbers at the Bad Homburg Congress in 1925, when
Rank gave his paper at machine-gun speed, in German. Word
of his defection spread so slowly, or the differences mattered
so little, that many leading Americans became his patients, students, and sources of referrals in the next few years.

In 1926, with Brill's ascension, the New York Psychoanalytic
Society had ruled against lay analysts; they could be admitted
only if they promised not to treat patients. Needless to say, from
that time on psychiatrists were under pressure not to be supervised or analyzed by Rank, nor to send him referrals. Boston,
Philadelphia, Washington, Baltimore—strongholds of the more
liberal American Psychoanalytic Association—were still free to
be different, but not for much longer.[28] The New York Society's

ban on lay analysts was as much a slap at Freud, in principle, as at Rank, but it did not hurt Freud financially.

The reorganized Boston Psychoanalytic Society was a hybrid, an amalgam of three separate study groups. In 1928–29 the Rankians dominated: Peck, Wilbur, and John Taylor had been Rank's patients and students; Leolia Dalrymple was analyzed by Peck that year. Those psychiatrists attended the Rankian seminars in New York. Forty-five years later Dalrymple recalled the lively sessions in Frankwood Williams's large living room in lower Manhattan. The fifteen to twenty participants came from hospitals and universities, from Philadelphia and Boston as well as New York. "Dr. Williams was a delightful host and the discussions were lively and stimulating. When Dr. Otto Rank was in town, he chaired the meetings, which were always most exciting. At the close, a sumptuous repast was served in the dining room on the lower floor."[29]

This good augury for Rank however, was only a small bright spot in a darkening scene. Establishing standards had become a consuming interest for the psychoanalytic organizations. In 1929 the New York Society made a didactic (training) analysis by a senior analyst mandatory. That year Brill, already head of the New York Society, succeeded William Alanson White as President of the American Psychoanalytic Association; he was to lead both groups until 1936.

Brill had reached a compromise with Freud before the Oxford (1929) Congress: The European training centers would accept no Americans who had not been cleared by their home Society, while the Americans would in principle accept qualified nonphysicians. Within a year the New Yorkers voided the compromise by requiring a year of psychiatric training—in other words, a medical degree.[30]

From that time on, psychoanalytic orthodoxy in America was characterized by selective inattention to Sigmund Freud. This was poetic justice, perhaps, given Freud's disdain for the Americans (except for the ill-starred Frink). But if there was disagreement about the death instinct, the importance of the ego, and pre-Oedipal issues, there was solidarity between Freud, Brill and Jones against the heresies of Adler, Jung, and Rank.

The Boston Society reorganized once again in 1930 and was no longer a lively, cordial amalgam of three schools and diverse professions. The Freudians took control; the Rankians had to convert or leave. Yet the Freudians exhibited less harmony, despite their shared ideology, than the group they supplanted.[31]

In February Rank had spoken in Chicago at the Midwest Conference on Character Development. His lecture, "The Training of the Will and Emotional Development," was submitted as the text for an important event in Washington, D.C., the week of May 5–10: The First International Congress on Mental Hygiene. Sponsored by the NCMH and related groups and funded by a large philanthropic gift, the event brought professionals and laymen from fifty-three countries to Constitution Hall, and to the Willard and Washington Hotels. Over 4,000 people attended one or more sessions of the Congress, held under the patronage of President Herbert Hoover. William Alanson White chaired the event, which was set up largely by Frankwood Williams and George Pratt of the NCMH: three men who were Rank's friends up to a point.[32]

When Rank got up to speak he departed from the formal paper and, following instructions, gave a ten-minute summary that was followed by extensive discussion: There were seven panelists in all, including Oskar Pfister, Jessie Taft, A. A. Brill, and Franz Alexander. Rank used his ten minutes to give the background of his paper (which had been distributed beforehand to the discussants) and "a glimpse of the personality expressed in this world-view." He introduced himself to those who did not know him, to "relieve some doubts and correct some misunderstandings on the part of those who think they know me or knew me in the past."

> I am no psychiatrist, no social worker, no psychoanalyst, not even an ordinary psychologist, and to tell you the truth I am glad of it. . . . The scientific approach to human behavior and personality problems is not only insufficient but leaves out the most essential part of it, namely, the human side, the characteristic of which is just that it can't be measured and checked and controlled. And yet it is the only vital factor not only in life but also in all kinds of therapy, mental hygiene in the broadest sense. What helps is not intellectual knowledge but human understanding, which is emotional and hence cannot be schematized and utilized.[33]

Rank charged the scientific approach with denial of the human side, accomplished in psychoanalysis by stigmatizing it as "transference." In so doing, paradoxically, psychoanalysis becomes unscientific. Rank repeated his point from the Yale talk that there was no single psychological truth, but rather varying interpreta-

tions of experience, inner and outer. Rank compared the conflict
in world-view expressed in scientific versus humanistic psychology to the medieval religious wars. Having declared science a
failure, he explained:

> The error lies in the scientific glorification of consciousness, of intel-
> lectual knowledge, which even psychoanalysis worships as its high-
> est god although it calls itself a psychology of the unconscious. . . .
> Its failure is clearly shown in the complete lack of the essential
> part of the Unconscious, namely the emotional life. . . . Intellectual
> understanding is one thing and the actual working out of our emo-
> tional problems another, as I brought forward for the first time
> in 1922. . . . The second step beyond the materialistic viewpoint
> of psychoanalysis I made in 1923 in *The Trauma of Birth* with
> the emphasis on an Unconscious absolutely inaccessible to any intel-
> lectual grasp; at the same time, I was still trying to carry the scien-
> tific approach to human problems even further than Freud but I
> realized that in doing so I was carrying it *ad absurdum*. It is only
> within the last two or three years that I have gradually overcome,
> with the increasing acknowledgment of the purely human factor
> in psychotherapy, the intellectual ideology that worships knowl-
> edge for the purpose of controlling and predicting human behavior.
> For in order to pretend that control and prediction are possible,
> one had to deny the individual's own will, his emotional instability,
> and the large part chance plays in the sphere of our psychical
> life even more than in our cosmic life. The scientific approach
> with its artificial emphasis on one truth and its aim to control and
> to predict strives ultimately only for security, but it is a false security
> which does not do away with the cosmic fear of the individual
> and hence does not make us any more happy.

Rank pursued the theme by raising the issue of experience
versus explaining, in therapy and life. Science tries to spare us
the suffering without which people cannot develop. For Rank,
the emotional, actual working out of a problem must precede
insight and understanding, not the other way around as psychoanalysis would have it. Real knowledge and understanding
cannot be transmitted by a purely intellectual process.

This talk and the one at Yale are the two recorded examples
of Rank at his expressive best. His ideas are complex and inter-
connected. Oral presentation forced him to be more simple and
direct than he was in most of his writing. (Unfortunately these
two presentations never became available to a large reading
audience.)

The most valuable factor in a gathering of a crowd like this from all over the world lies in the human element, in the meeting of people, in the contact with the personalities themselves and not with their written and read words. So I hope I have been true to the real human spirit of this conference in pushing the personal element into the foreground, not without feeling greatly obliged to the broadminded attitude of the leaders in mental hygiene who offered me the opportunity to do it.

As Rank sat down the atmosphere was tense. Jessie Taft was his only supporter among the formidable discussants, most of whom were members of the psychoanalytic establishment. Her own excitement blurred the details of what followed, but she recalled general turbulence, in the face of which Rank remained remarkably calm and self-possessed. The Reverend Pfister spoke at length about education and the Oedipus complex, without mentioning Rank's name or his paper. Taft was next, a powerful second to Rank, castigating some of her fellow psychologists who study people's responses "under conditions so artificial and meaningless that only the zeal of the experimenter could confuse them with emotion as it actually operates in daily life." Her eloquence remains fresh after fifty years.

> A theory of the emotions that not only recognizes, but embraces, their inevitability, that is not trying to escape them or to reduce them to conditioned reflexes or infantile patterns that ought to be abandoned, gives us a new basis for self-respect, a new standard of values, and a very different concept of growth and maturity. As long as emotions are feared and condemned, as long as we struggle to attain the lifeless ideal of a maturity that is not subject to the negative separating affects, so long are we bound to a standard that already spells defeat or success at the price of self-deception and a deadening of all feeling. . . .
>
> It soon becomes evident that what is actually meant by adjustment is a condition in which one is not subject to the disturbing affects so characteristic of ordinary people. This expectation of perfection is never more in evidence than in the attitude of the professional and personal friends of the newly analyzed. It takes courage and conviction for one just out of the analytic experience to admit even to himself that pain, depression, anger, jealousy, and physical illness are still realities for him. Perhaps even the analyst himself is not quite free from the illusion of a static cure. It should be a relief then—not only to the young social worker who has despaired of attaining to this emasculated maturity or has rebelled against its coldness, but also to the parents and teachers whom we have

tried to convert to an impossible objectivity in their relations to children—to find a theory of the emotions that permits us to have them. . . .

The parent is hereby freed from a mental hygiene that seemed to demand a hardness and a disinterestedness incompatible with parental love, as well as an immunity to fear and irritation conceivable only in cases where personal relationship is non-existent. The teacher, too, is to be allowed to be human, provided only he permits the child the same privilege.[34]

There could hardly be a stronger contrast between Taft's thoughtful support and the next speaker's tirade. Mary Chadwick, Fellow of the British College of Nurses and one of the few nonphysicians accepted by Ernest Jones, professed disbelief at reading Rank's paper. Virtually sneering, she said he could not really mean all that he had said. His talk about the will and the intellect reminded her of "some dear old ideas that we learned about when we were very young," and referring to the story of Aladdin, she accused Rank of substituting new lamps for old to test "whether we were going to see through the substitution. I don't think we are so easily taken in." She ended her talk with a plea not to exchange the Freudian lamp for a new one, and the audience applauded. The next speaker, a child guidance psychiatrist, expressed discomfort in being "in the midst of a theoretical argument that is a little bit out of my sphere" and made some unexceptionable comments.

By then the session had gone past the lunchtime break. The chairman had left and the remaining speakers were not formally introduced by his substitute. Brill was next. He said his reaction was like Miss Chadwick's but not as nice, and he told an insulting

ssed by one remark of Dr. Rank's—namely, psychoanalyst. I have known that for some d him say it before. That is why he can ual will" and "human elements." He makes they were pieces of cheese. . . . is that psychoanalysis falls short of its objec- to educate people is to let them acquire m personal experiences and suffering. Well, y of his followers ever offer psychoanalysis ring? How is that possible? Only an idiot ng. [Audience laughter] The same implica- aft, who is particularly pleased with Dr.

Rank's paper because, unlike us, he leaves room for love of children. Miss Taft knows better than that. We never said anything to the contrary; we never thought of anything else being possible. In fact, I feel that all the stuff to which Dr. Rank treated us this morning is but an indication of his own present maladjustment. I do not, of course, feel very pleased at having to talk against Dr. Rank, with whom I have been on terms of intimate friendship for many years. I have no doubt at all that Dr. Rank is perfectly honest in everything he says. Remember, however, that he has just told us that he has undergone a sort of conversion; and it must have been a terrible sort of conversion, considering the very important role played by Dr. Rank for many years in the psychoanalytic movement. A deep conversion invariably involves deep emotional upset. My feeling about Dr. Rank is that it is this emotional upheaval that is responsible for his present confusion. [Applause]

One reads in most histories of psychoanalysis about the hostility encountered by Freud in his lonely pursuit of truth. But did he ever encounter the likes of this? Rank, at the hands of the preeminent Freudian, was consigned to categories of illness and idiocy from the platform of a mental hygiene conference, to audience applause! One can only cringe at Brill's presumption and hypocrisy as he paid lip service to "intimate friendship," only to attack with relish.

The next speaker, Dr. Isador Coriat, was the leading Freudian in Boston. He thought Rank had just put "new words to old music." In one sentence, Coriat spoke volumes about the theoretical standoff: "Dr. Rank criticizes certain of the Freudian concepts, and yet he substitutes for them a metaphysical concept of the will, whereas analytically we know that the will is nothing but the wish." Perhaps more than any other theme, the Freudians' equating will and wish brought Rank to his independent stand: a pioneering ego psychology, and what became his "will therapy."

The last discussant, Franz Alexander, was perhaps the most brilliant of the young Berlin-trained European analysts. He had written a long, thoughtful critique of the Ferenczi-Rank book and, of course, was steeped in the anti-Rank attitudes of Abraham and Sachs. Alexander, who soon emigrated to the U.S., came to regard psychotherapy as "a corrective emotional experience," a quite Rankian view. That Thursday in Washington his comments were surprisingly mild—he alluded to "the interesting new theoretical ideas of Dr. Rank"—but he then claimed that the ideas were reformulations of Freud's concepts. He was applauded, as was Rank when he ended the discussion: "I have nothing to say. I take my lamp home from Washington, and leave the old lamps to everybody who wants to stick to them."

That afternoon and evening the American Psychoanalytic Association held its annual meeting in conjunction with the Mental Hygiene Congress. An overflow crowd of 500 attended the scientific session, to hear a galaxy of foreign analysts: Pfister, Alexander, Chadwick, Helene Deutsch, René Spitz, Sandor Rado. Two remarkable personal items came out of the business session. The resignation of H. W. Frink was accepted with regret; and, on a motion by APA President Brill seconded by Dr. Harry Stack Sullivan, Vice-President, the name of Dr. Otto Rank was dropped from the list of honorary members of the APA.[36] (Rank had been awarded honorary membership at his appearance in Atlantic City in 1924.) The action was more than perfunctory, and it heralded what was to come: Rank's analyses were no longer acceptable as meeting the entrance requirement for the APA. Not only did that destroy his referral base among would-be analysts, but those who had had the misfortune to be analyzed by him in recent years were required to undergo a *second* analysis in order to qualify! The Rankian heresy would be expunged at any cost.

CHAPTER 11

The Art of Life

Art is almost always harmless and beneficent; it does not seek to be anything but an illusion. Except for a few people who are spoken of as being "possessed" by art, it makes no attempt at invading the realm of reality.

—Sigmund Freud[1]

In the next two years (1931–32) Otto Rank published three books, including his magnum opus, *Art and Artist.* He also experienced a personal crisis involving separation from Beata, a lengthy period of self-searching, and an episode of deep depression. He became aware of the temptation to substitute creative projects like writing for the creation of a personality and the living of life.

Helene Deutsch, Rank's successor as Director of Training at the Vienna Institute, had been much in evidence in Washington as a discussant at four different presentations. A few days afterward she wrote to Felix Deutsch: "I hear a lot of bad about Rank—he suffered a real calamity at the Congress, and I felt very sorry, for I see fate holding sway here, and Tola's future really worries me."[2]

But if Otto Rank felt Washington was a calamity he did not show it. He kept his aplomb in the face of the vicious attacks by Brill and others, and made no mention of his expulsion from the American Psychoanalytic Association. By 1930 Rank no longer considered himself an analyst, and he had suffered the worst hurt three years earlier when Ferenczi, once his best friend, shunned him in New York.

UPS AND DOWNS

Information about Rank's life during the next two years comes chiefly from his correspondence with Cape Cod psychiatrist George (Jake) Wilbur, and from Jessie Taft. These two were his closest American friends and colleagues at the time and were working on a book presenting Rank's psychology to the American reader. Rank encouraged their effort and prepared an annotated bibliography of his major works, including various reviews and comments. This invaluable document—Rank's "Literary Autobiography"—is all that materialized: the "Boston" book was stillborn.

The fact that no American psychiatrist supported him in Washington was more telling than Rank realized. Jessie Taft, who saw the rapid erosion of his medical base, agreed to work on the "Boston" book despite her doubts about its future.[3] Although Boston analysts were more independent than the New Yorkers, Isidor Coriat's hostility in Washington augured poorly for Rank.

Martin Peck was Rank's best hope in Massachusetts. Analyzed by Rank in 1926, he was more productive than George Wilbur and had leadership qualities. Described as "the gentle Peck," he was compared to Putnam on account of his integrity and decency. Peck taught at Harvard and wrote *The Meaning of Psychoanalysis* (1930), a popular book (reprinted several times) that was dedicated to Freud. It describes Rank as a defector from the "purely Freudian" school, and praises his *Genetic Psychology:* "a psychological system which has not proved acceptable to the more rigid Freudians. Rank's work is brilliant in conception and gives a welcome unity to parts until now disconnected." Peck offers a cogent summary of the active, time-limited Rankian therapy, but suggests that it is most suitable for patients whose problems are not too serious. After a second analysis (and a second marriage), Peck took a solidly Freudian position, became President of the Boston Psychoanalytic Society in 1935, visited Freud, and then, in his prime, committed suicide during an episode of depression in 1940.[4]

George Wilbur, Rank's weaker but more lasting psychiatric contact, maintained an interest in the history of science, including psychology. He worked slowly—interminably—at his translation of Rank's *Seelenglaube* (Soul-belief). Geographically and temperamentally apart from the center of psychoanalytic politics, Wilbur was a feisty nonconformist. He wrote many letters and kept files of his abundant correspondence, but he published little. Wilbur eventually became editor of *American Imago*, a revival of the *Imago* founded by Rank and Sachs in Vienna. Wilbur was a Cape Cod neighbor and close friend (from Harvard days) of writer Conrad Aiken. They analyzed each other in person and correspondence; Aiken portrayed Wilbur as "Jacob" in his autobiographical *Ushant*. Rank probably met Aiken on one of his visits to Cape Cod.[5]

Just after the Washington Congress, Rank stayed with Wilbur, who did not come to appreciate the extent of Rank's ordeal until he read the *Proceedings*, published two years later. The visit was interrupted by an emergency call concerning a paranoid young man Rank was treating in New York. Rank had hoped to take a plane back—an unusual event in those days—but the midnight train was more convenient. On May 15th Rank was able to report that Frankwood Williams would write a chapter for the Boston book. From Paris, in June, Rank wrote, "The more I think of it and hear now about the psa movement the more important the book seems to be. I wish you could hurry up with it or at least push Miss Bowers [an assistant on the project]." Wilbur procrastinated more than he pushed, pressing Rank with theoretical and historical questions which excited him more than the book.

In July the Ranks entertained Jessie Taft and Virginia Robinson in Paris. "No one who has been there," wrote Taft, "will ever forget the beautiful, stately room in which Rank received guests and patients, with a photograph of Freud still in evidence, nor the small but perfectly equipped library that was his especial pride." Taft was delighted by "the emergence of a boyish, mischievous Rank, who could enjoy with abandon a window-shopping excursion through mysterious Paris streets and make the ordering of lunch an adventure."[6]

Rank was then finishing the third and last part of his *Technique*. (It became part of *Will Therapy*.) He wrote Wilbur about the next project, a return to the universe of the artist, where he would give "the other side of the neurotic's Psychology as well as a whole new world-view. Nothing seems to be left after that!" Apparently Rank had not even mentioned the hazing in Washington; in answer to a question from Wilbur, Rank summarized the four critiques quite dispassionately. (As a veteran of Freud's Wednesday group perhaps he took their rudeness in stride.) Arguing the importance of will (against Coriat), he offered Wilbur two quotations from Goethe: "Our volition is a prediction of what we are going to do anyway" and "Our wishes (desires) forecast our inner abilities, anticipating what we can achieve."[7]

By October 1930 Rank sensed a real stall in the Boston effort, but he could report that Alfred Knopf, who published Peck's book, had expressed some interest in the *Genetic Psychology*. Meanwhile, Ludwig Lewisohn, the respected German-born American author and critic (whose wife Rank treated in Paris), wrote Knopf urging an English-language edition of Rank's collected works:

> *Freud, great old man, is not likely to do much more; Jung is a fairly old story; the one idea that Alfred Adler has had has been exploited to death. In the meantime Otto Rank has enlarged and deepened the entire science of psychology and has, above all, applied its findings to other provinces of human thought and activity—to education, to literature and criticism, etc. I am soberly convinced that his ideas are destined to create several revolutions in several departments of thought and that he will make a far deeper and more permanent mark on civilization than, let us say, so infinitely more explosive a person as Spengler. There are many psychologists, psychiatrists and sociologists both in Europe and in America, where Dr. Rank is personally well known, who quite agree with me. But it is possible, or rather, probable, that you will be more interested in the reaction of a layman who, like myself, has been enormously stimulated and instructed by Dr. Rank's ideas. Nothing, for instance, is clearer to me than that he has reduced to pathetic rubbish all conventional biography and nine-tenths of descriptive and merely empirical criticism in all the arts. In brief, he has perfected a revolutionary organon of thought.*

Lewisohn told Knopf that Rank's new books on education and art were not being published yet in German, so as to give first option to an American publisher. "Nothing would give me more satisfaction," Lewisohn said, "than to write an introduction to that second work. The book on American Literature which

I am doing [*Expression in America* (1931)] will probably show on every page the influence of Rank's theories."[8]

Rank wrote *Art and Artist* with amazing speed, finishing twelve of its fourteen chapters in one month. Echoing Lewisohn, Rank boasted to Jessie Taft that his two forthcoming books "will turn all educational fashions of the present day and all literary and art critics of the past and present upside down." But he told her of other, less encouraging developments at the same time: Frankwood Williams was in Paris; he and his friend Professor Kimball liked Rank's work, but it was doubtful whether Williams could "defend this viewpoint on his own against the psychiatric and analytic crowd" in New York.

> *I myself feel that it will be a big job for me to stand up—with some help from a few friends—for the defense of this dynamic and human viewpoint although there is no use in making a martyr of myself in fighting for it. I am glad I am beyond that, but just the same I feel I have to come to America sooner or later to do what I can. Perhaps Mr. Knopf will help a great deal if he really becomes interested.*[9]

Two months later, in December, Rank's letters to Wilbur and Taft were subdued. Peck had resigned from the Boston book project and Rank encouraged Wilbur to do a book on his own: "What you say about not knowing the real significance of psychoanalysis I quite agree with you, only that I would also include most Europeans and first of all most of the psychoanalysts themselves, including Freud." He hoped to see the Wilburs in Paris—"most lovely in springtime"—since he did not expect to be in America that winter: "I think I need a little rest and maybe also America from me." Facing publication delays on the two books he cared about so much, Rank told Taft that he had lost interest in publishing in any language: "Please don't think that I am not interested in your translation [of *Technik* as *Will Therapy*], but I have a horror of looking at any of my books again after they are written, no matter in what language it is." He mailed her the proofs of the *Technik*, Part 3, with the comment that the last chapter was sketchy. "It ought to be worked out into a real social psychology, which I may write one day if I get old enough."[10]

Rank was in the forefront, along with Sandor Ferenczi, in developing the psychoanalytic psychotherapy that has dominated mental health practice for the past fifty years. As leaders, the two genial therapists encountered strong opposition, even ostracism, and by 1930, his sanity under attack as we have seen, Rank's name had been expunged from the lists of psychoanalysis. To have been Rank's student or analysand became a liability in American psychiatric circles. To Dr. A. A. Brill, acknowledging Rank's post-Freudian achievements was tantamount to praising a madman or an idiot. Brill was President of the American Psychoanalytic Association from 1929 to 1935, and of the New York Society even longer, from 1925 to 1936. His leadership tenure in the United States compares with that of Ernest Jones in the International and British psychoanalytic organizations. The two most powerful Freudians in the world took pains to dispose of Rank and Ferenczi, their erstwhile competitors.

Ferenczi, who finally turned his back on Rank, nonetheless suffered a fate similar to that of his old friend. The New York establishment virtually ignored him during his 1926 visit because he steadfastly (along with Freud) continued to train and support nonmedical analysts. Like Rank, Ferenczi found that some of the psychiatrists he trained in Europe shunned him in America for political (and therefore economic) reasons. Later, Ferenczi's ideas brought him into conflict with Freud, and he separated from the mainstream. Upon his death in 1933, Ferenczi was eulogized by Freud as one afflicted with too much therapeutic zeal. Jones labeled Ferenczi (his own analyst) mentally ill—as he did Rank.

Competition and jealousy thrive in the mental health field as in any other. Rank became taboo at the same time his ideas began to take hold. Ives Hendrick, an influential Boston psychoanalyst who trained with Sachs and Alexander in Berlin, was initially quite amenable to Rankian ideas. Hendrick described analytic practice in Berlin (after Abraham's death) as similar to Rank's. Indeed, he objected to Rank's characterization of Freudian analysis: "No competent analyst in Europe today practices such an outmoded technique"—a remark that indicated increasing acceptance of Rank's active treatment. Wilbur summarized a discussion with Hendrick in a letter to Rank: "He also said that there [in Europe] they were quite consciously indebted to you for certain innovations, moreso I gathered than appears in the literature."[11] It was possible to practice in Rankian style, then, if one couched it in Freudian terms.

Rank heartily disliked the infighting that he increasingly encountered. He stood up to opposition forthrightly when necessary but not avidly, and with surprisingly little rancor. "Pioneers are also the victims," he once said, and he saw no use martyring himself in battle over his "dynamic and human viewpoint."

CREATING A LIFE

In 1931 Rank entered a new phase: He gradually ceased to write. Since leaving Freud he had published two major works on developmental ego psychology and therapeutic technique, along with *Soul-belief;* he was awaiting publication of his books on education and art. While he wrote and published, he continued to treat patients, travel, lecture, and read widely. With five important books in as many years, Rank's *oeuvre* encompassed a universe of thought: art, education, religion, therapy, and developmental psychology. He had had enough for a while.

The ending of *Art and Artist* introduces this next stage of Rank's life.

> The new type of humanity will only become possible when we have passed beyond the psychotherapeutic transitional stage, and must grow out of those artists themselves who have achieved a renunciant attitude towards artistic production. A man with creative power who can give up artistic expression in favor of the formation of personality—since he can no longer use art as an expression of an already developed personality—will remold the self-creative type and will be able to put his creative impulse *directly* in the service of his own personality. In him the wheel will have turned full circle, from primitive art, which sought to raise the physical ego out of nature, to the voluntaristic art of life, which can accept the psychical ego as a part of the universe. But the condition of this is the conquest of the fear of life, for that fear has led to the substitution of artistic production for life, and to the eternalization of the all-too-mortal ego in a work of art. For the artistic individual has lived in art-creation instead of actual life, letting his work live or die on its own account, and has never wholly surrendered himself to life. In place of his own self the artist puts his objectified ego into his work, but though he does not save his subjective mortal ego from death, he yet withdraws himself from real life. And the creative type who can renounce his protection by art and can devote his whole creative force to

life and the formation of life will be the first representative of the new human type and in return for this renunciation will enjoy, in personality-creation and expression, a greater happiness.[12]

Rank saw the artist as the last in a historical sequence of individual and collective solutions to the problem of mortality. The next stage entails the creation of one's own life—within the limits imposed, and the possibilities granted, by the givens of biology and society. The creative type becomes the creator of a self. Rank would devote his energies to forming his own life.

Rank's new awareness of the role of individual creativity in forming a personality coincided with his introduction of the theme of will into psychotherapy and human development. In his book on therapy, Rank explained how neurosis and creativity relate to one another. First, he rejects the notion that one must be neurotic to be an artist. Second, he states that the sources of creativity cannot be found by analyzing the artist's childhood. Instead, he argues that the creative type and the neurotic type have in common a strong will. In the neurotic, inhibition holds sway and creativity withers.

Using an idea from Schopenhauer, Rank develops a metaphor: Life is a loan, death the repayment. The artist type takes the loan and spends or invests it—willingly. Such a person accepts the finite term of the loan, and makes choices in accordance with that reality. The neurotic, in contrast, cannot willingly accept the loan with its limit. He or she vacillates, paralyzed by anxiety and doubt, refusing to commit the life–loan. At repayment time, the neurotic hopes—pathetically—to flout the limit. "I haven't begun yet. I should not have to die—I have not really lived!"

Freudians would differ with Rank's analysis. They would seek neurotic quirks in the artist in order to explain creativity—or, in the hero, to explain action. Rank did the opposite: He sought creative and heroic strivings in the neurotic. Usually he found them. Indeed, Rank called the neurotic a failed artist, or *artiste manqué*.

Besides the artist and the neurotic, both endowed with strong will and strong impulse, Rank recognized the existence of an ordinary or average type who has neither, and a criminal type whose impulse is strong but whose will (which is in part a guiding and controlling force) is ineffective.

The neurotic then is a man whom extreme fear keeps from accepting this payment as a basis of life. . . . He refuses the loan (life) in order thus to escape the payment of the debt (death). . . . the human being seeks to subject death, this original symbol of the "must," to his will, and as it were, at his own instigation transforms the death punishment that is placed upon life into a lifelong punishment he imposes upon himself. On the other hand, the ancient idea of the sacrifice plays a part in this, the idea that one could escape the hardest punishment by voluntary assumption of lighter self-punishment. Applied to the neurotic type, it results in a deepened understanding not only of the symptomatology in particular cases but also of neurosis as a whole, showing it to be an individual attempt at healing, against the archenemy of mankind, the death fear, which can no longer be cured by the collective method of earlier ages.[13]

By "collective method" Rank refers in turn to religion, art, and science, each of which dominated a period of history, but none of which is adequate any more.

Implicit in the metaphor "Life is a loan, death the repayment" and explicit in Rank's work is the principle that human living involves creation—and that involves an investment in something, a spending of oneself that inevitably makes us aware of limits, including life's ultimate limit. Rank cites "a general life principle, on the basis of which no creating is possible without destruction, and no destroying without some kind of new creation." (He credits Dr. Sabina Spielrein with first demonstrating this.) At the peak of life we confront the vale of death: One is most aware of finiteness at moments of great joy. To live, to will, to choose, one must face death. To make choices one must willingly reject—kill—other possibilities.

Rank dealt with another problem of creative will: the expression of difference, the separation of oneself from the group. Will individuates and separates, evoking guilt for not merging with the group. But inhibiting the will is no solution: Guilt also attaches to the refusal to separate, to the denial of one's uniqueness. In short, living one's life as a free man or woman entails guilt because creativity *and* its denial both entail guilt. The creative type affirms this (existential) freedom and responsibility, separates from and unites with society, developing mind, soul, and meaning in relationships with others and within the self.

A lover of the arts, Rank felt the limits of the creative endeavor, and he saw how it could become a substitute for living. This realization came by the end of 1930, almost three years before he met his famous muse, Anaïs Nin. That she helped him live more fully is certain; that he had already begun to live is equally clear, although in the period of transition Rank suffered a major depression.

FINDING HIMSELF

In January 1931 Rank wrote to Wilbur with unaccustomed bitterness: "I can't see why Alexander or his representative [Hendrick] should be so important still for you, because for me he is certainly not. What does it matter what they think even if they agree or accept things tacitly as long as they have to fight me publicly?" From Berlin to Boston, Rank the man was ostracized by the same leaders who slowly embraced his ideas. In the same letter, Rank spoke of the influence of Nietzsche in psychoanalysis: "Lately I have emancipated myself from him, too. But in stressing his influence on my development don't overlook the tremendous influence he had on Freud inasmuch as he has influenced all European thinking. (Freud read Nietzsche only in his later years but was spiritually under his influence from the beginning—just as he was under Schopenhauer's, although he denied both.)" The letter ended grimly with a reference to Mr. Knopf, who was "bewildered" by talks he had with some staunch Freudians: "It seems that he was scared off by the usual New York gossip which is apparently still their only way of fighting."[14] Rank still had no contract for the American publication of his last several books.

The New York psychiatrists showed their ambivalence by failing to invite Rank to return from Paris for seminars. Frankwood Williams was personally cordial, yet he needed patients and could afford neither competition from Rank nor the stigma of Rankianism, since he wanted to stay on good terms with the Freudians. Understanding this, Rank relieved Williams of the burden of hosting the seminar. Rank shared his forbodings with Jessie Taft, telling her in January that he no longer felt like fighting and would like just to write if he could afford it. In Paris he saw a few patients in the mornings, while in the afternoons he wrote or read. Because he did mostly short-term therapy—"I do this too well too!"—if he did not have sufficient new cases he would starve. The income prospects were better in New York, but the necessary entry visa was difficult to get: He would need assurance of paid work. He had considered moving to Boston, but his supporters had dwindled in the face of the Freudian onslaught. There was an invitation to go out West: "I would probably do it if I were a few years younger, but now I don't know."[15]

Unlike the compulsive, energetic, and well-organized Otto Rank, his friend George Wilbur seemed to ramble through life, collecting facts and ideas but doing little with them. One fine exception was his review of Rank's *Seelenglaube* (*Soul-belief*: an English version of the book did not appear until 1950), which he read to the Boston Psychoanalytic Society. Wilbur's presentation, published in 1932, began:

> Some years ago Rank perceived that in psychoanalysis the present moment must be made the center from which to work outwards in order to obtain valid results in theory and therapy. This is in contrast to the previous method of reconstructing the given present from a hypothetical past, where the results obtained are conditioned by the therapeutic needs of the moment. By this conception Rank has been able to revalue the entire analytic situation and the conclusions to be drawn from it in a way that seems destined to make it possible to cope better with its inherent but hitherto unsolvable contradictions.[16]

Rank was pleased with Wilbur's review but disappointed with Martin Peck's Freudian book, *The Meaning of Psychoanalysis*: "I am fed up with a new presentation of the development of psychoanalysis—and I am afraid the public is too." The New York Freudians, Rank said, had tried to dissuade Knopf from publishing his books, and might even succeed in making it impossible for him to practice professionally there.[17]

From his correspondence with Taft we learn that Alfred Knopf met with Rank in Paris and expressed interest in the American publication of Rank's complete works. In a friendly conversation the two men decided to start with the two unpublished books. Knopf preferred professional translators and so Rank spared Taft that chore, which she would otherwise have undertaken. Rank's pupil Mabel Moxon translated *Modern Education*, while Charles Francis Atkinson did the bigger (450-page) *Art and Artist*. Even with the contract in hand Rank felt sluggish and depressed: "I must confess it did not help my resistances to publication, because since he left I have not touched the books that I have to go over." Rank concluded the letter: "Don't worry about patients for me, because it is as bad as, if not worse than, with the books: I am in need of them to make a living but I don't want them. I am just as glad if a patient does not turn up as if he does. But enough of my 'bad' self—the other one that still exists sends you warm thanks and greetings."[18]

Three weeks later Rank wrote to Wilbur in a more optimistic mood about several projects, including the American and German publication of the latest books, plus a French translation of *Don Juan* together with *The Double*. He had started to outline a new book on social psychology and also was working on a shortened third edition of *Incest Motif* from a social-anthropological point of view. (He mentioned having had discussions with the anthropologist Bronislaw Malinowski [1884–1942], who appreciated Rank's work.) Rank felt "the beginning burden of so-called 'fame'!" Meanwhile, Taft, now addressed as "Jessie," had written a long review of Part 3 of *Technique* for *Psychoanalytic Review;* it was reprinted by Frankwood Williams in *Mental Hygiene*. Rank valued such reviews, since his forthcoming books, he told Wilbur, were "too general to influence the Psychiatrists and Psychologists who presumably will draw from them the conclusion that I have left their field and gone into—god knows what!"[19]

Rank stayed in Paris most of the summer. He put in eight to nine analytic hours each day, and for the moment had no financial worries. A British publisher was even fighting Knopf for the rights to *Incest Motif*. "I never thought this could happen to my books," Rank wrote Taft.[20] But the project died, as did the prospect of publication of Rank's collected works. (A German typescript of the *Incest Motif*, rewritten as a "sociological history of the Oedipus complex," is among Rank's papers.) The book on social psychology was never written as such, but parts were incorporated in Rank's posthumous *Beyond Psychology*.

Rank had become preoccupied with what he called his "old" and "new" selves at this point. He never says just how he went about creating a new personality, but it was a difficult process. "I take it easy just the same, I am not going to be run any more by anything or anybody (including myself!)," he wrote Taft during July. Then in the fall Rank retreated to Antibes on the Riviera, resting from work and a bad cold. It was no ordinary vacation. Rank had left Beata to "find himself," their daughter (then 12) later recalled. That year Helene again attended boarding school in Switzerland. Otto and Beata met her there at Christmastime, and the marriage continued for a few years longer. Rank told Taft only that his wife did not want to go with him to America, one factor in his decision to forgo another Atlantic crossing then.

Another deterrent to Rank's returning to America was the Freudian purge of Rankians there, abetted by the sudden migration of European analysts: Franz Alexander to Boston, Sandor Rado to New York, and Herman Nunberg to Philadelphia: "a Freudian invasion," he wrote Wilbur, "which I had predicted and am not surprised at. Obviously other people too have to go through the same or a similar development as we did."[21] Rank saw himself well out in front of a moving tide. He wrote Jessie Taft:

> *I haven't done any writing lately but a great deal of thinking, which clarified and confirmed the feeling that I am "fed up" with psychoanalysis and with America as far as it is concerned with it.*
>
> *I foresaw, if you remember, a Freudian wave, which necessarily will last some time since it represents the "mechanistic psychology" which mechanistically trained minds only are capable of grasping!*
>
> *That's one reason for my not being in any hurry, neither for teaching nor for writing. I feel I am a few generations ahead anyway, so why widen that distance?*[22]

Taft fully endorsed Rank's estimate of his own importance. About this time she told Esther Menaker, a graduate social worker embarking for analytic training in Vienna: "Rank is as far ahead of Freud as Freud was of the hypnotists." Yet notwithstanding Rank's self-assurance, he was surprised at publishers' eagerness for his work. This combination of high self-esteem and low expectations for success exemplified his own theory of the artist. To the extent he was creative he was too far ahead of the pack to be accepted or even understood. The greater his vision, in effect, the less general would be his success. The artist's need for public recognition clashes with his contempt for the acclaim.

In this entire creative process, which begins with this self-nomination to be an artist and concludes in the fame of posterity, two fundamental tendencies—one might almost say, two personalities of the individual—are throughout in continual conflict: the one which wishes to eternalize itself in artistic creation, the other which wants to spend itself in ordinary life—in a word, the mortal man and the immortal soul of man. . . .

But fame not only threatens the personal immortality of the artist by making it collective; it is moreover directly hostile to life, since it forces the artist to stay officially in the groove that he has chosen for himself. This is seen in success . . . a sort of "return of the artist to life." It is a return which disappoints the artist because it does not give him freedom of experience, but compels him to further *artistic creation.* Success is therefore a stimulus to creativity only so long as it is not attained—which means, as long as the artist believes he can regain life by his success and so free himself from the bondage of creating. Bitterly, then, he finds out that success only strengthens the need for creating, and that fame, which is the end of it, leads to depersonalization during his lifetime and is of no use for life if it comes after death. The artist does not create, in the first place, for fame or immortality; his production is to be a means to achieve actual life, since it helps him to overcome fear. But he cannot get out of the bypath he has once trodden, which was to lead him back by means of his work to life. He is thus more and more deeply entangled in his creative dynamism, which receives its seal in success and fame.[23]

Like a richly woven tapestry that can be appreciated from both sides, this excerpt from *Art and Artist* expresses Rank's sense of paradox, his own vacillation. Rank goes on to develop the argument that artistic creation is antisexual. Even the artist shares the illusion that the self-sufficient, creative soul is bisexual. Yet among artists there are clear masculine and feminine types, while neither homosexuality nor bisexuality is an indicator of artistic gifts. Rank articulated an image of godlike independence, a creative power that would "bring forth the world and itself from itself and without help." Yet this splendid autonomy of the artist depends on the audience for completion (fame, success), even more than ordinary people need their sexual partners for completion. The artist pays for his (antisexual) independent creativity by exhausting himself in the work. Rank's stunning portrayal of the artist in society concludes:

Success and fame then supervene to assure the artist that for all his lordliness he is still dependent on the collective forces that he seeks to escape by autonomous creation. . . . Success and fame make him once more a collective being, take him from his divine creative role and make him human again; in a word, make him mortal. However much he may like to return to earth and become human, he cannot do it at the price of his own immortality; and the paradox of the thing consists in the fact that success and fame, which make him collectively immortal, make him personally human once more and restore him to mortality. His work is taken from him by the community, as the child is taken from its parents, and in place of it he receives his title to fame, rewarded like a mother by a state hungry for soldiers. The artist, too, looks for this reward, but he hopes to return by his success to life, whereas fame condemns him often enough to spiritual [soular] death.[24]

A chapter from *Art and Artist,* "Life and Artistic Creation," appeared in *This Quarter,* a Paris literary magazine, in December. Translated by Edward Titus, who edited and published *This Quarter,* the chapter brought Rank to the attention of expatriate and Anglophile readers. The same issue included work by Joseph Wood Krutch, Ludwig Lewisohn, E. E. Cummings, Selden Rodman, and Ernest Hemingway. They and Rank were all mentioned in a review of the issue in the Paris *Tribune.*

Edward Titus was a Polish-American, like his wife, Helena Rubinstein. Her cosmetic fortune subsidized his publishing ventures and his antiquarian bookstore; his advice helped build her art collection. Rank must have frequented his *librarie* "At the Sign of the Black Manikin," which was full of graphic treasures. Titus published Lewisohn's *The Case of Mr. Crump* (1926), a novel hailed by Thomas Mann, Sinclair Lewis, Freud, Mencken, and Dreiser.[25] The Black Manikin Press also published D. H. Lawrence along with a book about him—which was Anais Nin's first book.

CRISIS

At year's end George Wilbur reported to Rank on the continuing turmoil among Boston psychoanalysts who had been joined by one of Berlin's best, Franz Alexander. They debated what constituted a training analysis, required for membership in the Boston Society. In one argument the younger students of Alexander "got to going on the deficiencies of the Rankians. Whereupon Alexander spoke up and said they would have to be careful of their definitions as to what constituted a Rankian, since for some 15 or 18 years you had been the one-man training institute of Vienna and had consequently trained all the older group. Where then would they draw the line?"[26] Ultimately, those who had been analyzed by Rank were required to have a second analysis or leave the American Psychoanalytic Association.

Alexander himself had no need or desire to penalize the Rankians, and his open-mindedness persisted throughout his career. Strongly influenced by Ferenczi, he went to Berlin to be analyzed by Hanns Sachs as the first official Institute candidate with the first official training analyst. One of the most brilliant and admired graduates of the Berlin training program, Alexander remained free of doctrinaire conservatism. After just one year in Boston, he established himself in Chicago and later in Los Angeles. Alexander led important developments in psychosomatic medicine, inspiring many students as he became known for his thesis that psychotherapy is a "corrective emotional experience."

Once Alexander gave a presentation which could hardly be more Rankian, although it was a discussion of Ferenczi, who was then still acceptable to Freudians. Wilbur reported to Rank:

> *Many things in it sounded almost as if they were coming from you, particularly a statement that the patient's resistance was something not to be beaten down but taken account of as the force which enabled him to be cured. Another point which interested me was some discussion of the epistemological difficulties produced by a more active role on the part of the analyst. Alex. did not seem to realize exactly what he was up against but it seemed to me that he would not have far to go before he arrived at the position you attained some years ago and which led to the discovery of the denial of will.*

The Boston Society, Wilbur said, bridled under the "dictatorship of N.Y. . . . For a while it looked like us Rankians (Taylor and I) were going to be out in the cold but they relented." Having endured a "two hour quarrel about whether we should 'purify' the Society or not," Wilbur observed that "there is one thing about Rankians. They are able to submit with calmness to the terrifying experience of being in the presence of somebody who differs in analytic belief."[27]

In a remarkable letter (December 15, 1931), germane to the

rapidly rigidifying orthodoxy in psychoanalysis, Rank told Wilbur
about Freud's changing psychoanalytic views:

> *With regard to your paper on child analysis (castration phobia),*
> *a recent article of Freud's ["On Female Sexuality"] might inter-*
> *est you. Not that you could learn anything from it—because*
> *he "discovers" there the primal significance of the mother as*
> *the first object of libido and of inhibition (fear and hate, etc.)*
> *which I pointed out elaborately in the* Genetic Psychology; *he*
> *doesn't mention me, of course, only more recent articles of*
> *woman analysts whom he values now more than his man-pupils.*
> *He states there that most of the things which "we" (he means*
> *himself but says we) hitherto have traced back to the father-*
> *relation belong to the mother-level from which they are later*
> *on transferred to the father. Even the good old Oedipus complex,*
> *he admits, is thereby shaken considerably. Yet he prefers to*
> *hold on to it. Why not, it was his first and only love!*[28]

The beleaguered Wilbur replied that, despite the great importance of Freud's new position, "it will be mainly passed up
in silence, and the fiction that everybody adheres to a fixed
theory will be maintained." Wilbur, self-assured but angry and
frustrated at the response of the Society to his presentation of
a case, told Rank, "Your old question as to the relation of theory
to practice will only begin to occur to these people about 50
years from now." He mentioned a rumor that Alexander's wife
gave him only two more years as a Freudian. Wilbur looked
to Alexander for support as Hendrick stepped up his attack,
saying that the chief Rankians were "untrained women."
Rank answered promptly (on January 14, 1932):

> *In Germany the shortcomings of the Freudian philosophy are*
> *more and more clearly realized and stated not in hostile criti-*
> *cisms but rather with regret of Freud's limitations. . . . [In a*
> *pamphlet on* Civilization and its Discontents *appear] the same*
> *fundamental criticisms which I pointed at and [the writer]*
> *Kronfeld quotes my correct criticism of Freud's attitude towards*
> *fear. Karen Horney . . . uses my own argument (without quot-*
> *ing me) . . .*
>
> *The main criticisms of the whole Freudian philosophy are:*
> *first of all that Freudian doctrine does not take into consider-*
> *ation the actual experience, for instance in the faithful (reli-*
> *gious), which is independent of the content of either religion*

itself or any intellectual interpretations of it (e.g., father com-
plex, etc.). Secondly it is only interested in the genesis, i.e.,
emphasizes the repetition instead of seeing the importance of
the new (the actual) which is added to the old or transforms
it. 3. that the value of a phenomenon is measured by the intellec-
tual "truth" it contains or conveys and not by the emotional
needs it satisfies (this has to do with the first argument). 4.
(in connection with the interest in the genesis) that Freud sees
or emphasizes only the regressive tendencies, the negative, and
does not value the positive factors (e.g., in religion sees only
the dependence and not the liberation and so on).

As you see, arguments familiar to us. So it may take less
than 50 years for other people to see it; the present day Freudian
will probably never see it anyhow! . . .

With regard to the woman problem [Hendrick's attack on
"untrained women" Rankians]: the gossip might have very
likely started with Virginia Robinson's book A Changing Psychology in Social Casework, *which came out about a year ago.*
But it may also have some ground in the fact that there is
(since my last visit to the states) a small group at Columbia
(to which Martha Taylor and Martha Jaeger belong) the mem-
bers of which are analyzing. I think what gets their goat (the
N.Y. analysts I mean) is that some women whom I analyzed
make (at least potentially) good analysts as women, i.e., as
having accepted their femininity contrasted to most Freudian
female analysts who are compensating in a masculine role (for
that statement I have good real reasons). Be that as it may—
they will always find fault with me! But to come back to Freud
with whom it is different: his late appreciation of women ena-
bles him only now to see that they have their own makeup
and are not merely "castrated" man. [29]

Now Wilbur's contacts with the Boston group dwindled to
monthly visits to watch quarreling, which, he said, had nothing
to do with analysis, only human nature and politics. "The lineup
seems to be the old Boston gang against the newcomers." Martin
Peck, Rank's analysand who got "regularized" (Wilbur's term)
by a second analysis, was to replace Isador Coriat as head of
the Boston Freudians.[30]

After almost a two year absence, Rank arrived in New York
around March 1: "Everybody seems to know that I am here,"
he wrote Jessie Taft from the Gramercy Park Hotel, "and America is just as terrible as ever! But also I am not so well now—I

17

The Ranks settled in Paris in 1926, where for a few years Otto's practice and writing brought fame and a good income (17, 18). Rank's fee was five dollars less than Freud's but triple what most analysts in New York could charge (19). One of many American writers and artists in Paris who sought out Rank, Ludwig Lewisohn (20) championed Rank's work, writing the preface to *Art and Artist*.

18

20

19

June 1st _____ 1927

Mrs. Martin W. Peck
to
DR. OTTO RANK

9 rue Louis Boilly (XVIᵉ)

26 sittings at $15.—

$ 390 00/100

21

Impressed with Rank's books, Henry Miller (22) went to see him in Paris. Then the aspiring writer Anais Nin (23) came for psychotherapy. Her famous *Diary* describes Rank (21) vividly, if not always faithfully. First Rank was her muse, then she became his. In 1934 she accompanied him to New York to become an analyst herself; Miller came hurrying after to reclaim his lover. Nin gave up Rank and psychology to return to Paris.

23

22

24

25

Jessie Taft and Virginia
Robinson (24, rt.) became
Rank's staunchest colleagues in
America after his first visit to
New York in 1924. They
successfully raised two adopted
children while making the
Pennsylvania School of Social
Work —under Dean Kenneth
Pray (26)—a Rankian
stronghold. (Taft is at Pray's left,
Robinson at his right). Rank
visited psychiatrist George
Wilbur on Cape Cod (25) after
A. A. Brill purged Rank from the
American Psychoanalytic
Association in 1930. After that
Rank's analysands—Wilbur for
one—had to be reanalyzed by a
strict Freudian or else resign
from the APA.

26

27

An international summer institute held in
Paris in 1934 and led by Rank with Harry
Bone (left) and Pearce Bailey (27) was
highly successful, but worsening economic
conditions and the Nazi menace forced
cancellation of the 1935 session and made
the Ranks adopt a third homeland: the
United States. Their marriage had failed;
Otto met Estelle Buel (29), who became his
secretary and companion. Though no
sportsman, Rank enjoyed the outdoors
around Paris (28), on the Riviera, in
California and New Hampshire.

28

29

30

A warm and witty man, Rank increasingly drew away from academic writing to
develop a fuller life with people. In 1936 *Will Therapy* and *Truth and Reality*
appeared in English. Rank developed an approach which today is known as
existential or relationship therapy, with an emphasis on freedom within
boundaries, will, and a real encounter between patient and therapist.

Chateau
Crillon

Rittenhouse Square
Philadelphia

March 10th 1935

Dear Jake:

I was glad to hear from you at last! I have been back from the coast for about a week which I used to move to Philadelphia and settle down here at the above address.

About my trip I can only tell you briefly that it was successful from every point of view and that I am now contemplating to go out to Frisco to live there.

As to the translations I must confess that the last chapter of the incest I received from you did not satisfy me at all. I hate to say this considering all the work you put into it, but I am afraid it cannot be used as it is and I have neither time nor inclination to go through the whole thing over and over again.

I hope we shall have an opportunity to discuss the whole matter before I go back to Europe ,- some time in the latter part of May.

I was glad to hear that you are all well & preparing for the Spring which I hope will come soon.

With best regards to Joy and yourself -as well as Jakie,

as ever

Letters to George "Jake" Wilbur (32) and Jessie Taft (33) show Rank's strong attachment to America. After his first visit to California in 1935 he hoped to settle there. With Estelle and Jessie he began using the nickname "Huck," from

live in a home
of art and culture

telephone clarkson 2-1700

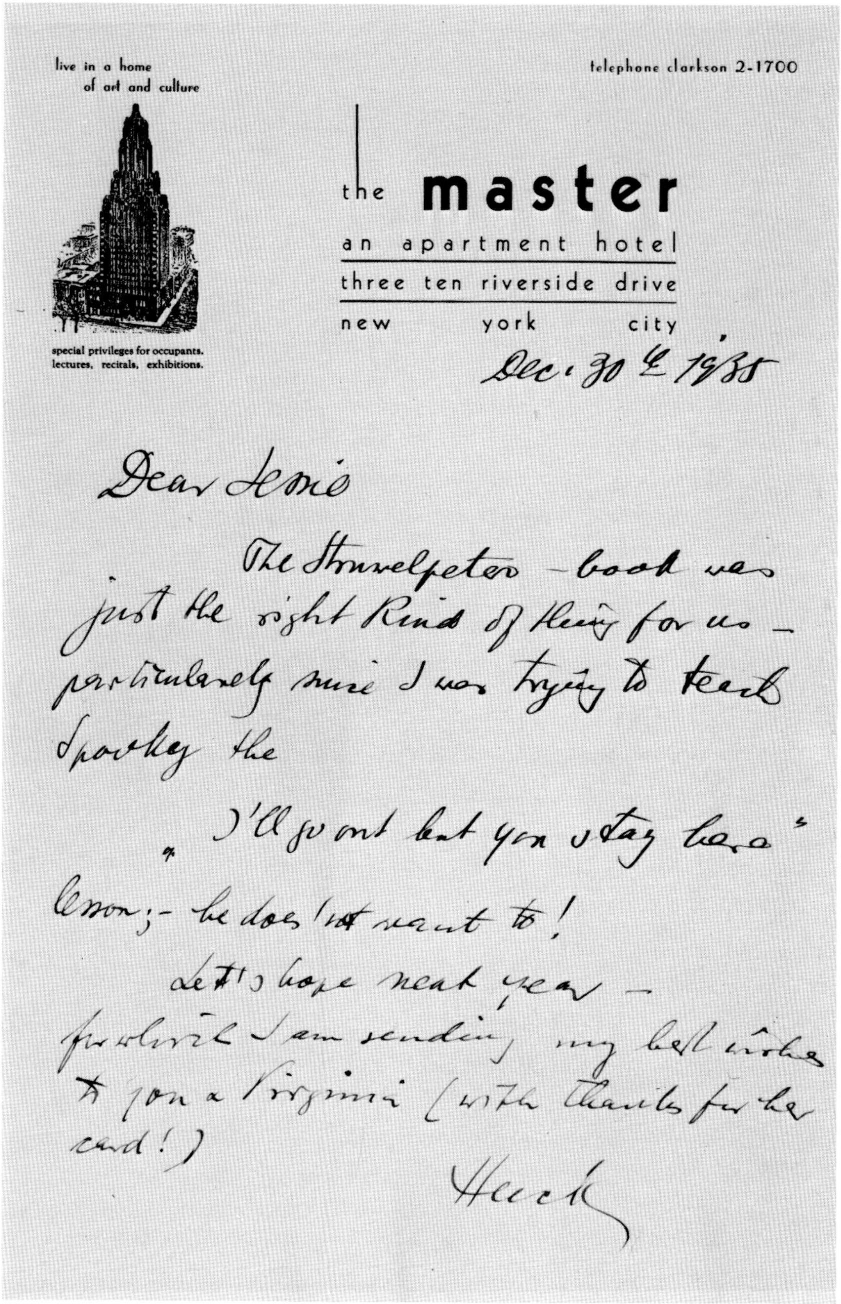

the master
an apartment hotel
three ten riverside drive
new york city

special privileges for occupants.
lectures, recitals, exhibitions.

Dec. 30th 1935

Dear Jessie

The Struwwelpeter-book was just the right kind of thing for us – particularly since I was trying to teach Sparky the

"I'll go out but you stay here"

lesson; – he does not want to!

Let's hope next year – for which I am sending my best wishes to you & Virginia (with thanks for her card!)

Huck

33

Mark Twain's great novel. From 1935 Rank lived at the Master apartment hotel (33). He married Estelle in 1939 just three months before his death.

Rank (34) remained popular and influential among social workers, psychologists, and artists but the powerful psychoanalytic community continued its vendetta. A story that Rank was mentally ill was perpetuated for years, as seen in the vicious *Time* magazine review of Jessie Taft's memoir (excerpt, 35), in which she told how Rank transcended his poor and unhappy family origins.

34

35

DISCIPLE RANK, MASTER FREUD
Sick, sick, sick.

psychoanalysis made its heaviest impact on psychiatry and education just after World War I, Rank was a respected eminence in the top hierarchy, with vast power as a molder of minds. In these same 20 years he ran the gamut from infantile adulation of Freud, through emulation, to a break with the Master on matters of doctrine.*

One of Rank's most devoted disciples: Jessie Taft, psychologist and professor in the University of Pennsylvania's School of Social Work. In *Otto Rank* (Julian Press; $6.50), Disciple Taft, 76 this week and retired, reveals the agonizing details of Rank's character that a dozen years of personal association and years of painstaking research have provided. In unsophisticated, pre-Freudian days, it would have been considered shocking that a man so disturbed should win such acceptance.

Sex at Six. Though Biographer Taft makes no claim to impartiality, she is painstakingly honest. Rank, she discloses,

* Of the eight apostles who at various times were closest to Freud, four eventually defected: Alfred Adler and Carl G. Jung (by far the most famed of his followers), Rank, and Sandor Ferenczi (who has been called emotionally disturbed).

have difficulties with myself—apparently the usual crisis that one reaches sooner or later." He had come to read proof pages and select the dozens of illustrations for *Art and Artist,* and to lecture in Philadelphia. To her great consternation, Taft would not see Rank for several weeks. When they finally met, she was shocked to find him in a profound depression. It was an effort for him to speak. He showed her the proofs, but his mood barely changed despite her efforts to give help to her former therapist. Two weeks later (April 2) they met for lunch. Although he was somewhat better, the meeting was painfully difficult for both of them.[31]

Rank was to begin a series of seminars the following week in Philadelphia, under Taft's aegis. On April 6, he sent her a telegram (and Wilbur a letter) announcing his abrupt return to France, necessitated by ill health. Taft was caught between compassion and rage: She had to cancel the lectures and therapy commitments Rank had made, while covering up what she called "the enormity of his behavior." Apparently it had not occurred to her that he might renege on his commitments, no matter how depressed he seemed to be. His trip to the South of France the previous fall had also been due to this illness, he wrote Wilbur, who penciled on the margin of Rank's letter: "A depression in which he was suicidal? and some trouble with a woman as I recall learning afterwards."[32]

Taft remained in limbo until Rank wrote from France at the beginning of June.

> I not only feel that I ought to apologize first for the disappointment and trouble I caused you but I really regret deeply the pain you must have felt on account of me—even before I left so abruptly. I knew you were my friend . . . and yet you couldn't help me then because you stood for something (at least with one part of yourself) which I had to get away from at that time. . . .
>
> What I did was terrible in a sense—not only to others but also to myself—but it was a necessity to my inner truer self, the human side, which is now free to turn to you. It was too bad that this need for a radical operation on myself occurred just in the midst of my activities in New York—but apparently otherwise I wouldn't have known how sick my soul was and what I needed for a remedy. . . .
>
> I am clear in myself now as to my personal problem, which

*I hope to work out in the right spirit to my own satisfaction
soon; it doesn't bother me nor does money worry me (although
I have not a cent); I am sure of my attitude toward life and
this will take care of everything else.*[33]

In *Art and Artist* Rank had written about the human need
for identification, "the echo of an original identity, not merely
of child and mother, but of everything living." This "identity
with the cosmic process" must be surrendered and re-established
continuously in the course of self-development. In this process,
Rank wrote, the neurotic takes the world inside himself and
uses it "as a protection against the real claims of life," paying
the price of "the feeling of world-sorrow which has to be taken
in with the rest. The artist, too, has this feeling of *Weltschmerz*"
but he can use the internalized world as material, so he is "never
wholly oppressed by it—though often enough profoundly depressed—but can penetrate it by and with his own personality."[34]
This passage may be the best clue we have from Rank himself about the nature and resolution of his own deep depression.

Dr. Wilbur was, like Taft, encouraged to hear from Rank
and wrote him, in the midst of the Hoover-Roosevelt campaign,
"Here we just mark time and watch our plants grow and our
assets vanish." He had just received the *Proceedings* of the 1930
Washington Mental Hygiene conference and expressed his
amazement at the "sneering ill-temper and deliberate misunderstanding" that Rank had endured so calmly.[35] Wilbur had experienced some of that vitriol in recent meetings of the Boston
Society and had taken pride in his Rankian calmness.

Rank seemed well in June, when he urged the Wilburs to
visit Paris. He planned to work there through the summer, and
confided that he had set aside other writing to work on a new
book on the "Jewishness" of psychoanalysis. A publisher (Harper's) was interested in the topic, which "opens up quite unex-
pected views on almost every subject we are interested in."[36]
Then he did not write until October 8, when he told both his
American friends that he had again not been well. Taft knew
this already; Rank had broken off treatment of a friend of hers
in Paris. "I am just now coming out of a crisis that lasted over
a year," Rank wrote Jessie, "and don't quite know where I am
at present although I feel well and am working."[37]

ART AND ARTIST

Rank was justifiably pleased with Knopf's release of *Art and Artist* in early October. Beautifully designed and illustrated and expertly translated, the book was introduced by Ludwig Lewisohn, who wrote a fine précis of the work and its significance.

> Freudian psychology created the first revolution . . . to it belongs the undying credit of having revealed the structure of the human psyche . . . [but] it was itself "sold" to nineteenth-century mechanistic doctrine; it, too, insisted on an unbroken chain of causality, of which all the links were to be the same in kind. It had the nineteenth-century passion for "reducing" all phenomena to a common denominator. . . . The Oedipus complex was used like an overdriven horse. If a man was an artist or a warrior or a neurotic or a tramp, he was convicted of having an Oedipus complex. But, as Dr. Rank admirably and convincingly points out, since all men have an Oedipus complex, since this relation and its difficulties are universal, the artist is still one who, by virtue of what he is in his own nature, reacts in a special way to this as to all other human experiences. . . .
>
> It is the brilliant and memorable achievement of Dr. Otto Rank to have . . . brought the psychological interpretation of cultural phenomena from the nineteenth to the twentieth century. Precisely as the new physics, in its analysis of the atom, has come upon a dynamic element in a universe now no longer like a machine, so Dr. Rank, again like the physicists rejecting causality in its rigidly and hopelessly deterministic sense, has come upon a dynamic element in the human psyche and has reinstated in its proper place and function the psychology of the will. . . . His arguments have no syllogistic structure. But anyone who has the creative experience will, like myself, read and ponder with a kind of awe the revelations concerning the character of that experience. . . . The free creative and self-representative character of all art, its tendency of liberation from the biological, its self-justificatory and immortalizing urge, its need of and yet resistance to the collective culture of its age, the artist's conflict within the dualism of creativity and experience, his need of Muse and mate and the difficulty of combining the two, his resistance to his art itself, his desire for fame and his fear of being depersonalized by that essentially myth-making process—all these explanations and revelations made by Dr. Rank I cannot conscientiously call otherwise than literally epoch-making. . . .
>
> He has been able to interpret the development of creature to

self-conscious creator in the course of the ages and, above all, the process whereby art gradually becomes differentiated from religion and tends finally to take religion's place. Thus he offers the first adequate explanation of that enormous preoccupation with art and with the artist which characterizes recent ages and, above all, the present age. He justifies and grounds both the artist's representative and his prophetic function, and will, I trust, free us, especially, again, in the English-speaking world, from that supremely silly and vicious notion that ranges art a little below flirting, a little—by courtesy—above baseball—among the pleasant ways of killing time. . . .

He solves the old riddle of "imitation" in art, proving that the creative activity is always a free and by intention a transcendent one, of which "imitation" is but a cultural mood and method. I may finally call the reader's attention to the extraordinary method of historical and psychological reasoning by which Dr. Rank reinterprets what the Romantics called "acceptance of the universe," and good and wise men of many ages "submission to the will of God" as "volitional affirmation of the obligatory" and thus shows us that the newest knowledge does but confirm the most ancient wisdom of mankind.[38]

Rank's "volitional affirmation of the obligatory" is less clumsy in German, from which the simplest translation is "willing yes to the must." Rank states again in this form the idea that to find meaning and fulfillment in life we must also embrace death. Forty years later, Ernest Becker celebrated Rank's achievement in his own signal work, *The Denial of Death*. But Ludwig Lewisohn, an American at home in German and French milieus, knew and probably understood Rank better than any reader of his time. Compared with his preface, the favorable review by Joseph Wood Krutch (*The Nation*, December 7, 1932) pales. Rank's most important book and the culmination of his genius as a writer and scholar, *Art and Artist* will eventually take its place among the great works on the history of art and the psychology of creativity. But surprisingly few reviews of the book appeared. Even more surprisingly, the German original has never been published.

INNER AND OUTER WEATHER

In January 1933, Franklin Roosevelt took the Presidential oath of office in Washington and Adolf Hitler was appointed Chancellor of Germany. But Rank and his correspondents wrote little about political or general economic conditions, which included the whole period of the Great Depression. In May the Nazis burned Freud's books, among others, in Berlin. Rank was then negotiating with a Viennese publisher who wanted him to revise the German version of *Art and Artist.* The project stalled. The shadow of Nazi power, which officially took psychoanalysis to be a "pornographic Jewish specialty," was surely a factor. Rank's *Modern Education* was published in the original German as *Erziehung und Weltanschauung,* (*Education and World-view*), by Reinhardt (Munich) a year after the English translation; that was Rank's last publication in his mother tongue.[39]

Herman Nunberg, a rival of Rank's from Vienna, had migrated out of the Nazi storm to Philadelphia. He established himself promptly with a book, *Principles of Psychoanalysis,* introduced and endorsed by Freud. It contains a section on birth anxiety, which mentions Rank only to dismiss him. Yet, it concludes: *"Birth anxiety, therefore, is an anxiety of separation. It is biological but it becomes the prototype of psychic anxiety."* Reading it, George Wilbur was bemused: "I am unable to make out whether this is supposed to be the last word in refutation of you or is the final acceptance of your idea." But Rank had no interest in Nunberg's version, suggesting that no one could understand his birth trauma theory because "when I wrote it I did not understand it myself. The book [*The Trauma of Birth*] is really a great vision of the idea of separation governing the universe." (Rank pursued this idea in *Art and Artist.*) He ended the letter: "The whole history of psychoanalytic thought has to be written one day and I am afraid that I am the only one who can write it."[40] Unfortunately, he never did.

In February Rank told Jessie Taft about his reading and writing. He liked *The Fantasia of the Unconscious* by D. H. Lawrence, calling him the "greatest psychological philosopher since Nietzsche because more human." He responded to her questions and comments about Anna Freud, Melanie Klein, and Karen Horney thus:

I think . . . this is the natural revenge of women against the "masculinized" psychology. Horney is the clearest and simplest example because she does it openly. . . . Freud is trying his best to accept those things, evidenced by an article on female sexuality (or sexuality of the woman), which he discovered only

now to exist. . . . For the time being I gave up writing—there
is already too much truth in the world—an overproduction
which apparently cannot be consumed.[41]

Meanwhile, in Berlin, a Hitler appointee had organized the
New German Society for Psychotherapy. Within the year, Ernst
Kretschmer resigned as President and Carl Jung took his place.
Although some say that Jung took this position to help Freud
and other Jews, the fact remains that Jung became an outspoken
apologist for Naziism, if not a proponent. He endorsed the National Socialist world-view attacking the "Jewish theory" of
Alfred Adler. He wrote "The factual and well-known differences
between Germanic and Jewish psychology should no longer be
blurred, which can only benefit science," decrying Freud's application of "Jewish categories" to Germans and Slavs. "The most
valuable secret of the German personality, its creative intuitive
soul, was declared [by psychoanalysis] to be a childlike banal
morass," Jung wrote as he hailed the Hitler phenomenon "upon
which the whole world looks with amazed eyes." Jung's ecstatic
early letters to Freud can be heard echoing in his salute to Hitler's charismatic movement, its "unprecedented tension and mo-
mentum" which was "hidden in the German soul, in its depth,
which is anything but a wastebasket for unfulfilled childhood
desires and unsettled family resentments. A movement which
takes hold of a whole nation must have become rife in each
person."[42]

Despite the forbidding situation in Europe—thousands of
Jews were fleeing their homes, jobs, kin, and heritage in Germany—Rank's personal life had improved. In August he said
he was "out of the crisis—not only of the last two years but of
the last ten years, that is, since I left Vienna in 1923." Rank
actually left for America in 1924; perhaps the slip refers to the
previous summer away, in which the birth trauma and therapy
books were finished and the Jones–Rank conflict exploded. The
diagnosis of Freud's cancer in that year was another factor. By
early 1933 Rank had lost interest in both therapy and writing,
but he carried on his practice to make a living. Publishers and
translators approached him; the less he cared about books and
writing—a condition he enjoyed—the more they wanted. Between May and August he crossed the threshold of indifference
to a new exuberance, which he shared with "Dear Friend Jessie:"

> *To give you an idea of my present state of mind: I put aside*
> *the book on the Jews (and Religion) that Harper's are urging*
> *me to do and am writing a humorous (not bitter) satire on*
> *our present civilization in which I am making fun of everything*
> *people take (too) seriously, including myself. If I can judge*
> *from the main ideas and the few things I put down already*
> *it is going to be a great book in the manner of Rabelais or*
> *rather of Cervantes, who killed a whole literature by one book.*
> *At any rate while doing it and reading some of the great humor-*
> *ists (the greatest, because most human, being Mark Twain) I*
> *am enjoying myself and I am laughing a great deal. Fortu-*
> *nately, in that mood not even the economic crisis (I mean my*
> *own!) seems to bother me very much—although I have to do*
> *something about it—as well as for my former Self whom I am*
> *afraid I shall have to support for the rest of my life.* [43]

Rank was setting up a training program instigated by Pearce
Bailey, an energetic young American psychologist (later a neurologist) who studied at the Sorbonne. They set out to raise some
money for the project, which would train people to carry on
Rank's ideas "not when I am dead but as of now so I can grace-
fully withdraw." Rank's humor book was being written in English, "which to me seems the language of humor"; it was to
remain secret, because he planned to publish it anonymously.
Rank's practice was smaller, "just enough to keep me financially
afloat," and doing it "as it were on the side" improved the quality
of his work. Taft expressed apprehension about the major
changes Rank talked about, and he assured her that he was not
much different from the person she knew. He explained that
his "new Self" was "the real identical twin of my old natural
Self." Rank had only recently outgrown the relationship with
Freud, he said, so that "my old natural Self (which even Freud
always recognized as a 'roguish boy') came back into its own." [44]

This remarkable comment shows that Rank's separation process from Freud, which began in 1923, lasted fully a decade.
The "roguish boy" which both Freud and Rank recognized in
the younger Otto was to emerge again as "Huck"—Rank's newly
discovered twin. We may recall that the devoted Secretary revealed a roguishness at times within the Vienna Society in his
willingness to engage Freud provocatively, as in the presentation
on lying and the truth fanatic. Rank's use of the tale of delayed
obedience was no accident, either. The other side of the coin,

delayed disobedience, was played out in the ultimate separation of Rank and Freud. The pain of that loss and the upheaval of independence obscured a part of Rank which now joyously unfolded.

Rank's major writing was complete. He wanted to devote himself to living, to humor, to the "formation of personality." Unlike Freud, who wrote that art was "harmless"—a mere illusion—Rank maintained that art, the creator, governed human reality as much as instinct, the creature. In *Art and Artist* he showed how, before the age of science, art could satisfy both the individual and social need for immortality. In working through this theme he freed himself from thralldom to art only to reaffirm that in order to live, human beings need illusions, meanings, ideologies: they are essential, and far from harmless.

In his youthful first publication *The Artist,* Rank predicted that an increase of self-consciousness would impede aesthetic creativity, the social and individual need for which would be met by the scientific healer of the soul, the psychotherapist. Looking back twenty-five years, Rank took pride in that prediction. Art had decayed in the past decades during which psychoanalytic psychology increased "enormously . . . but not entirely to the advantage of mankind as a whole."[45]

The modern artist, Rank felt, was diverted from creativity in part by science, especially psychology. Lacking the traditional cultural base of religion and community, unable to replace them with the new intellectual tools, the modern artist tries to shape art into science, to discover laws of creativity. Thus he moves from a formative to a cognitive mode, raising in himself the perennial conflict between beauty and truth.

Ironically but inevitably, this truth-seeking inhibits creativity. Rather than self-expression, the artist engages in self-analysis; "the more successful his discovery of truth about himself, the less can he create or even live, since illusions are necessary for both." The solution Rank saw was not in science—even cultural anthropology—but in what he called a new personality structure which can use creatively the psychological insight which is harmful when it exists mainly as introspection. After this personality structure—"a new type of humanity"—is created, new art forms may evolve.[46] These, always in the context of time and culture, will then support life with what Freud dismissed as the illusory and harmless.

FATHER AND SON: ANALYTIC RECIPROCITY

Freud and Rank both died in 1939, thirteen years after their relationship ended. Only infrequently after their break did they refer to each other in letters, conversation, or in print. Freud, Jones and others attributed Rank's actions to an unresolved father complex. Rank analyzed Freud as an ex-revolutionary who retreated from emotional reality on intellectual bypaths.

If he was aware of strong feelings over the loss of Rank, Freud could not acknowledge them, much less his share of blame for the separation. "Now, after I have forgiven everything, I am through with him," Freud said, but subsequent events show that Freud neither forgave nor was finished with Rank. Two years after the break, speaking of the Committee as an "analytical brotherhood," Freud said: "Rank then broke the magic spell; his secession and Abraham's death dissolved the Committee."[47]

Then, in discussing the painstaking practice of analysis, Freud contrasted his own mature approach with that of "a huckster like O. Rank who travels around maintaining that he can cure a severe obsessional neurosis in four months." In conversation he concurred with Jones: "Since leaving me Rank has been having periodic fits of depression, and in between, sort of manic phases . . . One could call him ill." (This was hearsay: neither Jones nor Freud saw Rank after the break.) At about the same time, in 1933, a visitor to 19 Berggasse noted Freud's bitter contempt for Adler and Jung; in contrast, Freud "had nothing but good to say about Rank—his imagination and brilliance— but simply stated 'he was a naughty boy.' "[48]

At that time the "naughty boy" was 49!

In print Freud denounced Rank's short-term therapeutic method. He called it "bold and ingenious"—as a device to profit from the haste and affluence of America. He likened it to a fire brigade which only removed an overturned lantern while letting the house burn. "The theory and practice of Rank's experiment are now things of the past," Freud's wishful thinking concluded, "no less than American 'prosperity' itself."[49] Freud vacillated on the question of whether Rank was mad or bad, "ill" or "naughty" and grasping. Regardless, Rank was considered unfit by his mentor and former peers.

In his last book, *Moses and Monotheism*, Freud credits a younger Rank—"at that time still under my influence"—for his *Myth of the Birth of the Hero.* But—without naming Rank—Freud reports the case of a young man who had a worthless father but who, in defiance, became "a capable, trustworthy and honorable person." In the prime of midlife, however, he changed and became the living image of the bad father. Although "repudiated, and even overcompensated," Freud wrote, the original father figure "in the end establishes itself once more." That Freud had in mind Otto Rank and Simon Rosenfeld was confirmed by Hanns Sachs.[50]

By treating Rank's mature development as a throwback to the bad father, Freud combined an insult with his gratuitous insanity defense for the wayward protégé. Freudian forgiveness allows the pardoner to feel magnanimous while consigning the miscreant to psychoanalytic purgatory. Others in the movement simply called Rank's departure folly, sickness or ingratitude. Self-respecting analysts would not read his books. Rank's training analyses were retroactively discredited; some of the psychiatrists he analyzed gladly went for a second analysis to meet the new requirement, but others felt it as a "forced conversion, a baptism by the sword."[51]

Actually Freud himself—especially in old age—manifested some of the pettiness of Ibsen's self-absorbed, self-pitying Hjalmar Ekdal (Rank's bad father). After cancer surgery Freud complained to Oskar Pfister: "You are the only one of my friends who does not mention my illness in your letters, but I assume you will be glad to hear that I am getting on with my work." Although Freud waved off profuse sympathy as insincere, the absence of sympathy stung him and he had to sting back. Another example: After meeting Albert Einstein (in 1926) Freud remarked, "The lucky fellow has had a much easier time than I have. He has had the support of a long series of predecessors from Newton onward, while I have had to hack every step of my way through a tangled jungle alone." Such whining does Freud no credit. Moreover it wipes out Breuer, Fliess, Jung, Rank and also predecessors like Nietzsche, whom Freud chose to ignore.[52]

Contrary to Freud's analysis, Rank did not revert willy-nilly to an identification with his "worthless" father. Rather, with a thoughtful, difficult act of will—a veritable trauma of birth— Rank broke with an embittered, cautious Freud who could not embrace his protégé's independent identity. Rank, who felt he was being sacrificed to his rivals, had endured as much as he could of Freud's compromise with the arch-conservative and anti-Semitic elements in the movement. Indeed it was Freud, not Rank, who reverted to an identification with paternal weakness: Sigmund accomodated anti-Semitism in a way reminiscent of Jacob Freud's meekness toward the bullies in the village street.

To Rank, psychoanalysis had become "as conservative as it appeared revolutionary; for its founder is a rebellious son who defends paternal authority, a revolutionary who, from fear of his own rebellious son-ego, took refuge in the security of the father role."[53] As the young Otto had come to accept the modicum of good in Simon Rosenfeld, so the mature Rank had to reject the bad—the obstructive narcissism—in his brilliant and beloved mentor.

Rank's concern with Freud as a father dates back to his own youth. Re-analyzing the Frau Doni dream, Rank had boldly concluded that Freud wanted no children but sought immortality in other ways. Paradoxically, Rank chose to be the foster son of a man he thought wanted no children. Much later, after their break, Rank argued that Freud—like Oedipus—wanted to be "neither father nor son, but simply self." Oedipus, Rank wrote in *Modern Education,* was the son of a man who wanted no successor, who "wanted to be his own immortal successor." To be a biological father, to accept paternity, means that one is mortal and will be supplanted.[54]

In *Soul-belief* Rank challenged Freud's assertion that the father's death is necessarily the most important loss in a man's life. Given Rank's background, his skepticism on this point comes as no surprise. But he goes further, contradicting Sigmund's view of Jacob Freud, whose death in 1896 triggered the discovery of the Oedipal factor.

Rank felt that Freud had long since let go of his 80-year-old father, writing: "There is scarcely any doubt which event in the life of the 40-year-old Freud was more significant: the death of his father or the *simultaneous* separation from Breuer, to whom he owed the key to understanding the neurotic and the basis of his own success, and from whom he was compelled to break in order to go the way of his own development."[55]

Thus Rank, after finally going his own way, interpreted the

mid-life crisis of Freud a generation earlier. Rank seems to be the only person to have noticed that Freud omitted Breuer from *Interpretation of Dreams* even where a "Josef" appeared in a dream! The separation from Breuer was so difficult that Freud had to deny it and displace it—onto the more commonplace relationship with his father.

As Freud's associate in revising *Interpretation of Dreams* Rank knew (and so asserts) that none of the disguised persons in the book represents Breuer. Freud's painful separation from his mentor was so recent, the memory so fresh, that Rank diagnosed the omission of Breuer as *denial*. For Freud it was easier to deal with a death wish toward his father than toward Breuer. Thanks to Oedipus, Freud could generalize and depersonalize his guilt: All boys are guilty. "Here we see the *birth of psychology* out of self-deception," Rank wrote.[56] Freud's system of causality depended upon his own need to displace present reality into the past.

Rank's theory, like his therapy, asserts the importance of the *present* encounter. He viewed the neurotic as one who escapes *into* the past; the Freudian neurotic was unable to escape *from* the past. Psychoanalysis could lessen individual guilt by asserting the primacy of instinct over will, or past over present. We are not bad, merely biological; we cannot choose our ancestors so don't blame anyone for showing the same flaws as his father. Psychoanalytic solace has its price: a profound pessimism attaches to the denial of will. To Freud the great achievements of consciousness and culture are only a thin veneer of sublimation covering our "true" animal nature. Rank challenged this with the idea that as creators, not creatures, we are most characteristically human.

One last point needs emphasis. Rank's artist, the creative type, cannot be stereotyped—for example as a great painter or composer. "The successful painter may be a thoroughly average man or a neurotic; the humble backwoodsman or simple housewife *may* be an artist," explained one interpreter.[57] Perhaps because of his humble origins and self-made soul Otto Rank was more democratic, less elitist, and more optimistic than Sigmund Freud. For Rank the ultimate artistry was living an affirmative life, ceaselessly creating that which one will be from that which is given—a personality which both respects and transcends the definitions, rules, and limitations of the past.

THE FREUDIAN DIASPORA

By the end of 1933, of the original Committee only Freud, Jones, and Rank remained in Europe. Abraham and Ferenczi were dead. Sachs had gone to Boston, Eitingon to Palestine. Given the incessant turmoil among the paladins and Freud's leaning toward women colleagues after Rank left, it is surprising that Jones concluded that the Committee "functioned perfectly for at least ten years" and succeeded "in its original aim of creating a bodyguard around Freud which dispelled the last traces of his loneliness and isolation."[58]

With the departure of Alexander from Boston after one year there was room for another European: Hanns Sachs. George Wilbur befriended him quickly in 1932 and wrote to Rank: "He had to admit that his affects were such that he could not read comprehendingly what you had written since [*Trauma of Birth*]."[59] Sachs was a minor figure in the literature of psychoanalysis, although an important and well-liked teacher. Now he had a sinecure in a major medical community as a lay analyst accepted by Harvard psychiatrists, working on ground prepared by Rank.

Sandor Ferenczi fell ill in 1932 with pernicious anemia. Despite his rejection of Rank as an apostate, Ferenczi eventually also pulled away from Freud. He was to succeed Eitingon as President of the IPA but withdrew because of growing differences with the psychoanalytic leadership. Freud said, "He is offended because one is not delighted to hear how he plays mother and child with his female patients." According to Jones, Ferenczi said that Freud had no more insight "than a small boy." Jones remembered this as a comment he first heard from Otto Rank. Sensing another defection, Freud wrote to Ferenczi: "Each of those who were once near me and then fell away might have found more to reproach me with than you of all people. (No, Rank just as little.) It has no traumatic effect on me. I am prepared and am accustomed to such happenings."[60]

In one of his last letters Ferenczi urged Freud to flee to England with Anna. Freud demurred, sure that Nazi brutality would be limited to Germany. On February 27, 1933, within a month of Hitler's appointment as Chancellor, the Nazis burned the Reichstag (Parliament), blaming the Communists. By the summer of 1933, Hitler reigned over a country with only one party. He extinguished freedom of the press, labor unions, and individual rights of all kinds and built concentration camps— Dachau, near Munich, was one of the first—where anyone suspected of opposition could be sent without trial. Hitler blamed the Jews for Germany's troubles and persecuted them accordingly. The Berlin stronghold of psychoanalysis dissolved, to be replaced by Aryan psychiatrists led by Jung. When in May the Nazis publicly burned Freud's books in Berlin, they also destroyed at the press 50,000 copies of a popular edition of his *Introductory Lectures.* Freud quipped, "What progress we are making. In the Middle Ages they would have burned me; nowadays they are content with burning my books." Freud's death in 1939 spared him a later judgment of that progress. Among the 65,459 Austrian Jews who would perish at Nazi hands were his four sisters.[61]

CHAPTER 12

Anais Nin

*I admit the tragic end to all absolutism, and I do fight the
tendency to extremes; extremes in life, debauchery because it
defeats its own quest for pleasure; extremes of love because they
defeat love; extremes of pain which defeat aliveness.*
— Otto Rank, as quoted by Anais Nin[1]

His personal life, the privacy of his friends, and the identity
of his patients were all scrupulously guarded by Otto Rank. For
example: Jessie Taft and Anais Nin, two former patients who
became close friends of his in the mid-thirties, did not know
of each other. "We never talked about his friends or introduced
them to one another," Nin recalled.[2] Not a single love letter
to or from Rank has yet surfaced.

The history of Rank's involvement with women remains obscure. He wrote an undated—probably youthful—romantic vi-
gnette, "Diary of a Stillborn," about a boy who meets a girl at
a lake and falls in love; consummation is thwarted by his shyness
and his preoccupation with remembering (controlling) the experience rather than living it fully. The theme reappears in Rank's
life and thought; very likely he was the stillborn lover who felt
he had lost his chance.

In Krakow during the war, Rank had met and courted Beata
Mincer, a beautiful and intelligent Polish-Jewish woman; he was
34 when they married, in 1918. Their first long separation occurred in 1924, when Rank spent six months in New York. Jel

liffe's comment three years later about Rank's traveling with a "secretary" coincides with Rank's inscribing one of his books "to the Twin" (April 1927). And in the Rank papers is a mysterious letter from the summer of 1933, in his hand, to "Niniusko." He uses the intimate "Du" form; in it he asks the recipient to get certain books and some tobacco for him in England. This was before Rank's first meeting with Anaïs Nin, who presented herself in her famous Diary as Rank's patient, apprentice, and muse. She does not say they were lovers, but that is generally assumed by readers of the Diary and by some of my informants.

The daughter of the Spanish composer Joaquin Nin and the Danish singer Rose Culmell, Anaïs Nin (1903–1976) was born in France. At the age of eleven, after her father deserted the family, she moved with her mother and brothers to New York. At 20 she married Hugh Guiler, an engraver and film-maker known by the name Ian Hugo. Like Lou Andreas-Salomé, Nin lived apart from her lifelong husband much of the time. She and Henry Miller (1891–1980), the struggling expatriate writer, began their intimate and lasting friendship in Paris in 1931. At the end of 1932 the two writers were avidly reading and discussing *Art and Artist*. In January 1933 Miller got up the courage to write Rank, and he finally saw him one afternoon in March: "I am going to Rank in full panoply, with questions and with indictments." Henry sent Anaïs ten pages of notes on his reading of Rank, and minutes before the appointment told her about his "terrible timidities."[3]

It was a titanic hour; Henry phoned Anaïs excitedly that night and penned a fourteen-page letter to her the next day. The gangling Brooklyn refugee felt that the little Viennese analyst had probed his core. Miller, 41 and working on *Tropic of Cancer*, was married to his second wife, June, who could be equally comfortable in bed with a woman, with Henry, or with both. For a time she and Anaïs were fast friends who commiserated about Miller; they intermittently succored and shook his large but vulnerable ego. Miller, who visited Rank with nothing to be cured but his timidity, achieved "no less than a brilliant, an artistic cure." Miller got "the high challenge, the acid test" that he needed. Impressed by Rank's "thirty years of struggle, diligence, research, exploration," Miller nonetheless felt equal to, if not above, the man whose work had intimidated him so recently.

He claimed that Rank's amazement at the encounter matched his own. They discussed the late D. H. Lawrence, whose intellect, they agreed, had not been equal to his intuition. They also agreed about what was best in Rank's work: the chapters "Microcosm and Macrocosm" and "The Formation and Creation of Speech" in *Art and Artist.* Miller said they even agreed that Rank had not gone beyond Nietzsche.

Henry excitedly explained to Anais Rank's discovery about the evolution of belief in the soul, the problem of bodily death and personal immortality which he explored in *Soul-belief.* It is only recently, in what Rank calls the sexual era, that art became eroticized. Miller found "simply marvelous" Rank's point that, even after primitive peoples learn the connection between intercourse and pregnancy, they cannot accept the idea. It is modified, exaggerated, sanctified—in religion, then in art—in order to protect the belief in the soul's permanence despite bodily death. Miller wrote to Nin:

> But all primitive art, wholly contrary to the general and vulgar belief, is devoid of sex emphasis; sex appears only incidentally, as it appears in actual life, and even less than that because it is allied to the hostile forces of life. . . . Here lies the root of all that evil and destructive aspect of woman which man has created through his varying culture patterns . . . directed not against woman per se but against that generative symbol which she expresses and which negates his cosmical view of life and birth, of creation and death.
>
> . . . And remember about the Renaissance that it was exceptional in its spawn of great individuals, men and women. . . . Men of eminence were discussing that very problem (perhaps not understood as herein) with those very women whom they admired. Remember all I have been trying to say about the masculine aspect of the civilizing process, that all culture is built up on an evasion (that's how I was putting it to myself, perhaps not so neatly as Rank) of that sex problem—that dilemma really. For when you consider woman, in her role of generator, of begetter, when you consider how analagous she appears, to man's mind, to the role of Nature, Nature which spawns ceaselessly and carelessly and destroys at the same time, how natural, inevitable it is that this artificial, this abstract, this thoroughly mental image of life which his Culture is should be opposed to the female view, the female principle. Woman is, man becomes—I think that was one of Spengler's phrases.[4]

Henry's exuberant sharing with Anaïs continues. He summarizes Rank's "great contribution," the insight that man establishes an ideology of creation which is nonsexual (or antisexual) by a splitting (division) of the self. When man finally accepts the sexual facts of life he seizes upon the Oedipal idea, which lets man be his own creator by returning to his mother's womb. Patricide symbolizes the awareness of mortality that comes with conscious acceptance of biological fatherhood. With the double crime (patricide and incest) there is a distorted acceptance of sexuality with its inevitable fatality. The distortion undoes the creative roles of mother and father in favor of the primitive idea of self-creation.

> [Man] *makes of his necessity an act of freedom again. He persists, in other words, in restoring the magic, the deeply religious quality to his creative faculties. His incestuous longing then is a sacred characteristic; it is this perhaps that Nietzsche meant when he spoke of the necessity of man to commit the unpardonable sin, to commit the crime against nature, against instinct. Man is the crime against nature—or that is, his representation of Life is such a crime. It is something he can only adhere to by a violation. Here, and am I happy to state it, lies what there must be of Orphic mystery! This incest route, traversing as it does all the ramifications of the sexual anomalies (the mating of man with mother, with sister, with animal, with goddess), this route leads man perpetually back to the fulcrum on which his universe rests—"the irrational phenomenon of fear," says Rank, "world-fear and dread," says Spengler, the tragic springs of life, from the Nietzschean point of view. Anyway, life reduced to its fundamental terrors, its horrors, its awfulness, its absurdity, its sublimity. But Life—even though the way be through Death.*

Miller ends his letter with gratitude, telling Nin she is the real teacher, the one who breathed life into the ideas of these great thinkers, the "guide who conducted me through the labyrinth of self to unravel the riddle of myself, to come to the mysteries."

After their meeting in March, Miller remained in contact with Rank (who, characteristically, left no indication that he ever knew Miller). Rank read and praised the manuscript of Miller's *Tropic of Cancer,* as did Nin.[5] Like all artists, Henry Miller,

Anais Nin, and Otto Rank had in common their self-nomination for that role. They actively integrated strong emotion with formidable intellect, a notable accomplishment for three very different people who were largely self-educated.

RANK THE IMPROVISER

Born into a musical family, Anais Nin had been an artist's model and a dancer. Her Diary began as a letter to her errant father when she was eleven; she kept it as a retreat, a sourcebook, a place of privacy for her second self. Volume I (1966) covers the years 1931–34 and her first encounter with Rank. Noted for its freshness and immediacy of expression, the Diary, more than her novels, made Anais Nin an international celebrity, a literary phenomenon. Her adult Diary extends to seven volumes, all of which mention Rank, although his death is recorded in the third. (The youthful—pre-1930—diaries have recently appeared in several further volumes.) She published only a portion of the manuscript original. Nin—like Rank with his youthful Diary—revised and rewrote material, sometimes months after the event. She said herself that "it was the fiction writer who edited the diary," which can therefore be regarded as a journal-novel.[6]

Nin concerned herself with psychological rather than historical truth. She names historical figures like Rank and Miller, but others—like her husband, Ian Hugo—were excluded from the published version. Even the dating of events serves only as a guide, not an exact calendar. Despite the confessional aspect of the work, Nin's real life remains veiled. For example, the volume of Miller-Nin letters omits her side of the correspondence. Rank did not keep personal letters or patient records; his letters to her have not been made available. They will undoubtedly modify and augment parts of the story she tells, which meanwhile must be taken as fictionalized biography.

After he met Miller and before Nin's first visit, Rank was developing a Psychological Institute in Paris, which would bring lecturers "from all parts of the world and all kinds of schools" the following summer. He encouraged Taft and Wilbur to attend (in 1934) and to send others to what would be a "living dynamic center instead of a Sunday school class where first the Old Testament (Freud) and then the New Testament (Jung) are taught mechanically." Referring to his recent identity crisis and sounding like Mark Twain, Rank described the Institute as "a kind of mausoleum of this past self, which in this way gets a beautiful and honorable burial whereas my natural Self is amused (that is the humorist) at seeing people believe it is in the Institute."[7]

Anais Nin had become dissatisfied with Dr. René Allendy, a Freudian therapist who had helped her to some extent. Having read "all" of Rank's books (presumably those in English and French), she made an appointment (with Miller's encouragement) and met Otto Rank on November 8, 1933. "He was short, dark-skinned, round-faced; but what stood out were his eyes, which were large, fiery, and dark. I singled out his eyes to eclipse the short Dr. Caligari body, the uneven teeth." Anais was petite and beautiful, a cultivated flower compared to her weedy friend Henry. She and Rank quickly achieved rapport. Soon she learned that there was more at issue in her relation to her father than a victory over her mother, that there was something beyond lesbianism, narcissism, masochism, and the other categories: There was creativity.

> What predominated was his curiosity, not the impulse to classify. He was not like a scientist intent on fitting a human being into a theory. He was not practicing mental surgery. He was relying on his intuition, intent on discovering a woman neither one of us knew. A new specimen. He improvised. . . .
> "What you call your lies are fiction and myths. The art of creating a disguise can be as beautiful as the creation of a painting [Rank said]. . . . Confusion creates art. Too much confusion creates unbalance."[8]

She spoke of her long-absent father and he told her about his study of incest myths. He dissociated himself from the psychoanalytic interpretation that they prove an unconscious incest wish, pointing out that characteristically (as in Oedipus) the child and parent do not know or recognize each other when they meet later in life. This fact "does not bother these psychological interpreters," who simply claim the incest wish is repressed. Rank thought that in the boy-hero myths the story is told from the son's point of view, and the young heroine's story from the father's. He concluded that men wrote the stories, since man "has always been keen to usurp all creation; and the proverbial passivity of the woman, who always appears as waiting or pursued, might have enabled him to depict her as he wanted her, *in her life story written by him.* And now I am glad to hear the woman's side of the story."

Rank surprised her at the end of the hour by requesting that she leave her diary with him. "He interpreted my carrying it as a wish to share it." She was alarmed because it contained some fictions she had prepared to tell him about herself. When later she told him the diary was originally written for her father, Rank thought that her writing was a response to inner guilt, a feeling of inadequacy which accounted in her mind for the loss of her father. The stories she told in the diary were to win him back, to hold onto him in the manner of Scheherazade.

For some time, Rank had understood the analytic situation as one in which the patient tells stories designed to please and hold the analyst. As long as one caters to the powerful authority, one can stay inside and be safe. The result of such prolonged analysis is endless gestation, or psychological stillbirth. Rank developed the technique of setting an ending to counteract the problem of interminable analysis. End-setting was gently provocative, not arbitrary or cruel. Therapist and client focus on a limit that is both chosen and inevitable. Birth terminates symbiotic life just as death terminates individual life: Both events are "musts" that can nevertheless be chosen psychologically—they can be *willed.* One's being and one's death cannot be prevented; but whether they are lived or just endured depends upon conscious acts of will.

Nin deserves credit for a profound insight about Rank's technique: He *improvised.* The root word means "not to foresee." While even good surgeons and Freudian analysts sometimes improvise, Rankian therapists do it constantly. Improvisation does not imply caprice; but it requires a capacity to withstand anxiety in oneself and the other. In therapy, as in music, improvisation requires a foundation in theory, deeply embedded skill, and a love of dynamic experience—that is, of life. "Dr. Rank," Nin wrote, "opposes the concept that all struggle in the neurotic is merely a perverse resistance to an infallible teacher. He apparently diminishes the supreme oracular role of the analyst in order to equalize the relationship."[9]

Rank added the imagination and discipline of the artist to those of the scientist, so that both are freed from static formulas.

If Freud discovered depth psychology, then Rank, to use his own adolescent phrase, had become a "soul diver." He had seen dogmatic analysis reduce the person to a specimen, a formula. He watched analysts dissect personalities, dry them out, color them with strange intellectual lights, and leave them lifeless. "I believe analysis has become the worst enemy of the soul," he said to Nin. "It killed what it analyzed. . . . I disliked medical language, which was sterile." Rank discovered that what restores life to science is art.[10]

NIN ON RANK: "HE IS INEXHAUSTIBLE"

At the time he began seeing Anais Nin, Rank had put aside writing in order to develop the summer "Training Institute for Practical Psychologists" in Paris. With the help of Jessie Taft, he hoped to attract a large contingent of Americans. In a letter to Taft he asked about a course she was giving on Lawrence and the creative personality and he mentioned Gertrude Stein: Rank had not read her books, but had read a review of her latest one (*The Autobiography of Alice B. Toklas*) in *The New Yorker*. "I liked it very much without any further desire to read the book. I think she is too sophisticated for me—and I crave simplicity (the other I have myself)." When later he read Gertrude Stein and heard her speak, Rank liked her emphasis on the present and on difference—themes of his own. But he thought she was the most self-conscious writer ever while his favorite, Mark Twain, was the most spontaneous.[11]

Having taken no real summer vacation—just "short flying trips around the country for extended weekends"—Rank spent the two weeks around the New Year visiting Vienna and Switzerland. This vacation allowed him to renew contacts with Eugene Minkowski, Edouard Claparéde, Charles Baudouin, and Jean Piaget.[12]

Anais continued in intensive therapy. Rank helped her disengage from her father, who abandoned her and then came back into her life. "Your father, as far as I can make out, is still trying to create you to his own image. . . . Man is always trying to create a woman who will fill his needs, and that makes her untrue to herself." Nonplused without her diary, Anais began writing a portrait of Rank.

Background: Books, shining and colorful books, many of them bound, in many languages. They form the wall against which I see him. Impression of keenness, alertness, curiosity. The opposite of the automatic, ready formula and filing-away. The fire he brings to it, as if he felt a great exhilaration in these adventures and explorations. He gets a joy from it. It is no wonder he has evolved what he calls a dynamic analysis, swift, like an emotional shock treatment. Direct, short-cut, and outrageous, according to the old methods. His joyousness and activity immediately relieve one's pain, the neurotic knot which ties up one's faculties in a vicious circle of conflict, paralysis, more conflict, guilt, atonement, punishment, and more guilt. Immediately I felt air and space, movement, vitality, joy of detecting, divining. The spaciousness of his mind. The fine dexterity and muscular power. The swift-changing colors of his own moods. The swiftness of his rhythm, because intuitive and subtle.

I trust him.

We are far from the banalities and clichés of orthodox psychoanalysis.

I sense an intelligence rendered clairvoyant by feeling. I sense an artist.

I tell him everything. He does not separate me from my work. He seizes me through my work.[13]

Her last lines have the cadence of Walt Whitman, befitting the poetic resonance of Rank and Nin. Others who knew Rank personally and through his teaching have said that his therapy sessions were like poems, joint works of art created in the moment by the union and the struggle of two souls.

Nin relates what Rank told her one day about his early life. Because of a lung problem a friend took him for treatment to Dr. Adler, who introduced him to Freud in 1905. "The men who surrounded Freud were awed and acquiescent. Not Rank. Freud enjoyed the disparities and the clashes of opinions. Rank learned, but he also questioned. . . . He became his research worker, his proofreader, his adopted son. Freud made him editor. . . . He gave Rank a ring (which Rank showed me and was wearing) and wanted him to marry his daughter, to be his heir, and continue his work."

Nin is eloquent, self-centered, sensitive, inconsistent, coy— and sometimes false. Her story contains errors: thus, Rank did not work as a glassblower, nor was his mother a widow. Nin says that people in Vienna thought Rank's pen name was Ferdinand Bruckner (pseudonymn of Theodor Tagger, 1891–1958), which hurt his reputation as a psychoanalyst! Nin was interested in Bruckner's psychological dramas, but seems to have erred in linking Rank with him. Nevertheless she says much that is credible and interesting.

> Freud tried to analyze Rank, but this was a failure. Perhaps because they were too closely bound, perhaps because Rank was the rebel son and he was beginning to disagree with Rank's ideas. Freud did not like the concept of the Birth Trauma, nor Rank's ideas on illusion and reality. Like all fathers he wanted a duplicate of himself. But he understood Rank's explorative mind, and he was objective. Even their disagreements on theories would not have separated them. The real cleavage was achieved by the others, who wanted a group united by a rigid acceptance of Freud's theories.[14]

This account could have come only from Rank. He may have told it only to Nin; Jessie Taft and others who questioned Rank about his past, like Wilbur, confirm his reticence to open this door. Nin's Diary reports the jealousy of Rank's colleagues as well as Freud's shift from support of Rank's innovations to censure. "After twenty years they had succeeded in banishing him. He not only lost a father but a master, a world, a universe."

Some passages in the Diary paraphrase, even almost quote from, Rank's writing. Others present a side of him not to be found in his books or even his letters, but are consistent with Rank's life and thought and illuminate him further. She quotes him:

> The new hero, still unknown, is the one who can live and love in spite of our *mal du siècle*. The romantics accelerated their suicide. The neurotic is the modern romantic who refuses to die because his illusions and fantasies prevent him from living. He enters a combat to live. We once admired those who did not compromise, who destroyed themselves. We will come to admire those who fight the enemies of life.[15]

Rank had taken the Diary away from Nin so that she would not use it as a "traffic island" (his words) from which to observe the analysis and control it. Apparently he did not tell her he had also kept a diary. Nin continued writing and Rank relented about the restriction, inclined as he was to respect the patient's will. Rank encouraged Nin to keep a sketchbook, "instead of being kept by a diary." He shared with her the dilemma of combining life and art in a way that enhanced both.

After 1933, the year he met Nin, Rank published little besides Taft's translations of his books on therapy. His writing had fallen off after 1931; the planned books on humor, on the "Jewishness" of psychoanalysis, and on social psychology were stillborn; fragments appear in *Beyond Psychology*, a group of essays published posthumously. After the post-Vienna frenzy of authorship—six books in six years (1926–32)—Rank turned from writing to living, reversing the balance of his earlier life. Nin seemed compelled to attempt both simultaneously: She lived to write and wrote to live.

With Anais Nin, Rank grappled with the problem of the woman as artist. Her ability to create in childbearing, a palpable act, sets woman apart from man; his role in this creation is tangential by comparison. Woman's immortality and her mortality both are expressed in pregnancy and parturition. The male, Rank thought, vacillates between the tangible immortality of parenthood and the symbolic immortality of a godhead. He thought that women's (maternal) creative realism left them less in need of artistic productivity. Rank never suggested, however, that a woman's creative life could be fulfilled biologically. Thus in speaking of the state's hunger for soldiers he deplored pressure on women merely to breed, rather than to create new individuals.

In one session, Anais was trying to understand her indulgence of Henry Miller. Rank expressed his thought that women can indulge men because they sense the child in the man. Men are less capable of seeing the child in the woman in a nurturing way. Rank allowed, however, that an especially paternal man might similarly indulge a woman. Rank, of course, could constructively indulge the child in Nin and his other patients, consistent with his discovery of the mother tie in the transference and its significance in human development generally.

Twice in the Diary Nin expresses Rank's view that a woman, cured of neurosis, becomes a woman, while a man becomes an artist. Some have found this attitude condescending toward women, but Rank valued living—the creation of personality— as the highest expression of creativity and he spoke of the overvaluation of the artist in recent times. Nin herself later criticized Rank on this point, "that all women who were analyzed and got rid of neurosis would go back into life and not create. Of course he was wrong." But she oversimplifies his position. He believed that the uncreative life is not worth living. He even said, "The man who acts in reality like a woman—who is a woman following her instincts—he alone is human."[16]

Observations on Beata Rank in these years are hard to come by. Rank made few comments about her to his correspondents, and no letters between her and Otto have come to light. Late in life Helene Deutsch reminisced about Beata, whom she met when both were young mothers in Vienna. She described the Ranks' married life in a small two-room apartment as "simple but obviously contented." To Deutsch, Beata Rank was an intelligent woman, much loved and admired, who underwent some kind of personality change: "She suffered from a painful though unjustified sense of inferiority."[17] Anais Nin also had some comments.

> Once, as I arrived, I caught a glimpse of a small, rather thin woman dressed all in black like a widow. I asked Rank who she was. He told me, "It is my wife. A short time before we married, she lost her father. I thought, then, that her wearing black and mourning was rather natural. But she has remained bereaved and grieving; she remained a widow. Compare this permanent mourning with your immediate efforts to create something in place of what you lost. That is the artist."[18]

Nin, whose own remarkable definition of neurosis was "a stuttering of the soul in life," found Rank a man of sensitivity, wisdom, and warmth whose energy and optimism grew out of and away from suffering. His presence, as much as his words, conveyed his wisdom. She could not recall many of his exact words, except his favorite, elated phrase, "You see? You see, eh?"

> He is inexhaustible. When he shrugs his shoulders, then I know that he has dismissed the unessential. He has a sense of the essential, the vital. His mind is always focused. His understanding never wavers. Expansion. A joyous fertility of ideas. The gift for elevating incident into destiny.
>
>   . . . .He defeats the past, its obsessive clutching hold, more by the fact of his enthusiasm, his interest, his adventurousness, his war against conventions than by any simple statement. It is his aliveness which sings the funeral rites of dead emotions, dead memories.
>
>   . . . .The average Freudian analyst is a purely analytical type, bored by the variations on eternal themes. Rank prizes the varia-

tions as precious indications of the character, color, nature of the neurotic's imagination, a key to be used later in helping him to construct his own world.

[Scientific, rationalistic analysis of the neurotic] deprives him of that very illusion and creative halo which is necessary to the re-creation of a human being. Instead of discovering the poetic, imaginative, creative potentialities of his disease (since every neurotic fantasy is really a twisted, aborted work of art), he discovers the de-poetization of it, which makes of him a cripple instead of a potential artist.[19]

According to Nin, Rank restored the neurotic to the mainstream of life by honoring his or her imagination, distorted though it is, as the wellspring of creativity. Creativity involves both will and imagination; in his writing on therapy Rank spoke of the denial of will by the neurotic. Rank distinguished between the process of willing and its content; neurotics tend to confuse the two—just as, in Freudian terms, they confuse wishing with doing. If a distorted imagination frightens the neurotic, he or she suspends or denies willing in order to escape guilt. Rank worked toward the restoration of willing and the harnessing of imagination, recognizing—as Nin learned—that guilt is inescapable, for it accompanies creation, destruction, and refusing to create.

Otto Rank dominated Nin's life between November 8, 1933, and the following February; she moved into Paris to be closer to him during the winter. In her Diary, Nin wrote that Rank was deeply moved by her portrait of him.

Rank. I have a blurred memory of vigorousness, of muscular talks. Of sharpness. The contents alone are indistinct. Impossible to analyze his way of analyzing, because of its spontaneity, its unexpectedness, its darting, nimble opportunism. I have no feeling that he knows what I will say next, nor that he awaits this statement. There is no "suggestion" or guidance. He does not put any ideas in my mind as the priests in the confessional put sin in my mind by their devious questions: "You have not been impure, my daughter? You have not enjoyed the sight of your own body? You have not touched your body with intent to enjoy, my daughter?"

Rank waits, free, ready to leap, but not holding a little trap door in readiness which will click at the cliché phrase. He awaits free. You are a new human being. Unique. He detours the obvious, and begins a vast expansion into the greater, the vaster, the beyond. Art and imagination. With joyousness and alertness.[20]

In March, probably after her therapy had ended, Nin invited the Ranks to dinner. Henry Miller enlivened the party, which Nin found rather disappointing. "Mrs. Rank is negative, and spent the evening snipping everybody's wings. . . . Rank talked volubly and fully, like his books. . . . Mrs. Rank cold and brittle. Rank put his peaches in his champagne, as they do in Vienna. He became very gay."[21]

During the spring, Nin decided to become an analyst herself. She was good at analyzing character, had a yearning to help people, and wanted to be financially independent. Rank told her she was identifying with him; he would test her mettle by having her study with him at the Cité Universitaire where his Psychological Center was located. "Rank is willful, firm, whole. I feel the dynamite in him, a great depth of emotion unified and concentrated."

THE SUMMER INSTITUTE

Rank, meanwhile, was devoting much energy to the teaching program, with the help of Pearce Bailey and Harry Bone, both Americans studying in Paris. He began a small seminar of five at the end of February, which included George Wilbur—thereafter, "Jake"—and Jane Shaw Ward, who had taught for many years in China. (Ward's fluent French and administrative experience greatly helped the Psychological Center.) But Rank was ambivalent about the seminar and its possibilities, as he wrote Taft:

> I haven't anything to "teach" and can't have any kind of a "school"—not even an undogmatic one—whereas most people (and "good" people for that matter) want that, need it! . . . And yet how pathetic it is to see him [Wilbur] struggle to match my theory against the Freudian when I haven't got one and he couldn't understand it anyway, because he doesn't know (what you know) that it is a question of being that theory oneself, of representing that viewpoint in one's attitude towards life. The message is as simple as was Christ's, but you get crucified before they get it![22]

Rank's English had improved with the study of Mark Twain; his letters now show colloquial verve, with few mistakes or Ger-

manisms. Rank told Taft he had done little in the first two months
of the year: A couple of patients enabled him to scrape by financially, while reading and writing lost their hold on him. He was
not depressed, but almost wished he were. For the first time,
Rank mentioned the political context, which had become more
prominent among Rank's concerns: "Of course times are difficult,
too, all over the world: people in America have no money to
come over and besides Europe seems to be threatened by war!"[23]

Rank thought about the possibility of teaching in Philadelphia—an assignment he canceled because of illness. He was tired
of analysis and wanted to do something else.

> *The other day I received a letter from Brazil asking permission
> to translate all my books into Portuguese. . . . Maybe I can
> find a place there near the Jungle: Europe's dying anyway! . . .*
>
> *Of course reading Mark Twain—as I do right along—does
> not make it any easier to write English; it was rather bad luck
> to choose as my favorite author a writer whom I think is the
> greatest word artist in modern times (only comparable, as far
> as the art of verbal expression goes, to the Bible and
> Shakespeare.)*[24]

This letter to Taft, dated February 28, contains a postscript
(omitted by Taft in her book): "Jung has gone overtly 'Nazi'
and propagated now a 'Germanic' psychology against the 'Jewish.' This he publishes in black and white as the new editor of
a Journal for Therapy which is admittedly based on Hitler's philosophy!" Rank's awareness of and distress about Jung's Nazi
sympathies were shared by surprisingly few psychologists and
psychiatrists at that time or since. Jung, who was both ambitious
and politically naive, served as President of a Nazi-dominated
psychotherapy society for six years. Jessie Taft probably omitted
Rank's comments to avoid conflict with Jung and his followers.

Apparently some patients paid their debts, enabling Rank
to go to the South of France in mid-March "to do nothing at
all" for three weeks. Before leaving he gave a "revolutionary"
lecture in French at the Sorbonne "on psychoanalysis as a bour-
geois ideology that has been killed by the failure of democracy
and individualism." The large, enthusiastic audience applauded
Rank, but some friends thought it too radical.[25] Rank's *Wahrheit
und Wirklichkeit* (1931) had just appeared in French as *La Volonté du Bonheur.* (Taft was translating it as *Truth and Reality.*)

George Wilbur left Paris in May for England and Cape Cod, intent on finishing *his* translations of Rank, who suggested he turn for help to Rank's friend Arthur Burckhardt, Professor of German Literature at Harvard.[26] Jessie Taft and Virginia Robinson arrived in Paris in June, well ahead of the six-week Institute, which began in mid-July. Taft recalled the fourth of July in Paris, marked by a celebration featuring the aged mother of President Franklin Roosevelt speaking fluent French. Jessie Taft's reunion with Rank was easy; the traumatic separation of April 1932 had been put behind them. She met with a group of seminar leaders at Rank's beautiful apartment and noticed that he had taken down the large photograph of Freud. Two other American lecturers were Dr. Frederick Allen and Miss Almena Dawley, chiefs of psychiatry and social work, respectively, at the Philadelphia Child Guidance Clinic. Rank was elated at the success of the summer program, which was praised in publications in France and the U.S.[27]

Nin describes in her Diary her sprightly interactions with two American students, Rank's assistant, Harry Bone and artist Hilaire Hiler, who was "almost insane" about *Art and Artist*. Most of the group were women; she singles out a pair (Taft and Robinson?—Like Rank, they were two decades older than Nin) who have "sagging breasts, and hair on their lips." Nin turns critical (if not always consistent) in the Diary: first, of the Americans for being too practice-oriented, unable to follow Rank's philosophical teaching. She was infuriated when the audience pestered Rank with elementary questions, but that also encouraged her to pursue analysis as a profession.[28]

At the same time, Nin found Rank *too* philosophical in his teaching: "By now, whatever gifts he had for life are atrophied." The truth he discovered, she writes, left him frightened, rather than helping him "to live, to heal, to teach." But a little later she writes in admiration of his strong leadership, his freedom from doubt: "He has doubts about ideas, but none about the significance of life and character and action." Nin faults Rank for being too serious, not knowing how to laugh or how to live; she contrasts his inexperience and inability to enjoy "the flower" with Henry Miller's passion for the details of life. "To living he brings nothing," she writes in a major turnabout; "his life is in abstractions." Yet in the classroom she found him brilliant, subtle, fond of paradox, a dangerous philosophical opponent of

Freudianism, with "tragedy at the bottom of his black eyes."
(And only a few pages later she calls Henry "pale and passive"
compared with the "active and explosive" Rank.) In the end,
Nin saw Rank lose his spark when confronted with the dullness
of the summer students. Finally she asked him to excuse her
from the course. Shortly thereafter he took her to meet a sculptor
he admired, Chana Orloff, who did a bust of him in wood and
a sculpture of Nin as well.[29]

A different view of Rank at the time comes from Nin's husband, Ian Hugo (Hugh Guiler). He also was Rank's patient, having seen him weekly for several months. He told me that he
considered Rank a great man, a major philosopher, but found
some fault with him as a therapist. Hugo thought Rank operated
with a formula that favored action and impulse over other, less
direct alternatives; thus Rank could facilitate a decision that
might have disastrous consequences. "If you came to a question
in your mind, he would say, 'Why don't you?' He would sort
of push you into action and that isn't always the best therapy,
is it?"[30]

In any case, Rank was not *always* overly serious; a humorous
sidelight at the time concerns a woman student who forgot her
umbrella at Rank's apartment after a reception. Having called
and gone to retrieve it from Emma, the maid, she apologized
to Rank the next day at the seminar. Quite embarrassed
by the episode, she was full of interpretations about what it
might mean. Rank said, "That's all right. Emma is not a
psychoanalyst."[31]

On the strength of the success of the first summer program,
a second Institute was planned for 1935. (Political and economic
conditions ultimately wrecked these plans.) Rank wanted to
come to America in the fall of 1934, but needed confirmed em-
ployment there in order to clear immigration restrictions. In
September, Helene, 15, attended a school outside of Paris while
Mrs. Rank packed up the family belongings. According to Nin,
the Ranks had to move from their elegant Paris home because
of financial pressures.

Nin relates that Rank offered to train her intensively in psychoanalysis. (Rank did not practice analysis any more, but the
term was commonly used—or misused—by laymen to include
psychotherapy.) He asked her to accompany him to New York
for a few months, to "give him the courage to make a new

start." Nin quotes him: "I denied myself life before, or it was denied me, first by my parents, then Freud, then my wife."

> He feels that I pushed him into life. . . .
>   For the first time I know the joy of a solid, reciprocal friendship. I touch an absolute of friendship. I like Rank's sadness, his tenacity, his caring about people. He cares. He cares tremendously about everything, and everything that happens to others. I am growing away from Henry's nonchalance and non-caring.[32]

When she wrote this Nin was pregnant. In August 1934 she delivered a stillborn child, a six-month female fetus, presumably conceived with Henry Miller. Both he and Rank came to her bedside. "You ought to die in warmth and darkness," she mused to her unborn child. "You ought to die because in the world there are no real fathers, not in heaven or on earth."[33]

IN NEW YORK

Rank sailed to Baltimore, arriving on October 18th. He stayed with Taft and Robinson in Flourtown, near Philadelphia, en route to New York. There he taught two courses at the Graduate School for Jewish Social Work (headed by Maurice and Fay Karpf, who had taken the summer course in Paris) and one at the Hartley-Salmon Clinic in New Haven. Rank's modest teaching positions engendered criticism and rumors from psychiatric and psychoanalytic opponents. Writing to Wilbur, Rank assured him that the Pennsylvania School was not training lay analysts but rather working to improve the psychological skills of the social worker.[34]

At Rank's request, Anais Nin agreed to follow him to New York for a two-month stay. She was willing to help him start a new life, as he had done for her. According to her Diary, Rank had bought Chana Orloff's bust of her for his library. She says, too, that he insisted she return to dancing. In the midst of this, she says, she had the urge to go to Zurich and seduce Jung! From America, she says, Rank then wrote "desperate" letters in November reminding her that he had canceled important meetings in London to come to her hospital bedside. "Well, I am dying now. Come to my rescue."[35]

But on November 10 he wrote Jessie Taft from the Adams Hotel to say how happy he was. "I don't hate New York at all—I suppose because I am different, probably hated myself before in it; in fact I like it—was always attracted to it—and if I had a little more leisure I could probably love it." Taft was surprised, being acutely aware of increased hostility to Rank and herself among Freudian analysts and psychiatrists. Rank knew about the retreat of his best supporters—people like Kenworthy, Williams, and Peck; even child psychiatrist Frederick Allen, an enthusiastic admirer, did not want to be labeled a Rankian. Taft recalled, "As long as I had not known how to help, Philadelphia psychiatrists were friendly and frequently referred cases that were annoying to them; now that I began to know what I was doing, a few were suspicious and even hostile." She noted increased hostility toward Rank in Philadelphia with the arrival and acceptance there of a Freudian analyst (Nunberg).[36]

Rank thrived on teaching intensively, which he found "a new revelation." Taft and Robinson had given him a copy of *Huckleberry Finn*, which he read "every night when I go to bed and enjoy it tremendously." (Was this man pining desperately for Anais Nin at the same time?) Rank heard that Ives Hendrick's new book, *Facts and Theories of Psychoanalysis*, was out, "in which I am treated (or mistreated) for the first time together with Jung and Adler (which I don't like)." Better news from Boston was that Harvard psychologist Henry Murray was interested in Rank's work.[37]

Nin was met by Rank at the pier; he had arranged through an influential patient to get her through the formalities quickly. She immediately became involved in his practice. Rank told her stories of patients and how to treat them; then he gave her rough translations of his books to put into polished English. She acted as his secretary and sat outside the closed door of his consulting room. Rank's patients included the rich and well-connected, whose gratitude was expressed with gifts of tickets to opening nights and opera performances, along with invitations to restaurants and foundation events. Nin learned about politicians, millionaires, impresarios, stage and film stars, and business executives from Rank. She and Rank enjoyed the status, the glitter and pomp. They went to the theater and afterwards did mock rewrites of dull Broadway plays. When Rank had a formal dinner or other solo engagement she wrote in the Diary in her small hotel room or went out with friends.

Rank scrupulously guarded his patients' identities, but Nin, as his secretary, was privy to their names. Part of her avowed motive for learning analysis was to gather material for her writing. She makes a naive aside to the reader: "I could not reveal their names (it would have been unethical), but their stories fascinated me as a novelist."[38]

Nin brought out something new in Rank. She pulled him away from his work for a night of jazz and dancing in Harlem; at first he had only wide eyes and clay feet, but soon she had him dancing. "I would have liked to dance with the Negroes, who dance so spontaneously and elegantly, but I felt I should give Rank the pleasure of discovering freedom of physical motion when he had given me emotional freedom. Give back pleasure, music, self-forgetting for all that he gave me." It was another revelation: Rank was so taken with the experience that he couldn't wait for the end of the work day. "I am tempted to prescribe it to my patients," he told her. "Go to Harlem! But they would have to go with you."[39]

The reader of Nin's Diary who is familiar with Rank is brought up short when she relates their talk of Mark Twain, especially *Huckleberry Finn* and the theme of freeing the Negro. Nin reverses the characters in Rank's favorite book: "Rank admired Mark Twain's parody of literature, Huck's search for complications, additions, circuitous ways."[40] She means Tom Sawyer: Huck was the pragmatic simplifier, the open-hearted, clear-headed lad who could dispense with the frightful complications that Tom needed and loved. Tom, with his insistence on the authoritative, tradition-bound, slow, painfully difficult approach to liberating Nigger Jim, makes a perfect Rankian parody of the classical Freudian analyst.

Rank identified strongly with Huck Finn; indeed, at the end of the year he began signing himself "Huck" in letters to Jessie. "Through Huck," he wrote, "I discovered a new and yet age-old philosophy that is my own, my very real self, and that made me happy." It is hard to explain why Rank embraced this great novel so late, considering his long-standing enthusiasm for Twain. Nin makes a surprising assertion: Rank must have been like Huck as a boy, "freckled, homely, tattered, rough-hewn, mischievous, adventurous, inventive . . . spirited and humorous." Rank's own Diary scarcely supports that idea, though perhaps, as she says, he liked to catch fish in a river with his bare hands.[41]

Rank wrote his lectures riding the train to Philadelphia or Connecticut; he asked Nin to write her comments in the margins, to supply a woman's point of view. "I have always been a prisoner of people's need to confess," he told her, yearning for a change in order "to live for myself." He felt full of "unused life," which she had discovered in him as Henry and June Miller had done for her. Rank cut down his busy practice somewhat, sending a few patients to Anais and giving himself more time for the theater, book collecting, and writing.[42]

Henry Miller was divorced from his second wife, June, on December 20. He was then free to marry Anais Nin Guiler—should she divorce Hugo. Anais had an income as a lay analyst and Henry felt that she could teach him the technique: He had no experience of analysis beyond one interview with Rank. Henry was shocked when Rank spirited Anais away to New York. He could barely survive a month without her, and in late December he sailed to meet her after she cabled the money for his ticket. He moved into the Barbizon-Plaza, where Nin was staying—she called it the "Hotel Chaotica"—but soon left for less expensive quarters.[43]

ARTIST AND MUSE

Anais Nin's published Diary does not say with whom she slept, but Nin tells with relish of some of those she turned down, including Theodore Dreiser and Waldo Frank. The notable figures in Nin's New York sojourn, some of whom may have met Rank, included Rebecca West, Norman Bel Geddes, William Carlos Williams, John Huston, and Raymond Massey. Late in her life she wrote: "I was more interested in love than psychology . . . I worked with Rank for the moment only . . . But this fragment was not wasted. Rank's work was part of his seduction. It outlived the seduction."[44]

The relationship between Miller and Rank must have been strained. As for Nin, one detractor believes that Rank's involvement with her was motivated by his fascination with incest, a major theme in her life. Another feels that she played the decisive role in breaking up Rank's marriage. The eventual release of Rank's letters to her, and of Nin's unedited Diary, will answer many questions. But we need no more information to conclude that these two people had a telling effect upon one another. Each gave to and took from the relationship a hearty share of innocence and experience.

At the end of January Rank (she never calls him Otto) left for three weeks in California. He was invited by Dr. Lovell Langstroth, who later wrote a neurological treatise based on Rank's ideas. Rank gave four lectures, including one at Stanford, arranged by President Ray Lyman Wilbur. On February 9 he spoke on "Self-inflicted Illness" at the California Academy of Medicine in San Francisco. There he was introduced as "Professor of Psychiatry, Paris, France." Altogether he stayed in the San Francisco area for the first two weeks of February, followed by three days in Los Angeles. In California Rank met Jessie's younger sister, Lorraine Taft Warner. "Rank has such a genuine childlike pleasure in little things you can't help warming to him," Lorraine wrote Jessie. "He is younger than I expected, not nearly so homely." Rank fell in love with California and wanted to make it his home.[45]

Rank's California trip redounded to Henry Miller's benefit financially, if not romantically. According to Jay Martin, Miller's biographer, Anais began referring patients to Henry, who was seeing four people daily by the end of February. There is no indication that Rank knew or would have approved of this, nor does Nin mention it in the Diary, which does note that she took Rank's phone calls—"This is Dr. Rank's assistant speaking"—and sorted his mail while he was away. Although Rank supported lay analysis, he was hardly cavalier about personal qualifications, training, and supervision. Nin had worked intensively with him, and—according to her report—she earned his confidence personally and professionally. A sign of his esteem for her consists of two unpublished prefaces he wrote, one for her early Diary, one for Nin's *House of Incest*, which he got her to finish. When Rank returned from the West he read Nin's reports on her patients and approved: "You have a gift for this." Henry Miller, however, combined a skeptical view of analysis with a cocksure sense of his own helpfulness. He administered mixed doses of Freudian jargon and his favorite philosophers to patients. But Miller tired of the business, aware that he was not really helping, and soon gave it up, despite his need for money.[46]

A description of Rank's unique encounter with one patient appears in Nin's Diary at this time. Anais sought Rank's help for Richard Osborn, who had suffered a breakdown and was hospitalized in Connecticut. A young American lawyer who worked in a Paris bank for Hugh Guiler, Osborn had rescued Henry Miller from near-starvation, and then introduced him to Anais. Osborn was torn between his day and night selves, between banking and bohemianism. Rank agreed to see him, and Nin thought Osborn would be responsive because he had liked Rank's books. The interview at the hospital, however, was very brief. When the two men were alone, Rank greeted the staring patient: "I am Doctor Otto Rank." Smiling, Osborn replied, "So you say," and walked out. Nin was disappointed but couldn't help laughing at the story.[47]

In another episode, Rank, once grateful for standing room at the Vienna Opera, transforms himself into patron, producer, and opera star.

> One night Rank was taken to the opera by an enormously wealthy man he had cured. At midnight he telephoned me from downstairs. Could he come up for five minutes? When I opened the door he was hidden by a giant basket of flowers he had been given and wanted to bring to me. He also wanted to display Dr. Otto Rank the Viennese, all dressed up in his new tailored evening suit with cape, top hat, and patent-leather shoes. He came in and like an actor, he leaped on the couch, took off his hat like a famous singer receiving an ovation, bowed and said: "The ovation should have been for me, because I made the singer sing his best, I made the rich man back the opera." He bowed to an imaginary, applauding public. He sang a fragment of a Viennese opera, leaped down, and vanished.[48]

Nin makes it clear in recounting this episode that the two were not living together. Rank was learning to play more, to enjoy life, but he was pressing some burdens of work upon her at the same time. He wanted her to condense and refine the translations of his books, particularly the *Incest Motif,* which struck Nin as a lifetime project. The novelty of the helping role, with patients and with him, began to pale for Anais. Tension grew between them as Nin felt pressured to subordinate her creativity to his.

A few pages later Nin speaks of a different Rank, "dark and heavy. He has no *joie de vivre.* His pleasures are of the mind." She contrasts the yielding needed for life with the autocratic imposition of will in creation, whether by artist or doctor. "Henry yields, accepts. Rank seeks to change, control. Henry is happier.

Wisdom gained from ideas, the effort to control life intellectually is disastrous. This is the *will* D. H. Lawrence railed against." Then, a little later: "I can see Rank differently now, the cause for his tragic personal life. If Henry has no will at all, Rank has too much." The romance that Henry hoped for with Anais did not flourish, nor did Rank's hoped-for collaboration with her.

Nin writes as a changeling: now the parent/author, now the child/subject of her Diary; here the patient, there the analyst of Doctor Rank. She interprets him eloquently at one point, then says something totally contrary to his spirit: "He never accepts experience as a substitute for wisdom." Yet this principle—setting emotion against intellect, living above knowing—was thoroughly his. Nor does it sound like Rank when she attributes to him the philosophy that "man was born to be happy, that pain is illness."

In May, after attending a dismal psychoanalytic conference, Nin decided to abandon that profession and to be a writer in her own way. She overcame her need for Rank and her sense of obligation to him, and set sail for France. (Henry Miller followed at the end of the summer.) Having freed herself, she viewed the attachment to Rank as the continuation of her need to find her father. Although generous, Rank wanted Anais to devote herself to his work, she said, "a lifelong task which would have destroyed the artist in me. He will never forgive me my return to Paris."[49]

But Rank did seem to forgive her leaving. She came back a year later (April 1936) for an hour visit with him in New York, like a patient, and says he envied her that freedom to live. Nin had emancipated herself from psychoanalysis.

> I entered with impunity the world of psychoanalysis, the great destroyer of illusion, the great realist.
> I entered that world, saw Rank's files, read his books, but found in the world of psychoanalysis the only metaphysical man in it: Rank. I lived out the poem and came out unscathed. Free. A poet still. Not all the stones tied around my psychoanalyzed and psychoanalyzing neck can drown the laugh. Life, for me, is a profound, a sacred, a joyous, a mysterious, a soulful dance. But it is a dance.[50]

Rank's preface to Nin's early Diary has only recently come to light. Its concluding words might apply to the end of his relationship with her.

This seems to me not so much an expression of the unconscious desire for incest as of the opposite tendency, namely, not to find the lost father who cannot be recaptured from the past, but to find her future man. Not the man of her choice, but the man of her destiny, the man who she finds by completing the eternal cycle of love, and from whom she has to take herself away again not because he turns out to be her father, but because separation is the force which governs all cosmic life of which woman is not only a part but still so much of an expression.

Her love, the woman love, as it grows out and expands from the maternal instinct, she offers to alleviate temporarily the pain of living that she bestows on man by giving birth to him.[51]

Apparently Rank and Nin did not meet after 1936 (when, notwithstanding her change of heart, she was still doing some counseling in New York). That she was not close to anyone in his social or professional circle is evidenced by the fact that she did not learn of his death until months afterwards. More about this relationship will come out with the opening to scholars of the Nin papers. But the tenor of the relationship and its significance can be gleaned from information currently at hand. Both Nin and Rank sought a life that was individual, creative, and meaningful. They shared a love of writing and the arts and opened each other to experience. She was his muse for the art of life, which he had undertaken before they met. His highest praise for her philosophy of living came when he said "It is the one I arrived at—on paper!" She was better for having lived it than he was for creating, he said with a trace of envy and resignation.[52] In *Art and Artist* Rank anticipated what happened in life with Anais.

For the artist to project on to the beloved woman his bisexual creative urge—of begetting and of bearing, or of self-begetting and self-rebirth, which he has fused into one—is not only his perfect right but a necessity of life for him. . . . But for psychologists to believe that they have therefore understood anything about the creative process or even about a work of art is a presumption. . . .

[With the modern artist] the woman is expected to be Muse and mistress at once, which means that she must justify equally the artistic ego, with its creativeness, and the real self, with its life; and this she seldom (and in any case only temporarily) succeeds in doing. We see the artist of this type working off on the woman his inward struggle between life and production or, psychologically speaking, between impulse and will. . . .

To make a woman his Muse, or to name her as such, therefore, often amounts to transforming a hindrance into a helper—a compromise which is usually in the interest of productiveness, but renders no service to life. . . . Usually, however, he needs two women, or several, for the different parts of his conflict, and accordingly he falls into psychological dilemmas, even if he evades the social difficulties. He undoubtedly loves both these persons in different ways, but is usually not clear as to the part they play, even if—as would appear to be the rule—he does not actually confuse them one with the other. . . . To the Muse for whom he creates (or thinks he creates), the artist seldom gives himself; he pays with his work, and this the truly womanly woman often refuses to accept.[53]

Although Rank speaks of the artist as male, in respect to Nin the roles were flexible, if not reversed. Much of the time she was the artist, he the muse. In friendship, as in therapy, he was not bound to a traditional male role. Knowing Nin, Rank could have modified his text to say, "She needs two men, or several . . ." Rank had noted that the artist must sometimes overcome and discard the muse, who "often comes off badly enough in real life." Nin claims to have cast him off, although whether the decision to separate was chiefly hers remains to be verified. Both Rank and Nin were artists, and both sought to escape the temptation to sacrifice life to art. "Between the two—artist and art—there stands Life," Rank wrote, "now dividing, now uniting, now checking, now promoting."[54]

Thus Rank maintained that between the creative person and the art work yawns a gulf that biography cannot bridge: life itself, the "usually dull facts" of which do not satisfy an idolatrous public. Biographers obligingly fill the gap so the creative "genius" comes to represent his or her creation. But this only misleads the audience to suppose there is a harmonious, comprehensible relationship between the artist's life and work. In *Art and Artist* Rank warned against such a tendency to seek parallels between experience and art. He stressed instead the opposition between them. Applying this principle to Rank himself, we can imagine that the dour philosopher we met in his adolescent diary may in fact have been (as Nin reports) a spirited, Huckish youth.

In *Art and Artist* Rank conveys a self-portrait without writing an autobiography. Coming a generation after Freud's self-analysis, Rank's book compares in import but contrasts in direction with *Interpretation of Dreams*. At the pinnacle of his career Rank sets forth the limits of art and of psychology, dealing with the interaction of the two from the unique perspective of one who grew up with Freud and outgrew Freud. If Freud was the pioneer of a new self-consciousness, Rank forged the way toward a new self-development.

It is not possible to resolve the dilemma of being versus knowing—of expending versus conserving life—in a book. To the intrepid reader Rank was remarkably successful, his success resulting from the recognition of paradox at every turn. Rank concluded his quest by proposing a new creative project: human personality.

Rank allowed Anais Nin to record a phase of his own pursuit of that goal. Students of his life, the details of which he rightly kept so secret, can be grateful to her for her effort. But Rank himself would direct the curious to Mark Twain's *Huckleberry Finn*, where aliveness, self-creation, will, and responsibility are joined in a personality upon which Rank—choosing to be "Huck"—evidently could not improve.

CHAPTER 13

Will

> *It even seems to me as if the Oedipus myth itself, if taken in the Greek spirit, were an experience of this same striving for independence in human development: namely, the deliberate affirmation of the existence forced on us by fate. That which is dimly but unequivocally preordained for the hero by his birth, in the mythical account, he deliberately makes his own by embodying it in action and experience . . . But the life of the individual hero will inevitably be destroyed, whether this human destiny be interpreted in terms of heroism, fatalism, or tragedy.*
>
> —Otto Rank, Art and Artist[1]

In April 1934, Otto Rank celebrated his fiftieth birthday as a world-renowned psychologist whose major works could be read in English, French, and German. Secure in his independence from Freud, Rank struggled for a place of his own in the world of ideas. But he had no interest in a "movement" or school of disciples. More important for Rank was the creative pursuit of life: relationships, personality, meaning.

Writing was no longer Rank's central concern, but he worked with Jessie Taft, who was translating his *Will Therapy* and *Truth and Reality*. These books express his mature post-Freudian psychology. One admittedly complex word, "will"—which almost disappeared from psychology after the time of Nietzsche and William James—contains the core of Rank's philosophy of helping and of life. Rank's theory, to the extent it can be articulated, was based on the notion of will.

355

WILL THERAPY

After World War I, the two great poles in psychology were psychoanalysis and behaviorism. One derived all causation from internal conflicts within the psyche, the other from conditioning by the external environment. These contrasting theories had in common a focus on the past, and contempt for the will. Rank stood apart from both.

In the nineteenth century, philosophers and psychologists divided the mind into faculties of emotion, intellect, and will. But with the appearance of Freud and even more "scientific" psychology like behaviorism, the will—discredited—disappeared. Freud reduced it to "wish"; others found it a species of delusion, or a holdover from dogmatic religion, which invoked it to hold sinners responsible for their acts, if not their thoughts. "Modern psychology," to quote one respected authority, "has tended to consider the concept of the will as an unscientific principle."[2] Will is perceived intuitively. Unlike emotion, intellect, attention, and some other phenomena of mind or motive, will cannot be objectified to the satisfaction of skeptical observers. Put another way, will cannot be proved or disproved in objective terms. It can be denied or rationalized away relatively easily; only with difficulty can it be fully accepted.

To say "free will" is redundant, since having a forced or very limited choice amounts to a negation of will. Of course, to aver will does not mean that human beings can start anywhere and do anything. Much in life, starting with birth and ending with death, is beyond our control. For Rank, the creative person comes to terms with the inevitable—the givens of life and death—by "willing affirmation of the must." In that way he or she exercises the *function* of willing, even though what is "willed" may be given. This is no empty exercise, since for Rank the essence of neurosis is denial of will. Acceptance of will means engaging life as a creative experience and death as its inescapable yet potentially creative end.

Otto Rank identified with Huckleberry Finn, one who did not fear his impulsive self. He was strong-willed and creative, meaning he succeeded in affirming life and creating self. This creative willing of inevitabilities along with initiatives was the hallmark of Rank's pragmatic idealism. We cannot prevent our own birth or death, but we can choose how to confront them.

The average person yields to the inevitable; the neurotic fights against it; the artist wills it actively. Rank therefore viewed the neurotic and the artist as similar in having a strong will, though it is expressed mostly as counter-will by the neurotic. "Psychological rebirth," giving birth to oneself or creating a personality, describes the way in which therapy breaks through to the constructive expression of will. "Will psychology" became Rank's own term for his stance against the overly intellectualized, deterministic, and mechanistic development of psychology as a science. Yet he was not unscientific. He derived great support for his ideas from developments in modern physics, including relativity theory and the uncertainty principle.

Defining will is like defining personality: Everyone knows what it is, but hardly anyone can *say* what it is. Jessie Taft, Rank's most trusted interpreter, explained the term in a review of his *Technik der Psychoanalyse*, which she translated as *Will Therapy*.

> Will, for Rank, is the integrated personality as original creative force, that which acts, not merely reacts, upon the environment. Rank's "will" has nothing in common with the Freudian "wish" in that it is actually effective, not a passive element in a deterministic chain. The will of the individual, as Rank conceives it, is in itself a first cause and produces something new. Its expression in the dreams of the patient goes beyond the wished for but unattainable to the newly affirmed capacity for control already realized. Will is not merely the drive of a predominant instinct or combination of instincts, it is that central integration of the forces of the individual which exceeds the sum of the parts, a unity which can inhibit as well as carry through to realization the instinctual urges. Only the individual whose will is locked in negativism is obliged to fear his own impulsive self. Once the patient has recovered the use of own will, he can bear to become conscious of denied impulses. They no longer threaten him any more than the objects of the outside world, since both have become material for the successful use of the will, as well as the possibility of defeat.[3]

The concept of will is difficult, but no more so than many that have become fashionable in the half-century since Rank published his *Will Therapy*. Each sentence—by Rank or Taft— is thoughtfully crafted. Her paragraph above elaborates his brief definition of will: "a positive guiding organization and integration of self which utilizes creatively, as well as inhibits and controls the instinctual drives."[4] If this does not immediately capture the imagination, let it be said that Freudian definitions of "libido," "ego," and "unconscious" are also inexact and bland, despite their usefulness.

To explain or define "will" carries additional burdens. Will represents the life center of the human being, something primal and ultimate. People have trouble acknowledging will personally, just as they had trouble at an earlier time accepting the unconscious and infantile sexuality. Will makes us at once free and responsible, godlike and guilty, ecstatic and aware of our limits—including, ultimately, death. Will belongs in psychology, and Rank's calling attention to its absence might well remind us of the boy who expressed what all could see—that the emperor had no clothes.

What is effective in therapy, Rank taught, is "the same thing that is potent in every relationship between two human beings, namely the will." This is neither Freud's instinct/drive or infantile wish (biological), nor Adler's will to power (sociopedagogical), but something psychological (i.e., soular). In psychoanalysis, will was pejoratively called "resistance." It was to be met and overcome. Willing has a bad name because it appears as willfulness, obstinacy, protest, insistence, and aggression, and its expressions could fill volumes of negative as well as positive human acts. It is hazardous as well as wonderful.[5] People tend to moralize about the *effects* of willing—its content—overlooking the *process*, with its potential for variety, creativity, and self-control. Will originates in the child's experience of opposing another's will. Thus it is first felt as "counter-will," a negative force. Depending on the parental response, a child's will—the basic expression of its personality—may be constructively developed, stifled, or distorted from the start.

Psychoanalytic theory and therapy ignore willing, but cannot banish it. With pointed and poignant humor, Rank speaks of the futile effort of the analyst to achieve "Buddhistic will-lessness." Rank saw that, paradoxically, therapy can be effective only because of the inevitable expression of will on the part of both helper and patient.[6] At the right moment the Rankian therapist can yield to the other, commending the patient for manifesting a strong will. Rank acknowledged the struggle of wills as such, rather than denying his own like the pure Freudian, who would try to tear down or stare down or outlast the stonewalling patient with trained neutrality, a pretended noninvolvement.

Rank used end-setting in treatment—not arbitrarily but in cooperation with the patient—to crystallize the inner will conflict. He brought out the ambivalence of life fear and death fear in the patient's conflict about ending or continuing therapy. Ambivalence shows "the human capacity for mobilizing will and counter-will at one time." Rank's goal was to transform counter-will into "positive and eventually creative expression."[7]

Compared with will, Freud's unconscious is a negative concept; yet it dominates the modern ideology of mind. Will is not merely consciousness; it partakes of drives while guiding them. Also, will "rules over the past and determines the attitude of the individual to it." This is a radical departure from Freud. It challenges historical, linear causality. Even when we take the royal road to the unconscious, through dreams and free association, we see only what we *will*. We remake the past individually, just as a family, tribe, or nation does collectively. Will shapes memory, and through forgetting can "free us from the past so that we can live in the present." Rank further characterizes will as the power of the ego or self and the unifying force in the individual. Intelligence, which guides the individual's command of reality, is "the executive organ of the will."[8]

Rank wrote a whole monograph on the difference between "truth" and "reality." Reaching into the past can be a simple escape from the present, just as the search for "historical truth" often evades psychological reality, which exists only in the "momentary, present, feeling experience." (Rank did not need Anais Nin to teach him this; he wrote it years before meeting her.) In therapy we strive for "immediate understanding of experience, consciously, in the very act of experiencing." And Rank defines experience as "emotional surrender to the present."[9]

Let us compare the task of therapy as conceived by Freud and Rank in terms of what is required for the process to be helpful. The traditional Freudian calls for the patient to verbalize freely, without censorship, to a professional listener who remains relatively unknown and distant. The patient is encouraged to disengage the critical ego, to let the unconscious flow. The analyst, a neutral screen who is there to receive and decipher the transference, interprets so that the patient can understand the otherwise confusing, apparently senseless content. By contrast,

Rank held that what is most valuable and most difficult in therapy is to assert what one already knows but cannot own: will. It is conscious but paralyzed or not fully appreciated, because willing is either overburdened with guilt or hidden in denial, rationalization, or justification. The Rankian therapist is not a stranger but an intimate, whose own will is also present in the encounter, first as "assistant ego," then as "assistant reality."[10]

The intense emotional experience of therapy cannot be unilateral; it must be mutual, as in teaching and learning, but not quite reciprocal, as in friendship. The therapist maintains a setting wherein the client can discover and use the strength that arises only when one is vulnerable. Rankian technique requires the therapist to meet the patient's creative needs, to serve as the material upon which the patient works to expand his or her shrunken will. So, as Rank said, the therapist must *be* the theory, not merely use a theory. Since every person is different, and every hour is different for both therapist and client, a certain spontaneity characterizes the approach. It does not fit any formula, and Rank once said he needed a new theory for every patient. It is a task of construction—psychopoiesis, let us say— rather than analysis. Unlike an engineer, architect, or preacher, the therapist does not design or build a life for another person but serves as a consultant who is retained and then let go.

AMERICA: LAST HOME

By 1930 the Freudian opposition had virtually exiled Rank from psychiatric and psychoanalytic circles: His nonmedical status combined with his maverick ideas made it a simple matter for establishment opponents to exclude him. So he taught at schools of social work in New York and in Philadelphia at the invitation of Fay Karpf and Jessie Taft, respectively. After his return from California in early 1935, he taught at the Pennsylvania School of Social Work. His course, "Theories of Personality Development," began with a series of guest lectures. Frederick Allen presided; speakers included Rank, William Alanson White, Adolf Meyer, and Franz Alexander. Rank alone led a smaller, weekly seminar for twenty-five advanced students. He enjoyed teaching a well-prepared group which could go beyond the usual questions about psychotherapy and his differences with Freud. Rank held his students "by virtue of the vitality and immediacy of his own thought processes and his complete freedom in their expression. Organization was so fundamental with him that it required no effort on his part to combine it with spontaneity."[11]

Rank had moved to the Chateau Crillon in Philadelphia for most of the spring, to accommodate a busy teaching and therapy schedule there and in New York. His dwindling correspondence with George Wilbur came to an end after Rank said he could not accept the psychiatrist's faulty translation of *Seelenglaube* and did not have time to work on it. Rank spent several hectic weeks in Paris in the summer; the Psychological Center's second summer Institute had to be canceled, as both faculty and students were too few. Rank applied for an immigration visa to the United States and by the end of the summer had settled in his last residence, The Master, an apartment building at 310 Riverside Drive, overlooking the Hudson.

Rank's immigration visa application, filed in Paris in July 1935, contains his answers to some thirty questions designed to exclude the subnormal, the insane, "persons with constitutional psychopathic inferiority," polygamists, criminals, anarchists, "persons afflicted with a loathsome or dangerous contagious disease," paupers, "persons likely to become public charges," etc. "Give me your tired, your poor . . ." says the inscription on the Statue of Liberty, but it was not quite so simple as that.

Rank's papers identified him as a professor teaching at the Pennsylvania School of Social Work. For "race" he answered "Hebrew." Rank submitted birth and marriage certificates and a French judicial (police) report. The one surprise to be found in the papers concerns Otto's parents, who are listed as Simon and Karoline *Rank*, instead of Rosenfeld.[12] Rank's mother still lived in Vienna but she died before the year ended. Simon Rosenfeld had passed away, unremarked and unmourned, in 1927.

Evidently the final separation of Otto and Beata took place in 1934. Rank's wife and daughter remained in Europe another two years. In Paris Rank had met Estelle Buel, an attractive, dynamic, intelligent American of Swiss parentage. Her father was a respected ophthalmologist in Cleveland, her birthplace. Estelle spoke German and French at home as well as English. A graduate of Western Reserve University, she had studied philology and art history in Switzerland and Italy and library science in Paris. At 32 Miss Buel became Rank's secretary, and thereafter his permanent companion. "No one could have provided more exactly and agreeably the help Rank needed," said Jessie Taft, "and to her cheerful efficiency and editorial skill he owed much of the comfort and satisfaction to be obtained from daily living."[13]

As conditions worsened in Germany, many Jews and most psychoanalysts fled their homeland. The Nuremberg Laws of 1935 deprived Jews of citizenship, forbade intermarriage, and made the swastika the official flag of Germany. Music of Negro or Jewish origin could no longer be played on German radio. Dachau had been in operation for two years as a concentration camp for Jews, Communists, and other opponents of the Hitler regime.

Unlike Carl Jung, who became a temporary mouthpiece for Nazi ideology, Ernest Jones eschewed any such role but did cater to Nazi demands rather than oppose them; he presided at a meeting in Berlin when Jewish members resigned so that the Society for Psychotherapy (which included analysts) could continue to operate. "Opinions have since differed about this step," Jones wrote, "and some have thought it would have been more dignified for all the members to resign in protest, as the Dutch colleagues did later on a similar occasion."[14] Whether because of or despite his compromises with Nazis as late as 1936, Jones won plaudits for helping a number of Jewish colleagues. That Jones accommodated fascism to save a remnant of psychoanalysis might be supportable, but there was a dark moment when he adopted Nazi tactics himself. In October 1934, confronted with a manuscript about Freud by Isidor Sadger which he could not abide, Jones suggested that Sadger be put in a concentration camp to prevent its publication. This was "beyond all normal limits" to Vincent Brome, but was cited only as an example of Jones's extreme protectiveness toward Freud by Paul Roazen. That others who knew—Federn, Eitingon, Anna Freud—made no more of an issue of it may be laid to their consuming passion for the image of psychoanalysis, and to their feeling that Sadger was a minor figure while Jones was indispensable.[15]

Back in America in early August, Rank was happy, enjoying a vacation at the Tokeneke Inn in Darien, Connecticut. He wrote Taft about his new dog, an Airedale named Spooky he received as a puppy from a patient. For some years the Ranks had owned a dog; Rank called Spooky "a very nice fellow and good friend.

. . . He knows everything without having to be told and he likes the car too . . . and likes horses as much as I do." Rank said with his dog and his car he was "really here," further evidenced by the presence of his secretary, "who is not only very efficient but does it pleasantly."[16]

When Will Rogers, an enthusiastic air traveler, died in a plane crash in Alaska, Rank remarked, "I liked Will Rogers very much and the only consolation is that this is the death he would have preferred anyway. Humorists don't like to die in bed. They live in it."[17]

After Labor Day, Rank had a busy schedule of nine patients daily. He needed money to move his library from Paris and still had long range plans to move to California. In October he gave a series of three lectures in Cleveland before an audience of about 100, organized by social workers but including leading psychiatrists as well. That month Rank introduced Miss Buel to Jessie Taft and Virginia Robinson, who were not aware of the special place she occupied in Rank's life. Rank hoped Estelle could ride horseback while the others discussed academic topics. "You'll say I spoil her," Rank wrote Taft. In late November his mother died, in Vienna "at the age of 80—the last tie there gone when I came here for good."[18]

Sometime in 1935 Rank spoke at Harvard. Henry Murray, who invited him, was a physician who turned to psychology after meeting Jung many years earlier. He headed the Harvard Psychological Clinic beginning in 1926; he also developed the famous Thematic Apperception Test (TAT). For a time Murray had been involved in the Boston Psychoanalytic Society, but he withdrew because he disliked the doctrinaire squabbles. A literary man who wrote on Melville, Murray knew George Wilbur through their mutual friend Conrad Aiken. On the occasion of Rank's visit, Murray asked him for a photograph of himself to put up in the Clinic along with those of Freud, Janet, Jung, and Adler. Rank declined, saying he never gave out his picture because he did not want patients to have his likeness.

This struck Murray as strange, since Rank did not seem to exemplify the analyst who had to be a blank screen upon which patients cast their transference. He checked with Jake Wilbur, who confirmed that Rank deliberately placed himself in a dark corner of the room where he could not be seen very clearly. Sometime later Murray learned that Freud had said Rank would not succeed in private practice because he was so homely. (Freud's concern about looks is expressed in *Interpretation of Dreams,* where he mentions a doctor who would have difficulty starting a practice because he was homely.) Murray concluded that Rank took Freud's words to heart and tried to minimize his exposure.

But Murray liked Rank's looks and found him more appealing than Hanns Sachs, who had come to Boston with Freud's imprimatur. Rank had "more imagination, more experience, a better grip on reality, and was a better talker." When Murray made a remark to Rank disparaging factions and cults in psychoanalysis, Rank replied that it was unavoidable. Freud advanced his ideas by means other than science, and it had to be that way. "I was thinking of science," Murray said; "Rank thought of scientists as human beings."[19]

GOOD WORK, POOR REVIEWS

Besides conducting a busy New York practice, Rank again led courses at the Pennsylvania School of Social Work and the Graduate School for Jewish Social Work during the first part of 1936. In February a young man he was treating committed suicide. Rank felt he had done all that was humanly possible, and the youth's parents were understanding.[20] In her memoir, Taft described this period:

> He came to Philadelphia at noon on Monday, spent the afternoon on appointments, conducted a class of fifty intensely interested social workers, the best to be found in Philadelphia, from 7:15 to 9 P.M., and either took a train back to New York or, when he was too tired, stayed overnight at the Hotel Crillon. There was seldom a free moment; someone always wanted to be seen and he could not afford to refuse. Yet tired though he always was, there was never a trace of weariness in the seminar. Something in his personality always took hold of the group and held it without apparent effort. He spoke directly, simply, without formality as if he were immediately related to every person present. He gave his best. His thinking was alive, as if generated at the moment and for that occasion, yet it welled from a depth of experience not to be exhausted and carried for everyone the sense of universality. Perhaps no one in the group had the background or capacity to

understand more than a fraction of what he heard, but for every individual there was an experience of meaning, of value, beyond anything he had expected.[21]

One member of the seminar recalled that the social workers called themselves "terrapins," deriving the nickname from Rank's pronunciation of "therapy." Another remembered him as a small man who "sat up there like a little frog on a leaf. He had a lot of personality, spoke clear as a bell. It should have been recorded: His books were much too heavy." In June Rank traveled to Rochester, New York, for several lectures. One of the audience upon whom he made a lasting impression was a young psychologist named Carl Rogers.[22] Looking forward to writing again—his long-dormant book on social psychology—Rank spent a week in Cleveland and then vacationed on a Connecticut farm in August.

The book takes on form and shape in my sub- or preconscious, a state that I like best and from which I have to force myself into the actual writing. I usually do that by getting a new notebook, scrapbook, pencils, and all the paraphernalia I've liked since my school days (when I stole them). But sometimes I don't get beyond that stage, as for example in the last five years. Maybe this time I'll go further. It will depend on finding a nice place for the summer to do the writing in—but not too nice either or I won't do it.[23]

Taft's translations of *Will Therapy* and *Truth and Reality* were published by Knopf in 1936. Literary critic Kenneth Burke reviewed it in *The Nation:* "Freud's and Rank's emphasis seem equally 'infantile' in the sense that they consider human relationships in terms of non-political or pre-political coordinates." Burke went on to credit Rank with indicating "one more way of doing what successful therapies have always done—i.e., it gives the patient an attitude, filled out with documentary substance, that enables him to be humble and self-reliant simultaneously." He concludes the rather negative review: "The Marxist challenge suggests that it does not encompass enough—hence the man who takes this philosophy as his father-principle may be like the man of whom it was said that he had a dumb pap." Rank's comment to Taft was that the review blamed him "for not being Marxist!"[24]

Helene arrived in September, in time to begin her junior year at Swarthmore College near Philadelphia; Beata stayed in Paris long enough to put most of the books and furniture in storage. When she reached America in October, she and Otto visited Helene at school. Then Beata moved permanently to Boston, where she became a leading member of the psychoanalytic community, despite her lack of a doctorate. She specialized in working with seriously disturbed children. Rank confided to Jessie Taft that he felt his wife was unaware of fighting him, which was all right because he did not have to fight her any more. He was pleased to see her again after she had settled in Boston and was having some initial success.[25]

Rank had suffered two severe colds in the previous year, and in the fall he became exhausted and depressed. He had money problems after the family's migration and told Jessie that he felt "dead"; if he did not get out to California to start a new life, "I will probably die anyway."[26] By November he felt better, as Taft and Robinson proposed a faculty position for him at the Pennsylvania School, something that would give him a base which he lacked in New York. Taft was also trying to help Helene and her father establish a better relationship, for which he expressed gratitude. Another cold or attack of influenza hit him in November, but he used the occasion to rest and write. The book he was working on, *Beyond Psychology,* was the only one he wrote in English.

An academic book had recently been published which upset, even infuriated, both Rank and Taft. Written by Yale psychologist John Dollard, it applied a new set of life history criteria to case reports by psychotherapists, anthropologists, and others. Adler, Freud, and Rank were represented, but Rank's "case" was actually one of Taft's, describing her treatment of an emotionally disturbed boy of 7. Taft wrote about the will, the importance of the present moment, and the problem of separation. But no one who understood Rank would have taken a surrogate—even Taft—as his representative. Besides, Rank did not treat children or write about their treatment.

Dollard calls Rank's position inadequate on the role of culture, social factors, and the family, apparently without having read *Modern Education,* which addresses all three. Dollard sets up a straw man. Patronizing her, Dollard excuses Taft from elaborating the patient's cultural context: "We would hardly expect to find it since the clinical psychologists are not handed, by their training, a clear workable concept of culture." To speak of Taft in such terms shows Dollard's ignorance, carelessness, or malice. Later: "The idea of culture is strikingly absent from Rank's psychology as exhibited by this document." Dollard assumes that Rankian theory slights culture, individual past history (except for the birth trauma!) and the father. Not surprisingly, Dollard has difficulty coming to terms with will.

In his preface Dollard expresses appreciation to, among others, Harold Lasswell, Harry Stack Sullivan, Hanns Sachs, Erich Fromm, and A. Kardiner. His treatment of Freud, not surprisingly, is very positive; that of Adler, negative.

Taft omitted this painful episode from her book on Rank, but Dollard's name and position made his work an important statement on Rankian thought—all the more so because few academics were available to redress the injustice done to both Taft and Rank. That Rank was outside the psychoanalytic establishment was a given; now he stood condemned by an academician whose allies included the most important "sociocultural" dissenters from Freud.

Responding to Taft, who felt the attack was unfair, Rank called Dollard's book "dishonest from cover to cover." Rank found Dollard's "life history" concept sterile, pointing out that novelists had long been doing what Dollard strained to present as original. "And it has been done also in every good biography— which is life-history—but only good if written alive and not cooked from a recipe which was abstracted from dishes"—Rank fumed—"after the meal was over."[27] But it was not Rank's way to raise a storm over such a matter, nor would it have done much good.

The last letter of the year to Jessie responds to her having sent a Christmas parcel which included some animal figurines and other gifts.

Tuesday, December 22

Dear Jessie,

I like the little book—and do you remember I had the ape on my mantelpiece in Paris!

The tobacco pouch is the softest I ever saw in my life, and I like softness!

The trouble is I am too soft myself for life.

The duck reminds me at present, in my present mood, of Ibsen's "Wild Duck," which used to be my favorite play—for various reasons.

The wild duck when wounded is supposed to go all the way down to the ground, bite into it and stay there till it dies.

It was nice anyway to get so many different things—it was like a stocking!

But at present I am going to the ground and I hope you'll wait till I come up again or till you fetch me.

> *My best to you and Virginia,*
> *Rank*

[PS] "Huck" likes the cabin in Vermont! I really wish I could retire and live a peaceful life-end. I had enough of the "world" and I have worlds and worlds within myself. I want to talk to you about the cabin in Vermont—please remind me if I don't when I see you.

> *With my real love to you*
> *Rank*[28]

It had been a difficult year, with some bright spots. Rank was settled and enjoying some fruits of renown. His work on therapy appeared in English. But he suffered negative reviews by Kenneth Burke and (on Taft's child therapy) by John Dollard. His daughter was nearby, but the relationship was not easy. Estelle Buel had come into his life. Jessie Taft remained his great ally, although the year ahead was to bring strain into that friendship once again.

Rank erupted in anger at Taft early in 1937, evidently because she pushed him to teach more than he felt he could. "I am not sure whether I'll be able to live up to your demands (or expectations) . . . If other people are too hesitant in stating what they want from me, you seem to be too explicit." Two days later he apologized: "It was really mean of me—you are right—but I didn't mean it! This is the worst part of my nature which always gets me into trouble! Please Forgive it!"[29]

Rank gave a week-long seminar for the Department of Sociology at the University of Buffalo at the end of January. The discussion with Taft about his teaching continued by mail.

I wish I had a little bit of your enthusiasm—but maybe I have too much wisdom for that and so have to counteract it by being foolish!

I also have no sense of perpetuation—that's why I don't like my books or my success with people nor any big following! But I am more willing to let things come as they do and at least won't oppose it as I used to do! I can't even get myself to buying a new suit of clothes that I need or anything like that. But I'd love to see you in your new outfit.[30]

Jessie Taft did not like Rank's self-effacement and bluntly told him so. His reply—"the only unpleasant letter ever to come to me from Rank"—came by return mail.

January 29 [1937]

Dear Jessie,

I don't see why you had to write me that terrible letter, unless you are at moments just as unreasonable as I am. But this time I didn't deserve it at all. My letter was written—though apropos of yours—out of my mood here which it reflected and in fact I felt very good about you while I wrote it.

Feeling my lack of enthusiasm in spite of the fuss people here are making over me I realized that I never had a real sense of perpetuation or continuation and was glad you had it for me! I don't doubt that you know all about me intuitively but when you put it down in words (almost terms) it becomes so inadequate & sounds so theoretical—to me at least. . . .

So, I propose we shouldn't be so silly and a little more reasonable since we don't seem able to be wise.

Things here are going all right, the group is not so bad and discussion is quite lively. On the other hand, the more people I talk to the more hopeless it seems to really get them any further. But I don't deplore this nor do I blame them nor do I feel badly about it.

Professor Canter—who is a hyper-intellectual of the Jewish caliber and therefore feels the need for the other side—emphasized again how contrary my viewpoint is to the whole mentality of our age and if I could complete my work (for which I need two lifetimes, he said) that I will be called in the future the Copernicus of the Social Sciences.

Still your Huck (incorrigible)[31]

Rank's consciousness of mortality and immortality seems indeed to have intensified, with a reference to *Wild Duck* and the need for two lifetimes to finish his work. According to Taft, the angry exchange of letters cleared the air.

RANK AS PROFESSOR

Franklin Roosevelt was inaugurated for a second term as President in January, having won a landslide victory in November. The world had been spectator in 1936 to the Olympic Games in Nazi Berlin; the start of Civil War in Spain, with Franco's insurgent government recognized by Hitler and Mussolini; the Italian fascist occupation of Ethiopia and the impotence of the League of Nations; and the outbreak of war between China and Japan. In Austria, Kurt Schuschnigg tried to maintain independence from Germany. Charlie Chaplin's *Modern Times* interpreted the mood in an artistic form which Rank appreciated.

At this time Rank began to show a greater interest in politics. He participated in a few meetings of the Social Workers' Union; initially uninformed about such issues as collective bargaining, he became sympathetic to the organizers' position, although Taft and Robinson were displeased, if not shocked, by this kind of student/professional activism. At a meeting on the Spanish Civil War Rank took a strong anti-fascist position.[32]

In February Rank discovered Thurman Arnold's *Symbols of Government* (1935). Called a cross between Voltaire and a cowboy, Arnold was a Wyoming native who became one of the most influential law professors at Yale; he served in the Roosevelt administration, after which he became a judge and then a founding partner of the famous Arnold, Fortas and Porter law firm in Washington. At Yale, Arnold enjoyed interdisciplinary seminars at which Harry Stack Sullivan, among others, participated. Like Rank a pragmatist who scoffed at the professionals' hope of achieving illusionless objectivity, Arnold was more concerned with myths and symbols than with facts. "Law," he wrote in the preface to his book, "is primarily a great reservoir of emotionally important social symbols." His appeal to a mind like Rank's can be seen from his concept of the rule of law: "the belief that there must be something behind and above government without which it cannot have permanence or respect. Even a dictator cannot escape the psychology of his time."[33] Rank wrote

Taft that he was "dazed" by the book, something which did not happen to him often.

> *But—believe it or not—I've found a book that does the same thing with (or to) law that I did for therapy and education: that is first separating all content from dynamics and then* stating *the fundamentally dualistic principle inherent in the dynamics: showing what it is and pointing out why it* has *to be that way, good and bad. It's profound psychology although he doesn't know it and calls it [an] "anthropological" approach!*[34]

With renewed interest in teaching, Rank began to develop a course based on the book. But in April he again taught seminars on therapy and development at the Pennsylvania School and saw clients in Philadelphia and New York. He traveled to Richmond to lecture and saw a little of the South. Periodically he suffered from colds or malaise, but, apart from total rest on these occasions, he kept an amazingly full schedule. Even Jessie Taft found it difficult to bear the paucity of personal time with him.

In one course he used students' cases to illustrate his method. One of his students remembers this course in social casework.[35] "He acknowledged doubt about this undertaking since, he said, he knew little about social agencies and their practice. It was his handling of my case, an interview with a child in foster care, that told me what a remarkable man he was. He grasped at once the setting, the specific nature of the social worker's role within the boundaries of their realistic connection, did not try to make a therapist of me or indicate doubt that I could, within my role, give the child the help needed. He was very sensitive to what I had done, to my deep concern, and direct in suggesting what more I might do."

This social worker, having found herself in two unsatisfactory job situations, went to see Rank for personal help, in New York. "For my second session I wore an expensive red hat, just bought to exactly match my coat. In 1937 a woman was not decently dressed without a hat. Suddenly a gust of wind came across the open top of the double-decker bus and took my hat away over Riverside Park." Despite the loss, and her embarrassment at being hatless, she felt what was to her "inappropriate relief."

When she told Dr. Rank what had happened, he smiled and said, "Why didn't you catch it?"

"At once I knew, as he of course did, that this was the big problem, tenacity, rigidity, letting go of nothing without too much struggle and, for once, a free letting go. Then I could laugh. It was the beginning for me of something different, and I have never forgotten it. This was a significant factor of his therapeutic genius, to know at once, out of the immediate situation, where the struggle lay, to meet it simply and directly, and to somehow release one's energies to deal with it."

Another student and client of Rank's made some interesting observations. While Freud gave us the anatomy of the psyche, Rank, Taft, and Robinson gave us the kinetics: They were the co-discoverers of twentieth-century psychodynamics, parallel to Einstein. "No two people describe him the same way. He was truly reflective: he let you find your reflection in him. We met face to face across a table. Once I was bitten by his dog; he was very embarrassed. . . . I find his books unreadable. . . . he was in such a period of discovery, but his books do not hang together. . . . I only saw him comfortable, happy-looking, never angry."[36]

In May the *New York Times* printed an intelligent, highly favorable review of *Will Therapy* and *Truth and Reality*. "Within the field of psychotherapy these books are without a doubt the most important and illuminating this year," said critic Livingston Welch. "In Dr. Rank's theory of therapy technique does not exist. If, however, one uses this term in its broadest sense, technique for the author is nothing more than a skillful balancing of the therapeutic level of play (which permits us to make reality our own, a creativity of everyday living) with the actual life plane."[37] Unlike Dollard, Welch had no difficulty handling Rank's concept of will, which he could relate to the thinking of Schopenhauer, Nietzsche, and Freud.

Another who greatly admired Otto Rank as teacher and therapist was Dorothy Hankins, who had taught school for three years before becoming a social worker. As different in background from Rank as possible, she had grown up among whites and blacks in Tazewell, Virginia, a town which had not one Catholic or Jew, and only one person who spoke a foreign language. An active reader, she had heard of Freud and went through all his works available in English before 1930. She found Freud's use of dreams fascinating and useful, but questioned whether he had observed babies and children. At that time most psychiatrists had their roots in neurology; there was no practicing analyst in Philadelphia, nor any training program in child psychiatry.

> *When I read [Freud] about id, ego, superego, with ego described as so weak and buffeted about by the other two, I couldn't take what was said seriously. I couldn't help thinking of Ego as "I," or Id as "it" and I considered what was being called "it" was as much me as "I" was, and the same for Superego. I did not feel tossed about by my unconscious, id, or superego in the ways that were being discussed. In retrospect I think I was ripe and ready for the concept of the will as I very gradually began to get hold of it.* [38]

Dorothy Hankins was indeed ready for Rank's philosophy when she read *Modern Education.* By then she had taken seminars with Freudians, including Nunberg, as well as with Taft, Dawley, and Allen. She found the chapter on "The Will and Emotional Development" a revelation.

There Rank points to the limitation of Freud's and Adler's causal approach to the child's emotional life. For Freud it originates in the sex drive, for Adler in a form of will which is compensatory—a reaction to inferiority feeling. The implications are this: Freud develops a therapeutic plan for adapting the child's emotional life, Adler a pedagogic plan. Both seem to be an advance over prior thinking—over the old religious, moralistic approach to child training. Yet both replace that with a new ideology, this time called "psychology" instead of religion, but no less pointed moralistically.

Rank's will, on the other hand, is expressed constantly in the child's emotional life—which, he notes with dismay, is put down by parents and pedagogues precisely because it is a manifestation of will and therefore repugnant. Hence the self-creative element is stunted even in modern education.

Dorothy Hankins decided to apply for therapy with Rank in 1935. Rank replied to her letter of inquiry by return mail. He told her later how important it was to respond immediately to a person who finally reaches out for help.

> *Until I began sessions with Dr. Rank in the spring, I was frequently overcome by the thought of my audacity in aspiring*

so high. The differences between us were so many and so ex-
treme. Of course, my main concern over the possible conse-
quences of these circumstances was for myself, but I felt some
for him as well. He was a genius and a creative artist. I was
neither. I had never studied or read philosophy, nor was I famil-
iar with mythology, whereas he was erudite in both. He thought
abstractly at a level well beyond anything I was capable of.
He could think, write, and talk in three languages, while I had
difficulty expressing my thoughts in my own American English.
Our entire life experiences could hardly have been more differ-
ent. . . . I would have felt less apprehensive if I had known
that he was an admiring reader of Mark Twain. Then there
was the fact that he treated writers, musicians, painters—artists
of all sorts. . . . I thought it quite possible that Dr. Rank would
find me rather dull as person and as patient. I remember think-
ing rather ruefully that maybe it would be a restful change
for him after all the gifted people he had worked with![39]

In a preliminary session she found Rank surprisingly easy
to talk to: "welcoming, natural, gentle, and practical." Once
she started seeing him—four times weekly—there was no sense
of foreignness. As she found by comparing notes with friends
who worked with him, he easily bridged the differences between
himself and patients. She introduced him in passing to Emily
Dickinson ("Nature rarer uses yellow than another hue") and
Popeye ("I yam what I yam . . ."); in response to the latter
Rank said he should begin reading the comics. But she found
him keenly aware of events and issues on the American scene.

In the spring of 1935 Rank was still seeing his patients on
the couch, but by the fall he conducted therapy face-to-face.
In lectures, Rank said Freud used the reclining position to encourage the patient's regression while allowing the analyst to
remain neutral and faceless, in order to facilitate development
of the transference. Freud was also more comfortable not being
looked at all day. Rank did not say why he stopped using the
couch, but clearly he did not wish to foster regression, and he
thrived on real emotional engagement rather than the faceless,
will-less, impersonal encounter of orthodox (Jonesian) analysis—
what might be called "technical emotional virginity."

Hankins usually remembered several dreams each night, and
they took a good share of the hour, although she tried to report
concisely. Rank told her that every dream is unique to one per-

son—could only have been dreamed by that person—but at another level, he found that most dreams were gender-neutral. Rarely did he find one that could have been dreamt only by a woman; at least one of hers (long since forgotten) seemed to fall in that category, and he asked her to write it out for him.

In the four years of their contact Hankins never heard him derogate Freud or anyone else; he did not engage in personal attacks. Once Rank asked her opinion of Freud. She thought he was a genius, but criticized his understanding of women. Rank replied, "You may not like his theory and are free to draw a different conclusion from his data, but his data are correct," defending his old mentor as a careful observer who could revise his theories in accord with new experience. Rank expressed wonderment at the fact that so many women accepted the Freudian psychology of women. Once he remarked that in the therapy setting women presented themselves as more masculine, men as more feminine, than in everyday life.

Hankins was a member of Rank's seminar on "Symbols of Government." Rank had invited Thurman Arnold, then in Washington, to visit the seminar. Too busy to leave his new post as Assistant Attorney General, Arnold declined, but urged Rank to telephone him on his first visit to Washington. Hankins recalled Rank telling the class about his attempt to make contact.

He had been passed through three secretaries, but eventually had been connected with Mr. Arnold, who obviously had no clue whatsoever as to who he was. In their brief dialogue Rank proved unable to remind Arnold of their prior contact. Arnold seemed a likable person, given the considerate manner in which he handled an apparent eccentric. Rank, realizing the futility of further talk, helped him end the conversation. By the time Rank finished his story, the whole class was laughing. He smiled, amused at himself, at Mr. Arnold, and at the absurdity of the situation.

Another example of Rank's enjoyment of the absurd arose after he had missed a class owing to illness. When a student expressed the hope that he was well again, Rank said he felt better, then revealed what the doctors had diagnosed: "They tell me I have the trouble because I am allergic to myself!" He was taking medicine for it. Obviously he (and his twin, the "old" self) enjoyed the irony of autoimmunity.

Although Rank emphasized the here and now, he was quite

interested in, and even determinedly sought, family data and past history along with extensive associations to dreams. He analyzed slips, lateness, and forgetting. If a patient had both dreams and a current conflict to report, he suggested the latter, saying, "Dreams will keep." Once he spoke of a former patient—perhaps Anais Nin—who went home and wrote down everything that happened in the hour. By way of contrast, Rank mentioned a man he had watched aboard ship on one of his Atlantic crossings. The man sat in a deck chair reading mystery stories. As he finished each page, the man tore it out and threw it over the side. Rank found the latter example an amusing antidote to the other extreme—the attempt to capture and hold onto experience.

Miss Hankins, accustomed to detailed recording of social work interviews, had thought of keeping a diary of her sessions with Rank but decided to savor the ephemeral experience rather than try to capture and hold it. As a result, forty-five years later she could remember vividly the outlines of the experience, a few episodes, and its general helpfulness—without being able to explain its power.

Unlike Freud, Rank rarely used clinical examples to illustrate his approach. We therefore depend on reports of his patients, students, and colleagues. Miss Hankins recalled some examples from his seminar.

A man came to see Rank who had already been analyzed by four men: two Freudians, a Jungian, and an Adlerian. The analysts had all agreed that his sex life was normal and satisfying. So the man said he did *not* need Rank's help with the sexual side of his life, but with practically everything else. He sounded quite desperate. After exploring his failed efforts in therapy, Rank told him that he must need help badly in order to seek it a fifth time. Although not certain he could help him, Rank offered to try under one condition: that they begin with his sex life and continue with that until Rank decided to change the subject. The man agreed.

With this example Rank illustrated how people sometimes seek help in ways that defeat both patient and therapist. Rank felt that the man had always set the rules under which his previous therapy would proceed. A need to control relationships was the central problem with this patient. By taking control at the beginning (though not without compassion), Rank made the in-

evitable struggle of wills immediate and obvious to both participants.

In another case, a child and mother were being seen separately in the child guidance clinic. The child was doing well,
thanks mainly to changes in parenting. The mother needed more
help for herself, but if she were told that, she would stop coming.
A staff disagreement ensued about "using" the child to keep
the mother in treatment. Rank saw nothing wrong with keeping
the child in therapy for that purpose. The child enjoyed his
sessions and was not being hurt by them.

"If you treat a patient you also affect the lives of other members of the family," Rank said, anticipating family systems therapy by decades. "With individual therapy you may be helping
or hurting people you never see." For example, a woman could
not stand her marital situation, but her husband refused to come
in for therapy. Rank invited her to come in alone, saying, "He
will not treat you the same if you make use of the sessions."
Treating one spouse, Rank explained, would affect the other
by changing the marriage relationship. Indeed, in this case after
a few sessions the husband decided to participate in therapy.

Although he did not see children in treatment, Rank enjoyed
discussing such cases in seminars. He brought in Ruth Shaw,
who pioneered in using finger paints in child therapy. With compassion for the individual, and the intellectual excitement of
an art historian and mythologist, Rank discussed children's paint-
ings and their accompanying stories.

Rank's involvement with the Philadelphia Child Guidance
Clinic was no less important than his influence at the Pennsylvania School of Social Work. The clinic was called "Rankian" by
some, although neither its director, Frederick Allen, nor Rank
himself wanted it so labeled. Once Rank told a student that
Allen was more Rankian than he himself![40] Dorothy Hankins
served at the PCGC for over thirty years, mostly under Dr.
Allen and Almena Dawley; she became chief social worker (when
Rankian psychiatrist John Rose succeeded Allen) and continued
from 1963 until her retirement in 1969, with renowned family
therapist Salvador Minuchin as Director. Thus Rank's direct influence endured through her work perhaps longer than in any
other institution.

Frederick H. Allen, six years younger than Rank, was a Cali-
fornian and a member of the United States Olympic track team

in 1912. He trained in psychiatry under Adolf Meyer at Johns Hopkins and organized the PCGC in 1925 with Phyllis Blanchard and Almena Dawley, the classic child guidance triad of psychiatrist, psychologist, and social worker. The three worked together for thirty years, training many—and affecting all—of the leading figures in American child psychiatry, child guidance, and "orthopsychiatry." Allen's two books became basic reading in the related professions; his "positive ego psychology" makes specific reference to Rank's definition of will. Allen was once asked to lecture in New York on Rank's philosophy and therapy, but declined on the grounds that Rank himself was available to do it. This indicates that audiences found Rank either taboo or difficult to understand. Allen was viewed as an approachable spokesman for Rank, though he declined that role.

Rank's influence was more easily felt than described or measured. His teaching and therapy were both much more personal than his books and more ephemeral. Virginia Robinson remained astonished that her six-week "analysis" with Rank could be the basis for "an understanding of the problem of relationship. . . . That it can be so remains always beyond explanation, often beyond belief, and certainly beyond proof when one approaches it intellectually or scientifically." Jessie Taft remarked that the relatively few social workers who had had therapy with Rank did not try to grasp and apply a "Rankian technique" in casework. "They had learned that help comes from something more than intellectual knowing, that it goes beyond the facts or even the traumas of a life history, that it is a dynamic, present, swift-moving experience with an ending."[41]

AGING

The summer of 1937 brought Otto and Beata Rank back into conflict. Despite her considerable early success, she was not happy in Boston. Some furniture was still in storage in Paris, which Rank was eager to retrieve for practical and emotional reasons. Tola was reluctant to cut the last tie to Europe; also, he wanted a divorce and she did not. To save money Otto moved to another apartment at "The Master" on Riverside Drive, this one without a terrace, but still facing the river.

Rank vacationed at the Finger Lakes, swimming and fishing,

but he felt poorly; it was discovered that he had three infected teeth. They were extracted at considerable expense—$300—in late August. Rank refused a removable denture or "beautification" and was pleased to have found a dentist who is "simple and honest and only does the necessary."[42]

September found him struggling against a feeling of futility about re-entering the world of work. By month's end Rank was exhausted from the packing and moving process and had caught cold again. Helene was with him for a visit that was hard for both of them: She was bored and he was impatient, but he also took the blame for not entertaining her. It was one of his worst periods.

Carl Jung was coming to deliver the Terry Lectures at Yale on "Psychology and Religion." Earlier in the year he had received an honorary doctorate at Oxford, as he did in 1936 at the Harvard Tercentenary celebration. (Freud coveted the Harvard award.) Rank observed on October 15, "Jung is coming next week to this country, seemingly as an apostle of Naziism. In today's issue of the *Saturday Review of Literature* he has an article on 'Wotan' justifying fascist ideology."[43]

Rank was thoroughly dismayed, if not totally surprised, by Jung's ideological stand. It was no secret: The universities that honored him either overlooked or accepted Jung's anti-Semitic "Aryan" psychology. Disgusted by professional and political events, Rank came to a wry and bitter conclusion, which he shared with Taft: Stupidity is "even more powerful than badness, meanness—because many actions or reactions that appear mean are simply stupid and even calling them bad is a justification." He felt that a great deal of psychology, the attempt to explain the complexities of human behavior, is "nothing but an attempt to give a meaning to one of the most powerful motives of behavior, namely stupidity!"[44] Rank must have viewed the genteel response to Naziism as stupid and no less powerful than Naziism itself.

By mid-October Rank felt better, despite a persistent rheumatic pain in his right arm. By early November his spirits were up after a good visit with Helene. But he noted that his circulation was poor and he felt "kind of foggy in the head . . . I am kind of ageing in one spot and the rest is young. But I am afraid that is not so good!"[45]

Rank wrote Taft about a patient she had referred to him, a

woman who had spent a year with Adler and three with Jung. She got more from him in five sessions than from the other two combined, Rank said:

> *She has a goodness and honest masochism (I mean sexual "per-version" of being beaten) that never was touched by her analysts apart from having been told to cut out those childish phantasies in favor of—one thing or another (social feeling [Adler], or anima [Jung]). It really is incredible, I never would have believed it was so bad. In connecting her problem with her woman-self in a positive and death-fear in a negative way, I produced an integration of herself that released real creative will which the others had trampled on.*[46]

Rank's right arm improved with "a few electric treatments" and he acquired a heat lamp for the winter months. He was busy, with eight patient hours every day except Sunday, and had no energy for *Beyond Psychology*. A few chapters were done and had been shared with Taft. Rank felt himself aging: "But I don't complain—it's all right, part of life and I had little of it. So I get my share now."[47]

From a review of Thurman Arnold's second book, *The Folk-lore of Capitalism*, Rank surmised that it showed how "economic ideologies are carried on beyond their validity in time and place." Thus it did for economics what Rank was doing for psy-chology. "I only mind," he added, with respect to Arnold's join-ing the government, "that he did it to defend the New Deal which in itself is all right, only just as full of 'mythology' as was the Old Deal."[48]

Beata and Helene converged in New York around the New Year (1938), and Rank enjoyed an improved climate in visiting with them. He saw them off to Cambridge and Philadelphia, respectively. Beata was working hard and having real success in Boston.

Rank had been treating a violinist, who played "well enough so that the critics said he has improved both in his technique and interpretation, but to me it seemed that he couldn't 'fill' Carnegie Hall not only not with an audience but not with his personality either!"[49] This rare mention of music recalls Rank's early, passionate interest in concerts and opera. At this point in his life, Rank needed to rest most evenings when he was not lecturing, owing to his busy work schedule and continuing health problems. He did enjoy the phonograph and radio.

Rank's spring semester course at the Pennsylvania School of Social Work on "Symbols of Government" required the students to read Arnold's book of that title plus at least two others from a list of thirty. Among the authors were Mortimer Adler, Kenneth Burke, Stuart Chase, J. H. Denison (*Emotion as the Basis of Civilization*), Morris Ernst, Ernest R. Groves, Carl Jung (*Psychology and Religion*), Alfred Korzybski, C. K. Ogden and I. A. Richards, V. Pareto, Talcott Parsons, Harry Scherman, William Sumner, Thorstein Veblen, and Alfred North Whitehead. Most of the books were very recent. The extent of Rank's interests and his reading, and the level of effort expected from his students in this course were formidable.

The brief but tantalizing minutes of the course suggest that Rank challenged conventional thinking and its Freudian underpinnings. He disputed the notion that people are civilized by gradual socialization of unruly drives, mainly via external threat and control. Instead, he argued that "law" symbolized a need already within us. Internal control projected on outer symbols results in the appearance of law and order imposed from without. Scherman's *Promises Men Live By* (1938) shows how the economic system depends on promises, and remarks how astonishing it is that we keep so many. Rank's comment: "In spite of our deviations to the contrary it is amazing how well we obey "The Law" that is in us!"[50] (This illustrates how people avoid coming to terms with individual will; by projecting what we do onto laws—societal or divine—we deny our own power, power which makes us responsible, anxious, and guilty, no matter how we use it.)

The seminar minutes also address Jung's latest book: "Jung conceives of dogma and ritual as a method of experiencing, but the irrational self breaks through in immediate experiences, and these are checked and rationalized by dogma and creed, not necessarily released thereby. Dr. Rank finds the irrational self is not half as irrational in a therapeutic situation as Jung describes it. Therapy is another framework within which the patient is no more irrational than he likes to be. But Jung encourages irrational expression as did Freud in his early days, and this brings out exaggerated expressions of it."[51]

Between this class and the next, on March 11, Hitler's troops entered Austria. Two days later Austria was declared part of the German Reich. If this came up for discussion, it was not in the minutes. Sigmund Freud, along with his wife, children, doctors, and maid and a few others, was invited to England through the efforts of Ernest Jones and released from Austria through the intervention of Marie Bonaparte. Freud left Vienna on June 3, having signed a paper required by the Gestapo certifying that he had been properly treated. At 82, Freud still had flair and fire, evidenced in the postscript he appended to his signature: "I can heartily recommend the Gestapo to anyone."[52]

Rank's class took up economic history, which included a discussion of Jews and moneylending in medieval times. Gentiles could not engage in moneylending until they had a theory which allowed it in the face of the canon against usury. "The Jews could lend money without endangering their future life—because they had no future life. Shakespeare's *Merchant of Venice* is a dramatization of this problem—painted upon the background of the Renaissance when the merchants began to lend and gamble and put it on the Jew."[53]

Rank brought in a discussion of Napoleon, whose battle was said to be against the banking (economic) system in England. He told his people, "You are penniless and I am going to take you to a new country." Recently, Rank said, Mussolini did the same thing when invading Ethiopia. "While wars are fought with military or political power, or with ideologies, as is the case nowadays, the basic underlying forces are economic and money power."[54]

On June 7, Rank had a thorough—one and one-half hour—physical examination, which revealed nothing more or less than a sore throat, attributed to excessive smoking (pipe and cigarette), which in turn was attributed to "nervousness and tension." Helene, not quite nineteen, graduated from Swarthmore the next day; Otto and Beata were present. Rank had a lighter schedule in the summer, which included two rainy but active weeks at a cabin in Vermont as the guest of Taft and Robinson. He enjoyed clearing sections of woods, and the dog, Spooky, was enjoyed by everyone. Rank was feeling the effects of cataracts in both eyes as he continued work on *Beyond Psychology*.

AN ENGLISH ADMIRER

Dr. Colin Campbell, a 34-year-old English psychiatrist in training at Dr. Allen's clinic, had developed an interest in Otto Rank's work. Both he and his wife, Kay, had some therapy with Rank and read some of his writings. In March 1938, Campbell wrote a long letter to a friend summing up his experience with Rank and Allen. The letter is especially important because Campbell did not live to pursue his obviously profound understanding of Rank's philosophy.

[Rank] *was with Freud for 20 years and, after he left him, took a line much more divergent than did Jung or Adler—a line more searching and creative involving a totally different approach to the other three, which might be described as dynamic instead of static—he does so describe it. He is concerned in therapy with the immediate present and the willing which is taking place in it—the actual therapeutic relationship is the curative factor. Content, the actual matter which spontaneously comes into consciousness, is of interest for what it shows of present patterns of willing, denial, evasion, not for its own sake or what it tells of the past. . . .*

The exploration of the past is not of importance for its own sake, though it is necessary in spots where great distortions result in the present. The object of therapy is to get free from the past ingrained patterns, to learn to bear the responsibility for present willing. The past is already over-emphasized in the neurotic's mind, he is too ready to evade responsibility by invoking the past to escape from the present into the past. Freudian cures are incidental to the exploration of the past and are due to the inevitable relationship with the therapist during that search, to the actual interaction or battle of wills. They are characteristically so long drawn out because of the emphasis of the past instead of the present and the misunderstanding and mishandling of the relationship. . . .

[Rank] is a charming man—a little German Jew—and he certainly is a brilliant and powerful thinker. His own treatments are for a deliberately limited period of time—something like 3 to 5 hours a week for 3 months. . . .

To Freud the neurotic is biologically subnormal, to Adler sociologically, to Jung spiritually. To Rank the neurotic is a person with strong creative urges who through having his will predominantly organized on the negative side, as counter-will rather than positive will—these two aspects are present in varying mutual adjustment in all willing—is unable to internalize his urges along creative channels. He is an "artiste manqué." His negative bias shows itself as denial instead of affirmation of himself, of his own powers. By exercising his will against the therapist's, who intentionally puts him in total control of the situation, he is able to find his own validity, turn his denial into affirmation, unfetter his positive will and carry his affirmation into his outside relationships. . . . There is no question of being below or above a hypothetical norm—if anything, as I have said, his difficulties are connected with his being potentially above the average. . . .

It is a whole philosophy in itself. It is directly opposed to—and I think sufficiently refutes—the determinism which is inevitable wherever the past is invoked to account for the present. . . .

Rank is, I think, beginning to have a considerable influence in this country. . . . I have never met such a live, enthusiastic, broad-minded, understanding collection of people anywhere as I have at the Clinic. . . . I came along with my half-fledged ideas and my disgruntlement with medical psychology and psychiatry and find myself immediately at home. . . . The demarcation between psychiatrist and social worker is narrow to vanishing. Really the latter are better trained. . . . The parent is seen for her own problems whether connected with the child or not. There is absolutely no probing, no instructing, no moralizing. The worker just helps her to work out her own salvation, find her own initiative. . . .

The modern educational idea of giving a child absolute freedom and expecting him to set his own limits is regarded as unnatural and already out of date—a reaction from the old restrictedness merely, too extreme and individualistic and failing to prepare the child for life in a community. . . . A child can exercise his feelings more freely and so learn to control them if he has the reassurance of a firm adult in the background who while allowing him the full range of his feelings can be trusted to curb his expressions of them. Too much freedom is just frightening.

Among American psychiatrists Allen is respected but he stands alone. He is very broad-minded and always sees the sound elements in other points of view. [55]

That summer Colin Campbell was killed in an automobile accident in England. His friend Marion Milner, a prominent English psychoanalyst and writer, gave the letter to his widow, Kay. To her Rank expressed his shock and sadness: "a definite loss to child guidance work, especially in England. . . . What it must mean to you to lose your husband before you had even time to establish a home I can imagine although I cannot express my sympathy in words." Rank had lost a real ally, and he commiserated with Jessie Taft about this "eager and sincere" man.[56]

Working feverishly on *Beyond Psychology*, Rank completed four chapters in August. "My eyes seem to give out and so I am trying to get as much preliminary working done as is necessary to dictate the whole book when Miss Buel returns (the last of September). She is my 'seeing eye'! (Competitor of Spooky)."[57] Estelle—Rank called her Sandra—actually returned on September 2, and Rank had finished his draft of the book.

HIS LAST YEAR

That fall Rank suffered two attacks of severe abdominal pain, finally diagnosed as due to kidney stones. Rank elected to leave them alone rather than undergo probing with sharp instruments. "I am a little scared, not that there is any real danger nor of the pain (I have morphine tablets now in reserve in case) but of a general letting down of my health, which is aggravated by the 'dark' prospect of having to have my cataracts removed within the next couple of years." Rank was torn between resting more and hurrying up "with the book and other things I want to do before I become a half invalid."[58]

Rank decided not to teach in Philadelphia in 1939 in order to lighten his schedule. He did complete a series of six lectures in New York. By March he was exhilarated over the book and himself and enjoying a "stratospheric" high. He described his creativity with a remarkable metaphor, considering his own experience of having been sculpted in wood by Chana Orloff: His books, he said, came out "like wood-shavings in shaping the self. They are splinters, not the self. . . . With me it was always that I was bigger than the work, not, as it is usually, the other way round."[59] Rank, true to his own conclusion in *Art and Artist*, wanted to be bigger in life than in his work products.

In March, psychologist Erich Fromm lectured on "The Social Philosophy of 'Will Therapy.'" Rank heard from a patient of his that Fromm had portrayed him as fascistic. In his presentation, published in the May issue of *Psychiatry*, Fromm summed up Rank's social philosophy as "authoritarian. . . . his disbelief in the existence and effectiveness of truth, his emphasis on the unimportance of reality, his concept of the necessity of submission and sacrifice . . . [suggest] a close kinship with the elements of Fascist philosophy." Fromm admits that Rank's emphasis on creativity contradicts the imputation of fascism, but then complains that Rank has too much "versatility and lack of consistency," and that the spirit of his work, though not intended to, echoes *Mein Kampf*.[60] Fromm's article does no credit to its author or to *Psychiatry*, a new journal edited by Harry Stack Sullivan.

In his analytic days Rank had been attacked from the right: His humanism, egalitarianism, and feminism were too liberal for Jones and Abraham. Now, as a post-Freudian whose ideas were being espoused by Clara Thompson, Karen Horney, and even Sullivan himself, Rank was savagely attacked from the left. Ironically, the only protest in response to Fromm's article came from psychoanalyst Karl Menninger in Topeka, who complained that *Freud* had been misrepresented! (In the article, Fromm—echoing Rank without realizing it—said that Freud was too pessimistic and that his technique suffered from his "neutral, distant attitude toward the patient.")

Menninger complained: "You will get plenty of long treatises from the Rankians. As a Freudian, I should think that you would want the more egregious errors corrected." Since the journal printed no letters, Menninger was invited to write an article, but he declined. Associate editor Ernest Hadley wrote him: "I am really perplexed by your letter. I thought that Fromm had effectively laid Rank to rest."[61]

According to Hadley and Sullivan, psychoanalysts should have been grateful to Fromm for dispatching Rank once and for all. The Jungians, too, should have been pleased, since Fromm made no mention of Jung's ongoing administrative and theoretical contributions to the Nazi cause.

There were no answering articles from Rankians. John Rose wrote one, but Rank discouraged its submission. (Rose eventually published a fine defense of Rank in 1942.)[62] Rank preferred not to enter the arena to fight what he had come to regard as stupidity.

Although he did not fight it openly, Rank expressed to Taft

his anger about being called "fascist—whatever that means besides 'I don't like it.' " In the same letter Rank told of his hopes to visit the West Coast, to look around and spend the summer in the mountains. The letter ended, "As Mahatma Gandhi said lately when interviewed and having uttered one sentence about peace to the reporter, 'Isn't that enough for once!' "[63]

Still Rank was feeling badly. In mid-May, he wrote, "The last diagnosis eliminated kidneys, liver and gall bladder and you may wonder what is left. The good old colon which—it is true—had been troubling me years ago but I felt different. Then it was only the colon and I knew it but now it's myself. I know I am sick." Besides this he faced the uncertainty of his eye surgery. "All I am thinking now and hope for is to finish the book within the next few weeks." At the end of May, he and Estelle set off for the West, driving across the country at a leisurely pace. They stayed for six weeks at Lake Tahoe, Nevada, so that Rank could meet the residency requirement for a divorce. Feeling "very well and happy" there, he worked on the book, enjoyed the beauty of Zephyr Cove Beach, and even did "lots of exercise—not done as exercise," after getting acclimated to the altitude.[64]

In the space of a month he had changed from sick and worried to well and happy. The trip west made palpable Rank's anticipation of a new life in California. The preface to *Beyond Psychology*, dated June 15, 1939, was apparently written on arrival at Lake Tahoe. The book itself was not quite finished then, and the published preface mysteriously differs from Rank's handwritten draft. His draft version is more spontaneous than the posthumously published one and includes two phrases, italicized here, that were omitted in the printed text.

> I merely wanted to give an impression of how I see human life, not only after having studied it for more than a generation in its various manifestations but after having achieved it myself,—achieved in an inner freedom from the compulsion to change it according to any man-made ideology. *The struggle of youth, the battles of manhood, the fights for success and against stupidity are all over.* My life work is completed too—*not because I have no more time to live but I have no more time for work.* The subjects of my former interest—the hero, the artist, the neurotic—all come back once more on the stage, not only as participants in the eternal drama of life but also after the curtain has gone down: unmasked,

undressed, unpretentious. Not debunked by any means, just human, while I myself do not pretend to pull their strings, to tell them what to do or say, nor to interpret them to the audience.[65]

The two omitted statements are among the most revealing autobiographical comments Rank ever made. He was resigning from struggle and from work, but not from life. Rank sent a greeting to Jessie on her fifty-seventh birthday, adding: "and yet it doesn't seem such a lot to my starting a new life at 55½!"[66]

Although Taft knew of his Nevada divorce, Rank's love life was outside her ken, "since he was incredibly reserved in regard to personal relationships. With him, each relationship was maintained within its own boundaries, not to be confused with or shared with any other." Taft had observed Rank in his first marriage as "amiable and considerate" in a relationship complicated by his wife's adherence to Freudian psychoanalysis. Taft thought he met his responsibilities as husband and father but doubted that "as a man driven by his own creativity" he could do more.

Helene, who was separated from her father to a considerable extent in her early years, remembers him as warm and supportive, capable of intense work but also quite sociable, with a good sense of humor. He loved playing bridge and going to the movies—including animated cartoons like Mickey Mouse. He was a good storyteller and delighted in sharing the latest technological wonders—cameras and assorted gadgets brought back to Paris from America. Helene was much closer to her mother. She knew of her father's involvement with Estelle well before their marriage, and also knew that Estelle was not the one (if there was one, it was probably Anais Nin) who had pulled him away from her mother.

Otto Rank and Estelle Buel were married on the last day of July. The announcement to Jessie Taft—a note from California signed, "Huck (still!)"—took her by surprise. The newlyweds stayed at the Clift Hotel in San Francisco for part of August while looking for a future home in California.[67]

They returned to New York before September 1, which marked the beginning of World War II. In his English domicile, Sigmund Freud, 83 and moribund, asked for the injections of morphine that released him finally from the torment of cancer on September 23. He had made a pact with his doctor to help him escape a lingering death.

At month's end Rank was hospitalized for removal of a kidney stone. He returned home after a few days but was debilitated by an infection with fever for two weeks. As he slowly returned to normal activity and feeling in mid-October, he wrote Jessie:

I remember the old story of the man whose execution was set for Monday morning and who on his way to the gallows remarked: This week does not begin too well! Starting in the fall with such a "hit" doesn't seem to me a good beginning for the winter season and so I decided to move out West as soon as I can wind up my affairs here—which will be by the end of the year! . . .

The book, which is going to flourish under the Western skies, will furnish a substitute for my personal appearance and may be a basis for future discussion of some world problems— if any should be left.[68]

Rank promised to visit her with his wife and Spooky before going out West. He told Virginia Robinson in his last known letter that he was proud of his contribution to the Pennsylvania School but was now turning his attention to things which had little bearing on either therapy or social work. "I have to come to some peace within myself and with the world at large, which is a purely personal matter. Not that others may not benefit therefrom but it is not primarily meant for that."[69]

On Friday, October 28, while dining out with Estelle, Rank complained of a sore throat. Resisting medicine as long as possible, Rank had to be persuaded to undergo examination as the night wore on and his fever rose. He was admitted to Polyclinic Hospital and his condition progressively worsened over the weekend. Helene, then just 20, and Estelle visited him in the hospital. Death came at 8:30 A.M. on Monday, October 31. *"Komisch"* (comical, strange, peculiar) was the last word he was heard to say.[70]

The cause of death was acute agranulocytosis (a diminution of the white blood cells which fight infection), a side effect of sulfanilimide, the antibacterial drug used before the introduction of penicillin.[71] Rank had been treated with sulfa drugs for the kidney trouble (pyelitis) he had experienced a few weeks earlier. Considering his illnesses of the past two years, with infections of the teeth, throat, and kidneys and a rheumatic heart, the administration of sulfa seems justified: he probably would have died of the infection otherwise.

At 2 P.M. on Wednesday, November 2, there was a final gathering of shocked and grieving family and friends. Estelle, Helene, and Beata Rank were joined by a crowd of over 100 which overflowed the funeral home. Jessie Taft stayed away but Virginia Robinson was there, along with John Rose, Frederick Allen, Almena Dawley, and Dorothy Hankins. The open casket rested in a side room, which was visited by many of the mourners. When it was time to leave, the crowd parted so the coffin could be carried out. Consistent with what Rank expressed in his adolescent diary (he left no other will), the body was cremated. The ashes were placed at Ferncliff Cemetery in Westchester County.

The lengthy obituary in the *New York Times* included an impressive précis of Rank's career and his concept of will. The *Times* reported that Rank had applied for U.S. citizenship and had expected to be naturalized soon.[72] He looked forward to a new life in California and the completion of what he intended to be his last book.

The death certificate, ironically, includes the decedent's *father's* name as "Otto Rank." Simon Rosenfeld had become "Simon Rank" in Otto's immigration papers. Now, posthumously, in the confusion of Estelle's grief, Rank's father was officially renamed, re-created in the image of his son.

Rank taught that the artist's development took him from creature to creator of himself in life.

Komisch.

CHAPTER 14

Epilogue

Estelle's grief deepened through November, notwithstanding the support of many friends and some other mourners who met her for the first time after Rank's death. "Oh Jessie I'm so sad I seem to be hitting rock bottom," she wrote on December 1. "The storage people are coming tomorrow morning to get the furniture and manuscripts. There will be no more excuse for me to go upstairs to the old apartment and so I must finally face the separation. Tell me is it true?" And she quoted two lines from Heine's *Lorelei:* "It seems like a fairy tale from long ago which will not leave my mind."

Estelle ("Sandra") and "Huck," as Rank liked to be called, mostly spoke German together. She remembered him after forty years as a great mind, immensely erudite, with a personality combining strength and kindness. Although not physically attractive, in a group he was like a "honey pot," surrounded by everyone, a magnetic personality. His eyes had power: They showed his sense of humor, his sadness, his warmth, and also his wrath. Their life together had been quiet; he needed to rest from work and was happy reading, writing, talking, or taking a walk with Spooky. When he died, Estelle could have been the center of a circle of his admirers, a dowager. It appeared that Beata wanted that role, and Estelle was astonished to hear an accusation that she, the new widow, had done Rank in. This created a break with Helene, who in her school years had been on good terms with Estelle.

"I did not deserve the halo. Let him have it," Estelle told me. She did not care to bask in Rank's glory, and the efforts of others to do so upset her. Having first met Rank in 1934, she knew him for six years, was the closest person to him for the last four, and was his wife for exactly three months. Estelle's mother had died in 1936; her father, Dr. Julius Buel, suffered a stroke before Rank's death and died in 1941. In a period of five years she lost her parents and her husband.

Rank left less than $3,000 in his estate. Rank's books were divided between his widow and daughter; Estelle gave most of hers to the Pennsylvania School of Social Work. Rank's manuscripts and files went to Jessie Taft. His divorce, medical expenses, and attendant debts left Estelle in need of a job. She was hired to counsel immigrants at the Christian Refugee Committee, where she earned praise for her work from professional supervisors. She cooperated with Jessie Taft and Almena Dawley, whom she especially admired, on the final editing of *Beyond Psychology*, which bore the dedication "To Sandra." Rank had not encouraged Estelle to read his books, but as his assistant she was familiar with his later writing. When she turned to his books many years later she found them quite readable.

The only child of older, cultured parents, Estelle had grown up with responsibility and freedom along with a good education, enriched by travel abroad and culture at home. The trauma of losing Rank made Estelle cut herself off from things of the mind, including professional library work. She wanted to get back to the earth, and with her patrimony bought a ranch in Northern California and moved there in 1941.

OBITUARIES

Rumors abounded about Rank's death. I have heard or read that he committed suicide, that he died insane, and that he lost his will to live after Freud's death. The circumstances of Rank's death are clearly documented. Equally clear is the evidence of his ongoing will to live, to live in California with his beloved Estelle without the burden of treating patients. No one who knew him at all well after his separation from Freud saw any evidence of the psychosis that Jones alleged. Rank's depressions, the severest being that of 1932, temporarily upset his career, family life, and friendships, but in general he withstood great stress with great strength.

The news of Rank's death was overshadowed by that of Freud's a few weeks earlier; also, Havelock Ellis had died in July 1939. The deaths of Freud at 83 and Ellis at 80 were expected. That of Rank at 55 came as a shock. Among the obituaries of Rank the most telling, perhaps, were those by Ernest Jones and Frederick Allen. Both knew Rank well and acknowledged his brilliance. Jones, of course, regarded Rank's Freudian period as his fruitful one and his exodus as a deterioration. Allen stressed the originality and creativity of Rank's post-Freudian work. But most startling is the contrast between Jones's view of the mature Rank as troubled and "ruthless . . . a sick man," and Allen's picture of "a scholar with ability and courage to be himself."

Jones admired Rank's erudition and his flair for interpreting unconscious material: "The ease of it actually bored him." In the obituary (1940) Jones reveals some of the meanness—he was a careful writer, not stupid—that permeated his treatment of Rank. He mentioned the Verlag as though it were part of Rank's secretarial position with Freud, admitting Rank's editorial role as an afterthought. Still worse, Jones said that he himself had to oppose Rank's post–World War I "plans of unfairly using England and America for the benefit of German scientific activities." This was a sleazy contrivance to link Rank with the enemy, given that Rank's activities in Vienna followed Freud's agenda, of which the sole German characteristic was language. Jones concluded:

> The melancholy that was to cloud his later years had already begun [at Salzburg in 1924] and he spent the rest of his life—in Paris and New York—alternating between feverish endeavors to find some short and efficient form of psychotherapy and moods of apathetic depression. It was a sad close to a fruitful career, one so full of further promise.[1]

Jones maintained his malicious libel of Rank throughout his Freud biography, only then to recant in part, stating that Rank was not to be regarded as insane (although "manic-depressive") and that Rank's years in New York were highly successful![2]

Frederick Allen differed from Jones, and was supported in

posthumous tributes by Jessie Taft and Almena Dawley. These three Americans had worked closely with Rank after 1925, when Jones no longer saw him. Allen, who understood Rank clearly, said:

> In that work [*The Trauma of Birth*] emphasis was laid on the significance of physical birth as providing the prototype of later anxiety patterns. But Rank's primary concern was the understanding of psychological birth, or the emergence of a self, and the interrelated reaction of that self with others as the individual moves toward the determination of his own destiny and ideals. . . .
>
> He believed in making constructive use of whatever an individual has, because he saw man as holding within himself the means of determining his own ego-ideal. Resistance, then, was not a force to be broken down but rather a force to be utilized in self-development. It is this positive emphasis on human development that will stand as one of the significant and increasingly productive monuments of his creative mind.[3]

Almena Dawley's tribute noted that Rank's contributions, so relevant to psychotherapy, were not so well accepted in that field as in social work, a new profession which lacked a unifying theory and was characterized by divergent streams of practice. Jessie Taft compared Rank and his recently deceased mentor:

> If Freud embodies the scientific attitude, the attitude of the student and experimenter who puts humanity outside of himself in order to observe and analyze objectively, Rank stands at the opposite pole, carrying into the field of psychotherapy the vision and scope of the artist, the man who includes within himself the opposition science sets up, who is at once doctor and patient, experimenter and subject, scholar and healer, helper and helped. . . . In life span he seems to have been cut off prematurely; in life experience, in creative achievement, in therapeutic contribution to humanity, he has completed many lives.[4]

Anais Nin returned to New York in December 1939 but, oddly, did not learn of Rank's death until the next February, when curiosity led her to make a phone call. "No flowers, no announcements, no letters of consolation," she wrote: "A void." She filled it with her own recollections, having no one to ask whether he had suffered, no one to tell her even that he had died. She wondered whether he knew he was dying, even whether he knew "how much or how deep was his gift, how vivid his human experience?" Her life with him had been so compartmentalized that she had no contact with anyone who was close to him at the end. But she remembered: "He did have sorrows, profound depressions, disappointments, frustrations, but he never became bitter or cynical. His faith never died, nor his capacity to feel, to respond."[5]

AFTERMATH

Marguerite Pohek, an American social worker who studied with Rank, worked in pre–World War II Vienna helping endangered Jewish children and families to emigrate. In 1940 she received a letter from a Viennese acquaintance, Isidor Sax, once the lawyer for the Vienna Psychoanalytic Society.

In September, 1939, it was exactly fifty years since Otto and his brother Paul, who died in January 1921, and I became friends, our association unbroken through all these years. I recall finding among my papers a letter from Freud which tells of the relationship between these two great men, and shows clearly the extraordinary esteem which Freud from the beginning had for him. This letter, which I cannot remember in all its detail, I had wanted to give to our beloved Otto upon my arrival in America, since I thought he might have forgotten how interesting it was and would rejoice to see it once more. I planned to bring it with me to England, but since the Nazis exercised rigorous control over all luggage and had such terrific hatred of psychoanalysis, I left it with my papers. . . .

Otto united, in rare degree, both inner calm and temperament. He was always an unassuming, beloved, related person— he had not much use for formal school pursuits. . . . he found a place in the locksmith industry, and had to wear the workman's suit of blue, and labor from early morning until evening in the workshop. But Otto was too filled with aspiration and thirst for knowledge to find joy in this occupation. . . .

As a psychoanalyst Otto always took pleasure in his comprehensive knowledge of his calling, and he was much resorted to because of his native power of attracting others. . . . Otto was a rarely gracious person, delighting in humor in an especially appealing form.

He was very fond of his mother, with an abiding love. . . . I shall never forget his way of helping me get out of Dachau. . . . When Otto came for the last time from New York to Vienna,

we spent many beautiful hours together. We were deeply happy
to be with each other again, and neither of us had any premoni-
tion that this was to be our last meeting.[6]

What Rank did to free Sax from Dachau can only be surmised.
Perhaps it was through Charles J. Liebman, President of the
Refugee Economic Corporation, which helped emigrés settle
in various parts of the world. Liebman, an American businessman
and philanthropist, had helped the Psychological Center in 1933
through the Emergency Committee for Aid to Displaced Scholars. Less fortunate than Sax was Rank's university friend Praeger,
whose son Frederick worked for Rank in Paris one summer.
Max Praeger was murdered at Auschwitz in 1945.[7]

In 1941 Rank's *Beyond Psychology*, written in English, was
brought out by a group of his friends. It is a social psychology,
with chapters on the double, on male and female psychology,
love, sex, and religion. In one surprising passage, following Theodor Lessing, Rank takes a narrow view of Judaism as a religion
of self-hatred and pessimism. He contrasted it with Christianity,
which he saw as based on self-love and optimism. The book
lacks the cohesion of his other post-Freudian works on therapy,
religion, art, and education and he did not see it to completion.
It does show Rank's grasp of contemporary writers—he quotes
Peter Drucker, Ashley Montagu, Crane Brinton, T. S. Eliot, and
Jacques Maritain, among many. Only 1,000 copies of the book
were published (privately), and a commercial reprint did not
appear until 1958, so for years the book was largely unknown.[8]

In the book, unlike Jung, who postulated the need for charismatic, authoritarian religious leadership and followership, Rank
looked for a religious connection with democracy and egalitarianism. The "beyond" of which he spoke referred to a basic
human need "for a religious philosophy broader and deeper
than any political or economic ideologies which happen to be
operating." Rank was concerned with meaning, and with the
human need to elevate ideology (even if illusory) above reality,
to expand beyond the self. "In this sense, the individual is not
just striving for survival but is reaching for some kind of 'beyond,'
be it in terms of another person, a group, a cause, a faith." In
the preface—but not in Rank's manuscript—appears the phrase
"in religious terms, through revelation, conversion, or rebirth."
Rank valued religion as a special ideology which helped make

life endurable, at least for some, but nowhere does he avow or preach a theistic doctrine. But because he asserted the importance, even the primacy, of will and responsibility, Rank's position did find favor with some theologians, including Catholics. In 1939 Rank was cited prominently in a pastoral counseling book by Rollo May, which was introduced by Dr. Harry Bone, a psychologist who worked with Rank in Paris and New York. Perhaps all this accounts for the comment of historian Henri Ellenberger that Rank "was moving toward a kind of religious psychotherapy."[9]

Carl Rogers, in *Counseling and Psychotherapy* (1942), called Rank's a "relationship therapy" that was not authoritarian like Freud's, but instead emphasized helping the client grow rather than solving a problem. It stressed feeling rather than knowledge, the immediate situation and the experience of the therapy itself rather than the client's past history and early childhood. Rogers, who also acknowledged the influence of Taft, Robinson, Dawley, Hankins, and Allen, had been present when Rank spent three days in Rochester. On that occasion Rogers recalled being more impressed with Rank's therapy than with his theory.[10]

In 1942, with the U.S. embroiled in the war against Hitler, Erich Fromm's charge of fascism was answered by a Rankian. The young psychiatrist John Rose, in an article called "Democracy and the Philosophy of Will Therapy," called Fromm's article a misreading of Rank, and his labeling of Rank as authoritarian a travesty. Rose, who had been in therapy with Rank when he died, declared that no real therapeutic philosophy could be fascist. Rose must have known about Brill and Jones: Some who "disagree with Rank have inferred in open scientific meetings that he was 'spiritually sick' at the time he was producing his most important works." Rose, who succeeded Frederick Allen in Philadelphia, developed Rank's perspective with distinctly American illustrations, if not as lucidly as Allen.

> To be banal, when a man pays taxes to support a police force and then gets mad because he gets caught for speeding, he typifies the complete projection of a function of government on to the outside, so that the man no longer feels the governing to be a part of himself; or oppositely, when the college football team wins a game, the alumnus feels as proud as if he had done it himself despite not having really contributed to the victory. It is just that when the human need to be free of a certain kind of self-conscious-

ness arises, man is able to project his will, and having done so, to deny or affirm it completely by his feeling for the institution on which it is projected. In doing this he does not have to bear it as part of himself and, therefore, is more free to live and feel. . . .

Rankian philosophy, advocating nothing, really understands that human culture at any given time mirrors both human striving and human need. Rank recognized that man reached his highest peak when he could bear his own difference and not just know it painfully; and it follows as a corollary that when a limit of self-consciousness is reached that the culture should have enough differences to be able to carry parts of the wills of men and yet permit them all the self-expression they can bear.[11]

In Germany, Rose said, Nazi ideology took over all responsibility paternalistically in exchange for complete obedience of the populace. Such a government appeals to people who fear growing up—i.e., being self-conscious and responsible. But a society of children is a society which cannot abide individual difference. "The Jews were, therefore, exterminated," Rose wrote in 1942, "as were any other groups who held out difference." Ironically, Rose's analysis has much in common with *Escape from Freedom* (1941), where Erich Fromm uses "willing" and other Rankian concepts but without mentioning Rank.

The end of the war coincided with a period of ascendency for psychoanalysis, especially in American medicine and culture. But everywhere psychoanalysis ignored Rank, except for what was written in his youth. Thus in England, when Edward Glover proposed to Ernest Jones that every psychoanalytic candidate learn about the major deviants, Jung, Adler, and Rank, Jones replied, "Why waste their time?" Glover wished only to equip students to criticize the "schismatics": Melanie Klein, he said, combined in her system "some of the errors of both Rank and Jung."[12]

The situation was similar in the United States, except for a time in Philadelphia and a few other places. In social work the Freudians were called the "diagnostic" school, Rankians the "functional," after a term introduced by Taft which Rank himself did not sanction. Besides Taft, Robinson, and other Rankians mentioned so far, prominent social workers who integrated Rank's thinking into their work included Anita Faatz, Ruth Gilpin Wells, Kenneth Pray, Callman Rawley (Carl Rakosi), Karl de Schweinitz, and Ruth Smalley. Taft and Robinson were powerful, demanding teachers; Taft was considered autocratic by some students, inspiring by most. They both retired from the Pennsylvania School in 1950.

RANK AND THE HISTORY OF IDEAS

Why has Rank been submerged for so long? Can the politics of psychoanalysis, the density of his writing, and his relatively early death explain his disappearance from the mainstream? All three factors have contributed and others might be added, including his own reticence and disinclination to rebut attacks, his confidence that he was far ahead of his time, and his lack of concern for wider acceptance. A surprising number of relatively informed people mistake Rank for Wilhelm Reich or Theodor Reik, both of whom made distinguished contributions but whose ideologies and problems were quite unlike Rank's.

University teachers would have had to move against the tide in assigning Rank's works to students; and each of his five later works might require a semester's work for advanced undergraduates. More often than not Rank has been badly summarized and then dismissed in textbooks and histories of psychology and psychiatry—by, for example, Clarence Oberndorf, Walter Bromberg, A. A. Roback, Patrick Mullahy, Marthe Robert, Reuben Fine, Henri Ellenberger, Gerald Sykes, Lucy Freeman, and even Clara Thompson, who once summarized Rank so beautifully. Favorable exceptions exist: Ruth Munroe, Paul Roazen, Ira Progoff, John Reisman, and Rolf Muuss have at least done justice, where others have ignored or maligned Otto Rank.

In 1953 Fay Karpf published the first book about Rank's work, a small volume entitled *The Psychology and Psychotherapy of Otto Rank*. She knew Rank well, having organized courses which he taught in New York, and she was a historian of psychology. She notes the denigration of Rank in Brill's introduction to *The Basic Writings of Sigmund Freud* (1938) and the exclusion of his later writings from surveys such as that of Otto Fenichel. A great admirer of Rank, she was unhappy with some of the positions he took in his last book, for example, on Judaism. "In any event," she wrote, "no one is bound to accept Rank as a whole, not even his interpreters, as his dynamic dualism and his authorization of different points of emphasis demonstrate.

You are invited to accept what you can use, provided it is accepted in the spirit of his basic pattern of thought, and to leave the rest to the test of time and further experience."[13]

The third and last volume of *The Life and Work of Sigmund Freud* by Ernest Jones appeared in 1957. As his preface states, Jones took pains to show how tolerant Freud could be of difference in the case of Otto Rank. This depiction was achieved, however, by portraying Rank as psychotic. Since then, writers like Roazen, Fromm, Sulloway, and Clark have questioned the tendency of Jones and other psychoanalysts to label dissidents mentally ill. But other writers have accepted the Jones text as gospel. Lionel Trilling said of Rank and Ferenczi in the *New York Times Book Review:* "Both men fell prey to extreme mental illness and they died insane." Trilling, a literary critic who later (with Steven Marcus) condensed the Freud trilogy into one volume, exceeded Jones himself in his treatment of Rank. Challenged by Virginia Robinson, Trilling printed a correction which could not even begin to offset the damage done in his review.[14]

Still more shocking was the *Time Magazine* review of Jessie Taft's *Otto Rank* (1958). It seems surprising that *Time* would notice such a book, but just two years earlier Ira Progoff's *The Death and Rebirth of Psychology* had received a good review there, emphasizing his favorable treatment of Rank. In the second *Time* review, certainly influenced by Jones and Trilling, Taft's book did not fare well.

> Adolescent Rank was successively infatuated with Schopenhauer, Nietzsche and Wagner. Lonely, understood by nobody (a fact that Psychologist Taft makes thoroughly understandable), Rank early and arrogantly declared himself an "artist"—a designation that he viewed as equivalent to a patent of nobility. . . .
>
> Among Rank's chief qualifications for membership in Freud's Wednesday Psychological Society were an inordinate interest in sex, a self-appointed expertness in the interpretation of dreams, and an infinite capacity for making vast, galactic generalizations about the nature of man without an atom of fact to support them. . . .
>
> Nothing interested Rank less than facts. . . . Freud became too busy to keep a tight rein on Rank; by 1923, the Master accepted the dedication of *The Trauma of Birth* without having half read the manuscript. This was the beginning of the end of Rank the Disciple, and marked his self-anointment as the messiah of a new cult. . . . Later he proposed the idea—monstrous to orthodox Freudians—that patients in analysis must exercise will power.

In Rank's later years his behavior was more appropriate to the role of patient than of therapist. He went through one emotional crisis after another (diagnosed by famed Freud Biographer Ernest Jones as a mild manic-depressive psychosis), even suffered artist's and writer's "block"—a symptom that analysts claim to relieve most effectively. . . . In the post-Freud patter of the cocktail hour, Otto Rank was "sick, sick, sick."[15]

The last three words of the unsigned review appeared under an accompanying picture of Rank and Freud. A similar review appeared in the *New York Post.* Both were by Gilbert Cant, medicine editor for *Time.* Thus millions of copies of one man's degrading commentary poured like a tidal wave over Taft's thoughtful book, which appeared in a few thousand copies, never in paperback. She was 76 at the time and died two years later. At least she had the solace of other, favorable reviews, including one by her (and Rank's) former critic, John Dollard.

Dr. Progoff's book enjoyed wider circulation and reprinting. Known as a Jungian, he stirred resentment among some of his friends for his strongly positive presentation of Rank. Jung himself acknowledged receipt of the book but never commented on it. Once in a personal meeting Progoff tried to learn Jung's opinion of Rank; having pressed the question three times without getting any answer, Progoff gave up.[16]

In 1959 a paperback edition of *Myth of the Birth of the Hero* with selections from three other Rank books appeared, edited by critic and novelist Philip Freund. This has been the only Rank title to be generally available since then; *Art and Artist, Beyond Psychology, Psychology and the Soul, Will Therapy,* and *Truth and Reality,* have been in print at times, the last two again recently. In 1960 an article by Jack Jones appeared in *Commentary* calling Rank perhaps "the best mind psychoanalysis contributed to intellectual history." The essay had little apparent impact. A decade later the same author praised Rank in another article, commenting that the birth trauma theory was only transitional, causing widespread misunderstanding of Rank, and "should be immediately dropped into the garbage pail. It has at best only a metaphorical relationship to Rank's later and actually characteristic ideas, of whose existence few are aware even now."[17]

One who was aware and who wrote for professionals—unfortunately again with limited impact—was Donald MacKinnon, who published a remarkable essay in 1965 on "Personality and the Realization of Creative Potential." Professor of psychology at the University of California at Berkeley, MacKinnon first read Rank in the 1920s at the Harvard Psychological Clinic, where Henry Murray taught. He read Rank's books on art and therapy as they appeared in the 1930s, but when he turned his attention to the problem of creativity decades later, Rank had faded out of awareness. MacKinnon thought about Freud, Jung, Adler, Kris, Kubie, Maslow, Rogers, and Allport, but not until his data were collected and partly analyzed did Rank's influence on his design become apparent to him. At that point MacKinnon reviewed the psychological literature on creativity and to his dismay found not a single reference to Rank. Perplexed and stimulated, MacKinnon renewed his acquaintance with Rank.

> In making *will* a central concept in his psychology, and in defining it as the integrative power of the self, and in explicating its role in the development of personality, Rank was a pioneer in the field of ego psychology. In being the first to set a time limit upon the duration of analytic therapy, he stimulated later widespread efforts to achieve briefer forms of psychotherapy. He described the therapeutic process in terms of relationship and wrote of interpersonal relations before Sullivan. . . . He was the first analyst to reject the narrow concept of psychoanalysis in favor of the broader and more widely employed term of psychotherapy, and he was the innovator of a new form of therapy which led to the conception of "helping a client" instead of "curing a patient." . . . I suspect that there are many psychologists today who do not know how much there is of Rank in Rogers, or how much in other ways his thought foreshadowed present-day emphases in the psychology of personality, most notably in the writings of Fromm and Maslow.[18]

MacKinnon had gathered data on architects, who could be categorized in a way which corresponded to Rank's typology: (I) the artist (creative), (II) the neurotic (conflicted; *artiste manqué*), and (III) the average (adapted). (Architects were chosen because they combine art with science, business, even psychology.) His research found significant differences among the three groups. Group I scored highest, in MacKinnon's analysis, on aggression, autonomy (independence), psychological complexity and richness, and ego strength (will); their goal was found to be "some inner artistic standard of excellence." Group II scored intermediate on independence, close to (I) on richness, and highest on anxiety; their goal was "efficient execution." Group III scored highest on abasement, affiliation, and deference (socialization); their goal was to meet the standard of the group.

On a self-image checklist, the adjectives chosen most frequently were (I) "imaginative"; (II) "civilized"; (III) "conscientious." From Rank's standpoint, one could hardly ask for a more congruent result from a research study of this kind. But there is an additional delight. MacKinnon reports the family and developmental characteristics of his subjects; his summary of the creative architects' life histories brings to mind some aspects of Rank's biography.

> Just as we have found in our test data a considerable degree of confirmation of the Rankian description of the stages of development of individuality and the realization of creative potential, so also in the life-history protocols of our subjects we have obtained supportive evidence for many of the kinds of early interpersonal experiences which Rank would have thought most strengthening of positive will and most conducive to the fullest development of the individual . . .: an extraordinary respect by the parent for the child, and an early granting to him of an unusual freedom in exploring his universe and in making decisions for himself; an expectation that the child would act independently but reasonably and responsibly; a lack of intense closeness between parent and child so that neither overdependence was fostered nor a feeling of rejection experienced, in other words, the sort of interpersonal relationship between parent and child which had a liberating effect upon the child; a plentiful supply in the child's extended social environment of models for identification and the promotion of ego ideals; the presence within the family of clear standards of conduct and ideas as to what was right and wrong; but at the same time an expectation, if not requirement, of active exploration and internalization of a framework of personal conduct; an emphasis upon the development of one's own ethical code; the experience of frequent moving . . . which provided an enrichment of experience, both cultural and personal, but which at the same time contributed to experiences of aloneness, shyness, isolation, and solitariness during childhood and adolescence; the possession of skills and abilities which, though encouraged and rewarded, were nevertheless allowed to develop at their own pace; and finally the absence of pressure to establish prematurely one's professional identity.[19]

MacKinnon wrote as a psychologist and historian, who, more than most, cared where ideas came from. His summary of Rank as research mentor shows that difficulties in grasping Rank are relative—it is a matter of how, when, and by whom the material is approached and digested. Any theory of personality and creativity that can find experimental validation receives an enviable boost, and MacKinnon did that for Rank. Alas, two decades later his own creative confrontation with Rank seems to have been lost in the literature. As Ernest Becker said, "The perversity of academic culture is that the truly vital work lies around crying for attention for years, and when we finally do belatedly discover it we are impelled by a necessary hysterical urgency to make up for lost time. But as children of our times we are not guilty of what is, after all, a cultural blindness and a historical lack of readiness. Rank himself saw that he was a generation or two ahead of his time, and so it falls to us to make full human gain out of him."[20]

The contrast between Freud and Rank was between pessimism and optimism, reason and emotion, past and present, science and art. Freud's therapy required love from the patient and surgical objectivity from the analyst. Rank's therapy envisioned a mutual relationship, with a balance of objective and subjective responses from both participants. He distinguished the present reality from the past "truth" and said we need illusions to live. We cannot look at death without blinking; we need solace, meaning, purpose, affirmation. Freud called religion an illusion and thought we would do better without it.

Just as Freud found in his own dreams the key to the mind's archives, the plan for a soular archeology, so Rank found in his own trauma of birth a model of psychological rebirth.

Although he did not use the term, Rank's approach can be called existential. Sartre's famous phrase, "Existence precedes essence," means we are not cut from a pattern like a coat nor made from a mold like a tool, but we determine our own essence by what we make of ourselves. Compare Rank's last definition of will: "an autonomous organizing force in the individual which does not represent any particular biological impulse or social drive, but constitutes the creative expression of the total personality and distinguishes one individual from another."[21]

If the watchword of traditional analysis was to make the unconscious conscious, or "where id was, there shall ego be," Rank's aim was to unify and free the crippled will. He taught that neurotics are failed artists. Treatment does not aim to make them paint or compose, but to develop a self, a distinct personality capable of making life a creative enterprise. The individual is not responsible for everything, but he or she must create an identity—a soul, if you will—given a particular genetic endowment and an environment, a reality, to push against. Where life and art conflict, or life and knowledge, Rank chooses life. Rank's first motto from Shakespeare never lost its depth for him: "Is it possible, he should know what he is, and be that he is?"

RANK TODAY

In November 1965 the Otto Rank Association was chartered in Pennsylvania to stimulate interest in Rank's ideas "and their meaning for art, literature, psychology, psychotherapy, and the history of culture." Virginia Robinson was President, Anita Faatz was Executive Secretary, and sponsors included Mme. Pierre Simon (Estelle Buel Rank), Helene Rank Veltfort, George Wilbur, and Anais Nin. The ORA published a *Journal* twice yearly and had a one-day annual meeting. The membership grew to over 600, then began to decline with the attrition of older members. In addition to a number of previously unpublished Rank essays and lectures, the *Journal,* ably edited by Anita Faatz, carried articles and reviews by Ernest Becker, Esther Menaker, Martin Grotjahn, Herbert J. Muller, Leslie Farber, Ira Progoff, Marianne Horney Eckhardt, Maxwell Geismar, Miriam Waddington, Carl Rakosi, Pauline Shereshefsky, and many of the Rankians already mentioned. The collection of thirty-one issues (1966–83) represents an invaluable resource for several fields.

Estelle Rank married Pierre Simon, a French citizen, several years after Rank's death and has lived in Paris since the end of the war; her husband died in 1972. She entrusted Rank's papers to Jessie Taft, who donated them to Columbia University in 1957. The papers of Taft, Robinson, and the ORA were added in 1983. They are open to qualified scholars without restriction. (The papers of Brill, Freud, and other relevant figures have been donated to the Library of Congress with restrictions on some portions for many years, ostensibly to protect former patients; but the result has been to impede objective study.)

Beata Rank never remarried. She died in 1967 after a distinguished career as a Freudian psychoanalyst specializing in the study of disturbed children. In her last years she mounted a photograph of Otto in her residence. Helene Rank Veltfort received her doctorate in psychology at Stanford and remained in the San Francisco area, where she today practices psychotherapy. She has two daughters from her first marriage. Although never a student of her father's work, Dr. Veltfort has spoken about him occasionally when asked by colleagues, in part to rebut the charge that he was mentally ill.

Ironically, while authoritative and cogent writing about Rank by Fay Karpf, Jessie Taft, Jack Jones, and Donald MacKinnon has given Rank only limited recognition, two better known writers whose presentations are less faithful to Rank's thought, albeit more vivid, have recently brought him prominence. The *Diaries* of Anais Nin have acquainted a large readership with Rank's name since 1966. And Ernest Becker's *The Denial of Death* (1973) rests heavily on Rank, "a mine for years of insights and pondering." Brilliantly written but somewhat uneven, the book won a Pulitzer Prize for its author, who was dying of cancer as he wrote. In places Becker makes Rank too much a prophet of doom and too much a religious preacher, but his writing engages Rank and the reader forcefully. Through Nin and Becker a large public has gained a partial, indirect knowledge of Rank, a stimulating introduction that, however, cannot substitute for a deeper, more direct acquaintance with Rank's own works. Becker's posthumous book, *Escape from Evil* (1975), was dedicated to Rank's memory.[22]

Although the Otto Rank Association ended with the retirement of Anita Faatz (then 80) in 1982, Rank's ideas are by now joining the mainstream, and he does not need the special emphasis of an organization or the liabilities that come with discipleship. Rank could be called the consummate eclectic, and it is no surprise that his influence extends now to leaders in social psychiatry (Robert Jay Lifton), group therapy (Irvin Yalom), family therapy (Carl Whitaker), Gestalt therapy (Paul Goodman and Fritz Perls), and child psychiatry (Frederick Allen and Paul Adams) as well as to Carl Rogers, Rollo May, Henry Murray, Jacques Choron, and important figures in social work. Though neglected by most studies on art and culture, he is recognized by William Johnston in his brilliant survey *The Austrian Mind* (1972), by Anton Ehrenzweig in *The Hidden Order of Art* (1967), and by poets and writers including James Agee, Mircea Eliade, Paul Goodman, Colin Wilson, Max Lerner, Floyd Matson, Stanley

Burnshaw, Carl Rakosi, and Miriam Waddington. In *Otto Rank: a Rediscovered Legacy* (1982), Esther Menaker presents the first major study of his place in the firmament of social and psychological thought.

Rank has also been given credit he would not care to claim. A respected popular writer on psychoanalysis, Lucy Freeman, recently said Rank's legacy was primal scream therapy. While proponents of that approach may cite Rank, to put the matter as she does is like saying that Gutenberg's legacy is the comic book. On a more serious note, psychoanalysis is awakening to Rank's influence. His work with Ferenczi has gained new readers after sixty years.[23] Turmoil within the profession can be expected to lead scholars to careful study of Rank's transitional and post-analytic writings in relation to current critiques of psychoanalytic theory and therapy.

Ernest Jones, the last of the Ring, died in old age (79) in 1958. He finished his monumental biography and led the 1956 centenary celebration of Freud's birth. It has taken another quarter-century for scholars to reassess the legacy and life of Freud from a more objective stance. In 1945 Jones published a paper on "The Psychology of the Jewish Question," which, while disapproving racial prejudice and anti-Semitism, betrays a startling anti-Jewish bias. Jones finds Jews stubbornly resistant to assimilation, referring to their "exclusive and arrogant" religious beliefs and their unjustified intellectual "superiority complex." To offset the unpleasantness of their moral mentorship, Jews would need "the mollifying influence of an endearing personality; no Gentile would maintain that this has been a prominent feature of Jews." He refers to the ancient Hebrews as "a pretty savage *Herrenvolk* [master race] . . . as ruthless and as marked by self-approval as anything we have known in later times." Yet, he says, the later Jewish aversion to violence "is despised as a sign of unmanliness," and however rare, avoidance of British military service by Jewish refugees strikes Gentiles as characteristic! Jones did not blame anti-Semitism entirely on the Jews; he only said they shared responsibility for it. "It is for both Jew and Gentile to search their hearts."[24]

This essay by Jones reveals blatant, aggressive bigotry on the part of the most powerful leader of the psychoanalytic movement after Freud himself—a movement peopled disproportionately with Jews who, except for Rank and Ferenczi, overlooked this outrage rather than assert their difference. Rank's argument with Jones was not as an observant Jew, but as a human being who felt the oppression of racism personally. As one who celebrated difference, individuality, and the artist, the uniqueness of the here and now and the limitations of scientific knowledge and generalization, Rank bridled at the mentality that enabled Jones to say, "If Jews are subject to the same social and historical laws as other people, and are not really unique, it follows that sooner or later assimilation will prove to be the definite solution of our problem. . . . Resistance to the decrees of Nature brings friction and discomfort, or even misery, in its train."[25]

In light of this position, one can understand the horror Jones felt at the tolerance of homosexuality expressed by Freud and Rank. To Jones, their acceptance of difference meant that they were aiding the forces of perversion against Nature. Because no one besides Rank and Ferenczi challenged Jones's anti-Semitism, and because he helped to rescue the Freuds from Nazi Austria, his domination of international psychoanalysis was not much questioned.

Anna Freud knew Jones for fifty years; her final tribute to him conveys respect tinged with criticism and suggests how she managed her ambivalence. Jones strongly disapproved of her approach to child analysis, complaining to her father about her publications. But these differences did not seem to affect their friendship. After the escape from Vienna, she marveled at Jones's ability to get the Freud entourage accepted forthwith into the British Psychoanalytic Society: "The memory of it influenced many of my later actions. Above all, I was always careful that none of my later activities in England should in any way constitute an embarrassment to our hosts." She paid tribute to three other rescuers of Viennese Jewish analysts: Marie Bonaparte, Walter Langer, and Muriel Gardiner. She defended Jones's biography of her father as truthful and denied any control over it: "No one ever directed Ernest Jones, or gave him permissions, or even criticized him to his face. It was always the other way round." Once launched on the writing of his biography, Jones availed himself of what he wanted of the Freud papers: "It made little difference whether we were always willing to part with them. . . . They did not even always return."[26]

Less than a year before her death at 86, Miss Freud graciously answered a few questions I put to her about Rank, whom she knew as a foster brother for twenty years. He was very often in the Freud home, she recalled, and was an indispensable help to her father and the Vienna Psychoanalytic Society for many years. The books he wrote before his departure were "much appreciated and probably of permanent value." Regarding the manic-depressive illness alleged by Jones, she declared that "there was no sign" thereof when she knew him![27]

Psychologist Esther Menaker, a student of both Jessie Taft and Anna Freud, recently wrote:

> It is little wonder that Rank became the psychologist of the will— and of the creative will at that. At a time when it was unfashionable to speak of "will," when a concern with the creative forces operating in the universe and in human psychology as well was considered trivially metaphysical, and when a strict determinism dominated the so-called scientific spirit of the times, Rank dared to express his awareness that not everything in human life is predictable on the basis of the knowledge of an individual's past history, as Freud had taught. For each individual is unique and carries within him or her the potentiality for creating something new, different and unexpected out of past experience: indeed of creating himself in a way that one might not have guessed just from the knowledge of a person's familial history. For who would have guessed that Rank himself at about the age of twenty, with no academic training at the time, could have written a treatise about the psychology of the artist (*Der Künstler*) based on his reading of Freud's work? It was this work which brought him in contact with Freud who helped him to get a higher education and ultimately to become a psychoanalyst. But the motivation to forge his own personality and his own destiny and the faith that his individuality would prevail is a manifestation of the same will that is expressed in the very existence of the Diary. Rank's decision to keep an account of his thoughts, feelings and reactions is in itself an act of will.[28]

The buffeting from left and right experienced by Otto Rank in his lifetime has continued through the decades since his death. For the most part he has been ignored, but gradually his influence has taken hold in the lives and work of a few therapists, teachers, artists, and thinkers of the generation that followed those who knew him. But his major works have not become staples of curricula even in departments of psychology, philosophy, art history, education, or literature. Banned from psychoanalysis, Rank died too soon to contribute the history of that epochal discovery that only Freud's adopted son could have written.

Among the contradictions displayed by this great mind and

endearing personality is that he felt no sense of perpetuity, yet he wrote and taught for perpetuity. Only a few in his audience could follow his argument, which in any case was generally felt more than it was grasped. Rank's argument might be summed up in the motto "Live as though you'll die tomorrow; learn as though you'll live forever." He loved books but knew their limits; he loved many people and many loved him; he loved work, solitude, music, art, games, language, dogs. Rank hated stupidity, bigotry, dishonesty, extremism, bloodshed. He cared about history and used it to understand individuals and epochs, but he counseled investment in the present.

Rank saw death as the price of life and self-consciousness. Then he yielded to the infinite and affirmed the inevitable: We need illusions to live. In religion, art, philosophy, literature, myth, and politics he found grandeur and pathos in partly successful efforts, individual and collective, to overcome the inevitable. It is enough, Rank taught, to live with it.

A deep student of history, Rank warned of its pitfalls—in psychoanalysis no less than in biography and politics. As explanation it can mislead, not just because historians are biased but because we confuse hindsight with insight; we tend, in the manner of nineteenth-century science, to look behind us for the primal cause, to make sequence the key to cause and effect. By looking to the past to solve riddles of human life we avoid death's glare ahead of us. Rank saw that the scientific pursuit of truth was, like others, a search for solace, for a consoling ideology.

We need illusion but we cannot keep our backs turned toward death without losing life itself—that is, the present. Freud's hysteric, who suffered from reminiscences, and Rank's neurotic, who clutches the life-lease in a death grip, are both evading the present moment, denying their own wills. They cannot be cured by understanding the past: That part they understand and relive compulsively. Anxiety and pain tell them that they are alive; joy heightens their awareness of life's limit, so joy must be muted. Artists recognize the paradox and use it, play with it. Rank's hard-won wisdom suggests we look carefully, not constantly, at death for the "explanation" of life, "the cause" of what we do. Why do so many people walk backwards or crab-wise along life's path? Because death waits up ahead.

Rank asked why people, from ancient clans to modern civilizations, have come to believe that the soul floats away or marches on after death to another, perhaps better, life. This belief at least enables them to face forward. The idea of nothing, the meaningless abyss, makes too many people turn their backs on life, or frightens them into making sacrifices of themselves and others to some essential though not always benevolent god. The godless have to find other ways to forge ahead so that they are neither surprised by death nor demoralized by life.

Having left his home, parents, and forbears behind, Rank gladly subordinated himself in exchange for the goodness and genius that Freud could bestow. Rank gained a new lease on life while learning a new way to think about living under Freud's tutelage. But the time came when Rank had to go out on his own or deny his own will, his individuality.

As Freud disturbed our sleep by probing his own dreams, so Rank disturbed our consciousness by probing his own will, his death-fear and life-fear. He outgrew Freud's initial explanation, that death represented punishment for sex, a symbolic castration for the Oedipal crime. Nor did he follow Freud's later conclusion, that there was a death instinct, a Thanatos to balance Eros. Instead, Rank viewed death as life's payment for itself. Life comes unasked, only to become indispensable to its bearer, who must ultimately give it back. Awareness of death is the price for awareness of life; the price goes higher as life gets better. Eternal life, in Eden, was unself-conscious. The pain of birth and the pleasure of sex, the push of love and the pull of loss, the finite spiral of union and separation followed the original sin of willing contrary to God, of knowing what only God knew.

Willful Adam and Eve, like willful Oedipus, broke a divine code. Solving the riddle, like eating the fruit, meant self-conscious living, with an end in sight. If Nietzsche fell into the abyss of existential dread, Rank, with Freud's help, managed to stay precariously balanced near the edge. He related to people singly and together, developed insight and foresight, and kept alive a vision of a more creative way of living for human beings.

In becoming independent from his mentor, Otto Rank suffered as much opposition and ostracism as had Freud himself as a pioneer. But the opposition to Rank came not from a hostile, uncomprehending society nor from a conservative medical establishment, but from the small yet increasingly powerful psychoanalytic movement which he had helped create. That movement is no longer a major intellectual or economic force; its ideas have been widely assimilated but its theories and practitioners no longer dominate psychiatry in the United States or elsewhere, and criticism from within and outside psychoanalysis has opened the way to reconsideration of the prescient ideas of Otto Rank.

His post-Freudian analysis of Hamlet awaits discovery by literary critics who have outgrown the psychoanalytic reduction of the play to a variant of the Oedipus complex. It will take time, some new translations, and the efforts of scholars from various disciplines to enable us to fully appreciate the teaching of this master of many fields. He began with ancient myth and came to an understanding of the indeterminacy principle in modern physics: It supported his view of will and his disdain for explanations rooted in the past. His love of Mark Twain, and his self-appointment as Huck's twin, reflect in Rank a frontiersman, an unpretentious philosopher of helping. He kept the soul elevated but knew how to nourish its hidden roots, and how to sustain its vitality in paradox. Both Hucks would improvise in order to free an enslaved soul. In doing so, each used his art and will to change some hallowed man-made laws of human nature.

APPENDIX

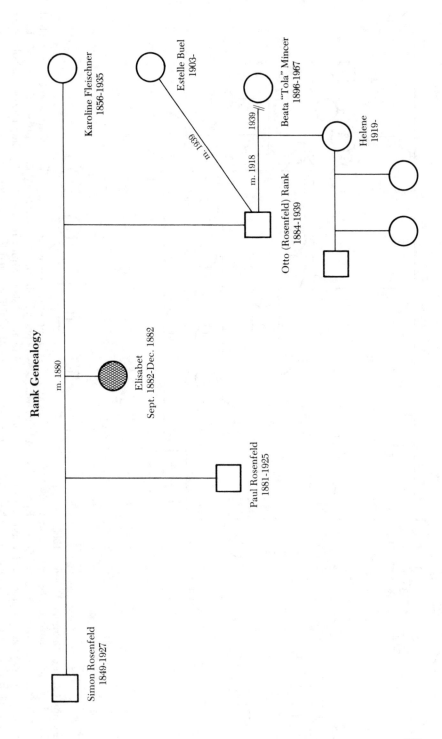

Rank Genealogy

Karoline Fleischner
1856-1935

Estelle Buel
1903-

m. 1939

Beata "Tola" Mincer
1896-1967

m. 1918

1939

Otto (Rosenfeld) Rank
1884-1939

Helene
1919-

Elisabet
Sept. 1882-Dec. 1882

m. 1880

Paul Rosenfeld
1881-1925

Simon Rosenfeld
1849-1927

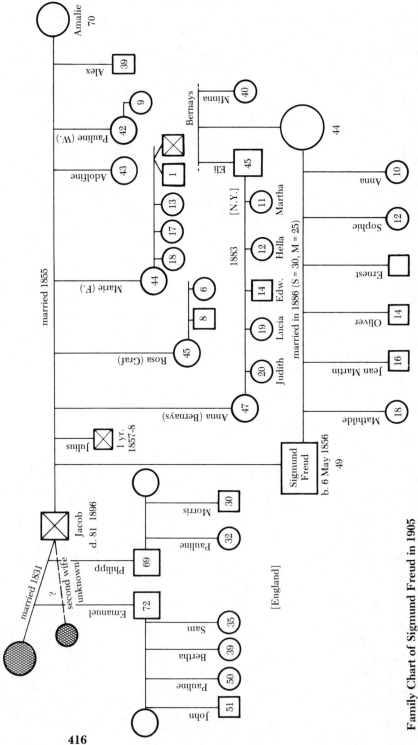

Family Chart of Sigmund Freud in 1905

Freud's father, Jacob, had two prior marriages; Sigmund had two half-brothers who were his mother's age. Emanuel's son John was Sigmund's "nephew" and closest playmate in early childhood. Sigmund had five sisters and a brother, twelve full and six half nieces and nephews. Married for nineteen years, Martha and Sigmund had six children, all younger than Otto Rank, who was then 21. Martha's unmarried sister Minna Bernays lived in the Freud household; their brother, Eli, married Freud's sister Anna.

Based on data in Ronald W. Clark, *Freud* (1980).

416

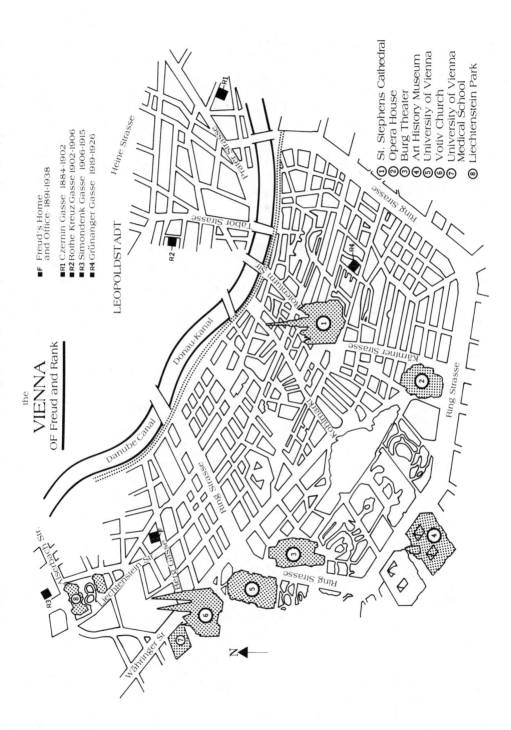

the
VIENNA
OF Freud and Rank

- **F** Freud's Home
  and Office 1891-1938

- **R1** Czernin Gasse 1884-1902
- **R2** Rothe Kreuz Gasse 1902-1906
- **R3** Simondenk Gasse 1906-1915
- **R4** Grünanger Gasse 1919-1926

LEOPOLDSTADT

① St. Stephens Cathedral
② Opera House
③ Burg Theater
④ Art History Museum
⑤ University of Vienna
⑥ Votiv Church
⑦ University of Vienna
   Medical School
⑧ Liechtenstein Park

A Bio-bibliographic Summary of Freud and Rank

(Central timeline: S. Freud, b. 1856; O. Rank, b. 1884; both d. 1939 — Freud age 83, Rank age 55)

FREUD'S MAJOR WORKS	RANK'S MAJOR WORKS	Year
		1855
		1860
		1865
		1870
		1875
		1880
		1885
		1890
Studies Hyst., 1895 w. Breuer		1895
Interpret. Dreams, 1900; Everyday Life, 1901		1900
Jokes, 1904; Sexuality, 1904; Int. Dr. ed. 2, 1909	The Artist, 1907	1905
Int. Dr. ed. 3, 1911°; Totem & Taboo, 1913; Gen. Intro. Lects., 1916-17	Hero, 1909; Eng. 1914; Inzest-Motiv, 1912	1910
	Signif. Psa. w. Sachs,'13; Eng. 1916; The Artist, 1918 ed. 2 & 3; 4 '25	1915
Pleasure Principle, 1920; Group Psych., 1921; Int. Dr. ed. 7, 1922; Ego and Id, 1923	Hero, 1922 ed. 2; Dev. Psa., 1924 w. Ferenczi; Trauma, 1924; Eng. 1929; The Double, 1925; Don Juan, 1924	1920
Inh., Sympt., Anx., 1926	Inzest-Motiv, 1926 ed. 2; Technik, 1926, '29, '31°; Genetische Psych, 1927, '28	1925
Int. Dr. ed. 8, 1929; Civ. & Discontents, 1930	Wahrheit,1929°°; Seelenglaube, 1930; Modern Educ., 1932	1930
New Intro Lects., 1933	Art & Artist, 1932; °Will Therapy, 1936	1935
Moses & Monotheism, 1939	°°Truth & Reality, 1936; Beyond Psychology, 1941	1940
		1945

°eds. 3-7 include two chapters by Rank

Psychoanalytic Congresses and Journals in Rank's Time.
Adapted from John Rickman, ed., *Index Psychoanalyticus* (1928).

Congresses		Jung	Stekel, Adler	Rank, Sachs	Ferenczi, Rank	Jelliffe, White	Jones	Editor(s)
		Jahrbuch	Zentralblatt	Imago	Zeit-schrift	Psa. Review	Int'l. Journal	Title
		Y	C	I	Z	PR	IJP	Abbr.
I Salzburg	1908	*Band* [Vol.]	*Band*	*Band*	*Band*	*Vol.*	*Vol.*	
	1909	I.						
II Nuremberg	1910	II.	I.					
III Weimar	1911	III.	II.					
	1912	IV.		I.				
IV Munich	1913	V.		II.	I.			
	1914	VI.		III.	II.	I.		
	1915			IV.	III.	II.		
	1916				IV.	III.		
	1917			V.		IV.		
V Budapest	1918				—	V.		
	1919			—	V.	VI.		
VI The Hague	1920			VI.	VI.	VII.	I.	
	1921			VII.	VII.	VIII.	II.	
VII Berlin	1922			VIII.	VIII.	IX.	III.	
	1923			IX.	IX.	X.	IV.	
VIII Salzburg	1924			X.	X.	XI.	V.	
IX Bad Homburg	1925			XI.	XI.	XII.	VI.	
	1926			XII.	XII.	XIII.	VII.	

CHAPTER NOTES

Most of the following references are of primary interest to scholars and are kept as brief as possible consistent with clarity. Longer notes which elaborate the text can be identified easily by scanning the relevant sections. Sources cited in abbreviated form are listed by author in Bibliography II except for Rank, whose works comprise Bibliography I.

Letters are cited in the following form: F–Ab., 294: 23 Nov 1919. Thus: Author-Recipient, page (*or* sequence) number if published: date of letter. This example is a letter by Freud from the published Freud-Abraham correspondence, page 294.

F/J 175J, 30 Jan 1910. This letter from Jung to Freud is published as #175 in chronological sequence (authorship shown by initial).

To lessen confusion—there are three different editions of the Freud/Jung letters—page numbers are not given. For the same reason, sequence numbers are cited rather than pages for the anthologized Freud letters (1960).

When only the date is given (*no* page *or* sequence number) the letter cited is unpublished and may be located in manuscript collections, most often the Rank Collection at Columbia University (see listing of special collections consulted in library acknowledgments). Having studied the original Rank–Taft (R–T) letters, I indicate where the published versions in Taft (1958) include substantially more or less than my own citations.

SHORT TITLE/ABBREVIATION LIST

AA = Rank, *Art & Artist,* 1932.

Ab. = Abraham

F = Freud

Fer. = Ferenczi

F/J = *The Freud/Jung Letters,* 1974. 87F = letter 87, by Freud.

F Ls. = *The Letters of Sigmund Freud,* 1960.

Ell. = Henri Ellenberger, *The Discovery of the Unconscious,* 1970.

I = *Imago* (Vienna)

I.D. = Freud, *Interpretation of Dreams* [1900], tr. Strachey, 1953.

IJP = *International Journal of Psychoanalysis* (London)

J 1,2,3 = Jones, *The Life and Work of Sigmund Freud,* Vols. I–III, 1953–57.

JORA = *Journal of the Otto Rank Association,* 17 vols. (31 issues), 1966–83.

Klein = Dennis Klein, *Jewish Origins of Psychoanalysis,* 1981.

Lang. Psa. = Laplanche and Pontalis, *The Language of Psychoanalysis,* 1973.

LA = Rank, *Literary Autobiography* [1930], *JORA* 16 (30): 3–38, 1981.

Lou = Lou Andreas-Salomé

MBH = Rank, *Myth of the Birth of the Hero* [1909], 1914.

MH = *Mental Hygiene* (New York)

M 1–4 = *Minutes of the Vienna Psa. Soc.,* Vols. I–IV, 1906–18.

Nin 1, 2 = *The Diary of Anais Nin,* Vols. 1, 2.

Ob. = Oberndorf, *History of Psychoanalysis in America,* 1953.

Pioneers = Alexander et al., *Psychoanalytic Pioneers,* 1966.

PR = *Psychoanalytic Review* (U.S.)

T = Taft, *Otto Rank,* 1958.

ToB = Rank, *Trauma of Birth* [1924], 1929.

Z = *Zeitschrift für Psychoanalyse* (Vienna)

Introduction

1. Tr. David Grene, U. Chicago Press, 1954, lines 1066–69.
2. Yale lecture, *JORA* 1: 1, 1966, p. 13.
3. J3, 220–21. Weiss 1970, 20–21.
4. Freud in *IJP* 7: 1, 1926; in *SE* 20: 277; in *Abstracts of the SE* 1926B, 20/277, USDHEW, NIMH, 1971.
5. Psa. as General Psychology. Lecture of 19 Jun 1924, in *MH* 10: 1, 1926, p. 13.
6. *Truth and Reality/Wahrheit und Wirklichkeit* 1929, p. 4, Tr. EJL. Cf. Taft tr. 1936, 210: "For in this act the psychic ego is born out of the biological corporeal ego and the human being becomes at once creator and creature or actually moves from creature to creator, in the ideal case, creator of himself, his own personality." And the original: "Denn in ihm wird nicht nur das Individuum, das seelische Ich, aus dem biologischen Körper-Ich geboren, sondern in ihm ist der Mensch Schöpfer und Geschöpf zugleich, oder eigentlich wird er aus einem Geschöpf zum Schöpfer—im idealen Falle seiner selbst, seiner Personlichkeit."
7. Psychoanalyst Lili Peller once suggested that we refer to parents as "birth" and "real" rather than as "real" and "adoptive." I am indebted to Minos Volanakis, Director of the Greek National Theatre's *Oedipus Rex* (1984), for pointing out that the self-blinding of Oedipus is 1) less severe a punishment than the chorus calls for; and 2) follows—belatedly—Jocasta's advice that it is better to live somewhat blindly than see too clearly who you are.
8. Ives Hendrick 1958, 336.
9. J3, 45, 47.
10. J3, 77. Trilling, *NYT Book Rev.* 13 Oct 1957, p. 7; Ibid. 17 Nov— Trilling's correction.
11. Gilbert Cant, *Time* see p. 400; *Post* 21 Jun 1958. Alvarez, "Schizoid Personality Revealed in Journal" *Los Angeles Times* 23 Mar 1959.
12. Robert, *Psa. Revolution* 1966, 339.
13. Menninger, *Psa. Tech.*, 156.
14. Stolorow and Atwood, *Faces in a Cloud.* Ch. 5.
15. Dyer 1983, 56.
16. Becker *Death*, 73 and xii.
17. Hampden-Turner, 1981, 66 (on Rank and Becker).
18. Yalom 1975 *Group*, ed. 2, 156–57. S. Arieti 1972, and Psychiatric Controversy: man's ethical dimension. *Am J Psychiat* 132: 39–42, 1975.
19. Marmor 1979, 150.

20. EJL, 1979, 1984. Int. with Mary Plowden.
21. Victor Rubenstein letter. To EJL, 24 Mar 1978.
22. Putnam, Personal experience with Freud's psa. method, 1910. Tr. O. Rank, C. 1: 533, 1911. Karpf, 1953, 55, indicates the link to William James whom Rank rarely, if ever, mentions.

Chapter 1

1. Rank, unpublished Diary, 1903–4. The order is thematic rather than chronological in places. Family genealogy from D. Klein, 108, 166; for Elisabet, letter from Israelitische Kultusgemeinde to EJL, 1983.
2. Letter of Isidor Sax to M. Pohek, 1940.
3. D. Klein, 34, n. 30; 110, 134 n. 25 on name change and religion. T. Reik, oral history, mentions *Hedda Gabler* but Rank appears only in *A Doll's House*. See also Roazen, 393. On other Viennese notables see Johnston, 1972.
4. Grollman, 56, 89; also see Rozenblit.
5. Twain, 1897.
6. Weininger died October 4, 1903. See Chapter 3.
7. Rank, "Diary Leaves of a Stillborn," 1904.

Chapter 2

1. James 1902, Lect. 8, 166.
2. Freud's reviews appeared 8 Feb 1903 and 4 Feb 1904: J2, 13, 335. The lecture is summarized by D. Klein, 159.
3. Johnston 1972: 232–33; on syphilis see Zilboorg & Henry, 526 ff; 544–45. On Nietzsche see Hayman, and Kauffmann.
4. B. Glass, 1967.
5. Quote: G. Clive, ed. *The Philosophy of Nietzsche* Mentor, 1965, xxx. On healing: Nietzsche *Dawn,* 1880; Hayman, 137, 302.
6. Quoted without source in *Infidels and Heretics,* Clarence Darrow & Wallace Rice, eds. Boston, 1929, 27.
7. Johnston 1972: 232–37.
8. Ell., 208; Whyte, 141, 160.
9. J2, 8; Nin 1, 278; F 1914, 25.
10. Clark, 227; R *Artist,* 16 n., *LA,* 3.

Chapter 3

1. F–Putnam 18 Aug 1910, in Hale 1971, 105. On Freud's letters see F Ls. 1960, preface; J1, 99. Main biographical sources are

Brome, Clark, Jones, Johnston, Roazen, Sulloway, and Wittels 1924. On Freud's output, see the *Concordance.*

2. J1, 8; *ID* 520–1. I prefer Jones's trans. to Strachey's.

3. J1, 10.

4. Wittels 1933, 32. The essay was written by G. Tobler: see Ell., 552 n. 52.

5. Clark, 37; J1, 24 and 28.

6. J1, 29.

7. Wittels 1933, 48; the extreme positivist was Laplace. On Meynert: Ackerknecht, 66; Ell., 434.

8. F Ls. #43, p. 107–108.

9. J1, 117.

10. J1, 111.

11. Ell., 486; F–Putnam (ed. Hale), 67.

12. Ell., 487; *ID,* xxvi (Preface to 2nd ed.)

13. F Ls. #110, 2 Apr 1896, p. 231–32.

14. J1, 112.

15. Vranich, 1976. Brandell makes a case for Ibsen as an influence on Freud. Several articles on Freud's reading leave unanswered the question, Did he know Hawthorne's *Scarlet Letter?* Published in 1850, it was popular in England in 1875, the year Freud visited. Oberndorf, Menninger, Ellenberger, and Lieberman have pointed out the (negative) likeness of "Dr." Chillingworth's soul-searching to psychoanalysis.

16. F Ls. #37. F *History,* 1914, 43.

17. J1, 357–41. Freud's title, Professor extraordinarius, meant he was not a regular faculty member and was not required to teach courses; he did lecture, usually on Saturdays, to a heterogeneous audience.

18. F–Fliess 22 Sep 1898, p. 264; cf. Sulloway, 218.

19. F–Fliess 7 May 1900, p. 318; cf. Sulloway, 220.

20. Sulloway, 222.

21. Eissler 1971 citing Swoboda (1906). Rank never commented on the record regarding the Weininger–Fliess uproar, which broke into print in 1906 (see Szasz 1976 on Karl Kraus). The Freud–Fliess correspondence has yet to appear in an unexpurgated version. Freud destroyed Fliess's letters to him. Weininger but not Freud impressed Swoboda as being a genius (Eissler interviewed Swoboda: personal communication to EJL). Quote: Weininger 1906, 7. Detailed information on Weininger in English is found in Abrahamsen, Brome 1967, Eissler 1971, Liptzin, and Sulloway.

Only Roback remarks on the similarity between Rank and Weininger.

22. Brome 1967, 7–12; Sulloway 223–29.

23. Brome 1967, 7–9; Sulloway 225–26.

24. Brome 1967, 9–10; Sulloway, 226.

25. Abrahamsen, 208; 54–55.

26. F Ls. #122 to Kraus, 12 Jan 1906.

27. F/J 70F, 17 Feb 1908.

28. J1, 312–15.

29. *ID*, 483–84. D. Klein, 126–28; Rank diary IV, 29 Apr 1905.

30. F *History*, 1914. Other primary sources on the Society are Stekel, Graf, Furtmüller, and Wittels 1924.

31. F *History*, 1914.

32. F Ls. #209 to Wittels, 15 Aug 1924.

33. F Ls. #169 to Putnam, 8 July 1915.

34. Martin Freud 1967, 203. Other sources on Freud's Jewishness: D. Klein, Graf, Cuddihy, Robert, Bakan, Grollman, Gay.

35. *ID*, 230.

36. Brome *Jones*, 186; Roazen, 351.

37. F/J 238F, 1 Mar 1911.

Chapter 4

1. Grollman, 94. General references for this chapter include Ell., and Fielding H. Garrison, *History of Medicine* 4th ed. 1929.

2. Re Anna: Roazen, 438; Nin 1, 279; re Martha: Stone, 543.

3. Klein, 167. Rank attended K.K. Staatsgymnasium XVIII.

4. Sulloway, 464–80; Ell., 791.

5. M1, 1–13. Re smoke: Wittels 1924, 44.

6. *Das Inzest-Motiv* 1912, 40–48 (Oedipus–Don Carlos); 188–91 (Murder of kin), tr. David Berger. Rank wrote most of this work before his 1906 presentation. The published book includes some later references and ideas, including "complex," first used by Freud in 1910. *LA*, 10–13.

7. Stone, 548.

8. Leupold–Löwenthal 1980, 26; M1, 52. I present this lengthy dialogue in the first person; usually I quote the minutes directly (third person).

9. M1, 21: 24 Oct 1906.

10. Ibid., 25.

11. Ibid., 29.

12. M1, 46–47: 7 Nov 1906.

13. M1, 60: 21 Nov 1906.

14. M1, 65: 28 Nov 1906; Roazen, 15.

15. M1, 75: 5 Dec 1906.

16. F/J 8F, 6 Dec 1906.

17. *All's Well That Ends Well. LA,* 3. The words "Is it" appear in reverse order in all editions of *Der Künstler.* Evidently the error never came to Rank's attention.

18. *Der Künstler* 1907, 38. The prior quotations come from *The Artist,* tr. of the 4th ed. (1925) which differs little from the first ed. *Art and Artist* (1932) is a completely different book.

19. F/J 17J, 31 Mar 1907. Review appeared in *Der Tag* before the meeting of 10 Apr 1907: M1, 159.

20. *LA,* 3.

21. M1, 81. *Pioneers,* 51–62.

22. M1, 90. *The Artist,* 7, 62. On libido, see *Lang. Psa.,* 239.

23. M1, 98–99: 30 Jan 1907.

24. F/J 11F, 1 Jan 1907.

25. Binswanger, 6–7. Also M1, 144: 6 Mar 1907.

26. Jung, *Memories,* 149. Brome 1967, 25–26.

27. M1, 175–79: 24 Apr 1907.

28. M1, 195–200: 15 May 1907.

29. F/J 27F, 26 May 1907.

30. F/J 28J, 30 May; 36F, 10 July; 38F, 18 Aug 1907.

31. F/J 40F, 27 Apr 1907.

32. F/J 42F, 2 Sep 1907.

33. F/J 45F, 19 Sep 1907.

34. F/J 49J, 28 Oct; 52F 15 Nov 1907. Binswanger, 6.

35. *LA,* 6–8. It was published in 1909.

36. *Der Künstler* 1907, 36; *MBH,* 8 (*Mythus* 1909: 7, 11).

37. *MBH* Ch. 3, par. 2, 65.

38. *Mythus* 1909, 68.

39. *MBH,* 76.

40. *De Natura Rerum* V, 222–27; *MBH,* 76.

Chapter 5

1. F–Abraham, J2, 51.

2. M1, 238–240: 13 Nov 1907.

3. M1 5 and 12, 298–317: Feb 1907.

4. Letter of 1 Dec 1788 in *Schillers Briefwechsel mit Körner*, 1847, in F/J, German ed., 144. Tr. rev. EJL. In 1909 Freud put the passage in *ID*, Ch. 2, 135, with credit to Rank.

5. F/J 77F, 5 Mar 1908; tr. rev. EJL.

6. Jung on Rank: F/J 17J, 31 Mar and 19J, 11 Apr 1907. Freud: 18F, 7 Apr 1907.

7. F/J 79J, 11 Mar 1908.

8. M1, 341–43: 4 Mar 1908.

9. M1, 361 (rephrased).

10. M1, 359–60: 1 Apr 1908. F on Nietzsche: Sulloway, 468; Ell., 271–78.

11. F 1914 *History of Psa.*, 48 (Std. Ed. 14: 13).

12. F/J 84F, 19 Apr 1908.

13. J2, 40–44.

14. F/J 86J, 30 Apr 1908.

15. F–Ab., 34: 3 May 1908; Clark, 252.

16. F–Ab., 83: 11 Oct 1908; F/J 92F, 10 May 1908.

17. F/J 94F, 19 May; 95J 25 May; 98J, 19 June 1908.

18. Carotenuto, 113 ff. F/J 134F, 9 Mar; 148J, 21 Jun 1909.

19. F/J 145F, 24 Jun 1909.

20. F/J 125F, 17 Jan; 139F, 16 Apr 1909; 72J, 20 Feb 1908; 138 J, 2 Apr 1909; 129F, 25 Jan 1909.

21. Ell., 802–803; 876 note #239.

22. Johnston 1972, 64–66.

23. Klein, 12, 167; 70–72 (Lueger); Grollman, 93.

24. Liptzin, 213–16.

25. Klein, 168.

26. M2, 25ff.: 8 Oct 1909.

27. M2 ibid.; 32.

28. M2, 120: 3 Mar 1909.

29. M2, 174: 10 Mar 1909.

30. M2, 193: 31 Mar 1909.

31. M2, 195–206: 7 Apr 1909.

32. R: ibid., 206; F: ibid. 203–204.

33. F/J 123F, 30 Dec 1908.

34. Hale 1971 *Freud*, 16–18. F 1910 *Five Lectures*. Schopenhauer motto in Sachs, 48.

35. Kardiner, Oral History, 117; James: Hale, ibid., 18–19.

36. F 1914 *History,* 64; see also F–Putnam letters.

37. J2, 60.

38. F/J 158F, 17 Oct; 159J, 8 Nov 1909.

39. M2, 286: 27 Oct 1909; Marmor, 1978, 150.

40. M2, 324: 17 Nov 1909; *ID* Ch. 6E, 436 (emphasis in original).

41. F/J 160F, 11 Nov 1909, tr. EJL; 162J, 15 Nov 1909.

42. F/J 175J, 30 Jan; 177F 2 Feb 1910 (tr. EJL). Freud's analysis of Anna is documented in E. Weiss, 81. On counter-transference, see *Lang. Psa.,* 92–93.

43. M2, 332: 24 Nov; M2, 338–52: 1 Dec 1909.

44. *LA,* 9. Abs. by Blumgart: *PR* 5: 230–34, 1918.

45. M2, 447.

46. Stekel, 129 (he mislocates the meeting to Weimar).

47. Jones *Free Associations,* 215.

48. F/J 178J, 11 Feb; 179F, 13 Feb 1910.

49. M2, 471: 6 Apr 1910. Of the 30 collaborating editors, Rank is the only one with no title or degree. See title page reproduction in Stekel, 140.

50. M2, 480: 20 Apr 1910.

51. F/J 185F, 12 Apr; 194F, 26 May; 199F, 19 June 1910.

52. F/J 218F, 31 Oct 1910.

53. Sachs, 60.

54. F/J 221F, 25 Nov; 223F, 3 Dec 1910.

55. F/J ibid.

56. M3, 142, 149: 1 Feb 1911.

57. M3, 172: 22 Feb 1911.

58. M3, 178: 1 Mar 1911.

59. F/J 238F, 1 Mar 1911. Rank's later views on Adler can be found in *Will Therapy* and *Modern Education.*

60. F/J 242F, 14 Mar 1911.

61. M3, 281: 11 Oct 1911.

62. Furtmüller, 350. See also Stepansky, 1984.

63. J3, 208; Roazen, 209.

64. F/J 253F, 27 Apr 1911.

65. M3, 247: 3 May 1911.

66. Oberndorf, 171. Kurt Adler, Alexandra Adler: telephone interviews, June 1982.

Chapter 6

1. F/J 87F, 3 May 1908.
2. J2, 85.
3. Brome *Jones*, 52; 74–75.
4. Ibid., 125, 131, passim.
5. J2, 86: F–Jones, 18 Dec 1910.
6. F/J 103F, 18 July 1908; 87 F, 3 May 1908.
7. Brome *Jones*, 67–68.
8. F/J 103F, 18 Jul 1908.
9. J2, 160.
10. Ibid.
11. Ibid.
12. Lou, 98.
13. M3, 310: 15 Nov 1911.
14. M3, 357–67; 20 Dec 1911. *Die Onanie*, 1912.
15. Ellis *Psychology of Sex* 1933, 134–35; *Lang.Psa.* 255–57 J2, 302–306.
16. *LA*, 8–9.
17. F *Psychopathology of Everyday Life*, 68; *Intro. Lects.* 33, 51.
18. Frederick Praeger to EJL, June 1983. M4, 265: 3 Jun 1914; a guest named Präger attended once only; Rank was present.
19. T. Reik, oral history, Columbia U.
20. F–R, 18 Aug 1912.
21. R *Inzest-Motiv*, 1–21, tr. David Berger. Ludwig Klages (1872–1956), philosopher and psychologist, addressed the Vienna Psychoanalytic Society 25 Oct 1911: M3, 293.
22. J2, 134–37.
23. Sachs, 62–63.
24. F/J 316F, 23 May; 321J, 2 Aug 1912
25. J3, 453; F–Lou, 195 (May or July, 1931).
26. F/J 323J, 11 Nov 1912.
27. F/J 338J, 18 Dec 1912.
28. F/J 342F, 3 Jan 1913.
29. Lou *Journal*, 98: 12–13 Feb 1913.
30. J2, 149.
31. J2, 102. Curiously Jones gives a different version in his autobiography, *Free Associations*, 224: "He sneeringly remarked to me: 'I thought you had ethical principles' (an expression he was fond of); my friends interpreted the word 'ethical' here as meaning

'Christian' and therefore as anti-Semitic." Jones's divergent reports and his inability to judge the matter seem significant.

32. Ibid., 227–28; J2, 152 ff.

33. F Ls. #163 to Fer. 9 Jul 1913; J2, 155.

34. J2, 163.

35. F–Ab., 110: 2 Nov 1911; 139: 13 May and 141: 1 Jun 1913.

36. Clark, 321; J2, 155.

37. Graf, 1942.

38. S. Rado, oral history, Columbia U. 1963–65.

39. E. Weiss, 1970.

40. A photograph of Rank's diploma appears in *Columbia Library Columns* 33:3, p.7, May 1984 (Rank Centenary Issue).

41. M4, 179: 12 Mar 1913.

42. M4, 189: 16 Apr 1913.

43. M4, 191: 23 Apr 1913.

44. M4, 210: 29 Oct 1913.

45. Sachs, 60–61.

46. Wittels 1924, 133 and 144–45.

47. F–Ab., 191: 25 Aug 1914; 195: 3 Sep 1914.

48. J2, 176: F–Fer. 2 Dec 1914.

49. F–Ab., 205: 14 Dec 1914; 207: 21 Dec 1914.

50. F–Ab., 225: 3 July 1915; J2, 181. F *Intro. Lects.*, 5.

51. J2, 187; T 67–68. See Warsaw ticket in Rank Coll.

52. *Der Künstler* ed. 2 & 3, 1918. Intro dated Sept. 1917, Luhatschowitz. Tr. Eva Salomon and EJL.

53. J2, 193; F–Ab., 267: 26 Dec 1917.

54. M1, xxii. See *Pioneers,* 54; Roazen, *Brother Animal.*

55. Klein, 169; Beata Rank interviews.

56. Roazen, 396.

57. Beata Rank interview 1954.

58. J3, 8, 30, 291; The statement that Rank analyzed children is doubtful; Jones may have meant *Beata* Rank. "I have never done any practical work with children," Rank said in 1927: *JORA* 3: 70, 1967.

59. J2, 160. J3, 12–13.

60. Roazen *Brother Animal,* 102; F–Lou, 98: 1 Aug 1919.

61. Roazen, 396.

62. Brome *Jones,* 123; J3, 46.

Chapter 7

1. J2, 182; on journals see Appx., p. 419. Johnston, 290.
2. F–Ab., 294: 23 Nov 1919.
3. J3, 21 (F–Jones, 12 Feb 1920).
4. J2, 189; F Ls. #177, 13 July 1917.
5. J2, 458 (F–Pfister 63: Oct 1918); Binswanger, 9.
6. See individual biographies in *Pioneers*.
7. J3, 19. F Ls. #185 F–Amalie 26 Jan & #187 F–Fer. 4 Feb.
8. R–Jones, 26 July 1920.
9. R–Jones, 20 July 1920.
10. Beata Rank interview 1954.
11. J3, 28.
12. J3, 31–32; 46.
13. R–Comm. 8 Oct 1920.
14. On *Rundbriefe* see *JORA* 8:2 (No. 15, 1973):5–91; overview, excerpts and comments by V.P. Robinson, M. Grotjahn and E. Salomon represent the fullest presentation of this vital material—387 letters—so far.
15. J3, 32; 78–79; F–Pfister, 79: 25 Dec 1920.
16. F Ls. #176, 5 Jun 1917.
17. In K. Menninger, *Theory of Psa. Technique,* 11; L. Durrell "Studies in Genius" VI, *Horizon* (England) 17: 384–403, 1948.
18. *Pioneers* 312–18.
19. *JORA* 3:2(5), 1968, p. 35; *Lang. Psa.* 6–8.
20. F–Pfister, 81: 23 Mar; 83: 3 Nov 1921.
21. Kardiner in Nelson, 48–49; Ob., 138–43.
22. Ob., 136.
23. J3, 81.
24. J3, xii. Jones itemizes his differences with Freud: Lamarkism, telepathy, child analysis, lay analysis, the death instinct, the theory of anxiety, and the identity of Shakespeare.
25. R & F to Comm., 11 Dec 1921 and 22 Jan 1922. Cited in "The Gay Rights Freud," by Herb Spiers & Michael Lynch, *The Body Politic* (Toronto) No. 33, May 1977, 8–10. (Research in the Rank Coll. by H. Ruitenbeek).
26. Ob., 195; R to Comm. 21 Oct 1921.
27. Kardiner, oral history, 114–20.
28. *JORA* 8:2, 1973, 57 ff.
29. Ibid., 63.

30. F–R 10 Jul 1922. Further excerpt in T, 75–76. *LA*, 18.
31. Beata Rank interview 1953, 12.
32. F–R 8 Sep 1922.
33. Ab.–Comm. 1 Nov 1922.
34. F–R 8 Sep 1922.
35. F–Comm. 26 Nov 1922; part quoted in T, 79–80.
36. F–Comm. 15 Dec 1922; in full in *JORA* 8:2, 69–72.
37. R–Comm. 20 Dec 1922.
38. *JORA* 8:2, 74; Jones–Comm. 15 Feb 1923.
39. R–Comm. 1 Feb, 18 Feb, 1 Apr 1923. *JORA* 8:2, 73–75.
40. Jones–Comm. 1 Mar; 5 Apr 1923.
41. J3, 89.
42. See Schur 1972 for fullest discussion of Freud's illness. Wilbur to John Taylor, 9 Feb 1947 (carbon copy, Wilbur papers) says Felix Deutsch told Rank of malignancy when tissue diagnosis was first made.
43. J3, 92.
44. Brome 1967, 176.
45. J3, 93–94.
46. J3, 55–56; Brome 1967, 177; Brome *Jones*, 139.
47. Clark, 443 (Jones–Comm. Nov 1924. Not in Rank Coll.).
48. J3, 96.

Chapter 8

1. Fer. & Rank, *Dev. Psa.* (Dec. 1923), 20. Rank wrote the chapter from which the citation comes. See translator's preface.
2. Ibid., 5.
3. Jones *Free Associations*, 227. Also J3, 55–57.
4. J3, 57 (F–Fer. 4 Feb 1924).
5. J3, 58.
6. J3, 58. Rank, 1923: "Toward Understanding Libido Development in Healing." (Grinstein 26515).
7. Rank, "Perversion and Neurosis," *IJP* 4: 282 (1923).
8. Ibid., 286–87.
9. Ibid., 287.
10. Ibid., 290–91.
11. Editha Sterba, telephone interview 22 Feb 1981. A manuscript of *ToB*, in the Rank Coll. indicates that the dictation was not unprepared; perhaps she actually typed Rank's part of *Dev. Psa.*

12. Beata Rank interview 1954, p. 7.
13. Paula Fichtl interview: London, 16 Aug 1982. Anna Freud–R, 31 Jul 1922.
14. Beata Rank interview 1953, p. 2; Roazen, 397.
15. F–R 1 Dec 1923; in T, 85.
16. Schur, 361–66.
17. R–Comm. 16 Nov 1923. *JORA* 8: 2, 77–79.
18. F–R 25 Oct 1923.
19. A fragment of this letter is in T, 78–79.
20. Sachs, 60–61; J3, 59.
21. Wittels 1924, 133.
22. Ibid., 223–24.
23. F–Comm. 15 Feb 1924. In F–Ab., 344–48 and J3, 59–63.
24. Fer. & Rank *Dev. Psa.*, 60; 3–4.
25. Ibid., 19–20.
26. J3, 56; F–Comm. ibid., F–Ab., 346.
27. F–Comm., ibid.
28. J–Comm. 18 Feb 1924; F–Ab. 349–51.
29. F–Ab., 349–51: Ab.–F. 21 and 16 Feb 1924.
30. Jones–Ab. 1 Jan 1923; Ab. Coll., Library of Congress.
31. R–F 14 Feb 1924; T, 89–90.
32. F–Ab., 346: F–Comm. 14 Feb 1924.
33. F–Ab., 349: 25 Feb 1924. *JORA* 8:2(14) 1973: 81–84.
34. F–Ab., 352–53: 4 Mar 1924.
35. Fer.–R (copy of Fer.–F) 18 Mar 1924. This is the only mention I have found of Jones's anti-Semitism by a Ring member.
36. F–Fer. 20 Mar 1924; T, 90–91.
37. Ibid.
38. R–Fer. 20 Mar 1924.
39. *LA* 19–32. F–Fer. 24 Mar, quoted Fer.–R 30 Jul; J3, 59. F–Fer. 26 Mar 1924, cited by Rank: *LA*, 31.
40. F–R 23 Mar 1924. T, 92.
41. R–F 24 Mar 1934. T, 93.
42. Marianne Hauser interview New York, 1983.
43. R–Fer 10 Apr 1924; T, 94.
44. F–Ab., 355: 31 Mar 1924.
45. Jones–Ab. 8 Apr 1924; (Ab. Coll.).
46. Sterba, 86.

Chapter 9

1. Notes and jottings to *The Wild Duck,* circa April 1884. In Dounia B. Christiani tr. & ed. *The Wild Duck* by H. Ibsen, Norton Critical Ed., New York, 1968, p. 84.

2. E. Jones. Report on the Eighth IPA Congress, *IJP,* 5: 391–408, 1924; partly reprinted in Székely-Kovács & Berény, 1955.

3. Bernays, 1965, 256ff. F–R 29 June 1924.

4. J3, 103; F–R, 23 May 1924; T, 95–96.

5. *Med. J. & Record,* 6 Aug 1924.

6. *PR* 11: 442, 1924.

7. T, x. "Bombshell" in Taft's notebook, 1924.

8. *ToB,* 181–82.

9. E. Weiss 37: F–Weiss 11 June 1922.

10. Ob. 171.

11. Kardiner, oral history.

12. Kardiner, ibid. *ToB,* 36–37.

13. *ToB,* 37.

14. C. Thompson, "Transference and Character Analysis," *Samiksa* 7: 260–70, 1953; rpt. in *Interpersonal Psa.* 1964, p. 234.

15. F–Ab. 361 (abridged): 4 May 1924. Sydenham: see Veith, 142.

16. Fer.–R 25 May 1924.

17. Burrow, 1958, 76–80.

18. F–Burrow, 31 July 1924; Lifwyn Fdn./Yale Univ.

19. F–R, 23 July 1924; T, 99.

20. R–F, 9 Aug 1924; T, 100–103.

21. F–R, 25 Aug 1924; F Ls. #210.

22. F–R, 27 Aug 1924; complete in T, 105–109.

23. Ibid.

24. R–Fer. 10 Aug 1924.

25. J3, 69–70; F–Fer. 6 Sept 1924.

26. J3, 71; F–Jones, 5 Nov 1924.

27. J3, 72; F–Jones, 16 Nov 1924.

28. Lou–F, 141–42: Nov 1924.

29. F–Lou, 143–44: 17 Nov 1924.

30. Beata Rank int. (K. R. Eissler) 1953, 1954.

31. J3, 72–73.

32. R–Comm. 20 Dec 1924; tr. W. Low; T, 110.

33. T, 110.

34. F–S. Viereck 23 Aug 1924; Brill Library.

35. Jones–R, 3 Jan 1925.

36. J3, 75 (departure date); R–Comm. 7 Jan 1925; T, 112–14.

37. F–Ab. 17 Oct 1924, p. 312. When the lady withdrew her offer, Freud repeated an old refrain of his: "Nothing will grow on Viennese soil."

38. F–Ab. 379: 29 Dec. 1924.

39. Brome *Jones,* 147; F–Jones 25 Sept 1924; Jones–F 29 Sept.

40. R–White, 21 Jan 1925; U.S. Archives.

41. Typescript minutes, Jan 1925.

42. James Strachey to Alix Strachey, 5 Oct 1924 (Walter Kendrick).

43. Jan 1925 minutes. See Menaker 1982 on Rank's relation to current theorists.

44. Aichhorn acknowledged Rank in his famous book *Wayward Youth* and is acknowledged in turn by Kohut. A Kohutian statement uttered by Rank in New York, 12 Feb 1925: "The primary narcissistic state is not analyzable and need not be analyzed. Even a neurotic needs it to exist. But we do have to analyze the way in which the impulses of this stage are used in mechanisms with relation to objects."

45. R–White, 2 Jul 1925; J3, 74; T, 119.

46. F–Ab., 3 Mar 1925 (LC, unpubl.).

47. J3, 75; Ab.–F 393–94: 8 Sep 1925. In *PR* 13:222 Jelliffe commented on Rank's "Gatling gun" reading of "The Genesis of Genitality" at Bad Homburg. "He first excused himself for not discussing the trauma of birth theory which seemed uppermost in the atmosphere of those most centrally interested in psychoanalytical theory, and promised to present his later reflections at a future time . . ."

48. F–Ab., 399: 5 Nov 1925, Ironically, after the Congress Abraham was treated by Wilhelm Fliess and told Freud "My illness has most strikingly confirmed all Fliess's views on periodicity [in WF's *Der Ablauf des Lebens,* The Course of Life, 1923]." 8 Sep 1925, 395.

49. *IJP* 7:1, 1926. Freud provocatively omitted the name.

50. R–White 11 Nov 1925. R–Jelliffe 2 July 1925. R–F cited in J3, 75 but not available.

51. Minutes, Jan 1925. Ferenczi's paper (Bad Homburg, 1925) was a clear sign of his separation from Rank (F–Ab., 393).

52. Bertin, *Bonaparte,* 124–25.

53. Roazen, 412, and 589, notes 12 & 13. I saw a 23-volume set of Nietzsche in the Freud library in Anna Freud's house, London, Aug 1982. There was no inscription. It is significant that Freud,

who could bring only part of his library out of Vienna, chose to include Rank's gift.

54. J3, 76 (F–Fer. 26 Apr 1925).

Chapter 10

1. F. Williams, *Proceedings* II, 149.
2. *S & S*, 5–7, tr. E. Salomon and EJL.
3. *Mental Hygiene* 11:176–188, 1927.
4. Review: *IJP* 8:93–100, 1927. Quote: T, xvi.
5. T, xi.
6. MK–R, 27 Aug; Peck–MK, 4 Sep; MK–Peck 25 Sep 1926. Kenworthy Coll., Columbia U.
7. Sullivan–White 9 Dec 1926: see D'Amore, 79–80.
8. Wilda (Mrs. Martin) Peck [later] Strong, 49 p. typescript diary of 31 interviews with Rank, 14 Apr-20 May 1927. Brought to my attention by Dr. Robert Kvarnes. Used by permission of her daughter, Wilda Peck O'Hanlon. Entries cited begin 30 Apr (session 14) and end 17 May (session 28). Photo No. 19. R–T 28 Feb 1927
9. Myron C. Nutting, oral history 1972, 351–62; UCLA.
10. R. Guthrie, "Yorick," *Maximum Security Ward* 1970, 1984.
11. Lodging: T, 133; R–T 12 Sep 1927. Quote: T, 134.
12. T, 135.
13. A list among Rank's papers included the following psychiatrists, many quite prominent: Frankwood Williams, Marion Kenworthy, Thomas Haines, George Pratt, Rita Parker, Elizabeth Adamson, Harry Tiebout, Leslie Luehrs, Lawson Lowrey, Joseph Eidson, Van Norman Emery, Martin Peck, John Taylor, and George Wilbur.
14. Burnham, *Jelliffe*, 226. A letter from Cavendish Moxon in San Francisco to White of 10 Apr 1928 invites referrals to Mrs. Moxon, "a woman analyst in New York using the Rankian technique."
15. V. Robinson, 1978, p. 11. Hilda Taft died some years ago. Everett Taft, who is retired after a successful career, is in agreement with Robinson's comment. (Interview with EJL, 1982).
16. *PR* 16: 1–11, Jan 1929. An unusually large crowd attended, 137 members and guests. Dr. Harry C. Solomon presided. Discussants included Drs. Macfie Campbell, John Taylor, Arthur Ruggles, and William Malamud. Minutes by Donald J. MacPherson, 19 Apr 1928. Harvard Medical School, Countway Library.
17. Beata Rank, Interview 1953, 9–13.
18. Brome, *Jones*, 176 (E. Jones–K. Jones, 1932).

19. Helene Deutsch, *Confrontations,* 146; Sachs, 150.

20. Peck, *MH* 14:500–503, Apr 1930. Dr. Kenworthy's article of 1928, p. 181, referred to Rank's *ToB* forthcoming in English and suggested that children born by Caesarian section are less "sensitized." But this kind of support only diverted attention from the more important psychological issue.

21. T, 140–41; R–T 1 Mar 1929.

22. Yale Lecture, *JORA* 1: 12–25, 1966; p. 17.

23. See works by Jerome Frank, Carl Rogers, Robert Carkhuff, H. Strupp.

24. *JORA,* op. cit., p. 24. H. Wilde, *William Penn* 1974, p. 46.

25. T, 141; R–T 10 Jun 1929.

26. T, 143; R–T 4 Sept 1929.

27. T, 144.

28. S. Gifford, "Psychoanalysis in Boston," 332.

29. Ibid., 370.

30. Ob., 181.

31. S. Gifford, op. cit., 333.

32. F. Williams *Proceedings* I, 46–49.

33. T, 147–51; Williams *Proceedings* II, 118–38.

34. Williams II, 142–43.

35. Williams II, 148–49.

36. *IJP* 9:513, 1930. Curiously, the paragraph about Rank does not appear in *PR* 17: 495 (1930), where the minutes of the May 9 APA business session in Washington are printed. For a nationally circulated report on the Congress see *Time* magazine, May 19, 1930, 32–34 (no mention of Rank).

Chapter 11

1. "The Question of a Weltanschauung [Worldview]" (1933) No. 35 in *New Intro. Lects.,* 160. An earlier translation titled this "A Philosophy of Life."

2. Helene to Felix Deutsch, N.Y. 13 May 1930, courtesy of Paul Roazen.

3. T, 152.

4. Peck, 1930; 51, 53, 83n., 156–58. S. Gifford, 336.

5. E.J. Lieberman, 1979; Conrad Aiken, *Ushant* 1971; Killoran.

6. T, 154.

7. R–Wilbur, 25 July 1930: EJL, op. cit., 9–10.

8. Lewisohn-Knopf 6 Oct 1930, in R–Wilbur papers. Knopf rejected Rank's *Genetic Psychology*, tr. Mabel Moxon, in 1931. Knopf papers, New York Public Library.

9. R–T 15 Oct 1930; T, 155–58. The twelve chapters were written between mid-September and mid-October.

10. R–Wilbur 5 Dec 1930; R–T 5 Dec; T, 158–59.

11. Wilbur–R 10 Jan 31: EJL, op. cit., 11.

12. *A&A* 430–31.

13. "Life Fear and Death Fear," *Will Therapy*, 126.

14. R–Wilbur, 21 Jan 1931: EJL, op. cit. 11–12.

15. R–T 26 Jan 1931; T, 159.

16. Read Nov 11, 1930; *PR* 19: 319–26, 1932.

17. R–Wilbur, 25 Jul 1931. R–T 26 Jan, 19 Feb 1931; T, 159–62.

18. R–T, ibid.

19. R–Wilbur 5 Mar 1931; Taft *PR* 18:454–62 and *MH* 15:845ff., Oct 1931.

20. R–T 14 Jul 1931; T, 166.

21. R–Wilbur 20 Nov 1931: EJL op. cit., 12–13.

22. R–T 3 Nov 1931; T, 168.

23. *A&A*, 408–409, "Success and Fame."

24. *A&A*, 410–411.

25. Hugh Ford, *Published in Paris*, 1975: 117–67.

26. Wilbur–R 2 Dec 1931: EJL, 13.

27. Wilbur–R 3 June 1932; EJL, 17. Alexander acknowledges that his work on briefer therapy and emotional reexperiencing was stimulated by Ferenczi and Rank; see *The History of Psychiatry*, 249.

28. R–Wilbur 15 Dec 1931; see also J3, 262–63.

29. R–Wilbur 14 Jan 1932: EJL, op. cit., 15–16 (fuller excerpt).

30. Wilbur–R 29 Mar 1932: EJL, op. cit., 16; S. Gifford, 333–36.

31. T, 171–72.

32. R–Wilbur, 1 Jun 1932. Wilbur's comment is dated Dec. 15, 1939. The initials "B.T." on the letter probably refer to Beatrice Taussig, who knew Rank and for a time helped with Wilbur's translation.

33. R–T 4 Jun 1932; T, 172–73.

34. *A&A*, 376–77, "The Artist's Fight With Art."

35. Wilbur–R 3 Jun 1932.

36. R–Wilbur 15 Jun 1932.

37. R–T 8 Oct 1932; T, 173–74.

38. Lewisohn, Preface to *A&A*, vi–xi.

39. R–T 12 May 1933; T, 176; Grollman, 133.

40. Wilbur–R 5 Jan 1933; R–Wilbur 26 Jan: EJL, op. cit., 18.

41. R–T 8 Feb 1933; T, 174–76.

42. In Alexander and Selesnick, 407–409. A fuller quotation and critique appears in Walter Kauffmann's *Discovering the Mind*, Vol. 3 (1980), 387–94. V.W. Odajnyk in *Jung and Politics* (1976) calls Jung's actions on behalf of the Nazis "stupid and callous" (p. 107). These critics do not call Jung anti-Semitic or pro-Nazi, but rather opportunistic, unprincipled, and/or naive. Defenders of Jung include Ernest Harms, E.A. Bennet and historian Henri Ellenberger, whose book minimizes Jung's involvement as no different from that of many who underestimated the Hitler menace (675–78). Joseph Campbell, editor of *The Portable Jung* (Viking, 1971), ignores the controversy, as did the extensive London *Times* obituary. A forthcoming book *Psychotherapy in the Third Reich* by Geoffrey Cocks (Oxford Univ. Press, 1985) may shed more light; however an article about it does not mention Jung (The New York *Times* July 3, 1984, C1).

43. R–T 28 Aug 1933; T, 176–78 [not *8* Aug].

44. R–T, ibid. and 18 Sept 1933; T, 179–80. Bailey *JORA* No. 3: 10–25, 1967. Obituary by V.P.R. in *JORA* No. 21: 53–54, 1976.

45. *A&A*, 389–90.

46. *A&A*, 390–91.

47. F–Ernst Simmel, F Ls. #236: 11 Nov 1928.

48. "Huckster" seems better than "mountebank:" F–Arnold Zweig, 13 Jun 1935, 107–108. "Ill" *(krank)*: Wortis, 121. "Naughty:" Grinker, 1940.

49. F, "Analysis Terminable and Interminable," 1937, cited in Roazen, 417–18.

50. *Moses*, 1939, 10, 125, cited in Roazen 417–18. He mentions Sach's confirmation via Wilbur (interview); see also Wilbur–John Taylor, 9 Feb 1947 (copy in Rank–Wilbur correspondence).

51. S. Gifford, 335.

52. F–Pfister 26 Feb 1924, 92–93. J3, 131: F–Bonaparte 11 Jan 1927.

53. *Modern Education*, 191. From Ch. 7, "Forms of Kinship" which is reprinted in the Rank anthology (Vintage); see p. 305.

54. Ibid., 193–94; anthol. 306. Sheleff, 310–11.

55. *Psychology and the Soul [Soul-belief]*, 130, tr. EJL; Turner's translation is inadequate overall: see *Seelenglaube*, 134. Rank adduces other evidence as to Breuer's significance in Freud's "non vixit" dream and an example of forgetting (English, 133; German, 137).

Roazen (p. 78) deserves credit for being perhaps the only historian of psychoanalysis to have noticed Rank's interpretation.

56. Ibid., Engl. 135, Ger. 138.
57. R. Munroe, 584. Her consultant on Rank was Lydia Burnshaw.
58. J2, 164 and J3, 184.
59. Wilbur–R 18 Oct 1932.
60. J3, 172–73 (F–Fer. 2 Oct 1932).
61. Grollman, 133. J3, 182. Josef Frankel, ed. *The Jews of Austria,* 545, note 21. One-third of Austrian Jews were killed by the Nazis.

Chapter 12

1. Nin 1, 283.
2. Nin 7 (1980), entry of 1966, p. 40. Nin mistook Anita Faatz for Jessie Taft in this passage. Nin attended some of Rank's lectures with Taft and Robinson in Paris, but told Rochelle Kainer many years later that her own relationship with Rank never touched on his relationship with them. Biographical information on Nin comes from Preface to Nin 1 by Gunther Stuhlmann.
3. Miller–Nin 5 Mar 1933, p. 80.
4. Ibid., 80–86; Martin, 267.
5. Martin, 279.
6. Nin, *The Novel of the Future* (1968), 85, cited in Franklin & Schneider, 171.
7. R–T 18 Sep 1933; T, 180.
8. Nin 1, 272–73.
9. Nin 1, 299.
10. Nin 1, 277.
11. R–T 5 Nov 1933; T, 182–83; R–T Easter 1934; T, 190.
12. R–T 7 Jan 1934; T, 185–86; P. Bailey (1967), 13.
13. Nin 1, 286.
14. Nin 1, 279.
15. Nin 1, 284.
16. Nin, *A Woman Speaks* (1972), 146. S. Brownmiller, among others, faults Rank on this (misunderstood) point. This Rank statement comes from a note he wrote which she kept in her diary, and hence is presumably verbatim.
17. H. Deutsch, *Reflections,* 145.
18. Nin 1, 293.
19. Nin 1, 295–98.

20. Nin 1, 289.

21. Nin 1, 320.

22. R–T 28 Feb 1934; T, 187–88.

23. Ibid., 187.

24. Ibid., 188–89.

25. R–T 17 Mar 1934; T, 189.

26. R–Wilbur 2 May 1934.

27. T, 194–97.

28. Nin 1, 325.

29. Nin 1, 329–32.

30. Interview by telephone, Jan 1982.

31. Interview with D. Hankins, 3 Jun 1982.

32. Nin 1, 336.

33. Nin 1, 338–49. Rupert Pole believes Miller was the father (interview, Nov 1982).

34. R–Wilbur 12 Aug 1934; sailing plan R–Wilbur 25 Sep 1934.

35. Nin 1, 359–60. Apparently in error, Jay Martin, Miller's biographer, dates Nin's analysis with Rank earlier than Miller's memorable meeting, and puts Nin on the same boat with Rank. Rank's letters to Wilbur and Taft came from The Adams, where Nin says he had his office as part of a three-room apartment. Martin locates Rank in the Barbizon Plaza with Nin (306–307).

36. R–T 10 Nov 1934; T, 200 n.

37. R–T 19 Nov 1934; T, 201.

38. Nin 2, 4.

39. Nin 2, 6.

40. Nin 2, 4.

41. Nin 2, 7.

42. Nin 2, 10.

43. Martin, 306–307. See note 35, above.

44. Nin 7 *Diary* 1966–74 (1980), p. 40.

45. Nin 2, 13 states he lectured in New Orleans also, but no other source indicates this; T, 202–203. Lorraine Taft Warner to T, Feb 1935.

46. Martin, 308. Nin 2, 16; Rank Prefaces in *JORA* 7:2 (13) 1972, 61–74. Some of the first preface appears almost verbatim in Nin 1.

47. Nin 2, 16–17.

48. Nin 2, 23–24.

49. Martin, 309. Nin 2, 46.
50. Nin 2, 69 (Jun 1935); 152 (Apr 1936).
51. Rank in *JORA,* op. cit., 67.
52. *JORA* ibid., 62; R–Nin 1935.
53. Pars. 1–3 from *A&A,* 378, 52, 59–61 respectively.
54. *A&A,* 59.

Chapter 13

1. *A&A,* 65.
2. *The Columbia Encyclopedia* 2nd ed. 1965, "will," p. 2148.
3. Taft review of Rank *Die Analyse des Analytikers* in *PR* 18: 454–62, 1931.
4. Rank, *Will Therapy,* 111–12.
5. Ibid., 7–11.
6. Ibid., 11.
7. Ibid., 14–15, 19.
8. Ibid., 28, 34, 177.
9. Ibid., 27.
10. Ibid., 105. Cf. EJL, Discovering Will Therapy. *JORA* 15: 2 (No. 29) 1–14, 1980.
11. T, 204–205.
12. Otto Rank Immigration identification card No. 842496 issued July 11, 1935. From U.S. Immigration and Naturalization Service. Although Rank listed his father as Simon Rank, the attached birth certificate shows his name as Simon Rosenfeld.
13. T, 205.
14. J3, 186.
15. Brome, *Jones,* 186, dates source letter, Jones to Paul Federn, 1934. Roazen, 351 says 1933. Ernst Federn, son of Paul, told me (letter, 1984) that he has no knowledge of such a letter to his father.
16. R–T 8 Aug [not *28* Aug] 1935; T, 206 (in part).
17. R–T 26 Aug 1935.
18. R–T 4 Oct 1935 (unpublished); 3 Dec 1935; T, 211.
19. Henry A. Murray interview, 18 Aug 1982. *ID,* 212.
20. R–T 8 Aug 1936.
21. T, 214–15.
22. "Terrapins," Dorothea Gilbert int.; "Frog," Max Silverstein int.; Carl Rogers, 1951 and other writings.
23. R–T 10 Jun 1936; T, 215–16.

24. K. Burke, *The Nation,* 18 Jul 1936. (He told me he never met Rank). R–T 28 Jul 1936.

25. R–T 4 Nov 1936.

26. R–T Oct 1936; T, 218.

27. Dollard, 1936. R–T 1 Dec 1936. Taft may have sent a protest to Dollard; copies are among her papers, and Rank commended it (3 Dec). Rank met Dollard at Yale (R–T 8 Nov 1935): "young sociologist . . . sophisticated intellectual." Dollard gave Taft's biography of Rank a mixed review in the *New York Times* 13 Jul 1958.

28. R–T 22 Dec 1936; T, 222–23.

29. R–T 11 Jan (unpublished) and 13 Jan 1936; T, 223–25.

30. R–T 26 Jan 1937; T, 225–26.

31. R–T 29 Jan 1937; T, 226–27 in part; signed "Huck," as most were to Taft thenceforth, though she usually indicates "Rank."

32. Max Silverstein, int. 9 Mar 1983 (a student and union organizer, he said Ethel Wannemacher Seidenman was also involved—another influential Rankian in Philadelphia).

33. Arnold, 1935, pp. 34 and v. See Gressley, p. 32 re Harry Stack Sullivan.

34. R–T 11 Feb 1937; T, 227–28.

35. Julia Ann Bishop, int. and letter Oct/Nov 1980.

36. Dorothea Gilbert int. Apr 1982. Died 1984.

37. *The New York Times* 9 May 1937.

38. Dorothy Hankins, int. and 36 p. ms., Apr 1982.

39. Ibid.

40. Clara Rabinowitz int., Dec 1982.

41. Robinson, *Dev. Prof. Self.,* 16 (includes Taft quote).

42. R–T 25 Aug, 4 Sep 1937; T, 234–35.

43. R–T 15 Oct 1937 postscript (unpublished). Freud complained to Henry Murray about not being honored by Harvard in 1936; Murray indicated that Harvard could not make an exception to its rule that honorees must come to Harvard, and Freud could not make such a trip. In those years Harvard and Yale were among the many institutions which had a quota (numerus clausus) limiting the number of Jewish students. The unprotested honors for Jung in that context are not surprising.

44. R–T 26 Sept 1937; T, 236.

45. R–T 3 Nov 1937; T, 239.

46. R–T 9 Nov 1937; T, 240.

47. R–T 18 Nov and 13 Dec 1937; T, 241–43.

48. R–T 6 Dec 1937; T, 242.

49. R–T Wed., Feb (n.d.) 1938; T, 245 omits a key phrase (in italics): "Apropos personality! I think I have an idea about the afternoon course: looking at precipitants of growth only from the environment (reality) and not psychologically, that is to say, happening vs. doing, which brings in 'therapy' as a secondary factor *and actually makes life the real 'therapeutic' factor,* i.e., precipitant of growth.

50. Mimeo. minutes of course, 28 Feb 1938.

51. Ibid., 7 March 1938.

52. J3, 226. Curiously, Jones says "Freud had of course no compunction in signing" the document. Rather, it appears that Freud expressed strong compunction with his ironic postscript.

53. Minutes of course, 14 March 1938.

54. Ibid., 21 March 1938.

55. Colin Campbell to Marion Milner (and Dennis); Joanna Field is her pen name. Letter, 20 ms. pp. 6 Mar 1938, excerpted with permission of Kay (Campbell) Braugham.

56. R–Kay Cambell, 16 Sep 1938.

57. R–T, 22 Aug 1938; T, 251.

58. R–T 7 Jan 1938; T, 254–55.

59. R–T 9 Mar 1939; T, 254–55. (Substitute "working" for "writing," line 12).

60. Fromm, *Psychiatry* 2:229–37 (May 1939).

61. Menninger–Hadley 6 Jul 1939. Hadley–Menninger 10 Jul. Access to the files of *Psychiatry* at the Washington School of Psychiatry made possible by the late Dr. Robert Kvarnes.

62. D. Hankins int. See Epilogue for extract of Rose essay.

63. R–T 20 Mar 1939; T, 257–59.

64. R–T 14 May 1939; T, 259–60. R–T 15 and 28 Jun; T, 261.

65. Preface to *Beyond Psychology* and ms., Rank Coll.

66. R–T 28 Jun 1939; T, 262.

67. R–T 13 Aug 1939, Clift Hotel; T, 262.

68. R–T 16 Oct 1939; T, 265.

69. R–Robinson 22 Oct 1939; T, 265–66.

70. M. Pohek, int. Estelle Rank visited her after Rank's death.

71. Death Certificate 22357, Dept. of Health, City of New York. "Informant: wife per W.B. Cooke, funeral director." An autopsy was performed.

72. *New York Times* 1 Nov 1939.

Chapter 14

1. E. Jones, "Otto Rank." *IJP* 21: 112–13, 1940. Jones claims that Rank was to come to England for analysis with him when World War I intervened. An unpublished letter R–Jones 24 Dec 1914 recently came to light, in which Rank says "I am able to continue my usual activity here (Sachs also). Subjectively I feel pretty badly and would like to come to you earlier than you suggest, if I could. Objectively all goes well, that is, I am working hard and well." War had already broken out, and perhaps Rank was hoping to avoid military service. I have seen no other mention of this matter. (Courtesy of Mervyn Jones via Andrew Paskauskas).

2. Jones–Lionel Trilling, 11 Oct 1957, Trilling papers, Columbia University (permission of Diana Trilling). Published in part in *The New York Times Book Review* 17 Nov 1957 in Trilling's response to Virginia Robinson's letter correcting his review, op. cit. 13 Oct 1957 (See Introduction). Trilling must have sent Jones an advance copy; Jones, who knew that Taft was about to publish her biography of Rank, saw that Trilling had exaggerated the libel beyond all bounds: "I hope you won't get into trouble for saying Otto Rank died insane. Manic-depressive insanity is only a psychosis in the medical sense, and only do very rarely certain phases, e.g. acute melancholia, become insanity in the lay sense. Rank had a very successful career for over 20 years [sic] in New York and wrote many books. His last one in 1939 is reputed to be of great philosophical value and a book recently appeared in New York devoted entirely to it. He died ultimately of a septic pneumonia." Jones apparently refers to *Beyond Psychology* (1941) and Fay Karpf's book of 1953 on Rank.

3. F. Allen. Otto Rank: an appreciation. *Am. J. Orthopsychiatry* 10: 186–87, 1940.

4. J. Taft. Otto Rank. *MH* 24: 148–49 (Jan) 1940. A. Dawley. Otto Rank's Contribution. *Social Work Today* 7: 19, 1940. See also V. Robinson, Otto Rank, 1884–1939. *The Family* 20: 303–304 (Jan) 1940.

5. Nin 3, 1939–44 (1969), 20–21.

6. Dr. Isidor Sax–M. Pohek, 19 Jan 1940, tr. M.P.

7. Information on Charles Liebman comes from the Rockefeller Foundation Archives, Rockefeller Archive Center, North Tarrytown, NY. Rank is mentioned in memo of 21 Oct 1933, D.P. O'Brien to Alan Gregg. I have been unable to trace Isidor Sax. Information on Max Praeger, whose firm was the R. Loewit Verlag, from Frederick Praeger (letter to EJL, 1983).

8. *Beyond Psychology*, 192. Reviewed by George Mohr, *Psa. Quar-*

terly 1944: 13: 371–76. On Freud's hatred of the self-hating Jew Th. Lessing see J3, 159–60.

9. Rank, *BP*, 194–95 and 16. Ell., 860. Rollo May, who often cites Rank, never met him. Catholic theologian J.F. Donceel 1955, 317: "The 'Will' which Rank rediscovered may not be the will of Scholastic philosophy; it is nevertheless a factor which brings the conception of man in some of the most recent trends in psychotherapy considerably nearer to the traditional doctrine."

10. Rogers 1942, 27–28, 439–40. R. Evans *Carl Rogers*, 28–29.

11. John Rose, in *PR* 29: 401–405, 1942.

12. E. Glover, *Freud or Jung?* 5, 21.

13. Karpf, 1953, 112–13.

14. See note 2, above.

15. *TIME*, 23 Jun 1958, 66–68; Cf. *TIME* 24 Dec 1956 on Progoff.

16. Telephone interview with Ira Progoff, 1982.

17. Jack Jones, Five Versions of "Psychological Man." In Boyers, 1975, 62. Reprinted from *Salmagundi* 20 (1972), 91. Jones also wrote the excellent Rank entry in the *Int. Encyc. Soc. Sciences* 1968.

18. D. MacKinnon, *The American Psychologist* 20: 274, 1965.

19. Ibid., 279–80. See Maddi 1968 on Rank and MacKinnon.

20. E. Becker–V. Robinson 30 Jun 1971; *JORA* 7:2(13), 99–101, 1972.

21. *Beyond Psychology*, 50. Also: "By will, I do not mean will-to-power as conceived by Nietzsche and Adler, or 'wish' in the Freudian sense, though it might include both these aspects."

22. Becker 1973, xii. Becker's interest in Rank was aroused by a comment in Perls et al., *Gestalt Therapy* 1951, 395: "*Art and Artist* is beyond praise." Isadore From informs me that Paul Goodman, who never met Rank but knew his work, wrote the above quotation and virtually the whole book, although he is listed as third co-author. Becker also corresponded with George Wilbur (ORA files).

23. Lucy Freeman, *Freud Rediscovered* 1980. Cf. EJL review, 1980. Leo Stone 1981. Menaker 1982.

24. E. Jones [1945] 1974, Vol. 1, 284–300.

25. Ibid. In *Pioneers*, 230–31 Lilla Veszy–Wagner says Jones "tried not to be influenced by his own philo-Semitism. . . . He did not try to gloss over factors by which the Jews themselves contribute to anti-Semitism. . . . He did not omit mention of their sharp practices or pushing ways, but he regarded these as the manner in which persons would react 'whose manliness has been impaired.' " She credits Jones with bringing "fifty German or Austrian" analysts to England— "a fulfillment of his humanitarianism, his personal

philo-Semitism, and his feelings of obligation to the cause." Hers is the only reaction I know of to his 1945 essay, although she does not cite it by name. Brome's *Jones* lacks a bibliography and makes no mention of her. Walter Kauffmann, a refugee himself, wrote that Jones was "far from anti-Semitic" unlike Jung, who was "not even content to be silent." *Discovering the Mind 1980*, Vol. 3. 182 and 387 ff. Kauffmann must not have read Jones's 1945 essay.

26. A. Freud. Personal memories of Ernest Jones. *IJP* 60: 271–73. Reprinted in her *Writings* Vol. 8, 346–53, 1981.

27. A. Freud–EJL, 6 Nov 1981.

28. E. Menaker. Impressions of the diaries. In Otto Rank Centenary Issue, *Columbia Library Columns* 33: 3, 18–19, May 1984.

BIBLIOGRAPHY

No complete bibliography of Rank exists. Except for the psychoanalytic indexes by Rickman and by Grinstein, the lists available concentrate on his books. These indexes present all of Rank's early contributions to the German-language journals. Grinstein includes Rank's reviews, translations, and abstracts, but not all of the relevant material in *JORA* nor information on reprint editions. All the publications which Rank annotated in his invaluable "Literary Autobiography" (1930; published 1981) are included below, with many more. This list, supplemented by Grinstein, provides the first comprehensive bibliography of Rank's work in all languages.

A general bibliography follows, and includes many more items than are cited in the notes. It is designed to help scholars locate significant references to Rank in the relevant literature. Only a few reviews of Rank's books are included; they are readily located in the journals of the period. Items marked with an asterisk (*) were considered important but do *not* deal specifically with Rank; this negative finding is significant and sometimes surprising.

Unless stated otherwise in the notes, all unpublished material referred to in the text is part of the Rank Collection, Manuscript and Rare Book Library, Columbia University. To locate other manuscripts see Sokal and Rafail (1982). Originals or copies of additional reference materials obtained by me and under my control will be placed in the Rank Collection, e.g., the Rank–Wilbur correspondence.

Many additional articles by and about Rank may be found in the *Journal of the Otto Rank Association* (*JORA*) 1966–1983. Edited by Anita Faatz, the 31 issues are a treasure. Only a few articles are included here (those cited).

Abbreviations in addition to those on the short title list:
Deuticke: Franz Deuticke, Leipzig and Vienna
IPV: Internationale Psychoanalytischer Verlag, Leipzig/Wien/Zurich
I.P.B.: Internationale Psychoanalytische Bibliotek (a series of 21 books published by IPV after 1918, under the editorship of Otto Rank).
NMDMS: Nervous & Mental Disease Monograph Series
JNMD: Journal of Nervous and Mental Diseases

THE WORKS OF OTTO RANK (CHRONOLOGICAL)

Diary leaves of a stillborn: Tagebuchblätter eines totgeborenen (1904). Tr. Gretl Cox and EJL. Two Early Poems, 1903–1904, tr. Miriam Waddington. In the Otto Rank Centenary Issue, *Columbia Library Columns* 33: 21–27, 1984.

(As Secretary). *Minutes of the Vienna Psychoanalytic Society,* tr. by M. Nunberg, ed. by Herman Number and Ernst Federn. NY: International Universities Press, four volumes, 1962–75. I: 1906–1908, sessions 1–53, 1962. II: 1908–1910, sessions 54A–112, 1967. III: 1910–1911, sessions 113–155. IV: 1912–1918, sessions 156–250, with cumulative index, 1975. The missing ms. of the session of 24 Feb 1909, Freud's presentation "On the Genesis of Fetishism," found in the Rank Collection will be published in German and English, with annotations by Louis Rose and Hans Lobner.

Der Künstler, Vienna: Hugo Heller, 1907. Eds. 2 & 3, 1918; Ed. 4, including 7 articles (1912–18), 1925. Tr. 4th ed. *The Artist* by Eva Salomon and EJL, *JORA,* 15: 1, 1980.

Der Mythus der Geburt des Heldens, 1909. Tr. by F. Robbins and Smith Ely Jelliffe *The Myth of the birth of the hero,* NMDMS No. 18, 1914. (In *JNMD,* 40, 1913.) Reprinted NY: Brunner, 1952. Italian tr. *Il mito della nascita degli eroi,* 1921. Spanish tr. by E. A. Loedel *El mito del nacimiento del heroe.* 1961. *MGH* (German), Ed. 2, IPV, 1922 (untranslated).

Ein Traum der selbst deutet. *Y* 2, 1910. Abs.: A Dream that explains itself. *PR* 5: 230–34, 1918.

Ein Beitrag zum Narcissismus. *Y* 3: 401–426, 1911. Abs.: A Contribution to the study of narcissism. *PR* 7: 100–103, 1920.

Die Lohengrin Sage, Deuticke, 1911. Rpt. Liechtenstein, 1970.

Das Inzest-Motiv in Dichtung und Sage, Deuticke, 1912. Ed. 2, 1926. Rpt. Darmstadt, 1974. Ms. of 3rd German edition in the Rank Collection.

Die Nacktheit in Sage und Dichtung. *Imago* 2: 267–301 & 409–446, 1913. Abs.: Nakedness in saga and poem. *PR* 4: 444, 1917; 5: 330–335, 1918.

(with Hanns Sachs) *Die Bedeutung der Psychoanalyse fur die Geisteswissenschaften,* 1913. Tr. C. R. Payne *The Significance of psychoanalysis for the mental sciences,* NMDMS No. 23, 1915. Also in *PR* 5 & 6, 1915–16.

Traum und Dichtung (Anhang 1). Traum und Mythus (Anhang 2). Chapters added to Section 6 of S. Freud, *Die Traumdeutung,* Deuticke, 4th ed., 1914; 5th ed., 1918; 6th ed., 1921; 7th ed., 1922, 346–367 and 368–380.

Psychoanalytische Beitrage zur Mythenforschung, I.P.B. 4, 1919. (Collected studies 1912–14). Rev. ed. 1922 includes different essays; some from the 1919 ed. reappear in *Der Künstler,* 4th ed. 1925.

Der Doppelgänger, *Imago* 3: 97–164, 1914; *Der Doppelgänger* IPV, 1925; French tr. from a new German version by S. Lautman, *Don Juan: Une étude sur le Double,* 1932. Eng. tr. by Harry Tucker *The Double,* Chapel Hill: UNC Press, 1971.

Homer. I. Psychologische Beitrage zur Entstehungsgeschichte des Volksepos. II. Das Volksepos. *Imago* 5: 133–169; 372–393, 1917.

Die Don Juan Gestalt. *Imago* 8: 142–196, 1922. *Die Don Juan Gestalt* IPV, 1922. French tr. *Don Juan et le Double,* 1932, rpt. 1974. English tr. by David G. Winter, *The Don Juan legend,* Princeton U. Press, 1975.

Perversion und Neurose. Z. 8: 397–420, 1922. Tr.: Perversion and neurosis. *IJP* 4: 270–92.

Eine Neurosenanalyse in Traumen, IPV, 1924.

(with S. Ferenczi) *Entwicklungsziele der Psychoanalyse,* IPV, 1924. Tr. Caroline Newton, *The Development of psychoanalysis,* NMDMS No. 40, 1925. Dover reprint 1956, with S. Ferenczi, *Sex in psychoanalysis.*

Das Trauma der Geburt und seine Bedeutung für die Psychoanalyse. I.P.B. 14, 1924. Tr. S Jankélévitch *Le Traumatisme de la naissance* Paris: Payot, 1928, 1968. Tr *The Trauma of birth.* London: Routledge, 1929; New York: Harcourt Brace, 1929. Reprinted NY: Brunner, 1952; Harper Torchbook, 1973. Tr. E. Davidovich, *O Traumatismo do nascimento.* Rio de Janeiro, 1934. Tr. N. M. Finetti, *El Trauma del nacimiento.* Barcelona, 1981.

The Trauma of birth and its importance for psychoanalytic therapy. *PR* 11: 241–245, 1924.

Zur Genese der Genitalität. Z. 11: 411–428, 1925. (Part of *Grundzüge* I, 1927).

Sexualität und Schuldgefühl: psychoanalytische Studien (1912–23), I.P.B. 21, 1926.

The Practical bearing of psychoanalysis. Four lectures given in 1924 and reprinted from *MH* 10 (1926): Psychoanalysis as general psychology; The Significance of psychoanalysis for social life; The Therapeutic application of psychoanalysis; Psychoanalysis as a cultural factor. NY: The National Committee for Mental Hygiene, 1927, 52 pp.

Technik der Psychoanalyse. Deuticke, 1926–31. I. *Die Analytische Situation,* 1926. II. *Die Analytische Reaktion,* 1929. III. *Die Analyse des Analytikers,* 1931. Tr. by Jessie Taft of II and III: *Will therapy,* N.Y.: Knopf, 1936; Norton pb., 1978. Tr. Yves Le Lay, *La Volonté du bonheur,* Paris: Stock, 1934, 1975. Combined ed. with *Truth and reality,* NY: Knopf, 1945, 1947, 1950, 1964.

Grundzüge einer genetischen Psychologie auf Grund der Psychoanalyse der Ichstruktur. Deuticke, 1927–29. I. *Genetische Psychologie,* 1927. II. *Gestaltung und Ausdruck der Personlichkeit,* 1928. III. *Wahrheit und Wirklichkeit,* 1929, tr. by Jessie Taft, *Truth and reality,* N.Y.: Knopf, 1936. Norton pb. 1978. Other chapters tr.: The Genesis of genitality. *PR* 13: 129–144, 1926. Psychoanalytic problems, *PR* 14: 1–19, 1927; Beyond psychoanalysis, *PR* 16: 1–11; Character formation and the task of education, NY: Comm. for Mental Hygiene, 1928. See also *JORA* 3: 1, 1968; 4: 2, 1969; 5: 2, 1970.

Seelenglaube und Psychologie, Deuticke, 1930. Tr. by William Turner *Psychology and the soul,* Philadelphia: U. Pennsylvania Press, 1950. Perpetua pb. (A. S. Barnes Co.), 1961. [Soul-belief and psychology]

Literary autobiography (1930). Rank's annotated bibliography of 21 works, citing background, reactions, and reviews. *JORA* 16(30): 3–38, 1981.

Modern education, tr. Mabel Moxon, NY: Knopf, 1932; Agathon 1968. *Erziehung und Weltanschauung: eine Kritik der Psychologischen Erziehungs-Ideologie.* Munich: Ernst Reinhardt, 1933. The Development of the emotional life, Ch. 2, appeared with discussion by Rank and others in *Proceedings of the First International Congress on Mental Hygiene,* Frankwood E. Williams, ed., 1932, Vol. 2, 118–150.

Art and artist, tr. by Charles Francis Atkinson, NY: Knopf, 1932, 1943; Tudor, 1948; Agathon, 1968, 1975. (Original German unpublished ms. in Rank Collection.)

Self-inflicted illness. *Proceedings of The California Academy of Medicine, 1935–1936.* CAM, 1937, 8–18.

Beyond Psychology. Privately published, Philadelphia (Printed by Haddon Craftsmen, Camden N.J.), 1941. Dover pb., 1958.

(Anthology) *The Myth of the birth of the hero and other writings,* ed. Philip Freund. From *Art and artist:* Introduction, Creative urge and personality development, Life and creation, The Artist's fight with art, Success and fame, Deprivation and renunciation. From *Modern education:* Sexual enlightenment and the sexual impulse; Forms of kinship and the individual's role in the family. From *Will therapy:* Life fear and death fear. From *Truth and reality:* Self and ideal. NY: Vintage pb., 1959, 1960, 1964.

GENERAL BIBLIOGRAPHY

Abell, Walter. *The Collective dream in art.* NY: Schocken, 1966; reprint of Harvard U. Press ed., 1957.

Abrahamsen, David. *The Mind and death of a genius.* NY: Columbia U. Press, 1946.*

Ackerknecht, Erwin. *A Short history of psychiatry.* NY: Hafner, 1959.*

Aiken, Conrad. *Selected letters,* ed. Joseph Killorin. New Haven: Yale U. Press, 1978.

Alexander, Franz. *Fundamentals of psychoanalysis.* NY: Norton, 1948.

_____. *The Scope of psychoanalysis: selected papers, 1921–61.* NY: Basic Books, 1961.

Alexander, Franz, Samuel Eisenstein, and Martin Grotjahn, eds. *Psychoanalytic pioneers.* NY: Basic Books, 1966.

Alexander, Franz and Sheldon T. Selesnick. *The History of psychiatry.* NY: Harper & Row, 1966.

Allen, Frederick H. *Psychotherapy with children.* NY: Norton, 1942.

_____. *Positive aspects of child psychiatry.* NY: Norton, 1963.

_____. Otto Rank: an appreciation. *Am. J. Orthopsychiatry* 10: 186–87, 1940.

Andreas-Salomé, Lou. *The Freud journal.* NY: Basic Books, 1964. (See also Binion.)

Arendt, Hannah. *The Life of the mind.* Vol. II, *Willing.* NY: Harcourt Brace Jovanovich, 1978.*

Arieti, Silvano. *The Will to be human.* NY: Quadrangle, 1972.*

Arnold, Thurman. *Symbols of government.* New Haven: Yale U. Press, 1935.* (See also Gressley.)

Assagioli, Robert. *The Act of will.* NY: Viking, 1973; Penguin Books, 1974.

Assoun, Paul-Laurant. *Freud et Nietzsche.* Paris: Press U. de France, 1980.

Aveling, Francis. *Personality and will.* NY: Appleton, 1931.*

Bailey, Pearce. Theory and therapy. *PR* 22: 182–211, 1935.

_____. The Psychological Center, Paris—1934. *JORA* 2: 2(3): 10–29, 1967.

Bakan, David. *Disease, pain and sacrifice.* Boston: Beacon Pb., 1971. Reprint of U. of Chicago Press ed., 1968.

Balmary, Marie. *Psychoanalyzing psychoanalysis: Freud and the hidden fault of the father.* Baltimore: Johns Hopkins U. Press, 1979.*

Becker, Ernest. *The Denial of death.* NY: Free Press, 1973.

_____. *Escape from evil.* NY: Free Press, 1975.

Bedford, Mitchell. *Existentialism and creativity.* NY: Philosophical Library, 1972.*

Bernays, Edward L. *Biography of an idea.* NY: Simon & Schuster, 1965.

Bertin, Celia. *Marie Bonaparte.* NY: Harcourt Brace Jovanovich, 1982.

Binion, Rudolph. *Frau Lou.* Princeton: Princeton U. Press, 1968.

Binswanger, Ludwig. *Sigmund Freud: reminiscences of a friendship.* NY: Grune & Stratton, 1957.

Blum, Gerald. *Psychoanalytic theories of personality.* NY: McGraw-Hill, 1953.

Bowlby, John. *Separation.* NY: Basic Books/Harper Colophon, 1974.

Brandell, Gunnar. *Freud: a man of his century.* Trans. Iain White. Atlantic Highlands, NJ: Humanities Press, 1979.*

Brammer, L. M. and E. L. Shostrom. *Therapeutic psychology.* Englewood Cliffs: Prentice-Hall, 1960.

Brill, A. A. *Lectures on psychoanalytic psychiatry.* London: Lehman, 1948.*

Broderick, Carlfred B. and Sandra S. Schrader. The History of professional marriage and family therapy. In *Handbook of family therapy,* ed. Alan S. Gurman and David P. Kniskern, 5–35, NY: Brunner/Mazel, 1981.

Bromberg, Walter. *From Shaman to psychotherapist.* Chicago: Regnery, 1975. First ed. *The Mind of man,* 1937; 3d ed. 1954 & 1959; 2d ed. *Man above humanity,* 1954.

Brome, Vincent. *Freud and his early circle.* NY: Morrow, 1968.

_____. *Ernest Jones: Freud's alter ego.* NY: Norton, 1983.

Brownmiller, Susan. *Against our will.* NY: Simon & Schuster, 1975.

Budman, Simon H., ed. *Forms of brief therapy.* NY: Guilford, 1981.

Buhler, Charlotte. *Values in psychotherapy.* NY: Free Press, 1962.

Burnham, John C. *Psychoanalysis and American medicine, 1894–1918. Psychological Issues* Monograph 20, NY: Int'l Us. Press, 1967.

_____. *Jelliffe: American psychoanalyst and physician.* Chicago: U. Chicago Press, 1983.

Burnshaw, Stanley. *The Seamless web.* NY: Braziller, 1970.

Burrow, Trigant. *A Search for man's sanity. Selected letters of T. B.* NY: Oxford U. Press, 1958.

_____. *Preconscious foundations of human experience.* NY: Basic Books, 1964.

_____. *The Biology of human conflict.* NY: Macmillan, 1937. Arno rpt. 1974.

_____. The World as will. Review of Rank's *Will Therapy* and *Truth and Reality.* In *J. Social Philosophy* 4: 162–173, (Jan) 1939.

Carkhuff, Robert R. and Bernard G. Berenson. *Beyond counseling and therapy.* NY: Holt, Rinehart and Winston, 1967; 2nd ed. 1977.

Carotenuto, Aldo. *A Secret symmetry: Sabina Spielrein between Freud and Jung.* NY: Pantheon, 1982.

Clark, Ronald W. *Freud.* NY: Random House, 1980.

Choron, Jacques. *Modern man and mortality.* NY: Macmillan, 1964.

Coan, Richard W. *Hero, artist, sage, or saint?* NY: Columbia U. Press, 1967.

Comfort, Alex. *Reality & empathy.* State U. of N.Y. Press, 1984.*

_____. "Existential" psychiatry and quantum logic. *Psychiatry* 46: 393–99, 1983.*

Cuddihy, John M. *The Ordeal of civility.* NY: Basic Books, 1974.

Cronbach, Abraham. *The Psychoanalytic study of Judaism.* Offprint from *Hebrew Union College Annual* 8–9: 605–740 (Cincinnati), 1931–1932.

Dalbiez, Roland. *Psychoanalytic method and the doctrine of Freud.* Tr. T. F. Lindsay, Intr. E. B. Strauss. London: Longman Green, 1941.

D'Amore, Arcangelo R. T., ed. *William Alanson White.* DHEW No. (ADM) 76–298. Washington: U.S. Govt. Printing Office, 1976.

Dawley, Almena. Otto Rank's contribution to social work. *Social Work Today* 7: 19, 1940.

de Forest, Izette. *The Leaven of love.* (On Ferenczi) NY: Harper, 1954.

Deutsch, Felix. *Applied psychoanalysis.* NY: Grune & Stratton, 1949.

Deutsch, Helene. *Confrontations with myself.* NY: Norton, 1973.

Dollard, John. *Criteria for the life history.* New Haven: Yale U. Press, 1935.

Donado, Stephen. *Nietzsche, Henry James, and the artistic will.* NY: Oxford U. Press, 1978.*

Donceel, J. F. *Philosophical psychology.* 3rd ed. NY: Sheed & Ward, 1955.

Dyer, Raymond. *Her father's daughter: the work of Anna Freud.* NY: Aronson, 1983.

Ehrenwald, Jan, ed. *The History of psychotherapy.* NY: Jason Aronson, 1976. Briefer version entitled *From Medicine man to Freud,* 1956.*

Ehrenzweig, Anton. *The Hidden order of art.* Berkeley: U. California Press, 1967.

Eissler, K. R. *Talent and genius.* NY: Grove Press, 1971.

Ellis, Havelock. *The Dance of life.* Boston: Houghton Mifflin, 1923.

———. *Psychology of sex.* NY: Long & Smith, 1933.

———. *Studies in the psychology of sex.* (1905–1928) 2 vols. NY: Random House, Modern Library, 1937.

Ellenberger, Henri F. *The Discovery of the unconscious.* NY: Basic Books, 1970.

Evans, Richard L. *Carl Rogers.* NY: Dutton, 1975.

Faatz, Anita. *The Nature of choice in casework process.* Chapel Hill: U. North Carolina Press, 1953.

Faber, M. D. *The Design within: psychoanalytic approaches to Shakespeare.* NY: Science House, 1970.

Farber, Leslie H. *The Ways of the will.* NY: Basic Books, 1966.

Federn, Paul. *Ego psychology and the psychoses.* NY: Basic Books, 1952.

Federn, Paul and Heinrich Meng, eds. *Das Psychoanalytische Volksbuch.* 3rd ed. Bern: Verlag Hans Huber, 1939.

Fenichel, Otto. *The Psychoanalytic theory of neurosis.* NY: Norton, 1945.

Ferenczi, Sandor. Contraindications to the "active" psychoanalytical technique (1925). In *Further Contributions to the theory and technique of psychoanalysis,* 217–230. London: Hogarth Press, 1926. (See also Gedo.)

Fine, Reuben. *The Development of Freud's thought.* NY: Aronson, 1973.

———. *A History of psychoanalysis.* NY: Columbia U. Press, 1979.

Fischer, Kurt Rudolph. The Existentialism of Nietzsche's Zarathustra. *Deadalus* 93: 998–1016, 1964.*

Flegenheimer, Walter V. *Techniques of brief psychotherapy.* NY: Aronson, 1982.

Flugel, J. C. *The Psychoanalytic study of the family.* London: Hogarth Press, 1957. First published 1921.

_____. *A Hundred years of psychology.* London: Duckworth, 1933.

Ford, Donald H. and Hugh B. Urban. *Systems of psychotherapy.* NY: Wiley, 1963.

Ford, Hugh. *Published in Paris.* NY: Macmillan, 1975.

Forrester, John. *Language and the origins of psychoanalysis.* NY: Columbia U. Press, 1980.

Fraenkel, Josef, ed. *The Jews of Austria.* London: Vallentine, Mitchell, 1967.*

Frank, Jerome D. *Persuasion and healing.* Rev. ed. Baltimore: Johns Hopkins U. Press, 1973.*

Frank, Lawrence. *On the Importance of infancy.* NY: Random House, 1968.

Frankl, Victor. Self-transcendence as a human phenomenon. *J. Humanistic Psychology* 6: 97–107, 1966.*

Franklin, Benjamin and Duane Schneider. *Anais Nin: an introduction.* Athens: Ohio U. Press, 1979.

Freeman, Lucy. *Freud rediscovered.* NY: Arbor House, 1980.

Freeman, Lucy and Marvin Small. *The Story of psychoanalysis.* NY: Pocket Books, 1960.

Freeman, Walter. *The Psychiatrist.* NY: Grune & Stratton, 1968.

Freud, Anna. *The Collected Writings* Vol. 8. NY: Int'l Us. Press, 1981.*

Freud, Sigmund. *The Interpretation of dreams.* Trans. James Strachey, incorporating all 8 edns., 1900–1930; Standard Edn. vols. 4–5. NY: Basic Books, 1955. Avon Books, 1965.

_____. *The Psychopathology of everyday life.* NY: Norton, 1960 (1901).

_____. The Origin and development of psychoanalysis. *Am J. Psychol.* 21: (Apr) 1910. In Std. Ed. as Five Lectures on psychoanalysis. Vol. 11: 3–58.*

_____. *The History of the psychoanalytic movement.* NY: Collier, 1963 (1914).

_____. *Introductory lectures on psychoanalysis.* NY: Norton, 1966 (1916–17).

_____. *Inhibitions, symptoms and anxiety.* Std. Ed. 20: 77–178, 1959 (1926).

_____. *New introductory lectures on psychoanalysis.* NY: Norton, 1965 (1933).

_____. *An Autobiographical study.* NY: Norton, 1952 (1935).*

_____. *Abstracts of the Standard Edition of Freud.* National Institute of Mental Health. DHEW Publ. No. (HSM) 72–9001. Washington, DC: U.S. Govt. Printing Office, 1972; also NY: Int'l Us. Press, 1973.

_____. Guttman, Samuel. *Concordance to the Standard Edition.* 6 Vols. 2nd ed. NY: Int'l Us. Press, 1982.

_____. *The Letters of Sigmund Freud.* Ed. Ernst L. Freud. NY: Basic Books, Harper Colophon, 1975.

_____. *A Psychoanalytic dialogue. The Letters of Sigmund Freud and Karl Abraham.* Ed. Hilda C. Abraham and Ernst L. Freud. NY: Basic Books, 1965.

_____. *Sigmund Freud and Lou Andreas-Salomé Letters.* Ernst Pfeiffer, ed. London: Hogarth Press, 1972.

_____. *The Freud/Jung letters.* Ed. William McGuire. Princeton: Princeton U. Press, 1974. *Freud/Jung Briefwechsel.* Frankfurt: Fischer, 1974. Abridged English ed., London: Picador Pan Books, 1979.

_____. *Psychoanalysis and faith: dialogues with Oskar Pfister.* Ed. Heinrich Meng and Ernst L. Freud. NY: Basic Books, 1963.

_____. (Freud/Putnam letters). *James Jackson Putnam and psychoanalysis.* Ed. Nathan G. Hale. Cambridge: Harvard U. Press, 1971.*

_____. *The Letters of Sigmund Freud and Arnold Zweig.* Ed. Ernst L. Freud. London: Hogarth Press, 1970.

Fromm, Erich. The Social philosophy of "Will Therapy." *Psychiatry* 2: 229–37, 1939.

_____. *Sigmund Freud's mission.* NY: Harper, 1959.*

Fromme, Allan. *Our Troubled selves.* NY: Farrar Strauss & Giroux, 1967.

Furtmüller, Carl. Alfred Adler: a biographical essay. In Alfred Adler *Superiority and social interest,* 3rd ed. Ed. Heinz L. Ansbacher and Rowena R. Ansbacher, 311–94. NY: Norton, 1979.

Gach, John. Culture and complex: on the early history of psychoanalysis in America. In *Essays in the history of psychiatry,* ed. Edwin R. Wallace, IV and Lucius C. Pressley, 135–160. Supplement to *The Psychiatric Forum,* Columbia, SC: Wm. S. Hall Psychiatric Institute, 1980.

Gay, Peter. Freud: for the marble tablet. Intro. to *Berggasse 19:* The photographs of Edmund Engleman. Chicago: U. Chicago Press, 1976.*

Gedo, John. The Wise baby reconsidered [Ferenczi]. *Psychological Issues* 9: 357–378, 1976.

Geismar, Maxwell. *Mark Twain: an American prophet.* Boston: Houghton Mifflin, 1970.

Gifford, Sanford. Psychoanalysis in Boston. In *Psychoanalysis, psychotherapy, and the New England medical scene, 1894–1944.* Ed. George E. Gifford. NY: Science History Publications, 1978, 325–46.

Glaser, Hermann, ed. *The German mind of the 19th century.* NY: Continuum, 1981.*

Glass, Bentley. Evolution and heredity in the 19th century. In *Medicine, science, and culture*, 209–48. Ed. L. G. Stevenson & R. P. Multhauf. Baltimore: Johns Hopkins U. Press, 1967.*

Glover, Edward. *Freud or Jung.* NY: Norton, 1950.

_____. *On the early development of mind.* London: Imago, 1956.

Goldberg, Carl. *In Defense of narcissism.* NY: Gardner, 1980.

Goodman, Paul. *Nature heals.* Psychological essays ed. Taylor Stoehr. NY: Dutton pb., 1979 (Free Life Editions, 1977). See also Perls, et al.

Gordon, William A. *The Mind and art of Henry Miller.* Baton Rouge: Louisiana State U. Press, 1967.

_____. *Writer and critic: a correspondence with Henry Miller.* Baton Rouge: Louisiana State U. Press, 1968.

Graf, Max. Reminiscences of Professor Sigmund Freud. *Psa. Quart.* 11: 465–76, 1942.*

Greenwald, Harold, ed. *Active psychotherapy.* NY: Atherton, 1967.

Gressley, Gene M., ed. *Voltaire and the cowboy: the letters of Thurman Arnold.* Boulder: Colorado Associated U. Press, 1977.*

Grinker, Roy. Reminiscence of a personal contact with Freud. *Am. J. Orthopsychiatry* 10: 850–55, 1940. (Rpt. in Ruitenbeek *Freud* 1973.)

Grinstein, Alexander. *The Index of psychoanalytic writings.* NY: Int'l Us. Press, 1956–1975.

Groddeck, Georg. *The Meaning of illness: selected psychoanalytic writings and his correspondence with Sigmund Freud.* NY: Int'l Us. Press, 1977. (See Grossman.)

Grollman, Earl A. *Judaism in Sigmund Freud's world.* NY: Appleton-Century, 1965.*

Grossman, Carl M. and Sylvia Grossman. *The Wild Analyst: the life and work of Georg Groddeck.* NY: Braziller, 1965; rpt. Delta pb., 1967.

Grotjahn, Martin. *Beyond laughter.* NY: McGraw-Hill, 1957.

_____. Notes on reading The Rundbriefe. *JORA* 8: 2(15), 35–88, 1974.

Groves, Ernest R. and Phyllis Blanchard. *Readings in mental hygiene.* NY: Holt, 1936.

Guntrip, Harry. *Psychoanalytic theory, therapy and the self.* NY: Harper Torchbook, 1973.

Hale, Nathan. *Freud and the Americans.* NY: Oxford U. Press, 1971.

Hampden-Turner, Charles. *Maps of the mind.* NY: Macmillan, 1981.

Hanna, Thomas. *The Lyrical existentialists: Nietzsche, Kierkegaard, Camus.* NY: Atheneum, 1962.*

Hannah, Barbara. *Jung: his life and work.* NY: G. P. Putnam's Sons, Capricorn Books, 1976.

Harper, Robert A. *Psychoanalysis and psychotherapy: 36 systems.* NY: Aronson, 1974. Reprint of Prentice-Hall ed., 1959.

Havens, Leston. *Approaches to the mind.* Boston: Little, Brown, 1973.*

_____. The Existential use of self. *Am J Psychiatry* 131: 1–10, 1974.*

_____. *Participant observation.* NY: Aronson, 1976.

Hayman, Ronald. *Nietzsche: a critical life.* NY: Oxford U. Press, 1980.*

Healy, William, Augusta Bronner, and Anna Mae Bowers. *The Structure and meaning of psychoanalysis.* NY: Knopf, 1930.

Heiman, Marcel, ed. *Psychoanalysis and social work.* NY: Int'l Us. Press, 1953.*

Hillman, James. *The Myth of analysis.* Evanston: Northwestern U. Press, 1972; Harper Colophon Books, 1978.

Hinz, Evelyn J. *The Mirror and the garden.* NY: Harvest, 1973.

Hoffman, Frederick J. *Freudianism and the literary mind.* 2nd ed. Baton Rouge: Louisiana State U. Press, 1957.

Holland, Glen A. *Fundamentals of psychotherapy.* NY: Holt, Rinehart & Winston, 1965.

Hollitscher, Walter. *Psychoanalysis and civilization.* NY: Grove Press, 1963.*

Honig, Albert M. *The Awakening nightmare.* NY: Delta, 1973.

Hook, Sidney, ed. *Psychoanalysis, scientific method, and philosophy.* NY: New York U. Press, 1959.

Horney, Karen. *New ways in psychoanalysis.* NY: Norton, 1939.

_____. Review of Rank's *Modern Education.* In *Psa. Quart.* 1: 349–50, 1932.

Ibsen, Henrik. *The Wild duck.* Trans. ed. Dounia B. Christiani. Norton Critical Edition. NY: Norton, 1968 (1884).*

James, William. *The Varieties of religious experience.* London: Longmans, 1902.*

Johnson, Richard E. *In Quest of a new psychology.* NY: Human Sciences Press, 1975.

Johnston, William M. *The Austrian mind.* Berkeley: U. California Press, 1972.

_____. *Vienna, Vienna: the golden age.* NY: Clarkson Potter, 1982.

Jones, Ernest. The Psychology of the Jewish question. In C. Newton, ed., *Gentile and Jew,* 1945. Reprinted in E. Jones, *Essays in applied psycho-analysis,* 2 vols. London: Hogarth Press, 1951. Rpt. *Psycho-myth, Psycho-history.* NY: Stonehill, 1974; I: 284–300.*

_____. *The Life and work of Sigmund Freud.* 3 vols. NY: Basic Books, 1953, 1955, 1957.

_____. *Free Associations.* NY: Basic Books, 1959.

_____. Otto Rank (Obit.) *IJP* 21: 112–13, 1940.

Jones, Jack. Otto Rank: a forgotten heresy. *Commentary* 30: 219–29, 1960.

_____. Otto Rank. In *Int'l Encyc. Social Sciences,* 1968, 1981.

_____. Five versions of psychological man. In Robert Boyers, ed. *Psychological man.* NY: Harper Colophon, 1975, 56–84. Earlier version in *Salmagundi* 20: 86–113, 1972, Skidmore College.

Jung, Carl. *Memories, Dreams, Reflections.* Rev. ed. NY: Random House, Vintage Books, 1965.*

Kainer, R. G. K. and Susannah Gourevitch. On the Distinction between narcissism and will. *PR* 70: 535–52, 1983.

Kaplan, Morton and Robert Kloss. *The Unspoken motive: a guide to psychoanalytic literary criticism.* NY: Free Press, 1973.

Kardiner, Abram. *Freud: the man I knew.* In Nelson 1957, 46–58.

Karpf, Fay B. *American social psychology.* NY: McGraw-Hill, 1932.*

_____. *The Psychology and psychotherapy of Otto Rank.* NY: Philosophical Library, 1953.

_____. Rankian will or dynamic relationship therapy. In *Progress in psychotherapy.* NY: Grune & Stratton, 1957, 132–39.

Kauffman, Walter. *Discovering the mind.* Vol 3: *Freud versus Adler and Jung.* NY: McGraw-Hill, 1980.

Kenworthy, Marion. The Prenatal and early postnatal phenomena of consciousness. In *The Unconscious: a symposium.* Intro. Ethel S. Dummer. Freeport, NY: Books for Libraries Press, 1966 (Knopf, 1928), Pp. 178–200.

Kiell, Norman, ed. *Psychoanalysis, psychology and literature: a bibliography.* Madison: U. Wisconsin Press, 1963.

Klein, Dennis B. *Jewish origins of the psychoanalytic movement.* NY: Praeger, 1981.

Klein, Viola. *The Feminine character: history of an ideology.* London: Kegan Paul, 1946.*

Klein, Melanie, Paula Heimann and Roger Money-Kyrle, eds. *New directions in psychoanalysis.* London: Tavistock, 1955.

Knapp, Bettina L. *Anais Nin.* NY: Ungar, 1978.

Kris, Ernst and Otto Kurz. *Legend, myth, and magic in the image of the artist.* Based on *Die Legende vom Kunstler,* 1934. New Haven: Yale U. Press, 1979.*

Kubie, Lawrence S. *Neurotic distortion of the creative process.* NY: Noonday Press, 1965. Reprint of U. of Kansas Press ed., 1958.*

Langman, Lauren. The Estrangement from being: an existential analysis of Otto Rank's psychology. *J. Existential Psychiatry* 1: 455–478, 1961.

Laplanche, J. and J.-B. Pontalis. *The Language of psychoanalysis.* NY: Norton, 1973.

Lerner, Max. Touch bottom. *The New York Post,* 15 Jun 1959; *JORA* 5: 1(8), 102–105, 1970.

Lessa, William A. On the Symbolism of Oedipus. In *The Study of folklore.* Ed. Alan Dundes. Englewood Cliffs: Prentice Hall, 1965, 114–25. Rpt. from W. A. Lessa, *Tales from Ulithi Atoll,* U. California Press, 1961.

Leupold-Löwenthal, Harald. The Minutes of the Vienna Psychoanalytic Society. *Sigmund Freud House Bull.* 4,2: 23–41, 1980. Trans. of postscript to volume 4 of the German edition of the *Minutes.*

Levine, Albert J. *Current psychologies.* Cambridge, Mass.: Sci-Art, 1940.

Lieberman, E. James. The Rank–Wilbur correspondence. *JORA,* 14: 1(26), 7–26, 1979.

_____. Discovering will therapy. *JORA* 15: 2(29): 1–10, 1980.

_____. Doctor of our discontents. Review of *Freud* by R. W. Clark and *Freud Rediscovered* by L. Freeman. *Book World, The Washington Post* 3 Aug 1980.

_____. Otto Rank in America (with Mary Plowden interview). *Columbia Library Columns* Otto Rank Centenary Issue, 33: 3, 1–11, 1984.

Lifton, Robert Jay. *The Life of the self.* NY: Simon & Schuster, 1976.

_____. *The Broken connection.* NY: Simon & Schuster, 1979.

Liptzin, Solomon. *Germany's stepchildren.* Philadelphia: The Jewish Publication Society of America, 1944.*

London, Perry. *The Modes and morals of psychotherapy.* NY: Holt, Rinehart & Winston, 1964.

Ludwig, Emil. *Doctor Freud.* NY: Hellman, Williams, 1947.

MacKinnon, Donald W. Personality and the realization of creative potential. *Amer. Psychologist* 20: 273–81, 1965.

Maddi, Salvatore R. *Personality theories: a comparative analysis.* Homewood, IL: Dorsey, 1968.

Malinowski, B. *Sex and repression in savage society.* NY: Harcourt Brace, 1927.

Marcuse, Herbert. *Eros and civilization.* Boston: Beacon Press, 1955.

Marks, Robert W., ed. *Great ideas in psychology.* NY: Bantam, 1966.

Marmor, Judd. Short-term dynamic psychotherapy. *Am. J. Psychiatry* 136: 149–55, 1979.

Martin, Jay. *Always merry and bright: the life of Henry Miller.* Santa Barbara: Capra Press, 1978. Penguin Books, 1980.

Marx, Melvin H. and William A. Hillix. *Systems and theories in psychology.* 2nd ed. NY: McGraw-Hill, 1973.

Matson, Floyd. *The Broken image.* NY: Braziller, 1964.

May, Rollo. *The Art of counselling.* Nashville: Abingdon Press, 1939.

———. *Springs of creative living.* NY: Abingdon Cokesbury, 1940.

May, Rollo, Ernest Angel and Henri F. Ellengerger, eds. *Existence.* NY: Basic Books, 1958.

McNeill, John T. *A History of the cure of souls.* NY: Harper, 1951.

Menaker, Esther and William Menaker. *Ego in evolution.* NY: Grove, 1965.

Menaker, Esther. *Otto Rank: a rediscovered legacy.* NY: Columbia U. Press, 1982.

Menninger, Karl. *Theory of psychoanalytic technique.* NY: Basic Books, 1958. Harper Torchbook, 1964.

Miller, Henry. *Letters to Anais Nin.* Ed. Gunther Stuhlmann. NY: Putnam, 1965.

———. *The Books in my life.* NY: New Directions, 1969.*

———. *My Life and times.* NY: Playboy Press, 1975. (See also Martin).

Mintz, Ira L. Some thoughts on the evolution of Otto Rank's theory of the birth trauma. *Int. Rev. Psa.* 2: 245–46, 1975.

Mitchell, Juliet. *Psychoanalysis and feminism.* NY: Random House, 1974.

Montagu, M. F. Ashley *The Direction of human development.* NY: Harper, 1955.

Mora, George. Historical and theoretical trends in psychiatry. In *Comprehensive textbook of psychiatry-II,* ed. Alfred M. Freedman, Harold I. Kaplan, and Benjamin J. Sadock, 1–74. Baltimore: Williams & Wilkins, 1975.

Moustakas, Clark. *Creativity and conformity.* NY: Van Nostrand Reinhold, 1967.

———, ed. *The Self.* (Includes Rank's "Fate and Self Determination" from *Will Therapy.*) NY: Harper, 1956; Harper Colophon 1974.

Moxon, Cavendish. *Freudian essays on religion and science.* NY: Badger, 1927. Includes "Freud's death instinct and Rank's libido theory," rpt. from *PR* 13: 294–303, 1926. Rev. *IJP* 1927 by R. Money-Kyrle.

———. The Bearing of Rank's discovery on medicine. *PR* 15: 294–99, 1928.

Mullahy, Patrick. *Oedipus: myth and complex.* NY: Hermitage, 1948.

Munroe, Ruth L. *Schools of psychoanalytic thought.* NY: Holt, 1955.

Murphy, Gardner. William James on the will. *J. History Beh. Sci.* 7: 249–260, 1971.*

Murray, Henry A. *Endeavors in psychology.* Ed. Edwin S. Shneidman. NY: Harper & Row, 1981.

Muuss, Rolf E. *Theories of adolescence.* 3d ed. NY: Random House, 1975.

Nash, Roderick. *The Nervous generation: American thought, 1917–1930.* Chicago: Rand McNally, 1970.*

Nelson, Benjamin, ed. *Freud and the 20th century.* NY: Meridian Books, 1957.

Nietzsche, Friedrich. *A Nietzsche reader.* Ed. & Trans. R. J. Hollingdale. NY: Penguin, 1977.*

Nin, Anais. *Diary.* Vol. 1, 1931–34; Vol. 2, 1934–39; Vol. 3, 1939–44. ed. Gunther Stuhlmann. NY: Harcourt Brace Jovanovich, 1966, 1967, 1969. (Cf. later *Diaries* and see also Hinz; S. Spencer; Franklin; Knapp.)

_____. *A Woman speaks.* Ed. Evelyn J. Hinz. Chicago: Swallow Press, 1975.

Nordau, Max. *Degeneration.* 7th ed. NY: Appleton, 1895.*

Novey, Riva. Otto Rank: beginnings, endings, and current experience. *J. Am. Psa. Assn.* 31: 985–1002, 1983.

Nunberg, Herman. *Principles of psychoanalysis.* Rev. ed. NY: Int'l Us. Press, 1955. (First ed. 1932).

Oberndorf, Clarence P. *A History of psychoanalysis in America.* NY: Grune & Stratton, 1953; Harper Torchbook, 1964.

Odajnyk, Volodymyr W. *Jung and politics.* NY: Harper Colophon, 1976.*

Peck, Martin W. *The Meaning of psychoanalysis.* NY: Knopf, 1931.

Perls, F. S. *Ego, hunger and aggression.* NY: Vintage, 1969 (1947).

Perls, Frederick S., Ralph F. Hefferline, and Paul Goodman. *Gestalt Therapy: excitement and growth in the human personality.* NY: Julian Press, 1951.

Perry, Helen Swick. *Psychiatrist of America: the life of Harry Stack Sullivan.* Cambridge: Harvard U. Press, 1982.

Phillips, William, ed. *Art and psychoanalysis.* (Includes Rank's "Life and Creation" from *Art and Artist.*) NY: Criterion, 1957.

Polster, Erving and Miriam Polster. *Gestalt therapy integrated.* NY: Brunner/Mazel, 1973.

Price, Lawrence M. *The Reception of United States literature in Germany.* Chapel Hill: U. North Carolina Press, 1966.*

Prinzhorn, Hans. *Psychotherapy.* London: Jonathan Cape, 1932.*

Progoff, Ira. *The Death and rebirth of psychology.* NY: Julian Press, 1956.

Quen, Jacques M. and Eric T. Carlson, eds. *American psychoanalysis: origins and development.* NY: Brunner/Mazel, 1978.

Rafferty, Frank T. and Paul J. Kachoris. The Trauma of birth and perinatal psychiatry. In *Basic handbook of child psychiatry* Vol. 4, ed. Irving N. Berlin and Lawrence A. Stone, 69–77. NY: Basic Books, 1979.

Rank, Beata. Interviews with K. R. Eissler. 30 Mai 1953 (German), 13 pp., 13 Feb 1954 (English), 12 pp. Freud Archive, Library of Congress (inaccessible until after 2000). Typescript copies courtesy of Helene Rank Veltfort.

Raphael, Frederic and Kenneth McLeish. *The List of books.* Includes Rank's *Myth of the Birth of the Hero.* NY: Harmony (Crown), 1981.

Rawley, Callman. Rank and Taft. *J. Jewish Comm. Service* 36: 390–95, 1960.

Reich, Wilhelm. *Character analysis.* 3rd ed. NY: Farrar, Straus & Giroux 1949; new trans. 1961; Pocket Books, 1976.

———. *Reich speaks of Freud.* Ed. Mary Higgins and Chester M. Raphael. NY: Farrar, Strauss & Giroux, 1967.

Reisman, John M. *A History of clinical psychology.* NY: Irvington, 1976.

Rickman, John. *Index psychoanalyticus 1893–1926.* London: Hogarth, 1928.

Riesman, David. *Individualism reconsidered.* Glencoe: Free Press, 1954.

Roazen, Paul. *Brother animal.* NY: Knopf, 1969.

———. *Freud and his followers.* NY: Knopf, 1974; Meridian Books, 1976.

———. *Erik H. Erikson.* NY: Free Press, 1976.

———. Reflections on ethos and authenticity in psychoanalysis. *The Human Context* (London) 4: 577–87, 1972.

———. Orthodoxy on Freud: the case of Tausk. *Contemp. Psa.* 13: 102–15, 1977.*

———. Reading, writing, and memory: Dr. K. R. Eissler's thinking. *Contemp. Psa.* 14: 345–53, 1978.*

Roback, A. A. and Thomas Kiernan. *Pictorial history of psychology and psychiatry.* Incorporates *History of psychology and psychiatry,* 1961. NY: Philosophical Library, 1969.

Robert, Marthe. *The Psychoanalytic revolution.* NY: Harcourt, Brace & World, 1966. Avon Books, 1968.

———. *From Oedipus to Moses: Freud's Jewish identity.* Garden City, NY: Doubleday/Anchor Books, 1976.

Robinson, Virginia. *The Development of a professional self: selected writings, 1930–1968.* Includes *A Changing psychology in social casework,* 1930. NY: AMS Press, 1978.

———, ed. *Jessie Taft: a professional biography.* Philadelphia: U. of Pennsylvania Press, 1962.

(———). Rankians unbowed. *The New Yorker* 11 Feb 1974, 30–32.

Rogers, Carl R. *Counseling and psychotherapy.* Cambridge: Houghton Mifflin, 1942. (See also Evans.)

———. *Client-centered therapy.* Cambridge: Houghton Mifflin, 1951.

Rose, John. Democracy and the philosophy of will therapy. *PR* 29: 401–405, 1942.

Rosenberg, Rosalind. *Beyond separate spheres: intellectual roots of modern feminism.* New Haven: Yale U. Press, 1982.* (Re: Taft).

Rosenberg, Samuel. *Why Freud fainted.* Indianapolis: Bobbs-Merrill, 1978.

Rozenblit, Marsha. *The Jews of Vienna, 1867–1914: assimilation and identity.* Albany: State U. N. Y. Press, 1984.*

Ruitenbeek, Hendrik M., ed. *Freud as we knew him.* Detroit: Wayne State U. Press, 1973.

———, ed. *The Analytic situation.* Chicago: Aldine, 1973.

Rychlak, Joseph F. *Discovering free will and personal responsibility.* NY: Oxford U. Press, 1979.*

Sachs, Hanns. *Freud: master and friend.* Cambridge: Harvard U. Press, 1944.

Sahakian, William S., ed. *Psychotherapy and counseling: studies in technique.* Chicago: Rand McNally, 1969.

Schafer, Roy. *The Analytic attitude.* NY: Basic Books, 1983.*

Schipkowensky, Nikola. *Psychotherapy versus iatrogeny.* Detroit: Wayne State U. Press, 1977 (German orig. ed. 1965).

Schmitt, Abraham. Otto Rank. In *CTP-II.* See Mora, 1975.

Schorske, Carl E. *Fin-de-Siecle Vienna.* NY: Knopf, 1980.*

Schur, Max. *Freud: living and dying.* NY: Int'l Us. Press, 1972.

Shands, Harley. *Thinking and psychotherapy.* Cambridge: Harvard U. Press, 1960.*

Sharaf, Myron. *Fury on earth: a biography of Wilhelm Reich.* NY: St. Martin's/Marek, 1983.*

Sheldon, William H. *Psychology and the Promethean will.* NY: Harper, 1936.*

Sheleff, Leon. *Generations apart.* NY: McGraw-Hill, 1981.

Sherman, Murray H. ed. *Psychoanalysis and old Vienna.* NY: Human Sciences Press, 1978. Also *Psa. Rev.* 65: 1, 1978.

Sievers, W. David. *Freud on Broadway.* NY: Hermitage House, 1955.

Slipp, Samuel, ed. *Curative factors in dynamic psychotherapy.* NY: McGraw-Hill, 1982.

Sokal, Michael M. and Patrice Rafail. *A Guide to manuscript collections in the history of psychology and related areas.* Millwood, NY: Kraus Int'l, 1982.

Spector, Jack J. *The Aesthetics of Freud.* NY: McGraw-Hill, 1972.

Spencer, Douglas. *Fulcra of conflict.* Yonkers: World Book Co., 1938.

Spencer, Sharon. Otto Rank's influence on Anais Nin. *PR* 69: 111–29, 1982.

Standal, S. W. and R. J. Corsini. *Critical incidents in psychotherapy.* Englewood Cliffs, NJ: Prentice-Hall, 1959.

Stein, Morris I., ed. *Contemporary psychotherapies.* NY: Free Press, 1961.

Stekel, Wilhelm. *Autobiography.* Ed. Emil A. Gutheil. NY: Liveright, 1950.*

Stepansky, Paul E. *In Freud's shadow: Adler in context.* Hillsdale, N.J.: Analytic Press, 1983.

Sterba, Richard F. *Reminiscences of a Viennese psychoanalyst.* Detroit: Wayne State U. Press, 1982.

Stolorow, Robert D. and George E. Atwood. An Ego-psychological analysis of the work and life of Otto Rank in the light of modern conceptions of narcissism. *Int. Rev. Psa.* 3: 441–59, 1976. Also Ch. 5, Otto Rank, in the authors' *Faces in a cloud: subjectivity in personality theory.* NY: Aronson, 1979. (Cf. Kainer and Gourevitch).

Stone, Irving. *The Passions of the mind.* Garden City, NY: Doubleday, 1971.

Stone, Leo. Some thoughts on the "here and now" in psychoanalytic technique and process. *Psa. Quart.* 50: 709–733, 1981.

Storr, Anthony. *The Dynamics of creation.* NY: Atheneum, 1972.*

Strupp, Hans H. *Freud and modern psychoanalysis.* Woodbury, NY: Barron's Educational Series, 1967.

_____. *Psychotherapy and the modification of abnormal behavior.* NY: McGraw-Hill, 1971.

Stuhlmann, Gunther. Remembering Dr. Rank [with excerpts from Rank and Nin]. *Anais* 2: 101–12, 1984.

Sulloway, Frank J. *Freud, biologist of the mind.* NY: Basic Books, 1979.*

Sutich, Anthony J. and Miles A. Vich, eds. *Readings in humanistic psychology.* NY: Free Press, 1969.

Sward, Keith. Self-actualization and women: Rank and Freud contrasted. *J. Humanistic Psychol.* 20, 2: 5–26, 1980.

Sykes, Gerald. *The Hidden remnant.* NY: Harper & Brothers, 1962.

———. *Foresights: self-evolution and survival.* Indianapolis: Bobbs-Merrill, 1975.

Szasz, Thomas. *Ideology and insanity.* Garden City: Doubleday Anchor, 1970.

———. *Karl Kraus and the soul-doctors.* Baton Rouge: Louisiana State U. Press, 1976.

Székely-Kovács, Olga and Robert Berény. *Caricatures of 88 pioneers in psychoanalysis.* NY: Basic Books, 1954 (1924).

Taft, Jessie. *The Dynamics of therapy in a controlled relationship.* NY: Macmillan, 1933. Reprint, intro. Virginia Robinson, Dover, 1961.

———. *Family casework and counseling: a functional approach.* Philadelphia: U. Pennsylvania Press, 1948.

———. *Otto Rank.* NY: The Julian Press, 1958.

Thompson, Clara. *Psychoanalysis: evolution and development.* NY: Hermitage House, 1950; Grove Press, 1957.

———. *Interpersonal psychoanalysis.* Ed. Maurice R. Green. NY: Basic Books, 1964.

Thompson, Clara, Milton Mazer, and Earl Witenberg, eds. *An Outline of Psychoanalysis.* Rev. ed. NY: Modern Library, Random House, 1955.

Turkle, Sherry. *Psychoanalytic politics.* NY: Basic Books, 1978.

Twain, Mark. *Huckleberry Finn.* NY: Webster, 1884.*

———. Stirring times in Austria. *Literary Essays.* In *Writings* 22: 200–249. NY: Harper & Brothers, 1897.*

VanderVeldt, James H. and Robert P. Odenwald. *Psychiatry and Catholicism.* NY: McGraw-Hill, 1952.

Veith, Ilsa. *Hysteria: the history of a disease.* Chicago: U. Chicago Press, 1965.*

Vesey, G. N. A. Volition. In *Essays in philosophical psychology.* ed. D. F. Gustafson. Garden City: Doubleday Anchor, 1964, 41–57.*

Vranich, S. B. Sigmund Freud and "The Case History of Berganza." *PR* 63: 73–82, 1976.*

Vygotsky, Lev S. *The Psychology of art.* Cambridge: M.I.T. Press, 1971.

Wallace, Edwin R. Freud's mysticism and its psychodynamic determinants. *Bull. Menninger Clinic* 42: 203–22, 1978.*

———. Historiography in history and psychoanalysis. *Bull. History of Med.* 57: 247–66, 1983.*

Wangh, Martin, ed. *Fruition of an idea: fifty years of psychoanalysis in America.* NY: Int'l Us. Press, 1962.

Watson, Robert I. *The Great psychologists*. 2nd ed. Philadelphia: Lippincott, 1968.

Weber, Samuel. *The Legend of Freud*. Trans. of *Freud-Legende*, 1979. Minneapolis: U. Minnesota Press, 1982.

Weininger, Otto. *Sex and Character*. NY: G. P. Putnam's Sons, 1906.*

Weisman, Avery D. *The Existential core of psychoanalysis*. Boston: Little Brown, 1965.*

Weiss, Edoardo. *Sigmund Freud as a consultant*. NY: Intercontinental Medical Book Corp., 1970.

Wellisch, Erich. *Isaac and Oedipus*. London: Routledge & Kegan Paul, 1954.

Whitaker, Carl. *From Psyche to system*. Eds. John R. Neill and David P. Kniskern. NY: Guilford, 1982.

White, William A. Review of Rank's *Modern Education*. PR 21: 109–10, 1934.

Whyte, Lancelot Law. *The Unconscious before Freud*. NY: Basic Books, 1960.*

Wilbur, George. Soul belief and psychology. PR 19: 319–26, 1932.

Willey, Malcolm M. Communication agencies and volume of propaganda. *Ann. Amer. Acad. Pol. Soc. Sci.* 179: 198–99 (May) 1935.

Williams, Frankwood, ed. *Proceedings of the First International Congress on Mental Hygiene*. 2 Vols. NY: Int'l Comm. for Mental Hygiene, 1932.

Wilson, Colin. *Origins of the sexual impulse*. NY: Putnam's Sons, 1963.

_____. *New pathways in psychology*. NY: Taplinger, 1972.

Wittels, Fritz. *Sigmund Freud*. London: Allen & Unwin, 1924.

_____. *Freud and his time*. NY: Liveright, 1931.*

Wolff, Werner. *Contemporary psychotherapists examine themselves*. Springfield: Charles C Thomas, 1956.

Wollheim, Richard. *Sigmund Freud*. NY: Viking Press, 1971.

_____, ed. *Freud: critical essays*. Garden City, NY: Anchor Books, 1974.

Wolman, Benjamin B., ed. *Psychoanalytic techniques*. NY: Basic Books, 1967.

Woodward, Robert and Mary Sheehan. *Contemporary schools of psychology*. 3d ed. NY: Ronald, 1964.

Wortis, Joseph. *Fragments of an analysis with Freud*. NY: Simon & Schuster, 1954.

Wyss, Dieter. *Psychoanalytic schools from the beginning to the present*. Tr. Gerald Onn, intro. Leston Havens. NY: Aronson, 1973 (Ger., 1961).

Yalom, Irvin. *The Theory and practice of group psychotherapy.* 2nd ed. NY: Basic Books, 1975.

_____. *Existential psychotherapy.* NY: Basic Books, 1980.

Zetzel, Elizabeth and W. W. Meissner. *Basic concepts of psychoanalytic psychiatry.* NY: Basic Books, 1973.

Zilboorg, Gregory, and George W. Henry. *A History of medical psychology.* NY: Norton, 1941.*

Zottl, Anton. *Otto Rank: Das Lebenswerk eines Dissidenten der Psychoanalyse.* Series "Geist und Psyche," Munich: Kindler Verlag, 1982.

Zweig, Stefan. *The World of yesterday: an autobiography.* NY: Viking, 1943.*

INDEX